D1046820

Clinical Psychology

2nd Edition

Clinical Psychology

THE STUDY OF PERSONALITY AND BEHAVIOR

2nd Edition

Sol L. Garfield

Washington University

PREZELL R. ROBINSON LIBRARY
SAINT AUGUSTINE'S COLLEGE
RALEIGH, NORTH CAROLINA 27611

Aldine Publishing Company
New York

616.89
G231
1983
C.2

About the Author

Sol L. Garfield is Professor of Psychology and was previously Director, Clinical Psychology Program, Washington University in Missouri. He received his B.S., M.A., and Ph.D. at Northwestern University and his diplomate, Clinical Psychology, in 1952 from the American Board of Examiners in Professional Psychology. Dr. Garfield has been widely published in the major journals. His books include *Handbook of Psychotherapy and Behavior Change* (co-edited with A. E. Bergin), and *Clinical Psychology: The Study of Personality and Behavior*. He is a former President of the American Psychological Association Division of Clinical Psychology, and has been Consulting Editor for the *American Journal of Mental Deficiency*, the *Journal of Abnormal Psychology, Clinical Psychology Review, British Journal of Clinical Psychology*, and *Professional Psychology*. He is currently the editor of the *Journal of Consulting and Clinical Psychology*. Professor Garfield is the recipient of two awards from the American Psychological Association for distinguished contributions in clinical psychology.

Copyright © 1983 by Sol L. Garfield

All rights reserved. No part of this publication may
be reproduced or transmitted in any form or by any
means, electronic or mechanical, including photocopy,
recording, or any information storage and retrieval system,
without permission in writing from the publisher.

Library of Congress Cataloging in Publication Data

Garfield, Sol Louis, 1918–
    Clinical psychology.

    Bibliography: p.
    Includes index.
    1. Clinical psychology. I. Title.
DNLM: 1. Psychology, Clinical. WM 100 G23li]
RC467.G3 1983   616.89   83-2649
ISBN 0–202–26094–1 Clothbound Edition
ISBN 0–202–26095–X Paperbound Edition

Table of Contents

Chapter Three

Diagnosis and Assessment

Chapter Four

The Clinical Interview and Case Study

Chapter Five

Psychological Tests and the Appraisal of
        Intellectual Functioning

Chapter Six

Personality Appraisal

Chapter Seven

Behavioral Observation and Assessment

Chapter Eight

Psychotherapy and Behavior Change

Chapter Nine

Variations in Psychotherapy: Traditional Approaches

Chapter Ten

Variations in Psychotherapy: Other Approaches

Chapter Eleven
Behavioral Therapies

Chapter Twelve
Group Therapy

Chapter Thirteen

Child and Family Psychotherapy

Chapter Fourteen

Psychotherapy: Research and Evaluation

Chapter Fifteen

Community Psychology and Mental Health

Chapter Sixteen

Professional Problems and Development

Preface

The second edition of *Clinical Psychology* provides the reader with an introduction to and survey of the field of clinical psychology. Although certain basic aspects of the field have undergone relatively little change since the publication of the first edition, there have been a number of noteworthy developments in this field. The continued impact of behavioral therapies and the influence of cognitive emphases on these therapies remain pertinent. There also has been increased interest and research on the effectiveness of psychotherapy. Still another area of expanding interest is that of family therapy, a description of which is included in the present revision. The area of diagnostic testing has shown relatively little change, with the exception of neuropsychology. Individual therapy with children is another area in which there has been little research. Brief psychotherapy, however, has become increasing popular in the past decade. Overall, the emphasis in this volume is on the area of psychotherapy and behavior change, which reflect the current interest and involvement of clinical psychologists.

There are also a number of significant changes that have taken place in the training of clinical psychologists. Although the scientist-practitioner model remains dominant, the number of Psy.D. programs and independent professional schools markedly increased. At present, the impact of these new training programs on the field of clinical psychology cannot be adequately evaluated, but there appears to be little question of their importance. Some discussion of this development and its implications are presented. Also discussed are recent developments in legislation for psychologists, legal rights of patients, the increase in the number of clinical psychologists, and issues related to these matters. New chapters have been added on behavioral observation and assessment, and on research in psychotherapy. Thus, the author has attempted to present a comprehensive survey and overview of the field of clinical psychology as it exists in the 1980's.

It is the Author's hope that this edition will be as well received as the last, and that it will continue to be a useful text for both advanced undergraduates and graduate students, as well as a reference source for practitioners in clinical and counseling psychology.

I would like to acknowledge the dedicated help of Marie McDonnell who, besides typing many of the chapters, maintained my reference card index and helped in the preparation of the index for this volume. I would also like to thank Sharon Bangert and Nancy Hawkins who helped with the typing and made my deadline attainable. I would like to express, in addition, my appreciation to all those whose work I have drawn upon. Finally, I would like to acknowledge the following for granting me permission to quote and use copyrighted or unpublished material: American Psychological Association, *Journal of Clinical Psychology,* Maurice Lorr, Richard McFall, Houghton-Mifflin, The Psychological Corporation, Hans Huber Verlag, and John Wiley & Sons, Inc.

Sol L. Garfield

Dedicated to the memory of
Rebecca and Julius Garfield

Introduction and Historical Development

Although clinical psychology has existed for more than 80 years, its most rapid and significant growth has taken place since World War II. Paralleling somewhat the general growth of the field of psychology itself, clinical psychology emerged slowly, playing an ever increasingly important role in the area of human adjustment. Although part of this development is undoubtedly due, in recent years, to society's increased interest in mental health and adjust- · ment, a substantial part rests also on the contributions made by psychologists and on the services they are seen as capable of providing.

This development, however, has not always proceeded smoothly. There have been conflicts between the professional and practical interests of clinical psychologists and the more research-oriented and scientific interests of others in the field. There have also been some real struggles within the area of clinical psychology itself concerning issues of training, professional roles, and the relative significance of the scientific and professional components of the clinical psychologist. There have also been some significant professional rivalries with older, established professional groups such as the medical profession. Clinical psychology has, however, continued to thrive and develop despite the fact that these problems have by no means been conclusively settled.

At present clinical psychologists are employed in a variety of settings engag-

1

ing in a great variety of diverse activities. The activities include the interviewing and testing of clients for assessment and diagnostic purposes; counseling and psychotherapeutic services for children, adults, college students, and families; consultation with schools, industry, government, and community groups; teaching in colleges and universities; administering clinics, hospitals, and various governmental programs; and engaging in basic and applied research pertaining to personality, abnormal behavior, and the evaluation of clinical techniques. As is evident from even this partial listing of activities, the clinical psychologist tends to interact with a variety of other professional groups. Moreover, it appears that, with such a diversity of activities and settings, the field of clinical psychology is of real interest to large numbers of people who have some motivation to work with others or have some curiosity concerning human behavior and adjustment. The latter assertion seems to be supported by the large number of individuals who every year inquire about and apply for graduate training in clinical psychology.

Various historical influences have had a strong impact on clinical psychology and have contributed to its development. It may be appropriate at this point, therefore, to examine the historical roots from which clinical psychology developed.

HISTORICAL BACKGROUND

Clinical psychology, as a specialty area within the broader field of psychology, is of course closely related to its parent field. We can, therefore, start this historical account with the beginning of psychology as a science, which is usually associated with the founding of the first laboratory by Wilhelm Wundt in Leipzig, Germany, in 1879 (Boring, 1929). The areas of research were chiefly concerned with sensation and perception. For many years thereafter, these and related problems were of primary interest to psychologists. However, as time progressed, other interests of a more practical nature became evident. Although still measuring mainly sensory functions, James McKeen Cattell, as early as 1894, attempted to appraise the mental abilities of incoming students to Columbia University, in New York City, with a battery of psychological tests. At the same time, other researchers were also experimenting with such approaches to mental measurement.

From the historical standpoint, the earliest direct contribution to the development of clinical psychology was made by Lightner Witmer. If anyone merits the claim of being the founder of clinical psychology, it was undoubtedly this man. He studied with Wundt and received his Ph.D. degree from the University of Leipzig in 1892. He was then appointed director of the laboratory of psychology at the University of Pennsylvania. In 1896, a date that is sometimes given as the beginning of clinical psychology, Witmer founded the first psychological clinic in the United States and gave the first formal course in clinical psychology. In fact, Witmer gave the new discipline its name, and although a number of those who followed him were not enamored of it, it has, nevertheless, been retained.

Witmer's clinical work began with the case of a child who had difficulties in spelling, and his interests continued to center on childhood disturbances. Although he was particularly concerned with sensory difficulties, mental retardation, speech disorders, and problems in school learning, he apparently also tried to work therapeutically with psychotic children (Sarason and Gladwin, 1958). Witmer also taught courses in Child, Clinical, and Abnormal Psychology and set up a training school and hospital to accompany his clinical teaching. In 1907 he founded the journal, *The Psychological Clinic,* and was active as editor and contributor to the journal until it ceased publication in 1935.

In spite of the fact that Witmer was an energetic worker and made significant contributions to the field of clinical psychology, his influence on later developments appears to have been limited. Several writers have speculated about the surprising lack of influence of Witmer's work on later developments. Some have pointed out that Witmer was mainly concerned with sensory and intellectual problems and that the child-guidance movement, which developed later, focused more on social and behavioral difficulties (Shakow, 1948: Watson, 1953). It is difficult to determine whether this explanation really accounts for the later expansion of the child-guidance movement and the more limited impact of Witmer's work. It is certainly conceivable that since psychology itself was in the early stages of its development, Witmer was considerably ahead of his time. In any event, Witmer was clearly a pioneer in the field of clinical psychology, and his clinic was one of the first to conduct psychological examinations. A somewhat more detailed account of Witmer's contribution and the early history of clinical psychology in the United States can be found elsewhere (Garfield, 1965).

More important, historically, was the work of Binet in France at the end of the nineteenth century. Faced with the problems of school retardation and mental deficiency, Binet and his colleague, Simon, developed the first workable test of intelligence, one which was the prototype for most present-day intelligence tests, including the well-known revised Stanford-Binet Scale. The advent of standardized individual intelligence tests was an important development in applied psychology. World War I subsequently provided an opportunity for the use of group tests on a wide scale; after the war, the group testing movement developed rapidly.

Closely related to the development of mental tests was the gradual application of such techniques to the study and care of the mentally retarded. Although psychologists such as Goddard and Witmer were working with defectives before the Binet Scale was introduced into the United States, the Goddard revision of the scale, in 1908, was readily applied to problems of diagnosis and classification. The Vineland School for feebleminded children in New Jersey, under the leadership of Goddard, pioneered in this work. It is interesting to note, too, that the early use of this scale was limited largely to retardates.

Although, as we have noted, Witmer founded the first psychological clinic in 1896 at the University of Pennsylvania, clinical psychology did not progress very rapidly before the introduction of the intelligence test. The following comments by Pintner (1931) attested to the influence of this test on clinical psychology:

> Although clinical psychology proper dates back at least to the last decade of the nineteenth century, it is undoubtedly true that the Binet Scale was the one most potent factor in its development and expansion. Shortly after the first work with the Scale in the institutions for the feebleminded, we find psychological testing of all kinds spreading rapidly to juvenile courts, reformatories, prisons, children's homes and schools. The psychological clinic did not and does not depend upon the Binet Scale, but it is unquestionably true that the appearance of the Binet Scale acted as a tremendous stimulus to this type of work. (Pintner, 1931)

In addition to tests of intelligence, other types of tests were also developed. At the same time that Cattell was testing Columbia students, Rice was working on comparative tests of spelling. This was the beginning of the testing movement in education, which was given real impetus a few years later by Thorndike and his students. Tests were devised for a variety of school purposes, including the measurement of achievement and diagnosis. Tests of special aptitude, such as the well-known Seashore Test of Musical Talent, also were developed before 1920. These developments were the forerunners of the school adjustment, guidance, and remedial services which today are accepted as regular functions of educational institutions.

To say that the testing movement was the sole important factor in the historical development of clinical work in psychology, however, would be to distort the actual significance of this factor. Several other movements were of decided, although sometimes indirect, importance. Some of these can be mentioned rather briefly as indications of the diverse influences on what we recognize today as clinical psychology.

OTHER EARLY DEVELOPMENTS

The growth of the mental-hygiene movement following the publication in 1908 of Beers' famous account of his own hospitalization in *A Mind*

That Found Itself (Beers, 1948) is noted here. Beers' book and his untiring activity in behalf of the movement helped greatly to stimulate public awareness to the problems of mentally disturbed patients. This work tended to emphasize two main aspects of the problem: (1) Improvement in the care and treatment of patients hospitalized for serious personality disturbance, and (2) prevention of such disorders. The concern with prevention of adult disorders led to planning for child-guidance clinics as active agencies for the early detection and treatment of deviant behavior patterns. These clinics were staffed by professional personnel competent to cope with such problems.

The first child-guidance clinic was founded in Chicago, in 1909, to work with delinquent children. Originally named the Juvenile Psychopathic Institute, it continues today as the Institute for Juvenile Research. At first the professional staff consisted of the psychiatrist, William Healy, as director, and the psychologist, Grace Fernald. Later, a social worker was added. It is of interest to note also that Healy introduced the use of the Binet-Simon scale into the clinic in 1910 (Healy and Bronner, 1948).

In 1912, in connection with the recently established Boston (Mass.) Psychopathic Hospital, another children's clinic was founded. In the following year, the Henry Phipps Clinic opened in Baltimore, Maryland, with a separate unit for children. A few years later, in 1917, Healy moved to Boston to set up and direct what is now known as the Judge Baker Guidance Center. Thus, in the United States, the child-guidance movement developed slowly at first, but continued to grow. Originally, the clinics appeared to be primarily concerned with problems of delinquency, but later they gradually enlarged the scope of their activities to include most types of adjustment problems. The psychologist's contribution was that of psychological testing, but included other activities, depending on the training of the psychologist and the specific setting in which he worked. As an historical footnote, it can be mentioned that Healy visited Witmer's clinic and Goddard's laboratory at Vineland in 1908, and thus they conceivably had some influence on the child-guidance movement.

Paralleling some of these historical trends was a growing interest in the problems of the mentally disturbed as a proper field of study and treatment. Not too long ago, psychotics, epileptics, and others were looked upon as anomalies and as persons afflicted with evil spirits. Many were herded into prisons and "asylums," and others were chained. Pinel, a French physician, was one of the first to regard them as individuals in need of sympathetic treatment. Along with a more humane attitude toward patients, there developed a greater knowledge and scientific interest concerning those unfortunates. Although a complete account of this story makes interesting reading (Deutsch, 1949; White, 1948), only a few aspects of it can be mentioned here, namely, those relating to the development of psychiatry and abnormal psychology.

In the latter half of the nineteenth century there was an increased interest in describing and classifying some of these behavioral disturbances in the field of medicine. Kraepelin's well-known classification of some of the frequently observed psychopathological patterns was one of the important contributions to psychiatry and helped to emphasize it as a special field of study. Although psychiatry is considered a specialty within the field of medicine, it is an area whose subject matter overlaps with that of abnormal and clinical psychology. There will be more said about this relationship later.

Although, as indicated, the care and treatment of hospitalized patients were confined to physicians, by the beginning of the present century psychologists began to conduct their own studies on psychotic patients. This work can be called "abnormal psychology," in that an attempt was made to apply psychological methods to the study of various mental functions in patients. There was little intensive study of individuals as specific cases for understanding and treatment. Rather than "clinical" contacts with patients, what was sought were studies of characteristic psychological reactions in various groups of patients. Such cross-sectional studies involved the appraisal of a given sample of subjects and emphasized the common or distinctive patterns found in the group rather than the study of individuals as individuals. Nevertheless, the application of psychological techniques to the study of personality and behavioral disorders was a natural forerunner to the later development of clinical psychology.

One other historical antecedent is also worthy of mention in this brief review. The development of psychoanalysis by Sigmund Freud (1938) and his followers introduced many new and significant concepts in psychopathology. Freud was among the first to emphasize the importance of psychological factors in the etiology and treatment of neuroses. Although some of his former followers such as Alfred Adler, Carl Gustav Jung, Karen Horney, and Otto Rank later deviated from many of Freud's basic postulates, they also emphasized psychological factors in the understanding and treatment of personality disturbances.

Many of the clinical deductions and theoretical concepts offered by the psychoanalysts have had tremendous influence on both the theory and practice of clinical psychological work with a wide variety of persons. One of the most important and influential concepts of Freud was that which concerned the unconscious determinants of behavior. He was impressed with the fact that many of his patients appeared to have motivations of which they were unaware. In understanding a patient and his personal difficulties, one was forced to go beyond what the patient initially volunteered about himself. The analyst must probe below the surface to uncover the dynamic and complicated motivational forces accounting for the patient's symptomatic behavior. Furthermore, in exploring these hitherto hidden aspects of personality, the psychoanalysts brought forth new views concerning the complex nature of human motivations and the factors associated with the "repression" of wishes and impulses dating from an earlier stage of the individual's development. The psychological treatment of such problems also was found to be a complicated matter, and much work was directed toward improving the psychotherapeutic process. Psychoanalysis became both an investigative theory of personality and a method of psychotherapy. We will have more to say about these matters in later chapters pertaining to personality theories and psychotherapy.

The result of these "dynamic" theories of personality was an increased emphasis on psychological or psychogenic factors in behavioral pathology. Stress was put on understanding the symptoms of the individual patient instead of being unduly concerned with the description and classification of behavioral symptoms. Thus, these earlier workers were important as contributors to personality theories which clinicians utilize in the understanding and modification of behavior and as assumptions underlying some of our clinical techniques, for example, word association and projective tests.

These diverse developments, some within the field of psychology and some in related areas, have all contributed in some way to the historical development of clinical psychology. It is from this unique background that clinical psychology has emerged as a specialized professional discipline within psychology. Although declaring allegiance to psychology, clinical psychology is differentiated from the more traditional areas of general experimental psychology. At the same time, because of its historical derivation from within psychology, clinical psychology, although an applied clinical area, is differentiated from other related clinical professions which deal with similar subjects, for example, psychiatry, psychoanalysis, social work. Because of its unique development, clinical psychology offers a distinctive contribution to applied psychological work which no other related discipline can completely duplicate. Before this point is more fully explained, however, let us complete our historical sketch of the development of clinical psychology.

Although, as we have noted, clinical psychology was given its start by Witmer at the University of Pennsylvania over 80 years ago, there was no rapid acceptance or expansion of such activities in the years which immediately followed. Psychology was still a very young scientific discipline in the early years of the present century and not too much effort was devoted to this embryonic clinical development. While some psychologists turned their attention toward clinical problems, and a few became enthusiastic followers of the psychoanalytic movement, the majority of psychologists were primarily interested in academic laboratory work. The increased use of standardized psychological tests in the 1920's, however, was instrumental in setting up some demand and interest in psychological examinations. Some psychologists functioned as examiners in schools, and others began to apply these new techniques in clinics and hospitals. While the expansion of activities in this area was modest, there developed a gradual acceptance of psychological testing, particularly the testing of intelligence; within limits, clinical psychologists were largely psychological examiners. The status, duties, and material rewards of such positions did not enhance the professional prospects of clinical psychology in spite of the fact that some psychologists in the field were already expanding the frontiers.

WORLD WAR II AND ITS IMPACT

Although the number of psychologists in schools, clinics, hospitals, and allied institutions steadily increased, the functions of such workers remained somewhat limited. Apart from courses in tests and measurements and abnormal psychology, the preparation of clinical psychologists differed little from the preparation of academic experimental psychologists. For the most part, professional experience and contact with clients was acquired after the student left the university. Internships in clinical work, for example, were available in only a few institutions and relatively few schools had full-time psychological clinics of their own. Ironically, it was not the science and profession of psychology itself, but World War II and its attendant manpower problems, that virtually revolutionized the training and scope of clinical work in psychology. For one thing, the amazingly high percentage of selectees rejected for military service because of psychological or emotional difficulties helped to focus the nation's attention on the severity of this problem. An early report on causes of rejection among eighteen- and nineteen-year-old selectees revealed that "mental disease" and mental deficiency were among the ten leading causes of rejection. In terms of combined figures for both black and white selectees, "mental disease" was a cause of rejection in 27.6 cases per 1000 examined and ranked second only to visual defects as a cause of rejection (Rowntree, 1943).

Even after such preliminary screening, the number of cases with psychological disabilities subsequently encountered in the armed forces, before and after combat, was extremely great. As the war progressed, and took its toll, the number of psychiatric casualties increased noticeably, and the personnel available for their care was limited. Although many psychologists were utilized in the armed forces at induction and reception centers for purposes of selection and classification of military personnel, few professional psychologists were actively employed in intensive clinical work. With the increased number of men requiring psychological care and rehabilitation and the limited number of physicians available for such work, the role of clinical psychologists was greatly expanded. In the army, for example, beginning in the fall of 1944, more than 200 clinical psychologists were commissioned from the ranks for duty in military hospitals and rehabilitation centers (Hutt & Milton, 1947). This not only helped to give clinical psychologists more adequate official status and recognition, but also acquainted many related professional groups with the services that could be performed by clinical psychologists. Because of the tremendous need for qualified personnel to take care of the large number of men referred for psychiatric observation and treatment, clinical psychologists were given an opportunity to perform a variety of professional duties previously not open to them. The fact that psychologists could take adequate case histories, contribute to the personality evaluation and diagnosis of the patient, help plan research studies, and effectively handle many types of patients in individual and group therapy, demonstrated that here was a professional group that had not been fully utilized in the past. The scope of clinical duties in psychology was thus broadened and clinical psychologists could be more clearly differentiated from psychological examiners or psychometricians whose duties mainly involved test administration.

This expansion of activities in clinical psychology has continued since the war, and many notable developments have contributed to it. The large number of veterans discharged with psychiatric disabilities necessitated a tremendous expansion of services in the Veterans Administration. In this expansion of hospital and clinic facilities, the help of clinical psychologists was eagerly sought and the enlarged role and functions of clinical psychologists were officially recognized. The Veterans Administration became the largest single employer of clinical psychologists, and, because of the scarcity of well-trained clinicians, the Veterans Administration embarked on a large-scale training program in clinical psychology in cooperation with the leading universities in the country.

The clinical psychology program administered and supported by the Veterans Administration was in many ways a radical innovation and played an important role in the post-war expansion of clinical psychology. In the early years of this joint program, students were expected to spend approximately half-time during each of their four graduate years at clinics or hospitals of the Veterans Administration and the remaining time at the university. In this way, practical work under supervision was combined with academic work, and the stipend received from the Veterans Administration enabled the student to attend graduate school.

This program was quite successful, particularly during this early period. A close relationship between the training universities and the Veterans Administration developed, university faculty served as consultants to the hospitals and clinics used for training, and a goodly number of the trainees took positions with the Veterans Administration upon completing their training. However, over the years, this training program underwent a number of changes. Currently, the Veterans Administration primarily provides internship training. Thus, support for students during the first few years of graduate training is no longer available from the Veterans Administration.

The U.S. Public Health Service also contributed to this expansion by providing grants to universities to expand their training programs, as well as training stipends to selected students to pursue graduate work in clinical psychology. This support of training was particularly important as the support from the Veterans Administration became limited primarily to advanced students only. Special committees of the American Psychological Association (APA) worked with these federal agencies as coordinating and certifying agencies. A Committee on the Training of Clinical Psychologists (American Psychological Association, 1947) recommended many changes in curricula and specified a supervised internship for clinical psychologists in training.

So many precedent-shattering innovations have been instituted with regard to clinical psychology since World War II that space limitations do not allow a complete account. Nevertheless, certain important trends should be noted. First of all, clinical psychology was recognized as a distinct area of specialization within professional psychology. Furthermore, specific training programs were developed leading to a Ph.D. degree in clinical psychology. A novel feature of these programs was the emphasis on professional clinical experience to be obtained by practicum work and a full year's internship. The federal government recognized clinical psychology as one of the professional disciplines in the mental health field along with psychiatry, social work, and nursing, and underwrote a huge training program. Finally, high academic and personal requirements were established for prospective clinical psychologists, and, for the first time, an accrediting agency was formed by the APA to certify universities capable of giving adequate clinical training. At the time of this writing, the number of universities fully accredited for such training has risen from 20 to 112 (APA approved doctoral programs in clinical, counseling, and school psychology: 1980).

TRAINING: THE SCIENTIST-PRACTITIONER MODEL

Because training and professional role models are closely intertwined, it is important to discuss in some detail the various conferences on training in clinical psychology and related developments that have taken place since World War II. As was mentioned earlier, the Committee on Training in Clinical Psychology, established by the APA, published a set of recommendations in 1947. Because these recommendations had a significant influence on the training programs that were developed subsequently, it is worthwhile to summarize their main features. In addition to broad pre-professional undergraduate education including psychology and related areas, the committee recommended an integrated program of graduate instruction. The program emphasized six major areas of study: (1) General Psychology; (2) Psychodynamics of Behavior; (3) Diagnostic Methods; (4) Research Methods; (5) Related Disciplines; and, (6) Therapy. The proposed four-year program included a one-year internship. The committee emphasized the continuity of clinical psychology with the general field of psychology and stressed the role of the clinical psychologist in research:

> A clinical psychologist must first and foremost be a *psychologist* in the sense that he can be expected to have a point of view and a core of knowledge and training which is common to all psychologists. This would involve an acquaintance with the primary body of psychological theory, research, and methods on which further training and interdisciplinary relationships can be built.
> Preparation should be broad; it should be directed to research and professional goals. Participants should receive training in three functions: diagnosis, research, and therapy, with the special contribution of the psychologist as a research worker emphasized throughout (American Psychological Association, 1947).

In addition to the didactic and practical program of study suggested for prospective clinical psychologists, certain other personal-professional requirements were also listed. Since the clinical psychologist's duties involve important problems of adjustment to others and the ability to evaluate such situations objectively, the personality and adjustment of the clinician are obviously important. Some students of superior ability, for example, might make poor clinicians because of personal difficulties, or because of an inability to work well with other people. The personality characteristics of the individual are, therefore, to be considered along with academic proficiency in judging suitability for clinical work in psychology. Although objective and validated criteria for personality selection were not available, the Committee on Training in Clinical Psychology listed the following specific personality characteristics as the kinds called for in clinical work: (1) superior ability; (2) originality and resourcefulness; (3) curiosity; (4) interest in persons as individuals; (5) insight into one's own personality characteristics; (6) sensitivity to the complexities of motivation; (7) tolerance; (8) ability to establish warm and effective relationships with others; (9) industry and ability to tolerate pressure; (10) acceptance of responsibility; (11) tact; (12) integrity and self-control; (13) sense of ethical values; (14) broad cultural background; and, (15) deep interest in psychology, especially the clinical aspects.

It is obvious from the foregoing list that the committee did not take the personal qualifications for becoming a clinical psychologist too lightly! One may even wonder if all clinical psychologists possess these desirable traits. It does reflect, however, the serious concern of a group of psychologists who were given the responsible task of helping to plan for the education and training of a newly expanding specialty within the field, and who desired to set high standards for the specialty.

In 1949 an important conference on training in clinical psychology was held at Boulder, Colorado. While there have been several subsequent conferences on clinical training, the Boulder Conference was unquestionably the one which set the pattern for graduate training for many years and whose subsequent influence on the field has been the most pronounced. In general, however, the participants drew upon and reaffirmed the principles and recommendations offered by the Committee on Training in Clinical Psychology two years earlier.

The Boulder Conference lasted for 2 weeks and was attended by representatives from each of the then approved university training programs as well as by some representatives from practicum and government agencies. Once again the three major areas of diagnosis, therapy, and research were designated as the major functions of the clinical psychologists, and once more the psychologist's unique role in the area of research was stressed. Probably of greatest significance was the firm decision to establish as a major goal the training of the clinical psychologist as *both* a scientist and as a practitioner at the Ph.D. level. Historically, this made sense since psychology was in great part an academic and research-oriented discipline. If academic departments were to train clinical psychologists it was to be at the highest academic level available to them; this was, of course, the Ph.D. degree, a traditional degree emphasizing research competence. For the clinical psychologist, therefore, additional courses of instruction emphasizing clinical skills and techniques were to be added to or superimposed upon the more traditional academic and research training in psychology. It was also emphasized again that the clinical psychologist was to be a psychologist first and a clinician second, thus affirming primary allegiance to the parent field of psychology. While this affirmation and this model of the clinical psychologist was clearly reaffirmed in all subsequent major conferences on training until 1973, the scientist-practioner model did not exist without a moderate amount of stress and strain. Because this matter is rather central to many other issues in clinical psychology, it is worth further discussion.

The scientist-practioner model was seen by the participants at the Boulder Conference as a unique one, and one which differentiated the profession of clinical psychology from most other (and by implication, most ordinary) professions. The point of view was expressed as follows:

The development of the profession of clinical psychology constituted something of an educational experiment, in that clinical psychologists are being trained both as scientists and as practitioners. Most professions base their practices on one or more sciences and train their future members in a separate professional school. In contrast, clinical psychologists are trained concurrently in both the theoretical (scientific) and applied (clinical) aspects of psychology. This training occurs not in professional schools but in the graduate schools of our colleges and universities (Raimy, 1950, p. v.).

Although the objective was a lofty one, it was not without its difficulties. A fundamental question was whether a single individual can combine the attributes required to be both a scientist and a practitioner and whether he/she can play both roles successfully. Can the "hard-headed" scientist also be a warm and empathic therapist? There is no clear answer to these questions at present although it appears that the interests and value orientation of researchers and practitioners are not necessarily compatible or congruent. At least on a number of occasions, there have been controversies between practitioners and the more scientifically and research-oriented psychologists within the clinical field concerning graduate training as well as other matters of more professional concern. The fact that these two emphases coexisted clearly had some impact on the professional identity of the clinical psychologist (Garfield, 1966). If he acceded to the dictum that clinical psychology was both a science and a profession, then he must embody both of these values. Many individuals, of course, identified mainly with one of the emphases. The divergent emphases of these two value orientations have thus been sources of conflict within psychology and clinical psychology. Before discussing this matter further, however, let us examine an interesting study related to this problem which was reported by Shaffer (1953).

In this study an attempt was made to evaluate the attitudes of clinical psychologists on the matter of intuitive versus objective viewpoints. In a general way, intuitive attitudes are viewed as more "clinical" in nature, whereas the objective attitudes are representative of a more rigorous research orientation. A scale, constructed to measure such attitudes, was given to a large sample of psychologists who were members of the Division of Clinical Psychology of the APA. In general, it was "evident that clinical psychologists as a whole cannot be labeled as intuitive or objective. They are both and neither" (Shaffer, 1953, p. 621). The average score of the group on the attitude scale was approximately at the midpoint of the scale. The dispersion of scores also was not very great. Nevertheless, while the essential unity of the group was reflected in these scores, some differences between the relatively intuitive and the relatively objective clinical psychologists were apparent. Such differences were noted when the most intuitive 27% of the sample were compared with the most objective 27% of the sample on selected items of the attitude scale. The items that were most discriminating were the following:

1. The time which graduate students of clinical psychology now spend learning research methods would be more profitably spent in obtaining first-hand clinical experience.

2. One good test of statistical significance is more convincing than a lot of clinical intuitions (Shaffer, 1953, p. 611).

Fifty-nine percent of the intuitive group agreed with the first item, while 94% of the objective group disagreed. Of the former group, 1% agreed with the second item as compared with 43% of the objective group. There also appeared to be a relationship between these attitudes and the type of position held by the psychologist. "Psychologists who reported that their main duty was diagnosis or psychotherapy held intuitively-tinged attitudes. Research was strongly associated with an objective attitude, teaching a little less so" (Shaffer, 1953, p. 615). A more recent study of clinical psychologists' responses to these two items found very similar results (Garfield & Kurtz, 1976).

The apparent conflict between clinical and research attitudes and values has remained a source of contention within clinical psychology, although the scientist-practitioner, or Boulder model remained as the official model for many years. In subsequent conferences on training, the Boulder model was usually affirmed with little opposition. At the 1965 "Conference on the Professional Preparation of the Clinical Psychologist," which was held in Chicago, the support for the Boulder model was almost unanimous—even though several alternative models for training clinical psychologists were considered (Hoch, Ross, & Winder, 1966). Among these were two possible programs for training professional clinical psychologists exclusively. One was that of a clinical psychologist trained primarily for a variety of professional functions, while the other emphasized training specifically for the practice of psychotherapy. In both of these proposals, the traditional research training required for the Ph.D. degree was omitted and a professional degree offered in place of the Ph.D. As already indicated, such proposals received a rather cool reception and the scientist-practitioner model was overwhelmingly approved.

There were two other matters considered at the Chicago Conference which are of particular interest in terms of the most recent developments in training. Apart from the general consideration of possible models for training a purely professional clinical psychologist, representatives from the University of Illinois also presented their own specific plans for a proposed four-year graduate program leading to a Doctor of Psychology degree (Psy.D.). The program proposed would omit the then traditional language as well as dissertation requirements of the Ph.D. degree and instead provide much more practical clinical training. The reaction to this innovative plan, designed in part to overcome the prevailing criticisms of conventional doctoral programs, was decidedly negative, even though the conference went on record as approving such experimentation in individual settings.

Another interesting feature of the conference, perhaps tied to the decision concerning training scientist-practitioners, was that there was little apparent support for considering training sites other than the graduate school of the university. The possibility of a separate professional school for training clinical psychologists, or for locating such training in medical schools, received little support from the conferees. Inasmuch as the Chicago Conference was probably the most widely representative conference in terms of the selection of participants from both academic and applied settings, the strong support for the scientist-practitioner model was somewhat surprising. Apparently, in spite of evident dissatisfaction with clinical training and the feeling that the concerns of a clinical nature were not always stressed in the university setting, few were willing at that time to give up the traditional model or the prestige of the Ph.D. degree for uncertain or untried alternatives.

It is interesting that despite the apparent support for the scientist-practitioner model manifested at the Chicago Conference in 1965, departures from this model made their appearance within a relatively few years. Before discussing these more recent developments, however, it is worth mentioning one other related matter—training psychologists at less than the doctoral level. At the Miami (Fla.) Conference, for example, considerable attention was devoted to the issue of also training psychologists at the master's degree level (Roe, Gustad, Moore, Ross, & Skodak, 1959). Such proposals were also presented at the Chicago Conference, but did not receive much support. The issues concerning the role and training of clinical psychologists at the master's degree level has continued until the present. Although only doctoral level training programs can receive accreditation from the APA, and although in most states only psychologists with doctoral degrees can be licensed or certified, a large number of master's degree psychologists are turned out each year and provide psychological services in a variety of settings.

TRAINING: OTHER MODELS

As indicated previously, although the scientist-practitioner model for the training of clinical psychologists remained the sole model for over 20 years after World War II, with the introduction of the Psy.D. program at the University of Illinois in 1968, a competitive model was presented (Peterson, 1969). Very briefly, the Psy.D. Program was a four-year program in which the formal research training and dissertation requirements were omitted and practical clinical training was substituted. The rationale was that most clinical psychologists were not interested in research, did not carry out any research once they left graduate school, that university faculty tended to overemphasize research training, and that the actual clinical training tended to be slighted.

It was also stated that a new professional degree, the Psy.D., was required to clearly identify the profession of clinical psychology. Whatever the reasons, a new program was developed and offered as an additional clinical program alongside of the traditional Ph.D. program.

The Psy.D. program at Illinois accepted a relatively small number of students each year, usually less than ten, and was comparable in size to the remaining Ph.D. program. Nevertheless, despite the small number of students involved, this program was important for initiating a radical departure from the traditional programs which had held sway during the post-war period. For a brief period, the University of Illinois program tended to be viewed as an isolated experiment conducted in a somewhat unusual university setting. However, within a few years, even more radical changes in training programs and settings began to appear.

Shortly after the Illinois program was instituted, a group of professional psychologists in California developed plans for a professional school of psychology with the support of the state psychological association (Pottharst, 1970). Although the original plans called for providing varied levels of training ranging from the two-year Associate of Arts degree up to the Ph.D. degree, as the California School of Professional Psychology has operated more recently, the lower level programs have been discontinued, and major attention has been devoted to the doctoral program.

The creation of the California School was in most respects a more radical departure from the Boulder Model than was the Illinois program, even though the Ph.D. degree was retained for reasons of acceptance and prestige. The California School of Professional Psychology did not become affiliated with any university, but instead became a free-standing, autonomous professional school. The faculty were largely practitioners, most of whom taught on a part-time basis. Also, in contrast to the small and generally highly selected class admitted to the university graduate programs, large classes have been enrolled. Instead of an average class of 8 to 12 students admitted each year in the university programs, classes were in the neighborhood of 100. Although some training in research was provided, as was true also at Illinois, and a doctoral project of a more clinical nature than the usual doctoral dissertation was required, the program was usually completed on schedule in four years, as contrasted with most university Ph.D. programs which tend to require five or more years for completion.

Since the appearance of these new programs, a number of others have made their appearance, and this development has also occasioned some concern on the part of individuals identified with the Boulder model and with more traditional programs of clinical psychology. At the 1980 APA Convention, for example, there were at least three scheduled symposia or debates on the general topic of the efficacy of training in a professional school versus training as a scientist-practitioner. There are a number of complex issues involved here and the recency of these new programs is such that no really adequate evaluation can be made at this time. However, a few of the concerns or issues involved can be mentioned briefly here.

One of the central issues really pertains more to the definition and potential identity problems of the clinical psychologist than it does to training per se (Garfield, 1966). As we have noted, in the Boulder model the research training and function of the clinical psychologist was considered a unique feature which distinguished the clinical psychologist from other mental health professionals. Such training also was characteristic of doctoral training in the other areas of psychology. Furthermore, clinical psychology students also took classes and interacted with students in other areas of psychology, thereby offering additional opportunity for broader views and enrichment. Particularly in the case of the free-standing schools of professional psychology, this type of situation is not possible. Thus, although all clinical students in the latter settings may still take courses in some basic areas of psychology, the educational environments and value systems of the two programs will be quite different, and conceivably, two different kinds of clinical psychologists will be produced.

Other concerns voiced pertain to the diversity of training settings, the different degrees offered, and the potential variability in the quality of training. At present there are professional schools of psychology affiliated with universities, most of whom offer the Psy.D. degree, and some have been accredited by the APA (Peterson, Eaton, Levine, & Snepp, 1980). There are also a few clinical psychology programs in medical schools, with some giving the Psy.D. degree and others the Ph.D. degree (Watson, Coddy, Johnston, & Rimm, 1981). There are also a much larger number of free-standing professional schools offering either the Psy.D. or Ph.D. degree. It is the latter group of schools which appear to generate the greatest concerns since they are new, are not affiliated with a university, have no educational history, generally have more limited resources, and are largely dependent on part-time instructors and students' tuition to keep functioning.

Thus, as can be noted from this brief description, a number of novel and unanticipated developments in the training of clinical psychologists have occurred in a very short period of time. Consequently, it is difficult to estimate or gauge the impact of these developments on the field of clinical psychology in the years ahead. Although the majority of the APA approved clinical programs are still Ph.D. programs espousing the scientist-practitioner model, most of these programs individually train a relatively small number of students as compared with some of the professional schools. Consequently, there may be a large influx of "professionals" or "professional-scientists" entering the field in the future and the scientist-practitioner clinical psychologist will no longer represent clinical psychology in its entirety. Whether this will be a positive or negative development remains to be appraised in the future. However, it is likely that there will be greater variability in both the content and quality of clinical training, and that the designation, clinical psychologist, will have less specifity than it had in the past.

Before leaving the topic of training, mention should be made of the most recent conference on training, held at Vail, Colorado, in 1973 (Korman, 1974). Reflecting some of the concerns already discussed, it was designated as a "National Conference on Levels and Patterns of Professional Training." However, issues pertaining to the participation of women and minority groups in American psychology also had some direct influence on the planning of the conference. As a result, the Vail Conference differed markedly from all previous training conferences in terms of the selection of participants. Previous conference participants consisted primarily of representatives of training universities, internship centers, and governmental agencies, who were almost exclusively psychologists, and to a large extent males. However, other criteria were used for this conference. Of the 116 invited participants at Vail, 14 were trainees, 40 were women, and 20 were male minority group members. Consumers of psychological services were also present. Thus, the criteria for selection differed noticeably from those used previously and may explain, at least in part, the relatively small impact of this conference on most university training programs. The recommendations of the Vail Conference to promote strong professional master's level training programs and to accord journeyman status to psychologists with the master's degree, have had little impact on the majority of APA members and on official APA policy. However, the conference did lend some official sanction to the more professionally oriented training programs and the awarding of the Psy.D. degree.

The preceding description of training developments in American psychology should give the reader some general understanding of the current situation. We will have a bit more to say about training requirements, applications to graduate school, accreditation, and related matters in a later chapter. Let us now turn our attention to a brief look at the current functions of the clinical psychologist.

CURRENT FUNCTIONS OF THE CLINICAL PSYCHOLOGIST

As previously stated, the clinical psychologist was identified early with the clinical use and application of psychological tests. The primary involvement with psychological examinations was augmented by the 1930's with vocational counseling, educational guidance, and remedial teaching, particularly in child-guidance clinics (Louttit, 1939). The status and stature of clinical psychology at that time was somewhat circumscribed. As already noted, however, World War II and its aftermath produced significant changes in the field. The demand for professional services with the accompanying support for training from agencies of the federal government led to an expansion of both the number and role of clinical psychologists. Three major functions were identified: diagnostic testing, psychotherapy, and research. The type of testing function performed was also quite different from the more psychometrically oriented testing of earlier periods. Instead of merely reporting an IQ or emphasizing quantitative results, the newer diagnostic role stressed a battery of tests, the utilization of personality theory as a frame of reference for interpreting test data and behavior, and the organizational and interpretative skills of the clinical psychologist in synthesizing his observations and in formulating his diagnostic findings. This diagnostic appraisal of the individual thus was not a routine mechanical operation but drew upon the clinical experience and understanding of the clinical psychologist.

One of the more novel features of the newer approach was a generally heavier emphasis on personality analysis and dynamics and on the use of projective techniques such as the Rorschach and the Thematic Apperception Test, techniques that were relatively new and rarely taught in the universities during the pre-war period. This new testing and diagnostic role became the primary activity of the post-war clinical psychologist as manifested both in the emphasis on such instruction in graduate training programs and in the amount of time devoted to such activities by clinical psychologists in clinical settings. It should be mentioned also that this newer diagnostic testing function tended to combine the traditional use of psychological tests with the more clinical use of dynamic theories of personality as integrated and interpreted by the clinical psychologist. In a sense, then, this was an elaboration of an historically established function or role of the psychologist.

A second function of the clinical psychologist, that of research, was also traditionally associated with the field of psychology, even though it tended to receive rather scant attention from most psychologists in clinics and hospitals. But, with the development of the new post-war Ph.D. programs in clinical psychology, following the Boulder model, the research function received specific emphasis. Since the training of clinical psychologists for the traditional Ph.D. degee stressed training in research methods and the completion of a research dissertation, the psychologist, more than any of his colleagues in the clinical disciplines, was equipped to plan and execute research. It was believed that the clinical psychologist, by the nature of his unique training, could probably make his greatest contribution in this research function to the fields of personality, psychopathology, and clinical techniques, since much of the work in these areas was poor in design, methodology, and evaluation. The clinical psychologist, then, appeared to have an unusual opportunity to increase our basic knowledge concerning human behavior. This, at least, was one of the hopes for the new clinical psychologist, and while definite contributions have been made in this area, it is also true that a large number of clinical psychologists, after successfully completing their doctoral dissertations, have thought no more about their research role.

The third function, that of psychotherapist, was, in many respects, the one most recently acquired by the clinical psychologist and the one beset with the greatest number of potential problems. In the first place, psychotherapy, unlike the other two main functions of the clinical psychologist, had no real historical roots within the field of psychology (Garfield, 1966). For example, in the 1930's in a survey by Louttit (1939) of 111 psychologists in child-guidance clinics, psychotherapy was ranked sixth among the activities engaged in by this group of practitioners. Furthermore, it was mentioned by less than one-third of this group as contrasted with a participation of over 86% in psychological testing. Comparatively little, if any, instruction was offered in psychotherapy at that time in the university psychology departments.

A second source of difficulty was that participation by psychologists in psychotherapeutic activities brought them into conflict with other professional groups, notably psychiatrists, who saw the therapeutic function as traditionally theirs. Whereas the testing and research roles of the psychologist in clinical settings had been accepted by their psychiatric colleagues, the new emphasis on the psychologist's role as psychotherapist was viewed with some alarm. While some clinics and agencies permitted psychologists to engage in psychotherapy, some implicit or explicit restrictions or safeguards tended to be set down. Only certain psychologists were permitted to function as psychotherapists, they could work only with selected cases, and their work should be supervised by medical personnel, preferably psychiatrists.

Although psychologists tended to chafe under such conditions, there were some reality aspects to this situation. As noted previously, psychologists generally had had little training or experience in psychotherapy prior to World War II. During the war, however, when the need for therapeutic services far exceeded the supply of trained therapists, psychologists began to participate more extensively in such activities and clearly expressed an interest in doing so.

The successful participation of psychologists in group therapy, as well as individual therapy with some of the milder behavior disorders, had led to partial recognition of the psychologists's role in therapy in the post-war era. The phrase, "partial recognition," is used advisedly, for the area of psychotherapy involved considerations that went beyond the field of clinical psychology. With regard to this problem, one had to consider also the attitudes of other professions, the agencies that hire psychologists, historical precedents, and even definitions of therapy. While the Committee on Training in Clinical Psychology (American Psychological Association, 1947) emphasized psychotherapy as one of the three main functions of the psychologist, a precise definition of the therapeutic function was not given. Mention was made, however, of the fact that the skill required for intensive therapy would have to be acquired after completing the requirements for the Ph.D. degree. On the other hand, the Veterans Administration attempted from time to time to clarify or define the therapeutic role of psychologists in its organization. An example of an early statement of this type is the following statement made by a former chief medical director of the Veterans Administration:

> The clinical psychologist will also have psychotherapeutic duties, but in carrying these out, we believe he must always operate within the medical framework. This arrangement will protect him, in legal questions concerning the practice of medicine, and also make certain that the multiform interrelationships between physical and mental diseases are under careful surveillance and control.
>
> Moreover, we believe that such therapeutic responsibilities should be delegated by psychiatrists only to clinical psychologists who are adequately trained in this field, and then only in the types of cases for which they are qualified, particularly in such fields as readjustment of habits; personality problems within the normal range: educational disabilities such as reading defects, speech impairments, or similar difficulties requiring reeducation; or relatively psychoneurotic conditions without important somatic components (Hawley, 1946).

PSYCHOTHERAPY, PSYCHOLOGY, AND OTHER PROFESSIONS

It is interesting in retrospect that the situation with regard to psychotherapy has changed so visibly since the preceding statement was made. Historically, the care and treatment of severe personality disturbances had been in the hands of the medical profession. Legally, the psychiatrist, as a physician, had the authority to treat patients and administer various therapies. In the past, as we have noted, psychologists were not concerned with such matters and confined their practical activities to test administration, re-education, remedial work, and various types of educational and vocational counseling. Even some of the leading clinical psychologists who contributed noticeably to the post-war development of the field were primarily concerned with diagnostic evaluations and research. However, the tremendous need for therapy, the use of psychologists as therapists in World War II, the subsequent expansion of clinical psychology, and certain specific movements within the latter helped bring psychotherapy within the field of psychology.

In addition to the legal and historical precedents for psychotherapeutic work in the field of medicine, there is also the complexity of psychosomatic problems which the physician regards as his domain. Many similar symptoms can be caused by either organic or psychological factors. In medical installations, of course, patients can be screened for possible somatic difficulties before being assigned to a psychologist for psychotherapy. In private practice, this cannot be accomplished so readily, although a large number of psychologists appear to have made some sort of collaborative arrangement with a physician and may require a physical examination or consultation before accepting a client for psychotherapy.

The enthusiastic expansion of clinical psychologists into what was regarded by psychiatrists as their domain was not without friction and conflict. At various times, considerable opposition was encountered from organized medical groups toward the practice of psychotherapy by clinical psychologists. Some of this was perhaps well-intentioned, but some was viewed by psychologists as unnecessarily restrictive and not necessarily in the public interest. Although it is not necessary here to review this history in any detail, it may be of interest to would-be clinical psychologists to at least make reference to one earlier pronouncement which illustrates the nature of the conflict. The pronouncement in question was issued as a joint resolution by the executive councils of the American Medical Association, the American Psychiatric Association, and the American Psychoanalytic Association. Their views were expressed, in part, as follows:

Psychiatry is the medical specialty concerned with illness that has chiefly mental symptoms. The psychiatrist is also concerned with mental causes of physical illness, for we have come to recognize that physical symptoms may have mental causes just as mental symptoms may have physical causes. The psychiatrist, with or without consultation with other physicians, must select from the many different methods of treatment at his disposal those methods that he considers appropriate to the particular patient. His treatment may be medicinal or surgical, physical (as electroshock) or psychological. The systematic application of the methods of psychological medicine to the treatment of illness, particularly as these methods involve gaining an understanding of the emotional state of the patient and aiding him to understand himself, is called psychotherapy. This special form of medical treatment may be highly developed, but it remains simply one of the possible methods of treatment to be selected for use according to medical criteria for use when it is indicated. *Psychotherapy is a form of medical treatment* and does not form the basis for a separate profession.

Other professional groups such as psychologists, teachers, ministers, lawyers, social workers, and vocational counselors, of course, use psychological understanding in carrying out their professional functions. Members of these professional groups are not thereby practicing medicine. The application of psychological methods to the treatment of illness is a medical function. Any physician may utilize the skills of others in his professional work, but he remains responsible legally and morally, for the diagnosis and for the treatment of his patient.

The medical profession fully endorses the appropriate utilization of the skills of psychologists, social workers, and other professional personnel in contributing roles in settings directly supervised by physicians. It further recognizes that these professions are entirely independent and autonomous when medical questions are not involved; but when members of these professions contribute to the diagnosis and treatment of illness, their professional contributions must be coordinated under medical responsibility (Resolution, etc., 1954; italics added).

The above statement is quite specific and clearly emphasizes the primary medical responsibility for the diagnosis and treatment of "mental illness." The problem of what constitutes mental illness and how it is defined or conceptualized is indeed a knotty one and certain aspects of it will be discussed in a later chapter. Nevertheless, a few points can be made here. On the basis of traditional social custom and legal prescription, the province of illness is the domain of the physician and few would argue wih this view. When we enter the field of "mental illness," however, we encounter a number of semantic and conceptual problems. If we agree that illness is the responsibility of the medical profession, then logically this would include all forms of illness including "mental illness." The concept of "mental illness," however, is a very nebulous and ambiguous one, and without specific delimitation or definition could include the entire range of psychological adjustment or maladjustment. To perpetuate what Szasz (1961) has called the "myth of mental illness" is to unnecessarily limit our views of behavioral disturbance and to exclude the potential contribution of other fields in coping with such problems. For example, many patterns of behavioral dysfunction can be adequately conceptualized as the results of faulty learning, and learning is clearly a primary concern of the psychologist. To state that psychologists cannot be concerned with psychological phenomena is clearly a ludicrous position in the light of their contributions to the fields of behavioral disorder and behavior modification. However, as we have pointed out before, the psychologist had moved into this arena more recently and had to assert his claims for participation and demonstrate his capabilities.

In any event, in spite of such negative and limiting pronouncements, clinical psychologists became increasingly involved with the practice of psychotherapy. In fact, by 1960, a drastic change in the patterns of professional practice had taken place (Kelly, 1961). Diagnostic testing, which had been the single most frequently engaged in activity of the clinical psychologist, had diminished in importance and psychotherapy had clearly become the primary activity in terms of the time devoted to it. This trend has continued. In a recent survey of a sample of clinical psychologists, psychotherapy was once again indicated as the primary activity in terms of the percentage of professional time devoted to it (Garfield & Kurtz, 1976). Along with this trend there has been an increase in private practice among clinical psychologists, and psychotherapy appears to be a primary activity of such psychologists. Furthermore, as will be noted in later chapters, the application of psychological theories of learning and behavior modification to a wide variety of clinical problems has indicated dramatically the psychologist's contribution to the broad field of psychotherapy and behavior change (Bandura, 1969; Bergin & Garfield, 1971; Goldfried & Davison, 1976; Yates, 1970). Furthermore, psychologists have assumed the leadership in terms of research on psychotherapy and the value of their research training has been clearly visible in this area (Garfield & Bergin, 1978; Gurman & Razin, 1977; Kazdin & Wilson, 1978).

Since in our discussion of psychotherapy we have alluded to problems of professional practice and relationships to the medical profession, it may be well at this point to make some brief mention of the related matter of legal certification and licensure. Prior to the 1940's there was comparatively little activity concerning legal definitions of the psychologist. As a consequence, anyone could call himself a psychologist and present himself as such to the public. However, with the increasing growth and professionalization of clinical psychology, more attention was given this matter.

In the 1940's a few states did pass certification laws for psychologists, and by 1955 nine states had enacted such legislation and had established examining boards to evaluate candidates for certification. Such laws limited the title, psychologist, to the individuals who met the stated requirements. These developments constituted additional recognition of the professional activities of the qualified psychologist and such legal recognition continued to increase. By 1973, 46 of the states had enacted some form of legislation, either certification of title, or licensure to practice. A few years later, all 50 states had enacted such legislation, although in two states the legislative acts were later allowed to become inactive. It is thus apparent that a great change took place in the role and status of the clinical psychologist in a relatively short period of time.

OTHER FUNCTIONS OF THE CLINICAL PSYCHOLOGIST

At the present time, although the three primary functions of the clinical psychologist emphasized in the 1940's continue as activities of some importance, their relative significance has changed. Some new activities have also emerged, several of which will be mentioned briefly here and their relative importance commented upon.

One of the relatively newer functions of the clinical psychologist is related to developments in what has been designated as community psychology or community mental health. The roots of this development are diverse. One aspect is related to the enactment of federal legislation to upgrade mental health services and to provide services for the patients in their home community. Greater emphasis was also placed on preventative and outpatient services in the hope of cutting down long hospitalization and chronicity of disturbance. Another aspect was the need for additional personnel in the mental health field and the utilization of whatever help could be recruited to assist with this task (Matarazzo, 1971). Because the limited number of professional personnel precludes much intensive work with any large number of disturbed people, and it appeared difficult to train enough professional workers to handle this task, considerable discussion took place concerning the best utilization of the trained manpower available (Albee, 1963, 1968; Felix, 1957). The increased emphasis on the possible prevention of mental disorders, along with utilization of nonprofessional personnel, had implications for the use of professional mental health workers in newer roles. In this way, their potential impact might be increased. A few examples may illustrate what is involved here. In terms of the prevention of disorder, for example, considerable importance would be attached to working with children. Since practically all children spend a large share of their waking time in school, teachers are potentially key individuals in fostering positive adjustment and preventing maladjustment. By working as a consultant to a school system and with individual teachers on specific problems, the clinical psychologist could have a potentially greater mental health impact than by working with a limited number of individual clients.

A somewhat comparable situation exists in our large mental hospitals where the ratio of professional staff to the number of patients precludes individual therapeutic efforts, except with a very small number of patients. The personnel who have the greatest contact with patients are such people as aids, practical nurses, volunteers, and the like. Again, by working with such people in a consultative and educational role, the psychologist may bring to bear his expertise in such a fashion that a more therapeutic milieu is established on the wards, and the patient–staff interactions also become more therapeutic. In a similar fashion, if increased attention is devoted to the fostering of positive personality adjustment and the prevention of future personality or behavioral disorder, modifications in the role and activities of the clinical psychologist would be called for. In particular, the training role of the clinical psychologist would continue to increase in importance as more "nonprofessionals" are trained to perform a variety of therapeutic and preventative functions. More will be said about such developments in a later chapter.

Another somewhat closely related occurrence has been the gradual increase in the amount of time devoted by clinical psychologists to administrative roles and functions. In the survey of clinical psychologists mentioned earlier, administration was the third most frequently engaged-in activity (Garfield & Kurtz, 1976). In fact, the time devoted to administrative activities was approximately half that devoted to individual psychotherapy. With the increase in community mental health centers, and with a more tolerant and permissive view toward who may administer such centers, there has been a decided increase in the percentage of psychologists who direct clinics or centers, who are responsible for the administration of significant state and federal mental health programs, and who even function as directors of state mental hospitals. Perhaps as many as 25% of clinical psychologists devote a major share of their professional time to responsibilities of an administrative nature. Although administration is thus one of the important functions of clinical psychologists, it is, of course, not a function unique to clinical psychology or is instruction in this function provided in most university training programs.

Another more recent development which can be mentioned briefly here is that of health psychology. Traditionally, clinical psychologists have been closely identified with personality and behavioral disorders, and have tended to work in psychiatric and similar installations. In recent years, however, a number of clinical psychologists have become interested in applying behavioral knowledge and techniques to more general areas of health and medicine. Thus, work to reduce smoking and obesity, to foster positive health behaviors, and related developments are part of this trend (Matarazzo, 1980).

At the present time, therefore, clinical psychologists are engaged in a variety of activities and function including diagnostic testing, psychotherapy, research, community consultation, training and administration, as well as being involved in research and practice in the general area of health. Thus, the roles and functions of the clinical psychologist continue to expand and change over time. The original involvement with diagnostic testing has diminished in relative importance and has been superceded by the expansion of interest in psychotherapeutic activities. In fact, it is probably fair to say that a large number of students who decide to enter the field of clinical psychology do so because of their interest in psychotherapy and their belief that clinical psychology is largely synonymous with psychotherapy. However, as has been indicated, clinical psychology embraces much more than psychotherapy. Furthermore, psychotherapy is by no means limited to psychologists. Psychiatrists, counseling psychologists, social workers, counselors, clergymen, and many others engage in various forms of counseling and psychotherapy. Thus, those individuals who seek a career as a psychotherapist have a number of professions from which to choose.

In the past, the main distinguishing characteristic of clinical psychology as compared with most of the mental health professions was its emphasis on research training and a research orientation. Although this emphasis has lessened, in part due to the emergence of the more purely professional programs, it is still nevertheless, an important feature of clinical psychology. Even the professional schools provide some training in research procedures and methodology so that their students can comprehend and appraise the research literature in clinical psychology. Thus, individuals interested in clinical psychology should expect at least some emphasis on research and can choose among prospective programs in terms of the importance placed on research training. For the research-oriented individual, clinical psychology in terms of the Boulder model offers a variety of professional activities, including the challenging opportunity of carrying out research on a number of clinically important activities. Apart from the important role that psychologists have played in research in the area of psychotherapy, there is the important area of psychopathology where psychologists have made, and can continue to make, important contributions. Helping to discover potential causes of mental disturbance is of greatest social importance for it opens the possibility of preventing such disturbance.

In any event, it is hoped that the reader now has some conception of what the clinical psychologist does and of the general emphases in his graduate training. The rest of the book will delve more specifically into the functions and techniques of the clinical psychologist, the theoretical orientations which prevail, and some of the professional and scientific problems he or she faces.

REFERENCES

Albee, G. W. American psychology in the sixties. *American Psychologist,* 1963, *18,* 90–95.

Albee, G. W. Conceptual models and manpower requirements in psychology. *American Psychologist,* 1968, *23,* 317–320.

American Psychological Association, Committee on Training in Clinical Psychology. Recommended graduate training program in clinical psychology. *American Psychologist,* 1947, *2,* 539–558.

American Psychological Association approved doctoral programs in clinical, counseling, and school psychology: 1980. *American Psychologist,* 1980, 35, 1116–1118.

Bandura, A. *Principles of behavior modification.* New York: Holt, Rinehart and Winston, 1969.

Beers, C. W. *A mind that found itself.* (7th Ed.) Garden City, NY: Doubleday, 1948.

Bergin, A. E., & Garfield, S. L. (Eds.), *Handbook of psychotherapy and behavior change.* New York: Wiley, 1971.

Boring, E. G. *A history of experimental psychology.* New York: Century Co., 1929.

Deutsch, A. *The mentally ill in America.* (2nd Ed.) New York: Columbia University Press, 1949.

Felix, R. H. The role of psychology in the mental health effort. In C. R. Strother (Ed.), *Psychology and mental health.* Washington, D.C.: American Psychological Association, 1957.

Freud, S. *The history of the psychoanalytic movement.* In *The basic writings of Sigmund Freud.* New York: Modern Library, Random House, 1938.

Garfield, S. L. Historical introduction. In B. B. Wolman (Ed.), *Handbook of clinical psychology.* New York: McGraw-Hill, 1965, Pp. 125–140.

Garfield, S. L. Clinical psychology and the search for identity. *American Psychologist*, 1966, *21*, 353–362.
Garfield, S. L., & Bergin, A. E. (Eds.), *Handbook of psychotherapy and behavior change.* (2nd Ed.) New York: Wiley, 1978.
Garfield, S. L., & Kurtz, R. Clinical psychologists in the 1970s. *American Psychologist*, 1976, *31*, 1–9.
Goldfried, M. R., & Davison, G. C. *Clinical behavior therapy.* New York: Holt, Rinehart and Winston, 1976.
Gurman, A. S., & Razin, A. M. (Eds.), *Effective psychotherapy: A handbook of research.* Oxford: Pergamon, 1977.
Hawley, P. R. The importance of clinical psychology in a complete medical program. *Journal of Consulting Psychology*, 1946, *10*, 292–300.
Healy, W., & Bronner, A. F. The child guidance clinic: Birth and growth of an idea. In L. G. Lowrey (Ed.), *Orthopsychiatry 1923–1948. Retrospect and prospect.* New York: American Orthopsychiatric Association, 1948, Pp. 14–49.
Hoch, E. L., Ross, A. O., & Winder, C. L. (Eds.), *Professional preparation of clinical psychologists.* Washington, D.C.: American Psychological Association, 1966.
Hutt, M. L., & Milton, E. O. An analysis of duties performed by clinical psychologists in the Army. *American Psychologist*, 1947, *2*, 52–56.
Kazdin, A. E., & Wilson, G. T. Criteria for evaluating psychotherapy. *Archives of General Psychiatry*, 1978, *35*, 407–416.
Kelly, E. L. Clinical Psychology—1960: Report of survey findings. *American Psychological Association, Division of Clinical Psychology Newsletter*, 1961, 14 (1), 1–11.
Korman, M. National conference on levels and patterns of professional training in psychology. The major themes. *American Psychologist*, 1974, *29*, 441–449.
Louttit, C. M. The nature of clinical psychology. *Psychological Bulletin*, 1939, *36*, 361–389.
Matarazzo, J. D. Some national developments in the utilization of nontraditional mental health manpower. *American Psychologist*, 1971, *26*, 363–372.
Matarazzo, J. D. Behavioral health and behavioral medicine: Frontiers for a new health psychology. *American Psychologist*, 1980, *35*, 807–817.
Peterson, D. R. Attitudes concerning the Doctor of Psychology program. *Professional Psychology*, 1969, *1*, 44–47.
Peterson, D. R., Eaton, M. M., Levine, A. R., & Snepp, F. P. Development of Doctor of Psychology programs and experiences of graduates through 1980. *The Rutgers Professional Psychology Review*, 1980, *2*, 29–39.
Pintner, R. *Intelligence testing.* New York: Henry Holt, 1931.
Pottharst, K. E. To renew vitality and provide a challenge in training-The California School of Professional Training. *Professional Psychology*, 1970, *1*, 123–130.
Raimy, V. (Ed.), *Training in clinical psychology.* New York: Prentice-Hall, 1950.
Resolution on Relations of Medicine and Psychology approved by the Board of Trustees of the American Medical Association, the Council of the American Psychiatric Association, and the Executive Council of the American Psychoanalytic Association (1954).
Roe, A., Gustad, J. W., Moore, B. V., Ross, S., & Skodak, M. (Eds.), *Graduate education in psychology.* Washington, D.C.: American Psychological Association, 1959.
Rowntree, L. G., *et al.* Causes of rejection and the incidence of defects among 18 and 19 year old selective service registrants. *Journal of the American Medical Association*, 1943, *123*, 181–185.
Sarason, S. B., & Gladwin, T. Psychological and cultural problems in mental subnormality: A review of research. *Genetic Psychology Monographs*, 1958, *57*, 3–290.
Shaffer, L. F. Of whose reality I cannot doubt. *American Psychologist*, 1953, *8*, 608–623.

Shakow, D. Clinical psychology: An evaluation. In L. G. Lowrey (Ed.), *Orthopsychiatry 1923–1948. Retrospect and prospect.* New York: American Orthopsychiatric Association, 1948, Pp. 231–247.

Szasz, T. *The myth of mental illness: Foundations of a theory of personal conduct.* New York: Hoeber-Harper, 1961.

Watson, N., Cobby, G. R., Johnston, J. H., & Rimm, D. C. Standards in the education of professional psychologists. The resolutions of the conference at Virginia Beach. *American Psychologist,* 1981, *36,* 514–519.

Watson, R. I. A brief history of clinical psychology. *Psychological Bulletin,* 1953, *50,* 321–346.

White, R. W. *The abnormal personality.* New York: Ronald Press, 1948.

Yates, A. J. *Behavior therapy.* New York: Wiley, 1970.

Personality and Behavior Theories

Personality or behavior theory of some sort plays a significant part in the clinical operations of the psychologist. Not only are the different diagnostic and therapeutic techniques related to specific views of personality and behavior, but the clinical psychologist as an interpreter, integrator, and evaluator of various types of clinical data and observations is himself influenced or guided by some explicit or implicit theory of human behavior. Because the theory or view of personality and behavior which the psychologist holds influences how he functions with regard to clients as well as the types of clinical techniques used and developed, it is important to examine some of the currently popular theories and to discuss their implications for clinical practice.

At the present time there are a variety of personality theories that have been developed to describe and explain human behavior. They have been derived from specific settings and contexts and from work with different populations. Thus, the various theories have tended to emphasize somewhat particular or circumscribed features of human functioning. The backgrounds and disciplines of the individuals who have developed these theories have also varied and, as might be anticipated, so have their concepts and terminology. Fairly comprehensive summaries of these theoretical views are available in several books and can be consulted by the interested reader (Bischof, 1970; Ewen, 1980; Hall & Lindzey, 1978; Maddi, 1980). This chapter presents only a few of these viewpoints, and they will probably be familiar to many readers. They have been selected to illustrate the diversity that exists, as well as being orientations which appear to be of more than passing significance as far as clinical psychology is concerned. Furthermore, the point of emphasis will be to illuminate the significance or relevance of the theory for clinical operations, rather than to provide a comprehensive presentation of the theory itself.

PSYCHOANALYTIC THEORY

Probably the most influential theory of personality developed thus far has been the psychoanalytic system developed by Sigmund Freud (1938a, 1949). Freud, who was born in 1856 and died in 1939, was trained as a physician. He had an interest in neurology and thus was concerned with the treatment of "nervous disorders." Among the patients in his medical practice in Vienna, he was particularly attracted to the problems of neurotic individuals who exhibited dramatic symptoms for which no organic basis could be found. It was primarily as a result of this experience that Freud developed his theory of unconscious motivation and his conceptions of personality development. In other words, it was as a practicing clinician working with a particular sample of disturbed people at a particular period of time that Freud drew his observations, derived his hypotheses, and eventually formulated his theoretical ideas.

While the Freudian system is a fairly complex one, we need only be concerned here with some of his main ideas which are particularly important for such matters as clinical diagnosis and therapy. One such view was the concept of *psychic determinism*. Influenced strongly by the deterministic and positivistic views of nineteenth-century science, Freud felt that all behavior has some cause or source of motivation. According to him, nothing happens by chance, and even such occurrences as common mistakes, accidents or forgetting are not happenstance; rather, there is a specific psychological cause for such events, even though we are not usually aware of them. In his *Psychopathology of Everyday Life* (1938b), Freud described such phenomena at length and provided a variety of common illustrations.

Such a guiding principle is easily applied to a variety of happenings in the clinical situation, and when combined with other related theoretical views, allows one to offer several explanations for the behavior exhibited by the client in his interaction with the clinician. Furthermore, since on the basis of other theoretical constructs, it is believed that the client is *unaware* of the true cause of his behavior, it becomes apparent that the clinician cannot take the client's explanation of his behavior at face value. For example, if the client is late for his appointment, he may apologize profusely and tell the psychologist that his bus was late, that he had trouble starting his car, or that his professor did not dismiss the class on time. Such socially acceptable and conventional reasons would be viewed as attempts on the part of the client to explain his behavior, but they would not necessarily be viewed as the true reasons. Hypotheses or explanations which might be offered by the clinician in this hypothetical situation might center around the client's negative view of the clinician or therapy and his unconscious desire to avoid the situation or to reduce the amount of time of the clinical encounter. The reasons for being late would thus center around motives out of awareness that reflected some negative or avoidance attitudes regarding therapy.

The deterministic viewpoint thus provides a general framework for clinically viewing the behavior of the client. Closely related to this conception is the principle, already alluded to, that the individual may be unaware of the true determinants of his behavior. Certain motives or ideas may exert a driving force on the individual's behavior, but the individual is unaware of them. Here we have another cardinal principle in the Freudian scheme, that of unconscious motivation. According to Freud's views, mental life was composed of three categories or types of phenomena—conscious thoughts, ideas, or wishes, and preconscious and unconscious thoughts, ideas, and wishes. At the conscious level, one is aware of ideational, cognitive, and motivational aspects that are going on within one's self. We are aware that we are hungry, or that we must study for an examination, or that we must hurry to get to work on time. One may also be aware of the fact that one's father is a real reactionary and that a fair amount of hostility and anger get stirred up in discussions with him about dress, sex, drugs, and the world situation. On the other hand, Freud hypothesized that certain ideas and wishes are so emotionally charged and potentially threatening to the individual that they are literally excluded from consciousness through a process labeled *repression*. Such material would be viewed as unconscious and not available to the individual's awareness. The term, preconscious, denoted memories which were not recalled immediately, but which, with some effort on the part of the individual, could be brought to awareness. In psychoanalytic theory, however, unconscious motivation receives the greatest emphasis and deserves further discussion. Nevertheless, to place the concept in proper perspective it is necessary to go into some other aspects of psychoanalytic theory.

PERSONALITY STRUCTURE

According to Freud, the basic structure of personality consisted of three major components or systems. These were viewed as dynamic and interacting systems and were designated the id, the ego, and the superego. In this structure the id was viewed as the primary and original system from which the ego and superego become differentiated through later development. The id is the source of psychological energy and instinctual strivings. Thus, it is the source of motives and drives—the motivating or driving force of the personality. While the id, therefore, is the repository for all sorts of instinctual strivings, some are accorded special significance—for example, sex and aggression. We shall have more to say about them later. In any event, the id is conceptualized as the primary source of psychic activity and as a source of tension which seeks release or discharge.

Closely related to the id, and derived from it, is the ego. It has frequently been referred to as fulfilling an executive or integrating function within the personality. It develops in part as a means or mechanism for satisfying the urges of the id. Whereas the id appears to operate primarily according to the *pleasure principle,* seeking the reduction of tension and the satisfaction of needs, the ego operates in line with the demands of reality, or the *reality principle.* The ego thus has the task of attempting to satisfy the instinctual strivings emanating from the id in accord with the realities of the situation the individual faces. A newborn infant cries when it is hungry in response to the organic tensions built up by the state of hunger. Id strivings or functions can therefore be inferred. Nevertheless, there is as yet no ego development evident in the infant. He is clearly unable to appraise the situation realistically and then to procede to satisfy his needs. Such ego activity is possible only at a later stage of development. Nevertheless, as the individual grows and matures, ego processes and functions develop and serve as mediators between the instinctive demands of the id, the reality demands of the environment, as well as certain inputs from the superego. As conceptualized here, the ego has to integrate these conflicting demands and, within the resources of the individual and the environment, attempt some resolution or course of satisfactory action. In Freud's scheme, the id appeared primary. Not only was the ego derived from the id, but the id remained the source of energy for all activity. More recently, some psychoanalysts have attempted a modification of this view in what has sometimes been referred to as "ego-psychology" (Hartmann, 1964). In this view, the ego is accorded its own conflict-free area of autonomy and a source of energy separate from the id. This is, however, a modification of the basic Freudian scheme.

The remaining component of the personality, the superego, is the last to be developed. Popularly equated with the term, conscience, the superego represents, according to Freudian theory, the internalization of the moral and ethical systems of the individual's culture as interpreted to him by parental figures. The superego develops as a result of parental prohibitions and rewards with reference to specific modes of conduct. The child learns what is good and bad, and gradually incorporates them into her own value system. This internalized system of values then also exerts an influence on the individual's behavior, specifically on the ego as it functions in relation to id impulses and the realities of the environment. The ego, theoretically, thus has to reckon with the superego as well as with the id. In terms of this conception, an individual with strong sexual drives and a fairly strong superego which prohibits the satisfaction of such drives, would be in a state of internal conflict and tension. Since sexual and aggressive impulses or drives are the ones most frequently prohibited by society at large, these tend to be potentially the greatest sources of internal conflict.

In line with this dynamic conception of personality, neurotic symptoms or disturbed behaviors were viewed as the outcome of internalized or repressed conflicts. In a sense, the symptoms were the manifestations of an internal conflict, and in some dramatic instances, the specific symptom itself symbolized the nature of the conflict. For example, a functional or hysterical paralysis of a person's right arm might be related to a conflict between the desire to strike one's father and the prohibition that one always respects the father and is deferential to him. The implications of this scheme for diagnosis and therapy are reasonably clear. One must look beyond the symptoms in order to discover the essential causes of disturbance. The disturbed individual himself will, of course, be unaware of what is causing his difficulty but will seek help primarily for his particular symptoms. Psychotherapy (in this instance psychoanalysis) will be concerned in part with helping the individual gradually to trace back the relationship from the symptom to the repressed conflict which underlies it. Although this is an overly simplified version of what may take place in psychoanalytic therapy, it does serve to show the relationship of the clinical operations to the theory on which they are based. In essence, an attempt is made to gradually overcome repressions and resistances to such probings in order to bring conflictual material to the level of awareness. When repressed material of this kind is unearthed in therapy, it is hypothesized that their threatening qualities and harmful effects are gradually diminished. The individual, with the understanding and help of the therapist, can face up to and understand the sources of his difficulties. Theoretically, in successful therapy his symptoms should decrease or dissolve since he is now more freely aware of his difficulties, and in a sense, has overcome the source of the problem. At least this is the psychoanalytic view.

PSYCHOSEXUAL DEVELOPMENT

During his lifetime, Freud promulgated several different views pertaining to basic drives underlying human behavior. One of his last schemas embodied two all-embracing and opposite forces—a life instinct and a death instinct.

The life force is behind efforts for self-preservation and the preservation of the species and generally motivates more constructive behaviors. The death instinct, on the other hand, leads to aggression and destruction. There is a particular energy source, the libido, which is part of the life force and which receives special emphasis in psychoanalytic theory. The libido comprises sexual energy, and as Freud viewed sexuality in a very broad way, it plays a central role in his theory. According to Freud's theory of psychosexual development, the sexual drive, or libidinal energy, is present in infancy. Sexuality in infancy and early childhood is, of course, quite different from sexuality in adulthood. Libidinal energy in the infant is centered in the mouth and the oral cavity and thus the first stage of psychosexual development is termed the *oral phase*. Later, the anal region becomes the focus, and still later the individual progresses to the phallic phase of development, somewhere around the age of five. During the first five years or so, which Freud considered to be the most important for personality development, the child progresses through these various infantile stages with libidinal energy centered on the various erogenous zones, the body parts or organs which provide pleasure.

The particular experiences the child has during these stages of development may affect significantly his developing personality. For example, during the anal stage, the type of toilet training utilized by the mother may reinforce certain patterns of response which influence certain types or traits of personality. If the mother is overly strict in this training the child may actually hold back on "doing his duty" and refuse to part with his feces. He may develop into an "anal-retentive" character, in Freudian terms, and later exhibit obstinate and miserly patterns of behavior. Other types of maternal handling at the various stages of development may lead to different kinds of personality formation.

During the phallic stage the sex organs become the center of libidinal energy and autoerotic activity ensues. During this phase also, the well-known Oedipus Complex makes its appearance, during which the child desires his opposite sexed parent and has hostile or negative feelings toward the other parent. The young boy, for example, becomes conflicted over his positive feelings for his mother and his negative feelings toward his father. As part of this, he may develop fears that his father may punish him and, more specifically, castrate him. Freud termed this phenomenon, "castration anxiety," and believed that it led to a repression of the sexual feelings toward the mother and an identification with the father. A somewhat comparable, but at the same time different, development occured with girls, with less strong repression being characteristic of the latter. How the Oedipus Complex was handled or resolved was considered of crucial importance for the later personality adjustment of the individual.

With the repression of the sexual strivings occurring during the Oedipus

Complex the individual then enters the *latency period*. This period is marked by the repression of sexual strivings and an outward lack of interest in such matters. With the arrival of adolescence, however, there is a reawakening or resurgence of such drives. At this time, at the genital stage, the individual turns his interests and energies to other people and away from himself and his own body. Libidinal energy becomes directed toward others. At first, there is a close attachment to members of the same sex; later, attention begins to focus more exclusively on the other sex as "object choices."

If development proceeds relatively smoothly, then the individual reaches and remains at a genital level of adjustment. He is able to maintain a normal heterosexual relationship which is most characteristic of the typical adult style of life. If, however, development has been blocked or impaired, the individual may not reach or remain at this level. Here, two other Freudian concepts may be introduced, *fixation* and *regression*. If a person's development has been characterized by a great deal of anxiety and insecurity, he may be fearful of new demands that require additional maturity on his part. As a result, he may become fixated at a given stage or level of development and fail to progress further. In another instance, an individual may progress to a higher stage of development, but upon finding it threatening or frustrating may retreat to an earlier developmental stage. Fixation and regression are also related, in that when a person regresses he tends to regress to a stage upon which there was some degree of fixation. A person who has been very dependent on her parents may return to the parental home whenever stress is encountered. In a similar fashion, some men are never able to fulfill the heterosexual role of marital partner, and after making a few attempts at relating to women, prefer to live with their mother or with some bachelor friends. Theoretically, such fixations and regressions can be understood in the light of the personality development of the individual involved.

ANXIETY AND DEFENSE

We have now reviewed briefly some aspects of psychoanalytic theory that have dealt with personality structure and development, as well as with some basic formulations pertaining to motivation. Closely related are some other concepts that relate to the adjustment process of the individual. One such key concept is anxiety, an apprehension or dread about some anticipated but unknown occurrence. As contrasted with fear, a response to some realistic danger, anxiety is more diffuse and generally the real stimulus for it is unknown. It is also a very painful state. As a consequence, the individual (or more precisely in psychoanalytic theory, the ego) attempts to avoid anxiety through a variety of acquired mechanisms, generally referred to as defense mechanisms (A. Freud, 1946). The general purpose of defense mechanisms is to reduce threat or anxiety, and to the extent that a particular mechanism is successful in doing so, it tends to be reinforced and to become an habitual part of a person's pattern of response.

Actually, we have already made reference to some mechanisms of defense—repression, fixation, and regression. They are means of handling anxiety and easing tension. The emphasis in the use of defense mechanisms is thus on anxiety reduction. Excessive use or reliance on defense mechanisms may impede other aspects of development, including the attainment of more mature patterns of behavior. Nevertheless, they bring some modicum of relief from unpleasantness and disquietude, and thus on a short-term basis are tension reducing and are consequently reinforced.

The variety of defensive maneuvers which the ego can employ in warding off anxiety would appear to be great. Nevertheless, some appear with such frequency and regularity that they have received particular attention. In addition to those already mentioned, a few others can be discussed because of the frequent reference to them in clinical work. One such mechanism is projection. In the use of this mechanism or defense the individual projects the negative feelings or ideas that he harbors onto someone else. If he has hostile and aggressive impulses toward others, he instead attributes such motives to others. Other people hate him instead of his hating them. This mechanism is presumed to occur to an extreme degree in the case of delusions of persecution where the individual believes everyone is out to get him, or that some conspiracy exists against him. Projection appears to be related to the rather common mechanism of rationalization which many of us employ in order to shift the blame for some of our shortcomings onto others. If we do poorly in a given course, we can say the professor was unfair or that it was an unusually boring course. In both mechanisms, the ego defends itself against self-blame or discomfort by shifting the blame elsewhere.

Another defense mechanism emphasized in psychoanalytic theory is that of reaction formation. Here, a negative feeling or thought is replaced by its opposite. A person with strong destructive impulses behaves in an unusually considerate and kindly manner. A person who may have tied tin cans to dogs' tails in his earlier years becomes a crusader against vivisection and research with animals. One of the problems here is the matter of the correct interpretation of a given individual's behavior. If a person appears consistently kind and considerate, should we suspect him of repressed hostile motives to which he is reacting by means of reaction formation? In some instances the problem is difficult and too many amateur analysts are willing to interpret a variety of underlying motives at the drop of a hat. On the other hand, there are some instances where the behavior of the individual appears to be overdone, inappropriate, and compulsive in nature. In such instances, conceivably, one has some basis for clinical inferences or hypotheses. If other data appear to support such an hypothesis or be congruent with it, then one may have more confidence in it. On the other hand, it should be apparent that if one hypothesizes unconscious dynamics, proof or disproof of the clinical hypothesis may be difficult to come by.

While the previous review of psychoanalytic theory is a very brief synopsis of some of the major tenets of the theory, it will suffice for our purposes. Enough has been said to provide a framework for illustrating the implications of the theory for clinical practice, and a few references to such have already been made.

The emphasis on the importance of early childhood for later personality development with the related stress on the infantile stages of psychosexual development and the resolution of the Oedipus Complex, would, of course, tend to focus the clinician's attention on such material. Thus, the early life history of the client, and particularly his relationships with his parents, would receive special attention in the clinical investigation of the client's difficulties. Conceivably, the current situation would be viewed as of lesser importance or as a repetition of earlier problems.

In line with this point of view, greater attention would be paid to unconscious motives and conflicts than to other types of material. Slips of the tongue, blocking, forgetting, and avoidance of certain kinds of topics would be attended to closely as sources of clinical inference and as leads for future explorations. This type of theoretical orientation can also be utilized for interpreting the behavior of the client in the interview situation as well as his performance on certain tests. For example, the behavior of an attractive female client who leans forward toward the therapist and looks at him rather intently may be judged to be seductive and related to earlier conflicts with her fahter. The way a person responds to items on a standard test of intelligence may also be interpreted, in varying degrees, from a psychoanalytic point of view, for example, when the subject incorrectly hears a word which the examiner has asked him to define and instead responds with a definition for a different but similar sounding word. Many other examples could be given but these can serve for the time being. They help to illustrate how the behavior and interpretaion of the clincian may be guided or influenced by the theoretical views he holds.

The types of techniques the clinician uses will also be influenced by his theoretical preferences, although other considerations such as validity and economy may also play a role in such decisions. Projective techniques such as the Rorschach or the Thematic Apperception Test, to be described in more detail later, are also more likely to be used for diagnostic work by psychologists with a psychoanalytic or dynamic frame of reference than they are by psychologists with a more behavioristic or scientific orientation. This is because these techniques, as developed and used by psychologists, are believed to provide data or cues about unconscious motives, conflicts, and defenses of the subject. Obviously, if one believes that such material is of primary importance in understanding the individual and his problem, then he will certainly be inclined to utilize techniques that he believes will help him in this regard. It should also be mentioned that the same techniques can be used or interpreted in different ways, depending on the theoretical preferences of the clinician.

The therapeutic procedures and goals of psychoanalytic or psychoanalytically oriented psychotherapists, as alluded to earlier, will also differ from most of those who follow other psychotherapeutic approaches. Although psychoanalytic therapy will be described in more detail in a later chapter, a few additional illustrations of how the therapy is related to the psychoanalytic theory of personality may be mentioned here. The attempt to recall forgotten or repressed material, the significance of childhood experiences, and the general framework for interpreting much of the client's behavior have already been touched upon previously. It can be added here that the therapist would assume that unconscious material is repressed because it is painful and threatening. It is also defended against by a variety of defense mechanisms. To proceed quickly or to offer interpretations to the client about some of his underlying motives before he is ready to accept them may increase his anxiety or induce him to leave therapy. Consequently, the therapist must gain the confidence of the client and proceed very cautiously. This, as well as other considerations in this type of therapy, implies that therapy will not be brief, but will last for some period of time. Since, theoretically, the therapist is not treating the symptom about which the client complains, but is exploring the factors that underlie them and have led to their formation, a basic personality change is sought via this approach to therapy. Since many aspects of the individual are investigated during the extended psychotherapy sessions, it is expected, also, that the client will gain newer and deeper insights into himself, and such insights are important features of the treatment.

In concluding this treatment of psychoanalytic theory, a few words on research are also in order. A good theory of personality should not only function as a guide for clinical practice but should serve also as a guide or stimulus for research. In this regard, psychoanalysis presents a somewhat mixed picture. Some specific aspects of the theory have received experimental research (Sears, 1943, 1944; Hilgard, 1952), and some parts have been a stimulus to research and have received some experimental confirmation. Yet, a number of problems have been encountered in this regard and conclusive validation of the theory has not yet been secured, or is it likely that such validation will ever be secured. The comprehensiveness of the theory and the conceptual terms used make it extremely difficult to really test the theory in any systematic way. Furthermore, the great majority of psychoanalysts have not been research oriented, have not seen fit to question or test the theory in any systematic fashion, and have not been eager to allow other research investigators to study their psychoanalytic work.

There is also a particular type of problem encountered in evaluating psychoanalytic theory that has been commented upon by several critics in the past. As stated by Heidbreder (1933, p. 401), the problem is as follows:

> This situation, in fact, is a special case of a logical difficulty which confronts any attempt to evaluate the theory from the standpoint of science: it is impossible either to prove or to disprove the psychoanalytic theories on the basis of scientific evidence. It is, in fact, impossible to prove them because it is impossible to disprove them. Science in the end appeals to experimental evidence, and a crucial experiment is one that gives a yes or no answer to some question. The experiment, therefore, must be put in such a way as to make possible an answer of either 'Yes' or 'No'; or of 'Yes—in a given percentage of cases.' It is for this reason that science insists on countng negative cases. But the psychoanalytic theory, as it is now formulated, makes a negative case impossible. For example, if the analysis discloses a sex complex, the theory is confirmed. If it does not, it has failed to do so because the analysis has encountered a stubborn resistance, hence a particularly serious sex complex; and again the theory is confirmed. This illustration is less subtle than many that might have been chosen, but it indicates the essential nature of the difficulty.
>
> From the standpoint of science, this question of evidence constitutes the most serious obstacle in the way of judging the theory.

Despite such problems, the theory has been influential in generating a moderate amount of research and in helping to stimulate investigations of specific areas in the field of personality. Without question, it has been the most influential theory of personality. However, it would appear that its popularity has already peaked.

DERIVATIONS AND VARIATIONS ON A THEME BY FREUD

As most students of psychology know, Freud had a number of early disciples who later broke with him and developed their own theories and schools of thought. In addition, there were other significant individuals who were at first influenced by Freud's thinking, but later went on to formulate theories of personality which diverged in important respects from psychoanalysis. It is not the author's purpose to present a review of all such views in this chapter. Courses in the psychology of personality, or more specifically, those labeled "Theories of Personality" cover these topics as their primary content and students who pursue a career in clinical psychology or related fields will normally take one or more such courses. Our present purpose, as indicated earlier, is merely to introduce the reader to some of these theories and to their significance for the activities and orientation of the clinical psychologist.

In part because of personality differences, as well as because of theoretical differences, a number of individuals who had earlier adhered to the psychoanalytic school, broke with Freud and went on to develop their own theoretical orientations. This development was an interesting and somewhat unique one as far as the history of psychology goes. Although there have been different theories and theoretical controversies within the field of psychology proper, the general tendency has been to resolve controversy by recourse to experimentation in the laboratory. The idea of devising a "crucial" experiment to support or fail to support a theoretical hypothesis, while not always carried out, has been the model for resolving theoretical differences. The history of psychoanalysis, however, has been rather different. In the first place, psychoanalysis tended to be viewed as primarily the creation of one man. Thus, Freud had the final say on what formulations were to be accepted as being consistent with psychoanalytic doctrine, and what were heresy. The resolution of conflict was essentially an appeal to Freud's authority and many disputations involved quotations from Freud and interpretations of his pronouncements on the part of both parties to the dispute. Because the early history of the psychoanalytic movement was marked by frequent attacks from those outside the fold, there developed a rather close-knit group feeling with Freud as the master surrounded by a small group of devoted disciples. Critical deviations could not be tolerated and in the early years of psychoanalysis, Adler and Jung, two of the most respected early followers of Freud, broke with him to set up their own schools of thought. Later, Rank and others also separated and went their own ways. Some of these events are presented by Freud (1938b) in his own history of psychoanalysis, which is a most interesting account of what occurred.

Since that time there have been other developments that differ in important respects from Freudian theory. In some instances, such as the movement designated as "ego-psychology," the modifications in theory are viewed simply as extensions of Freudian theory, and such individuals view themselves as psychoanalysts following within the tradition of Freudian psychology. Erickson (1963), Hartmann (1964), and David Rapaport (1959) are probably the best known in this category. Even Erickson, who has directed attention to stages of development beyond those conceptualized by Freud, and has been more sensitive to social and cultural factors in development, has still appeared to function within a Freudian framework. These psychoanalysts or "Ego-psychologists," as they are sometimes referred to, have tended to elaborate or extend psychoanalytic theory, while at the same time adhering to its basic tenets.

Their primary contribution has been to emphasize more the autonomous functioning of the ego. In this conceptualization, the ego is accorded its own source of energy and is not seen as primarily dependent on energy sources arising from the id. This view of ego functioning leads also to a somewhat greater emphasis on noninstinctual sources of motivation. It would appear that such modifications in theory would also have some implications for both the appraisal and therapeutic handling of the client. More attention would probably be paid to the coping mechanisms and the strengths and assets of the individual client, as well as to the situations that appear to arouse anxiety.

There are others, however, who while retaining some Freudian concepts, such as unconscious motivation, have generally seen themselves as outside the Freudian fold. The degree of disengagement or rupture varies. In some instances the person may view himself as a psychoanalyst but as a non-Freudian, whereas in other cases, the divergent approach has taken on a new name and a different identity. Freud attempted to make clear that the views and practices of Adler and Jung were not to be considered psychoanalysis, and that he welcomed their designation as Individual Psychology and Analytical Psychology, respectively, to indicate their separateness. Such individuals as Horney have frequently been labeled as "Neo-Freudians," whereas Sullivan's views have been referred to as the "Interpersonal Theory of Psychiatry" as well as Neo-Freudian (Bischof, 1970; Gilbert, 1970). Because of such ambiguity in terminology, the terms psychoanalysis, psychoanalytic theory, and psychoanalytically oriented psychotherapy lack precise meaning.

For the purposes of this presentation something will be said about the main difference between some of the viewpoints referred to above and psychoanalysis, rather than in providing any detailed presentations of any specific orientations.

Probably, one of the main differences between Horney, Adler, and some of the others and Freud is a greater emphasis on social and cultural influences on personality development and less of a stress on biological determinants. The libido theory of Freud and the emphasis on psychosexual development is either not accepted or given a place of lesser importance (Munroe, 1955). Adler, for example, placed greater stress on the social and family structure within which the individual lived as well as the place of the person within the family. Early memories, feelings of inferiority, compensation, and the struggle for power were also concepts or attributes that received considerable emphasis in Individual Psychology. Adler also emphasized the social nature of the person, his or her own purposes, and the "life-style." The individual normally desires social belongingness and displays an interest in others. At the same time, each person tries to reach some goal of superiority and in this process develops his or her own life style. Initially, Adler focused on the person's feelings of inferiority and his compensatory strivings for superiority. Thus, the person who fancied himself physically weak might be concerned or preoccupied with attempts at building up his physique. Adler later, however, stressed more the creative aspects of the individual in his adjustment to his social environment and the development of his life style.

In general, Adler's later views departed rather markedly from those of Freud. He was more optimistic about the human condition than was Freud. He saw the person as having social interest and feeling and as having a need to belong to some social group. The importance given to psychosexual strivings and development in the Freudian scheme clearly was not apparent in Adler's view and was another important difference between the two theoretical orientations. The implications for practice would appear to be quite apparent from the differences in viewpoint. There would be little concern with infantile psychosexual development, castration anxiety, or the oedipal complex. Rather, the position of the individual in the family, particularly as related to his experiences as a child, would become a focus for investigating personality and some emphasis would be placed on the earliest memories and recollections which the individual can recall. Therapy, in addition, would attempt to assess the individual's goals and style of life, and help him to understand himself and to attain a more realistic and social view of his life. As stated by a leading follower of Adler, Individual Psychology represents a social rehabilitation therapy (Dreikurs, 1963, p. 255):

> Psychotherapy is not a medical treatment but an educational process. The person learns to understand himself and his life. Psychotherapy implies a change of concepts, a change in the modes of finding one's place, an increase in the feeling of belonging through the diminution of self-doubt and of inferiority feelings. This is the basis for all correctional efforts: To overcome doubts about value and ability, and to develop a sufficient Social Interest to cope successfully with life and people.

HORNEY

Another significant figure among the Neo-Freudians was Karen Horney. While particularly critical of the Freudian emphasis on instinctive drives and of Freud's views on the psychology of women, she also took a negative view of his analysis of the structure of personality into id, ego, and superego. At the same time, however, unlike Adler, she still saw herself as a psychoanalyst and conceived of her own views as corrections of the scheme sketched out by Freud. More specifically, she did accept the basic psychoanalytic notions of unconscious motivation and psychic determinism.

Much of Horney's written work attempts to depict neurotic behavior and the conflicts and dynamics underlying this behavior (1937, 1939, 1945, 1950). Many of her descriptions were very clinically astute and one had the feeling that she was describing individuals we know, and that the behaviors described were not far removed from our own. Her books are more readable than much of the professional literature and have attained popularity with the informed lay readership interested in psychoanalysis and personality.

One of Horney's fundamental concepts was that of basic anxiety. This refers to the feelings a child has of being helpless and isolated in a world that is potentially hostile. A variety of environmental influences may produce this insecurity in the child, but the most important are those pertaining to the relationship of the child to his parents. The child who is insecure and anxious will tend to develop various defenses or coping strategies to deal with or alleviate this very painful state. At one extreme, the child may become overly ingratiating or submissive in order to win love and affection; or at the other extreme, he may strike out at those who have denied him what he seeks. Originally, Horney (1942) described ten neurotic needs that represent ten different ways or strategies that neurotics have developed to cope with their anxiety and which over time become rather stable personality patterns. Among these are the neurotic need for power, the need for prestige, the need for perfection, and the neurotic need for affection. These needs can be viewed as strategies for coping with anxiety. Because these needs tend to become insatiable, they can never be fully satisfied and thus conflicts develop and endure. To overcome them, the neurotic needs to learn the reasons for his insatiable and unrealistic needs and to gradually give them up and replace them with a more realistic view of self.

Later, Horney (1945) grouped these neurotic needs into three broader patterns: (1) moving toward people; (2) moving away from people; and, (3) moving against people. Moving toward people, for example, includes the need for love and affection whereas moving against people could include the need for power and the need to exploit others. Each of these orientations may produce a conflict within the person, but the degree of conflict and the rigidity of the person's orientation distinguish normal behavior from that of the neurotic.

The above theoretical emphases have implications for the clinical work that is carried on with the client, although specific therapeutic techniques have not been spelled out by Horney. Although the approach was considered as psychoanalytic in many respects, the orientation and what is focused on in psychotherapy would be expected to differ from the lines of investigation in classical Freudian psychoanalysis. More attention would be paid to the conflicts of the person and his methods of handling them in his contemporary life situation than to the "vicissitudes of the instincts."

THE INTERPERSONAL PSYCHIATRY OF H. S. SULLIVAN

Harry Stack Sullivan, the last of the group of personality theorists to be discussed here, also made significant departures from Freud through his emphasis of the social psychological matrix in which development and adult behavior occurs. His theory is often referred to as the interpersonal theory of psychiatry because he viewed personality as being derived from and having meaning only in terms of interpersonal relations. Apart from secondary sources and the general textbooks on personality theory referred to earlier, the best references to his ideas are found in two of his published works, *Conceptions of Modern Psychiatry* (1947) and *The Interpersonal Theory of Psychiatry* (1953). In the present context we can only allude to some of the more prominent and distinguishing features of his theory.

In contrast to the other theorists mentioned previously, Sullivan derived a great deal of his experience from clinical work with patients diagnosed as schizophrenic. Furthermore, unlike Adler who had been a close associate of Freud, and Horney who had been identified with psychoanalysis for many years, Sullivan's training was influenced more by the American psychiatrists William Alanson White and Adolph Meyer. He was also influenced by the writings of a number of social scientists among whom G. H. Mead was prominent.

To Sullivan, personality is an abstract concept which derives from the interpersonal interaction between an individual and significant others. More specifically, he defines personality as "the relatively enduring pattern of recurrent interpersonal situations which characterize a human life" (1953, pp. 110–111). Sullivan has a developmental scheme of personality that differs from most of the other theoretical views presented and which employs a new terminology that he introduced. In some ways this makes Sullivan's theory somewhat more difficult to comprehend, but his justification was that many of the more common terms used have taken on so many different meanings that he preferred to use his own.

Since Sullivan's interpersonal theory cannot be presented here in any detail, it may be sufficient to make brief reference to a few of his main ideas. Sullivan tended to emphasize two sets of drives or motivational variables. One consisted of basic organic needs, whereas the other dealt with anxiety and the need for security. Although in later life one appears to be greatly concerned with security needs, it should be pointed out that both sets of needs or tensions usually have some association with interpersonal relationships. The infant, for example, is dependent on others and the caring for his physical needs involves a relationship, usually with the mother, which brings into play such other needs or features as tenderness and intimacy.

Sullivan also paid attention to the importance of the self in the psychological adjustment of the individual. In his view, the "self-system" develops out of the desire of the child to comfort himself interpersonally so as to receive tenderness and positive reinforcement from the mother and to avoid anxiety. Sullivan appears to emphasize particularly the importance of the avoidance of anxiety in this development. The matrix, however, clearly involves interpersonal relationships. Furthermore, since the avoidance of anxiety is an important aspect of adjustment, the self, in Sullivan's terms, is an important "dynamism." "Thus we may expect, at least until well along in life, the components of the self-system will exist and manifest functional activity in relation to every general need that a person has . . ." (Sullivan, 1953, p. 166). Although the development of the self-system appears to be a necessary aspect of personality development, its close relationship to anxiety has potentially negative consequences. Events or stimuli that threaten the self may tend to be dissociated from it. In such instances, the self tends to limit the awareness and experiences of the person. An interesting attempt was made by Carson (1969) to reformulate Sullivan's ideas into a more systematic framework and in a format that provides empirically testable hypotheses.

Although our treatment of some of the theoretical views which have either supplemented Freud's or departed from his views have been exceedingly brief, it is hoped that the reader will at least get some of the flavor of these other theories and perceive some of the differences in emphasis. In some instances, the change has been one which has placed a greater emphasis on ego functions or integrative aspects of personality. In other cases, the reaction has been a more critical one, particularly to what has been viewed as an overemphasis on instinctual strivings, particularly sex, in the Freudian system. From another vantage point many of the later variants placed a greater emphasis on the social environment and particularly human interactions. Fuller accounts of these as well as other related theories are available in the writings of the theorists as well as in the more general textbooks referred to earlier in the chapter.

THE HUMANISTIC SELF-THEORY OF CARL ROGERS

Although there are a number of theories that are considered to be humanistic, we will consider here only the theory of Carl Rogers. There are two main reasons for this choice. The first is that Rogers' theoretical views stimulated a significant amount of research in the area of psychotherapy. The second is that it has been influential in a number of fields.

As was the case of the previous theories mentioned, the theoretical views of Carl Rogers were derived from his clinical work with clients. Rogers differed somewhat, however, from Freud and the others who have been discussed. He was a clinical psychologist who functioned as an influential university professor after some years of working in a community clinic. While at Ohio State University, and then at the Universities of Chicago and Wisconsin, Rogers was primarily interested in trying to study the psychotherapeutic process in a systematic fashion. As a result of listening to recorded therapy sessions of his own clients and those of his students and colleagues, and in analyzing them in a number of studies, Rogers developed his own theoretical views of how psychotherapy proceeds and the conditions that facilitate change in therapy. In this process he also tended to formulate a theory of personality. Rogers' orientation to psychotherapy, first termed "Non-Directive" and, later, "Client-Centered Therapy," thus provided the background and orientation for his views regarding personality. It is important to keep this fact in mind, for Rogers' theory of personality grew out of his therapeutic work with clients, and from his specific form of psychotherapy.

In part, perhaps, because of the particular focus of Rogers' interest, his theory of personality is primarily concerned with the self and pays comparatively little attention to such topics as stages of development, detailed analyses of the structure of personality, motivation, and so on. As Rogers himself pointed out, he did not embark specifically on the task of developing a theory of personality. Rather, "The theoretical system and the research program which are connected with client-centered therapy have grown from within themselves" (Rogers, 1959, p. 249). Thus, the theory, as noted, was derived primarily from the studies of clients undergoing a particular form of psychotherapy, and its main development was as a theory of psychotherapy. Rogers does emphasize that it is this part of the theory that is most closely related to observed facts and which has the most support in research data. Unlike some other theorists, he also emphasizes the tentative nature of his theories and his view that theories in general should not be taken "as a dogma of truth," but as a stimulus for further thinking.

In his most formal presentation of his theoretical views, Rogers has listed forty constructs grouped into eleven clusters (Rogers, 1959). We will not enter into any detailed discussion of this material here. Rather, some of Rogers' basic formulations and concepts will be presented.

THE ACTUALIZING TENDENCY, SELF-ACTUALIZATION, AND EXPERIENCE

Basic to Rogers' theory is his view of the actualizing tendency, "the inherent tendency of the organism to develop all its capacities in ways which serve to maintain or enhance the organism" (Rogers, 1959, p. 196). This is a broad tendency not only for securing the satisfaction of such needs as air, food, water, etc., but also for the growth and differentiation of the organism.

In this regard, it may be noted that this is the only motive posited by Rogers, and that it is the organism as a whole which exhibits this tendency. Rogers thus stresses the unity of the organism and its gestalt-like quality. This view of motivation is also a broad one that encompasses both drive-reduction and more positive qualities such as growth, curiosity, and the like. In the developing organism, some sort of self-structure develops. More will be said about this subject shortly. In any event, following the development of this structure, the general tendency for actualization is manifested also in the tendency for self-actualization.

Rogers also stressed the role of experience in personality. Influenced in part by Snygg and Combs (1949) and their concept of the "phenomenal field," and in line with some of the views of the existentialists, Rogers defined experience as all that is going on within the individual and which is potentially accessible to the individual's awareness. Experience also refers to the current situation, to that which stimulates the organism, regardless of whether these stimuli are in awareness or not. Ideally, the person should be open to his experience and to fully experience his feelings. If the individual, or rather the self, is congruent with his experience, then the actualizing tendency is relatively unified. If the self becomes organized over a period of time in such a way as to exclude major sources of needed information about its own processes or the behavior of others, this lack of congruence impedes actualization. Energy which is used to maintain fictions (that is, perceptions of self or others which cannot be confirmed by experience) cannot be turned to productive self-expression. Thus a conflict may arise between the basic tendency to actualize and the self-actualizing tendency.

At this point it may be well to elaborate further on two terms that have been referred to in the preceding discussion, namely self and congruence. As indicated earlier, the concept of self has received particular emphasis in Rogers's theory, and it has sometimes been referred to as a "self-theory." In his description of theoretical constructs, Rogers refers to self, concept of self, and the self-structure. "These terms refer to the organized, consistent conceptual characteristics of the 'I' or 'me' and the perceptions of the relationships of the 'I' or 'me' to others and to various aspects of life, together with the values attached to these perceptions" (Rogers, 1959, p. 200). The self or self-system is perceived as a fluid and organized process, but one that can be studied at any specific moment in time. The terms, self or self-concept, generally refer to the person's view of himself; self-structure more typically refers to the appraisal of self from an external frame of reference.

As defined and viewed by Rogers, the self is composed of conscious perceptions and values. Because the self, by definition, does not include aspects below the level of awareness, it can be defined more or less operationally, and can also be measured. Furthermore, as appraised during the process of psychotherapy, the self-concept is far from static and may fluctuate noticeably. Of particular importance is the relationship of the self to the individual's experience, and here reference is made to the term, congruence. Theoretically, in the fully self-actualizing person the self is congruent or consistent with the organism's experience. In some individuals, however, an incongruence may develop between self and experience. In other words, some discrepancy may develop between the self as perceived and the real experiences of the organism. The individual may perceive himself in one way or have a particular concept of self that is theoretically at variance with his actual experience. An individual may see himself, for example, as an extremely competent or confident individual, but his actual experience in this regard may be incongruent with this self view. Such incongruence or discrepancy is postulated to lead to tension or internal confusion, because the person's behavior is being influenced by two discordant tendencies—the actualizing tendency of the organism and that subsystem of the former, the tendency for self-actualization.

The last part of the preceding paragraph is in some ways reminiscent of Freudian views of repression and conflict, and it may be helpful to make some comparison of the two theories in this regard. To the extent that the individual's self-concept may exclude part of the individual's experience from awareness, and produce tension or maladjustment, the process would appear to have much in common with the Freudian notion of repression. The latter generally deals with negative or forbidden impulses, however, and according to Rogers, the feelings and impulses denied awareness were frequently quite the opposite, for example, feelings of love, tenderness, or self-confidence. The apparent explanation was related to congruence or consistency with the self. "Experiences which were incongruent with the individual's concept of himself tended to be denied awareness, whatever their social character" (Rogers, 1959, p. 202). A person, for example, who viewed himself as tough and "hard-boiled" would tend not to be aware of or to acknowledge feelings of tenderness. Thus, while Rogers's theory also explicitly recognizes that some of the individual's experiences may be below the threshold of awareness, and may contribute to a state of tension, his treatment of such phenomena does differ from that of Freud's, and a similar difference may be noted with reference to the concepts of threat and defense and how they are viewed in Rogers's system.

In psychoanalytic theory, the variety of defenses or mechanisms that individuals use to defend against anxiety and threat are viewed, within limits, as necessary for successful adjustment. For Rogers, however, such defensive operations and attempts to distort experience in terms of maintaining the current structure of self are essentially negative and interfere with the actualizing tendency. They lead to further incongruence between self and experience, and the goal of therapy as well as positive personality development is to bring the self and experience, the self-actualizing tendency, and the tendency for actualization into greater harmony and congruence. Thus, while there are some apparent similarities between the two theoretical systems in that both emphasize the significance of experiences that are not admitted to awareness, how such phenomena are conceptualized and related to other theoretical constructs differ significantly for the two theories.

POSITIVE REGARD AND RELATED CONCEPTS

Another group of significant constructs in Rogers' theory of personality basically involve the individual's relationships with significant others and their impact on the individual and his concept of self. Like most of the other constructs in this system, they were derived from the study of individuals undergoing client-centered psychotherapy. In these studies, certain therapist qualities were found to be related to the process and outcome of psychotherapy, for example, empathy, unconditional positive regard and genuineness or congruence. Rogers has attempted to utilize these concepts in sketching out a theory of personality, although he is quite explicit in pointing out that some of these theoretical propositions are rather inferential and furthest from experiential and empirical sources of data.

As indicated, research investigation in psychotherapy appeared to indicate that when the therapist manifests empathy, congruence, and unconditional positive regard toward the client, the latter shows positive change and growth. Thus, these therapeutic or relationship variables were seen as growth inducing or as related to positive personality change. In his development of a theory of personality, therefore, Rogers utilized and incorporated these concepts. The need for positive regard, in particular, was seen as a universal, although probably learned, need in all human beings. Furthermore, to the extent that the positive regard accorded an individual by significant others is unconditional, that is unconditional positive regard, then the individual is more likely to become fully self-actualizing and psychologically adjusted.

What has just been presented requires some elaboration. Unconditional positive regard means to value or prize another fully. "This means to value the person, irrespective of the differential values which one might place on his specific behaviors" (Rogers, 1959, p. 208). Thus, you do not differentially value or regard the experiences or behavior of the person—you value him or her unconditionally. If a significant other values some aspects of the individual more than others, then a condition of worth arises. If this occurs, the individual may assimilate this valuing system and then tend to place similar positive or negative values on the specific aspects of experience reacted to in this way. For example, if a parent values high academic performance or submissiveness above other attributes of the child, the child may incorporate such values into the self. The consequence of this process is that the individual then values specific experiences in terms of their worth to others rather than because the experiences enhance her own self or are congruent with her actualizing tendency. As a consequence, actualization is partially or wholly blocked. Unconditional positive regard, on the other hand, does not lead to conditions of worth and is a prerequisite for optimum psychological adjustment.

It is hoped that the above account will provide the reader with some understanding of Rogers' theory of personality and of some of his basic theoretical constructs. Although Rogers was influenced by Freud's thinking to some extent at an early stage of his career, he did not want to be confined by any rigid view. He preferred to be somewhat atheoretical and to be free to consider all views as well as to observe what actually took place in the psychotherapeutic situation. At later times he appeared to be influenced by the views of Rank, Maslow, Snygg, and Combs, as well as by the students and colleagues who worked with him. His theory, therefore, is quite different from Freud's as well as some of the others discussed, although there are some points of congruence or similarity. For example, although Rogers does not employ the concept of "the unconscious" or of unconscious motivation, he does distinguish and emphasize behaviors and experiences that are not in the person's awareness. In his discussion of the development of incongruence between the self and experience in relation to conditions of worth and in related discussions of the experience of threat and the process of threat, there is some similarity to the Freudian treatment of anxiety, defenses of the ego, and repression. Nevertheless, in spite of some similarities such as these, the language, the majority of concepts, and the general orientation of the two theories are quite different. There is generally a more positive outlook or view of the person evident in Rogers' theory than is true of many other theorists.

A few other comments can be offered about Rogers' theory before we conclude our discussion of it. In the first place, Rogers made very explicit the fact that he regarded his theory as one which was still in the process of being developed and that in no way was it to be viewed as a fixed and comprehensive theory of human personality. In fact, as noted, he emphasized that all theories should be viewed as temporary attempts to explain a given range of phenomena, to organize thinking, to stimulate further research, and eventually to be replaced by better and more inclusive theories. Second, Rogers attempted, particularly in his most formally organized statement of the theory (Rogers, 1959), to define his constructs in operational terms. Third, he attempted also to relate his theory to research evidence and to modify it in accordance with new research data. This was consistent with Rogers' early and important contribution to the field of psychotherapy, namely, using tape recordings of psychotherapy sessions for the purpose of analyzing the psychotherapeutic process and bringing it within the ken of scientific research. Finally, Rogers himself pointed out that his theory of psychotherapy was the one that was most closely tied to research evidence and which, therefore, had the most support. His theory of personality, however, was viewed as more tentative and derived from the theory of psychotherapy.

For a theory of personality which is so closely tied to formulations and research on the psychotherapeutic process, the implications for psychotherapy need not be spelled out in any detail. It is clear that the individual client is viewed as having the potentiality for positive change, and the task is to free the person so that his self and his experience are congruent. This, of course, is simplifying matters somewhat, but it contains the real goals of therapy. To free the individual so that she may more truly be open to her experience and to reduce distortion and lack of awareness, the therapist must possess and exhibit the necessary conditions for personality change and growth. The therapist must demonstrate unconditional positive regard toward the client, he must be genuine or congruent in the relationship—that is, he must be aware of his real feelings and truly be himself—and he must be empathic in terms of what the client is experiencing or feeling. If these three therapeutic conditions are present to a high degree, then, according to Rogers, the client will show positive movement and change in psychotherapy.

Although Rogers, in his recent writing, has not said anything specifically about the implications of his theory for diagnostic work, nor is it possible to draw any accurate inferences in this regard from these publications, he was very much opposed at an earlier time to any formal diagnostic evaluation of the client, except where it was used for research purposes. Rogers stated view was that diagnosis "is not only unnecessary but in some ways is detrimental or unwise" (1951, p. 223) and he gave some reasons for his views. One reason was that it fosters the role of responsibility on the part of the therapist, thereby increasing the dependency of the client on the therapist. Another reason concerned the social implications of control by the therapist over the patient's decision in important areas of his life. From this point of view, the directive or authoritative use of psychological tests is inconsistent with the basic philosophy of client-centered therapy and interferes with the patient's growth of self (Rogers, 1946). It would appear also that giving replies to any test may conceivably raise issues of worth and thus interfere with the actualizing process.

LEARNING AND BEHAVIOR THEORIES

All of the previously mentioned theories of personality have been derived from or are based upon the clinical study of disturbed or maladjusted individuals. The setting has been the hospital, clinic, or consulting room where persons with a variety of problems have presented themselves for help with their difficulties. The kind of theory (or theories) to be discussed in this section differs in significant ways from those already presented. This type of theory emanated from the psychological laboratory. Much of the earlier work was based on laboratory studies of animals and emphasized experimental procedures and controls. Thus, these theories came from the field of experimental psychology rather than from the world of the clinic and psychopathology, and stressed the processes of learning. It is to be expected, therefore, that they would differ in a number of ways from the theories mentioned previously.

Apart from the fact that learning appears to play a central role in most theories of human behavior, there are other reasons for emphasizing the importance of learning in relation to theories of personality. One very obvious one is that much of the individual's behavior is learned. Although heredity and maturation set certain limits on the potentialities for the development of an individual's behavior, most of what we observe of the individual, particularly in social interactions with others, appears to be largely influenced by previous learning. This is especially true when we consider such aspects of the person as goals, values, attitudes, language, and similar characteristics.

Thus, it is apparent that learning plays an important role in how the person develops and eventually becomes the particular kind of individual he or she is. From this point of view, therefore, it is easy to conceive of personality as being significantly influenced by learning and to view not only normal behavior as a product of learning, but maladaptive behavior as well. Furthermore, if maladaptive or maladjustive behavior is viewed as a product of learning, it is also conceivable that one might be able to make use of the principles and theories of learning for modifying such behavior and replacing it with more adaptive patterns of response. From such an orientation, it follows logically that learning viewpoints can contribute both to theories of personality and to methods for the modification of behavior.

Nevertheless, the application of learning theories and principles to clinical work with clients proceeded very slowly until quite recently. Most clinicians were primarily influenced by the theories of personality emanating from psychoanalysis and other dynamic orientations that appeared to view the person's psychic life as being rather complicated. The principles of learning and conditioning, on the other hand, appeared to be too simple and mechanistic. What might apply to the simple behaviors of the laboratory animal in the maze or the cage did not appear to be particularly relevant for the intricacies and complicated manifestations of human psychopathology. The situation, however, appears to have changed rather drastically in the past twenty years or so, and we delve into some of the possible reasons for this change in a later chapter when we discuss some of the behavior therapies. For the present, let us look briefly at some of the important theories of learning.

CLASSICAL CONDITIONING

Most students who have had an introductory course in psychology are familiar with Pavlov's famous experiments with dogs in his laboratory in which the animals were conditioned to salivate to a stimulus that normally would not elicit such a response. Thus, if a tone or light is consistently presented to a hungry animal just before he is fed, the dog will begin to salivate to these stimuli. The latter are termed conditioned stimuli because they do not ordinarily elicit salivation. Similarly, the response of salivation to the conditioned stimulus is termed a conditioned response. A conditioned response is a new response to a given stimulus and is essentially a learned response. The pairing of the conditioned and unconditioned stimuli has generally been referred to as reinforcement. When the association between the two stimuli and the response is regular and continued, the conditioned response is strengthened or reinforced. On the other hand, if the original or unconditioned stimulus is omitted and the conditioned stimulus is presented alone, the conditioned response gradually weakens and eventually disappears, a process referred to as extinction.

The experiments of Pavlov and others also demonstrated two other important learning processes, namely, discrimination and generalization. For example, if a particular tone has been used as the conditioned stimulus, a tone which is somewhat similar to it may also produce the conditioned response. But, with repeated trials where only the first tone is reinforced, the animal will learn to discriminate between the two tones and the conditioned response will be manifested only in relation to the first tone. The less similar the two tones are, the more easily is the discrimination obtained. In a comparable fashion, generalization of response also occurs. The more similar two stimuli are, the greater is the probability of response to the second stimulus and the greater the generalization. In a similar fashion, inhibition of response also generalizes—that is, if a response to one stimulus has been extinguished, the responses to similar stimuli will also be extinguished.

The experiments and theoretical views in the area of classical conditioning have had a decided impact on psychology. In addition to their specific importance for later developments pertaining to theories of learning, they also played an important role in the subsequent emphasis on a behavioristic psychology in America. Watson (1919), for example, was one of the early important behaviorists who found the concept of the conditioned reflex to fit in well with his own views. The use of the concepts of classical conditioning allowed the investigator to focus on the behavior of the organism and on the varied stimuli that led to the behavior in question. Since Watson's time, there have been a variety of developments and theories produced in the study of learning and behavior, but most of them have tended to focus on the relationship of stimulus and response, to emphasize observable behavior, and to limit, or to avoid entirely, the use of inferred personality structures or concepts. Such theoretical orientations are quite different from most of those discussed in this chapter, but they do represent another way of looking at behavior and trying to understand it. The implications for clinical analysis and the subsequent modification of behavior are obviously also quite different from those of the so-called dynamic theories of personality and more will be said about this later. It will be sufficient here merely to point out that it is possible to view and treat problems of human adjustment from such a viewpoint (Bandura, 1969; Guthrie, 1938; Slater, 1949; Yates, 1970) or to incorporate a learning orientation into a broader view of adjustment (Shaffer and Shoben, 1956).

OPERANT OR INSTRUMENTAL CONDITIONING

Another type of learning theory or approach to learning, operant conditioning, is associated with the work of Skinner (1938). While some of the operations and concepts derived from classical conditioning, such as generalization and extinction, apply also to operant conditioning, there are some differences between the two approaches.

In classical conditioning, one focuses on the stimulus conditions that produce a given behavior and one works with some behavior that is already available in the organism—that is, it is a part of the response repertoire of the organism. The kinds of reflexive behaviors studied in the earlier experiments on classical conditioning, such as salivation, eye blinks, and so forth, are natural responses of the organism to certain stimuli. The presentation of light will cause a constriction of the pupil and the association of a new stimulus with the unconditioned stimulus will gradually also call forth this response. Such behavior, called respondent behavior by Skinner, appears to be controlled by the stimulus. In operant conditioning, however, the situation is different. One is interested in producing a new behavior or in trying to shape the behavior of the subject. In this sense, the precise behavior sought may not be in the organism's behavior repertoire or habit system, but is within its capabilities.

Another important aspect of operant conditioning or instrumental learning concerns the effects of the individual's behavior. To the extent that a person's behavior "operates" on the environment it tends to have some effect on it. If the wind is blowing through the window and one feels that it may blow a lamp over, he may respond by going over and closing the window, thus, in effect, changing his environment. The consequences of the behavior are also stressed. If a certain behavior is reinforced, it will tend to continue and be strengthened. As in classical conditioning, if there is no reinforcement, then the operant behavior will diminish and extinction will result.

Reinforcement is a key concept in operant conditioning. If one wants to shape a certain behavior or strengthen a particular pattern of behavior, then the behavior must be reinforced. By reinforcing approaches or approximations to the desired behavior, the experimenter (or the behavior therapist) may gradually secure the result she seeks. The training of animals to perform in a variety of ways is one illustration of these principles of operant conditioning. In essence, therefore, operant conditioning refers to the strengthening of an association between a given stimulus and a given response by means of reinforcement. Once a given behavior is produced or emitted, it can be reinforced according to the principles derived from operant conditioning. To the extent that many of our everyday behaviors are operant behaviors and the result of learning, they can theoretically be modified by appropriate use of reinforcement, and thus would appear to have relevance for therapeutic endeavors which require either the modification of deviant behaviors or the substitution of new behaviors.

In the various experiments carried out in the area of operant conditioning, different schedules or patterns of reinforcement have been used. For example, a continuous schedule of reinforcement refers to rewarding or reinforcing a subject each time he or she demonstrates the desired behavior. When the reinforcement is withdrawn the subjects may increase their responding behavior briefly, but then the specific behavioral response decreases notably. In the fixed-interval schedule, behavior is reinforced after a specific period of time. Generally, performance under such conditions is low immediately after reinforcement but increases rapidly as the time for the next reinforcement draws near. In a fixed-ratio schedule an individual must reach a certain level of output or performance before he is reinforced and the resulting behavior tends to be more stable and can be kept at a relatively high level.

In addition to fixed and continuous scheduled of reinforcement, there are also intermittent or variable schedules of reinforcement. These can be divided into the categories of variable-interval or variable-ratio schedules of reinforcement. In the former, the length of time varies between the successive reinforcements, usually around some mean value. In the variable-ratio schedules, the number of responses per reinforcement usually varies around some mean ratio. Because of the variable and hence unpredictable rate of reinforcement, the type of patterns mentioned previously, whereby the rate of response varies with the time for the expected reinforcement, are not manifested. Rather, behavioral response to variable schedules appears more stable and more frequent. In general, the variable-ratio schedule of reinforcement appears to be the most effective in sustaining behavior (Bandura, 1969).

If the selective and judicious use of reinforcement can lead to significant modification, retention or extinction of specific behaviors, then such procedures and their underlying theories would appear to be important for a variety of applied endeavors, including clinical psychology. This, clearly has been the contention of a number of behavioral scientists and experimentally oriented clinicians (Bandura, 1969; Krasner, 1971), and they have been active in demonstrating the utility of their views. Such principles, derived initially from laboratory studies with animals, have been extended to experimental and clinical studies with humans in a variety of areas (Kazdin, 1978, 1980; Ross, 1978).

MODELING AND VICARIOUS REINFORCEMENT

Another type of learning which takes place is that which occurs when a person models his behavior after that of another person. As Bandura (1965) has demonstrated, such learning is not only common among people, but it is a highly efficient form of learning. Such learning has been referred to as vicarious learning or as learning by means of modeling. In these instances, the individual learns or modifies his behavior by observing some other person, rather than by his own direct participation in the behavior to be learned. Furthermore, this may apply also to the matter of reinforcement in that the observer is not directly reinforced for a change in behavior, although the model will receive some reinforcement for his behavior. Thus, the learning can be viewed as vicarious learning.

In our presentation here, reference can be made to two groups of experiments that illustrate this type of research and their theoretical implications. Brief summaries of this work are available in written reports by Bandura (1965) and Kanfer (1965). In research by Bandura and his associates a group of nursery school children observed an aggressive model who exhibited various forms of physical and verbal aggression toward a large inflated plastic doll. Another group observed the same model behave in a very controlled and subdued manner, whereas a control group was not exposed to any model. The children in the first two groups were allowed to watch the model's behavior but could not perform the behavior exhibited. Afterward, all of the children received some mild frustration and were then tested for the amount of imitative or aggressive behavior. "Children who observed the aggressive models displayed a great number of precisely imitative physical and verbal responses, whereas such behavior rarely occurred in either the nonaggressive-model group or the control group" (Bandura, 1965, p. 324). Children who observed the aggressive models tended to show about twice as much aggressive behavior as did the children in the other two groups.

According to Bandura, modeling may produce three rather different effects. First, the observer may acquire new responses or response patterns that did not exist previously in his behavioral repertoire. Second, exposure to a model may also strengthen or weaken inhibitory responses. For example, in the experiments referred to in the preceding paragraph, aggressive behavior was not a completely new type of behavior for most of the children. Thus, the increase in aggressive behavior can be viewed as the result of an increase in disinhibition, or a disinhibitory effect. Third, the experimental results may also be viewed as providing evidence for facilitation effects. Some of the behaviors, for example hitting a peg with a mallet, are socially sanctioned behaviors, but the increase in this behavior after observation of the model would appear to reflect an enhancing of this behavior.

Some experiments in the area of verbal conditioning by Kanfer (1965) and his associates are quite similar in their results and implications to those discussed previously. In experiments on verbal conditioning, the experimenter generally selects some class of words such as first person nouns, human words, or some other grouping, and reinforces the subject by saying "mm-hmm" or "good" when the desired class of words is emitted. In such experiments, which resemble the operant conditioning work with animals, somewhat similar types of learning curves can be obtained. But, because the human being does differ from animals and because Kanfer and his associates were interested in what might be going on within the subjects during an experiment, particularly with their reactions to the experiment, some novel experiments were devised and carried out. In these experiments, a group of subjects acted as observers of individuals who participated as the manifest subjects in a verbal learning experiment. In the first few experiments the words *I* and *We* were reinforced and the observers were asked to record their guesses concerning what the experiment was all about. Fifty percent of the observers were able to discern what the nature of the experiment was. The focus of the research then shifted from the matter of observer awareness of what behavior was being reinforced to whether or not the observers themselves were also being conditioned. Using similar procedures, groups of observers and participants were then studied to see the effects of vicarious reinforcement. In general, the observers, when tested, showed conditioning effects comparable to those for the participating subjects. Observers, however, generally were higher than participants in their awareness of the response-reinforcement contingencies.

The above experiments, like those of Bandura, indicate that individuals can learn from observing a model and that they do not have to be directly involved for learning to take place. The old adage "Do what I say and not what I do" also would appear to reflect the importance of modeling and, based on past experience, to suggest the relative ineffectiveness of simple verbal exhortation. It would appear that modeling is an important means of modifying behavior which has implications both for theories of learning and for clinical psychology.

The preceding introduction to theories of learning and behavior should give the reader some idea of both the diversity of viewpoints in this area and how such theories differ from those mentioned previously. The potential implications of learning theories for clinical practice are also different. To the extent that these theories tend to focus on behavior and the conditions that modify behavior, practitioners who hold such views would be expected to manifest little interest in the kinds of inferred and underlying personality constructs typical of psychoanalytic and related theories. A large battery of tests for the purpose of understanding personality dynamics clearly would not be called for. In a similar manner, the kinds of relationship variables stressed in psychoanalysis or client-centered psychotherapy also would not be stressed in a learning-oriented approach to the modification of behavior. Rather, the focus would be on the behavior to be changed and the establishment of the necessary conditions for such change. The role of the therapist, conceivably, would differ noticeably from the more nondirective role of the client-centered therapist. Learning-oriented psychologists and behavior therapists thus deal directly with the behavior in question, see little need for getting at "underlying causes," and attempt wherever possible to evaluate the extent of behavioral change.

More recently, a number of prominent behavior therapists have broadened their behavioristic views to include a recognition of the importance of social and cognitive factors in human learning and behavior (Bandura, 1977; Goldfried & Davison, 1976; Kendall & Hollon, 1979; Mahoney & Arnkoff, 1978; Meichenbaum, 1977). So-called cognitive therapies, which were developed for the most part outside of the behavioral or learning orientations (Beck, 1976; Ellis, 1962), have also shown an affinity for being combined or integrated with behavioral procedures. These developments have led to a greater emphasis on the importance of cognitive elements in therapy and to the gradual appearance of what is now referred to as cognitive behavior therapy or cognitive-behavioral modification (Kendall & Hollon, 1979; Meichenbaum, 1977). As stated in a recent volume, the cognitive-behavioral approach is "a purposeful attempt to preserve the demonstrated efficiencies of behavior modification within a less doctrinaire context and to incorporate the cognitive activities of the client in the efforts to produce therapeutic change" (Kendall & Hollon, 1979, p. 1). Although not all behaviorally oriented individuals approve of this kind of integration (Ledwidge, 1978), it does represent what appears to be a trend toward rapproachment or empirical eclecticism among different therapeutic orientations (Garfield & Kurtz, 1976, 1977; Goldfried, 1980). These are very recent but also very interesting developments, both theoretically and clinically, and more will be said about them later.

We shall go into the various therapeutic approaches derived from these and other theories in more detail later, and the reader will then be better able to understand and evaluate the important differences between the various approaches. The present objective has been to introduce the reader in a limited way to the diversity of theoretical views which exist in clinical psychology and to indicate some of the implications of these viewpoints for the practice of clinical psychology.

REFERENCES

Bandura, A. Behavioral modification through modeling procedures. In L. Krasner and L. P. Ullman (Eds.), *Research in behavior modification.* New York: Holt, Rinehart and Winston, 1965. Pp. 310–340.

Bandura, A. *Principles of behavior modification.* New York: Holt, Rinehart and Winston, 1969.

Bandura, A. Self-efficacy: Towards a unifying theory of behavioral change. *Psychological Review,* 1977, *84,* 191–215.

Beck, A. T. *Cognitive therapy and the emotional disorders.* New York: International Universities Press, 1976.

Bischof, L. J. *Interpreting personality theories.* (2nd Ed.). New York: Harper and Row, 1970.

Bower, G. H., & Hilgard, E. R. *Theories of learning.* (5th Ed.). Englewood Cliffs, NJ: Prentice-Hall, 1981.

Carson, R. C. *Interaction concepts of personality.* Chicago: Aldine, 1969.

Dreikurs, R. Individual psychology: The Adlerian point of view. In J. M. Wepman and R. W. Heine (Eds.), *Concepts of personality.* Chicago: Aldine, 1963. Pp. 234–256.

Ellis, A. *Reason and emotion in psychotherapy.* New York: Lyle Stuart, 1962.

Erickson, E. H. *Childhood and society.* (2nd Edition) New York: Norton, 1963.

Ewen, R. B. *An introduction to theories of personality.* New York: Academic Press, 1980.

Freud, A. *The ego and the mechanisms of defense.* New York: International Universities Press, 1946.

Freud, S. *The basic writings of Sigmund Freud.* New York: Modern Library, Random House, 1938a.

Freud, S. *Psychopathology of everyday life.* New York: Modern Library, Random House, 1938b.

Freud, S. *An outline of psychoanalysis.* New York: Norton, 1949.

Garfield, S. L. & Kurtz, R. Clinical Psychologists in the 1970's. *American Psychologist,* 1976, *31,* 1–9.

Garfield, S. L. & Kurtz, R. A study of eclectic views. *Journal of Consulting and Clinical Psychology,* 1977, *45,* 78–83.

Gilbert, G. M. *Personality dynamics. A biosocial approach.* New York: Harper and Row, 1970.

Goldfried, M. R. Toward the delineation of therapeutic change principles. *American Psychologist,* 1980, *35,* 991–999.

Goldfried, M. R., & Davison, G. C. *Clinical behavior therapy.* New York: Holt, Rinehart and Winston, 1976.

Guthrie, E. R. *The psychology of human conflict.* New York: Harper and Row, 1938.

Hall, C. S., & Lindzey, G. *Theories of personality.* (3rd Ed.). New York: Wiley, 1978.

Hartmann, H. *Essays on ego psychology.* New York: International Universities Press, 1964.

Heidbreder, E. *Seven psychologies.* New York: D. Appleton-Century, 1933.

Hilgard, E. R. Experimental approaches to psychoanalysis. In E. Pumpian-Mindlin (Ed.), *Psychoanalysis as science.* Stanford, CA: Stanford University Press, 1952. Pp. 3–45.

Horney, K. *Neurotic personality of our times.* New York: Norton, 1937.

Horney, K. *New ways in psychoanalysis.* New York: Norton, 1939.

Horney, K. *Self-analysis.* New York: 1942.

Horney, K. *Our inner conflicts.* New ork: Norton, 1945.

Horney, K. *Neurosis and human growth.* New York: Norton, 1950.

Kanfer, F. H. Vicarious human reinforcements: A glimpse into the black box. In L. Krasner and L. P. Ullmann (Eds.), *Research in behavior modification.* New York: Holt, Rinehart and Winston, 1965. Pp. 244–267.

Kazdin, A. E. The application of operant techniques in treatment, rehabilitation, and education. In S. L. Garfield and A. E. Bergin (Eds.), *Handbook of psychotherapy and behavior change.* (2nd Ed.). New York: Wiley, 1978.

Kazdin, A. E. *Behavior modification in applied settings.* (2nd Ed.). Homewood, IL: Dorsey Press, 1980.

Kendall, P. C., & Hollon, S. D. *Cognitive-behavioral interventions. Theory, research, and procedures.* New York: Academic Press, 1979.

Krasner, L. The operant approach in behavior therapy. In A. E. Bergin and S. L. Garfield (Eds.), *Handbook of psychotherapy and behavior change: An empirical analysis.* New York: Wiley, 1971.

Ledwidge, B. Cognitive behavior modification: A step in the wrong direction? *Psychological Bulletin,* 1978, *85,* 353–375.

Maddi, S. R. *Personality theories: A comparative analysis.* (4th Ed.). Homewood, IL: Dorsey Press, 1980.

Mahoney, M. J., & Arnkoff, D. B. Cognitive and self-control therapies. In S. L. Garfield and A. E. Bergin (Eds.), *Handbook of psychotherapy and behavior change.* (2nd Ed.). New York: Wiley, 1978.

Meichenbaum, D. *Cognitive-behavior modification. An integrative approach* New York: Plenum, 1977.

Munroe, R. L. *Schools of psychoanalytic thought.* New York: Dryden, 1955.

Rapaport, D. The structure of psychoanalytic theory: A systematizing attempt. In S. Koch (Ed.), *Psychology: A study of a science.* New York: McGraw-Hill, 1959, Vol.3. Pp. 55-183.

Rogers, C. R. Psychometric tests and client-centered counseling. *Educational and Psychological Measurement,* 1946, *6,* 139–144.

Rogers, C. R. *Client-centered therapy.* Boston: Houghton Mifflin, 1951.

Rogers, C. R. A theory of therapy, personality, and interpersonal relationships, as developed in the client-centered framework. In S. Koch (Ed.), *Psychology: A study of a science.* New York: McGraw-Hill, 1959. Vol. 3, pp. 184–256.

Ross, A. O. Behavior therapy with children. In S. L. Garfield and A. E. Bergin (Eds.), *Handbook of psychotherapy and behavior change.* (2nd Ed.). New York: Wiley, 1978.

Salter, A. *Conditioned reflex therapy.* New York: Farrar, Straus, 1949.

Sears, R. R. Survey of objective studies of psychoanalytic concepts. *Social Science Research Council Bulletin 51,* 1943.

Sears, R. R. Experimental analysis of psychoanalytic phenomena. In J. McV. Hunt (Ed.), *Personality and the behavior disorders.* New York: Ronald Press, 1944. Vol. 1, pp. 306–332.

Shaffer, L. F., & Shoben, E. J., Jr. *The psychology of adjustment.* (2nd Ed.). Boston: Houghton Mifflin, 1956.

Silverman, L. H. An experimental technique for the study of unconscious conflict. *British Journal of Medical Psychology,* 1971, *44,* 17–25.

Silverman, L. H. Psychoanalytic theory. "The reports of my death are greatly exaggerated." *American Psychologist,* 1976, *31,* 621–637.

Skinner, B. F. *The behavior of organisms.* New York: Appleton-Century-Crofts, 1938.

Snygg, D., & Combs, A. W. *Individual behavior.* New York: Harper and Row, 1949.

Sullivan, H. S. *Conceptions of modern psychiatry.* New York: Norton, 1947.
Sullivan, H. S. *The interpersonal theory of psychiatry.* New York: Norton, 1953.
Watson, J. B. *Psychology from the standpoint of a behaviorist.* Philadelphia: Lippincott, 1919.
Yates, A. J. *Behavior therapy.* New York: Wiley, 1970.

Chapter
Three

Diagnosis and Assessment

In the field of medicine it is traditional to speak of the diagnosis and treatment of illness or pathology. It is presumed, also, that a valid diagnosis of the illness is a necessary prelude to treatment. If one does not know what the illness is, then obviously it is rather difficult to treat it. The illness model generally presupposes some cause or etiology of disease, a particular course of the illness, some information about prognosis, and, hopefully, knowledge of possible treatments.

Early in the history of clinical psychology, problems of a diagnostic nature were generally focused on appraisal of intellectual abilities and educational accomplishments and deficits. With the advent of standardized tests and the emphasis on scientific objectivity, great importance was placed on test scores. Although the psychologist observed the subject's behavior in the testing situation and offered some interpretation of test performance, the quantitative scores such as IQ or Mental Age, percentile rank, or grade-level norms appeared to receive the greatest emphasis, and a psychological diagnosis was offered in relation to them. Psychologists working in mental hospitals appeared to be more concerned with how patients functioned on different mental tests than simply with an overall psychiatric diagnosis.

As clinical psychologists in the 1940's began to work increasingly in psychiatric hospitals and clinics, they not only began to be more concerned with the specific personality patterns and behavioral disturbances of the patients they were seeing, but they were very much influenced by the procedures and modes of thinking of their psychiatric colleagues. The latter had more experience in working with disturbed individuals; they had an officially recognized and sanctioned system for diagnosing and classifying patients and they were society's acknowledged agents entrusted with the care of the "mentally ill." In general, psychiatrists had more status in the field of abnormal behavior and held the positions of authority in the institutions in which psychologists were now being employed in increasing numbers. Under such conditions, it is not at all surprising that psychologists in their diagnostic work with patients were officially, and otherwise, greatly influenced by the procedures and modes of thought evident in the allied profession of psychiatry.

Because psychiatry is considered to be a specialty within the field of medicine, and because all psychiatrists are first trained as physicians, it is natural that they would be influenced by medical thinking and medical concepts of diagnosis. In fact, as already noted, the term, diagnosis, is most closely associated with the practice of medicine and has reference to identifying particular symptoms or a syndrome of dysfunction with a given course of illness or etiology. To make a diagnosis is thus to understand the illness by relating different symptoms or aspects of the case into a meaningful whole or understandable syndrome. In this manner, too, one is able to apply to the individual case the available knowledge pertaining to the particular disease or disorder. Because some similar symptoms, for example, fever, lack of energy, hyperactivity, and so forth, may be found in different syndromes or diseases requiring different types of treatment, careful diagnosis is important. This is particularly true in those illnesses where the more quickly treatment is begun, the better is the chance for recovery. If the physician can correctly diagnose the illness or disease of the patient, he is better able to prescribe or administer the appropriate treatment for the specific disease.

PSYCHIATRIC DIAGNOSIS AND CLASSIFICATION

For the most part, psychiatry, as a medical discipline, has tended to follow the medical tradition in matters of diagnosis. Following the Kraepelinian tradition, attempts have been made to diagnose or classify patients in terms of certain nosological categories (American Psychiatric Association, 1980; Committee on Nomenclature and Statistics of the American Psychiatric Association, 1968). Some of these diagnostic categories are based on known etiological factors, such as syphilis of the central nervous system. In other instances the etiology may be unknown, but the illness will have a reasonably defined clinical course such as Primary Degenerative Dementia. However, in a large number of instances, there is no known or commonly accepted cause of the disorder, and there may not even be a truly clearcut course that the disorder follows. In these instances diagnosis and classification of patients is based primarily on an appraisal of their symptomatic behavior. In other words, such a diagnosis is based essentially on descriptive aspects of external behavior. Much of what has been called "Descriptive Psychiatry" was concerned with such a diagnostic approach. From this point of view, certain rather frequently appearing symptoms were considered to be part of a disease process and given a particular diagnostic name, for example, schizophrenia or hysteria. Diagnostic terms of this type were used as convenient means of classifying patients in terms of selected patterns of behavior. Although such attempts at classifying behavior and symptomatology have served the purpose of bringing some order into our observations in the area of psychopathology, they have also had some unfortunate influences on clinical practice. A rather loose classification based on a variety of different symptoms has tended to be viewed as a distinct disease entity. As a consequence, diagnosis to many clinicians connoted merely the attaching to the patient of a label taken from a given system of psychiatric classification. For example, one might conclude his diagnostic appraisal of a patient by stating that "this patient is diagnosed as a case of schizophrenia." Such diagnostic work, however, is limited in scope and contributes relatively little to our understanding of the patient. The term schizophrenia includes a large variety of behavioral and personality symptoms, many of which may not apply to the patient at hand. Thus, this type of diagnosis does not identify the patient and his problems in any comprehensive or unique manner. All we can say on the basis of this diagnosis alone is that the patient is viewed as seriously disturbed by the examining clinician and that he may have exhibited one or more of the symptoms associated with such a diagnosis. Unfortunately, diagnostic study and diagnostic testing was oriented too frequently in the past around this nosological approach to diagnosis.

Too often, the assigning of a psychiatric diagnosis to patients in the traditional manner was considered an accomplishment or end in itself. Many diagnostic staff conferences consisted of lengthy and at times spirited discussions as to whether a patient was a schizophrenic or a manic depressive, or whether a patient was a paranoid or undifferentiated subtype of schizophrenia. Actually, as is known, many such diagnoses lack reliability and often are substitutes for a more meaningful appraisal of the patient. Quite frequently the final decision as to diagnosis, whether by democratic vote or by authoritarian decree, had little real influence on what was done for the patient. If he were unruly and agitated he would be assigned to the acute ward regardless of diagnosis, and sometimes treatment recommendations might also be made with little regard for the diagnostic classification of the patient.

If one goes through case records of patients with long histories of disturbance and hospitalization, he may find a variety of different diagnoses listed at various times for the same patient. This variation in diagnosis does not mean that the patient is suffering from a number of different diseases requiring different treatment, but rather that the diagnoses have reflected the varying symptoms which were most pronounced at a given time or the particular predilictions of a given clinician. A number of studies have now demonstrated the lack of reliability in psychiatric diagnosis (Ash, 1949; Beck, Ward, Mendelson, Mock, and Erbaugh, 1962; Hunt, Wittson, and Hunt, 1953; Kreitman, 1961; Malamud, 1946; Pasamanick, Dinitz, and Lefton, 1959; Schmidt and Fonda, 1956; Spitzer & Fleiss, 1974). Although several of these studies have some methodological limitations and the procedures used have varied from study to study, the general findings do point up some of the limitations in the reliability of psychiatric diagnosis. Not only have some of the studies shown important differences between psychiatrists in differentiating such broad categories as neurosis and psychosis, but most of them have shown large disagreements when precise diagnoses have been called for. In one study, for example, where the general findings were considered to show a favorable reliability among the diagnoses of a group of psychiatrists, the percentage of agreement between two psychiatrists for specific subtype diagnoses, excluding organic brain syndromes, ranged from .06 to .57 (Schmidt and Fonda, 1956). In another study comparing three psychiatrists working in the same hospital with comparable groups of patients, it was reported that one of the psychiatrists classified two-thirds of his patients as schizophrenic as compared with comparable percentages of 22 and 29 by the other two psychiatrists (Pasamanick, Dinitz, and Lefton, 1959). Frank (1969), in a review of a number of such studies, came to the conclusion that a new system of diagnostic classification was required and questioned the validity of research studies based on psychiatric diagnoses.

The material presented above does not inspire a great deal of confidence in the reliability and utility of psychiatric diagnosis. Although there is some variation in the diagnostic nomenclatures used in various parts of the world, American psychiatrists have used the classification systems developed by the American Psychiatric Association. These have been revised from time to time. The current, and greatly elaborated, system of diagnostic classification is the Third Edition of the Diagnostic and Statistical Manual of Mental Disorders, usually referred to as DSM-III (American Psychiatric Association, 1980). Because of the limited reliability of the previous DSM-II, serious attempts were made to improve the quality and reliability of DSM-III. The criteria for diagnosis were made more stringent and a number of field trials were held prior to its publication. The response by psychologists has not been very favorable (McReynolds, 1979; Miller, Bergstrom, Cross, & Grube, 1981; Schacht & Nathan, 1977), but the new diagnostic criteria have been included or referred to in recent textbooks on abnormal psychology.

It is probably too early to offer an adequate appraisal of the utility of the new diagnostic manual. Although it may be better in some respects than its predecessor, it does not appear likely that DSM-III will correct all of the problems associated with diagnosing those disorders which consist of a variety of symptoms and which may be viewed in different ways by individual clinicians (Cantwell, Russel, Mattison, & Will, 1979). Furthermore, some particular problems pertaining to categorizing certain behaviors as mental illness in DSM-III are readily apparent, and have been found objectionable by a number of psychologists. In the new diagnostic manual, for example, several new diagnostic categories were added which were not included in DSM-II. These include such new disorders as pathological gambling, identity disorder, developmental reading disorder, and developmental arithmetic disorder. Thus, a child who shows "a significant impairment in the development of arithmetic skills" can be given a psychiatric diagnosis if he or she is examined by a psychiatrist or psychologist. The same may hold true for college students with regard to identity problems. It should be evident that there are serious difficulties in deciding what really are diagnosable mental disorders, and that the issue is not just an academic one. Such decisions may have important social implications (Szasz, 1961). To most people, being diagnosed as "mentally ill" may have a very negative connotation, and in some situations it may lead to institutionalization. In other instances, it can be used as a defense in legal proceedings to avoid possible imprisonment. The matter is a complex one and, consequently, diagnostic labels should be used judiciously.

Before concluding this section, a few additional comments may be worthwhile. As indicated, formal diagnoses have been a part of medicine for some time, and all hospitals generally require that a diagnosis be placed in the patient's file. State and national statistics on mental disease also make use of diagnoses. More recently, with payments for psychological services provided by insurance companies in a manner comparable to that for medical services, a diagnosis is also required before payment is authorized. This would appear to put pressure on psychologists, as well as others, to provide a psychiatric diagnosis even when there are limited data upon which to base a diagnosis. Such a situation may also force a clinician to provide a diagnosis which is not accurate because the actual problems of the patient would not meet the requirements for reimbursement. For such reasons, as well as others, one must be cautious in placing undue emphasis on formal psychiatric diagnosis and in neglecting other attributes of the client which may be important for planning treatment.

DIAGNOSTIC TESTING

Even though psychologists working in psychiatric institutions were involved in helping to secure psychiatric diagnoses for the patients they examined, the limitations in this approach, along with the growing interest in personality dynamics, led to a somewhat different emphasis. One of the main influences in this new direction was contributed by the work of Rapaport and his colleagues, then at the Menninger Foundation (Rapaport, Gill, & Schafer, 1945, 1946). Essentially, this approach combined a psychoanalytic frame of reference with a large battery of psychological tests, and emphasized a rather extensive personality analysis of the individual being examined. Although Rapaport's thinking was still influenced by diagnostic categories, emphasis was placed on the "psychodynamics" of the different types of psychopathology. Diagnoses, per se, were somewhat secondary to the description and understanding of personality, the presumption being that a knowledge of personality structure and dynamics were of basic importance for the clinical disposition and treatment of the client.

Another relatively new feature of this approach was the use of projective techniques as an important part of the psychological test battery. These techniques were utilized particularly for insights about the individual's unconscious psychological processes, and unlike more traditional psychological tests, were less well standardized and relied much more upon the subjective interpretations of the examiner. The "newer" diagnostic role of the clinical psychologist thus combined the traditional psychometric procedures with the use of projective techniques, all interpreted by the psychologist in a clinical manner. In this process, personality theory, largely psychoanalytic, provided a frame of reference for interpreting test responses and for synthesizing the different types of data secured by the psychologist.

In the late 1940's and the 1950's, the approach mentioned above was in its heyday and students spent fairly large amounts of time studying the various diagnostic instruments and in learning how to write extensive personality appraisals. But, as noted in Chapter 1, there has been a gradual decline in the involvement with this pursuit and some changes have taken place in this area of activity. While it is difficult to give a fully adequate explanation for this phenomenon (Arthur, 1969; Holt, 1967), a few possibilities can be offered. One very practical problem concerned the amount of time devoted to this activity and whether or not the findings secured were worth the effort. An extensive battery of tests might require several hours for administration with many more hours for the scoring and interpretation of the findings, to say nothing of the time required to write a long, detailed report. Frequently, by the time the psychologist's report was ready to be added to the client's folder, the case had been disposed of entirely! Psychologists thus experienced some dissonance between the amount of effort they expended on their diagnostic testing and the use to which their work was put or the values placed upon it.

A second possible reason for the relative decline of this type of diagnostic work was that many of the reports appeared to abound in undue speculations about unconscious conflicts and dynamics without providing too much in the way of empirical support for such speculative assertions (Garfield, Heine, and Leventhal, 1954). Many of the psychological evaluations also were short on behavioral predictions and long on generalized statements, many of which could apply to most people.

Somewhat related to this was a growing psychological literature which seemed to raise considerable doubt about the validity of the instruments used and the accuracy of the conclusions derived therefrom (Garfield, 1957; Holtzman & Sells, 1954; Little, 1959; Little & Shneidman, 1959; Meehl, 1959; Murstein, 1965). Another possible reason may have been the fact that the psychologists' reports frequently had little impact on the treatment plans and disposition of the client. Furthermore, as psychologists began to participate more actively in psychotherapeutic activities, activities which were highly valued, their previous involvement with diagnostic testing began to decline. A final factor may have been the rise of the behavior therapies. As noted previously, these treatment approaches focused on the behavioral difficulties of the individual, and were not at all concerned with unconscious conflicts. From this orientation, diagnostic appraisal involved primarily behavioral assessment of the individual and his environment based on interviews, observations, and case history data.

The diagnostic role and activities of the clinical psychologist thus underwent some significant changes in a relatively short period of time. The involvement with diagnostic testing diminished, test batteries became less extensive, a more critical attitude toward diagnostic testing generally and projective techniques specifically was gradually manifested, and the amount of time devoted to instruction in this area in our graduate programs in clinical psychology gradually declined.

In spite of these changes, however, there is some continuity with past practices. Courses in the individual testing of intelligence, personality assessment, and projective techniques are still included in most graduate training programs, and batteries of tests are given and interpreted in hospital and clinical settings. The test batteries tend to be briefer and less extensive than formerly, and the reports are briefer. Nevertheless, although there are some newer tests used today, particularly in the area of neuropsychology, some of the old favorites are still used, and a certain amount of the psychologists' time is spent in diagnostic staff conferences. In a fairly recent survey of a sample of clinical psychologists, diagnostic and assessment activities were listed as the fourth most frequently engaged-in activity in terms of the total time devoted to it (Garfield & Kurtz, 1976)—almost 10% of the time of this sample was devoted to such activities. The range of participation for individual psychologists, however, is undoubtedly wide with some devoting a major share of their time to diagnostic activities and many devoting little or no time to such pursuits. Let us now proceed, however, to examine the kinds of diagnostic problems that are referred to the clinical psychologist for assessment.

TYPES OF DIAGNOSTIC AND ASSESSMENT PROBLEMS

Although some referrals may specifically include a request pertaining to the diagnosis or diagnostic classification of the patient, particularly in medical settings, other types of questions are probably more frequent. The specific referral problem or diagnostic question posited will depend on the particular clinical setting, the type of client served, and the philosophy or orientation of the staff. A psychoanalytic institute differs noticeably from a university counseling center or a large state hospital. Consequently, before going ahead with our discussion of diagnostic problems, it is worth describing briefly the procedures or activities that occur in a clinical setting before diagnostic decisions are made.

In most outpatient clinics, for example, the person who has applied for services is generally interviewed first by an intake worker. This frequently is a psychiatric social worker, but could be any staff person. This person will secure some biographical and historical data pertaining to the problem which brings the patient to the clinic, the patient's current life situation, his interest in treatment, and similar material. Some judgment will also be made as to the suitability of the particular client and his or her problem for treatment at the clinic. In some settings the new client may also be interviewed and examined by a psychiatrist, with some overlap in the material secured. In some children's clinics the child may be seen initially by a psychiatrist and the parent or parents by a social worker. Frequently, after the intake procedure is completed, a staff conference will be held to consider all new cases for disposition or assignment to treatment. If the client's problem appears to be relatively clear and unambiguous, the necessary staff decision can be reached without much difficulty, and the disposition of the case can be handled expeditiously. If the person is judged to be a suitable client, he is accepted for treatment and assigned to a specific therapist. If his problem is deemed to be one that is better served by some other agency, the proper referral is recommended. If, however, there is some concern that the patient may be more disturbed than he appears, if the staff feels he is likely to harm himself or others, or if, in general, the initial picture is unclear, the patient may be referred for a psychological evaluation. The psychologist thus would not routinely examine all new cases, but would work mainly with those cases that presented some particular diagnostic problem.

The situation at a large mental hospital might vary from that just presented. At present, when the combination of drugs and milieu therapy have produced a sharp increase in the rates of both discharge and readmission of patients in such institutions, many patients are already known to the hospital staff and do not require an intensive diagnostic assessment upon reentry to the hospital. The size of the hospital may also preclude the psychological evaluation of a large number of cases. In some instances attempts have been made to use group tests as screening devices for all new patients who are capable of cooperating with the test instructions. Individual referrals are reserved for those cases that present special diagnostic problems. A patient who appears particularly depressed might be examined for the purpose of evaluating the severity of depression and the probability of suicidal behavior. In another case, there may be a suggestion of possible brain damage that needs clarification. In still other instances there may be a question of whether the patient is psychotic or how severely disturbed he really is. In such cases, referrals may be made to the psychologist for help in appraising the patient and his difficulties. In a children's clinic or in a school situation there may be problems of erratic behavior, lack of attention, and hyperactivity, along with poor school performance. Questions of possible brain dysfunction or limited mental ability would usually lead to a request for psychological examination. In recent years there has been a growing interest and development in the area of neuropsychology. More extensive and refined procedures for evaluating deficits associated with brain damage have been developed, and a number of clinical psychologists have been active in training and research in this area (Boll, 1978; Heaton, Baade, & Johnson, 1978; Parsons & Prigatano, 1978; Reitan & Davison, 1974). A number of clinical centers now have the personnel and equipment to provide such evaluations.

The community mental health movement has also had an impact on the type of diagnostic services provided in many community clinics. One major emphasis in such clinics is on providing immediate service to clients who appear to be experiencing some kind of crisis situation (Darbonne, 1967; Harris, Kalis, & Freeman, 1963; Levine, 1966). In these "walk-in" or "emergency" clinics, the focus is on immediate and usually brief treatment. As a result, diagnostic testing and other related procedures are usually passed by in order to facilitate the initiation of therapy while the patient is still in a state of crisis. The rationale for this is that most individuals in such states respond positively and quickly to treatment which is provided at the time of crisis. Waiting lists and other delays in providing clinical services are viewed as not beneficial to the client. Thus, the type of clinical setting will generally influence the diagnostic role of the clinical psychologist and the type of diagnostic questions or referrals with which he will handle.

As was indicated in the previous chapter, the orientation of the clinical staff may also influence to some degree the types of diagnostic questions asked of the psychologist and the assessment techniques that will be used. These in turn will influence the kind of diagnostic or personality evaluation that is prepared. For example, in a psychoanalytically oriented clinic there may be considerable emphasis on personality dynamics including appraisals of ego strength, defenses, and unconscious conflicts. A lengthy description might thus be prepared based on the administration of several projective techniques. Clinics with a behavioral or cognitive orientation would generally forego such an appraisal and focus more on questionnaires and self-ratings of behavior, fears, and cognitions. Centers that rely heavily on medication in the treatment of their patients also would not require extensive psychological testing but rely more on interview, observation, or medical tests. Private practitioners would also vary, both in terms of the amount of time devoted to diagnostic testing, and to the type of examinations conducted.

Keeping in mind that clinical psychologists work and practice in a diversity of settings, it can be anticipated that they will encounter a variety of diagnostic problems. Of course, the average clinician would tend to be occupied with only a portion of these problems for not all occur in every setting and some degree of specialization develops with most clinicians. Clinical psychologists who work with children tend to see a different set of diagnostic problems and to use somewhat different diagnostic techniques than do those who work with adult clients. Similar specialization occurs for those who function in university counseling centers, walk-in clinics, neurological departments or medical schools, and so forth. The type of referral and clinic policy would also influence the kind of diagnostic appraisal considered appropriate. A few examples may be offered here for illustrative purposes.

Mild to moderately disturbed individuals who seek out psychological help will generally receive limited diagnostic study. Such help is usually sought in outpatient clinics or from private practitioners, and the intake interview may suffice for diagnostic purposes. However, if the intake interviewer or the therapist feel uncertain or concerned about certain aspects of the patient's behavior, the patient may be referred to a psychologist for a more complete examination. If the therapist is a psychologist, she may, of course, conduct the psychological examination herself. Most frequently, in the author's experience, the concern expressed in this type of situation is that the patient may be more disturbed and less well integrated than he appears to be on the surface. Psychotherapists generally believe that certain types of intensive or confrontative therapy may be potentially harmful to such patients and that different approaches are more desirable. However, where no particular concerns were expressed, such diagnostic appraisals would usually not be requested.

In cases of more serious potential pathology, or where the symptoms of the patient do not present a clearcut diagnostic picture, more intensive diagnostic appraisal would usually appear to be required. One of the most important diagnostic problems is that of differentiating a possible organic brain syndrome from a psychosis or severe disorder without known organic etiology. Since the care and treatment of patients with these two types of disorders are usually quite different, a diagnostic evaluation is more likely to be requested and such an evaluation may be quite extensive. Thus, medical centers which receive a high number of serious or problem cases in terms of diagnosis, will tend to provide more extensive and intensive diagnostic procedures than will outpatient clinics or hospitals that treat chronic cases.

In a similar fashion, cases in which a diagnostic decision is very important to the individual or to society will usually receive very extensive diagnostic examinations. A recent example is provided by the recent attempted assassination of the President of the United States. The young man who made this attempt is receiving extensive observation and examination while he is held in custody. The diagnostic conclusions offered will usually have some impact on the final judicial decision in such cases. In the author's own limited experience in this regard, the findings of his psychological examinations were given considerable weight by the courts, and, of course, decisions in such cases are not made lightly. Diagnoses concerning mental retardation, mental deficit, and psychotic behavior can be quite consequential, and thus considerable time may be spent in some diagnostic evaluations of this kind.

Children referred to clinics or to school psychologists also will present a variety of problems which range in complexity and severity. When children are brought for professional help it is frequently a function of the parents' perception of the child, their own anxiety levels, what they have read in the popular press, or other problems within the family, as well as the actual behavioral problems of the child. An only child may sometimes be seen as hyperactive because the parents expect the child to be quiet and well-behaved. A normal child may be viewed as dull or bright depending on the parents and the particular circumstances. In some instances, a relatively brief examination of mental ability may be sufficient to handle the problem situation. In others, more detailed appraisal may be necessary. These may include such problems as a marked decline in academic achievement, erratic behavior, overactivity, extreme fearfulness, social isolation, and the like.

From what has just been mentioned, it should be apparent that psychologists may be called upon to deal with a wide variety of diagnostic problems. It is difficult to group these problems into a few convenient categories. However, many of the diagnostic issues could be grouped into four general categories: (1) Appraisal of mental ability or intelligence; (2) diagnosis and appraisal of special defects or special strengths and aptitudes; (3) differential diagnosis; (4) personality assessment and appraisal. We shall say a few words about each of these categories, recognizing that the classification is arbitrary and that a diagnostic assessment may include all four emphases.

The appraisal of mental ability, as we noted in Chapter 1, is practically synonomous with the early development of clinical psychology. Historically, this is the oldest function of the clinical psychologist and the psychologist's role and expertise in evaluating mental ability is now well recognized. Any thorough assessment of possible mental retardation would include the administration of a standard test of intelligence by a trained psychologist. The type of test used would depend upon the client to be evaluated. Although some clinical psychologists today may view the administration of a test of intelligence as a somewhat lower level skill, the diagnostic importance of this procedure should not be undervalued. The appraisal of mental ability can also go beyond the overall evaluation of general intelligence to include an appraisal of particular mental deficits or strengths, since a test of intelligence attempts to measure a number of mental functions.

The examination of special defects or abilities would be conducted differently, depending on the clinical situation in which the psychologist works. In a counseling center, this might include the appraisal of various educational or vocational skills; in a school clinic, it might involve different reading skills, including rate of reading and degree of comprehension as well as auditory and visual perception; in a mental hospital, it could embrace memory, conceptual ability or ability to perform certain tasks. Such an appraisal of special assets and liabilities is of particular importance in the rehabilitation of disabled individuals. Previous abilities and skills may have been impaired by some disabling injury or disease and it becomes necessary to assess the individual in terms of planning a program of rehabilitation for him. This type of diagnostic appraisal usually is one of the first steps in the program of rehabilitating the person so that he can again assume a productive role in society.

The problem of differential diagnosis also would have a different orientation in the various clinical settings. Psychologists in psychiatric institutions are frequently concerned with helping to differentiate early psychotic disorders from less severe disturbances or with detecting cases with possible brain damage. Psychologists in children's clinics might be less concerned with such problems, and in cases of school retardation, for example, would have to evaluate the importance of physical, intellectual, and emotional factors contributing to this disability. The main emphasis in differential diagnosis is thus to delineate the problem in order that specific therapeutic efforts can be undertaken. Similar symptoms can be observed in cases which differ greatly in terms of etiological factors and the type of therapy required. Conversion or hysterical disorders and epilepsy, for example, would require radically different treatment efforts, although the overt symptomatology might be similar. Differential diagnosis in such cases can be extremely important.

It should be apparent that the matter of differential diagnosis follows and is derived from the medical model of illness. Although some criticism of the usefulness and reliability of psychiatric diagnosis has been made earlier in this chapter, and although the medical model has come under considerable attack by psychologists (Adams, 1964; Albee, 1967; Balance, Hirschfield, & Bringmann, 1970; Eysenck, 1961; Hobbs, 1963; Szasz, 1961), the kinds of problems presented above do have some reality. Some means of differentiating organic from nonorganic disturbance, for example, is clinically of great importance, even though one may not adhere fully to a given system of nosology. Furthermore, diagnosis, in the broader sense of specifying the problem as clearly as possible, would appear to have some clinical utility. This is different from merely trying to label a patient or to place him in some pigeonhole. In a similar sense, proper diagnosis or assessment of the individual seeking help would appear to be a meaningful approach to the planning of treatment, even though such an approach would not have to utilize a disease model or a particular classification system.

In other kinds of clinical cases, however, the problem of differential diagnosis as discussed above may not be of prime importance. The case may be clearly one of emotional conflict or disturbance previously described as neurotic. Nevertheless, a more complete appraisal of the patient's personality may be deemed important before assigning him to a specific therapist for treatment. This would be particularly true for clinical settings with a psychodynamic orientation. In such instances, the clinician is interested in understanding the possible conflicts, defenses, and resources of the patient and the implications these have for planning a program of psychotherapy. For example, how does the individual view himself and his world? What are his characteristic emotional patterns and how does he tend to relate to others in interpersonal situations? At this level, the clinician is concerned primarily with dynamic aspects of personality, although in some cases a knowledge of the patient's mental ability is also of value.

It is also pertinent to point out that while concern with understanding the dynamics of the individual's personality represents some progress beyond the mere assigning of a label to the patient, understanding for the mere sake of understanding does not fulfill a clinical function. The understanding of the patient is usually a means toward fulfilling some goal relevant to the patient's problems. It has become increasingly evident that a description of the patient's personality is not really adequate for assessment purposes unless it can be related meaningfully to the referral question or to some specific predictions about the patient. In other words, diagnosis and assessment must be related as much as possible to prognosis and treatment, and the diagnostic assessment of the individual's personality must contribute to the actual practical decisions that have to be made concerning a specific patient. The diagnostic findings, therefore, should provide information that is useful for devising answers to the problems presented by the case at hand. Such problems may involve a decision as to the type of treatment, the approach to treatment, commitment to an institution, assignment to a closed or open ward, discharge from the hospital, or assignment to a specific therapist. Frequently, even such diagnostic recommendations or conclusions may be too broad or lacking in specificity, as, for example, when psychotherapy is recommended for a given client. A more helpful outcome would be to specify what is wrong and what needs to be modified.

There is little question that the four general diagnostic categories overlap and that they have somewhat different applications in different settings. In some situations a complete evaluation of the patients's personality would include most of the other categories such as mental level, impairment, and specific defects, as well as an attempt to relate these to an understanding of the motivations, conflicts, and defenses of the individual. Although such intensive study is not necessary in most cases, it represents the most comprehensive and dynamic approach to the diagnostic assessment of the patient. Obviously this is a complex task which requires great skill on the part of the clinician. It is also a very time-consuming endeavor which, therefore, has to be justified by its clear usefulness and relevance for a particular problem.

In order to fulfill these functions, the psychologist relies on several types of tools or techniques. These include such different procedures as the interview, case study, observation of behavior, rating scales, and psychological tests. Although the psychologist in his professional duties will have occasion to use many of these techniques, he has tended in the past to become identified particularly with one of them—psychological tests. Consequently, more attention will be devoted to the use of psychological tests than to the other assessment techniques. But, in spite of this emphasis, which reflects the recent history of clinical psychology, the student must not assume that diagnosis in clinical psychology is synonymous with the use of tests. Tests represent only one of the diagnostic aids at the disposal of the psychologist, even though they represent a unique contribution of the psychologist. Here, once again, the type of clinic in which the psychologist works will determine the kind of techniques he will utilize most extensively. Where the psychologist works as a member of a team with the psychiatrist and social worker, the use of tests may be described as his particularly unique contribution to the study of the patient. In some university counseling centers, predominantly staffed by psychologists, or in a number of community mental health centers, interviews and related techniques may be used more frequently. Behavior therapists also appear to place little or no reliance on the use of projective techniques and a large battery of tests. Their focus is much more on the analysis of the client's specific behavioral difficulties with some attention devoted to the history of the problem.

PERSONALITY THEORY AND DIAGNOSTIC ASSESSMENT

It should be reemphasized that the assessment techniques used and the information secured by means of them do not provide us with automatic answers to the problems presented by the patient. What we have available from the tests, interviews, and observations of the patient essentially are bits of information and inferences relating to them. If we simply list these as our diagnostic report, we are merely combining items from different sources and at different levels of complexity in a somewhat additive fashion. We do not have a picture of an individual and how he or she functions as an integrated organism. To attain this end, we usually make some use of theory, whether it be social-learning theroy, phenomenological theory, or psychoanalytic theory. In other words, we draw upon some organized frame of reference within which to organize and relate our observations so that some meaningful synthesis can be obtained. This greatly enhances the possible significance of our data, for each part takes on more precise meaning when viewed in relation to the whole. This, essentially, is the process of clinical inference in which the clinician examines his data and orders or organizes them in some fashion. We ask ourselves, "What does this response mean?" "How does this impression fit in with our other information?" "Do the apparent fluctuations in the quality of responses and the suggested loss of control noted in this patient's test protocols signify an impending psychotic break with reality?" "Is the low level of mental functioning evident in this client's performance related to limited intelligence, or is it the result of severe disturbance?" We examine our data and then make inferences and construct hypotheses related to our clinical information and knowledge. We reject those hypotheses that appear not to be supported by all that we have available in terms of data and theory, and gradually relate those that do appear to be warranted. If we are reasonably successful we emerge with an interpretation or hypothesis about the individual which appears congruent with the material at hand and theoretically meaningful. This does not imply that we are always successful or that our interpretations and predictions are correct. It does illustrate, however, something of the process of clinical inference and the means by which the clinician reaches his diagnostic or assessment conclusions.

The diagnostic approach mentioned above has several important implications for the training and professional functioning of clinical psychologists. It implies that the clinical psychologist cannot be a technician, because there are no simple routine approaches to the assessment of personality. From this point of view, a mature understanding of the dynamics of personality and behavior is a prerequisite, not only for assessment, but for all functions of the clinician in psychology. A great deal of the psychologist's clinical assessment activities, for example, cannot be performed or interpreted adequately apart from this orientation. This point is stressed here because of the subsequent emphasis in the remainder of the book on the professional duties, functions, and techniques of the clinical psychologist. It is assumed, however, that maximum utilization of most of the techniques to be described is dependent on the individual's basic understanding of personality and behavior. Since such knowledge provides a frame of reference for the clinician's general understanding and interpretation of behavior, it should also play an influential role in his daily diagnostic work. This, however, is not always the case. Although a psychologist can function diagnostically at different levels of complexity—from the reporting of observed behavior, or psychological test scores to an interpretation of repressed conflicts—the critical use of available theoretical knowledge will enhance the quality of the work performed. This holds not only for the use of projective techniques, but for the more objectively scored tests as well.

An additional point that will be stressed later but which also deserves mention here concerns the clinical psychologists' knowledge of the relevant research literature on the techniques she uses. In addition to familiarity with the administration of appropriate tests and other techniques, the psychologist needs to be familiar with the research that has been done on these clinical tools. Such research may also provide a means of checking or validating popular clinical interpretations or hypotheses associated with the tests.

Many beginning students become primarily concerned with "practical" problems of test administration and stereotyped interpretations to the exclusion of theoretical considerations. To a certain extent this is understandable, because they are anxious to master techniques and perform creditably in the actual work situation. Perhaps, because of this, there has frequently been an undue emphasis in clinical work on diagnostic signs or patterns for various assessment techniques, even though they may have little validity. In the long run, the mature use and evaluation of theory and a knowledge of the research literature will differentiate the clinical psychologist from the test technician. This is true particularly if the psychologist is concerned with meaningful personality descriptions rather than with stereotyped and superficial psychological evaluations.

What is meant here is that the psychologist should concern himself with the understanding of an actual individual and his problems instead of an abstract report of test scores, stereotyped textbook test interpretations, or the placing of a label on a client. In other words, we should not be preoccupied exclusively with the intelligence classification of an individual or the fact that he performs at a level below his maximum or with reporting the presence of bizarre responses, but, rather, with the significance of such findings for understanding the person and helping him with his problems. A psychologist who is familiar only with tests is inclined to concentrate on the reporting of test data without being able to integrate these findings adequately with current theoretical knowledge to form a more meaningful picture of the individual.

An illustration may help to clarify this point. Let us suppose that we are examining an adult by means of a standard intelligence test. Our subject is obviously very bright and gives excellent, meticulous, and unusually detailed responses to our test questions. By focusing our attention solely on the test responses we might conclude only that the individual is an intellectually superior person with unusual verbal knowledge who is capable of producing very elaborate and detailed responses. Although this is of some value, we can learn or infer more about him by evaluating our test data in terms of a theoretical framework. Here is a person, for example, who is overly meticulous and detailed in responding to even the simplest questions. What is the significance of such behavior in terms of personality theory? If this performance can be viewed as a sample of his behavior, we might infer that he is an overly pedantic person who attempts to impress others with his intellectual formulations. This can be regarded as a personality pattern or possibly, a defense developed by the individual as a means of attaining some type of personal security. Things must be ordered and intellectualized by this individual for him to feel at ease and to handle interpersonal situations. A further inference might be that his overly intellectualized behavior results in a less flexible and free expression of feeling.

Although this brief example is taken out of context and may appear to be merely crude speculation, it is an attempt to illustrate how test data and behavior may be utilized more fully by interpreting them in the light of theoretical knowledge of personality. The interpreter, on the other hand, should not stray too far from his observations and data, or should he make his data fit his theories. There are obvious dangers in this regard and the clinician should regard his inferences as hypotheses that may have to be revised in the light of additional information. Nevertheless, the considered and judicious use of theory will tend to enhance the significance of test data.

To make the best use of psychological data, therefore, the clinician must interpret and relate the data in terms of available psychological facts and theories. He should also be aware of the theoretical implications and limitations of the various instruments he uses. Many personality questionnaires are based on a theory of rather specific traits. Some personality tests utilize unreliable nosological categories as variables in personality appraisal. Other theoretical assumptions are implicit in the use of the different projective techniques. The psychologist should also keep in mind that individuals respond in different ways to different situations. Apart from evaluating his own influence on the client, the psychologist also has to be wary of describing a static or abstract individual instead of a real person.

The type of diagnostic work engaged in by the clinical psychologist thus would appear to require a proper blending of abilities. The psychologist must be a sensitive observer and participant in the clinical situation, must be able to relate well to clients, must possess adequate knowledge of personality theory and psychopathology, and must be familiar with a variety of clinical techniques, including the research on their strengths and limitations. In addition, she must be capable of integrating her observations and data about the client so that they contribute in a meaningful way to the treatment or disposition of the case. This is no simple task and requires extensive training and experience.

REFERENCES

Adams, H. B. "Mental Illness" or interpersonal behavior? *American Psychologist,* 1964, *19,* 191–197.
Albee, G. W. Give us a place to stand and we will move the earth. *The Clinical Psychologist,* 1967, *20,* 1–4.
American Psychiatric Association. *Diagnostic and statistical manual of mental disorders.* (3rd Ed.). Washington, D.C., 1980.
Arthur, A. Z. Diagnostic testing and the new alternatives. *Psychological Bulletin,* 1969, *72* (3), 183–192.
Ash, P. The reliability of psychiatric diagnoses. *Journal of Abnormal and Social Psychology,* 1949, *44,* 272–276.
Balance, W. D. G., Hirschfield, P. O., & Bringmann, W. G. Mental illness: Myth, metaphor, or model. *Professional Psychology,* 1970, *1,* 133–137.
Beck, A. T., Ward, C. H., Mendelson, M., Mock, J. E., & Erbaugh, J. K. Reliability of psychiatric diagnoses: 2. A study of consistency of clinical judgments and ratings. *American Journal of Psychiatry,* 1962, *119,* 351–357.
Boll, T. J. Diagnosing brain impairment. In B. B. Wolman (Ed.), *Clinical diagnosis of mental disorders: A handbook.* New York: Plenum Press, 1978.
Cantwell, D. P., Russel, A. T., Mattison, R., & Will, L. A comparison of DSM-II and DSM-III in the diagnosis of childhood psychiatric disorders. I. Agreement with expected diagnosis. *Archives of General Psychiatry,* 1979, *36,* 1208–1213.
Committee on Nomenclature and Statistics of the American Psychiatric Association. *Diagnostic and statistical manual of mental disorders.* (2nd Ed.). Washington, D.C.: American Psychiatric Association, 1968.
Darbonne, A. R. Crisis: A review of theory, practice, and research. *Psychotherapy: Theory, Research and Practice,* 1967, *4,* 49–56.
Eysenck, H. J. Classification and the problem of diagnosis. In H. J. Eysenck (Ed.), *Handbook of Abnormal Psychology.* New York: Basic Books, 1961. Pp. 1–31.
Frank, G. Psychiatric diagnosis: A review of research. *Journal of General Psychology,* 1969, *81,* 157–176.
Garfield, S. L. *Introductory clinical psychology.* New York: Macmillan, 1957.
Garfield, S. L., & Kurtz, R. Clinical psychologists in the 1970s. *American Psychologist,* 1976, *31,* 1–9.
Garfield, S. L., Heine, R. W., & Leventhal, M. An evaluation of psychological reports in a clinical setting. *Journal of Consulting Psychology,* 1954, *18,* 281–286.

Harris, M. R., Kalis, B., & Freeman, E. Precipitating stress: An approach to brief therapy. *American Journal of Psychotherapy,* 1963, *17,* 465–471.

Heaton, R. K., Baade, L. E., & Johnson, K. L. Neuropsychological test results associated with psychiatric disorders in adults. *Psychological Bulletin,* 1978, *85,* 141–162.

Hobbs, N. Statement on mental illness and retardation. *American Psychologist,* 1963, *18,* 295–299.

Holt, R. R. Diagnostic testing: Present status and future prospects. *Journal of Nervous and Mental Disease,* 1967, *144,* 444–465.

Holtzman, W. H., & Sells, S. B. Prediction of flying success by clinical analysis of test protocols. *Journal of Abnormal and Social Psychology,* 1954, *49,* 485–490.

Hunt, W. A., Wittson, C. L., & Hunt, E. B. A theoretical and practical analysis of the diagnostic process. In P. H. Hoch and J. Zubin (Eds.), *Current problems in psychiatric diagnosis.* New York: Grune and Stratton, 1953.

Kreitman, N. The reliability of psychiatric diagnosis. *Journal of Mental Science,* 1961, *107,* 876–886.

Levine, R. A. Stand-Patism versus change in psychiatric clinical practice. *American Journal of Psychiatry,* 1966, *123,* 71–77.

Little, K. B. Problems in the validation of projective techniques. *Journal of Projective Techniques,* 1959, *23,* 287–290.

Little, K. B., & Shneidman, E. S. Congruencies among interpretations of psychological test and anamnestic data. *Psychological Mongraphs,* 1959, *73,* 1–42.

McReynolds, W. T. DSM-III and the future of applied social science. *Professional Psychology,* 1979, *10,* 123–132.

Malamud, D. I. Objective measurement of clinical status in psychopathological research. *Psychological Bulletin,* 1946, *43,* 240–258.

Meehl, P. E. Structural and projective tests: Some common problems in validation. *Journal of Projective Techniques,* 1959, *23,* 268–272.

Miller, L. S., Bergstrom, D. A., Cross, H. J., & Grube, J. W. Opinions and use of the DSM system by practicing psychologists. *Professional Psychology,* 1981, *12,* 385–390.

Murstein, B. I. (Ed.), *Handbook of projective techniques.* New York: Basic Books, 1965.

Parsons, O. A., & Prigatano, G. P. Methodological considerations in clinical neuropsychological research. *Journal of Consulting and Clinical Psychology,* 1978, *46,* 608–619.

Pasamanick, B., Dinitz, S., & Lefton, M. Psychiatric orientation and its relation to diagnosis and treatment in a mental hospital. *American Journal of Psychiatry,* 1959, *116,* 127–132.

Rapaport, D., Gill, M., & Schafer, R. *Diagnostic psychological testing.* Vol. 1. Chicago: Year Book Publishers, 1945.

Rapaport, D., Gill, M., & Schafer, R. *Diagnostic psychological testing.* Vol. 2. Chicago: Year Book Publishers, 1946.

Reitan, R. M., & Davison, L. A. *Clinical neuropsychology: Current status and applications.* New York: Wiley, 1974.

Schacht, R., & Nathan, P. E. But is it good for the psychologists? Appraisal and status of DSM-III. *American Psychologist,* 1977, *32,* 1017–1025.

Schmidt, H. O., & Fonda, C. P. The reliability of psychiatric diagnosis: A new look. *Journal of Abnormal and Social Psychology,* 1956, *52,* 262–267.

Spitzer, R. L., & Fleiss, J. L. A reanalysis of the reliability of psychiatric diagnosis. *British Journal of Psychiatry,* 1974, *125,* 341–347.

Szasz, T. *The myth of mental illness: Foundations of a theory of personal conduct.* New York: Hoeber-Harper, 1961.

The Clinical Interview and Case Study

The most widely used and ubiquitous clinical technique is undoubtedly the interview. All of us have had some personal experience with being interviewed in some connection or other. This method has been used in a variety of situations—personnel selection, social case work, medicine, law, education, vocational counseling, public opinion surveys, and so forth (Kahn & Cannell, 1957). Since the interview basically involves some form of communication between two or more persons, organized around a specific objective, it can be carried out without undue difficulties in most situations and can be adapted to serve a variety of purposes. In terms of the clinical psychologist, the interview is used mainly for three general purposes: diagnostic assessment, psychological testing, and psychotherapy. It is used in assessment to secure information about the client's problem and to assess the nature of his difficulty. In fact, the interview, in some guise or other, is usually the initial step in the clinical process. When an individual seeks help for his personal problems he is usually interviewed first to find out the nature of the problems and whether or not the clinic or practitioner can help him with it.

Individually administered psychological tests also can be considered a form of interview, in this instance a standardized form in which all clients are asked essentially the same questions in a carefully prescribed order and manner. Although psychologists have long been identified with this type of standardized interview, they also use other types and forms of the interview for other purposes. The interview situation is also used in different ways and with particular objectives in psychotherapy with particular emphasis placed on the communications and relationship between the participants. This third use of the interview, as commented upon previously, is shared by a number of professional groups. Since the clinical use of psychological tests and the therapeutic utilization of interview procedures will be covered in greater detail in later chapters our focus here will be on the more general and diagnostically oriented use of the interview.

Several kinds of information can be secured by means of the interview, and this information can be cataloged in a number of different ways. From one vantage point we can dichotomize the material secured during an interview into self-report information and behavioral observation. In the former, we include the information that the client himself gives to us, either voluntarily or in response to questions or suggestions from the interviewer. Such data are necessarily controlled and selected by the client. He may tell us much or little about any given feature of himself or his past history, he may omit reference to potentially important aspects of his personal life, and he may distort, consciously or unconsciously, what he relates to the clinical interviewer. Obviously, then, the clinician must weigh and evaluate the verbal report he receives from the client. Generally, the interviewer is guided by his theoretical orientation, his knowledge of abnormal behavior, and his own clinical experience both in terms of what information he seeks (and how he goes about it) and how he evaluates or interprets the information he secures.

In addition to the self-report of information by the client, there is another source of data available from the client which in many ways is quite different from the former. Here we have reference to the behavior which the client displays in the interview situation. Such behavior also provides cues to the interviewer, not only about the interpersonal behavior of the client as he interacts with the interviewer, but also in terms of helping him to evaluate what the client says or does not say. Furthermore, although the client has relative control over his verbal responses, so that he may inhibit or censor certain material, it would appear that it is more difficult to control his overt behavior (Rosenzweig, 1950). For example, if a person believes that it is not acceptable to verbalize certain hostile feelings toward other people, including the interviewer, then, he may say nothing about them or report that he has no difficulties in his interactions with others. On the other hand, his behavior may give him away. He may be unwilling to respond to all of the interviewer's questions, he may have unusual difficulty expressing himself, he may show an increase in tension, and so forth. If the client is unusually hostile, shy, or anxious, it may be exceedingly difficult for her to hide behavioral evidence of such feelings or characteristics. A person may say she is not at all anxious about her interview with the psychologist, but be visibly trembling or manifest very moist palms when shaking hands with the psychologist.

Thus, the behavior of the client in the interview situation frequently mirrors important behavioral patterns and is an important source of data in its own right. The clinical interviewer, therefore, must be a sensitive and astute observer of the variety of behaviors which are manifested by the client, in his interactions with him. We will say more about this later.

So far, we have discussed two more or less discernible aspects of the interview—the information about himself and others which the client verbalizes freely or in response to questions, and the behavior which he exhibits in this situation. In such an analysis the focus is necessarily on the client and what kinds of responses or behaviors he brings forth. It would be somewhat erroneous, however, to perceive the client's responses as uncontaminated or "pure" data, that is as solely organism determined and without being influenced to some extent by the situation at hand, particularly by the presence and stimulus value of the interviewer himself. In a real sense, there are no stimulus-free responses of the subject in the interview situation, and the situation itself, as well as the person of the interviewer, are influences in terms of how the subject responds. If the influence of the interviewer is kept at a minimum, then more reliance can be placed upon the behavior of the client as a "sample" of the latter's more typical behavior. At the same time, the interviewer has to entertain some hypotheses concerning the impact of the interview on the client and the possible expectations which the client brings to the interview situation. Perhaps a few examples will help to clarify these points. Is the client's behavior as observed during the interview typical of him in all situations or is it more restricted to situations where he relates to authority figures, where he does not know what to expect, or to situations which he regards as very threatening? An individual may be quite threatened at being interviewed by a psychiatrist or psychologist and may be overly compliant or overly controlled in such a situation. The case of an individual referred for a psychiatric or psychological examination by the courts in connection with a murder trial is an extreme example of where the specific situation must be taken into account when evaluating the client's performance in the interview situation.

Thus, some allowances have to be made for situational elements when studying the manifested behavior of the client. In a similar fashion, also, the interviewer must be able to appraise his possible influence on both the content and manner of the client's response. If the interviewer is an attractive female in a miniskirt, the responses from some subjects conceivably may be quite different from those given to a matronly interviewer or to a middle-aged man. Therefore, the interviewer has to have some awareness of his or her impact or stimulus-value for the client and for different groups of clients.

Enough has been said to indicate that the interview is not a mere routine procedure where anyone can ask questions and receive answers. Much more than that is involved and, as we have seen, the interviewer has to evaluate the possible impact of his personality and the situation as well as the expectations of the interviewee with reference to the information secured and the behavior observed. There is more to the interview, however, than what has already been discussed. The interviewer must know what to say, when to speak, when to be silent, and what to observe. He has to know when to push further in certain directions, when to reassure the client, and when to stop. Obviously, the specific purpose of the interview will also provide a frame of reference for what the interviewer looks for, what information he attempts to elicit, and what generally will be the focus of the interview. Even with different goals in mind, however, the interviewer's orientation concerning human personality and disturbed behavior will be his cognitive guide in terms of what he does and also in terms of how he evaluates whatever data he secures.

The importance of the interviewer's frame of reference, of his experience, and specialized knowledge for the interpretations that are finally placed on the material secured thus points up the fact that the interview is more than the mere sum of information plus observation. To the extent that individuals may diverge widely in orientation and background, some differences in the interpretation or outcome of the interview can be expected. To the extent, however, that criteria of disturbance are fairly clear and evidence of pathology is very apparent, the agreement between trained observers will tend to be high. Here, again, the type of disturbance or problem encountered will influence what takes place in the interview.

In the various clinical settings, all professional workers make some use of the interview method. Social workers rely heavily on the interview to secure information about the client's problem, his past history, family relations, job adjustment, and so forth. In addition to interviewing the client, they may also interview other persons as a means of securing further information about the client's situation. This occurs most frequently in those instances where the client is a child, a mentally retarded individual, or a psychotic, or where there are some unusual discrepancies in the client's presentation of data about himself.

Psychiatrists and nurses also use interviews in their interactions with patients. These interviews may be brief or lengthy, depending on their purpose. Those individuals who make daily ward rounds may conduct relatively brief interviews. A psychiatric examination will be more detailed and may consist of specific mental or physical tests in addition to the interview. If the patient is to be presented at a staff conference, he or she may be interviewed by a number of the professional staff present as well as by the patient's regular physician or therapist.

The manner or extent to which the interview is used by clinical psychologists will be determined in great part by the situation in which they work, by the ways their duties or roles have been defined, and by the specific objectives they may have for a given interview. In some community clinics, in educational institutions, and in university clinics, the psychologist may be the professional person responsible for conducting the initial intake interviews with the patient, as well as later interviews. In other settings, such as hospitals, child-guidance clinics, and psychiatric outpatient clinics, the initial intake interviews may be more frequently conducted by social workers or psychiatrists. Whatever the setting, however, all mental health workers will make use of the interview in some fashion—whether in conducting intake interviews, psychotherapy, or research, or as part of a more intensive assessment procedure. Thus, because of its broad diagnostic and therapeutic applications, the interview, more than any other clinical technique, may be considered a basic procedure in psychological work with disturbed individuals.

The form the interview takes will depend upon the diagnostic purpose it is to serve, the theoretical orientation and professional identification of the interviewer, the personality of the participants, and the setting in which the interview takes place. For example, such factors as whether the client comes voluntarily to the interview to seek help with his problem, or whether he is more or less under coercion to come, will determine how the interview begins and progresses. The type of situation may also determine how structured the interview will be and how many direct questions will be asked of the client. The expectations of the client and his/her perception of the clinician may also influence the outcome of the interview.

It should be apparent that there is no rigidly prescribed form that the interview must follow. It can and should be flexible in terms of the situation at hand and the purpose it is to serve. Although some agencies may provide a prescribed or suggested outline to guide the intake interview, in most instances this is not meant as a rigid procedure to be followed step by step by the interviewer, but rather is intended as a guide to highlight the types of information considered important.

THE INTERVIEWING PROCESS

Because the main purpose of this volume is to acquaint the student with the techniques and methods of clinical psychology rather than to make the student proficient in their use, the technical aspects of interviewing will be discussed only briefly. More extended treatments of this topic are available elsewhere (Bingham, Moore, & Gustad, 1959; Deutsch & Murphy, 1955;

Garrett, 1972; Kahn & Cannell, 1957; Matarazzo, 1965; Pope, 1979; Sullivan, 1954).

The interview, as indicated previously, is a verbal interaction between two persons, which usually has some specified purpose or goal. The latter determines how the process will proceed and the respective roles of the participants. In general, the direction of the interview is specified or guided by one of the participants, who is designated the interviewer. Thus, a medical interview consists of a physician and patient, it is directed or conducted by the former in a manner so as to elicit information from the patient which will provide a basis for a medical diagnosis and subsequent treatment. In an employment interview, the structure may resemble the former, but the content of the interview and the relationship of the two participants may be different. Conceivably, the person being interviewed in the employment interview might be less forthright in mentioning negative experiences and might strive more to make a positive impression on the interviewer than would be the case in the medical interview. One could easily predict which individual would give the longest list of physical complaints. Both interviews, however, despite their differences, might produce some tension or anxiety in the individuals being interviewed, since the outcome of the interviews is important.

As is true with most professional contacts with clients, the first step in the interviewing process is to put the client at ease. Most clients will tend to have some apprehension about seeing a psychologist or "shrink." For some it may be a decision that was put off for some time. Thus, the first contact is very important. Rapport is essential here as it also is in the administration of psychological tests. Although the interviewer should be friendly, displaying a sincere interest in the client and his problem, she should not overrespond in this regard and should not go out of her way to promise the client more help than is either feasible or possible. The clinical interviewer's main objective is to allow the client to participate as effectively as possible in the interview in order to eventually understand and help him with his problem.

After attempting to put the client at ease, one of the next steps in the interviewing process is to allow the client to state his problem as he sees it or experiences it and to present his reasons for consulting the agency or the practitioner at this particular time. In a related manner, the psychologist might clarify the functions of the clinic or his particular approach in terms of the expectations of the client. The interviewer should attempt to provide an atmosphere that allows the patient to express himself without fear of censure or disapproval. Issues of the confidentiality of the interaction can be clarified and the appropriate guarantees provided.

As was mentioned earlier, the interview situation also allows the clinician an opportunity to observe the behavior of the client including such aspects as gestures, verbal hesitancies, glances, and expressions of mood. Consequently, it is important to understand and consider not only what the client states verbally, but also the feelings and attitudes underlying her statements. This deeper understanding of the client is emphasized continually in the therapeutic use of the interview, but it is also of prime importance in the diagnostic interview. As much, or more, understanding of the patient's problems, conflicts and motivations may be gained by "listening" to her feelings as to her words. Furthermore, by indicating to the client that you do understand and accept her feelings, you are more apt than otherwise to set the stage for her to reveal relatively important aspects of herself and her problems. In other words, the client may become increasingly able to talk about and share her inner thoughts and feelings as she perceived that the other party can appreciate her views of the situation.[1]

In line with the above, the interview situation allows the trained psychologist to observe the client as he is telling his story. The interviewer can note at what points the patient blocks, where he becomes tense and restless, and when he suddenly changes the topic of conversation. Such observations, along with the general manner in which a given point is presented by the patient, may give the psychologist some clues to the patient's problems. What areas of the patient's life adjustment appear to be omitted in his discussion may also be noted by the psychologist as potentially significant areas. The astute observer can then utilize these observations and the material obtained to make inferences about the client and his problems. Usually, however, these inferences will not be communicated to the client. Apart from the fact that an individual is reluctant to divulge all aspects of himself to a stranger in one or two contacts, there are some aspects of his personality about which he may be quite defensive, about which he is unaware, or which, perhaps unconsciously, he has distorted in various ways. Consequently, although the interviewer may be able to make certain inferences or hypotheses about the client's underlying conflicts, he may only increase the client's defensiveness by verbalizing them to him during the early interviews. They may, however, provide the psychologist with material that can be useful in the diagnostic appraisal of the client.

Thus by listening to what the client has to say, how she says it, and what she does not say, by observing her behavior, and by being sensitive to the hidden or implied feelings of the client, the psychologist may be able to

---

[1] Some clarification of this process is presented in the chapters on the psychotherapeutic uses of the interview. It may be added here that diagnostic interviews may also have some therapeutic value for the client, since the latter can perceive that someone is sincerely interested in listening to his difficulties and in eventually initiating procedures to help him.

gain an understanding of the client's problem. It is also possible that the problem that is the source of difficulty may not be the one for which the client ostensibly has sought help. Sometimes clients cannot divulge what is really troubling them until they can really trust the clinician. In the author's opinion, it is probably wise in such cases to refrain from pushing or confronting the client; rather, the client should be allowed more time in order to feel more secure about bringing forth the problem that is really troubling him. However, the psychologist must be sufficiently alert and sensitive so that the real purpose of the meeting is not diverted into unproductive channels, even though at the same time he conveys full acceptance of the client as an individual. A well-conducted interview can be instrumental in clarifying the individual's difficulties and the issues involved, as well as in helping the individual to accept needed treatment.

The role of the psychologist in the interview situation, as already indicated, will be determined by a number of factors. Because of this, one interviewer may be inclined to allow the patient to tell his story in his own way with a minimum of questioning, while others may seek more direct answers to specific questions. Some may be interested in securing a moderate amount of factual information, whereas others may be more interested in allowing the patient greater freedom in the interview in order to see how the patient presents his story and what feelings are expressed. Dynamically oriented clinicians may focus more on early childhood experiences, whereas behavioral psychologists are more likely to concentrate on the history of the patient's problem, its antecedents, and the environmental events that appear to be related to it. The orientation of the interviewer, the local clinical ground rules, the nature of the referral, the type of patient, and the particular personality of the interviewer will all potentially interact to determine how the interview is conducted.

The matter of taking notes or of recording interviews will also vary depending on the individual and the setting. Some material of a factual nature can be recorded during the interview, although most of the impressions can be written down as soon as the interview is completed. Some persons believe that excessive note taking interferes with the direct personal relationship in the interview (Garrett, 1972), while others in the past have recommended taking verbatim notes if possible (Rogers, 1942). Sullivan (1954), in particular, feels that the interviewer should be as alert and sensitive as possible to what the patient says and how he reacts. From his point of view, if the interviewer is overly concerned about recording information, he cannot devote himself fully to the interviewing process. As a consequence, much will be lost and the interview will not be maximally successful. Many patients, also, may not feel as free to divulge personal information if they think everything they discuss is going to be recorded. The author has encountered a few patients who specifically requested that nothing be noted down or placed in their files about something they wished to discuss with him. The psychologist has to be particularly sensitive to such requests and to respond appropriately.

Some agencies may adhere to some type of formal outline for the study of each case, and workers in these agencies may feel a greater necessity to take down material on paper than people in other settings. The type of interview may also influence the manner in which data are recorded. Nevertheless, it should be remembered that the mere accumulation of verbal information is not the real goal of the clinical interview. Rather, the purpose of the interview is to secure an understanding of the patient, his problem, and those factors which appear to bear on his current maladjustment.

In recent years there has been a greater tendency to record interview material by means of audiotapes or videotapes. This is particularly true for purposes of research and training. This is the only precise way of obtaining truly verbatim material on what takes place in an interview. Nevertheless, this use of electrical recordings is not a routine procedure, because most clinicians do not have the time available to listen to the playback of their interviews. There is also the problem of securing the client's permission to have the interview recorded, and the possible influence of the recording procedure on the client's freedom of expression. These difficulties, however, are not insurmountable. Furthermore, for purposes of training and research, recordings of interviews are of inestimable value. The complete verbal interactions of the participants are available in the actual context in which they occurred. Inflections of voice, hesitations, anger, blocking, and similar aspects of the interview situation can all be interpreted with minimal distortion. The beginning clinician will profit greatly by having some of her interviews, as well as other clinical work, electrically recorded and then listened to attentively. Listening to one's own interview with a client is a most revealing and instructive experience. The following brief excerpts of medical interviews and the commentary by Kahn and Cannell (1957) illustrate very clearly both the value of recorded feedback of one's interviews and some of the common errors in conducting an interview.

Doctor: O.K. Now I want to take a history and I want symptoms primarily. I mean I don't want to know what diagnosis you have, I want to go more by symptoms. So what is the chief thing that's bothering you—at the present time?
Patient: I don't have any pains right now, I feel wonderful.
Doctor: Well, what trouble have you had in the near past?
Patient: Well, this summer I had days that I don't feel so good. Lots of days that I had to take it easy and kind of loaf around.
Doctor: Why did you have to take it easy? What has your main problem been?
Patient: I just felt—I really had no bad pain—I just—er—sort of feeling bad inside me for a long time. I felt—
Doctor: Didn't you have any pain *at all?*
Patient: I wouldn't really say it hurt, but it felt bad, like—
Doctor: *Where* did it feel bad?
As the above passage was played, the doctor who had conducted the interview became increas-

ingly tense. At one point he seized the arms of his chair and burst out, "I'm not letting the poor guy tell me what's the matter with him!"

The first medical interview concluded, and with noticeable relief the doctor who had been the major actor in that script turned his attention to the second interview, conducted by one of his colleagues.

The following excerpt is taken from the second medical interview to which the group was then listening:

Doctor: How many cigarettes do you smoke?

Patient: Oh, this package I have had pretty near . . . golly, almost—

Doctor: About a pack a week, perhaps?

Patient: Yeah, I guess about that. I am a pipe smoker—I have cigarettes here, but I smoke a pipe, probably more than I ought to.

Doctor: A pipeful a day?

Patient: Well, yes.

* * * *

Doctor: Have you had any operations?

Patient: No.

Doctor: How about your tonsils; have you had those out?

Patient: No.

Doctor: Have you had any injuries . . . falls or such like?

Patient: No.

Doctor: Sounds like you have been pretty healthy. Generally, you would say your health was pretty good?

Patient: Well, yes, I would say it was all right.

As the recorded tape continued to play, the second doctor began to show many of the same reactions previously displayed by his colleague. He listened intently, and obviously with some embarrassment, to the sound of his own voice and that of his patients, and finally said, "My gosh, I'm answering my own questions. I ask one, and then I don't let him alone." And then, a few minutes later, "Listen to that, will you? I really butchered that question. I gave him the answer."

By the time the evening was over, the two authors had noted a continuing succession of such comments as the following: "There I go with that medical terminology again. How could I expect that patient to understand that?" "I see *now* what she was trying to tell me. I just really wasn't listening to her." "That was a good lead he gave me. I should have followed it up and I missed it." "Why was I so short with that patient just then? I didn't mean to be, but it certainly shut him up, and I really wanted to hear more about that symptom." "That woman is scared to death to tell me what's bothering her. She has an awful lot of trouble getting the words out, and I certainly didn't do anything to help her."

Most of us, if confronted with a record of some of the extemporaneous dialogues in which we take part, would undoubtedly discover similar discrepancies between what we thought was happening and what was actually happening. What someone was trying to tell us would turn out to have differed from what we took in. What we made of our communication would appear on reexamination to have differed from what we intended to communicate. The doctors' experience demonstrates that even where the dialogue takes the deliberate form of an information-gathering interview, with the parties to it presumably bent upon a common purpose, the difficulties of communication persist. (pp. 4, 5)

The above illustrations indicate the difficulties some professional interviewers have in fully allowing the client to express himself concerning his difficulties in the interview situation. Two common faults are apparent: (1) not allowing the client to fully respond by cutting him off verbally, or (2) by providing a reply for the client. Although it is true that physicians are generally busy people who have to see a large number of patients and, consequently, cannot spend a large amount of time listening to a patient leisurely describe his or her symptoms, nevertheless, attempts to shortcut or unduly speed-up the procedure leads to a loss of accurate information. Furthermore, such behavior on the part of the clinician may also convey to the patient that the former is really not interested in him or his problems and wants to get the interview over as quickly as possible. Such impressions are particularly important in terms of the clinician's attempts at securing rapport and establishing an effective working relationship with the client. It should also be pointed out that if difficulties arise in securing information and rapport in the relatively more structured situation of a medical interview, the difficulties and complexities increase when we deal with disturbed individuals and where we seek to learn about feelings, perceptions, thoughts, and interpersonal relations. Although the clinical interviewer must not be simply a passive listener and allow the client to wander or digress unduly, at the same time she must be a sympathetic and empathic listener who allows the client to be himself and to gradually feel secure enough to discuss the problems that are causing him discomfort and concern.

Like other clinical techniques, the interview is merely one of the tools used to understand and help the patient. It is a flexible tool and can be adapted to serve the specific needs of a variety of situations. Its values in clinical psychology are related to the skill and understanding of the psychologist. Perhaps more than many standardized techniques, skillful use of the interview is dependent upon the psychologist's clinical experience and his knowledge of personality and psychopathology. The clinical interviewer must not only be sensitive to the feelings and hidden meanings underlying the spoken words of the patient, but he must be able to decide, and very quickly, how to respond to what is being said. Should he remain quiet, should he ask for additional information, should he reflect the patient's feelings, or should he confront him with the problem to be faced? These are some of the potential responses which the interviewer may have to consider in reacting to a patient. They illustrate the fact that interviewing is not a mechanical process with a simple list of rules. Rather, it involves a constantly interacting personal relationship and provides one method of clinical appraisal where the psychologist must concentrate completely on his patient and the interactions between the latter and himself. In diagnostic testing, the psychologist devotes a certain amount of his attention to the administration of his tests and the recording of responses. In some instances, psychological tests can actually be protective devices interposed as it were by the psychologist between himself and his patient. In the interview, on the other hand, one must deal directly with the individual and rely much more on sensitive observation and participation with another person.

STRUCTURED AND UNSTRUCTURED INTERVIEWS

Most of the previous discussion has been concerned with the interview as most commonly used in the typical clinical situation. As was indicated, most clinicians do not have any rigidly prescribed list of questions or order of questions that they follow in a specific form during the interview. Rather, the technique is used in a fairly flexible manner which allows the client to set his own pace during the interview and which permits him to explore some areas in depth. Although most clinical interviewers have some general scheme in mind when they interview a client, they do not necessarily cover exactly the same ground or the same material with every client. Generally, they may start the interview with the patient's problem as he sees it or with the reason he seeks help at this time and then allow the interview to proceed naturally in any one of a number of directions depending on the initial information and interaction. Certain specific information, however, usually will be sought by most interviewers in the initial interview. These might include such basic information as the age of the client, marital status, position held, current living situation, the beginning of the current problem, frequency of symptoms, and similar material. From this point on, however, there might be any order or sequence of topics in which the interview would proceed. Some interviewers may be more interested in certain aspects of the individual or his past history than others, and may more systematically explore these area. The Freudian psychologist, for example, might be relatively more interested in the person's sexual adjustment and history, in the person's childhood experiences, and in similar material. The Adlerian psychologist, on the other hand, would probably be more inclined to learn of the individual's birth order and place in his family than would others. The client-centered therapist would be less inclined to follow any specific pattern for interviewing the patient or for seeking certain kinds of information. Rather, it would be expected that she would be more interested in trying to understand the patient's perception of himself and of his situation. The behaviorally oriented clinician would tend to focus on the client's problems, their duration, the circumstance under which they were first manifested, and the possible environmental stimuli which appear to maintain the problematic behavior. Eclectic clinicians, those not committed to any single theoretical orientation, most likely would follow the plan or hypothesis which seemed to them to be most useful for the particular client and be less guided by one specific orientation.

In some institutional settings, a greater emphasis may be placed on securing certain types of basic information on all patients who apply or are referred for diagnosis and treatment. The individual who conducts the initial intake interview thus might try to obtain as much data as possible on job history, educational background, family history, marital relationships, previous hospitalizations, and similar material. In a similar fashion, the initial examining psychiatrist would try to secure a more detailed history and appraisal of the patient's specific problems and symptoms and to determine whether or not the patient has certain recognized symptoms of psychopathology. For example, in many mental hospital settings the examining psychiatrist is expected to conduct what has been called a "mental status examination." Such an examination basically involves an interview with the patient but in a more structured fashion. In essence, the psychiatrist attempts to interview and examine the patient in terms of diagnosing his psychopathology or "illness." Such a procedure is more common in the mental or psychiatric hospital than in a psychological clinic or counseling center and is also more likely to be used where there is some suspicion of severe psychopathology. In such an interview, the patient may be asked questions concerning whether or not he hears voices, whether he feels depressed, whether he has periods of feeling elated, whether he has fears, and so forth. He will also be asked if he knows who he is, where he is, the date, and similar questions in order to appraise the patient's reality orientation. In other words, this type of interview has a more structured quality and is organized around the objective of ascertaining both the degree and type of disturbance.

Apart from mental status and other comparable diagnostic examinations, there are other kinds of structured interviews but they generally are not used in traditional clinical practice. Public opinion polls and other survey techniques are essentially a more standardized type of structured interview in which a specific number of questions are asked of the sample selected for study. A personality questionnaire is really a form of structured interview and would actually be one if it were administered orally by the examiner. Except for research purposes, however, such interviewing techniques are generally not employed in most clinical situations. Nevertheless, they do have some utility for research purposes and a brief reference to some structured mental-status and diagnostic interviews can be mentioned here.

One such mental-status schedule was constructed for use with psychiatric patients (Spitzer, Fleiss, Burdock, & Hardesty, 1964; Spitzer, Fleiss, Endicott, & Cohen, 1967). The "Mental-Status Schedule" consists of eighty-two questions with fifty-one supplementary questions that may be used to probe or clarify the responses secured from the patient. These items cover the patient's complaints, feelings, thoughts, perceptions, and symptoms. The interviewer records the patient's responses as true or false on a 248-item inventory based on the patient's overt behavior and style and content of his oral communication. Thus we have in this instance a standardized interview which focuses on certain aspects of psychopathology. If this is the focus of a particular investigation, then it would appear that more systematic and reliable results could be secured by means of such a procedure than by an unstructured clinical interview. Measures for reliability have been secured for this instrument as well as certain information pertaining to the significance of the scores obtainable. Obviously the utility of such an instrument is determined by the objectives of the interviewer and by the population to be studied.

A more recent structured diagnostic interview guide has also been developed by some of the group that developed the Mental-Status Schedule. This is the Schedule for Affective Disorders and Schizophrenia (SADS) (Endicott & Spitzer, 1978). The SADS also includes rating scales pertinent to the specified diagnostic categories and has had rather wide use in research.

VALUES AND LIMITATIONS

The preceding material on the interview method has indicated in a general way the usefulness of this technique in clinical work with clients. Like the other techniques discussed, it has both special values and specific limitations, which depend on the type of problem presented and the clinical objectives sought. Among the main values of the interview are the opportunity it provides for the patient to tell his story, to participate in an interpersonal situation, and to be observed. From the interview one can secure a certain amount of factual information, some knowledge of attitudes and feelings, some observations of behavior, and, consequently, some basis for making inferences about the individual and his problem. To a certain extent, however, as we have noted before, the individual determines what he will say, how much he will say, and what he will refrain from saying. The client may also hide his true feelings because he wants to make a certain impression on the interviewer or because he is hesitant to express those experiences or views which he feels are socially unacceptable. Another problem, also commented upon previously, concerns those aspects of the personality that have been repressed or dissociated from consciousness, and consequently cannot be verbalized by the patient. For these reasons, the interview may contribute only partial and sometimes relatively superficial data concerning the individual's problem. In rather serious cases of personality disorder or where rather important decisions have to be made, the interview should be supplemented by other diagnostic approaches for a more comprehensive appraisal of the patient.

But, in cases of relatively minor difficulty, or where the diagnostic problems are minimal, the interview alone may suffice as both a diagnostic and a therapeutic tool, with little need for more intensive diagnostic investigation.

Because the interview has been used for so many purposes, it is difficult to generalize about its effectiveness for clinical work. The reported findings on the reliability and validity of the interview have varied considerably (Berg, 1966; Kelly, 1954). There is little question that the type of problem, as well as the training, skill, and personality of the interviewer, will influence the validity and reliability of the interview. As a consequence, it is to be expected that we will find varying viewpoints concerning the values of the interview. One writer, in evaluating some of the published material on the interview, reached the conclusion that where the problem is a fair one, and the required judgment is broad, "it may be said with confidence that the interview can be highly reliable and valid when used appropriately by skilled persons" (Berg, 1966, p. 30). Another reviewer, however, in discussing the values of the interview as a selection technique, reaches a somewhat opposed point of view. His position is that "all evidence available suggests that the technique is apt to have sufficiently low validity, even under optimal conditions, to make doubtful its general utility as a selection device" (Kelly, 1954, pp. 119–120). Although this statement has reference to the use of the interview in selection, a situation requiring specific predictions, it does have some relevance for the problem of clinical prediction as well. Worthwhile studies of the clinical values of the interview, however, are still scarce, and in the absence of conclusive data, it is not surprising to find different points of view. For example, in one book on interviewing, the author tends to be critical of the concern expressed by some of the reliability of the interview (Gorden, 1969). However, he does not present any research data on this matter, and it is not one that should be disregarded. If two interviewers come up with very different appraisals of the person interviewed, how much confidence can be placed in their appraisals? Another recent book on the clinical interview also says very little about the problems of reliability and validity and they are not listed in the index of the book (Pope, 1979).

Although these issues exist, it is well to keep in mind that the interview has been used in so many different ways for various purposes, by individuals with varying skills, that it is a difficult matter to make a final judgment concerning its values. Like other techniques, its usefulness will depend on the skill and perceptiveness of the clinician as well as for the purpose it is being used. It should also be remembered that the interview is a complex interpersonal technique. A great deal of worthwhile information may be secured from the interview which may be negated somewhat by an incorrect inference by the interviewer. Although it is true that the ultimate usefulness of the interview depends on the accuracy of the inferences or predictions made by the interviewer, as well as her observations, nevertheless, more detailed studies of the specific processes or steps in the interview situation might eventually increase its total effectiveness.

Before concluding our discussion of the clinical interview, reference can be made to two types of research on interview behavior which have provided additional insights into some of the operations involved in the interviewing process. One of these refers to experiments on verbal conditioning, and area of research to which reference has already been made in our discussion of learning theories in Chapter 2. The other deals with studies of specific interview behaviors.

Krasner (1958, 1962, 1965, 1971) has reviewed much of the literature on verbal conditioning with particular reference to its significance for psychotherapy. Although the studies reviewed have for the most part been laboratory studies of verbal behavior, the results obtained do appear to have relevance for the clinical use of the interview. In these studies such verbal units as emotional words, affect statements, a particular content area, and self-reference statements have been reinforced by means of such interviewer responses as head-nodding, smiling, and verbalizing of "mm-hmm" and "good." Among other things, it was found that the use of emotional words and specifically pleasant emotional words by the person being interviewed could be influenced by reinforcement from the interviewer. The production of unpleasant words was not influenced in this manner; however, some specific attitudes were influenced in a positive direction by means of the social reinforcement provided by the interviewer. On the basis of this work it was concluded that verbal conditioning "is prototypical of the social influence situation" (Krasner, 1965, p. 266) and is an important feature of traditional psychotherapy. Thus these studies allow one to perceive more clearly, the social influence of the interviewer on the client.

A somewhat different series of research studies reported by Matarazzo, Saslow, and their associates have also demonstrated how the interviewer may influence the verbal behavior of the client in the interview situation and vice versa (Matarazzo, Wiens, and Saslow, 1965; Matarazzo, Weitman, Saslow, and Wiens, 1963; Matarazzo and Wiens, 1972; Saslow and Matarazzo, 1959). These studies have focused on such behavioral aspects of the interview as the number of utterances per interview, their duration, number of interruptions, the duration of the client's silences, and similar features, rather than on the content of the verbalizations. The technique used initially for recording such observations was the Interaction Chronograph developed by Chapple (1949), but this was subsequently replaced by a newly developed and highly sophisticated Interaction Recorder. In essence, several discrete aspects or components of interview behavior "are objectively recorded by an observer who activates a series of electrically controlled counters that are connected to two keys, one for the interviewer, the other for the subject. Each key is depressed by the observer whenever the designated individual is talking, nodding, gesturing, or in other ways communicating (interacting) with the second person" (Saslow and Matarazzo, 1959, p. 127). The research of this group of investigators over the past two decades (Matarazzo and Wiens, 1972) indicates not only that the speech behavior of the interviewee and interviewer is highly stable and idiosyncratic for each *individual* human but, also, that there is a heretofore unsuspected two-way influence as well as "synchrony" in the give and take behavior of many interviewer-interviewee dyads.

Although many studies have been reported by these investigators on a variety of variables associated with behavior in the interview situation, we shall only note a few of these findings and focus our attention on the influence of the interviewer on the client's pattern of responses. It appears that in a nondirective interview of forty-five minutes most of the interviewees speak in utterances that, on the average, are well under a minute in length of time. The length of the interviewer's speech utterances, however, tends to influence the duration of the interviewee's verbal responses. In a series of studies where the interviewer systematically varied the duration of his utterances, a corresponding effect was noted on the part of the interviewee (Matarazzo, Wiens, and Saslow, 1965). When the interviewer increased his average verbalization from 5 to 10 seconds a corresponding increase was observed on the part of the interviewee. Conversely, when the interviewer reduced his utterances from 10 to 5 seconds, a comparable decrease was observed for the interviewee. Thus, within the limits of the experimental situation, the length (on the average) of the interviewee's response was related to the length of the interviewer's utterances. Comparable studies were also carried out to evaluate the effects of the interviewer's saying "mm-hmm" or nodding his head. While such behaviors individually also led to an increase in the duration of the interviewee's response, the increase was less than that produced by the increase in the interviewer's own utterances mentioned previously. A study of seven cases of psychotherapy by this group revealed that a number of these same relationships also occurred in psychotherapy interviews.

It is also of interest to mention that in a more recent report the investigators refer to several studies in which a significant relationship was found between empathy ratings of therapists and some of the speech measures studied (Matarazzo & Wiens, 1977). Therapists judged to be high in empathy were also found to talk and say more words during the therapy session and to less frequently use the tactic of not responding after the client has completed a comment.

The research just discussed demonstrates some of the ways in which specific behaviors of the interviewer may influence the response patterns of the clients. In these studies, the emphasis has been on quantitative influences pertaining to the duration of the interviewee's utterances, but similar methodology can be applied to a variety of other interview behaviors and used along with additional techniques to study other aspects of the interpersonal interaction in the interview. For example, the matter of the interviewer's or therapist's interpretation of the behavior and feelings of the client is a topic that has received much discussion in the psychotherapeutic literature, but relatively little research (Hammer, 1968). But, as the study by Kanfer, Phillips, Matarazzo, and Saslow (1960) illustrates, some aspects of the influence of interpretation on the interviewee's speech can be studied. In this study, an interviewer, limiting himself to speech segments of about 5 seconds, offered interpretations only during the middle period of a three-period, forty-five minute interview. Although the duration of the interviewer's speech did not differ significantly during the three interview periods, there was a significant decrease in the length of the interviewee's speech units of approximately 25% in the middle period. When the interviewer in period three discontinued his use of interpretations, the interviewee's mean duration of speech returned to the previous level. It should be apparent from this and the other research mentioned in the preceding pages that some start has been made in objectively studying some features of the interview and of the impact of selected behaviors of the interviewer on the response patterns of the interviewee. Much more research of this type is needed. Clinicians and researchers will have to become more involved in carrying out such research in order to increase our understanding of the variables that influence the behaviors in the interview situation.

At the present time, however, the interview is a widely used and preferred clinical technique. In fact, when the writer has asked clinical psychologists what diagnostic technique they would choose if limited to only one, the invariable answer has been "the interview." Until there is more definitive evidence at hand to contraindicate its use, it is safe to assume that the interview will continue as a widely used tool in the clinical study of the patient.

THE CASE STUDY

The use of interviewing procedures in the diagnostic study of the patient is closely linked to the case study approach in clinical work. The case study can be considered the most comprehensive evaluation of the patient, and includes data secured from many or all of the available techniques for understanding the patient and his problem. Although the case study is thus broader and more comprehensive than the interview, much of the information secured for the case study may be obtained from interviews.

The case study essentially involves the collection and organization of various kinds of information about the patient in relation to the problem at hand. This may include interviews with the patient, relatives, or other parties who may contribute worthwhile information, medical examinations, records of school achievement, work reports, psychological test results, reports from social or public agencies, and the like. For maximum effectiveness, the case study investigation should be planned to ensure adequate data and to avoid the accumulation of unnecessary trivia. The case study approach should not be confused with the mere compiling of large quantities of data. The material should be selected in terms of a planned inquiry. Not all information will be equally valuable, and, after it is secured, must be appraised and organized in a concise and meaningful manner. The plan of organization will vary, depending on the policies and functions of the setting (Burton, 1959; Burton & Harris, 1955; Menninger, 1952). Nevertheless, some available plan or outline will usually be followed for purposes of organizing and presenting the data secured for the case study.

Keeping in mind that the type of clinical situation and client will influence the relative emphasis of what is included in the case study, some suggested outline for a comprehensive case study can be offered. Other suggested outlines for the case study have been presented by a number of clinicians (Bernstein & Nietzel, 1980; Kanfer & Saslow, 1969; Korchin, 1976). The points to be emphasized here are the kinds of information to be secured rather than the particular plan of organization, which, necessarily, can be adapted in various ways to fit the needs of specific situations.

In general, a case study might include the major categories that are listed below. It should be emphasized again that the following outline and categories constitute just one possible way of integrating the data secured in the case study. As such, they will serve to give one a more concrete impression of this procedure.

A. *IDENTIFYING DATA*

The first section of the case study should include certain identifying information about the patient, such as name, address, telephone number, age, date of birth, marital status, employment, date of the interview, and similar material. The significance of such information is fairly obvious.

B. *STATEMENT OF THE PROBLEM OR REASON FOR REFERRAL*

The next section of the case study should include a concise statement of the patient's problem and/or his reason for seeking help at this time. It is important to explore the patient's reasons for seeking consultation or treatment because they may help the clinician to identify a current crisis in the patient's life as well as his possible motivation for seeking help. For example, does he frankly admit he is seeking help for some personal problems, or has he come to the clinic primarily because of pressure from his wife or family? Is his evaluation of his situation realistic, or does it appear biased and confused? It is also desirable to record the patient's problem as he perceived it, preferably in his own words, even though the basic difficulty may be withheld by the patient or may not be consciously known to him. If the clinician views the problem in a very different way from that of the patient, this can be noted separately. Such material will help to give others a more comprehensive appraisal of the patient's problem and his motivation for therapy.

C. BEHAVIORAL OBSERVATIONS

Some description of the patient and his behavior during the interview situation should be noted, whether it is recorded in a separate section or subsumed under other headings. This may include a description of bodily build, dress and appearance, and any unusual or outstanding characteristics. Observations of behavioral patterns and interactions with the interviewer during the interview should also be recorded. These include such things as cooperativeness, ability to relate to the interviewer, a reluctance to go beyond surface details, obvious tension and restlessness, submissiveness, mannerisms, etc. Such observations may also be reported upon in relation to specific topics or problems, but it is well to summarize these general features here, thus giving one some impression of the patient.

D. PRESENT LIFE SITUATION

Under this heading one can list and evaluate any of the factors that might be of some importance in providing us with a better understanding of the patient and his current environmental milieu, and which conceivably could be related also to the present disturbance as a possible precipitating or aggravating factor. Representative items in this category are:

1. The patient's immediate family, for example, wife, children, or in the case of a child, parents and siblings.
2. Housing conditions.

3. Present job and work situation.
4. Financial problems.
5. Present outlook.
6. Special stresses, strains, and events.

The reporting of such material necessarily includes a certain amount of factual information which has its value in providing a background of current events in which to place the patient in his everyday living and adjustment. As much as possible, however, trivial bits of information, which have little bearing on the patient's problem or adjustment should be omitted.

E. DEVELOPMENTAL PERSONAL HISTORY

What is sought here is a developmental history of the potentially important events in the individual's past life. The emphasis is on crucial determinants of personality, significant past events, behavioral patterns, and similar material with particular reference to the patient's current difficulties. How comprehensive this will be is determined by the clinical setting, the type of problem presented, and the purpose of the case study. If the latter is to be presented at a teaching conference, this section could be quite detailed. Possible topics to note here are the following:

1. Birth and early development.
2. Health.
3. Family relationships.
4. Educational development.
5. Social and recreational development.
6. Vocational history.
7. Sex and marital adjustment.
8. Onset and history of present disturbance. (This may be included as a separate unit or listed here.)

The categories listed above cover most of the important areas of the individual's past development and adjustment. Additional categories could be added if deemed necessary. The important objective is to secure a better understanding of the individual's past development, particularly as this is related to the development of the patient's problem. Each of the topics mentioned above could be elaborated upon in some detail. However, since the present description was prepared primarily to acquaint the student with the nature of the case study, no attempt will be made to list the many possible significant types of information that could be included under each of the topics. The student who is well grounded in psychopathology and personality development, however, will know what kinds of data would be pertinent.

F. *FAMILY BACKGROUND*

A section on the family history of the patient is usually included in most case studies. Whether it is treated separately or whether it is included as a part of the previous section is a matter of choice. In reviewing several case study outlines in use at various clinics, however, the author noted that the family background of the patient frequently was treated separately. The method of organizing the data, as always, should be determined by how well it served the purposes of the case.

Most frequently, the family history includes data about the patient's parents, grandparents, siblings, and other relatives who may have a bearing on the case. One reason for including such data concerns the possible hereditary factors in some disorders. It is also common practice in many clinics and hospitals to ascertain the incidence of serious personality disorder in the patient's family as one means of evaluating the prognosis for improvement in the case. Apart from the matter of hereditary predisposition, which in some disorders is suggestive, but still open to question, the data about the patient's family may throw some light on the development of the patient's personality or behavioral difficulties. Parental conflict, death of a parent, intense sibling rivalry, an unusually dominant or overprotective mother, parental abuse, and similar familial factors may be important in the ontogenesis of the patient's present behavior. It should be emphasized again that what are sought are meaningful data that can be used to better understand the individual's problem, and not simply a collection of numerous but insignificant facts. The dynamic aspects of interpersonal relationships are of greater value than the rather boring recitation of relatives, their names, ages, and so forth. The patient's Aunt Tillie may be an interesting "old gal," but the space devoted to her should be determined solely by her importance for understanding the disturbance of the patient.

G. *PSYCHOLOGICAL TEST FINDINGS*

How the psychological test data are organized and presented within the framework of the comprehensive case study will again vary from setting to setting. The findings may be subsumed under other headings of the case study in a somewhat segmental manner, for example, educational achievement, intelligence, personality, and so on, or they may be presented separately in an integrated fashion. Although the needs of a particular situation may dictate the method of reporting the test findings, the present writer, along with a number of other clinical psychologists, prefers a separate integrated report of the psychological test data. There are several reasons for this point of view. In the first place, the test data represent one type of material or source of inferences about the patient. Frequently, the material may be at variance with other information concerning some aspects of the patient's personality or psychopathology. If the purpose of the case study is to bring together data from many different sources and disciplines for a comprehensive integration and evaluation by the clinical staff, it is probably best to keep the different approaches to the problem distinguishable. In this way, certain inconsistencies can be highlighted for discussion and future clarification, and congruent patterns supported. For example, on a particularly difficult diagnostic problem, tentative hypotheses can be more clearly supported or negated in terms of the various existing types of clinical data presented.

Another reason for preferring a separate section for the psychological report rests on the tendency of psychologists to use some battery of psychological tests for assessment purposes rather than to rely on one test. An integrated report based on all of the test data plus the clinical psychologist's observations of the patient's behavior during the examination appears to be more potentially useful than separate test reports interspersed throughout the case study. This procedure also allows the psychologist to compare and evaluate inconsistencies in the patient's performance on different types of tests.

H. MEDICAL FINDINGS

What is included here naturally will be determined by the type of patient studied and the institution providing the clinical services. As might be expected, hospitals and other types of medical installations will provide the most complete and thorough examinations of this type. In addition to a general physical examination, such facilities may utilize a variety of special and laboratory examinations, including neurological evaluations, blood tests, X rays, urinalysis, spinal taps, electroencephalography, brain scans, etc. In many cases, extensive medical laboratory examinations may not be needed. Nevertheless, because many serious personality deviations or psychological symptoms may also be caused by organic factors, infections, poisons, and drugs, it is usually wise to have a thorough examination made to rule out such causes in these instances. In hospitals and psychiatric clinics, the medical personnel will, of course, routinely be charged with the responsibility for such evaluations.

In nonmedical clinic settings, it will be up to the psychologist or other professional persons to make the necessary referrals to the proper medical personnel. In some cases, for example, a neurologist may need to be consulted, and in others, perhaps, an ophthalmologist. In any event, pertinent medical findings in some instances may contribute significantly to a proper understanding of the case, and in some cases they may be of crucial importance for the determination of an accurate diagnosis.

I. SUMMARY AND FORMULATION

The preceding sections of the case study have emphasized certain types of information concerning the patient, his family, his past development, and his difficulties. Although each section has been guided by certain theoretical or unifying concepts, they have dealt with different aspects of the patient, or at least, the patient's problem has been viewed from different vantage points. However, after all this information has been collected and organized in as concise fashion as is possible, it is essential to evaluate the material, to attempt some meaningful synthesis, and then to offer some diagnostic formulation concerning the patient. This is one of the important goals and end products of the case study method. In other words, once we have collected and surveyed our data, we must proceed to reach some decision concerning the case under study.

How the overall evaluation of the patient and his problem is formulated will depend upon the setting and the professional identification and theoretical views of the person preparing the formulation. In many situations the final formulation may hinge around a specific psychiatric diagnosis. In the past, this would have been true mainly of psychiatrists and psychiatric institutions. However, as mentioned earlier, because insurance payments (so called third-party payments) may require a psychiatric diagnosis, even many psychologists will conclude their diagnostic evaluation with such a diagnosis (Miller, Bergstrom, Cross, & Grube, 1981). In some instances, of course, the psychiatric diagnosis, as we have pointed out before, may be of crucial significance. In other instances, however, its value is more limited. The evaluative summary, however, will be of greater value if it contains a concise and integrated appraisal of the key factors in the case. In brief, this would entail the factors considered to be significant in the patient's present adjustment, his past and present attempts at coping with his difficulties, his symptoms, his strengths and weaknesses, the severity of disturbance, and the prognosis. This more dynamic and comprehensive aproach would then constitute the diagnostic end product of the case study method.

J. RECOMMENDATIONS

Some recommendations for the treatment or disposition of the case should logically follow the diagnostic formulation. Sample recommendations of a very brief kind might include the following: The patient is considered dangerous to himself and to others and should be hospitalized immediately; the patient should be started on a course of drug therapy with participation in group psychotherapy and occupational therapy; the client should receive individual instruction in remedial reading and his school should be notified of our findings and recommendations; the client can profit from relatively brief psychotherapy in view of the situational character of her problem; this client's phobic behavior is best treated with a behavioral approach emphasizing *in vivo* exposure and modeling; in the light of the patient's limited personality resources and precarious hold on reality, a nonthreatening and supportive therapy approach appears to be the most appropriate one with an emphasis on reality factors—the therapist should be extremely sensitive to any "transference" manifestations in view of the patient's latent homosexual tendencies; the individual's problems primarily concern occupational matters and an appropriate referral should be made to the state employment service. Other possible recommendations, of course, might be made depending upon the kind of clinical problem presented and the resources available in the specific setting.

CONCLUDING COMMENTS

The present chapter has discussed some purposes, procedures, uses and limitations of the interview and case study methods in clinical diagnosis and assessment. Because these techniques are flexible and can be adapted to a variety of situations, no rigidly prescribed procedures have been advocated. One illustrative outline for organizing case history material has been presented in order to make the presentation more concrete and meaningful. In many practical situations, however, the case study of a client will be much briefer and less inclusive, due to the fact that there is usually a heavy load of cases assigned to the staff in most clinics and hospitals. Consequently, intensive diagnostic case studies are usually not made for most cases. As always, the problems presented and the purposes sought should determine what procedures will be used and how extensively they will be applied.

The interview and case study methods have been used widely in the clinical study and evaluation of patients. Although they do not appear to have received as much systematic or critical study by psychologists as has been the case with psychological tests, they have provided sources of data for research on psychopathology and personality. The study of life histories in particular has given us a rich source of information for our hypotheses and understanding with reference to the development of personality disturbances as well as normal development (Macfarlane, Allen, & Honzik, 1954; Roff & Ricks, 1970; White, 1966). Furthermore, when comparisons have been made between case history data and conclusions based on psychological tests, clinical predictions based on the former have generally fared better (Kostlan, 1954; Peskin, 1963). For example, in the study by Kostlan and the replication by Peskin, clinical psychologists using a battery of three tests could improve their predictions over those based solely on identifying information only when the social history was included along with the test data. The case study method thus appears to have considerable clinical utility.

At present, it appears that clinicians will continue to favor techniques in which they can observe the client and through which they may obtain information about him and significant aspects of his past development. Furthermore, if a comprehensive study of the individual person is sought, the case study is the most readily available technique.

REFERENCES

Berg, I. A. The clinical interview and the case record. In I. A. Berg and L. A. Pennington (Eds.), *An introduction to clinical psychology.* (3rd Ed.). New York: Ronald Press, 1966.

Bernstein, D. A., & Nietzel, M. T. *Introduction to clinical psychology.* New York: McGraw-Hill, 1980.

Bingham, W. V. D., Moore, B. V., & Gustad, J. W. *How to interview.* (4th Ed.). New York: Harper, 1959.

Burton, A. (Ed.), *Case studies in counseling and psychotherapy.* Englewood Cliffs, NJ: Prentice Hall, 1959.

Burton, A., & Harris, R. E. *Clinical studies of personality.* New York: Harper and Brothers, 1955.

Chapple, E. D. The interaction chronograph; its evolution and present application. *Personnel,* 1949, *25,* 295–307.

Deutsch, R., & Murphy, W. F. *The clinical interview. Vol. 1. Diagnosis.* New York: International Universities Press, 1955.

Endicott, J., & Spitzer, R. L. A diagnostic interview: The schedule for affective disorders and schizophrenia. *Archives of General Psychiatry,* 1978, *35,* 837–844.

Garrett, A. *Interviewing: Its principles and methods.* New York: Family Service Association of America, 1972.

Gorden, R. L. *Interviewing. Strategy, techniques and tactics.* Homewood, IL: Dorsey Press, 1969.

Hammer, E. F. (Ed.), *Use of interpretation in treatment.* New York: Grune and Stratton, 1968.

Kahn, R. L. & Cannell, C. F. *The dynamics of interviewing.* New York: Wiley, 1957.

Kanfer, F. H., Phillips, J. S., Matarazzo, J. D., & Saslow, G. Experimental modification of interviewer content in standardized interviews. *Journal of Consulting Psychology,* 1960, *24,* 528–536.

Kanfer, F. H., & Saslow, G. Behavioral diagnosis. In C. M. Franks (Ed.), *Behavior therapy: Appraisal and status.* New York: McGraw-Hill, 1969.

Kelly, E. L. An evaluation of the interview as a selective technique. In *1953 Invitational conference on testing problems.* Princeton, NJ: Educational Testing Service, 1954, pp. 116–123.

Korchin, S. *Modern clinical psychology. Principles in intervention in the clinic and community.* New York: Basic Books, 1976.

Kostlan, A. A method for the empirical study of psychodiagnosis. *Journal of Consulting Psychology,* 1954, *18,* 83–88.

Krasner, L. Studies of the conditioning of verbal behavior. *Psychological Bulletin,* 1958, *55,* 148–170.

Krasner, L. The therapist as a social reinforcement machine. In H. H. Strupp and L. Luborsky (Eds.), *Research in psychotherapy.* Washington, D.C.: American Psychological Association, 1962, pp. 61–94.

Krasner, L. Verbal conditioning and psychotherapy. In L. Krasner and L. P. Ullmann (Eds.), *Research in behavior modification.* New York: Holt, Rinehart and Winston, 1965, pp. 211–228.

Krasner, L. The operant approach in behavior therapy. In A. E. Bergin and S. L. Garfield (Eds.), *Handbook of psychotherapy and behavior change: An empirical analysis.* New York: Wiley, 1971.

Macfarlane, J. W., Allen, L., & Honzik, M. P. *A developmental study of the behavior problems of normal children between twenty-one months and fourteen years.* Berkeley: University of California, 1954.

Matarazzo, J. D. The Interview. In B. B. Wolman (Ed.), *Handbook of clinical psychology.* New York: McGraw-Hill, 1965.

Matarazzo, J. D., & Wiens, A. N. *The interview: Research on its anatomy and structure.* Chicago: Aldine, 1972.

Matarazzo, J. D., & Wiens, A. N. Speech behavior as an objective correlate of empathy and outcome in interview and psychotherapy research: A review with implications for behavior modification. *Behavior Modification,* 1977, *1.*

Matarazzo, J. D., Weitman, M., Saslow, G., & Wiens, A. Interviewer influence on durations of interviewee speech. *Journal of Verbal Learning and Verbal Behavior,* 1963, *1,* 451–458.

Matarazzo, J. D., Wiens, A., & Saslow, G. Studies of interview speech behavior. In L. Krasner and L. P. Ullmann (Eds.), *Research in behavior modification.* New York: Holt, Rinehart and Winston, 1965, pp. 179–210.

Menninger, K. A. *A manual for psychiatric case study.* New York: Grune and Stratton, 1952.

Miller, L. S., Bergstrom, D. A., Cross, H. J., & Grube, J. W. Opinions and use of the DSM system by practicing psychologists. *Professional Psychology,* 1981, *12,* 385–390.

Peskin, H. Unity of science begins at home: A study of regional factionalism in clinical psychology. *American Psychologist,* 1963, *18,* 96–100.

Pope, B. *The mental health interview. Research and application.* New York: Pergamon Press, 1979.

Roff, M., & Ricks, D. F. (Eds.), *Life history research in psychopathology.* Minneapolis: University of Minnesota Press, 1970.

Rogers, C. R. *Counseling and psychotherapy.* Boston: Houghton Mifflin, 1942.

Rosenzweig, S. Levels of behavior in psychodiagnosis with special reference to the Picture-Frustration Study. *American Journal of Orthopsychiatry,* 1950, *20,* 63–72.

Saslow, G., & Matarazzo, J. D. A technique for studying changes in interview behavior. In E. A. Rubinstein and M. B. Parloff (Eds.), *Research in psychotherapy*. Washington, D.C.: American Psychological Association, 1959. pp. 125–159.

Spitzer, R. L., Fleiss, J. L., Endicott, J., & Cohen, J. Mental status schedule: Properties of factor-analytically derived scales. *Archives of General Psychiatry,* 1967, *16,* 479–493.

Spitzer, R. L., Fleiss, J. L., Burdock, E. I., & Hardesty, A. S. The mental status schedule: Rationale, reliability and validity. *Comprehensive Psychiatry,* 1964, *5,* 384–394.

Sullivan, H. S. *The psychiatric interview.* New York: W. W. Norton, 1954.

White, R. W. *Lives in progress* (2nd Ed.) New York: Holt, Rinehart and Winston, 1966.

Psychological Tests and the Appraisal of Intellectual Functioning

As we have noted previously, psychometric tests and scales have been widely used techniques in clinical psychology. Literally, thousands of different tests have been constructed to measure a variety of psychological attributes—intelligence, interests, aptitudes, academic achievement, and personality traits (Buros, 1972, 1978; Anastasi, 1976). The emphasis in this development was on objective and standardized instruments. The advantages of such instruments over more informal tests or procedures were that they provided representative scores or norms with which the scores of a given individual could be compared, and the scoring was objective.

In addition to the standardized tests developed for administration to one individual at a time, tests which could be given to a group of subjects simultaneously were devised during World War I. Obviously, such tests are much more economical to give than are individual tests. In clinical work, however, the latter are generally preferred. The individual examination enables the psychologist to observe her client's behavior in a standardized situation and to make a more accurate psychological appraisal of him. Frequently, the psychologist is able to obtain some cues about the subject's personality by observing the individual's reactions in the testing situation and how he relates to the examiner. Reading or sensory difficulties can be detected more readily than in the group situation and there is less chance that misinterpretation of test instructions may go unrecognized. From the clinical point of view, group tests also restrict the subject's responses to a choice of answers given in the test form. Thus, individual tests provide the psychologist with more extensive information about the subject, allow the subject a greater freedom of response, and enable the clinician to evaluate more effectively the validity of his findings.

Before proceeding to a discussion of specific tests and their use in the clinical situation, it is important to review briefly two basic considerations in psychological measurement—*reliability* and *validity*. By "reliability," we mean consistency of results. Will the results secured from a test be roughly comparable to the results to be secured 6 months hence if the individual is retested? Obviously, without consistency or reliability of results, the test has little practical value. Since quantitative results are obtained from most psychological tests, actual coefficients of reliability can be computed.

There are several different methods of securing reliability coefficients. The comparison of scores obtained from two comparable forms of a test is usually considered the best method. Unfortunately, many well-known clinical tests do not have alternate forms and, therefore, this method cannot be used with them. The test-retest method is another means of evaluating reliability. From a practical standpoint it would appear that the actual retesting of a group of subjects with the same test after a reasonable time interval would be the most satisfactory approach. This method, however, is criticized because memory, maturation, and other factors may influence the scores secured from the retesting. Correlating the odd with the even items of a test is another frequently used method of estimating reliability, although this tends to give a spuriously high coefficient of reliability. Thus, the method used in computing reliability coefficients also needs to be considered in evaluating the reliability of a given test. A more detailed treatment of these problems may be obtained from other sources (Anastasi, 1976; Cronbach, 1970).

Validity in psychological testing means, in simple language, "does the test accomplish its purpose?" "Does it adequately measure what it is supposed to measure?" Although this is the most important consideration in measurement, it is at the same time the most difficult to handle adequately. Unfortunately, because of this, issues concerning validity have in the past received far too superficial treatment. While admitting the difficulty, we must still be sensitive to the problem and rigorously appraise any clinical instrument in terms of its apparent or purported validity.

Although the problems surrounding the validation of most psychological tests of interest to the clinician are difficult ones, some attempts have been made to examine this and related problems in some detail. The American Psychological Association (1954) joined with two other associations to appoint a committee to evaluate the matter of test standards. After some study, the committee produced a report in which four main types of validity were differentiated. Some years later, a similar committee was appointed to review the experience with the previous report and to revise the standards accordingly (Standards for Educational & Psychological Tests and Manuals, 1966). These standards were again revised in 1974 (Standards for Educational & Psychological Tests and Manuals, 1974). At that time four types of validity information were designated as follows: Content validity, criterion-related validities (concurrent and predictive), and construct validity. Content validity, useful primarily for tests of skills and knowledge, is indicated by showing how well the behaviors sampled by the test are representative of the behaviors to be exhibited in a desired performance domain. Criterion-related validities, on the other hand, are demonstrated by comparing the test scores with some external criterion that supposedly provides a direct measure of the variable or behavior in question. Statements about concurrent validity indicate the extent to which a test may be used to indicate how well the individual currently functions or performs on the criterion. Predictive validity refers to the "extent to which an individual's future level on the criterion can be predicted from a knowledge of prior test performance" (p. 26). While this type of validity appears to be the most meaningful, it is not easily obtainable. The last type of validity, construct validity, is the most difficult to explain briefly. Essentially, it involves determining the degree to which certain explanatory concepts or constructs account for performance on the test. Construct validity constitutes a check on the theory underlying a given test, and thus requires an accumulation of research results rather than a single study.

At our present stage of development we work with instruments that leave much to be desired. Admittedly, as clinical psychologists, we are dealing with complex and often intangible problems. It is exceedingly difficult, for example, to secure adequate criteria with which to validate tests of personality. Nevertheless, unless we strive for tests of adequate validity we may be deluged with inadequate tests. In this connection, the writer would like to emphasize the importance of carefully scrutinizing test manuals for information on reliability, validity, and method of standardization. In addition, the psychologist should follow the research literature on the tests he uses. The handbooks edited by Buros (1972, 1978) also are useful aids because they contain evaluative material on many widely used tests. Frequently, the claims of test manuals are not completely supported by other independent investigations. It is just as important to know the strengths and limitations of a given test as it is to know the procedures for administration and scoring. For these reasons, any evaluation of the clinical usefulness of a test should include an appraisal of its standardization, validity, reliability, and application to clinical problems.

With this brief introduction, let us now turn our attention to the clinical applications of several well-known tests. Obviously, no attempt will be made to review all the tests available to psychologists. Other references serve this need adequately (Anastasi, 1976; Buros, 1972, 1978; Cronbach, 1970). The main purpose here is to illustrate the use of psychological tests in clinical situations. Consequently, only a few tests, selected because of their wide use today, will be described and evaluated in terms of their clinical usefulness.

TESTS OF INTELLIGENCE

The concept of intelligence and the appraisal of intelligence or mental ability have been the cause of controversy both within psychology and the broader social arena. There are important issues concerning the definition of intelligence, whether or not so-called intelligence tests actually measure intelligence, whether the tests are biased against certain subgroups in our society, whether intelligence is influenced more by heredity or environment, and the like (Eysenck & Kamin, 1981; Garfield, 1970; Matarazzo, 1972; McNemar, 1964; Vernon, 1965; Wechsler, 1958). These are important and intriguing issues, but at present they remain unsettled or controversial. To discuss them in any detail would require considerable space and lead us away from our central purpose—the use of tests of intelligence or mental ability in clinical psychology. Furthermore, to treat these issues in a superficial or cursory manner would be disadvantageous. Therefore, there will be no general discussion of these matters, except as they impinge upon activities of the clinical psychologist. We will view intelligence tests as a standardized means of appraising mental functioning which have some utility in the clinical assessment of individuals with potential psychological dysfunction.

The administration and interpretation of intelligence tests, as indicated previously, has a long history in clinical psychology. Even in this traditional activity, however, a broader clinical view has developed concerning the functions and values of intelligence testing. The attainment of an IQ for a particular individual has come to be regarded as merely one purpose of an intelligence examination, instead of the only goal. In general, four main purposes may be served by administering a standardized test of intelligence.

1. AN APPRAISAL OF THE GENERAL INTELLECTUAL OR MENTAL LEVEL OF THE SUBJECT

This use of tests for the general purpose of estimating the subject's mental potentialities or level of functioning is probably the most common. Frequently, in this connection, the IQ or Mental Age of the subject is used to indicate the level or relative degree of mental ability. One must remember, however, that such tests are not absolute measures and that they possess no magical qualities. Many of them tend to be largely verbal in content and reflect the educational and cultural opportunities of the individual. Keeping these factors in mind, the psychologist can use the data secured from an intelligence test to help him understand the individual's mental ability or level of mental functioning. In many types of cases, such information may be of considerable value. The following case serves as an illustration of how such results may be of help in clarifying a given client's difficulties.

H. E., a student, was referred to a university psychological clinic because his grades were falling below the minimum required to remain in school. At the time of referral, H. E. was in the fourth semester of his college program and had been given probationary status. He was failing one subject and barely passing three others. An examination of his record during his first three semesters at college revealed generally poor work, with his grades evenly distributed between C's and D's. Since his academic performance was uniformly poor and no unusual trends were noted, it was decided to evaluate H. E.'s mental ability as a possible factor in his school failure. Consequently, an individual intelligence test was administered to him. The test results (IQ above 120) indicated that H. E. was capable of performing at a superior level of mental ability. Because the student obtained an IQ that was well within the range considered satisfactory for academic success, the test results helped to rule out lack of ability as a serious factor in his school failures. With this information, the psychologist was able to pursue his investigation in other directions and thus uncover other factors which were more important in explaining the client's current difficulties.

In this case, the matter of appraising the intellectual capabilities of the individual was an important aspect of the total clinical study. Such knowledge of the relative mental ability of the individual is also of definite importance in many different types of clinical problems. In cases of school retardation, of suspected mental deficiency, and even in cases of behavioral disturbance, the findings secured from intelligence tests help clarify our understanding of the problem. Many children who are failing in school and developing behavioral symptoms secure average or superior scores on intelligence tests, and lack of mental ability consequently can be ruled out as a factor in these failures. The difficulty may be related to lack of stimulation in school, unfavorable home conditions, or some other causal factor. In one instance, a child was referred to a university psychological clinic to be examined for possible mental retardation. On the Stanford Revision of the Binet Scale this child scored an IQ of 135, indicative of superior mental ability. In this case, the child was being compared unfavorably with an unusually brilliant older sibling by the parents. The test findings were of value in helping the parents understand and modify their attitude toward the child.

It is evident that the intelligence test is useful in evaluating cases of potential mental deficiency. Today, no study of a case of retarded mental development would be complete without an individual test of intelligence, unless the individual is severely impaired. The values of an objective standardized test are easily apparent in such an appraisal. In this connection, however, it is worth emphasizing that in the clinical study of an individual, more information is secured than just intelligence test scores. Tests are useful tools, but they do not give absolute answers to clinical problems. The results secured from psychological tests need to be interpreted and integrated with other data. If such interpretation and integration are handled carelessly, actual harm can be done to the individual client. *It is particularly important to proceed cautiously when low test scores are secured.* A competent psychologist would not diagnose an individual as mentally deficient without securing a history of his past development and social adjustment. In addition, the observation of the subject in the test situation, an analysis of separate responses to the various test items, and perhaps recourse to additional tests would be utilized by the psychologist before making a definite decision. With verbal tests, in particular, one must always keep in mind that such factors as the subject's educational opportunities, reading ability, sensory acuity, language handicap, and emotional disturbance may influence the score adversely.

The writer can recall several instances of individuals pronounced defective or borderline in intelligence whose test scores were lowered because of one of the reasons mentioned above. For example, an adolescent girl who was seen in a psychological clinic for possible vocational advisement obtained an IQ of 64 on an individual test of mental ability. Such a score falls in the range designated as mentally deficient according to the test norms. Although her performance on certain test items was decidedly poor, however, her performance on others approached an average level. This discrepancy, plus the examiner's observation that the subject appeared tense and gave up quickly on many items without really exerting herself, led to additional testing and study of the case. When this girl's case was presented at a staff conference, it was finally concluded that the girl was deeply disturbed emotionally, that her level of adjustment influenced her test performance—she was not mentally defective. Treatment for her personality difficulties was recommended.

Although intelligence tests are standardized instruments and therefore presumably possess the positive values of such instruments, they can also be a source of difficulty if improperly administered or interpreted. Not only must the examiner follow standard instructions for the administration and scoring of the test, but he must also be sure that the test is an appropriate one for the client being examined and that the client is properly motivated to perform

PREZELL R. ROBINSON LIBRARY
SAINT AUGUSTINE'S COLLEGE
RALEIGH. NORTH CAROLINA 27611

as well as possible in the test situation. A psychological examination requires the active collaboration and cooperation of the subject taking the test. Therefore, most books and manuals dealing with test administration stress the importance of securing the subject's rapport in the testing situation. The examiner is thus an important variable in this examination and it can be said with some truth that no test is better than the person who administers and interprets it. If the psychologist who administers an intelligence test, or any test for that matter, fails to secure the cooperation of the client, or if he is perceived as cold, aloof, threatening, or hostile, then less than an optimum performance may be secured from some clients. The resulting test score consequently will not be a valid reflection of the individual's mental ability.

Thus, it is important that the psychologist establish a friendly, but professional, relationship with the person to be examined; he should put the client at ease and discuss in a general way what is to take place and why. If the client refuses to cooperate, is inattentive, or acutely disturbed, then it may be difficult or impossible to evaluate him adequately, at least in terms of a standard formal evaluation of mental ability. Some examiners by virtue of their own rather negative interpersonal style, may tend to inhibit optimum performance and consequently to secure scores that are not accurate reflections of the person's real potential ability. Conversely, some other examiners may be so imbued with kindness and benevolence that they may unconsciously help the subject or otherwise be lax in following the standard instructions and time limits, thus securing scores which are spuriously high. In neither case are the client's interests served.

Apart from the matter of securing adequate rapport in the examination of a client, there are other examiner-related variables that may contribute to inaccuracy and error in this task. One simple but important source of error is inaccurate scoring of test responses. The writer has had enough experience in working with psychologists and students in training to know that at times some serious errors in scoring may result—sometimes simply as a result of faulty addition! Other errors may result from improper attention to a host of variables, alluded to previously, that may tend to lower a subject's test performance and lead to a faulty interpretation of his intellectual ability. Such matters as reading disability, visual and auditory defects, severe emotional disturbance, a crisis situation, lack of attention, misunderstanding of instructions, and inadequate opportunities for prior learning may all tend to affect test scores adversely. Obviously, in such situations, the test scores cannot be regarded as valid and the astute clinician needs to be sensitive to such problems.

Before concluding this section of our discussion it is worth emphasizing again a few of the points mentioned earlier. One of these concerns the matter of the client's previous opportunities for learning. Admittedly, there are a

PURSELL, R. ROBINSON LIBRARY
SAINT AUGUSTINE'S COLLEGE
RALEIGH, NORTH CAROLINA 27611

variety of views concerning the nature and development of intelligence or intelligent behavior. Nevertheless, the ability to perform well on a test is conditioned by the individual's previous experience. Furthermore, the norms of any single test are derived from a particular sample with certain previous learning opportunities, and if a test is used with a certain client there is an implication that this person resembles the standardization population and has had comparable opportunities for learning. If not, that is if the cultural opportunities and background of the subject and the normative sample are quite diverse, then the person cannot be meaningfully evaluated in terms of the test norms. An obvious example is that of a person taking a test that requires him to read when he has difficulty in reading. The score obtained in such an instance would not be a valid measure of the person's mental ability.

The point has already been made that a variety of factors can potentially depress intelligence test scores and that therefore low test scores must be interpreted with extreme caution. A low test score is not necessarily synonymous with mental retardation, although a number of examiners have apparently behaved as if this were so. Some years ago the author participated in a study at a state home for the retarded that revealed twenty-four cases who were initially institutionalized as retarded, but who, upon more detailed study, were found not to be retarded at all (Garfield & Affleck, 1960). An appraisal of the potential factors involved in these cases suggested inadequate examinations, an overreliance on the IQ as a primary or exclusive index of retardation, and a willingness to base important decisions on test scores with very young children when the predictive validity and reliability of such scores is known to be low. These findings illustrate some of the potential dangers and serious consequences that may result from the misuse of test data.

The preceding discussion illustrates both the potential value of mental tests, and the need to evaluate them carefully for clinical purposes. Thus far, the use of intelligence tests as measures of the general mental level of the individual has been described. As in the case illustration presented previously, however, other inferences about the client may also be made from intelligence test data.

2. INDICATIONS OF POSSIBLE PERSONALITY DISTURBANCE

In some instances the data secured from individual intelligence tests may suggest disturbed functioning in the client. This may be noted in a number of ways. If the individual's performance is unusually erratic, the clinician may be suspicious of possible disturbance. Erratic performance is evident when the subject's responses to various parts of the test are decidedly uneven, or if certain unusual discrepancies are apparent within a given subtest, for example, if the subject fails unusually easy items and succeeds on more difficult ones. The qualitative responses secured on the test also may be of diagnostic value. A series of unusual, highly personalized, or bizarre responses often are indicative of serious mental disturbance.

A few brief examples of one psychotic patient's responses on the Wechsler-Bellevue Intelligence Scale will help to illustrate what is meant by unusual or bizarre responses. In answer to the question, "Why are shoes made of leather?" the patient gave the following response, "So you can put on your shoes—leather shoes you know. I certainly should think of that. Slippers couldn't be called shoes. You're fairly well dressed." When asked in what way a dog and a lion are alike, this patient replied: "There are lions and tigers and dogs are the little animals. We often see that lions are great big animals and people aren't very close to them." It is apparent that this patient was not able to produce an adequate or precise response to the test questions. Instead, he brought forth some type of associational content that was related only peripherally to the questions and which was a manifestation of his disturbed functioning. The type of responses secured clearly were not the kind usually obtained with more normal subjects.

Again, it is emphasized that no conclusive diagnostic evaluation should be made on intelligence test data alone. Such data, along with observations of the subject's behavior, however, contribute to the total study of the individual. Such findings indicate that much more than an IQ or simple statement of the subject's intelligence can be secured from the administration of a standardized test of mental ability, and demonstrate the type of clinically important data that may be secured with some cases.

3. INDICATIONS OF SPECIAL ABILITIES OR LIMITATIONS

With some intelligence tests that sample a fairly wide range of functions, the clinician may be able to note certain specific defects or assets. If he is alert and sensitive to factors other than simply the IQ or MA, he may note that a particular client is poor in language usage, reads passages with difficulty, displays poor memory for recent or past events, and so forth. These observations constitute an important part of the total clinical examination. Poor use of language, for example, may be indicative of limited environmental opportunities for learning or possibly of some aphasic disturbance related to brain injury. In a similar way, specific memory defects may suggest the possibility of functional loss such as occurs with amnesia, or of mental impairment, associated with brain damage. Conversely, attention should be paid also to any particularly outstanding attributes of the individual. Unusual skill and rapidity in arithmetical computation or in reasoning may be observed, or the subject's responses may reveal an unusually rich vocabulary. Depending on the problem presented, such observations add to the overall appraisal of the client's skills and potentialities.

4. OBSERVATION OF THE SUBJECT'S BEHAVIOR

It has already been stated that one of the values of administering an intelligence test is that it provides the psychologist with an opportunity to observe the behavior of a client in a standard situation. Because in clinical work we are interested primarily in understanding the client, rather than in obtaining a given test score, any cues about the client that can be secured while observing him in the test situation may help us in this understanding. Frequently, valid inferences about personality trends may be made from astute observations. Does the client continually seek reassurance from the examiner? Is he apologetic about his responses? Are attempts made to impress the examiner? Does he display insight in terms of his test performance? Is he constantly ill at ease and tense during the testing period? Is attention difficult to hold? Such questions are illustrative of the kinds of clinically important behavioral trends that can be observed and reported via the testing situation. The observation and evaluation of behavior in the standard testing situation is also utilized in appraising the subject's mental level, special defects, and possible disturbance.

Obviously, if a person is distracted and does not appear to be attending fully to the requirements of the test, this behavior needs to be considered in evaluating the representativeness of the test results secured. Here again, the test scores are not fully meaningful unless accompanied by such an appraisal from the psychologist.

These considerations lead to a few statements concerning the actual administration of psychological tests. It is obvious, of course, that in order to obtain optimum results from psychological tests, the standard instructions and methods of administration must be carefully followed. This is necessary if the results of a given examination are to be interpreted on the basis of the norms obtained from the standardization group. This is a basic rule of all psychological testing and experimentation. When directions and methods of scoring are altered, the results secured cannot be interpreted in terms of the existing norms. One will find in his or her clinical work that standard instructions are sometimes incomplete, however, and that for certain cases they are inadequate. In such instances, the clinician must rely on his experience and judgment to make intelligent modifications. If, for example, it is apparent that a subject is failing a given test item because he has misunderstood the directions, it is foolish to continue simply because the standard instructions have been given once. The results secured actually will not be representative of the subject's capabilities. In this type of situation, it might be feasible to repeat the instructions and make sure that the subject fully understands them.[2] This, however, does not imply deviating from standard procedures in testing and should not be interpreted to mean that instructions will be repeated routinely when the subject gives a wrong response.

It is evident from these statements that psychological testing cannot be viewed as a routine mechanical process. If the examiner is not alert and sensitive to the behavior of the subject, not only will valuable clues about the latter go unheeded, but necessary information for making a more valid evaluation of the test data will be neglected also. Too often beginning students behave as if psychological testing were an end in itself, rather than one of the means utilized to study a given client. In the clinical frame of reference, the proper understanding of the client is a major goal toward the proper disposition of the case. Thus observation of behavior may be as significant as test scores, as well as a prerequisite for valid appraisal of such scores. This is particularly relevant in working with children as well as with very fearful or disturbed individuals. That clinical sensitivity and acumen are essential for adequate psychological appraisal is quite evident in the following statement made by Carter and Bowles (1948):

> The examiner must always watch for adverse effects on the examination which may arise from the testing situation. These often are subtle and develop from a variety of conditions on the part of the child, the examiner, or the test materials. The examiner must consider any unwitting effects he may have had upon the examination by failing to establish rapport, failing to elicit the child's best efforts, not understanding or not properly interpreting the child's responses, being brusque, impatient, or non-accepting. On the part of the child, hygienic conditions, fear, hostility, distrust, or excitement may influence the results (p. 126).
>
> In maintaining rapport, the examiner may need to vary the order of presentation of test items as the situation demands. When a child is shy or upset, for example, language tasks, or those highly interpersonal in nature should be postponed until he is more relaxed. The nature of the tasks should be varied if a child becomes bored, and if certain items stimulate withdrawal or avoidance, they should be employed cautiously (p. 131).[3]

---

[2] This statement has particular reference to test items involving general comprehension, information, and judgment in which the speed of response usually is not a crucial factor. Where test items involve speed or immediate recall, the psychologist must avoid routine repetition lest he in effect provide the subject with additional practice or time.

[3] It should be noted that such variation from the standard method of presentation is not a routine matter and requires considerable judgment on the part of the clinician. The final interpretation of the subject's performance calls for greater clinical understanding because the test norms

The above statements should not be interpreted as signifying that standard procedures should not be followed. Rather, they indicate that clinical observation and sensitivity to the client are matters of crucial importance. At the same time, we must repeat that recognized procedures of test administration are to be observed. The individual should be seated comfortably in a quiet room with little to distract him from the task at hand. Adequate explanation concerning the test should be given and attempts made to put the person at ease. Rapport with the person being examined is a basic prerequisite for reliable results.

THE CLINICAL USES OF INTELLIGENCE TESTS

The preceding pages have described some basic features of psychological tests and have discussed some general uses of intelligence tests in clinical practice. In this section we shall make reference only to those selected intelligence tests which are rather widely used by clinical psychologists currently, and describe them for illustrative purposes. In most graduate clinical programs, the student will usually have at least one course dealing with these tests as well as supervised experience in their use later on in the graduate program.

At the present time, the most widely used individual tests of mental ability are the various Wechsler Scales and the revised Stanford-Binet. The Stanford Revision of the Binet-Simon Scale of Intelligence has the longest history of any test in this field (Terman & Merrill, 1960). Originally published in 1916, this scale was the most widely used individual test of mental ability in the United States for over a quarter of a century (Lubin, Wallis, & Paine, 1971; Sundberg, 1961). It was also the standard of comparison used for other intelligence tests and frequently correlations with the Stanford-Binet were cited for other tests as indications of the validity of the latter. In more recent years, its popularity with clinical psychologists has declined somewhat as the Wechsler Scales have become more widely used. Nevertheless, the Stanford-Binet has consistently been mentioned as one of the ten psychological tests most widely used by clinical psychologists (Lubin, Wallis, & Paine, 1971; Sundberg, 1961; Wade & Baker, 1977) and in the training of clinical psychology interns (Garfield & Kurtz, 1973). Our description of the scale, however, will be brief.

---

are derived from tests administered under standard conditions, and strictly speaking, do not apply under changed conditions. On the other hand, adhering rigidly to standard conditions of test administration, when the subject obviously does not appear to be responding at an optimum level, will produce unsatisfactory or misleading results.

STANFORD-BINET SCALE

The original Stanford-Binet was revised in 1937 and in 1960, although the latter basically consisted in a detailed analysis of the older scale in which the best items of the two existing forms of the scale were combined. The 1960 version was restandardized in 1972 and used a more heterogeneous sample of subjects which included racial and cultural subgroups. However, with very minor exceptions, the items are the same as in the 1960 scale. The scale, following the work of Binet, remains a mental age scale in which groups of test items are arranged in terms of age levels—that is, there are items at the six-year level, the seven-year level, and so forth. For a variety of reasons, the way the items are arranged or weighted varies with the different ages. Below the age of 6 the items are grouped into half-year levels. From ages 6 to 14 the items are grouped at year levels. However, after age 14, the grouping of items becomes very different. There are four "adult" levels ranging from that of "Average Adult" to "Superior Adult III." The adult levels thus differ from the others in that they do not really conform to the concept of items grouped for specific ages or developmental levels. We shall refer to this later in making some appraisal of the scale.

The kinds of test items vary and, of course, are different for the different age groups. At the younger age levels, blocks, toys, and beads are used as well as purely verbal items, whereas at the adult levels the items are primarily verbal and emphasize problem solving and abstract thinking. The general procedure in administering the scale is to begin at a level consistent with the person's age level or just below it. If the individual passes all items at this beginning level, the examiner proceeds to the next higher age level and continues to a level at which the person fails all of the items. If the person fails to pass all items at the initial level, the examiner proceeds to the next lower level and continues downward until a level is reached, referred to as the basal level or basal age, at which the individual passes all items. After this, as mentioned above, the examiner proceeds upward on the scale until a level is reached where all items are failed. This range of test items administered to a person thus constitutes, as it were, a sampling of his mental ability from which an IQ is obtained. Before describing the Stanford-Binet Scale further, let us discuss the IQ briefly.

The IQ is an index or quotient indicating the relative rate of mental development. As traditionally defined, it was derived by dividing the obtained mental age by the individual's chronological age and multiplying the obtained quotient by 100. On a mental age scale each person secures a certain amount of mental age for each item she passes. By adding up all items passed and assuming the appropriate score for the items below the Basal Age, the person's mental age is secured. Dividing this by the chronological age and multiplying by 100 the person's IQ is secured. A child who is 8 years of age and obtains a mental age of 8 would have an IQ of 100. If the same child secured a mental age of 10 years, she would receive an IQ of 125, and so on. The IQ, therefore, can be viewed as indicating the rate of mental development or as reflecting the relative level of intelligence. As might be anticipated, individuals vary widely in mental ability and this is reflected in the range of IQ scores obtainable.

The procedure just described was the original one used for obtaining an IQ on the Stanford-Binet and other mental age scales. However, because differences in mental development at relatively higher ages appear to be less easily discriminated than differences at earlier ages, certain computations and procedures have been used to compensate for this phenomenon in computing the IQ. For example, the difference in performance between a 1- and 2-year-old seems greater and more readily apparent than is the difference between a 13-year-old and one who is 14 years of age. Thus, most current tests use a different procedure in which the subject's score is converted into an IQ based on the distribution of scores derived from the standardization sample. Tables for securing an IQ for the scores obtained are provided in the test manual.

The Revised Stanford-Binet, as well as most tests of intelligence, has been developed so that approximately 50% of the people obtain IQ's ranging from 90 to 110, with 25% securing scores above 110, and a comparable number getting scores below 90. Various schemes for interpreting and classifying IQ's have been offered by Terman and others, although it should be recognized that these are judgmental schemes and that there is very little difference in mental ability between individuals whose IQ's vary a few points. Thus, one should not judge an individual with an IQ of 109 to be average in intelligence and one with an IQ of 111 to be above average. Terman originally classified individuals with IQ's of 140 and above as being in the genius or near genius classification, but later recognized that much more than such an IQ was needed to indicate genius. Such individuals have scores that place them in approximately the upper 1% of the population and are clearly very bright. Genius, however, is another matter.

Now let us look at some of the items of the 1960 Stanford-Binet. Although, the types of items vary from the different age levels, there are certain types of items that tend to be used throughout the scale. At the two-year level the items include a form board with a circle, square, and triangle which the child is to replace correctly; the use of a large paper doll to identify parts of the body; the building of a tower with twelve 1-inch blocks; the evaluating of vocabulary by means of a series of pictures; and the identification by name of common objects depicted on a card. At the nine-year level, the items have increased in difficulty, and include the following:

1. *Paper Cutting.* This involves cutting out segments of 6-inch squares of paper which have been folded in certain ways and then asking the subject to make a drawing showing how the paper would look if it were unfolded.

2. *Verbal Absurdities.* This involves reading a series of "foolish" statements and having the subject respond by telling the examiner what is foolish about each of the statements. An example is, "Bill Jones's feet are so big that he has to pull his trousers on over his head."

3. *Memory for Designs.* A card with two designs is presented to the subject for ten seconds and then the subject is required to draw the designs from memory.

4. *Rhymes.* The subject is requested sequentially to tell the name of a color, a number, an animal, or a flower that rhymes with a specific word.

5. *Making Change.* As the name implies, this item includes questions which require the subject to perform the mental subtraction involved in making change.

6. *Repeating Four Digits Reversed.* The subject is given a series of four digits verbally and is required to say them backward.

To complete our brief sampling of items from the revised Stanford-Binet and to illustrate the range of difficulty evident at the different age levels, let us look at the items at the Superior Adult III level, the highest level in the scale. The first test item is the vocabulary test which is also included at many other levels. At this level, however, the subject must be able to define thirty words correctly. The vocabulary test begins with such simple words as *orange* and *envelope* and proceeds up to such words as *ochre, incrustation,* and *perfunctory.* The second set of items is made up of proverbs, for example, what does the proverb "Let sleeping dogs lie" mean? The third set of test items consists of "opposite analogies," for example, "A rabbit is timid; a lion is . . .". The next item involves the subject's orientation in relation to a set of given directions. This is followed by a reasonably complicated reasoning problem. The sixth and last item on this level involves the recall of a paragraph read to the subject.

The preceding paragraphs should give the reader some idea of the kinds of items that make up the Stanford-Binet and the range of difficulty evident in the scale. However, very little has been said about standardization, reliability, and validity of the test. Some brief mention of such considerations is in order.

The 1960 revision of the Stanford-Binet was based on testing approximately 4500 subjects ranging in age from 2½ to 18 years of age and an attempt was made to correct deficiencies in the 1937 version. Deviation IQ's were used with a mean standard score of 100 and a standard deviation of 16 for all ages, thus making the IQ's comparable at the different age levels. Only the best items from the two forms of the scale were incorporated into the revision. On the whole, satisfactory reliabilities, generally in the .90's, were reported for the 1937 revision in correlating the two forms of the test and the 1960 revision is perhaps slightly better (Terman & Merrill, 1960).

In the 1972 restandardization of the scale, approximately 2100 cases were tested. This sample was selected from a much larger sample used in the standardization of a group test, and, as indicated previously, was more representative of the general population. The later norms indicate what appear to be an increase in scores at all ages, but most noticeably at the preschool ages. It is suggested that the latter may be due to or reflect cultural changes that have occurred recently (Terman & Merrill, 1973).

The problem of validity is a more difficult one to answer adequately. This, of course, is a problem for all tests of intelligence since suitable criteria for test validation are not easily secured. Nevertheless, such matters have to be considered and evaluated by the competent psychologist in the selection and use of psychological tests.

The validity of test items in the revised Stanford-Binet Scales was evaluated by noting the increase in the percentage of subjects passing each item at successive chronological and mental ages. In other words, since intelligence develops with age, one can assume, up to a certain point, that older children are more intelligent than younger ones. Valid test items, therefore, should be passed by a greater percentage of children at successive age levels. The authors of the scale readily state that this is not conclusive evidence of validity. But, in the absence of suitable criteria of intelligence, more direct evidence is difficult to secure. The careful and comparatively extensive work on the standardization of the scale, the clinical usefulness of the previous scales, and the close agreement between the most recent scales contributed to the acceptance of the revised form.

There are two aspects or limitations of the Stanford-Binet Scale which should also be mentioned. Except for items at the early years, most of the items tend to be verbal ones. This may be a problem in examining some individuals who have limited language capability. The test also is not considered adequate for evaluating individuals over 18 years of age, since they are not represented in the standardization sample. For practical purposes, the test is probably best used for individuals in the age range of 5 to 15 years. In general, test results obtained before the age of 5 or 6 do not correlate very highly with those secured at later ages.

Where the problem presented by a child may be related to factors associated with intelligence, the Stanford-Binet Scale can be a useful diagnostic instrument. Often, in clinical work with children, the Stanford-Binet, or the Wechsler Intelligence Scale for Children, is administered even in cases where intelligence may not appear to be the most significant aspect of the problem referred for study and treatment. In such cases the practice is followed because it provides a general estimate of the child's ability and mental functioning, allows for observation of the child in a standard situation, and, in some instances, may even contribute to the establishment of a relationship between psychologist and child that may have some therapeutic value. An example may illustrate such use more concretely.

O. A. was referred to the writer because of poor work in school. The girl, 9 years old, was repeating the third grade a second time and having difficulty in her relationships with the teacher. The mother complained of animosity on the part of the teacher toward the child. On the other hand, it was also stated that the child was "not too good in school." The girl was somewhat thin and small in stature and appeared both docile and shy. After a short period of getting acquainted, the Stanford-Binet was administered to O. A. The examiner began with the items on the eight-year level, on which level O. A. failed to pass all the items. Nevertheless, the succeeding higher year levels were given until year eleven was reached, where all the test items were failed. During this period of testing, it was noted that the child lacked confidence in her abilities and apparently accepted failure as her accustomed lot. When praised for any minor success, she appeared happy and grateful. This was particularly evident when the test was continued at the seven- and six-year levels. On the latter, where the basal age was secured, she responded so warmly to the encouragement of the examiner that one could assume that praise and encouragement were rare in her past experience.

The IQ computed from the test responses was 88, indicating that O. A.'s mental level was roughly at the 25th percentile of children her age. She was thus somewhat below average in the abilities measured by the test. The observations during the test, however, revealed other findings of importance. Because of academic failure and the concomitant attitudes of others, the child was developing strong inferiority feelings and a self-attitude of inadequacy. She exhibited a great need for sympathetic encouragement and acceptance. These observations helped to clarify the problem, and, along with other information, provided the basis for the recommendations subsequently made to the parents and to the school. In this case it was important to know O. A.'s potentialities for academic work, but, in addition, an opportunity was provided to observe the reaction of the girl to her own limitations as well as to evaluate other aspects of her personality.

THE WECHSLER SCALES

The 1937 Stanford-Binet Scale, in spite of its merits, was not particularly well suited for work with adults. As we noted earlier, it was not standardized on any individuals over 18 years of age and some of the items tended to be viewed as relating mainly to children or to school. There was clearly a need for an individual test standardized and constructed for adults. The Wechsler-Bellevue Scale, which was first published in 1939, was developed specifically for this purpose. Although its initial standardization left much to be desired (Garfield, 1957; Gurvitz, 1952), it apparently met an existing need and was widely used. The scale was revised in 1955 (Wechsler, 1955) and the newer version was named the Wechsler Adult Intelligence Scale (WAIS). The WAIS retained the same format and many of the items of the original scale but was standardized in a much more careful and adequate fashion. This scale has been widely used since that time and a revised form of the WAIS (Wechsler, 1981) has just been completed and made available for professional use.

Apart from the fact that the Wechsler Scales were developed for use with adults, there are some other important differences between them and the Stanford-Binet. In the first place, the Wechsler Scales are point scales rather than mental-age scales. The items are not classified or grouped in terms of mental age. Rather, points (scores) are given for correct responses. These raw scores are then converted into scaled or standard scores which, in turn, can be related to IQ values. In this fashion, an average standard score tends to be equal to an IQ of 100. Another difference is that whereas a certain type of test item is interspersed through the Stanford-Binet Scale, occurring at different age levels, items of like kinds are grouped together on the Wechsler Scales to form subtests. On the Stanford-Binet, repeating digits consist of two digits at the 2½ year level and, increasing in difficulty, is found at various age levels until nine digits are required at the Superior Adult III level. In contrast, on the WAIS, all the memory for digit items are grouped together as one subtest and are administered in sequence from simplest to the most difficult.

The WAIS also differs from the Stanford-Binet in having age norms for adults. On the Stanford-Binet, all individuals above the age of 18 are compared to the norms for 18-year-olds in terms of computing their IQ. If mental ability reached a peak at this age and then remained constant, perhaps no harm would be done by means of this procedure. This does not seem to be the case, however, and at least several studies have indicated some rise and then a decline in mental ability at various ages after 18 (Bayley, 1968, 1970; Garfield & Blek, 1952; Matarazzo, 1972; Terman & Oden, 1959; Wechsler, 1958). Although the particular age at which the peak of mental ability appears to be reached will vary depending upon the population and the mental functions sampled, the data are such as to suggest that one is best compared with his or her own age group.

The entire area of mental growth and decline is a fascinating area in its own right and it would appear as if the nature of mental decline is not as clear-cut as earlier cross-sectional studies indicated. For our present purposes, however, we can state that it seems best to compare adult subjects to normative groups of their own age. In terms of the normative sample of the recently revised WAIS-R (Wechsler, 1981), the peak age of mental development is reached in the interval of 25 to 34 years. Thereafter, there is a slow but appreciable decline which is reflected in the IQ tables. For example, in terms of the WAIS-R manual, a total score of 115 at ages 25 to 34 is equivalent to an IQ of 100. At ages 35 to 44 the same score is equal to an IQ of 105, and at the ages 55 to 64 it equals an IQ of 113. In the age interval of 70 to 74, however, a score of 115 merits an IQ of 122. The decline in mental ability is thus most apparent in the very old-age categories of the sample, and one must keep in mind that the IQ reflects relative performance in terms of the age norm with which the individual is compared.

The WAIS-R consists of eleven subtests which are grouped into two scales. The Verbal Scale consists of six subtests: Information, Digit Span, Vocabulary, Arithmetic, Comprehension, and Similarities. The kinds of tasks involved in the Arithmetic, Digit Span, and Vocabulary subtests are reasonably obvious. The Information subtest, as might also be inferred, consists of items to test the subject's general fund of information. The Comprehension subtest attempts to evaluate practical judgment. A possible example would be, "Why should students read their textbooks?" The Similarities subtest consists of items that attempt to measure the ability to conceptualize or to engage in abstract thinking. One such item could require the subject to explain in what way an orange and an apple are alike. Most of these types of items are found in the Stanford-Binet as well as other tests of mental ability.

The second scale of the WAIS is called the Performance Scale and consists of five subtests. Although these are not all strictly performance or nonverbal items, they do not rely as much on verbal operations as do the subtests of the Verbal Scale. One subtest requires the subject to tell what part is missing in a set of pictures; a second involves arranging cutup parts into a meaningful whole; a third calls for the arranging of blocks in terms of specific designs; a fourth requires the subject to arrange pictures so they tell a story; and a fifth subtest involves the substitution of symbols for numbers. All of these subtests are also timed, whereas only one of the verbal subtests is so affected. By means of scaled scores, the examiner can quickly note the variability of performance among the various subtests. This allows him to look with relative ease for areas where the subject performs unusually well or poorly. In a similar fashion, separate IQ's are obtained for the Verbal and Performance scales which allow for comparison in this regard. In the WAIS-R the order of administration requires that verbal and performance subtests be given alternately.

Before discussing further the specific components of the WAIS-R and its potential clinical uses, something more can be said about the reliability and validity of the scale. Most of the test manual is devoted to a description of the scale, its basic standardization, changes made in the new revision, and instructions for administration and scoring. No specific data on the validity of the WAIS-R are provided. Instead, the point is made that since the WAIS-R measures the same abilities as the 1955 WAIS and the original 1939 Wechsler-Bellevue Scale (W-B) and overlaps in content with these earlier scales, "studies with the WAIS and W-B can be considered relevant to this revision" (Wechsler, 1981, p. 49). Reference, therefore, is made to the construction of the previous scales, to the large amount of published research on the earlier scales (Buros, 1978), and to important reviews of such work (Matarazzo, 1972; Zimmerman, Woo-Sam, & Glasser, 1973). Specific mention is made of the relationship of academic success and level of education to IQ's secured with the scales. The results of an early study comparing the original WAIS and the Stanford-Binet which was mentioned in the 1955 manual is also listed in the 1981 manual. In this study, based on 52 male prison inmates, a correlation of around .85 was obtained for both the Full Scale and the Verbal Scale.

Other comparable studies have been reported in the literature and a number of these studies are discussed in reviews of the Wechsler Scales (Guertin, Ladd, Frank, Rabin, & Hiester, 1966, 1971). There is some variability in these findings depending on the test used, the type of subjects studied, the range of mental ability and similar considerations. In general, the correlations between the two scales is in the neighborhood of .80, and if the Stanford-Binet is considered as the criterion in terms of construct or concurrent validity, the correlations are respectable. It is of interest to note, also, that a large number of other tests have used the WAIS as a criterion measure.

In terms of reliability, most of the available data appear to be quite satisfactory. In terms of data provided for two subsamples ages 25–34 and 45–54, the test-retest reliabilities for Full Scale IQ's were .95 and .96, respectively. The reliabilities for the Verbal IQ's are approximately the same, but those for the Performance IQ's are five to seven points lower. The reliabilities of the Full Scale and of the Verbal and Performance scales are generally higher than those for the specific subtests that make up the scales.

Clinical Applications. The general uses of the Wechsler Scales are essentially the same as those mentioned previously for all intelligence tests and illustrated in part for the Stanford-Binet. However, the unique format of the Wechsler Scales allows for clinical appraisals of performance which are not as easily made on the Stanford-Binet.

Since the total scale consists of separate verbal and performance scales as well as eleven weighted subtests, various attempts have been made to use differences in the patterns or profiles of subtest scores for diagnostic purposes. On the basis of his experience with the Wechsler-Bellevue Scale,

Wechsler offered diagnostic patterns of response for groups designated as follows: "Organic Brain Disease, Schizophrenia, Neurotic, Adolescent Psychopaths, and Mental Defectives." Certain of these diagnostic groups, for example, were reported to perform better on the Verbal Scale than the Performance Scale, or to exhibit a greater degree of interest variability or "scatter." In addition, certain groups purportedly score higher on some specific subtests and lower on others. The extent of significant subtest deviation was frequently calculated from the mean of all the subtest scores for a given subject. For example, if the mean subtest score for an individual were nine, a score of six on the Information subtest would be considered a significant deviation. Although Wechsler devoted an entire chapter to such diagnostic uses of his scale, and provided illustrative cases, no statistical evaluations of these techniques were presented in his manual.

Rapaport published an even more extensive analysis of Wechsler patterns in certain nosological groups and provided an elaborate rationale for the psychological functions measured by the scale (Rapaport, Gill, and Schafer, 1945, 1968). Although original and provocative in many respects, Rapaport's work had several limitations. It was oriented in terms of specific diagnostic groupings that were not in extensive use in either practice or research; some diagnostic patterns were based on very few cases; the standard scoring and administrative procedures of some tests had been modified in part; and many statistical errors were found (McNemar, 1946; Thompson, 1946). In addition, some of his hypotheses and conclusions were not supported by other investigations (Cohen, 1952; Garfield, 1949; Monroe, 1952; Wittenborn, 1949). Although these factors seriously limited the general applicability of the test patterns reported by Rapaport, many of his more qualitative appraisals of test performance revealed keen insights into intellectual functioning and disturbance.

The diagnostic interpretations of the Wechsler Scales mentioned above were by no means the only ones advanced by clinical psychologists. Other workers also reported diagnostic patterns for a variety of behavior disorders (Garfield, 1949; Rabin, 1945; Rabin and Guertin, 1951). There is little need to review all the data that have been reported, because comprehensive reviews of this work are available (Frank, 1970; Guertin, Frank, & Rabin, 1956; Guertin et al., 1962, 1966, 1971; Matarazzo, 1972; Rabin & Guertin, 1951). One striking finding by Wechsler (1944) and Rabin (1941) that schizophrenic patients obtain higher scores on the Verbal Scale than on the Performance Scale was not confirmed by others (Garfield, 1948; Olch, 1948). Similar contradictory findings for other indices also have been reported. In addition, Garfield (1948, 1949) early emphasized the variability of test patterns secured in the studies of one diagnostic group—schizophrenia. Other investigators also called attention to the conflicting results and patterns reported for various clinical populations (Carter and Bowles, 1948; Guertin, Rabin, Frank, and Ladd, 1962; Harper, 1950; Hunt and Cofer, 1944; Rabin, 1945; Rabin and Guertin, 1951).

In spite of such conflicting findings, Wechsler (1958) and other clinical psychologists have continued such diagnostic uses and investigations with the WAIS (Matarazzo, 1972). The first comprehensive review published after the WAIS had been in use for some 6 years generally reflected a similar picture. "The additional work on 'scatter,' profiles, and patterns has not led us on more solid diagnostic ground. The results with the several nosological categories are inconclusive" (Guertin, Rabin, Frank, and Ladd, 1962, p. 21). More recent reviews, while indicating some improvement in the quality of research in this area, still do not show truly reliable or valid patterns of ratios for specific diagnostic groups (Guertin et al., 1966, 1971).

The beginning student of clinical psychology may be somewhat confused and disheartened by such conflicting and negative findings in the use of a well-known clinical technique. Such discrepancies, by no means unique in the field of psychology and not limited alone to Wechsler scatter patterns, may be explained to some degree at least by two major assumptions underlying such diagnostic research. The first assumption is that various groups of subjects tested at different centers and bearing the same diagnostic name are directly comparable; or, to state it another way, that the test patterns derived from a modest sample of a given nosological group are applicable to a different sample. This assumption is implicit in most studies that report a "schizophrenic" or "neurotic" pattern based on a sample at one institution and implying that such patterns have general applicability. Upon analyzing the problem carefully, however, it is evident that several factors make such an assumption untenable. Foremost among these factors is the problem of the reliability and comparability of psychiatric diagnoses. This issue has already been discussed in a previous chapter. There is evidence available that indicates that diagnostic criteria and procedures vary, not only from institution to institution, but between psychiatrists in the same institution (Edelman, 1947; Malamud, 1946; Pasamanick, Dinitz, and Lefton, 1959). Thus the criterion used for pattern analysis is itself unstable. Besides this, there is the related problem of the marked variability of behavior within any given nosological group. The duration of illness, severity of disturbance, momentary motivations, and degree of rapport are all considerations that hamper comparability of patient populations and which have received inadequate attention in diagnostic research. In addition, there are basic sampling and research considerations that have been neglected in many diagnostic studies. These include such simple considerations as the age, sex, education, and mental level of the subjects studied. The importance of such variables was emphasized in an early paper by the author (Garfield, 1949), and is related to the second major assumption to be discussed next.

The second assumption underlying the study and use of diagnostic patterns from the Wechsler Scales is that certain intellectual functions are characteristically impaired in specific nosological groups. This assumption implies that performance on verbal or manipulative tasks is influenced in specific or uniform ways by the personality disturbance of the individual. It is also apparent, if one follows this line of reasoning, that much more emphasis is placed on the patient's nosological status as a factor influencing his test performance than on other factors. Because we are aware of the influence of age, education, socioeconomic status, and other factors on mental-test performance, it would appear that such variables have been neglected in much of the work on diagnostic testing. Some attention has been given to the influence of age on Wechsler patterns (Birren and Morrison, 1961; Doppelt and Wallace, 1955; Hulicka, 1962; Olch, 1948; Weider, 1943; Whiteman and Jastak, 1957), and such studies have shown some differences in the psychometric patterns obtained for different age groups. The author has also reported a study of Wechsler patterns in 109 schizophrenic patients in which separate analyses were made in terms of such variables as age, IQ, and education (Garfield, 1949). The findings indicated a definite relationship between performance on certain subtests and such factors as level of IQ and education. Thus, although all of the subjects in this study were diagnosed as schizophrenics by the hospital staff, those with some college education obtained their highest subtest scores on the Arithmetic subtest, whereas the opposite was true for patients whose educational progress terminated with the eighth grade. On the basis of such results, it is plausible to conclude that other variables besides the psychiatric classification influence the mental-test patterns of individual patients.

In summary, then, one is inclined to agree with the following conclusion by Frank (1970) concerning the use of diagnostic scatter patterns with the Wechsler Scales:

> The overview of the now more than twenty-five years of research, therefore, presents us with studies that are inconsistent, contradictory, and hence, inconclusive. What does seem clear, however, is that the specific predictions regarding the performance of subjects in the major diagnostic categories, viz., schizophrenia, neurosis, or the brain-disordered, as postulated by Wechsler and Rapaport, have not received support. Indeed, the research *does* reveal that there is *no* characteristic pattern of performance on the subtests for, for example, the schizophrenic *or* the neurotic (p. 177).

Although existing data on Wechsler subtest patterns do not give much support to such a diagnostic approach, even for purposes of psychiatric classification, this does not mean that the scale has no diagnostic values. The material reviewed emphasizes primarily the limitations of a purely psychometric pattern approach to diagnosis. In this connection, it may be well to remember that the scale was basically constructed to discriminate among individuals in terms of intellectual ability and not in terms of personality. The general values ascribed to standardized mental tests in the first part of this chapter, however, apply as well to the Wechsler Scales as to the Stanford-Binet. Furthermore, because there are eleven separate subtests, certain evaluations and comparisons of mental functioning and disturbance can be carried out easily. An unusually poor performance on a given subtest is quickly noted, and an analysis of separate responses as well as other data can be made in order to understand the significance of the particular deviation. The "scatter" of subtest scores thus will be of some use in our diagnostic work, but in a broader way than referred to previously. In a sense, it is a symptom that calls for scrutiny and analysis on the part of the clinician. For example, some low scores on verbal subtests in one case may be a reflection of limited educational opportunity. In other cases, similar patterns may be due to an inability to attend to verbal stimuli, to emotional blocking, or to patterns of withdrawal. In addition, such variations are important in evaluating the total IQ obtained with patients. Where marked variation exists between subtests, a low score may be indicative of some impairment in mental functioning rather than limited mental endowment.

In using the Wechsler Scales in clinical work, however, the psychologist relies on more than subtest scores. Unusual responses, qualitative analysis of responses, the types of items failed, particular methods of responding, and the general observation of the subject's behavior will all be utilized in an intergrated manner in diagnostic evaluations. Here again, the clinician's professional astuteness, his knowledge of psychopathology and personality theory, and his experience with the test will influence the diagnostic values secured from use of the test. More detailed illustrations of these points may be left to specific courses and practicum instruction in diagnostic testing, and clinical assessment. However, it can be stated here that simply diagnosing a patient as a schizophrenic or neurotic does not really tell you very much about the patient.

THE WECHSLER INTELLIGENCE SCALES FOR CHILDREN

In addition to the adult intelligence scales, Wechsler also constructed a similar type of scale for use with children, appropriately designated the Wechsler Intelligence Scale for Children or WISC. This scale, like the others, consists of a verbal and performance scale and the items are essentially similar to those found in the adult scales. "In fact, most of the items in the WISC are from Form II of the earlier (adult) scales, the main additions being new items at the easier end of each test to permit examination of children as young as five years of age" (Wechsler, 1949, p. 1). Because of the many similarities between the adult and children's scales, no extensive description of the latter will be provided.

The WISC was revised in 1974 and our brief description here will deal mainly with the revised form, the WISC-R. Like its predecessor, the WISC-R consists of twelve subtests, six of which are classified as verbal and six as performance. However, only ten tests are usually given. With the exception of one subtest, the subtests resemble those that are included in the adult scales. The WISC-R is also a point scale and scores are interpreted in terms of norms for specific age groups. The inclusion of nonverbal or performance types of items makes it, perhaps, of greater utility than purely verbal tests in appraising some types of subjects, although the WISC-R cannot be considered a "culture-free" test.

The test was standardized on 2200 American children selected so as to be representative of the U.S. national census in 1970 (Wechsler, 1974). The standardization sample included 100 boys and 100 girls at each age level ranging from 6½ through 16½ years of age. White and non-white children were included in the standardization sample in the same proportion as that for the 1970 census. In terms of individual intelligence tests, the sample may be the most representative of the U.S. population (Anastasi, 1976).

The data presented in the test manual indicate very satisfactory test-retest reliability with most correlations in the .90's. Verbal and Full Scale IQ's tend to show greater stability than the Performance IQ which showed an average increase of 8 to 10 points when children were retested 3 to 5 weeks later. No validity data are provided in the manual. However, the correlation of WISC-R IQ's and Stanford-Binet IQ's (1972 norms) for small samples of children at four different ages is given. The average correlation is .73 and the mean IQ's are quite comparable.

The revised WISC contains a number of new or substantially modified items as well as items from the original scale. The order in which the tests are administered was also changed. Verbal and Performance tests are now given in alternating order. The age range was changed from 5 to 15 years to 6 to 16, so as to reduce the age overlap between the WISC-R and the Wechsler Preschool and Primary Scale of Intelligence (WPPSI), which was developed for children from 4 to 6½ years of age. The IQ range of the revised scale extends from 40 to 160 with a standard deviation of 15.

The original WISC was well received by psychologists and a considerable number of research studies were published (Buros, 1965, 1972; Littell, 1960;

Zimmerman, & Woo-Sam, 1972). A number of these investigations were comparisons of the WISC and the Stanford-Binet. The latter has a greater range and ceiling in terms of IQ, and brighter individuals tend to do better on it. Such differences may be reduced with reference to the WISC-R.

As indicated, the Wechsler Scales have become very popular clinical tests. The WAIS is the most widely used individual test of mental ability for adults and it has no rival. The WISC has also appeared to exceed the Stanford-Binet in usage in clinical settings (Garfield & Kurtz, 1973; Lubin *et al.*, 1971; Brown & McGuire, 1976). In discussing the Wechsler Scales, Anastasi (1976) offered the following appraisal:

> In comparison with other individually administered tests, their principal strengths stem from the size and representativeness of the standardization samples, particularly for adult and preschool populations, and the technical quality of their test construction procedures. The treatment of reliability and errors of measurement is especially commendable. The weakest feature of all three scales is the dearth of empirical data on validity (p. 264).

CONCLUDING COMMENT

In the preceding pages we have discussed some general characteristics of standardized psychological tests, possible clinical uses of individual tests of intelligence, and have also described the most widely used intelligence tests in clinical practice. There are other tests of mental ability, but the ones described here are the ones that are clearly preferred by clinical psychologists.

Early in the development of clinical psychology, a number of nonverbal tests were devised for use with special groups of subjects for whom a highly verbal test was inappropriate, e.g., the deaf, non-English speaking groups, illiterates, and the educationally deficient. It would appear, however, that most of these tests are rarely used today, or if they are, they are used in very specialized settings. It seems very likely that the appearance of the Wechsler Scales, which consist of a performance as well as a verbal scale, may be greatly responsible for this diminished use of the older performance scales. Consequently, nothing further will be said about such tests here.

TESTS OF SPECIAL MENTAL FUNCTIONS AND IMPAIRMENT

The tests described in the preceding pages were designed to appraise general intellectual ability. However, as we have noted, intelligence tests also provide the clinical psychologist with opportunities for observation and appraisal of other aspects of the individual's overall functioning or performance. Nevertheless, there are a number of clinical problems where special assessment devices have been developed for a more thorough or precise appraisal. Particular attention in the past was devoted to diagnostic problems pertaining to organic brain damage and to the appraisal of cognitive impairment in such disorders as schizophrenia. Tests were developed to appraise mental efficiency or deterioration, memory functions, specific language impairment, and abstract or concrete thinking. Some of these tests were devised specifically to appraise clinical problems, whereas others were originally used for research investigations and then later applied in the clinic or hospital. Some of the previously popular tests appear to be little used today, and a few new or additional tests have made their appearance. In some instances, new specialities have been emerging which require expertise in some particular procedures. We shall now explore briefly some of the developments and techniques of this type.

TESTS FOR APPRAISING MENTAL IMPAIRMENT

Reflecting the interest of psychologists in evaluating mental functioning and the impairment of such functioning, a number of specific tests were developed in past years. One of the major hypotheses that guided the development of some of the tests in this area was based on the differential rate of decline of different mental functions with age. For example, some researchers reported that verbal skills, such as vocabulary, remained relatively stable and were little affected by increasing age (Fox, 1947; Shakow, Doekart, & Goldman, 1941; Weisenburg, Roe, & McBride, 1936). Conversely, speed of response and selected areas of nonverbal reasoning were observed to decline with age. Thus, while vocabulary may remain relatively stable over the lifespan, other functions may show a decrement with age (Wechsler, 1958). In a somewhat similar vein, it was assumed that functions such as vocabulary were not as much affected by psychosis or brain damage as were tests that involved speed of response, abstract reasoning, or concept formation. From this point of view, the vocabulary score (or the score on a test of any stable ability) could be viewed as an indication of the optimal level of functioning of the patient, whereas the scores on the other types of tests could be viewed as measures of the level of present functioning. Theoretically, normal individuals should show only small differences in level of functioning between various types of tests, whereas the seriously disturbed mental patient or client with an organic brain syndrome should be expected to perform much better on a test of vocabulary than on tests of recent memory or abstract reasoning. In general, the greater the difference in favor of the vocabulary, the greater the extent of impairment.

Several of the early tests of mental impairment were based on this theoretical premise. On one such scale the scores on a number of timed tests were compared with a vocabulary score derived from the Stanford-Binet. The resulting "Efficiency Index" indicated the efficiency of functioning or degree of impairment (Babcock & Levy, 1940). A much simpler test was the Shipley Scale which consisted of two 10-minute tests, a vocabulary test and an abstraction test (Shipley, & Burlingame, 1941). The abstraction score is compared with the vocabulary score to secure a Conceptual Quotient (CQ). CQ's below a certain value were considered to be suggestive of mental impairment. Although the Shipley was easy to administer and score, it also had some limitations (Yates, 1954, 1972). No age norms were provided and thus no provisions were made for the normal decline of mental functioning with increasing age. Older subjects, therefore, were more likely to be diagnosed as mentally impaired (Garfield & Fey, 1948).

Another measure of mental impairment that was rather popular with clinicians was based on several subtests of the Wechsler Adult Intelligence Scales. Wechsler devised a particular index of deterioration based on the ratio obtained from selected subtests. The general assumption regarding differential rate of decline of mental abilities already identified with other tests of this type was also utilized for the Deterioration Index. According to Wechsler's first formulation based on the Wechsler-Bellevue Scale, four subtests—Information (or Vocabulary), Comprehension, Picture Completion, and Object Assembly—appeared to be little affected by normal decline with age. Conversely, abilities measured by four other subtests—Arithmetic, Digit Span, Block Design, and the Digit Symbol—declined more rapidly with age than other subtests. For the WAIS, Wechsler (1958) substituted the Vocabulary subtest for the Comprehension subtest in the "Hold" tests, and the Similarities for Arithmetic in the "Don't Hold" group. A ratio derived from the two groups of subtests provided the Deterioration Index or estimate of mental decline. This index, in turn, was compared with the norms for the average or normal decline with age. Significant deviations from the normal pattern for a specific age group were then considered indicative of deterioration.

Because the Wechsler Scales have been so widely used by clinical psychologists in their assessment and diagnostic work, and because the Deterioration Index is easily calculated, this particular measure of deterioration was at one time rather widely used. In Wechsler's earlier publications (1944; Levi, Oppenheim, & Wechsler, 1945), however, no data were provided on the reliability or validity of the measure. Since that time several studies have been reported and, in general, considerable doubt has been cast on the validity and diagnostic usefulness of the measure (Garfield, 1957; Matarazzo, 1972). Although Wechsler acknowledged that other studies have tended not to support his claims for the utility of the Deterioration Index, he still maintained that it was useful when employed clinically along with other data. "In spite of the lack of supporting data from other studies the writer can report that in his own experience the 'Hold'-'Don't Hold' index is very useful in clinical diagnosis" (Wechsler, 1958, p. 213). The evidence, however, would appear to be otherwise, for among the possible explanations for such negative findings are the limited reliabilities of the subtests and the use of poorly defined clinical subjects in the research investigations. Whatever the reasons, one must seriously question the uncritical use of such tests in the clinical evaluation of the patient.

TESTS OF ABSTRACT AND CONCEPTUAL THINKING

As indicated previously, a variety of different tests, developed over the years, has reflected the special interests of their authors in particular aspects of psychopathology and mental functioning. A number of these were basically clinical instruments and were never really standardized; yet, they were used in clinical settings, particularly in appraising mental functioning in patients with apparent or suspected brain damage, or in that highly variegated group of patients classified under the rubric of schizophrenia. Patients in these categories not only constitute a large proportion of those hospitalized in mental hospitals, but also reveal a wide variety of impaired and deviant patterns of thought. As a means of better understanding such patients, many individuals have studied specific aspects of their mental functioning. One of the characteristics noted in patients diagnosed as schizophrenic, for example, was a disturbance in their ability to think along abstract or conceptual lines. The patients' thinking appeared to take on a more concrete and less-organized character. In order to study these patterns of thought more precisely, specific tests were developed by various workers. A similar approach was evident also in the study of patients with organic brain dysfunction. These patients, too, showed some characteristic impairments in their intellectual functioning. Although their performance was qualitatively different from that of the schizophrenic patients, defects in abstract thinking were also apparent. Again, investigations with special tests were designed and carried out.

Although once widely regarded by a number of clinicians, tests of this type have declined noticeably in popularity. For example, the Vigotsky or Hanfmann-Kasanin Test (Hanfmann & Kasanin, 1942), devised for studying the conceptual thinking of schizophrenic patients and once regarded as an important evaluative procedure, is rarely used today, if at all. The Goldstein-

Scheerer tests of abstract and concrete thinking, however, are apparently still used by some clinicians (Anastasi, 1976).

As a consequence of their study of mental functioning and impairment in cases with organic brain pathology, Goldstein and his collaborators developed a series of special tests for use with such cases (Goldstein & Scheerer, 1941). The primary guiding concept of Goldstein and his co-workers was that an impairment of the capacity for abstract thinking presumably occurs in organic patients. Although the normal individual is able to function on both a concrete and an abstract level, shifting his approach to meet the demands of the situation, some disorganization in this process occurs in cases with brain pathology.

A series of five tests were used by Goldstein and Scheerer. Probably best known is the Object Sorting Test introduced first by Gelb and used later by Weigl (1941), Goldstein, and Scheerer. Rapaport, Gill, and Schafer (1945) also included it in their testing battery. This test consists of thirty-three objects of varying utility, form, color, and material. After a sample try, the examiner selects an object and asks the patient to group all the other objects that belong with it. The objects can be grouped according to use (for example, tools), color, form, material, and so on. When the grouping is completed, the patient is asked why he grouped the objects in that particular way. As another part of the test, various groups of objects are presented to the subject and he is asked to explain the groupings. The examiner may also ask the subject if other groupings are possible in order to see if he can shift his approach.

Although the emphasis in evaluating the patient's performance is in terms of what approach is favored and whether the patient can shift his approach from a concrete to an abstract one, many qualitative gradations can be observed. A patient may function on such a concrete level that he will either refuse to group other articles with the initial one, or will select only one or two articles. For example, a patient will group matches with a cigar but not include other smoking materials. On the other hand, the same objects can be grouped in terms of a conceptual view (class of objects, for example, tools), or from a functional concrete view (things for carpentry). Thus, it is not merely the groupings that count, but the thinking or approach used to make the grouping. The following brief report by a psychologist of a patient's performance on the Object Sorting Test may help the reader to grasp more fully what is involved in the test performance:

> The patient utilized principles of classification based largely on personalized and functional uses. The following are examples: 'I have used all of these things in the hospital, and these I have not.' 'These I have in my tool chest at home, these I do not.' 'A child plays with these, and not with these.' 'These I would use in relation to my mouth, these

in relation to my hand.' 'These are things a man who smokes would use, these he would not.'

The patient could not shift independently from such principles of sorting to those of a higher or more abstract nature. Instead, such sorting was maintained throughout the entire test. When instructed to sort them according to color (or material, etc.), however, he was able to grasp and utilize these abstract categories of classification quite well. Following the instructed sorting of this type, the patient was asked once again to sort the objects according to principles he had not used previously. Rather than proceeding to use some other abstract or higher conceptual principle for sorting, he reverted to the more personalistic and lower-level functional characteristics which the objects held for him. When sorted material was presented to him later with the request that he give the basis of classification, the patient again succeeded in rapidly grasping the principles involved, for example, color, size, and so on. Thus, while the patient voluntarily performs on a concrete level, he is able to grasp and react to abstract principles of classification. The total test performance does not suggest a disorder of an organic nature.

Four other tests are also used in addition to the Sorting test. One is similar to the block design subtest of the WAIS, but uses additional trials and materials. The three remaining tests are a color sorting test, a color form sorting test, and a stick test. The first comprises woolen skeins of different colors and shades in order to see if the subject can sort according to definite color concepts. At least twelve different shades of each color are present. The color form test consists of four equilateral triangles, four circles, and four squares. In each set of four there is a red, green, yellow, and blue figure. The purpose of the test is to see whether the patient can first sort the objects according to either form or color and then shift to the other principle of classification. The final test is made up of a group of two different sized sticks. First the patient copies patterns made by the examiner, and later the patient reproduces patterns after the figure has been exposed for a given time.

These tests have been used most extensively in research investigations of patients with brain damage, but they have also been applied with other types of cases. Goldstein (1943) has used some of the tests in studying schizophrenic patients, while others have utilized the sorting test in work with diverse patient groups (Rapaport, Gill, and Schafer, 1945). The essentially qualitative use of the tests has limited an adequate objective evaluation of their validity.

MEMORY TESTS

Tests of memory functions, retention, and recall have long been used in the clinical investigation of hospitalized patients, because memory defects are one of the frequently noted symptoms in a variety of psychiatric disorders.

Retrograde amnesia, a failure to recall recent experiences adequately, is a common finding in senile psychoses, cerebral arteriosclerosis, Korsakoff's syndrome, and general paralysis. Although cases with functional psychoses may also show some impairment of memory functions, as a general rule, the deficit is not as marked as in the organic psychoses. But, as we have pointed out in our discussion of mental impairment, there is another aspect to this problem which in the past has not received adequate recognition. This is the influence of aging on memory functions. Since senile psychoses occur in an older age group than does a psychosis such as schizophrenia, the poor performance in the former may be due in part to advanced age. Some research by Shakow and others (Shakow, Doekart, and Goldman, 1941) supports this view. Not only did they note marked memory deficit after age 60, but when the psychotic groups were compared with normals of comparable age, the deficit in the former did not appear as marked as formerly. Aging, therefore, appeared to affect memory functions significantly. Gilbert's classic study (Gilbert, 1941) also supported these findings, as have other studies (Harwood and Naylor, 1969; Schonfield, 1965; Talland, 1968).

THE WECHSLER MEMORY SCALE

Although some test or examination of memory functions has usually been included in the mental status evaluation of patients, such tests usually have been informal and unstandardized. The Wechsler Memory Scale (Wechsler, 1945) represented an attempt to remedy such deficiencies. The scale consists of seven subtests. The first test is made up of six simple questions of Personal and Current Information (for example, subject's age, name of the President, and so forth). The second test consists of five questions to evaluate the subject's orientation for time and place. Mental Control, the third test, includes counting backward from twenty to three and counting by threes. The fourth test, Logical Memory, consists of two memory passages. The fifth test, Memory Span, is the well-known recall of digits forward and backward. Visual Reproduction and Associate Learning are the remaining tests. The former requires the reproduction of geometric figures and the latter the learning of paired associates. "Provisional Norms" were based on 200 normal subjects, ages 25 to 50. Each raw score is corrected for age and then can be translated into the corresponding Memory Quotient (MQ).

Although a standardized memory scale has definite utility in examining cases of suspected brain damage or in evaluating the effects of electric shock therapy, the Wechsler Memory Scale has certain deficiencies. No adequate or validated interpretive scheme is offered the clinician for evaluating the significance of memory deficit. Apparently, if the MQ is noticeably lower than the IQ in a given patient, this is evidence of deficiency in memory. But no adequate data are offered on this point, or is there information concerning normal variation of MQ's. In addition, the test manual provides no data on the reliability of the scale as a whole or of any of the subtests.

An alternate form of this scale has also been published which enables one to evaluate changes in the patient over time (Stone, Girdner, & Albrecht, 1946). Data on eighty-seven cases were reported in comparing the two forms of the scale. Only slight differences in means were noted, although further research with average or below average subjects is recommended since the ceilings of the scales were somewhat low for the above average subjects used in the comparison.

BENTON VISUAL RETENTION TEST

The Benton Visual Retention Test differs considerably from the Wechsler Memory Scale. The test was designed to assess memory, perception, and visuomotor functions, and has been revised several times (Benton, 1963, 1974).

The test currently consists of three forms of ten cards each, with each card containing one or more simple geometric designs. In the standard procedure the designs are exposed for 10 seconds and then the individual is required to reproduce them from memory. A good performance, therefore, depends on visual perception, immediate recall, and also on visuomotor reproduction of the designs. The score on the test is based on the number of designs reproduced correctly and the total number of errors. The designs can also be administered in different ways.

The main utility of the test is considered to be in helping to diagnose cases of brain damage. Although some normative material is given in the manual and some distribution of scores for both brain injured and control subjects is also provided, it is somewhat difficult to appraise adequately the clinical utility of this test from the information provided. For example, the author mentions that the test correlates .7 with measures of intelligence. This is a rather high degree of correlation between a general measure of mental ability and a more specific diagnostic instrument. Another point to keep in mind is the kind of control groups that are used in making comparisons with specific diagnostic categories. Differences tend to be more easily obtained when a clinical group is compared with a normal control group than if they are compared with some other clinical group.

At present this test is used to some extent as an aid in problems of suspected brain damage. Its advantages are its ease of administration and the short period of time required to complete the test. On the negative side, most of the comparisons of brain-damaged and control patients show some degree of overlap with only 36% of the brain-damaged patients being identified if one sets cutting scores to exclude false positives. The previous research reported on the test leads one to be somewhat cautious in its use. Although groups of organic brain-damaged patients can be differentiated from controls at statistically significant levels (Brilliant & Gynther, 1963; L'Abate, Vogler, Friedman, & Chused, 1963; Wohler, 1956), in one study the test did not do as well as the base rates in the hospital (Brilliant & Gynther, 1963).[4] In another study, length of hospitalization appeared to be the most significant variable in accounting for the distribution of scores on the test (L'Abate, Boelling, Hutton, & Mathew, 1962).

Finally, it can be noted that Benton in his 1974 manual, provides a review of recent research studies, a commendable practice which is not always followed by those who publish psychological tests. This is decidedly useful to the individual who is contemplating the use of the test.

MEMORY-FOR-DESIGNS TEST

A test that has certain similarities to that of the Benton is the Memory-For-Designs Test devised by Graham and Kendall (1960). This test consists of fifteen designs which the subject is to reproduce after an exposure time of 5 seconds. As compared with the Benton, the designs are less complex, and the manual provides more comprehensive information on standardization and related matters. The main purpose of the test is also as an aid in diagnosing cerebral brain disorder.

[4] The matter of base rates warrants a special note. If a test or other procedure is to merit use, it must demonstrate its ability to exceed the base rate in a given population for diagnosing the specific pathology or type of case in which the clinician is interested. For example, if one has a test for diagnosing schizophrenia which correctly identifies 65% of such patients, the value of the test depends among other things on the base rate in that institution. If 67% of all patients admitted are actually diagnosed as schizophrenic, then the test does not do as good a job of selection as would the use of the base rate. That is, if one simply diagnosed all patients admitted as schizophrenic he would be correct 67% of the time, whereas, by using the test he would be correct only 65% of the time. In cases of rare occurrence, such as suicide, which occur perhaps four times per thousand in hospitalized patients, it is exceedingly difficult to improve on the base rates. For a more extended discussion of this problem and its complexities, the reader is referred to the paper by Meehl and Rosen (1955).

In their manual, Graham and Kendall present data on two cross-validational studies of brain-damaged and control subjects. Utilizing a cutoff score that produces 4% false positives in the control group, approximately 40–50% of the brain-damaged patients are correctly identified. Somewhat comparable findings have also been reported by other investigators (Garrett, Price, & Deabler, 1957; Howard & Shoemaker, 1954; Korman & Blumberg, 1963), with the percentages varying somewhat depending on the age range and psychopathology of the groups compared. Intelligence, as measured by standard tests in the case of children and vocabularly scores for adults, showed a low but significant correlation with scores on the Memory-For-Designs Test ($-.39$ to $-.31$). Corrections are provided in the manual for age and intelligence level, but corrected and uncorrected scores are highly correlated (.90 to .92). Nevertheless, it should be remembered that age, particularly after 60, is an important variable in terms of level of mental functioning, and most tests, including this one and the Benton provide very little data for such subjects.

The Memory-For-Designs Test at present appears to be a relatively popular test of its type (Lubin, Wallis, & Paine, 1971). It probably works best in cases of severe brain damage, but the test may have some utility if used judiciously along with other assessment data. If the base rates in a given setting are very low for cases of brain damage, however, the practical utility may be limited.

There are relatively few other standard tests of memory (Buros, 1972; Klebanoff, Singer, & Wilensky, 1954). Many of the intelligence scales include some tests of memory and the psychologist may use these as a rough measure of such functioning of the patient. If the patient performs poorly on memory items in comparison with other types of items, the discrepancy should be noted in the clinical appraisal of the patient, and more extensive testing can be performed later.

Although memory functions are noticeably impaired in some clinical conditions, there is evidence that memory tests are also highly correlated with tests of intelligence (Benton, 1963; Brilliant and Gynther, 1963; Eysenck and Halstead, 1945). Wechsler (1958) also makes the point that all mental functions decline with age, not just memory. The question may be raised, therefore, as to whether or not there is a unitary memory factor. Other factors may also be involved in poor performance on tests of memory functions (Matarazzo, 1972). It has been suggested, for example, that "many disturbances of immediate memory may actually reflect difficulties in attention to presented material" (Klebanoff, Singer, and Wilensky, 1954, p. 11). In a similar vein, Benton (1963) has also cautioned the users of his test about similar factors that interfere with test performance and which conceivably may lead to erroneous interpretations when they are overlooked. Acutely disturbed, distractable, or apathetic patients are particularly vulnerable in this regard.

THE BENDER-GESTALT TEST

Another interesting and widely used test is the Bender-Gestalt (Bender, 1938). In fact, it has been one of the most popular tests (Garfield & Kurtz, 1973; Lubin, Wallis, & Paine, 1971; Sundberg, 1961; Wade & Baker, 1977), and has been used in a variety of ways for a variety of purposes. It is a simple test to administer for it consists merely of nine designs which the patient is asked to reproduce on a blank sheet of paper. The patient can reproduce the designs in any size or sequence that he or she wants and on any part of the paper. Particular attention is paid to the accuracy of reproduction, the spacing and ordering of designs, rotations, distortions, and similar phenomena.

This visuomotor test has been used as an aid in appraising possible brain damage, as a test for evaluating learning disabilities, and also as a projective technique for evaluating some aspects of personality (Koppitz, 1964, 1970; Tolor & Schulberg, 1963; Tolor & Brannigan, 1981). Because of the ease of administration and the brief amount of time required for taking the test, it has been used frequently by clinical psychologists as part of a testing battery. Interpreters of test results have utilized both clinical intuition and quantitative psychometric data, but empirical support for the validity of either approach has been mixed (Tolor & Schulberg, 1963; Koppitz, 1964).

As indicated, the Bender-Gestalt test has been used for diverse purposes with a variety of populations. It has been used clinically with both children and adults and, apart from evaluating brain damage and possible emotional disorders, it has been used in studies of learning problems in school, mental retardation, differential diagnosis, and as a screening test for research purposes. However, its usefulness and validity for these purposes has not been uniformly demonstrated.

At the present time there is a diverse and extensive literature dealing with this test in several hundred publications. An early review of the literature was published by Tolor and Schulberg (1963); a more recent one has been published by Tolor and Brannigan (1981). The reader who is interested in a more detailed evaluation of the test is referred to these volumes as well as one by Koppitz (1975) which is primarily concerned with the use of the test with children. No attempt will be made here to offer a definitive evaluation of the test. It is well to emphasize, however, that a test may have some utility for one purpose and limited utility for another. This would appear to be particularly true for the Bender-Gestalt since it has been applied to so many different populations and problems.

Although most clinicians probably use the test in a subjective manner in evaluating the drawings of the subject, there are several scoring systems that have been developed. One early and widely used system was developed by Pascal and Suttell (1951) for adults; another system was developed by Koppitz (1964) for children. Each of these systems has a list of particular kinds of responses, generally oriented toward the negative or pathological side, which are scored by the examiner. Reports of both systems indicate that there can be a high degree of inter-scorer reliability.

Although the test has been used rather extensively as an aid in diagnosing possible organic brain damage, applications in this area appear to have some limitations. In focusing solely on a global view of organic brain damage, we tend to lose sight of the fact that such factors as the site of the lesion, the extent of damage, the hemisphere involved, and the age at which traumatic brain injury takes place may all influence the clinical picture of the patient and his level of performance. Although the Bender-Gestalt Test appears to have value as a diagnostic screening device (Heaton, Baade, & Johnson, 1978; Lacks, 1979; Tolor & Brannigan, 1981), more definitive research concerning specific perceptual-motor disturbances in particular types of brain dysfunction would improve the value of the test and our understanding of impaired brain functioning. For example, in one study, which compared brain function in problem children and controls, different patterns on the test were noted between hyperactive and nonhyperactive children (Wikler, Dixon, & Parker, 1970). However, with the possible exception of chronic schizophrenics, the Bender-Gestalt does tend to differentiate organic cases from other clinical groups with what appears to be an acceptable degree of accuracy. In this regard it matches at least the results of other such tests in this area (Heaton et al., 1978; Tolor & Brannigan, 1981).

A few concluding comments can be offered on the Bender-Gestalt Test. The test appears to have utility when used appropriately with clinical problems involving visuomotor difficulties. It is easily administered, requires relatively little time to administer, and can be used along with other appropriate diagnostic techniques in appraising a particular problem. The test, however, should not be relied upon as the sole means for individual diagnosis, or should a particular score or a particular diagnostic sign on the test be interpreted as indicating a particular diagnosis such as brain damage. As Koppitz (1964) pointed out, "All diagnoses of brain injury made with the Bender-Gestalt Test should always be regarded as hypotheses which should then be validated against supporting evidence from developmental, medical, and other psychological data" (p. 106). Some clinicians are prone to offer diagnoses on the basis of limited or even conflicting findings, and such practices are really misuses of diagnostic procedures. Thus, a technique, which may have some utility for particular problems when used appropriately and critically, may be misused when it is applied in a gross fashion to complex problems. This point is also clearly made in a recent paper by Koppitz (1970) in discussing the use of the Bender-Gestalt with cases of reading disability. The test is a useful diagnostic tool in such cases only if the problem derives in part from visuomotor difficulties. If, however, the reading problem is caused by language disability or memory deficits, then the situation is different. In the last analysis, a test can be used most constructively for specific problems, and its usefulness will depend in large measure on the skill of the person using it.

A new primary visuomotor test has also been published (Haworth, 1970). This test, consisting of sixteen designs, resembles the Bender-Gestalt Test, but was designed for use with children 4 through 8 years of age. The current form of the test was standardized on a sample of 500 white children, ages 4 to 8. The manual also contains data on a sample of mentally retarded subjects with comparisons offered between the normal and retarded groups. Additional research with the test with children under age 13 indicates it may be useful as a screening device for psychotic patterns of functioning (Haworth, 1981).

THE HALSTEAD AND REITAN BATTERY

One of the more comprehensive attempts to devise tests for the identification of brain lesions is provided in the work of Halstead (1947) and Reitan (1966a, 1967). Halstead devoted considerable experimental work and naturalistic observation to the study of human subjects with cerebral lesions and in this process utilized a wide variety of test materials and procedures. Building upon his work, Reitan, his one-time student, has added over the years other techniques in his own research, and in essence has consolidated an extensive battery of tests for the evaluation of brain damage in humans. Although the Reitan Battery is more complex than the tests commonly used by psychologists in clinical settings, a certain number of centers have secured the necessary apparatus and test materials and have utilized the battery for clinical and research purposes. Some of the main procedures used will be described briefly.

The neuropsychological test battery used by Reitan includes Halstead's tests, a modification of the Halstead-Wepman Aphasia Screening Test (1949), the Wechsler-Bellevue Scale, the Trail Making Test, and a series of sensory-perceptual examinations involving tactile, auditory, and visual functions (Reitan, 1966c). As is evident, the battery is a comprehensive one that requires a full day for administration, and thus is not likely to be used in a routine fashion by most clinicians. Unlike the tests previously described, which are used largely for differential diagnosis, the Halstead Reitan Battery has been used in research investigations of brain–behavior relationships (Parsons & Prigatano, 1978; Reitan & Davison, 1974).

According to Reitan (1966b), one of the most useful and valid tests is the Halstead Category Test. This test uses an apparatus for the successive projection of 208 stimulus-figures on a screen viewed by the patient. In response to each of the stimulus-figures the patient selects an answer by depressing one of four levers. If a wrong lever is depressed, a harsh buzzer sounds; if the correct answer is chosen, a pleasant bell sounds. The patient is told that in each group of items a single principle underlies the correct response for each of the items. The subject obviously can only guess at the right answer in responding to the first item in a group, but as he continues, the type of sound accompanying each of the responses he makes allows him to test possible principles until the correct solution is secured. The test thus requires the ability to reason, abstract, and conceptualize.

The Halstead Finger Tapping Test and the Halstead Tactual Performance Test are also used by Reitan as part of his battery. Fine motor function, as reflected in the tapping test, is apparently often impaired by brain damage. Comparing the performance with each hand is also of some diagnostic importance, since a significant departure from the usual superiority of the preferred hand conceivably could indicate some impairment of the cerebral hemisphere contralateral to the slow hand. The Halstead Tactual Performance Test utilizes such traditional test materials as blocks and a form board, but requires the subject to be blindfolded. Consequently, he must depend upon tactile and kinesthetic cues for performing this task. In addition, the subject is required to do this three times, first with his preferred hand, then with the nonpreferred hand, and finally with both hands. It is believed that the latter procedure evaluates incidental learning, which may be one of the important deficits that result from brain lesions.

Although other tests are also used in the battery, we will only mention two others here. One is the Trail Making Test which was developed by the U.S. Army as a performance test during World War II and later used in testing patients with organic brain damage (Armitage, 1946). The test is a relatively simple one, consisting of two parts. In part A, the subject is to connect circles on a page as rapidly as possible in their numbered order from 1 to 25. In part B, both numbers and letters are given and the subject must alternate between them—1, A, 2, B, and so on. While Reitan has modified the original instructions, he also has used the time for completion as the raw score on the test. Finally, Reitan also uses the Wechsler-Bellevue Scale (Form I) as part of his battery. In general, an impairment index derived from the Halstead Battery appears consistently more effective than the Wechsler-Bellevue in identifying patients with brain lesions (Reitan, 1966b). This scale, however, was also used to study the differential effects of left and right cerebral lesions. While the Wechsler-Bellevue appeared to have some utility for such differentiation, its value was also found to be limited by a number of variables including chronicity of damage, age and education of patients, and the type of lesion (Reitan, 1966c).

Reitan and other investigators have conducted a large number of studies with the various tests in this battery (Filskov & Goldstein, 1974; Reitan, 1967; Reitan & Davison, 1974). This approach appears to have real utility for the study of problems associated with brain damage. On the other hand, the battery is a long one and the full day required for its administration would appear to limit its usefulness in most ordinary clinical situations. Furthermore, in two studies it was reported that this battery did not differentiate adequately between organic and schizophrenic patients (Lacks, Colbert, Harrow, & Levine, 1970; Watson, Thomas, Anderson, & Felling, 1968), although these studies were criticized because the issue of schizophrenia as a nonorganic disorder is still moot (Goldstein, 1969). Thus, one should maintain caution in evaluating the potential clinical utility of this or any other test. Nevertheless, the continued detailed study of the effects of the site of lesion, the type of lesion, and related problems, should eventually contribute to a fuller understanding of the psychological deficits resulting from such lesions as well as providing an improved means of diagnostic assessment.

THE LURIA-NEBRASKA BATTERY

Another test for appraising possible brain disorders which has appeared very recently is the Luria-Nebraska Neuropsychological Battery (Golden, Hammeke, & Purisch, 1978). Based on the clinical procedures of Luria and on the previous work of Christiansen (1975), Golden and his co-workers have published a number of reports on this battery to indicate its potential utility in appraising such disorders (Golden, Hammeke, & Purisch, 1978; Golden et al., 1981; Purisch, Golden, & Hammeke, 1978). Most of the published work on the test has come from Golden and his colleagues thus far, although some critical appraisals have been made by other investigators (Adams, 1980a; Spiers, 1981). The rather high diagnostic accuracy of 88% reported by the test authors has been questioned (Adams, 1980a,b), although some confirmation was published recently (Malloy & Webster, 1981). On the basis of Golden's work, the test does appear promising, but additional cross-validational studies from other centers would be desirable in more fully appraising the usefulness of this battery.

In this chapter we have reviewed some general features of psychological tests as well as a number of well-known and widely used tests of mental ability and special mental functions. We will withhold further discussion of the clinical uses and limitations of these tests until we have examined other widely used psychological tests, specifically, tests of personality. These are discussed in the next chapter.

REFERENCES

Adams, K. M. In search of Luria's Battery: A false start. *Journal of Consulting and Clinical Psychology,* 1980, *48,* 511–516. (a)

Adams, K. M. An end of innocence for behavioral neurology? Adams replies. *Journal of Consulting and Clinical Psychology,* 1980, *48,* 522–524. (b)

American Psychological Association. Technical recommendations for psychological tests and diagnostic techniques. *Psychological Bulletin,* Supplement, 1954, *51,* 201–238.

Anastasi, A. *Psychological Testing* (4th Ed.). New York: Macmillan, 1976.

Armitage, S. G. An analysis of certain psychological tests used for the evaluation of brain injury. *Psychological Monographs,* 1946, *60* (Whole No. 277).

Babcock, H., & Levy, L. *Manual of directions for the measurement of the efficiency of mental functioning.* (Rev. Exam.) Chicago: C. H. Stoelting Co., 1940.

Bayley, N. Behavioral correlates of mental growth: Birth to thirty-six years. *American Psychologist,* 1968, *23,* 1–17.

Bayley, N. Development of mental abilities. In P. Mussen (Ed.), *Carmichael's manual of child psychology* (Vol. 1). New York: Wiley, 1970.

Bender, L. *A visual motor Gestalt Test and its clinical use.* American Orthopsychiatric Association, Research Monographs, 1938, No. 3.

Benton, A. L. *The revised visual retention test* (3rd Ed.). New York: Psychological Corporation, 1963.

Benton, A. L. *Revised visual retention test: Manual.* New York: Psychological Corporation, 1974.

Birren, J. E., & Morrison, D. F. Analysis of WAIS subtests in relation to age and education. *Journal of Gerontology,* 1961, *16,* 363–368.

Brilliant, P. J., & Gynther, M. D. Relationships between performance on three tests for organicity and selected patient variables. *Journal of Consulting Psychology,* 1963, *27,* 474–479.

Brown, W. R., & McGuire, J. M. Current psychological assessment practices. *Professional Psychology,* 1976, *7,* 475–484.

Buros, O. K. (Ed.), *The sixth mental measurements year-book.* Highland Park, NJ: Gryphon Press, 1965.

Buros, O. K. (Ed.), *The seventh mental measurements year-book.* Highland Park, NJ: Gryphon Press, 1972.

Buros, O. K. (Ed.), *The eighth mental measurements year-book.* Highland Park, NJ: Gryphon Press, 1978.

Carter, J. W., Jr., & Bowles, J. W. A manual on qualitative aspects of psychological examining. *Journal of Clinical Psychology,* 1948, *4,* 109–150.

Christensen, A. L. *Luria's neuropsychological investigation.* New York: Spectrum, 1975.

Cohen, J. A factor-analytically based rationale for the Wechsler-Bellevue. *Journal of Consulting Psychology,* 1952, *16,* 272–277.

Cronbach, L. J. *Essentials of psychological testing* (3rd ed.). New York: Harper & Row, 1970.

Doppelt, J. E., & Wallace, W. L. Standardization of the WAIS for older persons. *Journal of Abnormal and Social Psychology,* 1955, *51,* 312–330.

Edelman, I. S. Problems in psychiatric classification. *Diseases of the Nervous System,* 1947, *7,* 171–174.

Eysenck, H. J., & Halstead, H. The memory function. I. A factorial study of 15 clinical tests. *American Journal of Psychiatry,* 1945, *102,* 174–180.

Eysenck, H. J. versus Kamin, L. *The intelligence controversy.* New York: Wiley, 1981.

Filskov, S. B., & Goldstein, S. G. Diagnostic validity of the Halstead-Reitan neuropsychological battery. *Journal of Consulting and Clinical Psychology,* 1974, *42,* 382–388.

Fox, C. Vocabulary ability in later maturity. *Journal of Educational Psychology,* 1947, *38,* 482–492.

Frank, G. H. The measurement of personality from the Wechsler tests. In B. A. Maher (Ed.), *Progress in experimental personality research.* New York: Academic Press, 1970. Pp. 169–194.

Garfield, S. L. A preliminary appraisal of Wechsler-Bellevue scatter patterns in schizophrenia. *Journal of Consulting Psychology,* 1948, *12,* 32–36.

Garfield, S. L. An evaluation of Wechsler-Bellevue patterns in schizophrenia. *Journal of Consulting Psychology,* 1949, *13,* 279–287.

Garfield, S. L. *Introductory clinical psychology.* New York: Macmillan, 1957.

Garfield, S. L. Intelligence and intelligence testing. In J. R. Davitz and S. Ball (Eds.), *Psychology of the Educational Process.* New York: McGraw-Hill, 1970. Pp. 519–561.

Garfield, S. L., & Affleck, D. C. A study of individuals committed to a state home for the retarded who were later released as not mentally retarded. *American Journal of Mental Deficiency,* 1960, *64,* 907–915.

Garfield, S. L., & Blek, L. Age, vocabulary level, and mental impairment. *Journal of Consulting Psychology,* 1952, *16,* 395–398.

Garfield, S. L., & Fey, W. F. A comparison of the Wechsler-Bellevue and Shipley-Hartford scales as measures of mental impairment. *Journal of Consulting Psychology,* 1948, *12,* 259–264.

Garfield, S. L., & Kurtz, R. M. Attitudes toward training in diagnostic testing—A survey of directors of internship training. *Journal of Consulting and Clinical Psychology,* 1973, *40,* 350–355.

Garrett, E. S., Price, A. C., & Deabler, H. L. Diagnostic testing for cortical brain impairment. *A. M. A. Archives of Neurology & Psychiatry,* 1957, *77,* 223–225.

Gilbert, J. G. Memory loss in senescence. *Journal of Abnormal and Social Psychology,* 1941, *36,* 73–86.

Golden, C., Hammeke, T., & Purisch, A. D. Diagnostic validity of a standardized neuropsychological battery derived from Luria's neuropsychological tests. *Journal of Consulting and Clinical Psychology,* 1978, *46,* 1258–1265.

Golden, C. J., Moses, J. A., Fishburne, F. J., Engum, E., Lewis, G. P., Wisniewski, A. M., Conley, F. K., Berg, R. A., & Graber, B. Cross-validation of the Luria-Nebraska neuropsychological battery for the presence, lateralization, and localization of brain damage. *Journal of Consulting and Clinical Psychology,* 1981, *49,* 491–507.

Goldstein, K. The significance of psychological research in schizophrenia. *Journal of Nervous and Mental Disease,* 1943, *97,* 261–270.

Goldstein, K., & Scheerer, M. Abstract and concrete behavior: An experimental study with special tests. *Psychological Monographs,* 1941, *53* (No. 239), 151.

Goldstein, S. G. Strategies of research in human neuropsychology. *Journal of Learning Disabilities,* 1969, *2,* 403–406.

Graham, F. K., & Kendall, B. S. Memory-For-Designs Test: Revised General Manual. *Perceptual and Motor Skills,* 1960, *11,* 147–188.

Guertin, W. H., Frank, G. H., & Rabin, A. I. Research with the WB Intelligence Scale: 1950–1955. *Psychological Bulletin,* 1956, *53,* 235–257.

Guertin, W. H., Rabin, A. I., Frank, G. H., & Ladd, C. E. Research with the Wechsler Intelligence Scale for adults: 1955–1960. *Psychological Bulletin,* 1962, *59,* 1–26.

Guertin, W. H., Ladd, C. E., Frank, G. H., Rabin, A. E., & Hiester, D. S. Research with the

Wechsler Intelligence Scales for adults: 1960–1965. *Psychological Bulletin*, 1966, *66*, 385–409.

Guertin, W. H., Ladd, C. E., Frank, G. H., Rabin, A. I., & Hiester, D. S. Research with the Wechsler Intelligence Scales for adults: 1965–1970. *Psychological Record*, 1971, *21*, 289–339.

Gurvitz, M. S. Some defects of the Wechsler-Bellevue. *Journal of Consulting Psychology*, 1952, *16*, 124–126.

Halstead, W. C. *Brain and intelligence. A quantitative study of the frontal lobes.* Chicago: University of Chicago Press, 1947.

Halstead, W. C., & Wepman, J. M. The Halstead-Wepman aphasia screening test. *Journal of Speech and Hearing Disorders*, 1949, *14*, 9–15.

Hanfmann, E., & Kasanin, J. *Conceptual thinking in schizophrenia.* New York: Nervous and Mental Disease Publishing Co., 1942.

Harper, A. E., Jr. Discrimination between matched schizophrenics and normals by the Wechsler-Bellevue Scale. *Journal of Consulting Psychology*, 1950, *14*, 351–357.

Harwood, E., & Naylor, G. F. K. Recall and recognition in elderly and young subjects. *Australian Journal of Psychology*, 1969, *21*, 251–257.

Haworth, M. R. *The primary visual motor test.* New York: Grune and Stratton, 1970.

Haworth, M. R. Visual motor performance of psychotic children. *Journal of Consulting and Clinical Psychology*, 1981, *49*, 947–958.

Heaton, R. K., Baade, L. E., & Johnson, K. L. Neuropsychological test results associated with psychiatric disorders in adults. *Psychological Bulletin*, 1978, *85*, 141–162.

Howard A., & Shoemaker, D. J. An evaluation of the Memory-for-Designs test. *Journal of Consulting Psychology*, 1954, *18*, 266.

Hulicka, I. A. Verbal WAIS scores of elderly patients. *Psychological Reports*, 1962, *10*, 250.

Hunt, J. McV., & Cofer, C. N. Psychological deficit. In J. McV. Hunt (Ed.), *Personality and the behavior disorders* (Vol. 2). New York: Ronald Press, 1944. Pp. 971–1032.

Klebanoff, S. G., Singer, J. L., & Wilensky, H. Psychological consequences of brain lesions and ablations. *Psychological Bulletin*, 1954, *51*, 1–41.

Koppitz, E. M. *The Bender Gestalt Test for young children.* New York: Grune and Stratton, 1964.

Koppitz, E. M. Brain damage, reading disability and the Bender Gestalt Test. *Journal of Learning Disabilities*, 1970, *3*, 6–10.

Koppitz, E. M. *The Bender-Gestalt Test for young children. Vol. II. Research and application, 1963–1973.* New York: Grune and Stratton, 1975.

Korman, M., & Blumberg, S. Comparative efficiency of some tests of cerebral damage. *Journal of Consulting Psychology*, 1963, *27*, 303–309.

L'Abate, L., Boelling, G. M., Hutton, R. D., & Mathew, D. L. The diagnostic usefulness of four potential tests of brain damage. *Journal of Consulting Psychology*, 1962, *26*, 479.

L'Abate, L., Vogler, R. E., Friedman, W. H., & Chused, T. M. The diagnostic usefulness of two tests of brain damage. *Journal of Clinical Psychology*, 1963, *19*, 87–91.

Lacks, P. B. The use of the Bender-Gestalt Test in clinical neuropsychology. *Clinical Neuropsychology* (Third Quarter), 1979, 29–34.

Lacks, P. B., Colbert, J., Harrow, M., & Levine, J. Further evidence concerning the diagnostic accuracy of the Halstead organic test battery. *Journal of Clinical Psychology*, 1970, *26*, 480–481.

Levi, J., Oppenheim, S., & Wechsler, D. Clinical use of the mental deterioration index of the Bellevue-Wechsler. *Journal of Abnormal and Social Psychology*, 1945, *40*, 405–408.

Littell, W. M. Wechsler Intelligence Scale for Children. *Psychological Bulletin*, 1960, *57*, 132–156.

Lubin, B., Wallis, R. R., & Paine, C. Patterns of psychological test usage in the U.S.: 1935–1969. *Professional Psychology,* 1971, *1,* 70–74.

McNemar, Q. Review of Rapaport, D., Diagnostic psychological testing. Vol. 1. *American Journal of Psychology,* 1946, *59,* 306–311.

McNemar, Q. Lost: Our intelligence? Why? *American Psychologist,* 1964, *19,* 871–882.

Malamud, D. I. Objective measurement of clinical status in psychopathological research. *Psychological Bulletin,* 1946, *43,* 240–258.

Malloy, P. F. & Webster, J. S. Detecting mild brain impairment using the Luria-Nebraska neuropsychological battery. *Journal of Consulting and Clinical Psychology,* 1981, *49,* 768–770.

Matarazzo, J. D. *Wechsler's measurement and appraisal of adult intelligence* (5th ed.). Baltimore: Williams & Wilkins Co., 1972.

Meehl, P. E., & Rosen, A. Antecedent probability and the efficiency of psychometric signs, patterns, or cutting scores. *Psychological Bulletin,* 1955, *52,* 194–216.

Monroe, J. J. The effects of emotional adjustment and intelligence upon Bellevue scatter. *Journal of Consulting Psychology,* 1952, *16,* 110–114.

Olch, D. R. Psychometric patterns of schizophrenics on the Wechsler-Bellevue Intelligence Test. *Journal of Consulting Psychology,* 1948, *12,* 127–136.

Parsons, O. A., & Prigatano, G. P. Methodological considerations in clinical neuropsychological research. *Journal of Consulting and Clinical Psychology,* 1978, *46,* 608–619.

Pasamanick, B., Dinitz, S., & Lefton, H. Psychiatric orientation and its relation to diagnosis and treatment in a mental hospital. *American Journal of Psychiatry,* 1959, *116,* 127–132.

Pascal, G., & Suttell, B. *The Bender-Gestalt Test.* New York: Grune and Stratton, 1951.

Purisch, A. D., Golden, C. J., & Hammeke, T. A. Discrimination of schizophrenic and brain-injured patients by a standardized version of Luria's neuropsychological tests. *Journal of Consulting and Clinical Psychology,* 1978, *46,* 1266–1273.

Rabin, A. I. Test-score patterns in schizophrenic and nonpsychotic states. *Journal of Psychology,* 1941, *12,* 91–100.

Rabin, A. I. The use of the Wechsler-Bellevue Scales with normal and abnormal persons. *Psychological Bulletin,* 1945, *42,* 410–422.

Rabin, A. I., & Guertin, W. H. Research with the Wechsler-Bellevue Test: 1945–1950. *Psychological Bulletin,* 1951, *48,* 211–241.

Rapaport, D., Gill, M. M., & Schafer, R. *Diagnostic psychological testing* (Vol. 1). Chicago: Year Book Publishers, 1945.

Rapaport, D., Gill, M. M., & Schafer, R. *Diagnostic psychological testing.* (Rev. ed. by R. R. Holt, Ed.). New York: International Universities, 1968.

Reitan, R. M. A research program on the psychological effects of brain lesions in human beings. In N. R. Ellis (Ed.), *International review of research in mental retardation.* New York: Academic Press, 1966. Pp. 153–218. (a)

Reitan, R. M. Problems and prospects in studying the psychological correlates of brain lesions. *Cortex,* 1966, *2,* 127–154. (b)

Reitan, R. M. Diagnostic inferences of brain lesions based on psychological test results. *Canadian Psychologist,* 1966, *7a,* 368–383. (c)

Reitan, R. M. Psychological assessment of deficits associated with brain lesions in subjects with and without subnormal intelligence. In J. L. Khanna (Ed.), *Brain damage and mental retardation: A psychological evaluation.* Springfield, IL: Charles C. Thomas, 1967.

Reitan, R. M., & Davison, L. A. *Clinical neuropsychology: Current status and applications.* New York: Wiley, 1974.

Schonfield, D. Memory changes with age. *Nature,* 1965, *28,* 918.

Shakow, D., Doekart, M. B., & Goldman, R. The memory functions in psychotics. *Diseases of the Nervous System,* 1941, *2,* 43–48.

Shipley, W., & Burlingame, C. C. A convenient self-administering scale for measuring intellectual impairment in psychotics. *American Journal of Psychiatry,* 1941, *97,* 1313–1326.

Spiers, P. A. Have they come to praise Luria or to bury him?: The Luria-Nebraska Battery controversy. *Journal of Consulting and Clinical Psychology,* 1981, *49,* 331–341.

Standards for educational and psychological tests and manuals. Washington, D.C.: American Psychological Association, 1966.

Standards for educational and psychological tests and manuals. Washington, D.C.: American Psychological Association, 1974.

Stone, C. P., Girdner, J., & Albrecht, R. An alternate form of the Wechsler Memory Scale. *Journal of Psychology,* 1946, *22,* 199–206.

Sundberg, N. D. The practice of psychological testing in clinical services in the United States. *American Psychologist,* 1961, *16,* 79–83.

Talland, G. A. (Ed.), *Human aging and behavior.* New York: Academic Press, 1968.

Terman, L. M., & Merrill, M. A. *Stanford-Binet intelligence scale.* Boston: Houghton Mifflin, 1960.

Terman, L. M., & Merrill, M. A. *Stanford-Binet intelligence scale: 1972* (norms ed.). Boston: Houghton Mifflin, 1973.

Terman, L. M., & Oden, M. H. *The gifted group at mid-life: Thirty-five years' follow-up of the superior child.* (Genetic studies of genius, Vol. 5). Stanford, CA: Stanford University Press, 1959.

Thompson, C. W. Review of Rapaport C., Diagnostic psychological testing. Vol. 1. *Journal of Genetic Psychology,* 1946, *69,* 123–128.

Tolor, A., & Brannigan, G. G. *Research and clinical applications of the Bender-Gestalt Test.* Springfield, IL: Charles C. Thomas, 1981.

Tolor, A., & Schulberg, H. C. *An evaluation of the Bender-Gestalt Test.* Springfield, IL: Charles C Thomas, 1963.

Vernon, P. E. Ability factors and environmental influence. *American Psychologist,* 1965, *20,* 723–733.

Wade, T. C., & Baker, T. B. Opinion and use of psychological tests: A survey of clinical psychologists. *American Psychologist,* 1977, *32,* 874–882.

Watson, C. G., Thomas, R. W., Anderson, D., & Felling, J. Differentiation of organics from schizophrenics at two chronicity levels by use of the Reitan-Halstead organic test battery. *Journal of Consulting and Clinical Psychology,* 1968, *32,* 679–684.

Wechsler, D. *The measurement of adult intelligence* (3rd ed.). Baltimore: Williams and Wilkins, 1944.

Wechsler, D. A standardized memory scale for clinical use. *Journal of Psychology,* 1945, *19,* 87–95.

Wechsler, D. *Wechsler intelligence scale for children.* (Manual) New York: Psychological Corporation, 1949.

Wechsler, D. *Manual for the Wechsler adult intelligence scale.* New York: Psychological Corporation, 1955.

Wechsler, D. *The measurement and appraisal of adult intelligence* (4th ed.). Baltimore: Williams and Wilkins, 1958.

Wechsler, D. *Manual for the Wechsler intelligence scale for children—revised.* New York: Psychological Corporation, 1974.

Wechsler, D. *WAIS-R Manual. Wechsler Adult intelligence scale—revised.* New York: Psychological Corporation, 1981.

Weider, A. Effect of age on the Bellevue Intelligence Scale in schizophrenic patients. *Psychiatric Quarterly,* 1943, *17,* 337–345.

Weigl, E. On the psychology of so-called processes of abstraction. *Journal of Abnormal and Social Psychology,* 1941, *36,* 1–33.

Weisenburg, T., Roe, A., & McBride, K. E. *Adult intelligence.* New York: Commonwealth Fund, 1936.

Whiteman, M., & Jastak, J. Absolute scaling of tests for different age groupings of a state-wide sample. *Education and Psychological Measurement,* 1957, *17,* 338–346.

Wikler, A., Dixon, J. F., & Parker, J. B. Brain function in problem children and controls: Psychometric, Neurological, and Electroencephalographic comparisons. *American Journal of Psychiatry,* 1970, *127,* 94–105.

Wittenborn, J. R. Bellevue subtest scores as an aid in diagnosis. *Journal of Consulting Psychology,* 1949, *13,* 433–439.

Wohler, H. J. A comparison of reproduction errors made by brain-damaged and control patients on a Memory-For-Design Test. *Journal of Abnormal and Social Psychology,* 1956, *52,* 251–255.

Yates, A. J. The validity of some psychological tests of brain damage. *Psychological Bulletin,* 1954, *51,* 359–379.

Yates, A. J. Review of Shipley-Institute of Living Scale for Measuring Intellectual Impairment. In O. K. Buros (Ed.), *The seventh mental measurements yearbook* (Vol. 1). Highland Park, NJ: Gryphon Press, 1972.

Zimmerman, I. L., & Woo-Sam, J. Research with the Wechsler Intelligence Scale for Children: 1960–1970. *Journal of Clinical Psychology,* April, 1972 (Monograph Supplement 33).

Zimmerman, I. L., Woo-Sam, J., & Glasser, A. J. *The clinical interpretation of the Wechsler adult intelligence scale.* New York: Grune and Stratton, 1973.

Personality
Appraisal

Early in the history of psychological tests, attempts were made to appraise other attributes and functions besides intelligence. Of particular interest to clinical psychologists have been the techniques developed to appraise personality and individual adjustment. Over the years a variety of techniques and approaches with different assumptions have made their appearance on the psychological scene.

These techniques can be categorized in a number of ways. Some of these methods have been derived or applied from a specific theoretical orientation and in essence are attempts to apply the theory in a particular manner. Other techniques have been derived primarily on an empirical basis in terms of how well test items and scores differentiate specifically designated groups of subjects. Still others may be oriented around observable behaviors or diagnostic categories derived from the fields of psychiatry and psychopathology.

The various methods also differ in terms of the materials or procedure used. The most widely used procedures in clinical psychology have been personality questionnaires and projective techniques. These popular techniques will be discussed and described in this chapter. Other methods which have had somewhat more specialized usage will be presented in the following chapter.

Before we proceed to describe some of the current procedures for appraising personality and adjustment, it is important that the reader keep in mind the different conceptions of personality that have been espoused and developed from the different theories of personality referred to in Chapter 2. Although not all methods of personality appraisal have been derived from explicit theories of personality, most in some fashion or other are at least tied to some implicit view of personality. Some of the methods are used to obtain a comprehensive picture of the individual's personality, while others deal with selected aspects of personality or adjustment. The techniques vary also in terms of what aspects of personality are evaluated. Some are primarily concerned with behavioral manifestations, some with the individual's introspective analysis of his own behavior, feelings, and attitudes, and others with structural and ideational components of personality of which the individual is relatively unaware. It is apparent, therefore, that the terms "personality" or "adjustment" do not mean precisely the same thing with regard to the various tests that purport to measure such variables. Not only are there many different definitions and views of personality, but any specific definition selected would not apply equally to the various methods devised for its study. The clinical student, therefore, should have some familiarity with the major theories of personality in order to understand and evaluate the various approaches to personality appraisal.

Generally, the term, "personality," refers to the integrated and organized behavior of the individual that characterizes him as a unique person. As used in the area of personality testing, the term usually indicates nonintellective or conative aspects of the individual. This is not a clear-cut demarcation inasmuch as personality also includes intellectual components. The former, therefore, is more inclusive, and in discussing the personality and adjustive aspects of the individual, we are concerned with such matters as unique patterns of response to social situations, how the individual gets along with others, whether he is tense or irritable, whether he tends to withdraw or is overly aggressive, his view of self, and similar categories of behavioral response. Frequently, such manifestations have been considered in relation to drives, dispositions, situational factors, and conflicts, so that ideally one more fully understands the individual's unique behavior. Actually, as we have seen, even standard tests of intelligence give us information about certain aspects of the individual's personality in terms of how he answers different kinds of problems as well as the adequacy of his solution. There are, however, differences between the approaches, purposes, and methods used in measuring intelligence and those utilized in tests of personality. Although it may be said that all tests and most contacts with the patient serve to give us some clues about his personality reactions, there are differences between these methods with regard to the aspects or facets of personality studied. The tests to be discussed in this section are those which have been specifically devised by psychologists for the purpose of evaluating certain aspects of personality.

One final and complex issue should be mentioned before proceeding to the next section. This concerns the relative stability of personality, the existence of such constructs or characteristics as personality traits, and the importance of situational factors on the behavior of the individual. This issue (or issues) has been a topic of controversy for many years and we will make no attempt to settle it here (Allport, 1937, 1961; Epstein, 1977, 1980; Mischel, 1968, 1977). The implications of this issue, however, are important for the appraisal of personality and the interpretations made by the clinical psychologist. Are there a number of traits such as aggressiveness, shyness, introversion, and the like, by means of which the person can be meaningfully appraised and understood? Are such traits stable and enduring over time? Is the person's personality and behavior thus stable and predictable, or is behavior primarily a response to environmental stimuli and contingencies? If both personality and the environment interact in producing certain behaviors, how much emphasis should be placed on appraisals of individual personality?

It should be apparent that different answers to the questions raised in the preceding paragraph will be received from psychologists with very different theoretical orientations. Psychoanalytic psychologists generally will tend to emphasize individual intrapsychic variables, whereas behaviorally oriented psychologists will be more sensitive to variables in the current environment of the individual. Such considerations will also influence the choice of methods used for the appraisal of the individual. However, a variety of procedures are available, and the clinical psychologist should be able to evaluate them in terms of their explicit or implicit theory of personality, as well as for their psychometric properties. Now, let us proceed with our presentation of methods of personality appraisal.

PERSONALITY QUESTIONNAIRES

Probably the most widely used method of evaluating personality devised by psychologists is the personality questionnaire or self-report inventory. Such questionnaires have been constructed to measure a wide range of personality attributes. Some have attempted to measure broad categories, including such aspects as emotional adjustment, social adjustment, neurotic tendency, and emotional instability. Other personality questionnaires have focused their attention on more specific personality traits, including such traits as introversion, extroversion, self-sufficiency, and ascendancy or dominance. Still other inventories have been developed from specific theoretical conceptions of personality or have essentially utilized different psychiatric categories. Nevertheless, personality questionnaires or inventories, while differing in some ways, have certain important characteristics in common.

In general, personality inventories are instruments made up of a number of questions or test items which are to be answered by the subject. Usually, the person is requested to indicate his/her response to the various test items by choosing between a "yes" or "no" answer. In some instances, a third category, designated either as a question mark or as "cannot say" may also be utilized, while in others the subject is asked to choose between two statements. The number of test items may range from less than 100 to over 500. The test items are scored for one or more personality variables by means of a key which may give differential weighted scorings to the various responses, and the scores obtained are interpreted in terms of the norms provided by the test author. Although the scoring of the test or inventory is objective and is carried out with the aid of a scoring key, or by means of a computer, the actual responses given by the subject are determined by her own subjective feelings or experiences.

Most of the better known personality questionnaires report split-half reliability coefficients of around .80, a method that tells us more about the consistency of one-half of the scale in relation to the other half than about the actual stability of scores with the passing of time—that is, test-retest reliability, which is the more crucial concern of the clinician. Nevertheless, within these limits, acceptable reliability has been established statistically for many of these scales. As is the case with most psychological instruments, however, validity—the extent to which the test scores are a true measure of some one or more personality variables—has not been established with any degree of conclusiveness. The test manuals rarely give truly adequate data for demonstrating the validity of the test. A common procedure is to compare the scores of a known maladjusted group with the scores of a group of subjects considered to be well adjusted in terms of the absence of overt pathological symptoms. It is important, however, to know how well the scale will differentiate future samples from various populations. Frequently such data are not contained in the test manual and must be secured from independent investigations reported later in the different applications of the scale. Thus one sees again how important it is for the clinical psychologist who utilizes psychological tests to acquaint herself with the literature on evaluation of the various clinical techniques. As mentioned previously, independent follow-up investigations are extremely important in fully testing the validity and utility of a given instrument.

Although one cannot pass judgment on all such tests, since some are better than others, it is fair to state that personality questionnaires in the past have been viewed as having somewhat limited value for individual diagnostic work in clinical practice (Buros, 1972; Cronbach, 1970; Gynther, 1972). Where extensive data exist on given questionnaires, they indicate that such instruments may differentiate groups of subjects but have less predictive validity where individual subjects are concerned. Some of these personality scales, therefore, may have value for the rapid screening of individuals who are grossly maladjusted, but may be of less significance in the intensive study of the individual case.

In the last analysis, the value of any instrument is largely determined by the goals or purposes for which it is used. It is for this reason that most published personality scales have been of limited value in clinical situations such as psychiatric hospitals or clinics. If an individual is committed to a psychiatric hospital, there is little apparent value in administering a personality inventory that will reveal only whether or not he is maladjusted. This can be evaluated quickly by other means. Similarly, when a patient comes to a mental hygiene clinic with definite symptoms of maladjustment, there is little need to discover whether or not he has "neurotic tendencies." On the other hand, if one were functioning as a psychologist in a large school system, it might be advantageous to administer personality scales to the entire school population in order to quickly identify children with a potential personality disturbance. Such screening values, of course, would be limited by the validity of the measuring instrument. Furthermore, in such situations any child identified by a personality inventory as deviant should be thoroughly examined by other means of personality appraisal and no consequential decisions made without considering all available data. In other words, a personality inventory may identify as disturbed a child who upon closer examination may be well within the normal range.

The mention of administering personality questionnaires to an entire school system (or even a segment of the school) illuminates another problem that has received considerable attention the past few years. This concerns the matter of personality testing and the invasion of privacy. In recent years there have been strong reactions by congressmen, lawyers, and others to the invasion of privacy as represented by the administration of personality tests in certain situations. This is a complex issue that cannot be dealt with here in any extensive way. The reader should be aware, however, that the testing services of psychologists, once taken for granted as helpful, or at least not harmful, are now viewed more critically and even with suspicion (Haney, 1981).

It can be pointed out that items on some personality questionnaires concern the private beliefs and experiences of the individual being tested. If a person is asked to reveal his own views about himself, or to express his opinions or his experiences in such areas as sex or religion, he may be realistically concerned about the consequences of his self-disclosures. If the completion of such questionnaires is a requirement for employment, the prospective employee may be decidedly uncomfortable about actually revealing his personal, innermost thoughts and behaviors conducted in the privacy of his home. He may, in fact, perceive the necessity for doing so as an unwarranted invasion of his privacy.

As a result of the strong reaction to forced self-disclosure, there has been some soul-searching on the part of psychologists and personnel specialists concerning the circumstances and situations where personality testing may be appropriately applied. Does a psychologist, for example, have a right to examine an individual intensively and give the report of his findings to someone else, for example, an employment officer? Can a school psychologist administer personality tests to a child in school without securing the permission of the parents? Although the professional psychologist does have a code of ethics to guide her professional behavior, not all issues can be clearly anticipated and new problems do occur (Anastasi, 1976).

Where the clinical psychologist is consulted directly by a person who seeks his help or has a client referred by another professional practitioner for consultation, most of the problems discussed above do not usually arise. The psychologist's services are sought by the client and a relationship involving confidentiality usually develops. Whatever material of a highly private nature is divulged by the client in this situation is offered with the expectation that it will be of value in terms of helping him with his problem. This is clearly different from the personnel selection situation where the psychologist is hired by someone other than the person being examined, and problems of conflict of interest or ethical responsibility may occur. Nevertheless, the clinical psychologist should be informed about and sensitive to the issues involved. Two special issues of *American Psychologist* have been devoted to discussions of such matters and contain a diversity of reports including hearings of congressional committees (Testing and Public Policy, 1965; Testing: Concepts, Policy, Practice and Research, 1981). This material makes for fascinating reading and the hostile and critical views of personality testing expressed may come as a real shock to the reader.

There are some other general issues which should be mentioned in discussing personality questionnaires. One, mentioned previously, concerns the psychological reality of the traits measured. Are there unitary traits such as aggressiveness, dominance, and so forth, that can be measured? How general or stable are such traits? If a person is shown to be "dominant" on a personality questionnaire, does this mean he is dominant in every situation? If not, it would be important to know which situations produce such responses and such information is not available from the test. This issue is also highlighted by the fact that some tests that purport to measure the same trait show little relationship to each other—that is, "construct validity" of personality variables is difficult to achieve (Fiske, 1971).

One additional criticism of personality questionnaires is that a unified and integrated picture of personality usually cannot be secured with this type of technique. Not only is the personality picture limited to the particular traits sampled by a given questionnaire, but these traits are evaluated in an isolated manner. Knowledge of the interplay of personality trends and their significance in terms of the total pattern is usually missing. There have been attempts to overcome this deficiency, however, by relating profiles of scores on the various scales to certain types of personality patterns (Gilberstadt & Duker, 1965; Hathaway & McKinley, 1951; Hathaway & Meehl, 1951; Marks & Seeman, 1963). Here attention is focused on the actual patterning of scores and not merely on the scale values for each of the separate scales.

Another novel suggestion, designated "configural scoring," was offered by Meehl (1950). This refers to the analysis of patterns of responses to groups of test items. According to this view, individual items by themselves may not discriminate between criterion groups. However, groups of items may reveal patterns of response that do have discriminatory value. For example, three test items taken individually may not differentiate between two criterion groups of subjects. A pattern of *True, False, True* to the three items, however, may hold for one group of subjects and not for the other. In other words, this pattern of response would differentiate the two groups, whereas each item separately would not. Such an approach, potentially, could be integrated more adequately with theories of personality dynamics than the more traditional questionnaire scores, which are simply the sums of large groups of test items.

More recently, attention has centered on the importance of certain kinds of response patterns to personality questionnaires. Very briefly, two aspects have been stressed. One concerns the subject's tendency to respond to test items in a socially desirable manner rather than in the way that best describes his actual behavior or mood, a problem already commented upon previously. Although several studies have attempted to evaluate the matter and considerable controversy has ensued, the issue has not been conclusively settled (Block, 1965; Edwards and Diers, 1962; Lanyon and Goodstein, 1982; Mischel, 1968). Furthermore, although the social desirability of responses to items in a particular questionnaire undoubtedly influences how the respondent answers the items, it is difficult to evaluate fully the extent of the influence. As Mischel has pointed out, "It is difficult to choose between the social-desirability interpretation and the characterological or trait interpretation of self-report scores on psychiatric inventories. The choice among interpretations is difficult because even an accurate self-report of problematic, idiosyncratic, or debilitating behavior invariably requires endorsing a socially undesirable item (Block, 1965)" (Mischel, 1968, p. 84).

Another type of response set that has been emphasized has sometimes been referred to as response style. This refers to the tendency of subjects to respond in certain characteristic ways, regardless of the content of the specific test item. Some people, for example, appear to answer most items in the affirmative, while others respond in the reverse manner. Again, it has been argued that such response styles account for a significant part of the variance secured with personality inventories (Bass, 1955; Messick and Jackson, 1961). McGee (1962), however, concluded that the generality of such response tendencies has not been firmly established. Thus, although several investigations have emphasized the importance of such problems as social desirability and response style, no conclusive answers to these problems have appeared.

Since we have now discussed some of the attributes, methods, assumptions, and problems of personality questionnaires in general, let us examine an actual questionnaire. The Minnesota Multiphasic Personality Inventory has been selected because it has been, and is currently, the most widely used personality questionnaire in clinical psychology.

THE MINNESOTA MULTIPHASIC PERSONALITY INVENTORY (MMPI)

The MMPI, like most other inventories consists of a series of questions and statements to which the subject responds with either a "yes," "no," or "cannot say." Consisting of 550 test items, it is by contrast with most inventories a lengthy test. The test can be given to groups as well as individuals. In content, the MMPI resembles other personality inventories, although it is oriented more toward psychopathology and psychiatric diagnosis, thus reflecting its original use as a screening device in a medical setting. A novel feature of the scoring of this inventory is the use of several special keys to evaluate the validity of the patient's responses to test items. One such score, the Question Score, is made up simply of the number of items the subject places in the "cannot say" category. A large Question Score invalidates the other scores. Another validating score, the Lie Score, gives some measure of the subject's attempt to falsify his scores by placing himself in a more socially acceptable light. A third check is the Validity Scale. A high Validity score usually indicates that the other scales are not valid, while a low score is considered "a reliable indication that the subject's responses were rational and relatively pertinent" (Hathaway and McKinley, 1943, p. 4). Later, an additional scale was developed to increase the validity of the clinical scales making up the inventory. This scale, called the K Scale, is used as a correction factor on some of the other scales. The authors thus have attempted to correct or lessen some of the obvious distortions that may be found in the use of personality questionnaires.

The Inventory, in addition to the various validity scales, is composed of nine separate clinical scales. These were devised originally to evaluate personality characteristics deemed to be important in identifying psychological abnormality. Actually, eight of the nine scales are designated by psychiatric diagnostic categories, for example, hypochondriasis, depression, hysteria, psychopathic deviate, paranoia, psychasthenia, schizophrenia, and hypomania. The remaining scale is designed to measure the "tendency toward masculinity or femininity of interest pattern." Scores from different scales are converted into standard score equivalents, and those above a specified value are in most cases considered to be indicative of abnormal trends. The significance of deviant scores, however, varies for the different scales and, in addition, the interpretation will be influenced by the pattern or profile of scores.

The MMPI has been developed and standardized more thoroughly than most of the inventories that preceded it. The manuals are more detailed and explicit than was usually the case, and the research data are more extensive (Butcher, 1969, 1972; Dahlstrom, Welsh, and Dahlstrom, 1972, 1975). The actual values of the MMPI, however, must be determined by the uses to which it can be put. In evaluating the inventory, therefore, such criteria must be kept in mind.

The various scales of the MMPI have been developed by contrasting normal groups with selected clinical cases. "The chief criterion of excellence has been the valid prediction of clinical cases against the neuropsychiatric staff diagnosis, rather than statistical measures of reliability and validity" (Hathaway and McKinley, 1943, p. 3). Reliability coefficients, however, are reported for some of the scales and range between .71 and .83. These correlations were obtained by retesting a group of forty normal individuals at various time intervals. With regard to validity, the authors report in the original manual that "a high score on a scale has been found to predict positively the corresponding final clinical diagnosis or estimate in more than 60 percent of new psychiatric admissions" (Hathaway and McKinley, 1943, p. 3).

Although it is stated that the MMPI has been designed "to provide . . . scores on all the more important phases of personality" (Hathaway and McKinley, 1943, p. 2), most of the original material on the test is closely related to psychiatric diagnosis. Actually, the main purpose of the inventory as originally conceived was to help in the diagnostic classification of the patient. Consequently, let us first evaluate the MMPI from this point of view.

Some of the problems of diagnostic work in clinical psychology have already been discussed in Chapter 2 and need not be repeated here. We can state again that the attaching of a nosological label to a patient in many cases is of limited value. Usually, clinical reports go beyond this in appraising the personality of the individual. If psychiatric classification is a primary goal of the MMPI, it would then appear to be of limited value and fraught with potential error in categorizing patients. Several older studies attempted to evaluate the diagnostic accuracy of the inventory and the results have been somewhat equivocal. Leverenz (1943) found the MMPI to be a valid diagnostic instrument with various patient groups, but other studies have not reported such favorable findings (Benton, 1945). Another investigation (Benton and

Probst, 1946) found significant agreement between psychiatric ratings of personality trends and the MMPI on three of the clinical scales but not on the remaining six. The findings from additional diagnostic studies of various groups of patients (Michael and Buhler, 1945; Rubin, 1948) have not been impressive. It was noted, too, that the profile or patterning of scores will distinguish normal from pathological groups, but differentiation among the different clinical groups is not sharply defined (Meehl, 1946; Kleinmuntz, 1967). Zelin (1971) also found rather low correlations between the specific scales of the MMPI and ratings of psychiatric symptoms. Furthermore, in at least some investigations, approximately 20% of normal control subjects have received at least one abnormally high score on the MMPI (Modlin, 1947).

The above analysis, as well as a more recent appraisal (Lanyon and Goodstein, 1982), indicates that the validity of the MMPI as a diagnostic instrument in terms of psychiatric classification is still to be adequately demonstrated.[5] Furthermore, it is doubtful whether an approach based on psychiatric categories can be really successful in attempts at diagnostic classification because of the weaknesses in the criteria upon which it rests. There is also some overlap among the various clinical scales which also limit diagnostic differentiation. Because of these limitations, the MMPI has been used in other ways more recently. In several instances, the three scales, Hysteria (Hy), Depression (D), and Hypocondriasis (Hs), have been viewed together as an indicator of neurotic patterns (see Fig. 1). Combinations of other scales have been designated as psychotic profiles and behavior problem profiles (Hathaway & McKinley, 1951). Although this use of the MMPI may be of value in certain kinds of screening and research, by itself it is of rather limited value in the clinical study or understanding of the individual patient. Such characterizations of the patient contribute relatively little to our understanding of the patient's problems, and in cases where it would be important to rule out a possible psychosis, many clinicians would want to base their evaluations on more than the MMPI.

Recently, greater attention has been placed on the use of profile and pattern analysis for interpretative purposes (Gilberstadt & Duker, 1965; Marks & Seeman, 1963). In this approach, attention may be focused on the profile of scores above a given value, on the pattern of scores for all the scales, or more frequently on the highest two or three scales. The scales are coded or numbered and interpretations are based on the patterning as much as on

[5] It should be mentioned that the authors of the MMPI clearly indicate the limitations of the scales for this purpose and discuss how the scales may fluctuate with time. They also emphasize the fact that the profile must be evaluated by the clinician in terms of many factors, for "the MMPI profile does not directly provide definitive evidence as to disability or diagnosis even with the majority of psychiatric patients" (Hathaway and McKinley, 1951, p. 22).

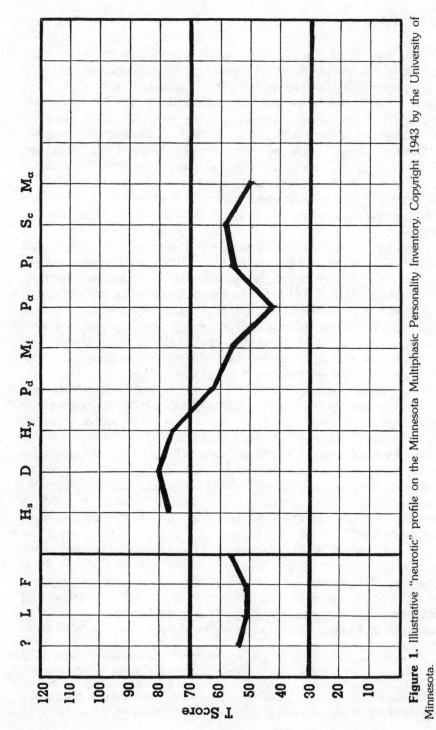

Figure 1. Illustrative "neurotic" profile on the Minnesota Multiphasic Personality Inventory. Copyright 1943 by the University of Minnesota.

the particular scale scores. Different patterns are considered indicative of certain types of personality.

An example may be given of the coding procedure utilized by Hathaway and Meehl in their *Atlas for the Clinical Use of the MMPI* (Hathaway & Meehl, 1951). Eight of the nine clinical scales are represented by arabic numerals. The Masculinity-Femininity (M-F) Scale was not included with this group for specific reasons, but it is included in the total code by the actual weighted score. In coding, the scale with the highest score comes first and is followed in order by the numerals representing those scales with scores above 54. All such values are followed by a dash. All scales with values below 46 are then coded after the dash. A prime (') is placed to the right of all scores above 70, and all scores above 54 which are within one point of each other are underlined. These coded values are followed by the actual score of the M-F Scale in parenthesis and by the raw scores of three of the validating scales.

A specific illustration will make this procedure more comprehensible. For this purpose let us look at the following code:

$$1'3\underline{82}—96 \ (55) \ 4:3:18$$

This coded profile indicates that a score of 70 or above was obtained on the Hypochondriasis Scale, which is represented by the numeral, 1. Scores above 54 but under 70 were obtained on the three scales. Hysteria, Schizophrenia, and Depression (382), and the scores on the latter two scales were within one point of each other. Scores below 46 were obtained on the Manic and Paranoid scales, the M-F score was 55, and the raw scores on the Lie, Validity, and K scales were 4, 3, and 18, respectively. Coded patterns approximating this one have been secured from patients with hypochondriacal complaints. By comparing closely related patterns secured from known groups of patients, one is able to note similarities between patients and to group the coded patterns accordingly. Other systems of interpretation have also been developed, and computerized scoring and interpretation of MMPI test records are available from a number of sources.

Pattern analysis differs from the traditional approach of simply interpreting scores in terms of the test manual's description of various traits or scales. This appears to call for more clinical judgment and experience than have usually been required with personality questionnaires. For such reasons, a number of special short institutes on the MMPI have been offered in recent years.

At the present time the MMPI appears to have a body of faithful and devoted adherents as well as some critics. It has been used in a large variety of studies with the usual conflicting findings. The use of computers for scoring the inventory and providing personality descriptions according to several different empirically derived sets of rules has, indeed, made it a very popular test (Buros, 1972, 1978). Although its use in clinical situations has perhaps been exceeded by projective techniques, it still ranks as one of the most widely used clinical tests of personality (Lubin, Wallis, & Paine, 1971; Wade & Baker, 1977) and, as we have noted, several handbooks for the interpretation of the test have been published. One report has indicated that psychologists on the West Coast appear to prefer the MMPI over projective techniques, whereas the reverse appears to hold for their colleagues on the East Coast (Peskin, 1963). Generally, it appears that there are different groups of clinicians with different preferences and biases. Those with a somewhat more objective or psychometric point of view seem to prefer such instruments as the MMPI, while those with more psychodynamic leanings rely more on projective techniques. Those psychologists, on the other hand, who favor a learning theory orientation, would appear to favor neither approach to personality evaluation. This was borne out in a recent survey, although personality inventories were used more frequently than projective techniques by a sample of behavior therapists (Swan & MacDonald, 1978).

PROJECTIVE TECHNIQUES

The second category of methods for personality appraisal to be discussed in this chapter are the projective techniques. These methods have had an interesting history. At first, they were given a rather cool reception by psychologists, for they were not viewed as being tests in the more conventional sense. They depended on the subjective interpretative skills of the examiner, they were not standardized instruments, there were little or no normative data available, and so on. But, with the great growth of clinical psychology in the 1950's and the emphasis on dynamic theories of personality, the use of projective techniques spread widely. In many ways, projective techniques, particularly the Rorschach Test, became almost synonymous with clinical psychology, and courses in such methods became a basic part of practically all curricula in graduate training programs.

In the past few years, as noted previously, there has been a noticeable decline in the clinical psychologists' involvement with extensive diagnostic testing and, consequently, with projective methods. These techniques have continued to be a topic of controversy among psychologists of different theoretical persuasions. They have been criticized most strongly by psychologists with research oriented, objective, or behavioral orientations and have been most staunchly supported by those who espouse psychodynamic points of view. Before making any other generalizations, let us look at some of the projective methods and some of their underlying assumptions.

A variety of materials and hypotheses for evaluating various components of personality have been utilized in the various projective tests. Some, like the Rorschach, make use of inkblots; others use ambiguous pictures; still others use blocks or drawings by the subject (Murstein, 1965; Rabin, 1968). Although there are differences between the various projective methods, some similar theoretical assumptions are made for most such approaches to personality appraisal. The basic assumption is that the subject reveals something of his personality in the way he responds to the stimulus material. In reacting to the relatively nonstructured test materials, the subject is free to respond in many different ways. How he constructs or organizes his responses, how he perceives the stimulus, what comments he makes, and similar response patterns are viewed as being related to the motivations, conflicts, and defenses of the individual. Thus, the individual's constellation of responses is interpreted as reflecting characteristic aspects of his personality. It is in this sense that the individual is considered to project his personality into the test situation. The greater the latitude allowed the client in his mode of response, the more likelihood his individuality or uniqueness of personality will be revealed in his productions. Some of the client's responses obviously may be stereotyped or largely culturally determined, but others will reveal unique aspects, in terms of both conscious attitudes and unconscious tendencies.

In addition, since the client is considered to be unaware of the significance of her responses to the relatively neutral stimuli presented, it is expected that she will reveal certain aspects of personality more freely and with less conscious control than is the case with other techniques. It is also implied that, within certain limits, the responses given by the client are manifestations of stable aspects of personality.

On the basis of the assumptions mentioned above, many psychologists believe that projective tests of personality have values that are not found in other tests of personality. The test materials are less structured, the client is free to respond in any way that he wants, there is less chance for deliberate distortion and for responding in what the client believes is a socially approved manner, more leads to the motivational and conflictual aspects of personality can be secured, and a better understanding of the total personality may be obtained. These are some of the values claimed for the use of projective techniques.

For such reasons, projective techniques were considered to be of great potential value in the clinical appraisal of individuals with personality problems. Furthermore, the disappointing results secured from other tests of personality, the increased emphasis on dynamic interpretations of personality, and a closer working relationship with psychiatry all tended to influence the use and acceptance of projective techniques. In terms of the last, for example, projective tests appeared to offer useful data for psychiatric diagnosis and for considerations of therapeutic planning and disposition. Much of the earlier published work on the Rorschach was related to problems of psychiatric diagnosis, and there were numerous papers on the use of the Rorschach Test in diagnosing schizophrenics, neurotics, epileptics, mental defectives, depressives, and cases with organic brain damage. Many clinical psychologists not only believed the Rorschach to be a tremendous aid in diagnostic matters (Klopfer & Kelley, 1942), but also saw mastery of the technique and the preparation of diagnostic reports as their major professional functions. Furthermore, besides providing information relevant to the problem of psychiatric diagnosis, the psychologist also was able to offer data about the individual's personality structure that might be of help in understanding the patient and in planning a therapeutic program for him.

Projective techniques, therefore, were viewed as devices capable of penetrating below the surface aspects of personality, of revealing significant clues about the individual's personality structure and underlying dynamics, and thereby, of contributing to the effective resolution of problems of diagnosis and disposition. Since they appeared to meet the assessment needs of the clinical psychologist in relation to clinical problems, projective techniques rapidly became highly preferred tools in the armamentarium of clinical psychologists. Such projective techniques as the Rorschach became standard parts of the psychological test battery and still are rather widely used today (Lubin, Wallis, & Paine, 1971; Wade & Baker, 1977). This is particularly true of clinicians with psychodynamic orientations. Let us now examine some of these techniques.

THE RORSCHACH TEST

The Rorschach Test has been the most popular projective test of personality. Developed by Hermann Rorschach, a Swiss psychiatrist, the test consists of ten symmetrical inkblots printed on separate cards (Rorschach, 1942). Five of the cards are fully or partially colored, while the remaining five are achromatic, including only shadings of grey to black. These particular blots were selected on the basis of extensive clinical investigation by Rorschach. Although inkblots had been used in some psychological research studies at an earlier date, Rorschach explored the possibilities for personality study offered by this method. His published results and hypotheses are based on test data secured from more than 400 subjects. It is to Rorschach's credit that he emphasized the preliminary nature of his work and the need for further experimentation. Some of the later adherents to the method seemingly have not shared this view.

There are numerous hypotheses and empirical findings associated with the Rorschach Test. In addition to the general observation that the pattern of responses to this perceptual and interpretive task varies with different groups of subjects, many observations and hypotheses have been offered for selected types of responses. These, in turn, have led to complicated scoring and interpretive schemes for the test (Exner, 1974, 1978).

Since some of the general assumptions underlying projective methods of personality have already been discussed, we shall consider some of the special features of the Rorschach. In analyzing and interpreting responses to this test, major emphasis has been placed on certain formal aspects of the response, although the content of the response is also considered. For example, different psychological meanings are given to a response which integrates the entire blot, as contrasted with an interpretation that involves only a large or minute detail of the blot; a response that reverses the figure-ground relationship of the blot is judged differently from a conventional one. No one manner of responding to the blot is, by itself, considered to be better than others. One must view the total pattern of responses, for each response assumes significance in terms of its relationship to the totality of responses. Thus, while a response that integrates the entire blot is assumed to reflect superior organizational ability, an individual who responded only in this way might reflect a certain rigidity or compulsive need to impress others. A normative aspect also enters into the interpretation of responses. For example, since it has been found that a majority of people respond most frequently to certain large details of the blot rather than to wholes, the individual who responds in the manner described above is neglecting the stimuli in the environmental field judged most obvious by most people. The reasons for an atypical pattern, however, must be sought in an analysis of the entire record.

In addition to the size and location of the blot segments responded to by the subject, one investigates also the factor or factors that determined the response. In the Rorschach Test there are several different "determinant categories," of which only a few will be mentioned. The most frequent determinant of a response is the shape or form of the blot or blot segment. Form on the Rorschach is equated generally with intellectual activity and, among other things, denotes intellectual control, clarity of perception, reality contact, and "ego strength." Thus, when form is a factor in the subject's response, the examiner must decide whether the form quality is good or poor, that is, how well does the percept correspond to the stimulus? Ratios have been used to express the relative frequency of clearly perceived percepts (good form) in a patient's record and are among the most important indices derived from the Rorschach Test (Beck, 1968). In line with these hypotheses, studies have shown that the percentage of responses with good form is lower among psychotic patients than in normals, although there is some overlap between the two groups. As is true with other Rorschach variables, however, there is an empirically determined optimum of well-perceived forms and a subject whose entire record is made up of such responses also deviates from the norm. In the latter instance, according to some clinical views, the individual may be overly cautious, conventional, or fearful, and as a result may be trying to maintain strong control over his behavior with a resulting loss of spontaneity. Again, however, we remind the reader that the final interpretation given to such a pattern would be influenced by the total test protocol.

In addition to form, other aspects of the blots may influence or determine the subject's responses. Color also can be a determinant of a response, either in conjunction with form or separately. Again, there are many hypotheses relating to the interpretation of responses which include color as a determinant. Although some of these postulate a precise relationship between a certain type of color response and a specific personality trend, in most instances interpretations of such responses are conditioned by the context in which they appear. Response to color as a determinant generally is considered to represent capacity for emotional response to external stimuli. When it is associated with form but is not the primary determinant of a response, the latter is said to indicate that the emotional responsivity of the subject is well controlled. Conversely, if the response is determined primarily or solely by color, then it is considered to reflect varying degrees of inadequate control over emotionality and could be indicative of impulsivity, lability, sensitivity, or immaturity. Generally, adults are expected to have their emotional responses relatively well controlled and thus would react to color in most instances as a secondary determinant, whereas a young child would be expected to reveal less intellectual control and to be more responsive to color as a primary determinant. Rigorous experimentation to test these hypotheses, however, is lacking. The general trends have been supported in some studies of children and adults, but not in others (Beck, Rabin, Thiesen, Molish, and Thetford, 1950; Exner, 1978; Ford, 1946). Furthermore, a factor analytical study of Rorschach responses in normal subjects could find no support for differences between the different types of responses to color (Wishner, 1959).

One other important determinant in the Rorschach Test should also be mentioned because it is closely related to those already indicated. This involves the perception of human movement in the blots. In such responses, the movement perceived is designated the determinant of the response. There are so many hypothetical assumptions made for the movement response that it is difficult to categorize it here. In a broad sense, it is conceived to be indicative of "inner promptings" within the personality and thus is viewed as a balance to color responses, which represent reaction to outer stimulation. According to Rorschach, it is characteristic of people "whose interests gravitate more toward their intrapsychic living rather than toward the world outside them-selves" (Rorschach, 1942, p. 64). Thus, "introversive" patterns are linked with movement responses. In addition, the latter may signify fantasy activity, imagination, originality, and, in part, intelligence. Other hypotheses link the movement activity on the Rorschach with unconscious tendencies, instinctual drives, and wish-fulfillment activities. Once more, however, it can be noted that the varying hypotheses associated with the perception of human move-ment on the Rorschach lack extensive validating support. Furthermore, since the movement response is considered an indicator of many complex aspects of personality, it is more difficult to evaluate than a simple unidimensional variable.

The determinants already discussed, although of basic importance, are only some of the many Rorschach test components. Others include the use of shading, texture, depth, and white space in the subject's response. Moreover, in addition to the more formal scoring categories of the Rorschach, other aspects of the patient's responses are also considered in the total test interpreta-tion. These include the patient's behavior during the testing period, questions of the examiner, handling of the cards, time taken to respond, random com-ments, the type of content offered, and the symbolic references in his responses (Exner, 1978; Holzberg, 1968; Phillips and Smith, 1953; Schafer, 1954). It is obvious, therefore, that this projective method is more difficult to score, interpret, and evaluate than the traditional personality questionnaire. Not only is it difficult to set up experimental situations that adequately test the multitude of hypotheses related to the different Rorschach factors, but in many instances it is exceedingly difficult to delineate precisely the psychological functions underlying each factor. In addition, since each component is best interpreted in relation to other components within the framework of the entire test record, the isolation of variables for systematic study is frequently criticized by propo-nents of the method. This emphasis on the Gestalt qualities of the test is at the same time one of its greatest strengths and most serious limitations.

Over the years there have even developed divergent "schools" of the Ror-schach method with consequent variations in methods of administration, scor-ing, and interpretation (Beck, Beck, Levitt, and Molish, 1961; Exner, 1974; Hertz, 1970a; Klopfer, Ainsworth, Klopfer, and Holt, 1954; Klopfer and David-son, 1962). Thus, there is really no one way to give or interpret the test. The ten test cards, however, are given to the patient in a prescribed sequence with instructions to tell what the cards look like, what they suggest, or what they might be. The test administration consists of two main parts: (1) the free association period, and (2) the inquiry. In the former, the subject's re-sponses to all ten cards are recorded, with no comments or questions by the examiner. All responses, comments, exclamations, and so on, are recorded verbatim by the examiner. In addition, the time taken to produce the first response to each card as well as the total response time are noted.

After the free association period is completed, the inquiry is begun. This entails looking at the cards again to ascertain from the patient which parts of the card he responded to and what factors led him to perceive the blots as he did. The inquiry thus is used to ascertain the *location* and *determinant* of each response. These two factors, plus some designation for the actual content of the response—that is, whether the subject sees a human being, an animal, or an object—constitute the minimum scoring for one response. A fourth scoring element may also be added in those instances where a particular response is considered to be a popular (P) or frequently seen response. Various shorthand symbols have been used to designate these scored elements, and the single responses can then be combined into a psychogram which is a summary of all of the scored responses. These features of the Rorschach Test are illustrated in part in Figs. 2 and 3.

The scoring and interpretation of the Rorschach Test are rather difficult and complex matters. Although there are several scoring guides and manuals available (Beck *et al.*, 1961; Exner, 1974, 1978; Hertz, 1970a; Klopfer and Davidson, 1962), most are not completely adequate for practical purposes. One notes, for example, that identical responses may be scored differently according to the manuals, and that the latter reflect varying frames of reference with regard to scoring procedures. A great many responses also are not included in the present manuals and must be scored subjectively by the examiner. There still exists a need for comprehensive norms for the various subject groups with whom the test is used, although some work has been done in this regard (Ames, Learned, Mitroux, and Walker, 1952, 1954; Ames, Mitroux, and Walker, 1971; Beck, 1968; Beck, Rabin, Thiesen, Molish, and Thetford, 1950; Ford, 1946; Francis-Williams, 1968; Ledivith, 1959). More recently, Exner (1974) has attempted to meet this need by combining several methods of scoring the test and securing some normative data. However, I have some question about the possible variation in the way the data may have been secured and the adequacy of the samples used. In addition, as has been noted, the test interpretation is based on more than the scored elements of the test and thus there is additional room for subjective variation. In this sense, the test is subjective and dependent in great part on the skill, experience, and knowledge of the individual examiner.

Although the initial use of the Rorschach emphasized the analysis of basic personality structure, the client's responses have also been examined for leads concerning related aspects of personality such as attitudes, motives, aspirations, and conflicts. The use of the Rorschach Test as an aid in psychiatric diagnosis also has been one of the reasons for its wide acceptance in clinical work. Numerous investigations have utilized the test with a variety of patient

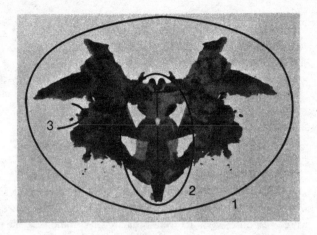

Free Association	Inquiry	Scoring
1. 38″ That reminds me of a butterfly—yes—a large butterfly.	The entire blot (what suggested it?) The way it's shaped—the wings here, the body in the center.	W F+ A P W—Whole blot. F+—Form as a determinant and the quality is good. A—Animal content. P—Popular response.
2. The center part looks like a woman with arms raised.	This part here (points)— The shape of it.	D M+ H D—Normal or common detail. M—Movement response. H—Human content.
3. Hm—a cliff I would say—right here—I guess that's all. 112″.	This part is what I saw as the cliff—the outline— (anything else?)—No.	Dd F— Ls Dd—Rare or unusual detail. F—Form as a determinant and the quality is poor. Ls—Landscape as content.

Figure 2. Card I of the Rorschach Test and three sample responses. From Hans Huber, Publishers, Berne, Switzerland.

R 23

W	6	M	2	H	3	F+%	75
D	15	CF	1	Hd	2	A%	43
Dd	2	FC	2	A	8	P	7
	——	FV	1	Ad	2	M/C	= 2/2
	23	FY	1	An	2	T/1R	= 46″
		F+	12	Bot	2	T/R	= 42″
		F−	4	Ls	2		
			——	Sci	1		
			23	Biol	1		
					——		
					23		

Figure 3. Rorschach Psychogram. The first column of the psychogram summarizes each response in terms of location. For example, out of a total number of 23 responses (R), 6 were whole responses (W), 15 were ordinary or common details (D), and 2 were rare details. The second column is a list of the determinants used and the symbols indicate that 2 of the responses contained human movement (M), 3 included color (CF, FC), one vista or depth (FV), one shading (FY), and 16 were determined by form only (F+, F−). The third column is used to indicate the content of the responses. H and Hd stand for human and human detail responses, respectively, A for animal responses, etc. The fourth column includes ratios, popular responses, and reaction times.

groups and diverse diagnostic criteria have been published. The literature on this topic is too voluminous to be presented here, although a few general observations may be offered.

The values of the Rorschach Test as an aid in diagnosis are related to one's philosophy of diagnosis. Assuming that by means of the Rorschach we can "correctly" classify patients in terms of a given nosology, one may still question the ultimate clinical values derived from this approach. In selected diagnostic problems, however, the Rorschach may have some potential value at a clinical level, for example, in cases of incipient psychosis. Sometimes, the severity of disturbance is not apparent in initial interviews with the patient, and the Rorschach data may provide clues for a more thorough evaluation of the patient. A brief reference to an actual clinical case may serve to illustrate this use of the Rorschach Test.

The patient was hospitalized on a medical ward in a general hospital because of sustained but rather vague complaints about certain parts of his body. All medical and laboratory examinations were essentially negative, revealing no physical basis for these complaints. Consequently, a consultation was requested from the psychiatry service in the hospital. The psychiatrist who examined the patient felt that there was something peculiar about him, but was not able to make a definitive diagnosis. As a result, the patient was referred for psychological examination. He was given the Rorschach along with several other tests.

The responses to the Rorschach Test indicated that the individual had superior intellectual ability, but that definite disorganization of intellectual functioning was present. His perception of reality, as reflected in the form quality of his responses, was decidedly poor and not in keeping with his intellectual level. Furthermore, there were only a few popular responses, which indicated that the patient was not responding to the most commonly perceived stimuli in a manner typical of normal individuals. Along with several rather bizarre responses, this pattern suggested an incipient withdrawal from the world about him. There were also a number of responses where the use of color also suggested a lessening of control over emotional reactions. Several of the responses were exceedingly vague and were seen as an indication of disturbance in the individual's perceptual processes. In addition, there was noted an overpreoccupation with sexual content and rare details which were interpreted as an excessive reliance on obsessive compulsive defenses, although the latter were no longer fully effective. Along with the other data available, these features of the test were suggestive of a developing and potentially serious disintegration of personality in this individual, one which is associated most frequently with an incipient psychotic process. As a result of this clinical appraisal, the patient was transferred to the psychiatric service of the hospital for further study and treatment where he was eventually diagnosed as a case of paranoid schizophrenia. The test data thus were of help in clarifying the underlying features of the individual's personality and in the eventual diagnosis of treatment of the patient.

The Rorschach also has been considered by some clinicians to be of help in differential diagnosis. However, a number of the earlier studies which reported diagnostic signs on the Rorschach for various psychopathological categories (Klopfer & Kelley, 1942) were poorly designed and have not been substantiated by subsequent studies. In addition, the test has also been used as an aid in therapeutic planning. Knowledge of the individual's personality structure is of some value in psychotherapy, and, traditionally, only certain types of relatively well-integrated individuals have been considered as really suitable for intensive psychotherapy. Thus, the kind of patient described in the preceding paragraph would not be judged as a good candidate for intensive psychotherapy and would require a different approach to treatment. The Rorschach has been used also in studies pertaining to prognosis and outcome in psychotherapy, with somewhat conflicting results (Garfield, 1978).

For various reasons, the Rorschach and other projective tests cannot be appraised in traditional ways as easily as other tests (Cronbach, 1949; Anastasi, 1976). Objective and adequately quantified scores are lacking, each card in the test has special qualities, separate components are most meaningfully interpreted in relation to the rest of the test, and there are so many different elements to consider.

Another problem of central importance is at what level validating research should be carried out. Shall such research concern itself only with total or global personality appraisals, or is it more fruitful to work with specific aspects of the test in relation to more specific traits or aspects of personality? If the former approach is used, how rigorous can our experimental design be? If we isolate smaller components for study, can we obtain meaningful results without relating the part to the total unit? There is also the problem of the level of personality at which appraisals can be made. If through the Rorschach one secures data about the individual's inner psychological structure and personality dynamics, with what criteria can these data be compared? Do hidden or repressed motivational systems have to be manifested in behavior? If not, how does one evaluate the correctness of the interpretations made about such aspects of personality? These issues are far from settled but are of decided importance for research on the Rorschach Test (Zubin, Eron, and Schumer, 1965). Actually, many of these problems are not limited to the Rorschach Test, but are of significance for the entire area of personality diagnosis and assessment.

In spite of these difficulties, several attempts have been made to evaluate the reliability and validity of the Rorschach. The methods used in this work have varied from attempts at experimental verification to reports of agreement with other clinical criteria. Much of this work is covered in several past reviews (Ainsworth, 1954; Hertz, 1951, 1970b; Rabin, 1951; Suinn and Oskamp, 1969; Zubin, Eron, and Schumer, 1965) and, only some of the overall findings will be discussed here.

Reliability. Much skepticism has been expressed concerning the application of standard methods of estimating test reliability to the Rorschach. Since the test cards differ, the split-half method is not considered applicable (Cronbach, 1949; Goldfried, Stricker, and Weiner, 1971). The absence of an alternate form precludes this possibility. The test-retest method also has limitations. If the test is readministered after a short interval, recall, practice, and related factors may contribute to spuriously high coefficients. If the time interval is long, actual changes in personality may have occurred which will be reflected on the test and lower the correlation. Finally, there is the problem of how to treat statistically the numerous scoring variables which contribute to the overall test interpretation (Cronbach, 1949). Nevertheless, research with some of these methods has been reported.

Studies utilizing the test-retest approach report somewhat different results for the reliabilities of the test determinants. Ford (1946) secured reliabilities ranging from .38 to .86 for various test components with young children, but the interval between tests was only 1 month. Kagan (1960) in a study over a 6-year period reported low but significant correlations for some Rorschach categories such as human movement and number of responses, but not for human percepts. The median number of responses for most of the categories studied, however, was around zero. One early study (Fosberg, 1938), in which the test was repeated with instructions changed, did not find significant changes in the Rorschach, although others have found the test responses influenced by the situation (Henry and Rotter, 1956; Kimble, 1945).

Studies of projective methods also have compared the reliability of the interpretations offered by different examiners. Some claim that this procedure is more pertinent to the evaluation of projective techniques than are other measures of reliability (Zubin, Eron, and Schumer, 1965), although it is apparent that what is being appraised here is the reliability of the examiner rather than the stability of test factors. Admittedly, information on the former is of value in appraising the extent of subjective factors in Rorschach interpretations. Such studies have shown agreement between examiners for general personality appraisal and for selected scoring categories. Generally, we can expect that individuals trained together will show greater comparability of interpretation than those who adhere to different schools.

There is certainly no simple appraisal possible concerning the complicated matter of reliability as it pertains to a technique like the Rorschach. Although Hertz, an outstanding student of the Rorschach method, stated some years ago that, "by and large, the method is accepted today as satisfactorily objective and reliable" (Hertz, 1943, pp. 70–71), one would not find such a view accepted by all psychologists (Zubin, Eron, and Schumer, 1965). Certainly the problem of reliability in terms of personality is a complex one and traditional conceptions may not be fully adequate. For example, is it reasonable to expect that all aspects of personality will remain stable with the passing of time? If some personality features do change or reflect varying environmental forces and experiences, is it not desirable to try to gauge these changes? If reliability, in the conventional sense of stability, forces us to pay attention only to those factors that are relatively stable, will this limit our appraisal of personality? In other words, is test reliability, as usually defined, a desired characteristic in the appraisal of personality? In many instances, psychologists are interested in appraising even subtle changes in personality as a result of therapy, and an instrument that is sensitive to such change will be preferred over one that is less sensitive. On the other hand, under normal circumstances, we also expect some consistency in the basic features of personality, and thus would expect this consistency to be reflected in our tests. Traditional statistical approaches for appraising reliability, therefore, may not be adequate for appraising projective tests of personality. Perhaps, as Macfarlane and Tuddenham have suggested, "since reliability is implied by validity, it is . . . possible to circumvent the difficulties involved in measuring reliability, provided that one can demonstrate that his test makes possible valid predictions with respect to other variables" (1951, p. 42). Certainly, if it becomes difficult to decide whether a test is unusually sensitive or whether it is merely unreliable, a most important consideration would be how well predictions can be made in relation to criterion variables.

Validity. Some of the general problems already discussed are particularly important with reference to the attempts at validating the Rorschach. How well can one validate a total personality pattern? If the separate components of the Rorschach cannot be studied apart from their relationships, how can one adequately validate the underlying assumptions for the different test factors? If the Rorschach is supposed to provide us with a penetrating analysis of the basic personality structure, with what kinds of criteria shall we evaluate our findings? How much can be generalized about the test apart from the clinical skill of the psychologist? These represent only a few of the many difficulties encountered when one considers carefully the matter of validating the Rorschach.

Many studies have attempted to appraise the Rorschach in terms of how well it helps to differentiate groups classified according to psychiatric diagnosis (Goldfried, Stricker, and Weiner, 1971; Hertz, 1951; Suinn and Oskamp, 1969). While several such reports have indicated a high percentage of agreement between test interpretations and clinical diagnosis, this criterion is necessarily limited and negative results have also been reported (Guilford, 1948; Suinn and Oskamp, 1969; Wittenborn and Holzberg, 1951; Zubin, Eron, and Schumer, 1965). Related studies have compared groups of normals with various groups of abnormal subjects to discover differentiating characteristics in Rorschach patterns. This literature, too, is somewhat equivocal. The technique of matching test protocols with other types of information about subjects has also been employed in the past with both positive (Benton, 1950; Hertz, 1951) and negative results (Newton, 1954). Such studies, particularly those in which behavioral clues are eliminated by "blind" analysis of test data, were seen as providing potential validating data on behalf of the Rorschach. Possible criticisms of these global evaluations of the test are a reliance on criteria that may lack validity, and insufficient attention to the more specific hypotheses underlying the test factors. For example, correct matchings of Rorschach protocols and case history data may occur as the result of one or two unique or outstanding features of personality. But, many of the other descriptions of personality trends secured from the test may be in error or lack verification. The evaluation of the test might be improved if more research were directed at the prediction of behavior in actual situations.

In spite of the criticism made that research on the separate Rorschach components neglects the interaction of these factors and their role in the total personality appraisal, investigations of this type have been made. It is exceedingly difficult to give a condensed account of this research here since it includes many different scoring components and, to be meaningful, would require a more extensive treatment of the test factors than is intended. For our purpose a few examples may give the student an introduction to the problems involved. As mentioned previously, the percentage of good form responses (F + %) is an important factor in the Rorschach Test, being associated with intellectual functioning, perception of reality, and intellectual control. In several studies the F + % has been correlated with intelligence test scores. While practically all such research indicates a positive relationship between the two sets of scores, the coefficients range from around zero to over .60. Some of the studies, it should be noted, included small numbers of subjects and sometimes highly selected ones. The general impression is that F + % on the Rorschach is related positively to intelligence test scores, but that the relationship is a modest one.

Over the years there have been many attempts at appraising different aspects of the Rorschach (Beck and Molish, 1967; Goldfried, Stricker, and Weiner, 1971; Suinn and Oskamp, 1969; Zubin, Eron, and Schumer, 1965). Although some have been largely clinical appraisals of selected subjects in terms of the relationship of Rorschach factors to predicted personality features, others have attempted to employ more refined experimental and statistical procedures. Some have changed the properties of the test cards in order to test selected hypotheses relating to color (Baughman, 1959; Buker and Williams, 1951; Siipola, 1950), and others have been concerned with problems of scoring test responses and with the influence of the examiner on Rorschach protocols (Lord, 1950; Sanders and Cleveland, 1953). Some of the latter studies have indicated that the subjects' responses to the Rorschach cards are influenced to some extent by the personality of the examiner and related variables.

An adequate appraisal of this research cannot be presented here because it would involve some discussion of the methodology employed in the various studies, as well as more extensive information about the variables investigated. However, much of this material is available to the interested reader in other reviews (Ainsworth, 1954; Frank, 1976, 1978; Hertz, 1951; Rabin, 1951; Suinn and Oskamp, 1969; Zubin, Eron and Schumer, 1965). It can be stated, however, that even though the findings are not conclusive, several of the specific hypotheses from the Rorschach have been questioned. The research data on the influence of color on Rorschach responses are illustrative of this point (Baughman, 1958; Benton, 1952; Frank, 1976; Siipola, 1950). Some of the findings strongly suggest that responses thought to be influenced by the color on certain cards are influenced by factors other than color. For example, it had been noted clinically that some subjects reacted differently to the colored than to the achromatic cards. Among the reactions observed were delayed response time, poor form perception, restriction of response, exclamations, and so on. On the basis of these observations, certain hypotheses were advanced concerning the psychological significance of color and its influence on the reactions of the subject. It was hypothesized that certain types of subjects, particularly neurotics, were upset by the colored cards as emotional stimuli and, consequently, were unable to respond as well to them as to the other cards. Subsequently, attempts were made to test some of these hypotheses experimentally. In some studies, two sets of Rorschach cards were adminstered to groups of subjects by projecting the cards on a screen (Benton, 1950). One set was the traditional set while the other was made up of the same cards, but the colored cards were now achromatic. The findings were essentially negative and suggested that some of the reactions previously ascribed to color could be accounted for by the form qualities or complexity of the cards. Another study utilized two sets of cards which were administered individually to schizophrenic patients (Buker and Williams, 1951). One set of cards was the traditional Rorschach set, while the other was a set of achromatic cards. The findings, in general, corroborate those previously mentioned. With the exception of an increase in initial response time, none of the other test variables was affected significantly by the removal of color.

In another study, it was determined that the reactions previously considered to be a response to color were primarily a matter of the congruence of specific colors with the form of the card segment responded to by the subject (Siipola, 1950). In other words, where the color naturally fitted in with the shape of a blot segment, there were no unusual reactions to the color per se. If the color and the shape were incongruous, however, this was a more difficult task for the subject and led to lengthened response time and a somewhat different pattern of response. It thus appears that the influence of color on the Rorschach is not as specific or as simple as previously thought (Baughman, 1958; Benton, 1952). In fact, Frank (1976) in a recent review of the research on this topic finds little support for the presumed relationship between color and affect.

There have been other interesting studies in which Rorschach test data have been used for predictive purposes or for appraising clinical validity. In a large-scale study by Kelly and Fiske (1951), the Rorschach was used as one of the techniques for selecting clinical psychologists. In this investigation, ratings made by well-known clinical psychologists on the basis of Rorschach protocols bore only limited relationship to the criterion ratings, with median correlations ranging from .20 to .33 (Morris, 1952; Samuels, 1952). In another study, nineteen experienced psychologists utilized a group adaptation of the Rorschach to predict which aviation cadets would be successful in flight training and which would be eliminated because of personality disturbance. In general, the overall predictions did not differ significantly from chance (Holtzman and Sells, 1954). One other study compared the ratings of adjustment made by three psychologists experienced in Rorschach procedures with outside criteria of adjustment secured in a developmental study of children. The findings here were also disappointing as far as the Rorschach was concerned, for there was no evidence of a significantly positive relationship between the Rorschach ratings and the criteria measures of adjustment (Grant, Ives, and Ranzoni, 1952).

The preceding paragraphs indicate some of the kinds of research that have been performed on aspects of the Rorschach Test, particularly during the period of its greatest popularity. Several thousand studies now have been reported. Unfortunately, in spite of this massive outpouring of research and clinical reports, many of the findings leave much to be desired, and issues concerning validation still remain. In fact, it is the author's impression, after reviewing a number of volumes that have attempted some appraisal of the research literature on the Rorschach Test, that research on basic aspects of the test has diminished noticeably in the past 15 years or so (Beck and Molish, 1967; Goldfried, Stricker, and Weiner, 1971; Kleinmuntz, 1967; Suinn and Oskamp, 1969; Zubin, Eron, and Schumer, 1965). Most of the studies referred to tend to have been published before 1960. Whether this is due to the conflicting findings reported earlier, which may have discouraged other investigators from pursuing such lines of inquiry, or whether it is a more general reflection of the decline in involvement with diagnostic testing, is difficult to say. Several reviewers in the *Seventh Mental Measurements Year-book* (Buros, 1972), however, reported similar impressions. Rabin (1972) stated that "There can be little doubt that research productivity with the Rorschach method has dropped off in recent years." Knutson (1972) also commented on the decline in the use of the Rorschach in research and predicted "that Rorschach use will follow a gradual but accelerating decline in the next decade." Data consistent with these pronouncements were reported in a study by Crenshaw, Bohn, Hoffman, Matheus, and Offenbach (1968) of the research use of projective methods from 1947 to 1965. Their findings show that the use of projective methods as a group peaked in the year 1955, dropped sharply in 1956 and 1957, and remained rather stable through 1965. In the case of the Rorschach, a peak of eighty-six citations in the journals studies was reached in 1954 and then dropped noticeably to a low of twenty citations in 1961.

Nevertheless, in spite of this diminished research interest in the Rorschach, it continues to be used to some extent in a variety of investigations and it remains a popular technique in clinical and internship settings (Lubin *et al.,* 1971; Wade and Baker, 1977). In a survey of directors of training in APA approved internship centers, for example, the Rorschach was considered as a "very important" technique by 86% of the respondents (McCully, 1965).

In a comparable survey, conducted a few years later, the Rorschach was designated as the most emphasized psychological test in internship training (Garfield & Kurtz, 1973). On the other hand, studies of university training faculty indicate that the latter hold a more critical or negative view toward instruction on the Rorschach (Jackson and Wohl, 1966; Thelen, Varble, and Johnson, 1968), and that there is a lessened emphasis on training in projective techniques in general.

Somewhat contrasting views of the Rorschach are also expressed in the two reviews of the test in the latest issue of the Mental Measurements Yearbook (Buros, 1978). While noting the more questioning and limiting view of the Rorschach evident in recent years, Dana (1978) points to the use of the Rorschach as a source of information, or structured interview, and to the increased sophistication in research. Peterson (1978), however, although noting that the test is still widely used, feels that the test's lack of predictive validity raises "serious question about its continued use in clinical practice" (p. 1045).

Before concluding this discussion of the Rorschach, it can be pointed out that one serious attempt has been made to develop and standardize a more psychometrically sound version of an inkblot test. This is the Holtzman Inkblot Technique (Holtzman, Thorpe, Swartz, and Herron, 1961) which consists of two forms of 45 inkblots each. In contrast to the Rorschach, the subject is limited to one response per card and the inquiry is conducted after the response is given. A limited number of major variables were selected for scoring, such as, Location, Form Appropriateness, Color, Shading, Movement, and Form Definiteness. Thus, while attempts were made to tap and evaluate some of the major variables utilized with the Rorschach Test, the test procedures and standardization were more rigorously controlled and followed the more conventional procedures for test construction than was true for the Rorschach. Clearer scoring guides and normative data were also provided.

Although the Holtzman Inkblot Technique was developed to overcome some of the psychometric limitations of the Rorschach, it has not received a very wide acceptance on the part of clinical psychologists. In a survey of psychological test usage in 487 clinical settings, the Holtzman was used frequently in only one center and in no instance was it used in a majority of the cases seen. In contrast, the Rorschach was used frequently in 62 centers and with a majority of the cases seen in an additional 88 centers (Lubin, Wallis, and Paine, 1971). Whether this reflects the views of clinical psychologists toward the relative merit of these two techniques or whether it reflects the rigidity of practice and training in this field is difficult to say. One might also speculate that those clinical psychologists who are attracted to the Rorschach test are not swayed by psychometric considerations or research findings. Although the research on the Holtzman Inkblot Technique is quite limited as compared with that of the Rorschach, one review of the literature (Gamble, 1972), as well as a response to that review, have been published (Swartz, 1973).

THEMATIC APPERCEPTION TEST (TAT)

Another widely used projective test is the TAT. It consists of 29 pictures and one blank card, from which four different combinations of 19 pictures and the blank card are provided for separate administration to adult males and females and boys and girls. Most of the pictures are of human subjects and vary in terms of how clearly the activity or mood of the characters are portrayed. The test materials are at least partially structured, although there is enough latitude to allow for varying individual interpretations. The client is asked to make up a story about each of the pictures, describing what is taking place, the antecedent events, how the people are thinking and feeling, and how the story ends. It is assumed, of course, that the client will project aspects of his own personality into his stories and identify in varying degrees with some of the characters portrayed.

To illustrate the type of material secured from the TAT, several stories made up by different patients for the same card are given below. The reader will note some of the individual patterns in the stories, even though they are in response to the same card. The stories were based on Card 4, which is described in the test manual as follows: "A woman is clutching the shoulders of a man whose face and body are averted as if he were trying to pull away from her" (Murray, 1943a). In the background of this card there is also a picture of a somewhat scantily clad woman.

> Looks as though a mirror there. Torn between two things—two women. One upright trying to keep him from other—on bed naked. Fellow in bedroom with two women. One is sort of prostitute. Doesn't seem to be married to either one. Seems to be going berserk, on verge of it—eyes dilated. One girl pleading with him—other is trying to entice him. He is leaning toward bed. (*How does it end?*) I wouldn't say—undecided.

> He's a criminal—just escaped. This is his wife. Convicted of something he didn't do. Is very apprehensive here. Came to tell her something—can't stay—has to get out. She's pleading with him to go back to authorities, he doesn't hear her. How it ends, I don't know. He disappears, never hears from him again.

> I was struck with extreme harshness of this individual—but now something about his eyes a little blank. Of course the woman obviously loves him very much. He's indifferent to her. Boy, am I telling about myself! But he doesn't want to hurt her feelings, but if they ever got together they'd make mad passionate love, then he'd leave her. Those are the grounds on which he'd be with her and he's tried to tell her that only on those grounds

would he go with her. But he's afraid of her tenacity and isn't particularly attracted by her. (*Turn out?*) He hurts her feelings and walks away, but he's slightly haunted by it. You can see that haunted look in his face already.

Looks like a scene that started out to be a happy married couple and something was told to them that maybe wasn't the truth, caused a misunderstanding, and made them unhappy. Looks like she's trying to explain to him what is up. (*Q*) He was told this and she's trying to explain that it wasn't true. In the end they separate.

He's definitely very angry—angry enough to kill. She seems to be pleading with him. So far as I can see there must be a woman involved because of this portrait—a woman of evil, low cut dress, legs crossed. The fact that this woman has eyebrows like this and a low cut dress shows she isn't of the highest type. He's longing to tear away from her, but by the look in her eyes she would knife him if he turned his back. He looks like the type who goes with other women. His eyes are the most terrifying part of the picture, aren't they? "Let me alone," he says; then he tears away and she throws a knife into his back.

It is apparent that the stories created by these five male patients in response to the same card differ considerably. Furthermore, some individual manifestations of personality appear to be evident in these creations. Although no detailed analysis of these stories will be attempted, a few comments may be offered for purposes of illustrating how some of the more obvious individual personality trends can be inferred from the stories.

In the first story, there appears to be some conflict within the man concerning his relationship to the two women mentioned. The picture of the scantily clad woman is perceived as a prostitute who is trying to entice the man. The latter is unable to make any decision or act and appears on the verge of some kind of breakdown. Whether or not the two women symbolize the "good" and "bad" aspects of sexuality is not certain. But, some conflict and indecision in this area are suggested.

In the second story the picture of the second woman is not utilized. The man is a criminal and is apprehensive about his escape. He does not respond to the pleading of the woman, however, and disappears. Although certain elements of the story may have personal significance in suggesting guilt over past misdeeds, it is also likely that the plot comes from a Class B movie. One would have to look to the other stories given by this subject for additional information.

The third story is quite different from the preceding two. In this one, probably the outstanding pattern concerns the male's attitude toward women. There is expressed some indifference to women, a view of women as merely necessary for satisfying man's needs, a fear of close relationship, and some guilt about these attitudes. The pattern suggests definite difficulties in heterosexual adjustment. (The individual who gave this story actually did reveal very significant features of his own personality on the test and has some awareness of this.)

The fourth story does not appear as revealing as the preceding one. There is mentioned the husband's distrust of the wife on the basis of gossip. The man refuses to listen to his wife and a separation occurs. The significance of this story, with its theme of distrust, also has to be evaluated in terms of a rather stereotyped plot and the somewhat structured character of the picture.

The last story in the group is, in many ways, the most unusual or atypical. Here we have material that is peculiar and bizarre. The emotions expressed are also much stronger than is usually encountered. The man, for example, is seen as angry enough to kill, and the woman has a similar look in her eyes. The other woman is characterized as "evil," and the story is concluded with a violent act. Furthermore, the latter is not at all suggested by the picture. Not only is there a definite suspicious and paranoid flavor to the story, but all persons seem to be characterized rigidly in terms of evil and violence. The story is thus strongly suggestive of a serious paranoid personality. Together with other aspects of the story, one might also infer strong conflicts in heterosexual adjustment and possible symbolic or unconscious concern with homosexual strivings.

The instructions for the TAT state that it should be given in two parts separated by at least one day. But, in clinical practice most psychologists administer the test in one setting and use only a selected number of cards. In most instances, the examiner attempts to record, by hand, the stories, comments, and behavior of the subject. This is a difficult undertaking, even when the examiner has worked out some form of personal shorthand. Consequently, some use of sound recording equipment has been made and some psychologists have also had their subjects write out their own stories. In the latter instance, the stories appear to be reduced in length and descriptive richness.

The test was first introduced by Morgan and Murray in 1935 as a means of investigating fantasies (Morgan and Murray, 1935). In addition to general instructions for administration, a means of analyzing the test stories was offered by Murray based on theoretical views of personality developed by him (Murray et al., 1938; Murray, 1943a). Since that time there have been several different interpretive and scoring schemes proffered by others (Aron, 1949; Dana, 1956; Henry, 1956). Many clinicians in actual practice, however, do not follow any prescribed or systematic procedure in analyzing TAT stories. Particular attention may be paid to the frequency or uniqueness of particular themes, to the degree of affect evident in the stories, to omissions or distortions of figures in the card, and similar kinds of material.

Although there are diverse methods of analyzing and using TAT material, some of the general features of the test may be discussed. As noted, the TAT is used to secure fantasy material, and the subject can create a story in any way that he wishes, using the picture as a starting point. It is assumed that the subject will identify with some of the figures in the picture and will associate some of them with important persons in his own life. Aspirations, motives, conflicts, attitudes, and similar aspects of personality can be inferred from the content of the subject's stories. Are the "heroes" of the stories constantly seeking wealth and fame, or are they always in need of advice and succor from others? Are the female figures usually seen as threatening people, or as a means of gratification? Are the stories realistic, is there a strong element of indecision in many stories, must the central character always give in to the demands of others? Such patterns can be noted in the subject's stories for purposes of personality evaluation.

The matter of securing an integrated picture of the individual's motives, conflicts, attitudes, and patterns of reaction is not as simple as might be inferred from the preceding questions. For example, with which character is the subject identifying? Which material is actually of personal significance and which can be viewed as culturally determined responses of a stereotyped nature? Which stories reflect the patient's fantasies and which his actual tendencies or behavior? How can one distinguish the repressed from the overt levels of personality? How does one evaluate the actual significance or depth of the patterns noted in the TAT stories? How far can one go in interpreting the stories as symbolic manifestations of personality conflicts?

Securing adequate answers to such questions is not a simple task although a certain amount of research has been done in seeking answers to some of them. In an important longitudinal study, Skolnick (1966) attempted to appraise the relationship between fantasy imagery reflected in TAT stories and actual overt behavior. In general, it was not possible to make any definitive statement between TAT fantasy and behavior that would hold true for all motives, ages, and both sexes, although the predominant effect appeared to be direct rather than inverse.

In addition to the problems listed above, there are the related problems of standardization, norms, reliability, and validity. Thus far there have been only a few sporadic attempts at securing various types of normative data. A few studies have evaluated the frequency of occurrence of different themes, designation of characters, and the predominant mood of the stories (Eron, 1948, 1950, 1953; Garfield and Eron, 1948; Rosenzweig, 1949; Rosenzweig and Fleming, 1949). The classification of themes in some investigations has been quite broad, and important individual variations may be hidden by the overly general classifications. Nevertheless, such material is necessary in order to provide a more objective frame of reference for test interpretation. Some studies of the mood of TAT stories, for example, have indicated a close relationship between this attribute and the structural qualities of the test pictures. Certainly one must understand the stimulus values of each of the test cards before he can adequately interpret the TAT stories.

Reliability and Validity. Many of the problems in this area are similar to those already discussed in terms of the Rorschach, although the lack of an accepted and complex scoring method leaves fewer specific hypotheses to be tested. Although some tentative scoring schemes have been brought forth, most psychologists have not used them in their regular clinical work. Rather, interpretations of test data have been made on the basis of general projective hypotheses, the clinical reports of some investigators, and the specific theoretical orientation and experience of the individual psychologist. Thus, even more than the Rorschach, the TAT is a "clinical" instrument whose validity in the testing situation is dependent primarily upon the individual examiner.

Much of the research on the reliability and validity of the TAT also resembles that reported for the Rorschach. Useful reviews of such work are available and our comments will be brief (Buros, 1965, 1972; Harrison, 1965; Murstein, 1963; Zubin, Eron, and Schumer, 1965). Studies of reliability have emphasized the degree of correspondence between the interpretations of different examiners. Although agreement has been high, there have been important individual variations. One study (Combs, 1946) evaluated the consistency of interpretations of the same examiner on the same test data after a 6-month interval. The obtained finding of 68% agreement is comparable to the agreement reported between different examiners (Harrison, 1965). There has been comparatively little work on retesting subjects with the TAT (Skolnick, 1966), and the problem is complicated by the methods of analysis to be used as well as the specific time interval. The reliability of the test, therefore, has been based primarily on the agreement reached between different examiners. Obviously, when the examiners are trained in similar methods of interpretation, the agreement will be higher than might otherwise be the case (Kleinmuntz, 1967).

Only a few statements will be made concerning the attempts at validating the test. Clinical studies have compared TAT interpretations with case history data and psychiatric diagnosis and the results have been contradictory (Eron, 1950; Foulds, 1953; Shneidman and Farberow, 1958). In one study in which clinicians were asked to distinguish between "stable" and "disturbed" boys on the basis of TAT protocols, a large majority of the "stable" boys were classified as "disturbed" (Cox and Sargent, 1950). Most of the studies, however, have not been cross-validated. There have also been some experimental studies of the projective hypothesis as manifested in the TAT (Feshback, 1955; Murray, 1943b). Such studies have shown that experimentally induced aggression and fears were reflected in TAT stories, although they were more easily produced in response to some pictures than others. Lindzey (1952) has also appraised some of the logical considerations and empirical evidence bearing on basic assumptions of TAT interpretation. In general, while there is some support for many of the assumptions upon which interpretations are based, there is still need for more explicit information about the specific conditions under which the various TAT assumptions are applicable.

> For example: what are the means by which the important story in a series can be determined? How can we determine whether or not a given fantasy impulse will receive overt expression? In what way do we determine whether or not a given response has been determined by the stimulus material? What are the circumstances under which symbolic transformations must be engaged in? How do we determine the empirical referent of a given symbol? Answers to these and a host of related questions are necessary before we can hope to provide the TAT user with an explicit, repeatable set of operations for inferring motivational states. (Lindzey, 1952, pp. 20–21)

The status of research on the TAT is thus comparable in several respects to that on the Rorschach. We may state that there is some evidence, largely clinical, in support of the reliability and validity of the test, although negative results have also been reported (Eron, 1972; Harrison, 1965; Kleinmuntz, 1967). Although somewhat less popular than the Rorschach, over 2000 publications dealing in some fashion with the TAT have been published (Buros, 1978). It is also rather "amazing that (the) TAT, introduced over 40 years ago, still can be sold with the original 20-page manual, a publication that gives no data whatsoever on validity" (Swartz, 1978, p. 1127). This is an interesting commentary from a recent review of the test. However, the reviewer, in a manner that may be shared by other clinical psychologists, appears quite ambivalent in his appraisal. Although he wonders "about the ultimate usefulness of an instrument that yields such mixed results after 40 years of investigation," he concludes that current research activity "does appear to indicate that, despite its shortcomings, TAT remains a viable assessment tool" (Swartz, 1978, p. 1130). One's own view of assessment will undoubtedly influence one's perception and evaluation of the test.

OTHER PROJECTIVE TESTS

The marked interest in projective methods in past years led for awhile to various attempts at devising new techniques for appraising personality. This expansion of projective approaches was reminiscent of the tremendous spurt in the testing movement after World War I. This enthusiasm, however, has diminished noticeably, and at present, only a few projective techniques besides the Rorschach and TAT are used to any extent.

One technique that has had steady usage is the sentence completion test

(Rhode, 1946; Rotter and Rafferty, 1950; Stein, 1947). This entails the use of a number of incomplete sentences which the subject is to complete with whatever thoughts come to his mind. The following are typical of the kinds of items found in most sentence completion tests:

1. When I was young . . . .
2. I sometimes feel . . . .
3. My mother . . . .
4. Compared to others, I . . . .
5. Most people . . . .
6. When by myself . . . .
7. Women are . . . .
8. One's fellow workers . . . .

The incomplete sentences are usually selected to cover certain areas of importance in understanding the individual, for example, attitudes toward self and others, family relations, aspirations, and sexual adjustment. Although the client is free to respond in any way that he chooses, he is able to distort his responses and thus present himself in either a favorable or unfavorable light. This criticism is the same as that already made of personality questionnaires. But, because the clinician usually analyzes each response, he is more readily aware of patterns that appear extreme, and can therefore try to interpret such patterns in the light of other data. Research on this technique has been complicated by the appearance of many different sentence completion tests, each with different items, different norms, and different scoring criteria. In recent years, however, the form prepared by Rotter (1950) appears to be the most widely used.

One other projective method also deserves some special mention because of its great popularity—the Draw-A-Person or Figure Drawing Test. Machover (1949) and Hammer (1958) are among those who have helped to popularize this method. Buck (1948) extended the procedure with his House-Tree-Person Test.

Undoubtedly, the extensive use of the Draw-A-Person Test is related to the simplicity of the task, its brevity, and to the fact that many clinicians believe it contributes something of value. Like the other projective techniques, the Draw-A-Person Test has its devotees and its critics. The former believe the test provides clinical leads concerning personality dynamics through the judicious interpretation of the many different clues contained in any freehand drawing. Among the features noted in appraising figure drawings are the sex of the person drawn first, the size of the figure, its location on the paper, facial expression, shading, particular or unusual features concerning various facial or body parts, clothing, and the like. A variety of hypotheses and interpretations can be generated from figure drawings ranging from the subject's self-concept to latent homosexual strivings and paranoid aggression. The literature on this technique, however, has mainly produced conflicting or negative findings. In the first comprehensive review, Swensen (1957) cast considerable doubt on the value of the method for personality appraisal. Since then there have been at least two additional reviews, one by Swensen (1968) and one by Roback (1968). Although Swensen in his later review stated that the quality of research with figure drawings had improved since his earlier review, questions concerning the validity of inferences derived from the test still remain. The question of the importance of artistic or drawing ability in relation to clinical judgments of personality remains unanswered. Swensen also concluded that except for global ratings, the interpretation of specific structural and content variables on the Draw-A-Person Test "have reliabilities that are too low for making reasonably reliable clinical judgments" (1968, p. 40). Roback (1968) was even more critical. He concluded that most of the studies reviewed "generally failed to support Machover's hypotheses," and he also criticized the quality of the research studies.

Projective techniques thus have had a rather interesting development in clinical psychology. After a somewhat slow acceptance prior to World War II, these techniques were quite warmly received in the postwar period. They have been used extensively and to a great extent were identified with the postwar professional development in clinical psychology. In more recent years, however, a much more critical attitude has been manifested toward these techniques, and many of the assumptions that were more or less accepted previously have gradually come to be viewed as hypotheses that need to be tested. Although the views and opinions of clinical psychologists on projective techniques vary widely, there is a greater recognition today of the need for systematic formulation of the hypotheses related to these tests and their validation. Even though projective techniques have held much appeal for clinicians, their worth eventually must be appraised in terms of well-conducted studies that take into consideration the special problems posed by these techniques. For a variety of reasons, the involvement with projective techniques, as with the broader function of diagnostic testing in general, has diminished over the past decade.

It is apparent that the various techniques reviewed emphasize different aspects of personality and are manifestations of different theoretical conceptions of personality appraisal. The choice of techniques thus will depend upon the purpose to be served by them, the setting in which they are used, and the experience and predilections of the examiner. Personality questionnaires, probably used more widely than any other technique in the past, appear somewhat limited in terms of individual diagnostic appraisal. Although they may give one a picture of how the client views himself, they are susceptible to possible distortion by the client. In general, they have been developed to appraise overall adjustment, to measure generalized personality traits, or to categorize the patient in terms of a particular nosology. Within the framework of understanding the total individual personality, each of the above falls a bit short of the goal, although the use of profile analysis has enhanced their potential utility in this regard. Such tests, however, can be of some value in comparing groups of subjects, as screening procedures, and in research.

Projective techniques originally appeared to have the greatest potentiality for helping us to understand the total personality, the interaction of various drives and motives, and the aspirations and conflicts of the individual. They are less subject to manipulation or distortion by the subject, but depend greatly on the skill of the examiner. With all their promise, however, basic problems of validity and reliability have not been conclusively answered and, despite some recent contributions (Exner, 1974, 1978), there are comparatively little adequate normative data. Evident also is an overemphasis on psychopathology in personality appraisals based on projective techniques. The multitude of hypotheses advanced with the techniques still await rigorous verification. Although enthusiastically used, they leave us with many questions to be answered. Also, as a greater emphasis on behavior and the social environment has emerged with correspondingly less emphasis on internal psychodynamic formulations, there has appeared to be a diminished reliance on projective techniques.

Thus, there are no perfect instruments for evaluating personality. The tests at hand are being used in a variety of ways and in time may be improved or supplanted by others. They are products and manifestations of the present level of development in clinical psychology. Further advancement will depend upon progress in our theories and conceptual knowledge. This is perhaps of more crucial importance in the area of personality than in any other. Such problems as the consistency of personality and the generality or specificity of personality patterns crop up in our discussions of all types of personality tests because they are theoretical problems that are still unresolved. As we increase our knowledge of personality, we shall probably improve the quality of our diagnostic techniques.

SOME CONCLUDING COMMENTS

We have now reviewed a number of tests that are used by clinical psychologists in the diagnosis and assessment of clinical problems. The specific techniques used by particular psychologists, and the frequency of their use, will, of course, vary, depending upon the clinical setting, the type of referral problem presented, and the theoretical orientation and predilections of the individual psychologist. Nevertheless, over the past 20 years there has been evident a clear preference among clinical psychologists for using certain specified tests and most of these have been described in the preceding pages (Sundberg, 1961; Lubin et al., 1971; Wade & Baker, 1977). In many instances several of these tests have been used as a battery for the appraisal of patients referred for psychological evaluations. For adult patients, these have included the Rorschach, TAT, WAIS, Human Figure Drawings, Bender-Gestalt, MMPI, and, perhaps, a sentence completion test. Where the question of brain damage has been raised, tests of memory, mental impairment, or concept formation may also be included. In the case of children, appropriate substitutions are made [for example, WISC-R, Children's Apperception Test (Haworth, 1966)], and some other tests added. For example, children who have personality or behavioral problems frequently also have academic or school difficulties. In such instances, the psychologist may also want to administer some educational achievement or diagnostic tests.

Even though a number of negative or critical findings have been reported on some of these tests, and although there has been something of a decline in the extent to which diagnostic testing has been utilized in recent years, the reliance on these popular tests has continued.

The pattern described above is an interesting one and one for which the explanation is probably complex. Undoubtedly, part of the reason for this pattern of test usage is related to the diagnostic training that students receive in both their university programs and in their internship training. Instruction is generally provided on the more popular diagnostic techniques and the assumption is implicit that all clinical psychologists need to be familiar with these techniques. Thus, students receive both didactic and practicum training with these procedures. Therefore, it is not surprising that they will also tend to use the same instruments when they are called upon to perform diagnostic or assessment functions.

Another possible reason for the relative concentration on these tests is that they have been given to a wide variety of patients and various diagnostic patterns have been reported for these groups of patients. Thus, there is the belief that, with a few exceptions, the common battery can be used with most of the patients seen in clinical settings. In a similar vein, there appears to be the belief that a particular battery can be used to help answer a variety of referral problems. The opposite approach, of course, would be to select particular techniques in the light of the specific problems presented by a particular client (Gathercole, 1968; Jones, 1961). The latter approach appears to be used more frequently by British psychologists than is the case with American psychologists.

Before concluding our discussion of diagnostic testing and assessment, some comments on a related aspect of this activity seem in order. Throughout this section of the book, a number of comments have been made concerning the use and interpretation of tests in clinical practice despite the fact that negative or critical findings have been reported in the literature. One may reasonably ask why clinical psychologists, who have been largely trained as scientists-practitioners, continue to use rather faulty instruments. This is a knotty, complex, and emotional issue in psychology, but it is worth examining some of the possible explanations.

There are several potential hypotheses that appear tenable as possible explanations for this situation, and these can be mentioned briefly. One seemingly reasonable explanation is that clinicians are reluctant to give up the techniques that they learned to use during their university and internship training. Having expended considerable time and effort in mastering these techniques, these psychologists are not about to discard them easily. One can readily understand and empathize with such a view.

A second possible hypothesis is that practicing clinicians do not keep up with the research literature, and thus, consciously or otherwise, avoid contact with the results of critical studies. In this instance, they are simply uninformed. A related view is that probably a majority of clinicians are more interested in reading about how to use and interpret clinical techniques than they are in reading critical studies that cast some doubt on the validity of these techniques. Another hypothesis takes note of the individual clinician's ability to effectively dissociate himself from findings of a negative nature. This process, speculatively, may go something like this: Negative findings are based on various samples of clinical psychologists. Some are made up of students in training who are not yet fully proficient in the use of clinical techniques; some are composed of mediocre clinicians, and some cover the whole range of clinical ability. In fact, a few studies have indicated that experienced clinicians as a group were unable to make predictions or judgments which were better than chance, but they have also indicated that a few clinicians did function at a better than chance level (Chambers & Hamlin, 1957; Holtzman & Sells, 1954). Thus, there are poor, mediocre, and good clinicians. The latter obviously are under-represented but they have the ability to secure valid results. Consequently, it is possible for some clinical psychologists to reason as follows: "I am a good clinician; therefore, the negative results do not apply to me." Obviously, this is a speculative interpretation of a process that some clinical psychologists may engage in to resolve the dissonance between their own beliefs and the conflicting findings reported by others.

There are also some other aspects to this problem about which one can speculate. From time to time one examines a patient and the test findings appear to be unusually revealing and worthwhile. It is possible that such instances make a deep impression on the clinician and their effect may be similar to that of intermittent reinforcement. That is, such highly rewarded or "peak" experiences tend to be vividly remembered whereas the more frequent and less spectacular instances of disconfirmation may have less impact. Although instances in which tests are accurately predictive or unusually informative may be in the minority, they tend to convince the clinician of the adequacy of his efforts regardless of other data. This type of interpretation has some apparent support in the findings of one study that many clinicians pay little attention to negative research data "because their opinions of a test's value derive principally from their personal experience with that test" (Wade & Baker, 1977, p. 879). Another possible explanation is that the kinds of interpretations offered by clinical psychologists are couched frequently in language that is not denotative and hence is virtually impossible to validate, or in descriptive terms that are so general they apply to practically everyone (Marks & Seeman, 1962). Consequently, validation or negative feedback is essentially avoided.

Finally, there is the possibility of *illusory correlation,* which has been suggested by Chapman (1967) and which has been studied by means of some interesting experiments (Chapman & Chapman, 1967, 1969). Illusory correlations appear to be based on a systematic error in reports of observations of supposed correlation between the occurrences of two classes of events. In actuality, however, the two classes of events are not correlated, are correlated to a lesser extent than reported, or are correlated in a direction opposite to that which has been reported. A brief summary of one of the studies by the Chapmans may illustrate what is involved here.

In this study (Chapman & Chapman, 1969), certain responses from the Rorschach Test judged to be associated with homosexuality were investigated. The study was organized around the twenty Rorschach signs reported by Wheeler (1949) for male homosexuality. First, a questionnaire was sent to a number of practicing clinical psychologists concerning their own experience in examining individuals with homosexual problems and asking them to list the kind of Rorschach content they had observed with these cases. Replies were received from 32 clinicians who reported a mean of 9.1 years of psychodiagnostic experience. A tabulation of the responses of these clinicians indicated that the five Wheeler-Rorschach signs listed most frequently were signs which had not received confirmation from research. On the other hand, only two clinicians listed one of the two Wheeler signs that have received some research support.

The next part of the study was an attempt to test an hypothesis derived from a previous investigation (Chapman and Chapman, 1967). This hypothesis was that the popularity of the "invalid" signs of homosexuality is based on verbal associative connection of the test signs to the symptom, rather than on valid clinical observations. For example, certain signs on the Rorschach, such as "buttocks" or "sexual organs," might be viewed as signs of homosexuality because of their obvious verbal associative connection with sexual matters than because they have actually been found to identify consistently cases with homosexual problems. To test this hypothesis a group of undergraduates were asked to rate the strength of associative connection between homosexuality and a number of items. The latter included the popular "invalid" signs, the two valid signs, and two neutral filler items. The results showed the "invalid" signs were rated significantly higher than the unpopular valid signs or the filler items by these subjects, and the findings were judged as supporting the hypothesis.

The authors then designed three laboratory studies "to determine whether naive observers, presented with contrived statements of patients' symptoms and their Rorschach responses, would make the same errors of observation that the clinicians appear to have made in their observational reports" (p. 274). Since these individual experiments are too detailed to be related here, only the general nature of the experiments and the major findings obtained will be presented.

A total of 693 undergraduates were tested in groups ranging from 37 to 66 under 13 conditions. Each group viewed thirty Rorschach cards on each of which was designated a patient's response and his two alleged symptoms or emotional problems. In one experiment thirty percepts were shown so that six fell into each of five categories: (1) One "invalid" sign; (2) and (3), the two valid signs; and (4) and (5), two filler items (a geographical feature or an item of food). The results in general supported the prediction significantly for four of the five illusory correlates. In another experiment in this series, the clinically valid signs were actually presented more frequently in association with the symptom statement of homosexuality than were the "invalid" ones, yet the latter were more frequently selected by the subjects than were the valid signs.

This series of experiments was interpreted by the authors as showing a marked similarity between the reports of clinicians concerning their own observations in clinical work and those of the naive observers in the contrived experimental situations. In essence, both groups ignored relatively valid signs, but selected relatively invalid ones that had a strong verbal associative connection to the symptom of homosexuality. "One of the most striking findings of these studies is the persistence of illusory correlation in the face of contradictory reality. Even in the two conditions in which all of the percepts of the two valid signs were paired with homosexuality, these two valid signs were reported as correlates of the symptom less often than the associatively based invalid signs" (Chapman and Chapman, 1969, p. 280). Whether or not illusory correlation can adequately explain some of the discrepancy between clinically held views and the results of research findings in diagnostic testing remains an open question. It is a provocative hypothesis and has stimulated some research, most of which has tended to support the hypothesis (Golding & Rorer, 1972; Kurtz & Garfield, 1978).

Because of emotional involvement, personal attitudes, and similar considerations, it is indeed difficult to resolve some of the controversies and contradictions in this as well as other areas of clinical psychology. There does appear to be a definite difference in the points of view held by university based psychologists and those in the field (Garfield and Kurtz, 1973; Thelen, Varble, & Johnson 1968), with the former having the more critical view. For a variety of reasons, as commented upon earlier, the emphasis on diagnostic testing has diminished and perhaps with it a lessening of the importance attached to the matter of diagnosis and assessment in general. This, in the author's opinion, would be a rather premature state of affairs. If our diagnostic techniques and conceptual systems are faulty, then clearly we need to develop better ones. To do away with assessment would imply that either treatment does not depend on the particular condition of the client or that we have only one treatment for all cases. Neither of these situations seems tenable or desirable, and the technical skills of psychologists seem potentially adequate to the task of improving our techniques and approaches in the assessment area. In the meantime, the techniques at hand must be used with awareness of their strengths and limitations.

REFERENCES

Allport, G. W. Personality. A psychological interpretation. New York: Henry Holt, 1937.

Allport, G. W. Pattern and growth in personality. New York: Holt, Rinehart and Winston, 1961.

Ainsworth, M. D. Problems in validation. In B. Klopfer, M. D., Ainsworth, W. G. Klopfer, and R. R. Holt (Eds.), Developments in the Rorschach technique. Vol. 1. Yonkers, NY: World Book Company, 1954.

Ames, L. B., Learned, J., Mitroux, R. W., & Walker, R. N. Child Rorschach responses. New York: Paul B. Hoeber, 1952.

Ames, L. B., Learned, J., Mitroux, R. W., & Walker, R. N. Rorschach responses in old age. New York: Paul B. Hoeber, 1954.

Ames, L. B., Mitroux, R. W., & Walker, R. N. Adolescent Rorschach responses. Developmental trends from ten to sixteen years. New York: Brunner-Mazel, 1971.

Anastasi, A. Psychological Testing. (4th ed.). New York: Macmillan, 1976.

Aron, B. A manual for analysis of the Thematic Apperception Test. Berkeley, CA: Willis E. Berg, 1949.

Bass, B. M. Authoritarianism or acquiescence? Journal of Abnormal and Social Psychology, 1955, 51, 616–623.

Baughman, E. E. The role of the stimulus in Rorschach responses. Psychological Bulletin, 1958, 55, 121–147.

Baughman, E. E. An experimental analysis of the relationship between stimulus structure and behavior in the Rorschach. *Journal of Projective Techniques,* 1959, *23,* 134–183.

Beck, S. J. Reality, Rorschach and perceptual theory. In A. I. Rabin (Ed.), *Projective techniques in personality assessment.* New York: Springer, 1968.

Beck, S. J., & Molish, H. B. *Rorschach's Test II. A variety of personality pictures.* (2nd ed.). New York: Grune & Stratton, 1967.

Beck, S. J., Rabin, A. I., Thiesen, J. W., Molish, H., & Thetford, W. N. The normal personality as projected in the Rorschach Test. *Journal of Psychology,* 1950, *30,* 241–298.

Beck, S. J., Beck, A. G., Levitt, E. E., & Molish, H. B. *Rorschach's test: I. Basic processes.* (3rd Rev. ed.). New York: Grune & Stratton, 1961.

Benton, A. L. The MMPI in clinical practice. *Journal of Nervous and Mental Disease,* 1945, *102,* 416–420.

Benton, A. L. The experimental validation of the Rorschach Test. *British Journal of Medical Psychology,* 1950, *23,* 45–58.

Benton, A. L. The experimental validation of the Rorschach test. II. The significance of Rorschach color responses. *American Journal of Orthopsychiatry,* 1952, *22,* 755–763.

Benton, A. L., & Probst, K. A. A comparison of psychiatric ratings with MMPI scores. *Journal of Abnormal and Social Psychology,* 1946, *41,* 75–78.

Block, J. *The challenge of response sets.* New York: Appleton-Century-Crofts, 1965.

Buck, J. N. The H-T-P technique, a qualitative and quantitative scoring method. *Journal of Clinical Psychology Monograph,* 1948, *5,* 1–120.

Buker, S. L., & Williams, M. Color as a determinant of responsiveness to Rorschach cards in schizophrenia. *Journal of Consulting Psychology,* 1951, *15,* 196–202.

Buros, O. K. (Ed.), *The sixth mental measurements yearbook.* Highland Park, NJ: Gryphon Press, 1965.

Buros, O. K. (Ed.), *The seventh mental measurements yearbook.* Highland Park, NJ: Gryphon Press, 1972.

Buros, O. K. (Ed.), *The eighth mental measurements yearbook.* Highland Park, NJ: Gryphon Press, 1978.

Butcher, J. N. (Ed.), *MMPI: Research developments and clinical applications.* New York: McGraw-Hill, 1969.

Butcher, J. N. (Ed.), *Objective personality assessment: Changing perspectives.* New York: Academic Press, 1972.

Chambers, G. S., & Hamlin, R. The validity of judgments based on "blind" Rorschach records. *Journal of Consulting Psychology,* 1957, *21,* 105–109.

Chapman, L. J. Illusory correlation in observational report. *Journal of Verbal Learning and Verbal Behavior,* 1967, *6,* 151–155.

Chapman, L. J., & Chapman, J. P. Genesis of popular but erroneous psychodiagnostic observations. *Journal of Abnormal Psychology,* 1967, *72,* 193–204.

Chapman, L. J., & Chapman, J. P. Illusory correlation as an obstacle to the use of valid psychodiagnostic signs. *Journal of Abnormal Psychology,* 1969, *74,* 271–280.

Combs, A. W. Validity and reliability of interpretation from autobiography and Thematic Apperception Test. *Journal of Clinical Psychology,* 1946, *2,* 240–247.

Cox, B., & Sargent, H. TAT responses of emotionally disturbed and emotionally stable children: Clinical judgment versus normative data. *Journal of Projective Techniques,* 1950, *14,* 61–74.

Crenshaw, D. A., Bohm, S., Hoffman, M. R., Matheus, J. M., & Offenbach, S. G. The use of projective methods in research: 1947–1965. *Journal of Projective Techniques & Personality Assessment,* 1968, *32,* 3–9.

Cronbach, L. J. Statistical methods applied to Rorschach scores: A review. *Psychological Bulletin,* 1949, *46,* 393–429.

Cronbach, L. J. *Essentials of psychological testing.* (3rd ed.). New York: Harper & Row, 1970.

Dahlstrom, W. G., Welsh, G. S., & Dahlstrom, L. E. *An MMPI handbook.* Vol. I. *Clinical interpretation.* Minneapolis: University of Minnesota Press, 1972.

Dahlstrom, W. G., Welsh, G. S., & Dahlstrom, L. E. *An MMPI handbook.* Vol. II. *Research developments and applications.* Minneapolis: University of Minnesota Press, 1975.

Dana, R. H. Cross validation of objective TAT scoring. *Journal of Consulting Psychology,* 1956, *20,* 33–36.

Dana, R. H. Review of the Rorschach test. In O. K. Buros (Ed.), *The eighth mental measurements yearbook.* Vol. 1. Highland Park, NJ: Gryphon Press, 1978.

Edwards, A. L., & Diers, C. J. Social desirability and the factorial interpretation of the MMPI. *Educational and Psychological Measurement,* 1962, *22,* 501–509.

Epstein, S. Traits are alive and well. In D. Magnusson and N. S. Endler (Eds.), *Personality at the crossroads: Current issues in interactional psychology.* Hillsdale, NJ: Erlbaum, 1977.

Epstein, S. The stability of behavior. II. Implications for psychological research. *American Psychologist,* 1980, *35,* 790–806.

Eron, L. D. Frequencies of themes and identifications in the stories of schizophrenic patients and nonhospitalized college students. *Journal of Consulting Psychology,* 1948, *12,* 387–395.

Eron, L. D. A normative study of the Thematic Apperception Test. *Psychology Monographs,* 1950, *64,* No. 9 (Whole No. 315).

Eron, L. D. Responses of women to the Thematic Apperception Test. *Journal of Consulting Psychology,* 1953, *17,* 269–282.

Eron, L. D. Review of the Thematic Apperception Test. In O. K. Buros (Ed.), *The seventh mental measurements yearbook.* Highland Park, NJ: Gryphon Press, 1972.

Exner, J. E. *The Rorschach: A comprehensive system.* Vol. 1. New York: Wiley, 1974.

Exner, J. E. *The Rorschach: Current research and advanced interpretation.* Vol. 2. New York: Wiley, 1978.

Feshbach, S. The drive-reducing function of fantasy behavior. *Journal of Abnormal & Social Psychology,* 1955, *50,* 3–11.

Fiske, D. W. *Measuring the concepts of personality.* Chicago: Aldine, 1971.

Ford, M. *The application of the Rorschach Test to young children.* Minneapolis: University of Minnesota Press, 1946.

Fosberg, I. A. Rorschach reactions under varied instruction. *Rorschach Research Exchange,* 1938, *3,* 12–38.

Foulds, G. A method of scoring the TAT applied to psychoneurotics. *Journal of Mental Science,* 1953, *99,* 235–246.

Francis-Williams, J. *Rorschach with children.* Oxford, England: Pergamon Press, 1968.

Frank, G. On the validity of hypotheses derived from the Rorschach: I. The relationship between color and affect. *Perceptual and Motor Skills,* 1976, *43,* 411–427.

Frank, G. On the validity of hypotheses derived from the Rorschach: III. The relationship between shading and anxiety. *Perceptual and Motor Skills,* 1978, *46,* 531–538.

Gamble, K. R. The Holtzman Inkblot Technique: A review. *Psychological Bulletin,* 1972, *77,* 172–194.

Garfield, S. L. Research on client variables in psychotherapy. In S. L. Garfield and A. E. Bergin (Eds.), *Handbook of psychotherapy and behavior change.* (2nd ed.). New York: Wiley, 1978.

Garfield, S. L., & Eron, L. D. Interpreting mood and activity in TAT stories. *Journal of Abnormal & Social Psychology,* 1948, *43,* 338–345.

Garfield, S. L., & Kurtz, R. M. Attitudes toward training in diagnostic testing: A survey of directors of internship training. *Journal of Consulting and Clinical Psychology,* 1973, *40,* 350–355.

Gathercole, C. E. *Assessment in clinical psychology.* Baltimore: Penguin, 1968.

Gilberstadt, H., & Duker, J. *A handbook for clinical and actuarial MMPI interpretation.* Philadelphia: Saunders, 1965.

Goldfried, M. R., Stricker, G., & Weiner, I. B. *Rorschach handbook of clinical and research applications.* Englewood Cliffs, NJ: Prentice-Hall, 1971.

Golding, S. G. & Rorer, L. Illusory correlation and subjective judgment. *Journal of Abnormal Psychology,* 1972, *80,* 249–260.

Grant, M. Q., Ives, V., & Ranzoni, J. H. Reliability and validity of judges' ratings of adjustment on the Rorschach. *Psychology Monographs,* 1952, *66,* No. 2 (Whole No. 334).

Guilford, J. P. Some lessons from aviation psychology. *American Psychologist,* 1948, *3,* 3–11.

Gynther, M. D. Review of MMPI. In O. K. Buros (Ed.), *The seventh mental measurements yearbook.* Vol. 1. Highland Park, NJ: Gryphon Press, 1972.

Hammer, E. F. (Ed.), *The clinical application of projective drawings.* Springfield, IL: Charles C Thomas, 1958.

Haney, W. Validity, vaudeville, and values: A short history of social concerns over standardized testing. *American Psychologist,* 1981, *36,* 1021–1033.

Harrison, R. Thematic apperceptive methods. In B. Wolman (Ed.), *Handbook of clinical psychology.* New York: McGraw-Hill, 1965.

Hathaway, S. R., & McKinley, J. C. *Manual for the Minnesota Multiphasic Personality Inventory.* New York: Psychological Corporation, 1943.

Hathaway, S. R., & McKinley, J. C. *Minnesota Multiphasic Personality Inventory Manual.* (Rev. Ed.). New York: Psychological Corporation, 1951.

Hathaway, S. R., & Meehl, P. E. *An atlas for the clinical use of the Minnesota Multiphasic Personality Inventory.* Minneapolis: University of Minnesota Press, 1951.

Haworth, M. R. *The CAT: Facts about fantasy.* New York: Grune and Stratton, 1966.

Henry, E., & Rotter, J. B. Situational influences on Rorschach responses. *Journal of Consulting Psychology,* 1956, *20,* 457–462.

Henry, W. E. *The analysis of fantasy: The Thematic Apperception Technique in the study of personality.* New York: Wiley, 1956.

Hertz, M. R. The Rorschach method: Science or mystery. *Journal of Consulting Psychology,* 1943, *7,* 67–79.

Hertz, M. R. Current problems in Rorschach theory and technique. *Journal of Projective Techniques,* 1951, *15,* 307–338.

Hertz, M. R. *Frequency tables for scoring Rorschach responses.* (5th Ed., Rev.) Cleveland, OH: Press of Case Western Reserve University, 1970(a).

Hertz, M. R. Projective techniques in crisis. *Journal of Projective Techniques & Personality Assessment,* 1970(b), *34,* 449–467.

Holtzman, W. H., Thorpe, J. S., Swartz, J. D., & Herron, E. W. *Inkblot perception and personality. Holtzman Inkblot Technique.* Austin: University of Texas Press, 1961.

Holtzman, W. H., & Sells, S. B. Prediction of flying success by clinical analysis of test protocols. *Journal of Abnormal & Social Psychology,* 1954, *49,* 485–490.

Holzberg, J. D. Psychological theory and projective techniques. In A. I. Rabin (Ed.), *Projective techniques in personality assessment.* New York: Springer, 1968.

Jackson, C. W., Jr., & Wohl, J. A survey of Rorschach teaching in the university. *Journal of Projective Techniques and Personality Assessment,* 1966, *30,* 115–134.

Jones, H. G. Applied abnormal psychology: The experimental approach. In H. J. Eysenck (Ed.), *Handbook of abnormal psychology.* New York: Basic Books, 1961.

Kagan, J. The long-term stability of selected Rorschach responses. *Journal of Consulting Psychology,* 1960, *24,* 67–73.

Kelly, E. L., & Fiske, D. *The prediction of performance in clinical psychology.* Ann Arbor: University of Michigan Press, 1951.

Kimble, G. A. Social influence on Rorschach records. *Journal of Abnormal & Social Psychology,* 1945, *40,* 89–93.

Kleinmuntz, B. *Personality measurement. An introduction.* Homewood, IL: Dorsey Press, 1967.

Klopfer, B., & Davidson, H. H. *The Rorschach technique: An introductory manual.* New York: Harcourt, Brace and World, 1962.

Klopfer, B., & Kelley, D. *The Rorschach technique.* Yonkers, NY: World Book Co., 1942.

Klopfer, B., Ainsworth, M. D., Klopfer, W. G., & Holt, R. R. *Developments in the Rorschach Technique.* Vol. 1. Yonkers, NY: World Book Co., 1954.

Knutson, J. F. Review of the Rorschach. In O. K. Buros (Ed.), *The seventh mental measurements yearbook.* Highland Park, NJ: Gryphon Press, 1972.

Kurtz, R. M. & Garfield, S. L. Illusory Correlation: A further exploration of Chapman's Paradigm. *Journal of Consulting and Clinical Psychology, 46,* 1009–1015.

Lanyon, R. I., & Goodstein, L. D. *Personality assessment.* (2nd ed.). New York: Wiley, 1982.

Ledivith, N. H. *Rorschach responses of elementary school children: A normative study.* Pittsburgh: University of Pittsburgh Press, 1959.

Leverenz, C. W. Minnesota Multiphasic Personality Inventory: An evaluation of its usefulness in the psychiatric service of a station hospital. *War Medicine,* 1943, *4,* 618–629.

Lindzey, G. Thematic Apperception Test: Interpretive assumptions and related empirical evidence. *Psychological Bulletin,* 1952, *49,* 1–25.

Lord, E. Experimentally induced variations in Rorschach performance. *Psychology Monographs,* 1950, *64,* No. 10 (Whole No. 316).

Lubin, B., Wallis, R. R., & Paine, C. Patterns of psychological test usage in the United States: 1935–1969. *Professional Psychology,* 1971, *2,* 70–74.

McCully, R. S. Current attitudes about projective techniques in APA approved internship centers. *Journal of Projective Techniques and Personality Assessment,* 1965, *27,* 271–280.

MacFarlane, J. W., & Tuddenham, R. D. Problems in the validation of projective techniques. In H. H. Anderson and G. L. Anderson (Eds.), *An introduction to projective techniques.* New York: Prentice-Hall, 1951.

McGee, R. K. Response style as a personality variable: By what criterion? *Psychological Bulletin,* 1962, *59,* 284–295.

Machover, K. *Personality projection in the drawing of the human figure.* Springfield, IL: Charles C Thomas, 1949.

Marks, P. A., & Seeman, W. On the Barnum effect. *The Psychological Record,* 1962, *12,* 203–208.

Marks, P. A., & Seeman, W. *The actuarial description of abnormal personality.* Baltimore: Williams and Wilkins, 1963.

Meehl, P. E. Profile analysis of the Minnesota Multiphasic Personality Inventory in differential diagnosis. *Journal of Applied Psychology,* 1946, *30,* 517–524.

Meehl, P. E. Configural scoring. *Journal of Consulting Psychology,* 1950, *14,* 165–171.

Messick, S., & Jackson, D. N. Acquiescence and the factorial interpretation of the MMPI. *Psychological Bulletin,* 1961, *58,* 299–304.

Michael, J. C., & Buhler, C. Experiences with personality testing in a neuropsychiatric department of a public general hospital. *Diseases of the Nervous System,* 1945, *6,* 205–211.

Mischel, W. *Personality and assessment.* New York: Wiley, 1968.

Mischel, W. The interaction of person and situation. In D. Magnusson and N. S. Endler (Eds.), *Personality at the crossroads: Current issues in interactional psychology.* Hillsdale, NJ: Erlbaum, 1977.

Modlin, H. C. A study of the Minnesota Multiphasic Personality Inventory in clinical practice. *American Journal of Psychiatry,* 1947, *103,* 758–769.

Morgan, C. D., & Murray, H. A. A method for investigating fantasies: The Thematic Apperception Test. *Archives of Neurology and Psychiatry,* 1935, *34,* 289–306.

Morris, W. W. Rorschach estimates of personality attributes in the Michigan assessment project. *Psychology Monographs,* 1952, *66,* No. 6 (Whole No. 338).

Murray, H. A. *Manual for the Thematic Apperception Test.* Cambridge: Harvard University Press, 1943(a).

Murray, H. A. The effect of fear upon estimates of the maliciousness of other personalities. In S. S. Tomkins (Ed.), *Contemporary psychopathology.* Cambridge: Harvard University Press, 1943(b).

Murray, H. A., et al. *Explorations in personality.* New York: Oxford University Press, 1938.

Murstein, B. I. *Theory and research in projective techniques (emphasizing the TAT).* New York: Wiley, 1963.

Murstein, B. I. (Ed.), *Handbook of projective techniques.* New York: Basic Books, 1965.

Newton, R. L. The clinician as judge: Total Rorschachs and clinical case material. *Journal of Consulting Psychology,* 1954, *18,* 248–250.

Peskin, H. Unity of science begins at home: A study of regional factionalism in clinical psychology. *American Psychologist,* 1963, *18,* 96–100.

Peterson, R. A. Review of the Rorschach test. In O. K. Buros (Ed.), *The eighth mental measurements yearbook.* Vol. 1. Highland Park, NJ: Gryphon Press, 1978.

Phillips, L., & Smith, J. G. *Rorschach interpretation: Advanced technique.* New York: Grune and Stratton, 1953.

Rabin, A. I. Validating and experimental studies with the Rorschach method. In H. A. Anderson and G. L. Anderson (Eds.), *An introduction to projective techniques.* New York: Prentice-Hall, 1951.

Rabin, A. I. (Ed.), *Projective techniques in personality assessment.* New York: Springer, 1968.

Rabin, A. I. Review of the Rorschach. In O. K. Buros (Ed.), *The seventh mental measurements yearbook.* Highland Park, NJ: Gryphon Press, 1972.

Rhode, A. A. Explorations in personality by the sentence completion method. *Journal of Applied Psychology,* 1946, *30,* 169–181.

Roback, H. B. Human figure drawings: Their utility in the clinical psychologist's armamentarium for personality assessment. *Psychological Bulletin,* 1968, *70,* 1–19.

Rorschach, H. *Psychodiagnostics: A diagnostic test based on perception.* (Trans. by P. Lenkau and B. Kronenberg.) Berne: Hans Huber, 1942. New York: Grune and Stratton.

Rosenzweig, S. Apperceptive norms for the Thematic Apperception Test. I. The problem of norms in projective methods. *Journal of Personality,* 1949, *17,* 475–482.

Rosenzweig, S., & Fleming, E. Apperceptive norms for the Thematic Apperception Test. II. An empirical investigation. *Journal of Personality,* 1949, *17,* 483–503.

Rotter, J. B., & Rafferty, J. E. *Manual for the Rotter Incomplete Sentences Blank, College Form.* New York: The Psychological Corporation, 1950.

Rubin, H. The Minnesota Multiphasic Personality Inventory as a diagnostic aid in a veterans hospital. *Journal of Consulting Psychology,* 1948, *12,* 251–254.

Samuels, H. The validity of personality-trait ratings based on projective techniques. *Psychology Monographs,* 1952, *66,* No. 5 (Whole No. 337).

Sanders, R., & Cleveland, S. E. The relationship between certain personality variables and subjects' Rorschach scores. *Journal of Projective Techniques,* 1953, *17,* 34–50.

Schafer, R. *Psychoanalytic interpretation in Rorschach testing.* New York: Grune and Stratton, 1954.

Shemberg, K., & Keeley, S. Psychodiagnostic training in the academic setting: Past and present. *Journal of Consulting and Clinical Psychology,* 1970, *34,* 205–211.

Shneidman, E. S., & Farberow, N. L. TAT heroes of suicidal and non-suicidal subjects. *Journal of Projective Techniques,* 1958, *22,* 211–228.

Siipola, E. M. The influence of color on reactions to ink blots. *Journal of Personality,* 1950, *18,* 358–382.

Skolnick, A. Motivational imagery and behavior over twenty years. *Journal of Consulting Psychology,* 1966, *30,* 463–478.

Stein, M. I. The use of a sentence completion test for the diagnosis of personality. *Journal of Clinical Psychology,* 1947, *3,* 47–56.

Suinn, R. M., & Oskamp, S. *The predictive validity of projective measures.* Springfield, IL: Charles C Thomas, 1969.

Sundberg, N. D. The practice of psychological testing in clinical services in the United States. *American Psychologist,* 1961, *16,* 79–83.

Swann, G. E., & MacDonald, M. L. Behavior therapy in practice: A national survey of behavior therapists. *Behavior Therapy,* 1978, *9,* 799–807.

Swartz, J. D. Gamble's review of the Holtzman Inkblot Technique: Corrections and clarification. *Psychological Bulletin,* 1973, *79,* 378–379.

Swartz, J. D. Review of Thematic Apperception Test. In O. K. Buros (Ed.), *The eighth mental measurements yearbook.* Highland Park, NJ: Gryphon Press, 1978.

Swensen, C. H. Empirical evaluations of human figure drawings. *Psychological Bulletin,* 1957, *54,* 431–466.

Swensen, C. H. Empirical evaluations of human figure drawings: 1957–1966. *Psychological Bulletin,* 1968, *70,* 20–44.

Testing and Public Policy. Special Issue. *American Psychologist,* 1965, *20,* 857–993.

Testing: Concepts, Policy, Practice, and Research. Special Issue. *American Psychologist,* 1981, *36,* 997–1189.

Thelen, M. H., Varble, D. L., & Johnson, J. Attitudes of academic clinical psychologists toward projective techniques. *American Psychologist,* 1968, *23,* 517–521.

Wade, T. C., & Baker, T. B. Opinions and use of psychological tests: A survey of clinical psychologists. *American Psychologist,* 1977, *32,* 874–882.

Wheeler, W. M. An analysis of Rorschach indices of male homosexuality. *Rorschach Research Exchange,* 1949, *13,* 97–126.

Wishner, J. Factor analysis of Rorschach scoring categories and first response times in normals. *Journal of Consulting Psychology,* 1959, *23,* 406–413.

Wittenborn, J. R., & Holzberg, J. D. The Rorschach and descriptive diagnosis. *Journal of Consulting Psychology,* 1951, *15,* 460–463.

Zelin, M. L. Validity of the MMPI scales for measuring twenty psychiatric dimensions. *Journal of Consulting and Clinical Psychology,* 1971, *37,* 286–290.

Zubin, J., Eron, L. D., & Schumer, F. *An experimental approach to projective techniques.* New York: Wiley, 1965.

Chapter
Seven

Behavioral
Observation
and
Assessment

In the two preceding chapters we have discussed the use of psychological tests in the clinical appraisal of individuals seeking help with a variety of problems and disorders. As has been noted, psychological tests constituted the unique contribution of psychologists to the clinical study of the individual and were almost synonomous with the diagnostic and assessment function of the clinical psychologist. However, during the last 20 years or so, this diagnostic role has been influenced to some extent by the viewpoints and contributions of behaviorally oriented psychologists. These psychologists have focused much more on appraisals of behavior and the client's environmental influences and have been critical of the previous emphasis on intrapsychic variables and generalized personality traits. As the popularity of psychodynamic viewpoints diminished, and as behavioral and social emphases became more prominent, there was evident also a relative decline in the importance of projective techniques and the use of extensive psychological test batteries.

Behavioral psychologists, although critical of some of the emphases of traditional psychological testing, have actually stressed the importance of adequate assessment of the client as well as the important environmental stimuli influencing the client's behavior. Such assessment is considered essential before a sound program of therapy can be instituted. Thus, they are not opposed to proper assessment as such. Rather, behaviorally oriented psychologists see little value in the more traditional assessment approaches of the past which they believe do not contribute significantly to treatment planning. They instead have emphasized what has been termed behavioral assessment.

It should be noted also that behavioral assessments per se did not originate with behavior therapists. A variety of rating scales had been used in the past in clinical research in psychology and psychiatry, as well as in personnel selection and evaluation. These procedures were not used very much by clinicians for ordinary diagnostic assessment, but they were used in a variety of ways for evaluating the effects of various treatments. The behavioral psychologists, however, have emphasized the importance of behavioral assessment for both the planning and evaluation of treatment, and have greatly expanded the development and use of such procedures. We shall first discuss some of the previous development and application of behavior rating scales, and then examine briefly some of the procedures developed and used by behavioral psychologists.

RATING SCALES

Rating scales of various kinds have been devised in the past to appraise many different aspects of personality adjustment and behavior (Lorr, 1954; Lorr, Bishop, and McNair, 1965; McNair and Lorr, 1965; Mischel, 1968). All such scales utilize a selected list of behavioral traits or personality characteristics which are to be rated in terms of a given set of values by one or more judges. Most frequently, five to nine values have been utilized for rating purposes, with the middle value representing the modal or average rating. Sometimes the different rating categories are expressed simply as numerical values, sometimes in descriptive terms, and occasionally in terms of frequency or percentage of occurrence in a given population. The separate ratings also can be arranged to form a profile for the graphic portrayal of the individual's personality traits.

In order to secure some practical value from rating scales, each attribute or characteristic to be rated must be defined as clearly as possible. If the descriptive terms used are ambiguous or left to the interpretation of the rater, the ratings obtained are likely to be of limited value. For example, characteristics such as "cooperativeness" or "dependability" should be exemplified in behavioral terms and, if possible, each value in the rating scale clearly differentiated. Instead of merely listing a trait name followed by five numerical values ranging from lowest to highest, the characteristic to be rated and the scale of values can be defined somewhat as follows:

Dependability: Worthy of being depended upon or relied upon, trustworthy, reliable.

1. Completely unreliable—cannot be depended upon to carry out any responsibilities.
2. Occasionally can be depended upon to fulfill his responsibilities without additional reminders, but frequently needs to be prompted.
3. Neither outstanding nor grossly deficient in regard to dependability; carries on in an average manner.
4. Can be relied upon to carry out most of his duties with little prompting; above average in this regard.
5. Always dependable in all that is required of him.

In addition to defining the personality variables and the rating values, some instruction in rating procedures and opportunity for practice should be given prospective raters. This will tend to minimize subjective bias and distortion. The more specific or overt the attributes for rating are, the greater the possibility of increasing the reliability of the ratings.

Different types of rating scales have also been developed for use in special situations. One such variation was the man-to-man scale used during World War I. With this device, actual persons known to the raters are used as reference points for the purpose of rating or comparing other individuals. Thus, individuals considered to possess or exhibit varying personality characteristics can be used in evaluating such characteristics in others. Also, if one is interested in rating a group of people, a simple ranking method may be used whereby each individual's rating on a given trait is his rank order in the group. Other modifications in the use of ratings may be developed for specific purposes.

Although rating scales can be constructed without undue effort, and have proved useful in many areas of clinical research, as mentioned previously, they have not been employed extensively in the clinical evaluations of individual clients. There are a number of possible reasons for this. In the first place, the ratings secured are subjective and can be distorted easily by the bias of the judges. The ratings also are dependent on the rater's knowledge of the subject and his opportunities for observing behavior in a variety of situations. If the variables to be rated are rather general personality attributes, it is especially important that the judges observe the individuals to be rated in many different situations. When this is not done, the rating of a behavioral variable may be overly influenced by specific situational elements. For example, a man might be rated as aggressive by his fellow employees who see him only in a limited work situation, yet the same person might be rated as rather submissive when viewed only in relation to his wife at home. The problem of the generality versus the specificity of a given behavioral trait or characteristic is, of course, a more general issue in the field of personality, and some workers seriously question whether there are generalized traits of personality that can be reliably appraised (Mischel, 1968, 1977).

Another shortcoming of rating scales is distortion due to the "halo" effect. A rater's overall impression of a person or his rating on one personality variable may influence the ratings on the other characteristics. Thus the latter ratings are to an unknown degree affected by other judgments, hence objectivity is lessened. For these reasons among others, the inter-judge reliability of ratings on a given individual may be low even though each rater by himself is reasonably consistent. Training and practice in rating, as well as clear definitions of the characteristics being rated, will tend to increase the reliability of ratings. But, even when high reliabilities are obtained, one may sometimes question how much of this is due to the sharing of common biases or even common errors. In such instances, conceivably, we may have high reliability, yet the ratings may have limited validity. This, of course, is something that must be evaluated with all clinical techniques, and not just with rating scales.

One additional problem should be mentioned. This concerns the tendency of many raters to restrict their judgments to only a few of the rating categories. For example, in terms of the writer's experience with ratings of clinical psychology trainees and interns secured from many different sources, it has been apparent that most supervisors tend to check the "average" rating and the one just above it. Below-average ratings, in particular, are given very infrequently. This tends to reduce a five-point scale in actuality to a three-point scale, with the "above-average" rating becoming the mean rating. As a consequence, the scale values take on meanings somewhat different from their stated values.

Generally, it may be said that rating scales are not well suited for evaluating the more covert or inferred aspects of personality—the motives and underlying dynamics of behavior. It is apparent that greater reliability of ratings can be secured with the more overt and readily observable aspects of behavior. If these are relatively stable, there is less opportunity for subjective distortion. To the extent that such features of personality are viewed as unimportant in the understanding and treatment of the client, however, the use of rating scales would be correspondingly limited. A psychoanalytically oriented person would be more concerned with underlying conflicts and motives than would other more eclectic or behaviorally oriented clinicians.

Other theoretical problems relating to the nature of personality organization enter into the evaluation of rating scales, although such problems are by no means limited solely to rating scales. We have already mentioned the possibility of error in identifying as generalized features of personality the reactions determined in great part by situational factors. Another aspect of the problem concerns the stability or fluidity of personality patterns and processes. Many techniques for personality appraisal are based on one or the other of such implicit assumptions, with comparatively little consideration given to careful evaluations of the underlying assumptions. Finally, in developing and using rating scales, the psychologist must consider whether the personality variables being rated are meaningful psychological attributes, or whether they are merely vague abstractions—again, a theoretical issue which transcends a particular method of appraisal.

In spite of these limitations, rating scales may be used with definite profit in several kinds of clinical situations. Carefully constructed by a sophisticated psychometrician, they provide a means of increasing the objectivity of clinical judgments and observations (Lorr, 1954). Ironically enough, clinical judgments or ratings that would be eschewed by a clinician in his practice have been used, directly or indirectly, as criteria for testing the validity of psychological tests he uses with confidence. Many times, clinical ratings are the only data easily obtainable for appraising or partially validating new diagnostic or therapeutic techniques. They may be used also to supplement other means of studying individual patients. For example, in a hospital, the actual behavior of the patient on the ward, in the examining room, and in the occupational therapy program may be of significance in appraising his progress. Rating scales have been developed for evaluating such behaviors as cooperation in group tasks, interest in recreational activities, initiative in performing routine duties, withdrawal from others, fluctuation in mood, and so forth. Consequently, rating scales can be used as adjunctive measures in diagnosis and in the evaluation of therapy, as a means of increasing the objectivity of clinical observations and judgments, and as a method of studying behavior in relation to other personality variables. Several rating scales, in fact, have been developed to serve such purposes in psychiatric hospitals (Lorr, 1954), and a number of them have been used in clinical research, particularly with reference to the evaluation of psychoactive drugs.

Rating scales for appraising patient behavior in hospitals and clinics may be classified in a number of ways. One method of classification is in terms of the type of person who does the actual ratings; for example, those designed for use by such ward personnel as nurses and aides utilize descriptive terms that are commonly used in their everyday work. Other scales, however, have been devised for use by trained clinicians. In the latter instances, the items to be rated may contain technical terminology and require some knowledge of psychopathology. Examples from both types of rating scales will be given to illustrate the type of items used and the behaviors rated. The first group of items is taken from the Fergus Falls Behavior Rating Sheet developed by Lucero and Meyer (1951). This is a brief rating form consisting of eleven categories of descriptive behavior for use in psychiatric hospitals. Three of the items are reproduced here:

B. *Response to Meals*

____Has to have special attention, as eats too much, spoon fed or tube fed.

____Eats by self, is sloppy—may need coaxing.

____Eats by self using knife, fork, and spoon properly. May show some finickyness.

____Passes and asks for things to be passed, but will not carry on table conversation.

____Would not stand out among normal people for eating habits.

D. *Response to Psychiatric Aides and Nurses*

____Negativistic—hostile (can include striking)—doesn't do anything requested.

____Will do a few things if asked or pushed—shows no open hostility.

____Will do most things when asked—will ask for simple things—"I want my toothbrush."

____Extremely cooperative—will do anything when asked.

____Normal give and take relationship. Speaks spontaneously to nurses about things of not immediate importance (weather, baseball games, etc.).

J. *Speech*

____Mute or speaks a lot but it doesn't make sense.

____A few words that make sense ("yes" or "no").

____Speaks in short, clear sentences—"Can I have my toothbrush?"

____Speaks normally except a little fast or slow.

____Speaks normally.

(If mute or senseless talk, which one.)

These sample items are ranked from the most deviant or pathological behavior at one end of the scale to normal behavior at the other. Two opposite but equally deviant types of behavior also may be grouped together. Values of one to five can be assigned to represent the varying levels of behavior.

A somewhat similar type of scale was prepared by the author to study the effects of chlorpromazine on the behavior and functioning of emotionally disturbed children. Certain target behaviors were eventually condensed into an eighteen-item behavior rating scale. The form was developed so that aides and nurses on two shifts in the inpatient service of a psychiatric hospital could complete the ratings. Sample items and instructions are as follows:

"This is a scale for rating the behavior of children. All ratings should be based on your own observations of the child as you have observed him at the hospital. These ratings will be utilized in a research study and will in no way affect the treatment of the child being rated. *Check only one item in each section.*"

II. *Activity-Inactivity*

____1. Extremely nonactive, never initiates activity, stays in one place.

____2. Rarely active, occasionally institutes activity, usually inactive.

____3. Neither outstandingly active nor passive.

____4. Quite active, initiates most of his activities, infrequently still.

____5. Overactive, on the go practically all the time.

III. *Verbal Behavior*

____1. Completely quiet, practically no verbalization.

____2. Talks only rarely; primarily responds to questions from others.

____3. Seemingly average in verbal activity, talks with others.

____4. Overly talkative and verbal, monopolizes discussion.

____5. Extremely overtalkative, talks practically all the time, difficult to keep quiet.

VI. *Mood*

____1. Appears to be extremely depressed, sad, blue, very moody, down in the dumps.

____2. Rather depressed, unhappy, rarely cheerful.

____3. Appears to have no particular ups or downs.

____4. Quite jovial, happy, rather carefree.

____5. High, up in the clouds, euphoric.

Rating scales for more sophisticated observers are well illustrated by the Inpatient Multidimensional Psychiatric Scale (IMPS) developed by Lorr, Klett, McNair, and Lasky (1962). This scale was basically designed to measure ten psychotic syndromes derived by means of repeated factor analyses. It consists of seventy-five items. Some of the items are rated on a nine-point scale which ranges from "not at all" at one end, to "extremely" at the other. Others are rated on a five-point scale and some items are simply recorded in terms of "yes" or "no." The ratings are based on the observations of the patient's behavior and his own verbal reports of his beliefs and feelings as obtained in a clinical interview. As indicated earlier, the scale was constructed for use by trained interviewers who have some background and experience in interviewing psychiatric patients. The scale was designed primarily for use with functional psychotic patients or severe psychoneurotics who can be interviewed. Thus its use is not applicable to patients who are very withdrawn and uncommunicative, or who are very minimally disturbed. According to the manual, this scale can be completed in less than 15 minutes following the interview with the patient.

This scale, therefore, is most clearly applicable to work with rather disturbed but still cooperative patients. Ten specific syndromes have been identified by means of factor analysis, and scores for these syndromes can be secured along with certain kinds of normative material. Among the syndromes sampled are Excitement, Paranoid Projection, Perceptual Distortion, Retardation and Apathy, and Motor Disturbance.

The IMPS is one of the most carefully worked out behavior rating scales, and, unlike most of the other scales discussed previously, is a relatively well-standardized instrument. It has been rather widely used in the past to study the effects of both experimental drugs and those used regularly with psychiatric patients. The first seven items of the scale, which are rated on a nine-point scale, are reproduced below for illustrative purposes:

COMPARED TO THE NORMAL PERSON TO WHAT DEGREE DOES HE (that is, the patient being interviewed) . . .

1. Manifest speech that is slowed, deliberate, or labored?

2. Give answers that are irrelevant or unrelated in any immediately conceivable way to the question asked or topic discussed?

Cues: Do not rate here wandering or rambling conversation that veers away from the topic at issue (see item 4). Also do not rate the coherence of the answer.

3. Give answers that are grammatically disconnected, incoherent, or scattered, that is, not sensible or not understandable?
Cues: Judge the grammatical structure of his speech, not the content which may or may not be bizarre.

4. Tend to ramble, wander, or drift off the subject or away from the point at issue in responding to questions or topics discussed?
Cues: Do not rate here responses that are obviously unrelated to the question asked (see item 2).

5. Verbally express feelings of hostility, ill will, or dislike of others?
Cues: Makes hostile comments regarding others such as attendants, other patients, his family, or persons in authority.
Reports conflicts on the word.

6. Exhibit postures that are peculiar, unnatural, rigid, or bizarre?
Cues: Head twisted to one side; or arm and hand held oddly.
Judge the degree of peculiarity of the posture.

7. Express or exhibit feelings and emotions openly, impulsively, or without apparent restraint or control?
Cues: Shows temper outbursts; weeps or wrings hands in loud complaint: jokes or talks boisterously; gestures excitedly.

The illustrations from these scales should give the reader some idea of clinical rating scales and the types of behavioral attributes that are appraised. There are, of course, other rating scales that vary somewhat from those described here, but the general pattern is similar. For some of the scales there are also data available that indicate acceptable reliability. For example, on the Fergus Falls Scale, 34 raters agreed 90% of the time on the basis of 866 ratings on 51 patients (Lucero and Meyer, 1951). Nevertheless, there is need for additional data on such matters from other investigators, for in one study of a rating scale, it was found that the amount of agreement between different raters on individual patients was unacceptably low (Pumroy and Kogan, 1955). Either additional training or the use of several raters may increase the reliability and, hence, the usability of the ratings secured. It may be mentioned also that norms for certain categories of patients are available for some of the scales (Lorr, 1954; Lorr et al., 1962).

The uses of rating scales obviously will depend on the situation in which they are applied. There does appear to be, however, a large number of situations where rating devices may contribute information of value. As mentioned previously, they have been utilized successfully as quick and meaningful indexes of behavior changes resulting from the administration of drugs. A variety of rating measures have also been used in studies of disturbed behavior, professional performance, changes resulting from different treatments, psychotherapeutic process and outcome as well as other areas of interest to the clinician. Such techniques do have limitations and can be misused, but they can also be of clinical and research value if constructed carefully and used judiciously.

BEHAVIORAL ASSESSMENT

As indicated earlier, behavioral psychologists and therapists were critical of traditional testing approaches to diagnostic assessment and, in terms of their theoretical orientation, emphasized what they termed, behavioral assessment (Barlow, 1981: Ciminero, Calhoun, & Adams, 1977; Hersen & Bellack, 1981). Although this approach to assessment was considered to be a departure from traditional approaches, in many respects, perhaps, the main difference was in the framework and rationale of assessment rather than on techniques per se. For example, behavioral clinicians tend to rely a great deal on the interview as a source of information and observation, instead of utilizing a regular battery of psychological tests. Part of this difference in assessment pattern, I believe, may be due to historical events. In the 1940's and 1950's, the clinical psychologist's main function was diagnostic testing and assessment. After the rather formal diagnostic appraisal by the psychologist, the patient was usually assigned to someone else for treatment. In the case of behavioral therapy, there did not appear to be such a differentiation or separation of function between diagnostician and therapist. The behavior therapist was also the assessor of the patient, and assessment and treatment were closely related.

Although behavioral psychologists rely greatly on the interview for assessment purposes, what is stressed and attended to in the interview will generally differ in certain ways from what psychodynamic or other nonbehavioral therapists might emphasize. One objective of the behaviorally oriented clinician is to be able to specify the target behaviors which bring the client to seek therapy and whose change will constitute the goals of therapy. The clinician does not necessarily select the first identifiable complaint or problem, but explores major areas of the client's life "because identification of all problematic areas is crucial to assessment and successful intervention" (Nelson & Barlow, 1981, p. 16). The focus, however, is to try to get as specific information as possible concerning the potential target behaviors of the client. Vague descriptions are pursued by the interviewer until there is a clearer understanding of the specific behaviors involved. Most behavior therapists also do not limit their inquiry simply to motor behaviors, but include cognitive (verbal) behavior as well as affective (physiological) behavior. Some guidelines for more structured types of interviews are also available as aides to the interviewer (Lazarus, 1973; Morganstern, 1976; Wolpe, 1969).

Many of the areas explored and some of the questions asked in the interviews will be similar to those already discussed in Chapter 4. Regardless of the clinician's theoretical orientation, there are certain items of interest which will be explored by most competent clinicians. These include the patient's complaints, symptoms, life events, significant relationships, and the like. In this sense, some form of "behavioral assessment" may be carried out by nonbehaviorally oriented clinicians. Behavioral psychologists also are sensitive to the importance of establishing rapport with the client in the interview situation (Roberts & LaGreca, 1981). However, in spite of some similarities, there will also be some differences. Behavioral clinicians ordinarily would not be particularly interested in the early childhood experiences of the adult client unless these appeared to be quite clearly related to target symptoms. The interpretation of certain reported events as well as behaviors manifested in the interview situation may also be viewed differently than would be the case with other clinicians.

In securing information about the client's difficulties and in trying to evaluate the potential target behaviors, several considerations tend to guide the behavioral clinician's conduct of the interview. The first objective is to secure a clear description of the *problematic behavior*. Such descriptive terms as "feeling anxious," "depressed," "nervous," "sexual difficulties," and the like, must be clarified so that the specific behaviors, cognitions, and affects involved are described and understood. For example, does feeling anxious include a strong apprehension that something terrible is going to happen, rapid heart beats, sweating, dizziness, and a gulping for air, or does it signify a rather brief and mild fear related to some reality-oriented stimuli?

Besides obtaining a clear picture of the problem behavior, the behavioral clinician is also interested in learning of possible variables that may be related to these behaviors. Thus, he/she may inquire as to where the behaviors occur, the frequency of such occurrence, and whether or not certain people are present or involved when the problematic behaviors occur. In pursuing an adequate and precise description of the behavioral problems which bring the client to seek therapy, the clinician, therefore, also seeks to find out about possible *antecedent conditions* or events which may be important in triggering the behavior in question. Do the latter appear to arise mainly in certain situations, in the company of certain people, at certain times? Many individuals are overly preoccupied with their subjective states and problem behaviors, and may not be close observers of the antecedent events or stimuli which preceded the onset of these states and behaviors. Consequently, recall of such events is not an automatic process and the interviewer must be persistent and skillful as well as empathic and encouraging. In some instances, of course, there may be no clearly discernible antecedent events to account for the emergence of the client's disturbing behavior.

If the psychologist has made an adequate attempt at ascertaining such antecedent events and no specific events are identified, then he will have to proceed without such information. However, the interview should be conducted carefully and in a thorough manner. In some instances, for example, it is possible that the event immediately preceding a specific problematic behavior is actually a cognitive one, and not a specific event occurring in the immediate environment. Thus, a variety of situations which on the surface appear to be different, may actually have similar effects on the client by causing him to make self-derogatory statements. These in turn, produce painful affects and withdrawing behaviors. The clinician, therefore, may have to consider variables within the organism as well as variables without in evaluating possible antecedent stimuli.

Besides focusing on potential target behaviors and antecedent events, behavioral psychologists are also interested in finding out about the possible *consequences* of the client's behavior. As we should know from our earlier discussion of operant conditioning, the consequences which follow given behaviors may act as reinforcers for those behaviors. It is to be expected, therefore, that behaviorally oriented psychologists would be interested in identifying the consequences which follow the behavior in question. The immediate consequence, or even a series of consequences may be found to be associated significantly with the problematic behavior. The consequences may pertain to the behaviors of significant others, or they may pertain to the cognitions, affects, and motoric behaviors of the client. In some instances, the consequences are of short duration or of limited effect, but because they reduce anxiety, the client persists in the problem behaviors which actually have long-term negative consequences. An individual, for example, who experiences severe anxiety attacks when leaving his home, may reduce the level of anxiety by returning home immediately. However, the long-term consequences of not being able to leave one's abode are to restrict severely the individual's way of life. Therapy, in this instance, would have to help the individual to change his behavior so that the more positive long-term consequences were realized.

Behavior therapists also stress that their assessment and therapeutic procedures are intimately connected. In fact, one of their criticisms of conventional psychological assessment is that it contributes little to the actual planning and implementation of therapeutic strategies. Consequently, behavior therapists are particularly alert to treatment implications when the assessment of the client is conducted. Assessment measures and devices are selected in terms of the particular problems presented by the client. Furthermore, the measurements and appraisals made at the initial assessment can be repeated at intervals during the course of therapy and at termination to check on the progress of the client.

After the behavioral clinician has completed his initial behavioral assessment, the next step is that of planning a treatment program or program of intervention. Using his knowledge of the problematic behaviors and the potentially important stimuli influencing or reinforcing these behaviors, the therapist selects or devises specific treatment procedures or strategies in terms of his therapeutic goals. In terms of recommended procedures, the therapist also will plan to monitor whatever changes may be taking place as treatment occurs.

In terms of what has been described thus far, it is apparent that behavioral psychologists believe that their approach to assessment has definite advantages over the conventional procedures used previously. Their approach is more ideographic, focusing on the individual's problems and unique situation; it deals with actual behaviors instead of inferred constructs; it helps the clinician determine the actual therapeutic plan and procedures; and assessments are carried out to evaluate the process and progress of therapy. In general, there seems to be at least some support for their claims, although it is hard to know what actually occurs in clinical practice. Behavior therapists emphasize assessment and evaluation more than most other therapists and have developed several procedures for securing a more systematic appraisal of the individual case, which will be described later in this chapter. From the author's own perspective, individualizing assessment and therapy and evaluating the effectiveness of treatment are positive features to be sought by all clinicians. However, before attempting to make any further appraisal of behavioral assessment, let us examine some of the assessment devices and procedures developed and used by behavioral clinicians.

Behavioral psychologists, like other psychologists, also use various self-report instruments and questionnaires. However, although they may make some use of such standard personality questionnaires as the MMPI or the Beck Depression Inventory, they tend to favor instruments which are geared more to specific target complaints or behaviors. As a general rule the latter have not received as much in the way of psychometric analysis and standardization as have the more generally used scales such as the MMPI. Thus, questions of reliability and validity may not be fully answered with regard to a number of questionnaires and inventories used.

As has been indicated already, the objectives of behavioral questionnaires also differ from the more conventional questionnaires. Behavioral therapists tend to be critical of assessment devices which attempt to measure broad, generalized, and stable personality traits and dispositions.

Rather, behavioral inventories are designed to assess the patient's specific reactions to a sample of problem situations. The items are generally constructed to be very specific and behaviorally based in order to sample a variety of relevant situations. As with other behavioral assessment procedures, the main intent of checklists and inventories is to assess factors that maintain the patient's problems and behaviors, and to suggest a treatment focus (Roberts & LaGrece, 1981, pp. 307–308).

Behavior therapists, consequently, have developed a variety of instruments to aid in the assessment of their clients and to help them decide on an appropriate program of treatment. Many of these procedures have not been standardized, but have been developed by individual clinicians to assess more adequately specific problems of individual clients, although a small number have received more systematic study and have been employed in research investigations. Various inventories and check lists have been developed and used to evaluate fears and phobias, problems of assertive behavior, obesity, social skills, and marital and sexual difficulties, among others. As can be noted, these instruments tend to focus on specific problem areas and behaviors, and reflect the kinds of problems on which behavior therapists have been actively involved.

Among the self-report forms or inventories which have received application in several research studies are the Fear Survey Schedule II (Geer, 1965), the Rathus Assertiveness Scale (Rathus, 1973), the Reinforcement Survey Schedule (Cautela & Kastenbaum, 1967), the Conflict Resolution Inventory (McFall & Lillesand, 1971), and the Marital Adjustment Scale (Locke Wallace, 1959). The conflict Resolution Inventory, for example, was developed to study problems of assertion. It includes eight items which require global impressions of assertion. Two of these items are reproduced below:

CONFLICT RESOLUTION INVENTORY

1. How assertive do you think you usually are compared to other people your age in this culture? To indicate how you would honestly rate yourself, place a checkmark on the following scale.

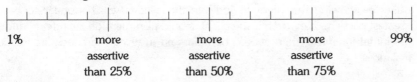

| 1% | more assertive than 25% | more assertive than 50% | more assertive than 75% | 99% |

2. Compared to other people your age in this culture, how assertive would you like to be in order to feel satisfied with yourself.

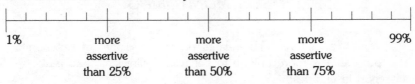

| 1% | more assertive than 25% | more assertive than 50% | more assertive than 75% | 99% |

The rest of the inventory consists of 35 specific situations involving refusal responses on the part of the individual. The client is asked to indicate which of five possible responses he/she would be most likely to make if the situation actually occurred. The following is a brief illustration taken from the scale:

Alternatives

A = I would *refuse* and would not feel uncomfortable about doing so.

B = I would *refuse* but would feel uncomfortable doing so.

C = I would *not refuse* but would feel uncomfortable because I didn't.

D = I would *not refuse* even though I might prefer to, but would not feel particularly uncomfortable because I didn't.

E = I would *not refuse* because it seems to be a reasonable request.

___1. Suppose you want to sell a book for $5. A mere acquaintance of yours says that he/she really needs the book, can't find it anywhere, and can only pay $3 for it. You are sure that you can easily get $5 for it.

___2. Suppose it were a friend who needed the book, but you were broke and needed $5 to pay off a debt.

___3. Suppose it were a mere acquaintance who needed the book, but you were broke and needed the $5 to pay off a debt.

Another self-report questionnaire which appears to have had wide usage is the Fear Survey Schedule. Used and reported in a study by Lang and Lazovik (1963), it was revised as the Fear Survey Schedule II by Geer (1965). This version has 51 different fears listed on a check list which the client rates on a seven-point scale with the following categories: "None, Very Little, A Little, Some, Much, Very Much, and Terror." The list of fears covers a wide range including fears of objects (dead bodies, hypodermic needles), insects and snakes, social situations, specific situations such as crowded places, heights, and the like. Although the rating values are not defined and clients may have different interpretative schemes, the scale has potential clinical utility in allowing the client to indicate those fears which appear to be of greatest concern. However, if the client should also mention such fears during the initial interview, there would be little gain in using the check list in such instances.

SELF-MONITORING

A somewhat different, but related procedure is that of self-monitoring. This procedure is more unique to behavioral clinicians than is the use of self-report inventories.

Self-monitoring, as the name implies, refers to the observation and record-ing of one's own behavior in a reasonably systematic manner. It is used in situations where external observation or monitoring of the patient's behavior is not feasible or possible, and thus the responsibility for the behavioral moni-toring falls on the patient. Its potential value, therefore, depends to a large extent on the adequacy and veracity of the patient's monitoring and reporting.

Nevertheless, it is a procedure which a number of behavior therapists have used with apparent success to monitor a variety of behaviors.

It seems evident that clearly defined behaviors that also are easily counted can be monitored most successfully. For example, the number of cigarettes smoked, the number of calories consumed, the number of dates one has had, and the number of alcoholic drinks one has consumed are fairly easy to record and thus to monitor. However, it is possible also to monitor specific thoughts, preoccupations, fights, and arguments as well. In order to ensure the greatest accuracy in self-monitoring, the recording of a given behavior should be made concurrently with the occurrence of the behavior(s) being monitored, or immediately thereafter. Trusting one's memory when one is trying to reduce or extinguish a given undesirable behavior is probably a precarious procedure. Various record-keeping forms for self-monitoring a variety of behaviors have been developed and used by behavior therapists.

Although the emphasis thus far in terms of self-monitoring has been on the counting and recording of specific behaviors, attention also needs to be given to the circumstances under which the behavior was performed and the possible consequences. In essence, as indicated earlier in this section, the antecedent events and the consequences of the target behaviors also need to be monitored. Thus, in monitoring eating habits, the obese person needs to monitor the specific times food was eaten, the setting and location, and possible thoughts and feelings as well as the quantity and type of food consumed. Consequently, although the monitoring of certain behaviors and situations may appear to be fairly simple and straightforward, in other instances considerably more information may have to be recorded.

Self-monitoring has also been used by behavior therapists as a therapeutic procedure. In such instances, it is believed that the self-monitoring by the client provides feedback to her and can also function as one type of reinforcement. As the individual becomes more aware of the factors influencing the undesirable behavior and is able to use self-control methods to reduce the frequency of the behavior, the result is a positive change in the individual's behavior and adjustment. Although self-monitoring may have a positive impact on the client, therapeutically speaking, such an occurrence also highlights the possible inadequacies of self-monitoring as an assessment device. This would be particularly true in the use of self-monitoring procedures to evaluate the efficacy of a particular therapeutic procedure. To the extent that the self-monitoring procedure itself influenced the client's behavior, the results secured could not validly be ascribed to the particular therapeutic approach. This type of process has been called "reactivity" by psychologists to denote the influence of particular assessment devices on the behaviors being studied. Obviously, accuracy of reporting is also important, and is a potential problem with all self-report measures.

BEHAVIORAL OBSERVATION

As might be expected, a major emphasis and potential source of data for behavioral psychologists are behavioral observations. Although the observation of behavior also would appear to be a rather straightforward affair, there are some potential difficulties in gathering valid and reliable data. As was noted in our previous discussion of behavior rating scales, situational elements, opportunities for observation, the possible intrusiveness of observers, and the reliability of observers all present potential problems. Nevertheless, behavioral observations provide an important type of data and have received particular emphasis from behaviorists.

In terms of face validity, the observation of the client in his natural life situation would be the preferred procedure. However, in most situations, this is difficult to carry out. People work, go to classes, attend parties, and go out with their boyfriends and girl friends, and it is not feasible, if at all possible, to observe them as they interact in these situations. This is particularly true of adults. Children offer potentially more opportunities to be observed in preschool, school, or playground situations. However, such observations require considerable time on the part of the clinician to arrange, and unless the clinician is working with individuals in an institutionalized setting, such as a hospital, such efforts are usually not made. Even in institutional settings, there have been questions raised recently concerning the necessity of securing the consent of those being observed for research purposes, thus making unobtrusive observation difficult. Perhaps more than others, however, behavior therapists have developed procedures which do require having the patient "behave" in a natural situation, although the focus may be on therapy rather than assessment.

Different guides or response codes have been developed to ensure as objective and reliable observation as possible. One such code for studying children in a classroom setting described eight different behaviors (Bijou, Peterson, Harris, Allen, & Johnston, 1969). These included such behaviors as "disruptive noise, aggression, gross motor behaviors, verbalizations and relevant behaviors." Each of these was defined, and a symbol used to designate them.

Another observation code was developed for identifying hyperactive children (Abikoff, Gittleman-Klein, & Klein, 1977). This behavior code consisted of 14 specified behaviors such as interference, off task behaviors, gross motor movements, physical aggression, noncompliance, and out-of-chair behavior. In the study reported by Abikoff et al. (1977), 12 of the 14 behavior codes differentiated normal from hyperactive children.

In addition to the observation of behavior in the natural situation, behavior therapists have also devised or adapted a number of structured situations to assess the client's initial behavior as well as the progress in therapy. For example, in dealing with marital problems, the actual interactions of the marital partners can be observed by the therapist in the therapy situation. However, such a situation may restrict the spontaneous responses of one or both of the clients, and the observations of the therapist most likely will not be very systematic. Videotaping the session and then having independent observers rate the frequency of defined behaviors will increase the objectivity and systematic nature of the observations. A structured situation also can be presented to the couple in which they are asked to resolve certain problems or conflict situations which have been identified as major areas of difficulty. Their interpersonal and problem-solving behaviors can be observed through a one-way mirror and also videotaped for later appraisal (Eisler, Hersen, & Agras, 1973). Raters or coders can be trained to record the specific behaviors manifested by the couple.

Probably the most widely used structured technique has been the Behavioral Approach Test (BAT) (Lang & Lazovik, 1963). This structured technique has been used in a number of research studies to appraise a variety of fears and phobias. It has been used to provide a behavioral assessment of specific fears (e.g., snakes, animals, insects) at the beginning of therapy and again to evaluate progress at the termination of therapy. The BAT has been adapted also for use with a variety of other types of approach-avoidance problems. In appraising clients who have a strong fear of snakes, for example, the BAT consists of the following steps. An examining room is set up in which the snake is placed in a visible container at the far end of the room. The distance between the entrance to the room and the snake is marked off and the client is asked to proceed with a series of possible tasks. These may include such behaviors as approaching the snake, looking at the snake, touching and holding the snake, removing it from the cage, replacing it, holding it close to one's face, and the like. Immediately before each task and during it, clients are also asked to rate the intensity of their fear. How far clients can proceed with the tasks constitutes a behavioral measure of their specific fear. Thus, some clients may only advance two-thirds of the way toward the snake, whereas others may go as far as looking at or touching the snake. At the end of treatment, the client's final performance would indicate what progress was actually made.

Although the BAT and its variations have been widely used in research investigations of the effectiveness of behavioral therapies, it may not be fully valid as a measure of specific fears and phobias. The laboratory-like situation used has certain demand characteristics which are not found in natural situations, and clients or subjects may believe that the therapist actually will not let them get hurt. Being in this kind of situation is not exactly like being alone in a setting where snakes are believed to be plentiful. Individuals, for example, may exhibit successful approach behaviors in the test situation, but rate themselves as being quite anxious. Nevertheless, techniques of this kind are worthwhile attempts to secure behavioral measures of avoidance behaviors and have some advantages over self-report instruments. They do require some type of performance instead of merely verbalizing a response or checking an item on a checklist.

A number of other types of structured situations have been devised by behavior therapists to evaluate a variety of problem behaviors. These include parent–child interactions, psychotic behaviors, assertive behaviors, play behaviors of children, and alcohol consumption. For some of these, lists of carefully defined behaviors have been developed that can be coded and rated. In many instances, simply the frequency and duration of specific behaviors are all that need be recorded. Some assessment situations have been worked out carefully and applied in several research investigations, whereas others have been developed by clinicians to meet the needs of a specific client. However, all such attempts typify the emphasis of behavior therapists on securing behavioral assessments.

Before concluding this chapter, mention can be made of one other procedure that has been taken over from other sources and used for behavioral assessment and treatment, namely, role-plays. In role-playing the therapist structures a situation for the client and asks the client to act out the situation with the therapist or with some other person. For example, if the client has difficulty in being assertive with her boss, the therapist may play the role of the boss and ask the client to play-act a scene in which the latter comes in and asks for a raise. The therapist is then able to appraise the client's behavior in this simulated situation, and to highlight particular behavioral deficiencies. Role-plays have also been used by both behavior therapists and other therapists as a therapeutic procedure to allow the client to practice more positive behaviors before trying them out in real life situations. However, behavior therapists have perhaps emphasized their assessment potential more than others and have tried to make such procedures more objective and systematic.

Behavior therapists have tried to emphasize the appraisal of behavior in their assessment procedures and, as we have noted, have developed a variety of procedures toward meeting this goal. Most of the more systematic attempts have been used more frequently in research appraisals than in routine practice, although individual therapists have used them in working with clients as well. This is in line with the stress behavior therapists have placed on assessment of the individual's problems and in designing specific therapeutic procedures to fit the individual case. However, it should be emphasized, that behavior therapists have also utilized self-report instruments, physiological measures, standard tests, and other procedures in order to secure comprehensive assessments of their clients.

REFERENCES

Abikoff, H., Gittleman-Klein, K., & Klein, D. J. Validation of a classroom observation code for hyperactive children. *Journal of Consulting and Clinical Psychology*, 1977, *45*, 772–783.

Barlow, D. H. (Ed.), *Behavioral assessment of adult disorders*. New York: Guilford Press, 1981.

Bijou, S. W., Peterson, R. F., Harris, F. R., Allen, K. E., & Johnston, M. S. Methodology for experimental studies of young children in natural settings. *Psychological Record*, 1969, *19*, 177–210.

Cautela, J. R., & Kastenbaum, R. A reinforcement survey schedule for use in therapy, training, and research. *Psychological Reports*, 1967, *20*, 1115–1130.

Ciminero, A. R., Calhoun, K. S., & Adams, H. E. (Eds.), *Handbook of behavioral assessment*, New York: Wiley, 1977.

Eisler, R. M., Hersen, M., & Agras, W. S. Videotape: A method for the controlled observation of non-verbal interpersonal behavior. *Behavior Therapy*, 1973, *4*, 420–425.

Geer, J. H. The development of a scale to measure fear. *Behavioral Research and Therapy*, 1965, *3*, 45–53.

Goldfried, M. R., & Kent, R. N. Traditional versus behavioral personality assessment: A comparison of methodological and theoretical assumptions. *Psychological Bulletin*, 1972, *77*, 409–420.

Hersen, M., & Bellack, A. S. *Behavioral assessment: A practical handbook*. New York: Pergamon, 1981.

Lang, P. J., & Lazovik, A. D. Experimental desensitization of a phobia. *Journal of Abnormal and Social Psychology*, 1963, *66*, 519–525.

Lazarus, A. A. Multimodal behavior therapy: Treating the BASIC ID. *Journal of Nervous and Mental Disease*, 1973, *156*, 404–411.

Locke, H. J., & Wallace, K. M. Short marital-adjustment and predictor tests: Their reliability and validity. *Journal of Marriage and Family Living*, 1959, *21*, 251–255.

Lorr, M. Rating scales and check lists for the evaluation of psychopathology. *Psychological Bulletin*, 1954, *51*, 119–127.

Lorr, M., Klett, J., McNair, D. M., & Lasky, J. J. *Manual. Inpatient Multidimensional Psychiatric Scale*. Veterans Administration, 1962.

Lorr, M., Bishop, P. F., & McNair, D. M. Interpersonal types among psychiatric patients. *Journal of abnormal Psychology*, 1965, *70*, 468–472.

Lucero, R. J., & Meyer, B. T. A behavior rating scale suitable for use in mental hospitals. *Journal of Clinical Psychology*, 1951, *7*, 250–254.

McFall, R. M., & Lillesand, D. B. Behavior rehearsal with modeling and coaching in assertion training. *Journal of Abnormal Psychology*, 1971, *77*, 313–323.

McNair, D. M., & Lorr, M. Differential typing of psychiatric outpatients. *Psychological Record*, 1965, *15*, 33–41.

Mischel, W. *Personality and assessment*. New York: Wiley, 1968.

Mischel, W. On the future of personality measurement. *American Psychologist*, 1977, *32*, 246–254.

Morganstern, K. P. Behavioral interviewing: The initial steps of assessment. In M. Hersen, & A. S. Bellack (Eds.), *Behavioral assessment: A practical handbook.* New York: Pergamon Press, 1976.

Nelson, R. O., & Barlow, D. H. Behavioral assessment: Basic strategies and initial procedures. In D. H. Barlow (Ed.), *Behavioral assessment of adult disorders.* New York: Guilford Press, 1981.

Pumroy, S. S., & Kogan, W. S. The reliability of Wittenborn's scales for rating currently discernible psychopathology. *Journal of Clinical Psychology,* 1955, *11,* 411–412.

Rathus, S. A. A 30-item schedule for assessing assertive behavior. *Behavior Therapy,* 1973, *4,* 398–406.

Roberts, M. C., & La Greca, A. M. Behavioral assessment. In C. E. Walker (Ed.), *Clinical practice of psychology.* New York: Pergamon Press, 1981.

Wolpe, J. *The practice of behavior therapy.* New York: Pergamon Press, 1969.

Chapter
Eight

Psychotherapy
and
Behavior
Change

With this chapter, we turn our attention to another major activity of clinical psychologists. As discussed in the first chapter, the psychotherapeutic function, although a relatively new one for clinical psychologists, has become their primary professional function. Consequently, we shall devote a considerable portion of the rest of the present volume to examining, discussing, and evaluating this aspect of the work of the clinical psychologist. It should be emphasized, however, that psychotherapy is not an exclusive professional function of the psychologist. Psychiatrists antedated the clinical psychologist in performing such functions, and at the present time a number of other professions, as well as groups which may or may not be viewed as professions, are also engaged in such activities. Among them are counseling psychologists, school psychologists, psychiatric social workers, psychiatric nurses, rehabilitation counselors, ministers, group workers, indigenous mental health workers, counselors of various types, and others. Thus, although many undergraduate, as well as graduate, students apparently see clinical psychology as synonymous with psychotherapy, it should be clear that this view is not an accurate one. There are many different roads that a person may take in order to engage in psychotherapeutic activities.

Another interesting, and sometimes bewildering, aspect of psychotherapy is that there are so many orientations or schools of psychtherapy. Among others, for example, there are the therapeutic approaches of Freud, Adler, Jung, Rank, Horney, Sullivan, Rogers, Frankl, Ellis, Kelly, Thorne, Wolpe, Stampfl, and A. T. Beck. There are also different varieties of group therapy, play therapy, brief therapy, marital therapy, and family therapy. Although these are merely a partial listing, they do provide the reader with some conception of the numerous types of psychotherapeutic orientations that exist. The type of theoretical orientation the individual psychologist favors will obviously influence her preference for a particular therapeutic approach and the specific emphases that will characterize her own individual mode of operation. Nevertheless, despite this variation, there are some general characteristics of psychotherapeutic activity that cut across the different approaches and which have served to identify this particular form of activity. To a certain extent, also, some of these features would apply as well to the more recent behavioral approaches in this area.

Psychotherapy in some form is probably as old as language or interpersonal communication between persons. That is to say, that one may hypothesize that in the distant past of man's history someone sought encouragement, reassurance, or advice from another, or told his tale of frustration and woe to some sympathetic listener. One can view these interpersonal interactions organized around some person's problems as the probable beginnings of psychotherapy. Some sensitive, perceptive, and empathic individual undoubtedly functioned in a manner that helped the troubled person adjust better to his life situation—in other words, in a therapeutic manner. It is probably true, also, that such individuals received no special training for their therapeutic endeavors or did they have any systematic theoretical rationale for what they did. In primitive societies the role of the healer or shaman became more formalized, and such individuals developed their particular rituals and methods of treating various types of human afflictions (Frank, 1961; Kiev, 1964). A more systematic and planned approach to psychotherapy, however, did not appear until much later. In fact, the latter development did not occur until the latter part of the nineteenth century. As a consequence, psychotherapy is a relatively recent development. Perhaps at this point, it would be worthwhile to describe what is meant by psychotherapy and what the psychotherapeutic process entails.

Psychotherapy can be described as a planned interpersonal interaction in which one individual, the therapist, attempts to help, modify, or improve the behavior of another person. Usually, psychotherapy involves an interview in which verbal communication plays a significant role. It should be made clear, however, that mere conversation is not synonymous with psychotherapy, or is the giving of advice or the admonition to someone to "stop worrying" or "buck up." Basically, psychotherapy involves the particular relationship that develops between therapist and client, a relationship that tends to differ in certain respects from most other relationships that the client has had with other people. Although the client, of necessity, must relate to the therapist as he tends to relate to others, the purpose of the relationship, the opportunities for self-expression, the sincere interest of the therapist in the client, and the understanding of human behavior, which the therapist brings to the setting, make this an unusual and distinctive relationship. Although the patient may react to the therapist as he has reacted to other significant figures in his life, the responses of the therapist are different from those that would be forthcoming from such persons or anticipated in other interpersonal situations. The therapist is not there to judge the patient as others might do, but to try to fully understand him and his problems and to provide a setting in which the patient may be able to explore his difficulties and modify his behavior. It is not only the therapist's knowledge of human difficulties that distinguishes him from other persons, but the way he relates to the patient, his sympathetic desire to help, and his creation of an atmosphere for self-exploration and change.

We shall have more to say about the process of psychotherapy later. But, from what has been said, it should be apparent that the therapeutic session does not consist of something akin to a private lecture in which the therapist, after listening to the patient, diagnoses his difficulties, and tells the patient what is wrong with him. It is not the imparting of superior knowledge to the patient. The emphasis in most forms of psychotherapy is on the interpersonal experience through which the patient, in interaction with the therapist, is able to become more hopeful about his situation, to reorganize his perceptions, to gain some understanding of his problem, to attempt new modes of response, and, hopefully, to modify his behavior in a positive direction.

THE PATIENT OR CLIENT

Psychotherapy usually takes place because an individual has some problem or difficulty in adjustment that causes him discomfort or is upsetting to those with whom he lives. The person who experiences only the minor difficulties unavoidable in life and resolves these problems satisfactorily is not likely to seek (or need) psychotherapy.

The circumstances under which psychotherapy is initiated varies with the type of problem and the specific environmental setting. The problems for which individuals seek psychotherapeutic help vary widely and include almost every type of human problem, symptom, or complaint. The following constitute only a small illustrative sample: inability to concentrate, failure in school, excessive shyness, vocational dissatisfaction, nervousness, tension, depression, anxiety, marital disharmony, frigidity, homosexual concerns, truancy, stealing, enuresis, social isolation, morbid thoughts, fire setting, sleeplessness, amnesia, feelings of hostility, headaches, chest pains, and a variety of other types of somatic and related symptoms. Perhaps, it should be added here, as a note of caution, that while individuals with the above presenting complaints have in fact been referred for psychotherapy, it is not implied that psychotherapy can effectively "cure" all such complaints.

It is probably obvious from the above list that referrals for psychotherapy come from diverse sources and that there is some relationship between various types of symptoms and referral source. Complaints of a medical or somatic nature usually lead the individual to consult his physician. When no organic basis for the symptoms are found, or when the symptoms do not respond to the usual medical treatments, the individual may be referred for psychotherapy or psychiatric evaluation. Problems of truancy, academic failure, stealing, and the like, may be referred for psychotherapeutic help by the school, court, or social agency. Referrals for other symptomatic problems may come from the minister, family physician, friends, newspaper columnists, or from the individual himself. During the past decade or so, there has been much popularization of psychotherapy through articles in newspapers and magazines and dramatizations on the motion picture screen and television. As a consequence, relatively more people today have some knowledge of psychotherapy and are inclined to seek such help for problems they believe are psychological in origin. Such individuals, for the most part, tend to come more frequently from the relatively better educated and higher socioeconomic strata of our society (Hollingshead and Redlich, 1958; Kadushin, 1969). Although lower social class individuals are less likely to seek psychotherapeutic help voluntarily, this has changed somewhat in recent years.

In any event, the individual seeking or referred for psychological help is motivated by a problem or symptom that is *personally* discomforting to him. As far as he is concerned, this is his difficulty and this is what he wants modified or removed. He is not particularly concerned with the reasons for his symptoms or what theoretically they may represent. He is not interested in talk, but in reducing the pain or emotional disturbance he is experiencing. In terms of this, many individuals fail to see how psychotherapy, perceived as mere talking, can possibly help them with their symptoms. This is particularly true of patients with somatic complaints and individuals of limited educational background and low socioeconomic status. More will be said about this problem later. Generally, in terms of most psychotherapeutic approaches, the client must be motivated to seek and begin psychotherapy. If he is not sufficiently motivated, or sufficiently distressed, he either will not seek out psychotherapeutic treatment, or will drop out of treatment shortly after it has begun (Garfield, 1978; Garfield & Affleck, 1959; Hollingshead & Redlich, 1958). This, again, is a matter which will be discussed later.

WHO PRACTICES PSYCHOTHERAPY?

At the beginning of this chapter, some reference was made to the variety of individuals with diverse backgrounds of training and professional affiliations who engage in some type of psychotherapy. The types of persons to be included will depend in great part on our definition of psychotherapy. In the past, psychotherapy was carried out primarily by psychiatrists, clinical psychologists, and psychiatric social workers, the traditional mental health professions. The training of each of these groups has included some instruction and experience in varying amounts in the areas of psychopathology, personality theory, interviewing, and psychotherapy. The extent of the training provided in psychotherapy varied from institution to institution, regardless of discipline. There were also other groups engaging in various types of "counseling activities," however, which may also be viewed as forms of psychotherapy. As already noted, these include guidance counselors in schools and universities, vocational and rehabilitation counselors, counseling psychologists, school psychologists, and similar types of persons. Some ministers also secured special training in psychotherapy and counseling and devoted a share of their time to "pastoral counseling." Some physicians, aware of the psychological aspects of illness, also attempt to relate to their patients in a manner that is psychotherapeutic, and some of them have received brief periods of training designed specifically for them. Nurses, trained in psychiatric nursing, or working in psychiatric hospitals and clinics also have participated in activities of a psychotherapeutic nature. Thus, a number of individuals with diverse professional backgrounds and types of training have been engaged to some extent in activities which might be viewed as psychotherapeutic.

Since the 1960's, this situation has become even more complicated. In part because of the shortage of trained mental health workers, a variety of programs were developed to train individuals in briefer programs to perform various clinical functions. These included 2-year programs in junior colleges, 1-year programs for selected college graduates, and even 6-month programs to train "psychiatric technicians." Although not all of the individuals in such programs were trained specifically to function as psychotherapists, many did function in therapeutic or quasitherapeutic roles. Besides such developments, the popularity of encounter groups led some individuals to function as group leaders, and a number of them were not fully trained psychotherapists. Since it was claimed that such groups were organized to increase the self-actualization of "normal" individuals and were not really therapy groups, such a practice was essentially unregulated. However, some of these activities were quite intense, resembled several of the features of psychotherapy, and even produced some casualties (Parloff, 1970). We shall have more to say about these and related developments in later chapters, but they are mentioned here to indicate the diversity that exists in our society among those who call themselves psychotherapists or who in some fashion provide services that appear to fall within the rhubric of psychotherapy. What is clear is that there is no single profession of psychotherapy.

While it is apparent that many professional and nonprofessional groups with diverse types of training and orientation engage in some form of psychotherapeutic activity, there still exist many problems concerning what constitutes psychotherapy, who may engage in psychotherapy, what is adequate preparation for psychotherapy, and the desirable or necessary personal prerequisites of the psychotherapist. Some of this controversy centers around how psychotherapy is defined. A related problem is in terms of what professional groups can engage in psychotherapy. Some of these discussions have little to do with scientific definitions of psychotherapy and of the psychotherapeutic process. They essentially represent professional and social conflicts, which perhaps go beyond the issue of psychotherapy. As a consequence, this matter will not concern us beyond our making a reference to it and giving an illustration or two of the issues involved.

Through the years, various terms have been used to denote the therapeutic activities of psychologists, for example, remedial work, guidance, counseling, and psychotherapy. It may be worthwhile, therefore, to say a few words about these terms. In the past, certain of the psychologist's efforts with cases referred to him were called remedial work in that they centered about the attempt to correct or improve specific disabilities. Examples of the latter are reading difficulties, speech disorders, and related problems implying some need for reeducation. Cases requiring remediation were frequently referred to psychological or psycho-educational clinics in universities, or to psychologists on the staffs of community guidance clinics. This reflected both the views then held concerning the treatment functions of the clinical psychologist and the type of training accorded psychologists.

Although some mention of training in remedial work was included in the recommended program of the American Psychological Association's Committee on Training in Clinical Psychology in 1947, most university training programs made little provision for such training. In most instances, university courses in remedial reading or speech therapy are given in departments outside of psychology, and specialization in these areas is viewed as belonging to professional groups other than clinical psychology, for example, remedial reading teachers, speech pathologists, school psychologists, and the like. Clinical psychologists since World War II have not concerned themselves much with remedial efforts in a designated function or skill. Rather, they have worked in psychotherapy with problems of personality maladjustment, and have focused on the individual's overall adjustment. Accompanying this was the dominant point of view that one treats patients, rather than symptoms. Thus, a speech or reading problem may be but one symptomatic manifestation of an underlying personality problem. Consequently, psychotherapy aimed at alleviating the underlying causes of the person's difficulties might be more effective than modification of the symptoms alone. In some clinical settings, for example, remedial efforts in an area like reading might be utilized along with other approaches, such as play therapy and interviews with the parents. Such an appraisal involves a greater attention to the personality factors attending a given case and a necessarily broader background of clinical training (Sobel, 1948). This type of approach, of course, reflected the then dominant psychodynamic emphasis in clinical psychology. It should be apparent that the more recent developments in behavior modification would not be congruent with this point of view, since the modification of specific behaviors do receive serious attention.

A more difficult problem is that of differentiating counseling from psychotherapy. There have been several discussions about the difference between these two activities, and there is no unanimity concerning these differences (Bordin, 1955; Garfield, 1957). Recognizing that both are techniques for helping individuals with personal problems and that they both utilize the interview situation with a client, we can try to emphasize a few aspects or dimensions in which they differ.

Counseling is, of course, a term that is used to describe a variety of relationships with a client. The lawyer gives counsel to his client and is ofttimes referred to as "counselor." There are marital counseling, employment counseling, vocational counseling, rehabilitation counseling, guidance counseling, pastoral counseling, and similar categories of counseling activities. When counseling is referred to in relation to psychotherapeutic activities, however, it usually has more specific reference to help with problems of personality adjustment. As contrasted with psychotherapy, it refers most frequently to nonmedical settings and nonmedical personnel. Traditionally, counseling of this type has largely occurred in university or school settings, but also in agencies concerned with family and marital problems. Psychologists and educators have used the term most frequently to designate their activities with clients. Counseling has also been used to designate psychological work with more "normal" or less disturbed individuals. Usually, also, counseling has had reference to a somewhat briefer and less intensive interpersonal process than psychotherapy, although this is not always the case. Intensive psychotherapy has emphasized more the dynamic and emotional interplay between therapist and patient than is true of the counseling process, and more attention has been paid to unconscious factors in the former than in the latter. As stated by Bordin, "The counseling relationship is characterized by much less intensity of emotional expression and relatively more emphasis upon cognitive and rational factors than is the relationship in psychotherapy" (Bordin, 1955, p. 15).

In recent years, however, the term, "counseling," has been used also to denote a type of activity that differs from the older type of guidance and counseling referred to in the preceding paragraph. The more recent trend with regard to counseling activities reveals a greater sensitivity to the counselor–client interaction in the interview situation. This is reflected in a more general emphasis on the interpersonal aspects of counseling, particularly the attitudes and feelings of the client, and a correspondingly lessened emphasis and reliance on test data. Associated with this has been a greater recognition of the importance of personality factors in all types of counseling problems. Also more attention has been paid to counseling individuals with personal problems of adjustment. This type of counseling, in turn, overlaps with the type of activity called psychotherapy, and is exemplified by the approach of Carl Rogers, whose first book in this area, interestingly enough, was called *Counseling and Psychotherapy* (1942).

Because there is some overlap between counseling and psychotherapy, there is little to be gained by attempts at detailed differentiation of these concepts or by discussing counseling activities separately. As has been indicated, some differences exist and are reflected in the divisional organization of the American Psychological Association. It can be assumed that the term, "counseling," is utilized more frequently by psychologists in the Division of Counseling Psychology than is true for psychologists in the Division of Clinical Psychology. With regard to psychotherapy, the reverse would be true.

In terms of the preceding discussion, most "counselors" would be seen as engaging in counseling activities rather than therapy and would not view themselves as psychotherapists. Nevertheless, as has been pointed out, some of them may engage in counseling activities that are difficult to distinguish from psychotherapy.

There is, however, another aspect of the matter of who does psychotherapy, which is somewhat different from the one just discussed. This has to do with legal and professional problems concerning what psychotherapy is and who may engage in it.

As already noted, many professional groups have participated, and continue to participate, in psychotherapy or in activities which overlap with psychotherapy. Nevertheless, as was discussed in Chapter 1, there has been a tendency on the part of psychiatrists and others in the past to see psychotherapy as a form of medical therapy. The view of organized medical groups is that illness, including all forms of "mental illness," is the province of the physician.

Legally, and traditionally, this has been their responsibility. While few qualified people would question the physician's proper role in cases of illness, psychologists and other professional groups have questioned the efficacy of viewing adjustment difficulties as illness and have opposed the view that "psychotherapy" falls exclusively within the province of medicine (Adams, 1964; Balance, Hirschfield, & Bringmann, 1970; Szasz, 1960). Instead of viewing psychotherapy as a form of medical treatment, they see it as a psychological or reeducative procedure involving learning and interpersonal processes. The latter, being psychological and behavioral, thus fall within the psychological and behavioral sciences fully as much as within the field of medicine. In any event, this is an issue that, while generating considerable heat in the past, does not appear to be of great importance today. In practice, many psychologists and other nonmedical groups who engage in psychotherapy with emotionally disturbed individuals work in psychiatric clinics or hospitals. In these instances, there is usually little conflict about who does psychotherapy, since the setting is a medical one and, if problems of a medical nature arise, appropriate consultation is available. In terms of private practice or practice in nonmedical settings, the responsibility is clearly on the psychologist to work with cases within his domain of competence, and to seek consultation or make the appropriate referral when this is indicated. The professional psychologist has a code of ethics to guide his practice and the enactment of certification and licensure laws in most states also tends to provide minimum standards for practice.

REQUISITES OF A GOOD PSYCHOTHERAPIST

Apart from the specific training required for the different professions engaged in psychotherapy, there are some general qualities that seem to be required of a good psychotherapist. In terms of intellectual knowledge and understanding, it is apparent that the psychotherapist needs to know a great deal about psychopathology and the various manifestations of maladjustive behavior. Not only does the therapist need to know what kinds of cases may be helped by psychotherapeutic methods, but he must be aware of problems in the accurate diagnosis of disturbed behavior, when to utilize additional resources, and when to make appropriate referrals elsewhere. He must be informed concerning theories of personality and development, not only in terms of their relationship to psychopathology but, also, in terms of understanding the behavior and conflicts of the individual. Such knowledge provides a base for the therapist's approach to the patient and his expectancies concerning the patient's behavior in therapy. This is of some importance because there is really no specific set of techniques that the therapist can routinely apply in all cases of personality disturbance. For example, an individual whose integration is seriously threatened may need strong support from the therapist and frequent contact with her. A too rapid attempt at psychological probing to secure "insight" may actually be disruptive rather than therapeutic. On the other hand, in another case, the supportive approach could lead to the fostering of prolonged dependency on the part of the patient, thus impeding his progress to more independent and mature functioning. In the fullest sense, therefore, the therapist needs to understand human behavior.

In addition to an understanding of behavior, the therapist also needs to be well informed concerning therapeutic procedures, major theories of psychotherapy, and the kinds of problems encountered in psychotherapy. Although the therapist may eventually prefer one type of therapeutic approach over others (Fey, 1958), he should be reasonably informed of other approaches lest he be too rigid in his orientation to therapy (Wolberg, 1967). An individual who follows exclusively, and somewhat inflexibly, one particular therapeutic procedure essentially requires the patient to adapt to his approach rather than attempting to modify his approach and procedures to meet the needs of a particular patient (Garfield, 1980).

In addition to specific knowledge in the areas of psychopathology and psychotherapy, it is probably important that the therapist be a reasonably well-educated and informed individual in the broad sense of the term. The emphasis is not on the acquisition of a wide array of erudite, esoteric bits of information. Rather, reference is made to a broad knowledge of how people live, differential patterns of response in the various subcultures of our society, and some understanding of particular adjustment problems in these groups. For example, if the therapist is to fully understand what the patient tells him about his life situation and his perception of the world, he must have at least some information and knowledge concerning them. How such knowledge can best be secured is far from settled, and one is not at all sure that courses in the social sciences will necessarily accomplish this task. Nevertheless, there are some research data that suggest the importance of such understanding for the psychotherapist (Lorion, 1978). For example, can a therapist from an upper class social background and milieu fully understand and appraise what a patient from a much lower strata of society conveys to him in terms of the values and patterns of his own group (Hollingshead and Redlich, 1958)?

Thus far the importance of specific types of knowledge for the psychotherapist has been emphasized. There is little question that both broad and specific knowledge are important and are a basic part of the preparation of any professional person. Nevertheless, there is obviously more to being a good psychotherapist than merely having a mind crammed with all sorts of psychological knowledge. As has been indicated, psychotherapy is an interpersonal process. As a consequence, the personality of the therapist is an integral part of the therapeutic process for much more than mere verbal knowledge and intellectual discussion is involved. The feelings of both participants also enter into this interaction. Although we still need much more scientific knowledge about the types of personality that seem best suited for specific types of therapy with specific groups of patients, there is little question that some individuals appear to be better therapists than others. Thus, the personality of the therapist, particuarly in interaction with a client, is one of the significant variables in psychotherapy. This aspect has, of course, been apparent to many students of psychotherapy. As a result, certain personality traits have been mentioned frequently as prerequisites for the competent therapist. One of these qualities appears to be the ability to empathize with the patient and his difficulties. From one therapeutic school in particular, the ability of the therapist to put himself in the place of the patient in order to experience as fully as possible what the patient has experienced has been particularly stressed (Rogers, 1959), and a certain amount of research has been reported in partial support of this view (Gurman, 1977; Kurtz & Grummon, 1972; Mitchell, Bozarth, & Krauft, 1977; Truax & Carkhuff, 1967; Truax & Mitchell, 1971). This ability to empathize is important not only in terms of understanding the patient, but also for communicating to the patient that the therapist really does understand him and is interested in helping him. This particular aspect of the therapeutic relationship has been deemed of great importance by a number of therapists.

Somewhat related to the above is the need for sensitivity on the part of the therapist. This attribute has also been stressed by many therapists. The therapist must be sensitive not only to the verbal communication of the patient, but also to all aspects of interpersonal communication. How the patient says something, how he looks at the therapist, his gestures, and the like, all communicate something of his feelings, to which the therapist must be sensitive. If the therapist is a person who lacks this quality of sensitivity, it is likely that he will be unable to fully understand the feelings and perceptions of the patient, what the patient is attempting to communicate to him, and how the patient in general reacts to him as a person.

Since the personality of the therapist is so intimately involved in the interpersonal process of psychotherapy, many therapists adhere to the view that the therapist needs some knowledge of himself as a person, of his impact on others, of how he reacts to stimuli that are threatening to him, and his own major conflicts and defenses. Some self-knowledge is thus considered to be an important prerequisite of the therapist. The therapist must be sensitive to his own feelings and behaviors as well as those of the patient. Because of this, many psychotherapists believe that every psychotherapist should undergo personal psychotherapy (Fromm-Reichmann, 1950; Garfield & Kurtz,

1976; Holt, 1971). In this way, the would-be therapist not only secures some understanding of what the patient experiences in psychotherapy, but gains important insights and understandings about himself. It is believed that such personal therapy will help the therapist understand some of his own blind spots and thus allow him greater awareness and objectivity in working with comparable problems with patients. The importance of personal therapy for the therapist has perhaps been emphasized most by the various psychoanalytical training institutes. Following the views of Freud, these institutes require a personal psychoanalysis for each of their training candidates.

Whether every psychotherapist needs personal psychotherapy in order to be a competent psychotherapy is at present a matter of personal opinion or conviction (Garfield, 1977; Holt, 1971). Scientific studies of this problem, as well as many others in this field, are a rarity and conclusive evidence to support or reject this view is lacking (Garfield & Bergin, 1971; Garfield & Kurtz, 1976; Rotter, 1960; Strupp, 1955). The writer has known competent therapists who have had no personal therapy, and also many that have. This observation, however, is obviously too limited to form the basis of any sound generalization. One can probably state, though, that some therapists have less need for personal psychotherapy than others. They have led richer personal lives, appear more sensitive and more perceptive of others, are more mature, and relatively more stable than other individuals. Because of this, such persons appear to profit more readily from their training and supervised experience with patients than do others. In other instances, individuals exhibit personal problems that clearly appear to interfere with their therapeutic work with patients. Sometimes these personal difficulties interfere with the individual's work with most of his patients. In other cases, the therapist's problems affect his work with certain types of patients, for example, aggressive patients, overly dependent ones, or cases with latent homosexual conflicts. In the latter instances, personal therapy for the therapist may be considered necessary if he is to overcome these personal difficultes and become a more effective therapist. There are, of course, instances where individuals simply lack the necessary qualifications for becoming an effective therapist and need to consider other alternatives.

In discussing the importance of the therapist's knowledge of himself as a person, some allusion was made also to other desired personality attributes of the therapist. Ideally, he should be a person who is mature emotionally, has reasonable security of self, and whose life situation outside of therapy provides him with adequate personal satisfaction of his needs. His own conflicts and tensions should be minimal and not enter or unduly influence his psychotherapeutic work with patients. He should be reasonably well integrated and able to attend to the problems of the patient without becoming unduly involved emotionally in these problems or having his own problems intrude.

While sympathetic and sensitive to the feelings and thoughts of the patient, the therapist also needs to maintain an objective orientation.

Finally, the therapist should be a person of integrity with a deep sense of responsibility for his patients. Since it is expected that the patient will discuss intimate aspects of his own personality with the therapist, it is essential that the latter be a person in whom the patient can place the utmost faith and trust. What the patient reveals in the therapeutic hours must be treated as extremely confidential. Except under extraordinary circumstances, the patient's confidences are private and are not to be revealed to any other person. Any departure from this pattern is bound to have negative consequences for psychotherapy. In a related vein, the therapist must be able to accept what the patient tells him with no attempts at moral evaluation. The therapist is not a person who judges the patient in terms of moral and social conventions, but is one who is sincerely interested in understanding the patient and helping him with his problems. In assuming therapeutic responsibility for the patient, the therapist takes on a certain obligation to see the patient through his difficulties. He thus must be a responsible person who has enough psychological resources to fulfill his role and his obligations. In accepting a patient for psychotherapy, the therapist consequently assumes a real responsibility, which in some forms of therapy, may last for several years.

Some of the desired qualities of the therapist just discussed have been specifically defined and studied by adherents of the Rogerian or Client-Centered approach to psychotherapy. They have emphasized three therapist characteristics as being essential for positive movement and outcome in psychotherapy—accurate empathy, genuineness, and nonpossessive warmth or positive regard (Rogers, 1959; Truax and Mitchell, 1971). We have already commented upon the matter of empathy. Genuineness refers to the therapist being nondefensive and authentic in his interaction with the client, whereas nonpossessive warmth has reference to the therapist's providing a nonthreatening and trusting atmosphere in therapy through his own acceptance and valuing of the client. While other orientations to psychotherapy have also emphasized similar qualities in the therapist, the Client-Centered therapists have defined these attributes, developed scales for their measurement, and investigated their importance by means of research (Truax and Carkhuff, 1967).

Although the above list of attributes of the therapist may appear to depict a somewhat superhuman individual and, parenthetically, a person whom one rarely encounters in actual experience, it is well to remember that these are desired characteristics of the good therapist. Probably few therapists have all these attributes, although the best may have many of them. The preceding statements also should not be interpreted to mean that the best adjusted individual necessarily makes the best therapist. It is conceivable that the latter individual may be relatively insensitive to the problems of others or react to them mainly in an intellectual fashion, since they are beyond any of his own experiences. On the other hand, the individual who is severely disturbed himself, probably cannot view the patient's problems in proper perspective or keep his own difficulties from intruding into those of the patient. The findings in one small study did show a positive correlation between the adjustment level of the therapist and outcome in psychotherapy (Garfield & Bergin, 1971).

In spite of some consensus concerning desirable qualities for the psychotherapist (Holt, 1971; Holt and Luborsky, 1958), however, it still is a difficult task to do an adequate job of selecting and predicting those who will turn out to be good therapists. The intensive investigation of psychiatric residents at the Menninger School of Psychiatry by Holt and Luborsky (1958) illustrates how much more we need to know in this regard. Generally, predictions of therapeutic competence based on interview or psychological test data were low. While other studies have compared experienced as contrasted with inexperienced therapists (Auerbach & Johnson, 1977), and a few have appraised some selected personality variables of therapists, our description of desired qualities in the psychotherapist are based largely on opinions of experienced therapists (Garfield, 1977, 1981; Parloff, Waskow, & Wolfe, 1978). At present we are undoubtedly greatly influenced by our own therapeutic experience but as has been pointed out, we still know comparatively little about what type of therapists secure the most favorable results with particular patients (Bergin, 1971; Kiesler, 1971; Knupfer, Jackson, and Krieger, 1959; Paul, 1967). As we know more about this problem, we shall undoubtedly discover also that certain therapists are relatively more successful with some categories of patients than others.

TRAINING FOR PSYCHOTHERAPY

At the present time there is no one generally accepted program of training for the person who is to function as a psychotherapist. As has been mentioned previously, individuals from different professions engage in psychotherapy and represent very different backgrounds in terms of their professional preparation and training. Currently, one cannot be trained solely as a psychotherapist because training in this activity usually constitutes only a part of the training program for particular professions, and specialized training programs in psychotherapy are available primarily for those who are already qualified in a particular field. In other words, physicians, social workers, and psychologists, as well as some others, may receive specialized training in psychotherapy *after* they have completed the training required for their own profession.

Some didactic and practicum training in psychotherapy and/or behavior therapy is included in most graduate programs in clinical psychology. The extent of instruction in psychotherapy for clinical psychology students will vary from program to program. In some programs there may be several courses in psychotherapy including fairly extensive experience with clients under close supervision. In these courses, sound or video recordings of patient interviews may be secured and discussed in detail with the supervisory faculty. In addition, the clinical psychology student will receive both seminars and supervised experience in psychotherapy in most approved internship training programs.

Although training in psychotherapy is provided in graduate clinical psychology programs, some individuals feel that additional training in psychotherapy is needed to ensure a desired level of competence. Postdoctoral training in psychotherapy has been one of the recommended courses of action. A number of psychologists have pursued postdoctoral programs of training, and such programs usually emphasize additional supervised training in psychotherapy. However, as training in psychotherapy in graduate clinical programs has increased, the demands for such postdoctoral training may have lessened. It should be made clear, however, that instruction in psychotherapy constitutes only one segment of the total training program in clinical psychology.

COMMON ASPECTS OF PSYCHOTHERAPY

As noted before, there are many different theories and techniques of psychotherapy. Consequently, the present heading may seem to be somewhat surprising. Nevertheless, in spite of what appear to be significant theoretical and technical differences among the different schools of psychotherapy, there are also indications that successful psychotherapy of one or the other varieties may have ingredients or elements that are also found in other types of successful psychotherapy. What may appear to be a dilemma can be explained in several possible ways. Ostensible differences among therapeutic orientations may result from the fact that certain particular or unique aspects of a given approach are unduly emphasized in identifying or delineating that approach. Thus, what is distinctive about a given orientation tends to be emphasized. The adherence to specialized terms and concepts that have been associated with a particular approach to psychotherapy also tends to stress what appear to be unique features of a given brand of psychotherapy. When a particular approach thus tends to focus attention on concepts defined within a given orientation, the particular operations or behaviors engaged in by the therapist appear to be lost within the conceptual and theoretical structure that the therapist is supposedly following.

Perhaps we can approach the matter best by beginning with some of the more obvious and simple aspects of psychotherapy. Basically, we can ask what apparent factors in psychotherapy each of the psychotherapies have in common. At this level, we might respond by stating that most psychotherapies consist of a therapist, a patient, some clinic or office setting, and some type of interaction that goes on between therapist and client. The client or patient, regardless of the orientation of the therapist, is seeking some type of help for his particular psychological difficulties. The therapist, whatever his theoretical persuasion, attempts to offer the patient a setting in which the latter may hopefully solve his problems, overcome his difficulties, and increase his level of adjustment. Although this analysis may seem obvious or superficial, it does point to some aspects of psychotherapy that appear to be common to most of the psychotherapies. Let us now proceed to other aspects of psychotherapy that appear to operate or be present in practically all effective psychotherapeutic approaches.

One important psychological aspect of any type of psychotherapy is the implication it has for helping the patient with his problems. In essence, the initiation of psychotherapy offers some hope to the individual who is psychologically disturbed. While we have, as yet, little in the way of research data concerning the importance of this aspect of psychotherapy, it would appear to be of some importance in the initial stages of psychotherapy (Frank, 1961). In initiating psychotherapy with a psychotherapist, the patient is being offered, directly or by implication, some hope for the amelioration of his problem. Whether the psychotherapist is an analyst, a behavior therapist, or an Adlerian, would seemingly have only relative importance in this area. As far as the patient is concerned, the therapist is a potential source of help. This view of the therapist, then, would appear to be common to most psychotherapies.

Another common feature to be found in all psychotherapy is that all forms of psychotherapy begin because the patient has some problem or feelings of discomfort. The type of symptom or difficulty may vary widely, but regardless of what it is, it is this discomfort that initiates the desire for treatment. Related to this, as noted previously, is the matter of motivation for psychotherapy. The patient must have enough subjective distress or discomfort to motivate him to seek therapy or it will not begin. In some instances, particularly with children, the pressure for seeking treatment may come from others. Generally, however, most individuals seek psychotherapy because they want to be helped with some particular problem or something that they experience as discomforting.

The problem of motivation for psychotherapy is also a problem that is of common concern to different therapeutic approaches. In contrast to other forms of treatment, most psychotherapies require some participation on the part of the patient. If the patient is not motivated to seek out therapy it is quite likely that he will not participate actively and, as it were, fail to fulfill his role in the therapeutic situation. This reluctance on the part of individuals to participate actively or fully in psychotherapy can be manifested in many different ways. An obvious one, of course, is to fail to keep appointments and to discontinue therapy after only relatively few contacts with the therapist. This happens with a large number of patients (Garfield, 1978). The patient's resistance to treatment may also be manifested in more covert ways. He may demand specific services, advice, or medication from the therapist or in other ways fail to engage actively in the therapeutic interaction. We will have more to say about such problems later, but at this stage it is sufficient to point out that the matter of motivation for therapy and the readiness of the client to participate in psychotherapy or to adopt a therapeutic role are problems of somewhat general importance for most of the psychotherapies. Various therapeutic systems may deal with these matters in different ways, but the problem itself is common to most.

Another aspect of psychotherapy that is common to most psychotherapies involves the setting of a specific time and place for psychotherapy. Generally, there is some orderly sequence of interviews so that whether these be weekly, daily, or monthly, there is a specific time set aside for the psychotherapy meeting. In most situations the amount of time set aside has also become somewhat conventional. Fifty minutes, give or take a few minutes, appears to be the most frequent time utilized for a psychotherapeutic session. In fact, the therapy session is usually referred to as the therapeutic or 50-minute "hour."

Most psychotherapies also utilize some kind of communication between the participants. Generally, most emphasis is placed on verbal communication, although attention is also given to gestures and similar types of nonverbal communication. In the case of children, play may be used as a means of communication and interaction between the child and the therapist. In behavior and cognitive therapies, some emphasis will be placed on the performance of tasks and "homework." However, communication is involved also in the directions given and in the reporting of progress. Thus, ease and clarity of communication between therapist and client would appear to have some importance for most psychotherapeutic orientations.

Once the patient has presented himself for psychological help, he is given an opportunity to state his reasons for consulting the therapist. This usually involves some discussion of the patient's symptoms or problems as he sees them. Most likely the patient will have several queries concerning what is wrong with him, whether the therapist can help him, how long therapy will take, and so on. During the first interview, arrangements will be made for other interviews, unless deemed unnecessary; and such matters as appointment time, frequency of interviews, fees, possibility of help, and probable length of treatment will also be discussed. The therapist should be honest in appraising the patient's case. Frequently the precise duration of therapy cannot be stated, or is it feasible or ethical to promise a complete cure. Usually, too, the patient will be given some orientation to therapy in terms of what is expected of her as well as what she can expect from the therapist. Although different therapists will vary in how these matters are discussed, some attention to them will be given by most therapists.

In the first interview or so, the therapist will attempt to evaluate the patient in terms of her personality resources, her complaints, her past history, attitudes toward therapy, and her potentialities for the type of therapy available. Sometimes several interviews may be utilized to secure additional information from the patient before any definite decision about specific arrangements for therapy are made. Special diagnostic examinations may also be called for at this time before final conclusions concerning therapy are reached. The patient referred to a psychotherapist, for example, may be so disturbed that the therapist recommends hospitalization. But, if there are no ostensible counterindications at this time, then plans can be made along the lines mentioned above for continuing treatment.

During the initial interviews the therapist thus has to make an appraisal of the patient in terms of the latter's suitability for psychotherapy and in terms of the particular approach to be used with him. In general, patients with average to above average intelligence and verbal ability, whose symptoms are more acute rather than chronic, who are not too advanced in age, and who do not appear to be deriving indirect satisfactions or benefits from their symptoms, are considered to be potentially better patients for psychotherapy (Colby, 1951). Psychotic patients and those with long-standing character disorders are most difficult to treat. Some tentative plan of treatment, therefore, has to be formulated for each specific patient.

In most therapeutic approaches, as therapy proceeds, greater emphasis is placed upon the relationship that develops between therapist and patient. Although this relationship may be conceptualized and utilized in somewhat different ways, depending upon the theoretical orientation of the therapist, it still is given a role of crucial importance in most therapies (Garfield, 1980; Strupp, 1977). Whether it be called rapport, transference, or some other name, the specific interpersonal relationship that develops in therapy is considered of basic importance by practically all therapists. How this relationship is viewed or utilized theoretically may vary in terms of specific therapeutic orientations. But unless a good relationship is secured between therapist and client, one which can be used to further the therapy, the results will usually be less than satisfactory. Certain aspects of this relationship, as well as the somewhat unique atmosphere of the therapeutic situation, would appear to provide a common thread among therapeutic approaches and to have a somewhat comparable impact on the patient. Generally, this will be more true of those therapeutic approaches which do not rely primarily on a directive or authoritarian role for the therapist. In what follows, an attempt will be made to describe in somewhat nontechnical language what these generalized attributes of the therapeutic relationship appear to be.

One can state at the outset that the therapeutic relationship is a somewhat unique one that differs from other relationships in a number of potentially significant ways. First of all, the therapist is, or should be, someone whom the patient can trust and respect. Regardless of the therapeutic orientations, this would appear to be an aspect of therapy that is basic and important to all forms of psychotherapy. From this point of view, it would be hypothesized that successful psychotherapy would not result if the therapist is someone in whom the patient cannot place his trust and confidence. In fact, this feature of psychotherapy has much in common with many other forms of healing. Frank (1961) has commented upon some of the apparent similarities between more primitive healers, such as shamans and witchdoctors, and psychothera-pists. In terms of the perceived role of the healer, the same problem can be viewed from another perspective. For example, the expectancies of the patient in terms of being helped, his attitudes toward the healer, and such phenomena as the placebo effect are all pertinent to the particular problem. The therapist is seen as an expert healing person in whom the patient can have confidence. Some of the attitudes in this regard are culturally determined, and may be reinforced by certain culturally accumulated beliefs. This is particularly evident in the healing rites of certain primitive societies, but can also be noted in some groups in our own society (Frank, 1961). The role of expert may vary considerably between a more medically oriented or directive therapist, on the one hand, and that of the very permissive psychotherapist, on the other. Nevertheless, both of these roles would have in common that of the person to whom the client brings his problem and from whom he seeks help. This particular attribute has many complex aspects that appear to be important, particularly, in the early stages of psychotherapy.

The placebo effect, for example, usually refers to the effect produced by the use of some nonspecific drug or therapy (Shapiro & Morris, 1978). In medical research a specific drug is compared with a placebo, which may look like the drug in question, but which supposedly is inert or has no specific effect on the condition under study. The drug is compared with a placebo in order to ascertain the specific effects of the drug. Placebo effects are pre-sumed to be more generalized effects related to the patient's being given some apparent medication or pill by a socially sanctioned healer. Thus, an individual who is helped by a placebo would appear to be helped by something other than a specific pharmacological agent. What is involved here is a complex phenomenon involving the prestige of the healer, his socially sanctioned role, and the patient's expectations about being helped.

The relationship between therapist and patient has thus far been stressed and yet it may appear somewhat mystical or magical to the reader. What is so important about the therapeutic relationship? How does this differ from other relationships? What is responsible for the improvement in the patient? Why cannot a person receive the same therapeutic help from discussion with a friend or parent? These are some questions that might be raised. Although it is difficult to give a brief yet adequate description of what psychotherapy entails without distorting the complex processes involved, some such description will be offered.

The psychotherapist's role differs from that of a friend's or parent's role in that his only association with the client relates to that of the client's problems and his need for help. In addition, he is supposedly a person with some knowledge of and experience with these types of human difficulties. As we have indicated, the therapist is a sympathetic, yet objective, person who is not involved in all the complexities of the patient's existence, except as they relate to therapy. The therapist thus helps to provide an environment in which the client feels increasingly free to reveal the innermost aspects of his personality. Contrary to what may have occurred elsewhere, or to his own expectations, the patient is not condemned for revealing negative aspects of himself. The therapist accepts him as a person, appears to understand him, and is interested in working with him. As a consequence, the patient is provided an opportunity for discussing many things that he might ordinarily not feel free to discuss with a parent or a friend. For example, he may have performed certain acts which he feels that his parents would not condone, or he may have feelings of hostility and aggression toward a particular parent which he would hesitate to verbalize to parents or others. The therapeutic situation thus allows the individual to bring forth and appraise these disturbing aspects of himself.

In this connection, the author recalls one client with whom he worked in psychotherapy. The client was a college student who had voluntarily sought professional help with his personal difficulties. When he entered the office he appeared very anxious and acutely disturbed. In appearance he was untidy and disheveled—and this was at a time when such an appearance was not typical of his peers. He started out by stating that he was emotionally upset, was doing poorly in school, and was on the verge of withdrawing from the university. As he discussed these matters, he became very critical of himself and stated that he was not doing as well as he should. He had a scholarship and felt he should perform at a very high level to justify retaining this scholarship. He believed he was unworthy and that he was letting the people down who were responsible for this scholarship award.

The author at first experienced some concern about the potential seriousness of the client's problem, since there was so much guilt, anxiety, depression, and self-recrimination. In order to understand the client better and to make a more adequate appraisal of him, however, the client was given several appointments and allowed to discuss his difficulties freely in an atmosphere of acceptance. After a few interviews, the client appeared to get a better grip on himself, apparently as a result of the acceptance and support provided by the therapeutic situation. It was apparent that some relationship had been established between therapist and client and that the therapist was seen as a person who could be trusted. In terms of this relationship the client felt increasingly free to explore his difficulties and to reveal some of the deeper problems that were of concern to him and responsible for his current level of adjustment. The major emphasis in these interviews was on providing a warm and accepting situation for the client. As a result, in the sixth interview the client brought up a problem that was of real concern to him. This concerned his masturbatory activities and the extreme feelings of guilt and shame that were associated with these activities. In terms of his previous experience, masturbation had been viewed as a wicked, sinful, and degenerate activity. It was only in an accepting and nonmoralistic situation that he finally felt free enough to unburden himself about this problem. As he gave free expression to his feelings of shame and ventilated his fears about the consequences of his masturbation, he achieved tremendous relief. There was a noted change in his view of himself and his situation. The fact that everything he brought forth was accepted with no surprise and with no condemnation provided an atmosphere in which he could express himself and see his problem in a much different light. From this point on, he made rather marked improvement in therapy and in his subsequent adjustment.

As is apparent in the preceding illustration, if a positive relationship is established, the client also secures some kind of support from the therapist and the therapeutic situation. If he has been beset by troublesome anxieties and fears, he may feel that he now has someone to whom he can turn and with whom he can discuss his innermost feelings. There is little question that the patient can distort the role of the therapist, but generally he can derive some support from his presence. In other words, he is not alone with his problems. There is some chance for improving his situation. Thus hope is fostered by the therapeutic relationship. The therapist also provides him with the courage to examine some of negative aspects of his personality. If the relationship is a good one, he can sense the sincere interest of the therapist, which tends to make this experience unique, that is, the therapist is interested in him as a person with no ulterior motives or demands on him.

As the patient feels more secure in therapy, he is able to bring forth and appraise many more facets of his personality and his difficulties. With varying degrees of activity, the therapist helps him to face his important feelings and some of the conflictual aspects of his personality. After first accepting such aspects of his personality as parts of himself, the patient can later explore their development and their significance for him. In this sense, therapy is also a learning or growth experience. In a sympathetic and sometimes firm manner, the therapist may help the patient face realistic problems that he has tended to avoid. As a result of this experience, the patient may be able to modify his perception of himself and also his perception of others. In this connection he may throughout therapy see the therapist in a number of different roles and gradually be able to also perceive him more realistically. For example, the patient may react to the therapist as he reacted to other significant figures in his past life. He may be subservient, or hostile, or demanding, regardless of the behavior manifested by the therapist. In other words, he responds in terms of his learned and characteristic patterns of interpersonal relations. If the patient characteristically has been hostile to authority figures, he may react this way to the therapist. He responds to the therapist as if the latter were an authority figure in his past experience. Such manifestations have been referred to as transference reactions or parataxic distortions. As they are manifestations of the patient's difficulties in relating to others, they can be dealt with directly in therapy. Thus, discussions in therapy do not deal with abstract or general material, but with the actual behavior of the patient in the therapeutic situation.

One case comes to mind which illustrates some aspects of what psychodynamic therapists have termed the transference relationship, but what may be viewed simply as the patient manifesting his characteristic patterns of behavior in relation to the therapist. At one stage in therapy, the patient in this case began to make excessive demands of the therapist, requesting special examinations, medications, extra appointments, and similar types of preferment. When attempts were made to discuss this pattern of behavior, the patient immediately accused the therapist of having no interest in him, of being rejecting, and of not really trying to understand him. In this instance the patient was exhibiting patterns of behavior which he had manifested previously in other life situations. He was relating to the therapist as he had related previously to other significant persons in his past life, and was perceiving the therapist as he had perceived other figures in his life who could not comply with his insatiable demands. Part of the therapeutic task was to help the patient to clearly perceive and understand this behavior and its negative consequences.

It has been stressed that psychotherapy is not mere intellectual discussion. It is not simply that the therapist points out to the patient some of his defects, and then the patient modifies his behavior accordingly. Of much more significance are the total patterns, including emotional ones, which are manifested in therapy and which are being described here. In other words, it is not that the therapist tells the patient what is wrong and what he should be, although some therapeutic approaches may contain such an emphasis (Ellis, 1962); rather, it is that in the therapy situation, the patient is provided an opportunity to explore along with the therapist many aspects of himself. As the patient, himself, perceives and experiences these aspects of self, he can more readily accept them and go on to attempt some modification with the therapist's guidance. It is obvious that words cannot completely describe this kind of process. It should be made clear, however, that this is not a matter of magical mumbo jumbo. The patient must feel secure enough to acknowledge the realities of his current behaviors and to eventually modify his perceptions, cognitions, and behaviors.

There are certain other features that can be expected with some variations in most successful psychotherapy. The patient usually will get some emotional release or catharsis as he tells his story to an interested participant-observer. As the patient unburdens himself of certain conflicting or negative feelings in the accepting therapeutic environment, he experiences some relief. This is comparable to the feeling one experiences when he "gets things off his chest." In most therapies, catharsis or release, alone, is not considered adequate. Nevertheless, it is one of the common factors in psychotherapy and does have some positive value.

In addition to the emotional relief that the patient may experience by simply unburdening himself of painful or conflictual material, he also gains something from the fact that what he relates is accepted by the therapist without censure. Feeling free to discuss negative or repressed components of his personality, the patient's reactions to these matters change as he continuously discusses them in the therapy situation. Previously disturbing aspects of his life situation tend to become less disturbing and more acceptable to him. In other words, as he discusses his problems in therapy, he may tend to become less sensitive about them. This has sometimes been referred to as the process of desensitization. From the viewpoint of learning theory, the stimuli associated with the patient's anxieties gradually diminish or become extinguished as factors evoking anxiety, as they become attached to the non-threatening and supportive elements of the therapeutic situation (Shoben, 1949). More systematic use of desensitization procedures are particularly emphasized in the behavioral approach of Wolpe (1958, 1969).

As therapy progresses, the patient usually will gain a better understanding of himself, his apparent problems, and his behavioral patterns or defenses. Such understanding is frequently referred to as "insight" by psychoanalytically oriented therapists and is viewed as a significant aspect of therapy. However, what is meant by insight may vary widely. Not only will the matter of insight be viewed in relation to particular theoretical orientations—so that what is real insight from one view is simply superficial talk from another—but there will also be differences in how insights are perceived by the patient and

their place in therapy. Nevertheless, there appears to be rather common acceptance of the fact that in successful therapy the individual gains new insights,
understandings, or perceptions about himself and his relations to others. As
a result, there is greater self-awareness on the individual's part of the antecedent's of his behavior and its possible consequences.

Although the writings of some psychotherapists appear to indicate that
insights occur in a highly dramatic fashion with the patient suddenly understanding his entire personality problem, in the author's experience the attaining
of a better understanding of one's self is frequently a long and tedious experience. Nevertheless, definite perceptual reorganization and increased understanding of self can take place.

The writer recalls one patient who was preoccupied with his somatic complaints and who could see little likelihood of any psychological explanation
for his symptoms. He was entering psychotherapy as a last resort, since he
had received little benefit from countless medical examinations and treatments
and, as a consequence, his own anxiety about himself had increased. After
some fifty interviews there was a slow but perceptible change in the patient's
attitude toward the psychological aspects of his difficulties. He began to see
that his relationships with others were related in some fashion to his symptoms.
In an additional seventy-five interviews other more significant changes occurred. The patient was able to grasp that both his perception of other people
and his expectancies in relation to them were dictated by his own needs
and behaviors. Due to certain traumatic events in his earlier life, he was
exceedingly insecure in his relationship with others and had developed a
pattern approaching obsequiousness in an attempt to please others and win
their approval. As a result of this pattern, he went out of his way to be
nice to people and to do favors for them. He even carried this into his
business relationships, where he performed extra services that were not really
demanded. When such services were not overtly recognized, he was acutely
disappointed. Furthermore, for fear of losing approval, he could not assert
himself and demand the things that were due him. When people would not
pay their bills he had extreme difficulty in asking them to do so. As a consequence, he developed a view that everyone was selfish and that most people
would try to take advantage of him.

As a result of this complex pattern of development, the patient was caught
up in a net from which he could not extricate himself. He constantly had
to suppress his feelings of hostility and anger toward others as they did not
comply with his unverbalized and unrealistic expectancies, and, at the same
time, he was unable to satisfy his intense cravings for recognition and succor.
He began to experience various kinds of somatic symptoms, and when no
physical basis was discovered for them, his anxiety increased. But, over a
period of time in therapy he was able to gain some insight into his pattern

of interpersonal relations and eventually to perceive both himself and others in a more realistic manner. After these changes occurred, he was able to modify his behavior accordingly and to function much more efficiently, both in his work and in his interpersonal relationships generally. Most of the somatic complaints disappeared and the remaining ones greatly diminished in severity. It should be pointed out, too, that securing insights into one's behavior is only one step in progress toward improved functioning. Behavioral change must also occur.

As implied above, another possible common feature claimed for all of the psychotherapies, and illustrated in the preceding case, concerns the matter of personality and behavioral change. All imply that some such change should and does take place. As the patient comes to grips with his problems and discovers his distortions, he is encouraged to react to the realities of the therapy situation and to his own life situation. Not only are distortions modified, aspects of self understood, and understandings gained, but these new understandings and perceptions supposedly are accompanied by some reorganization of personality and modification of behavior. Even where a special fear is removed or a disturbing habit modified, more general personality changes may also take place, such as increased self-confidence or self-regard. Whether viewed as learning, reeducation, corrective emotional experience, or growth, the process is one of change to a more mature and realistic pattern of adjustment. Although many such positive changes do occur in successful psychotherapy, it should be emphasized, too, that sudden and dramatic changes in personality are not the rule. As Colby puts it, "a psychotherapist should not expect great transformations equivalent to a psychological rebirth or a complete reorganization of the patient's personality" (Colby, 1951, p. 3). These statements are not meant to detract from the values of psychotherapy, but are offered as a note of caution. If the beginning therapist does not expect magical changes, he or she will be less frequently disappointed. The beginning therapist should also be aware that successful cases tend to be better remembered than the less successful ones, and it is the former which are usually referred to in the writings on psychotherapy.

Nevertheless, if current reports of therapeutic outcome are accepted at face value, most patients, regardless of the type if therapy, will show some improvement. This fact alone would suggest that there must be some common variables operating in the different approaches to psychotherapy. The matter of appraising therapeutic results, however, is such a complex matter that it will be discussed in more detail later. In conclusion, however, we can add that some research data exist that indicate that experienced therapists of different schools exhibit more similarities than do the novices and experts of the same school (Fiedler, 1950a,b). Furthermore, another study has shown that patients receiving psychotherapy from therapists representing three different theoretical orientations report similar changes and also tend to credit similar factors as having been responsible for these changes (Heine, 1953). Additional investigators also have concluded that there are possible common factors operating in different forms of psychotherapy (Barrett, Hampe, & Miller, 1978; Frank, 1971; Sloane, Staples, Cristol, Yorkston, & Whipple, 1975). These findings lend some support to the view that there are some common factors which may play an important role in most successful forms of psychotherapy.

REFERENCES

APA Committee on Training in Clinical Psychology. Recommended graduate training program in clinical psychology. *American Psychologist,* 1947, *2,* 539–558.

Adams, H. B. "Mental Illness" or interpersonal behavior? *American Psychologist,* 1964, *19,* 191–197.

Auerbach, A. H., & Johnson, M. Research on the therapist's level of experience. In A. S. Gurman and A. M. Razin (Eds.), *Effective psychotherapy: A Handbook of research.* Oxford: Pergamon Press, 1977.

Balance, W. D. G., Hirschfield, P. P., & Bringmann, W. G. Mental illness: Myth, metaphor, or model. *Professional Psychology,* 1970, *1,* 133–137.

Barrett, C. L., Hampe, I. E., & Miller, L. Research on psychotherapy with children. In S. L. Garfield and A. E. Bergin (Eds.), *Handbook of psychotherapy and behavior change.* (2nd ed.). New York: Wiley, 1978.

Bergin, A. E. The evaluation of therapeutic outcomes. In A. E. Bergin and S. L. Garfield (Eds.), *Handbook of psychotherapy and behavior change.* New York: Wiley, 1971.

Bordin, E. S. *Psychological counseling.* New York: Appleton-Century-Crofts,`1955.

Colby, K. M. *A primer for psychotherapists.* New York: Ronald Press, 1951.

Ellis, A. *Reason and emotion in psychotherapy.* New York: L. Stuart, 1962.

Fey, W. F. Doctrine and experience: Their influence upon the psychotherapist. *Journal of Consulting Psychology,* 1958, *22,* 403–409.

Fiedler, F. E. A comparison of therapeutic relationships in psychoanalytic, nondirective and Adlerian therapy. *Journal of Consulting Psychology,* 1950, *14,* 436–445. (a)

Fiedler, F. E. The concept of an ideal therapeutic relationship. *Journal of Consulting Psychology,* 1950, *14,* 239–245. (b)

Frank, J. D. *Persuasion and healing.* Baltimore: Johns Hopkins Press, 1961.

Frank, J. D. Therapeutic factors in psychotherapy. *American Journal of Psychotherapy,* 1971, *XXV,* 350–361.

Fromm-Reichmann, F. *Principles of intensive psychotherapy.* Chicago: University of Chicago Press, 1950.

Garfield, S. L. *Introductory clinical psychology.* New York: Macmillan, 1957.

Garfield, S. L. Research on the training of professional psychotherapists. In A. S. Gurman and A. M. Razin (Eds.), *Effective Psychotherapy. A handbook of research.* Oxford: Pergamon Press, 1977.

Garfield, S. L. Research on client variables in psychotherapy. In S. L. Garfield and A. E. Bergin (Eds.), *Handbook of psychotherapy and behavior change* (2nd ed.). New York: Wiley, 1978.

Garfield, S. L. *Psychotherapy: An eclectic approach.* New York: Wiley, 1980.

Garfield, S. L. Critical issues in the effectiveness of psychotherapy. In C. E. Walker (Ed.), *Clinical practice of psychotherapy. A guide for mental health professionals.* New York: Pergamon Press, 1981.

Garfield, S. L., & Affleck, D. C. An appraisal of duration of stay in outpatient psychotherapy. *Journal of Nervous and Mental Disease,* 1959, *129,* 492–498.

Garfield, S. L., & Bergin, A. E. Personal therapy, outcome and some therapist variables. *Psychotherapy: Theory, Research and Practice,* 1971, *8,* 251–253.

Garfield, S. L., & Kurtz, R. Personal therapy for the psychotherapist: Some findings and issues. *Psychotherapy: Theory, Research and Practice,* 1976, *13,* 188–192.

Gurman, A. S. The patient's perception of the therapeutic relationship. In A. S. Gurman and A. M. Razin (Eds.), *Effective psychotherapy: A handbook of research.* New York: Pergamon, 1977.

Heine, R. W. A comparison of patients' reports on psychotherapeutic experience with psychoanalytic, nondirective and Adlerian therapists. *American Journal of Psychotherapy,* 1953, *7,* 16–23.

Hollingshead, A. B., & Redlich, F. C. *Social class and mental illness.* New York: Wiley, 1958.

Holt, R. R. (Ed.), *New horizon for psychotherapy. Autonomy as a profession.* New York: International Universities Press, 1971.

Holt, R. R., & Luborsky, L. *Personality patterns of psychiatrists. Vol. 1.* New York: Basic Books, 1958.

Kadushin, C. *Why people go to psychiatrists.* New York: Atherton, 1969.

Kiesler, D. J. Experimental designs in psychotherapy research. In A. E. Bergin and S. L. Garfield (Eds.), *Handbook of psychotherapy and behavior change.* New York: Wiley 1971.

Kiev, A. *Magic, faith and healing.* New York: Free Press of Glencoe, Macmillan, 1964.

Knupfer, G., Jackson, D., & Krieger, G. Personality differences between more and less competent psychotherapists as a function of criteria of competence. *Journal of Nervous and Mental Disease,* 1959, *129,* 375–384.

Kurtz, R. R., & Grummon, D. L. Different approaches in the measurement of therapist empathy and their relationship to therapy outcomes. *Journal of Consulting and Clinical Psychology,* 1972, *39,* 106–115.

Lorion, R. P. Research on psychotherapy and behavior change with the disadvantaged. In S. L. Garfield and A. E. Bergin (Eds.), *Handbook of psychotherapy and behavior change.* (2nd ed.). New York: Wiley, 1978.

Mitchell, K. M., Bozarth, J. D., & Krauft, C. C. A reappraisal of therapeutic effectiveness of accurate empathy, nonpossessive warmth, and genuineness. In A. S. Gurman and A. M. Razin (Eds.), *Effective psychotherapy: A handbook of research.* New York: Pergamon Press, 1977.

Parloff, M. B. Group therapy and the small-group field: An encounter. *International Journal of Group Psychotherapy,* 1970, *20,* 267–304.

Parloff, M. B., Waskow, I. E., & Wolfe, B. E. Research on therapist variables in relation to process and outcome. In S. L. Garfield and A. E. Bergin (Eds.), *Handbook of psychotherapy and behavior change.* (2nd ed.). New York: Wiley, 1978.

Paul, G. L. Strategy of outcome research in psychotherapy. *Journal of Consulting Psychology,* 1967, *31,* 109–118.

Rogers, C. R. *Counseling and psychotherapy.* Boston: Houghton Mifflin, 1942.

Rogers, C. R. A theory of therapy, personality, and interpersonal relationships, as developed in the client-centered framework. In S. Koch (Ed.), *Psychology: A study of a science. Vol. 3.* New York: McGraw-Hill, 1959.

Rotter, J. B. Psychotherapy. In P. R. Farnsworth and Q. McNemar (Eds.), *Annual review of psychology.* Palo Alto, CA: Annual Reviews, 1960.

Shapiro, A. K., & Morris, L. A. The placebo effect in medical and psychological therapies. In S. L. Garfield and A. E. Bergin (Eds.), *Handbook of psychotherapy and behavior change.* (2nd ed.). New York: Wiley, 1978.

Shoben, E. J., Jr. Psychotherapy as a problem in learning theory. *Psychological Bulletin,* 1949, *46,* 366–392.

Sloane, R. B., Staples, F. R., Cristol, A. H., Yorkston, N.J., & Whipple, K. *Psychotherapy versus behavior therapy.* Cambridge, MA: Harvard University Press, 1975.

Sobel, F. S. Remedial teaching as therapy. *American Journal of Psychotherapy,* 1948, *2,* 615–623.

Strupp, H. H. The effect of the psychotherapist's personal analysis upon his techniques. *Journal of Consulting Psychology,* 1955, *19,* 197–204.

Strupp, H. H. A reformulation of the dynamics of the therapist's contribution. In A. S. Gurman and A. M. Razin (Eds.), *Effective psychotherapy. A handbook of research.* New York: Pergamon Press, 1977.

Szasz, T. The myth of mental illness. *American Psychologist,* 1960, *15,* 113–118.

Truax, C. B., & Carkhuff, R. R. *Toward effective counseling and psychotherapy.* Chicago: Aldine, 1967.

Truax, C. B., & Mitchell, K. M. Research on certain therapist interpersonal skills in relation to process and outcome. In A. E. Bergin and S. L. Garfield (Eds.), *Handbook of psychotherapy and behavior change.* New York: Wiley, 1971.

Wolberg, L. R. *The technique of psychotherapy.* (2nd ed.). New York: Grune and Stratton, 1967.

Wolpe, J. *Psychotherapy by reciprocal inhibition.* Stanford, CA: Stanford University Press, 1958.

Wolpe, J. *The practice of behavior therapy.* New York: Pergamon, 1969.

Variations in Psychotherapy: Traditional Approaches

Despite the similarities in psychotherapy mentioned in the preceding chapter, there are some specific and what appear to be contradictory differences between various approaches to psychotherapy. Although such differences are sometimes perplexing to the student, they can be viewed as representing an early stage in the development of more commonly acceptable and verifiable procedures.

How frequent the interviews will be, when therapy will be concluded, and the particular role of the therapist in therapy will be determined by the specific orientation and views of the therapist. If he is a psychoanalyst, the therapy may take place three to five times a week for a period of years. With a different approach, therapy may occur once per week or irregularly, as desired by the patient, and may last for only a relatively few interviews. These differences not only reflect divergent views concerning the therapeutic process and techniques of psychotherapy, but also are manifestations of significant theoretical differences in the realm of personality dynamics and psychopathology. At the present time, relatively little in the way of adequate data exists to support the efficacy of one approach over another. Until such time as conclusive research findings are available, the preference of one approach over another may be viewed as a manifestation of faith in a particular therapeutic orientation.

In addition to differences in training and theoretical orientation, another potential factor which may influence outcome in psychotherapy is the personality of the therapist. Since psychotherapy is an intimate interpersonal experience, the personalities of both therapist and patient are important considerations and should enter into any discussion of therapy. Such considerations make it exceedingly difficult to speak of a specific therapeutic approach or to evaluate various techniques apart from the personal variables involved. Nevertheless, with this in mind, it is worthwhile to survey some of the techniques and approaches of psychotherapy.

SUPPORTIVE AND RECONSTRUCTIVE PSYCHOTHERAPIES

In discussions concerning psychotherapy in clinical case conferences as well as in published reports, a distinction has frequently been made between supportive and reconstructive modes of psychotherapy. This has been particularly so in centers emphasizing a psychodynamic point of view. In a general way, the first category of psychotherapy refers to a variety of techniques designed to help the patient without delving into the hypothesized underlying, or dynamic causes within the patient's personality. As the name implies, supportive approaches to psychotherapy aim at giving the patient some support or help so that he can better cope with his current symptoms or difficulties. Rather than attempting to get at what may be viewed as the fundamental problem or to overcome the patient's defenses and resistance to therapy or self-evaluation, the objective is to align oneself with the patient in strengthening his defenses or coping mechanisms. It is hoped that with this type of help, in which the patient can rely or lean on the therapist to gain additional strength, he may be better able to surmount his difficulties and adapt to his life situation. From a psychoanalytically oriented viewpoint, the supportive process can be perceived as attempts to bolster or strengthen the patient's ego, that is, the integrative components of the patient's personality. Supportive techniques frequently are related to the symptoms or complaints of the patient and may center around his current life situation and problems. The content of the therapeutic interviews consist primarily of conscious material, although unconscious aspects may be involved through the relationship developed in therapy. The types of techniques in this category are indeed many. Among them are persuasion, advice, encouragement, sympathy, exhortation, and the giving of information. Some of these obviously are similar to so-called common sense attempts to help people with personal problems, but they also have been and are used in various types of psychotherapy (Levine, 1948; Garfield, 1980). Closely related are such procedures as occupational therapy, medication, drugs, and the like, which may also be used as adjuncts to psychotherapy.

There has been a tendency on the part of many psychotherapists to view supportive psychotherapy as somewhat less desirable and less challenging than so-called reconstructive psychotherapy, which has as its goal the patient's attainment of insight concerning his problems along with significant personality reorganization. Frequently, patients who are considered to be relatively poorly integrated, to have limited intellectual and emotional resources, and who are judged as not highly motivated to undergo intensive psychotherapy, are considered more suitable for a supportive type of psychotherapy. Conversely, reconstructive psychotherapy will more frequently be recommended for patients with better personality resources and a better prognosis for personality change. There has been a tendency also to associate the term, "intensive," with a reconstructive or uncovering type of psychotherapy. Cases seen more frequently than once a week for psychotherapy are more apt to be viewed as cases in intensive-reconstructive therapy, whereas, patients seen less than once a week are usually viewed as cases of supportive psychotherapy. It is the writer's impression that the terms, "supportive" and "intensive," reflect somewhat the ends of a hierarchial arrangement of the value systems of some psychotherapists. Whether this can be justified is questionable. Certainly, a number of recent developments in the field of psychotherapy appear to offer a challenge to this conventional way of dichotomizing psychotherapy.

One may also question whether these two approaches to psychotherapy are as mutually distinctive and nonoverlapping as many seem to imply. What therapists actually do in therapy may differ from what they say they do or what might be inferred from their theoretical orientation. Certain designations or terms tend to be endowed with more virtue or status than others. So-called supportive techniques have been viewed as rather superficial by dynamically oriented therapists and as tending to neglect the underlying causes of the patient's difficulties. Such procedures, therefore, were seen as offering mainly temporary symptom relief instead of a more permanent type of improvement. Reconstructive therapy, on the other hand, which aims at modification of the patient's personality, is considered to involve some uncovering or exploration of repressed material. This has been viewed as offering the greatest possibility for significant improvement therapeutically, since the factors responsible for the patient's symptoms are uncovered and, in light of this, changes in behavior can follow. Research evidence to support this view, however, is extremely scant. No direct comparison of the efficacy of supportive or reconstructive therapy has been made utilizing comparable patients and equally skilled therapists. However, the results of the long-term study conducted by the Menninger Foundation did not indicate any conclusive superiority of reconstructive therapy over so-called supportive therapy (Kernberg, Burstein, Coyne, Applebaum, Horwitz, & Voth, 1972). Patients judged to have high "ego-strength" secured positive outcomes with both supportive psychotherapy and psychoanalysis, whereas patients with poor ego-strength secured relatively poor outcomes with both of the forms of psychotherapy.

Although the higher value accorded reconstructive therapies in the past reflects traditional views associated with dynamic theories of personality, it should be emphasized that reconstructive therapies are not necessarily the best for all patients. As already indicated, a supportive therapeutic approach may be more efficacious for certain types of patients. In fact, attempts at reconstructive or "deep" therapy may be harmful, particularly when attempted by inexperienced therapists. It is worth remembering that regardless of the therapeutic approach, the competence and personality of the therapist are crucial variables in any therapeutic endeavor.

As has been mentioned, reconstructive or uncovering psychotherapy has been represented as an intensive type of psychotherapeutic involvement. The goal in this type of psychotherapy is to go beyond the amelioration of symptoms and to uncover the causes or roots of the individual's personality difficulties. Considerable attention is paid to the attainment of self-understanding and insight by the patient concerning himself and his difficulties. Also emphasized is the interpersonal interaction and relationship between therapist and patient. Although all psychotherapy involves such an interpersonal relationship, the emotional and interpretative aspects of this relationship are most highly stressed and utilized in reconstructive psychotherapy. The feelings of the patient toward the therapist, the behaviors of the patient in the therapy situation, and interpretations of these behaviors and motivations in therapy are significant aspects of reconstructive therapy. One may add, too, that most reconstructive therapeutic approaches will focus more on the unconscious conflicts and motivations of the patients and will dwell relatively more on past events and earlier childhood experiences than is the case of other therapies. The goals of reconstructive therapy, as implied by the name, are also more ambitious than other therapies. An extensive alteration of personality with understanding of unconscious motivations and conflicts is sought. Evaluating the attainment of such goals, however, is another matter. Thus far, more attention seemingly has been devoted to stating the goals of treatment than in studying how well they have been met.

Although long-term reconstructive psychotherapy has been highly valued by some psychotherapists, it has also been recognized that such therapy is not well suited for many patients. Most patients want to be treated quickly and long-term therapy has little appeal. It is also very costly. In cases of mild or transient personality difficulty, it may also be unwise or unnecessary to attempt deep reconstructive therapy. Here a few sessions of supportive or problem-centered therapy may suffice to help the individual over his current hurdle and allow him to continue with his previously adequate mode of adjustment. In the case of an individual with fairly severe personality disturbance who appears to be poorly integrated, it may also be unwise to attempt to offer intensive psychotherapy aimed at uncovering basic conflicts. Instead, support, and the attempt to strengthen social skills and existing coping mechanisms may be much more appropriate. On the other hand, some types of cases which lie between these two extremes conceivably may profit from a more reconstructive therapeutic approach. This becomes a matter of making the most appropriate clinical decision, keeping in mind the patient's attitudes and preferences.

With the advent of some new developments in psychotherapy in recent years, the emphasis on intensive reconstructive therapies and the differentiation between such approaches and supportive therapies appears to have lessened. The appearance of the behavior therapies in particular has affected this type of distinction. These therapies focus on the particular symptoms or complaints of the client and pay little or no attention to underlying conflicts, early childhood experiences, or to the attainment of insight. Rather, they aim specifically at modifying the behavior of the client. As such, they might be classed by some as supportive therapies, although this designation does not appear too meaningful. Recent approaches to crisis intervention, emergency therapy, and brief and time-limited therapy also differ from so-called reconstructive approaches. The rationales developed for these types of therapy, however, do not appear to fit easily under traditional classifications of supportive therapy. Such activities as marathon and encounter groups are additional new developments that require much less time than traditional reconstructive approaches, and also differ from what has been termed supportive therapy, because they are relatively intense periods of interaction in which strong feelings may be expressed and certain insights obtained. Thus, the traditional distinction between supportive and reconstructive therapies may not apply.

A few other observations can be offered before concluding this section. One important variable in selecting a particular approach to psychotherapy is the client himself. Some clients appear particularly well suited for long-term intensive therapy. The matter of motivation is one very important aspect in this regard. If the client is motivated and interested in a long and demanding period of self-exploration, he is better suited for such therapy than is someone who lacks these qualities. Along with motivation would go other personal attributes such as relative integration, intellectual and verbal ability, and the ability to pay for such treatment. Clearly, not all individuals who have problems and seek help meet such criteria. Therapists and clinics who prefer reconstructive therapies also tend to be selective in the type of client they will accept for therapy. Thus, only certain patients will be offered this type of therapy

(Garfield, 1978; Kadushin, 1969). On the other hand, there are individuals who have serious difficulties in adjustment, who are not motivated for such long-term treatment and self-appraisal, who look for more definitive guidance from the therapist, and who want to be helped more quickly. Such prospective clients either are not selected for long-term therapy or, if they begin a course of such therapy, will tend to terminate it prematurely. A large number of patients who begin psychotherapy terminate it after only a few interviews, and thus traditional approaches have not been effective with large numbers of patients (Eiduson, 1968; Fiester & Rudestam, 1975; Garfield, 1978; Garfield & Affleck, 1959; Rosenthal & Frank, 1958; Rogers, 1960). Social class variables appear to be related to such patterns of early termination and to the type of therapy that is given to various groups in our society. The upper social classes, and apparently those with less disabling disorders, are generally those who receive reconstructive or intensive psychotherapy.

PSYCHOTHERAPEUTIC APPROACHES

Attempts at systematic psychotherapy began about the turn of the century. This is not to say that prior to that time no psychotherapy of any type had been used. Such psychological techniques as persuasion and reassurance undoubtedly were used early in human history, along with the development of language. But, the significant development of planned psychotherapeutic procedures to alleviate psychological distress and improve behavior occurred in the latter part of the nineteenth century. This was associated with a greater scientific interest in abnormal behavior and in an increasing awareness of the role that psychological factors played in such behavior.

In the 1880's a great deal of interest was centered on the problems of hysteria. While the prevailing view of medicine favored an organic explanation of hysterical phenomena, or else considered the latter to be mere simulation of illness, several outstanding physicians and neurologists were considering the possibility of psychological factors in hysteria. Among the best known of these workers were Charcot, Bernheim, and Janet in France, and Breuer and Freud in Vienna. Freud, after working with Charcot, Bernheim, and Breuer, went on to develop his own therapeutic and theoretical views, which he termed "psychoanalysis" (Freud, 1949).

Since the development of the psychoanalytic method by Freud, and also concurrent with it, other approaches to psychotherapy have been brought forth. Several of these are essentially variants of Freud's approach and frequently are called psychoanalytic methods, even though some theoretical differences occur. Other therapies, however, have evolved somewhat more distinctly, and accordingly differ more from the traditional psychoanalytic approach.

PSYCHOANALYTIC THERAPIES

Earlier in this volume a brief review of psychoanalytic theory and some of its implications for the clinical activities of the psychologist was presented. In the discussion to follow, we will be concerned primarily with the therapeutic procedures that have been identified with this approach.

In line with the discoveries and formulations of Freud, psychoanalysis and psychoanalytically oriented therapy tend to be lengthy and intensive forms of psychotherapy. Although most analysts differentiate psychoanalysis from psychotherapy, the difference is not always clear. That is, psychotherapy, which is technically not psychoanalysis, may still occur several times a week, last for a number of years, and utilize a psychoanalytic frame of reference. The client in the latter instance, however, would usually face the therapist in a chair instead of reclining on a couch.

In traditional psychoanalytic treatment the patient is expected to meet with the analyst from three to five times per week, although some reduction in the frequency of meetings may occur after treatment has progressed for some time. An analysis today may last from 4 to 7 or more years, and, thus, this form of treatment is quite expensive. The number of trained analysts is also limited, which tends to restrict the number who can receive psychoanalysis, although here again there may be a lack of agreement concerning who are analysts. The program of training involves didactic seminars in psychoanalytic theory and technique, a personal analysis, and actual psychoanalytic work with patients under close supervision. According to the American Psychoanalytic Association, a person cannot be called a qualified analyst unless she has received training in a recognized training institute for psychoanalysis (Kubie, 1950). Those training institutes that have been recognized by this association have generally been controlled by medical analysts and primarily psychiatric physicians have been the graduates of these institutes (Knight, 1953). As a result, very few psychologists in the past have been able to secure training in these recognized psychoanalytic institutes in this country. For a number of reasons, which need not be discussed here, this has been the trend in the United States, although Freud himself was strongly opposed to limiting psychoanalysis to physicians. Nevertheless, a selected number of psychologists have received analytical training and have become well-known psychoanalysts, some even joining the staffs of psychoanalytic training institutes as training analysts. Many other psychologists have received personal analyses and have applied psychoanalytic concepts and techniques to their own therapeutic work. In more recent years, a number of independent training centers, set up outside the fold of the American Psychoanalytic Association, espouse a psychoanalytic point of view or emphasize psychoanalytically oriented psychotherapy (Rachman & Kauff, 1972). These tend to be interdisciplinary in nature and vary somewhat in their emphasis. The National Psychological Association for Psychoanalysis, established under the leadership of the late Theodore Reik, is one such organization that follows a Freudian point of view and offers a training program for both medical and nonmedical members.

As is well known today, most analysts direct the patient to recline on a couch with the analyst out of his line of vision. One of the reasons for this is to allow the patient to be as relaxed as possible in order to relate thoughts freely as they enter her mind. This procedure was also followed originally so that it would be easier for the analyst. Not only is it tedious to be in direct visual contact with patients for 8 to 10 hours a day, but by being somewhat removed from the patient the analyst does not have to be as constantly concerned about any facial or other reactions that she might exhibit to the patient. In addition, it is felt that the analyst should influence the patient's reactions as little as possible, and, by remaining in the background, she can be more impersonal. The analyst, in a way, is to be a screen upon which the patient can project her personal feelings and thoughts. As Freud stated it, "The physician should be impenetrable to the patient, and, like a mirror, reflect nothing but what is shown to him" (Freud, 1950b, p. 331).

One of the main techniques of psychoanalytic therapy is free association. Freud developed this technique after being dissatisfied with the use of hypnosis as a therapeutic method. In free association, the patient is encouraged to bring forth whatever thoughts or ideas come to his mind regardless of whether they are in any way related or even intelligible. According to Freud's deterministic view, each of these associations eventually leads to some significant or repressed area of the patient's life. In an atmosphere free of criticism—indeed one in which he is encouraged to drop conventional controls over thoughts and feelings—the patient's defenses are lessened, and his associations, therefore, may lead gradually to significant material. The nature of associations, blocks, slips of the tongue, emotional reactions, and related phenomena also provide clues toward understanding and unraveling the patient's personality difficulties.

Another important aspect of psychoanalysis is the use of dreams and dream interpretation in therapy (Freud, 1938). Freud himself felt that dreams were a particularly useful means of studying repressed material and called them the "royal road to the unconscious." A great deal of study has been done by Freud and other analysts on dreams and dream symbolism. As a result of such study, it is hypothesized that during sleep the patient relaxes his controls and thus some previously repressed material escapes and is manifested in a dream. Conscious controls are never fully relaxed, however, for if the unconscious material came forth openly it would tend to waken the dreamer because of its disturbing content. Therefore, the repressed material that emerges in the dream is distorted, and this enables sleep to continue. This process of distortion is referred to as the "dream work." Other aspects of the dream were also delineated by Freud. The actual dream as we know it was called the "manifest content" by Freud and represented the distorted dream. The true or unconscious meaning of the dream has been referred to as the "latent content." By having the patient associate to his dreams, and by the use of analytic knowledge of symbolism, the analyst then strives to uncover the unconscious or real meaning of the dream. For example, a person who had some conflicts about power, might dream of a lion, which would be symbolic of power.

Still another basic phenomenon or concept in psychoanalysis is resistance. As we have already noted, the individual in terms of his ego functioning resists or controls forbidden thoughts and impulses from the unconscious id. In a similar way, the patient in analysis resists the attempts at coming to grips with his repressed conflicts. This phenomenon has been referred to as resistance and is manifested in different ways during therapy. Examples are failure to keep therapy appointments, failing to hear what the analyst says, being late for appointments, treating the analysis lightly, and even "getting well." Resistance encountered in psychoanalysis must be overcome if therapy is to proceed satisfactorily. To dissolve resistance, the analyst relies on interpretations associated with the transference relationship, which we will discuss next.

Transference is one of the key conceptions in psychoanalysis and involves the feelings or attitudes which the patient develops toward the analyst (Freud, 1950a; Thompson, 1946). Some reference to transference was made in our previous discussion of the psychotherapeutic process, but transference reactions should be mentioned again within the context of psychoanalytical therapy. As viewed by Freud, these reactions, either positive or negative, are emotions or attitudes which the patient has previously held toward parent figures and which he now transfers to the analyst. For example, the female patient may fall in love with the analyst or be seductive in therapy; these are viewed as transferred reactions which she may have held toward her father or other significant male figures in her past development (Freud, 1950d). In a similar way, the therapist may be accused of all sorts of negative attitudes or behavior which he has not actually revealed, but which are distortions by the patient in terms of transference. Technically, the analyst maintains a neutral stance. Consequently, qualities which the client attributes to the therapist are viewed as distortions emanating from the transference relationship. The therapist initially relies on positive transference to keep the patient in therapy and to overcome resistances. In this process, the analyst interprets the resistance and transference attitudes and attempts to help the patient to see their true meaning and derivation.

Just as the patient may transfer earlier or characteristic patterns of response to the therapist, the therapist also may react to the patient in a manner determined by motivations other than those emanating from the therapy situation. The therapist can also project and distort. For example, he may react angrily or submissively to a patient because of his own developmental past or his own unconscious needs, rather than in terms of what is required in therapy. These emotional attitudes or feelings, which the analyst may have toward the patient, have been designated as counter-transference in psychoanalysis. In order to minimize the effects of counter-transference, a personal analysis is deemed necessary for all analysts. In this way it is felt that the analyst will gain deeper insights and understanding about himself and, consequently, distortions on his part will be greatly reduced. There is little question that the therapist's behavior in psychotherapy is a factor of prime importance. Freud and his followers were the first to emphasize this aspect of therapy.

In discussing transference we also mentioned the matter of interpretation by the analyst. This, too, is an important aspect of analytic therapy. Interpretation is withheld early in therapy, but usually begins with interpretations of resistance and transference phenomena. In this sense, it is related to interpreting the actual behavior of the patient in the therapeutic situation. The therapist later may use interpretation more broadly in terms of other aspects of analysis, including dreams and free associations. The matter of timing is important; if the patient has not progressed far enough in therapy and is not ready for certain interpretations, he will reject them. Freud clearly emphasized this aspect of interpretation by the analyst. "Even in later stages of the analysis one must be careful not to communicate the meaning of a symptom or the interpretation of a wish until the patient is already close upon it, so that he has only a short step to take in order to grasp the explanation himself. In former years I often found that premature communication of interpretations brought the treatment to an untimely end . . ." (Freud, 1950c, p. 361). The accuracy of interpretation is also of obvious significance. In making interpretations the analyst draws upon his knowledge of psychoanalytic theory and his own training and experience.

Since some reference has been made to the importance of interpretation in psychoanalysis, it may be well to add a few words about this topic generally. Interpretations of the client's responses or behavior are used in a variety of psychotherapeutic approaches, although such usage probably has received most emphasis in those approaches that utilize some psychoanalytic or psychodynamic orientation (Hammer, 1968). Client-centered or Rogerian therapy generally has deemphasized the use and importance of interpretation, and the focus in learning theory approaches to psychotherapy has also been on other variables for affecting change in the client's behavior. How interpretations are used and applied will also vary from therapist to therapist, and it may not, therefore, be too useful to view interpretation as a unitary phenomenon (Snyder, 1968). In a similar vein, what one judges to be a correct interpretation will of necessity vary, depending on the therapist's own theoretical orientation. What may be interpreted as an Oedipal complex by a Freudian may be interpreted as something quite different by someone with a different orientation or belief system. It is the writer's view that too much significance has been attached to interpretation, its accuracy, and timing. Rather, from the author's viewpoint, the impact of what the therapist says depends on the total context of the relationship in therapy. Thus, an "incorrect" interpretation may be received positively by the client if he views it as reflecting the interest of the therapist in understanding and helping him (Garfield, 1968). But, let us now return to our discussion of psychoanalysis.

The role of the analyst may vary from a fairly passive one to a much more active one involving frequent interpretation of behavior and symbolic material. Unquestionably, as is true of most therapeutic systems, the actual handling of a case will vary from analyst to analyst (Obendorf, 1943; Obendorf, Greenacre, and Kubie, 1948), but certain general features of therapy will be similar. Case reports of therapy are available in the psychoanalytic literature, and five case studies are reported in one volume by Freud (1950e).

Since psychoanalytic theory emphasizes the importance of early childhood experiences in the formation of the individual's personality, attempts are made in psychoanalysis to uncover previously repressed material associated with earlier periods of development. It is believed that only in this way can conflicts and distortions be brought to light and examined in terms of the client's current reality. By reconstructing past events and reexperiencing them in the present, the client is enabled to perceive them differently and more realistically. Theoretically, also, by becoming aware of past experiences and understanding their impact, the client becomes better able to cope with his difficulties. As he attains insight into such matters, the past events lose their threatening or disrupting quality. The individual is able, theoretically, to expand his awareness of himself, to reintegrate his past experiences in a more meaningful manner, and, hopefully, to function more adequately. This kind of reconstructive process, however, is a lengthy one.

Even from our brief description of psychoanalysis as a form of psychotherapy, it appears that it is not an ordinary method of treatment and that it might not be suitable for all or most people. Freud himself believed that psychoanalysis was not suitable for treating psychotic individuals (1950g), and that even among the neuroses, certain conditions had to be met. The patient in order to be a good candidate for psychoanalysis must first of all be willing to make the necessary effort and sacrifice to undergo the tribulations of analysis. He must be able to form a relationship with the analyst and observe the fundamental rule of free association. He must also have a relatively intact ego, be in touch with reality, attend to what is going on around him, and also be capable of thinking accurately and logically. He must also be able to relate his subjective experiences as they occur. Clearly, there is some selectivity in terms of which individuals are best suited for psychoanalysis. As Freud stated, "It is gratifying that precisely the most valuable and most highly developed persons are best suited for these creative measures. . . ." (1950f, p. 259). In other words, only a relatively select group of individuals are considered to be suitable or desirable candidates for psychoanalysis. Generally, these are relatively intact, intelligent, motivated, and upper-class individuals. Lower class and less bright persons are not generally seen as suitable candidates for reasons enumerated above. Although it does seem reasonable that the demands of psychoanalytic psychotherapy require very select clients, it is also true that poorly integrated and less motivated clients generally are not viewed very positively by therapists of other therapeutic persuations as well (Garfield, 1978).

Although psychoanalysis is an intensive, lengthy, and expensive form of psychotherapy which aims at significant personality change, comparatively little in the way of research evaluation has been reported (Luborsky & Spence, 1978). Psychoanalysis in the past has been identified with a small "in-group" of practitioners, who have not been inclined to conduct systematic studies of its effectiveness or allow others to do so. In fact, the whole history of psychoanalysis since its inception has been one of determined effort to strengthen the internal loyalty of its adherents, to prevent mingling with adherents of other theoretical views, and to show little interest in attempts at objective scientific evaluation. Discussions of the efficacy of psychoanalysis have tended to take place on an emotional or belief basis rather than in terms of systematic and empirically derived data on outcome. There have been some changes in this attitude in very recent years, but the above description is still accurate (Marmor & Woods, 1980; Wachtel, 1977).

MODIFICATIONS IN PSYCHOANALYTIC THERAPY

The important and unique features of psychoanalysis, which we have discussed, will usually distinguish it from other approaches (Alexander, 1948; Lorand, 1944). Nevertheless, both during and since the time of Freud, numerous modifications of psychoanalytic theory and practice have been presented in the literature. Some of these have been absorbed within psychoanalysis, while others have been rejected by Freud and his adherents. To survey all of these developments would take us beyond the intended scope of the present volume. But, mention of important figures in this development should be made, and brief descriptions of a few significant movements can be presented to illustrate some of the divergent trends.

The variations of psychotherapeutic approaches which are offshoots or derivatives of psychoanalysis differ in numerous ways. Although Freud stated that only his system could be termed psychoanalysis, a number of these variations are frequently referred to as psychoanalytic therapies. This is particularly true in those cases where the differences have centered primarily around modifications in therapeutic techniques, with little change in the basic Freudian theory. Some groups, however, have distinctly differentiated themselves from the psychoanalytic school, and have used other names to designate their particular systems. In such instances, significant differences in theoretical orientation have occurred with concomitant variations in the specific procedures of therapy. Foremost among the latter group are the approaches developed by Adler and Jung, called "Individual Psychology" and "Analytic Psychology," respectively. One cannot do justice to either of these therapeutic systems without discussing the important theoretical differences in each point of view. Since such a presentation will not be attempted here, we can only refer to a few points of special interest, using Individual Psychology for illustrative purposes.

The Adlerian approach places less emphasis on sexual problems and psychosexual development in its theory of neurosis than is true of the Freudians. Instead, feelings of inferiority and compensatory strivings for power and masculinity are stressed (Adler, 1929). In therapy an attempt is made to study the individual's life style, his neurotic goals, the gains secured by the patient's symptoms, and the distortions utilized in the struggle for power. His symptoms are considered to serve the patient's own egoistic goals. For example, a person may use his neurotic symptoms actually to dominate and control the life of another person. From this point of view, the neurotic is viewed as an essentially egocentric person who needs to become more socially altruistic.

Also emphasized as of some importance in the development of neurotic behavior are the family constellation and the patient's place in the family. Such factors as being the youngest child in the family, the only son among seven children, the only child, the sick child, or in being a child in a poverty-stricken home have potentially different influences on how a person develops. Individual Psychology, therefore, also points to the importance of the individual's past life experiences in personality development, but does so in a manner that differs from that of psychoanalysis.

While many of the same techniques developed by Freud are used by Adlerians, they are used in somewhat different ways in terms of the different theoretical emphases. For example, dreams, memories, and other material are interpreted in terms of the individual's life style, egoistic goals, and so on, rather than in terms of the repressed conflicts emphasized by the Freudians. In addition, the proponents of Individual Psychology emphasize the importance of the early memories as giving the therapist some clue to the individual's personality structure and attitudes (Adler, 1972). The length of treatment is usually shorter than that of psychoanalysis, and more emphasis is placed on conscious material. Conscious and unconscious material are not seen as primarily opposite forces in the personality, but rather as different manifestations of the neurotic patient's struggle for power.

In addition to the historical departures of Jung and Adler from psychoanalysis, there have been other developments within and away from classical psychoanalytic therapy. These include the earlier therapeutic theories and modifications of Stekel, Ferenczi, and Rank (Thompson, 1950), and the more recent contributions of Horney, Sullivan (1953), Fromm-Reichmann (1950), Rado (1953), and the Chicago Institute of Psychoanalysis (Alexander and French, 1946). Some of these workers were primarily concerned with modifications of psychoanalytic techniques, while others developed new theoretical views that differed significantly from traditional psychoanalytic theory. Karen Horney (1937, 1939), for example, criticized the biological and genetic emphasis in psychoanalysis and developed a theoretical orientation in which cultural factors were given greater prominence. She also stressed the importance of understanding the basic character structure of the neurotic, with its conflicting tendencies or trends. Sexual problems were viewed as only one manifestation of the neurotic's basic difficulties in relating to himself and others. In addition, greater emphasis was placed on the patient's current functioning and adjustment. Some mention was also made in the chapter on theoretical orientations of the recent developments in Ego-Psychology. While these changes in psychoanalytic thinking have been viewed as important for the theory of psychoanalysis, their impact on the techniques of therapy seems somewhat less (Hartmann, 1964). However, more recent emphases have been devoted to clinical writings on work with so-called borderline and narcissistic conditions (Kernberg, 1975; Kohut, 1971). Less emphasis may be placed on interpretation and more on resistance and need gratification (Kirman, 1980; Spotnitz, 1976).

No attempt will be made here to review the various modifications and innovations contributed by the many noted analytical workers. An excellent historical review of some of these developments in analytic theory and techniques is presented in the work by Thompson (1950), and summaries of several of these orientations are given in the volume by Ford and Urban (1963) and in that of Wolman (1967). However, the earlier innovative efforts of the Chicago Institute of Psychoanalysis with a somewhat abbreviated analytic therapy are worth mentioning since they were viewed as very radical and contained components that are quite contemporary (Alexander & French, 1946). Although departing from traditional psychoanalytic procedures, the Chicago Institute group identified itself historically and theoretically with the Freudian movement.

The modifications suggested by this group pertain essentially to an analytic therapy that is much more flexible than classical psychoanalysis. Rather than applying the same long-term treatment to each case, what is recommended is a flexible adaptation of treatment to fit the needs of a specific case. In a large number of cases this means a much briefer course of therapy. In addition, the work of the Chicago group has indicated that relatively few cases require strict adherence to classical psychoanalytic techniques throughout the entire course of treatment.

While emphasis was placed on choosing the techniques in terms of the therapeutic problem presented, the frame of reference was still psychoanalytic theory. In fact, Alexander and French (1946) pointed out that the psychodynamic knowledge obtained through years of psychoanalytic investigation can now be applied toward the end of a shorter and more flexible therapy. The point was also made that classical psychoanalysis was best suited for severe chronic neurotics and that such a method is not the best one to use with milder types of maladjustments.

In this approach, stress was placed "on the value of designing a *plan of treatment,* based on a dynamic-diagnostic appraisal of the patient's personality and the actual problems he has to solve in his given life conditions" (Alexander and French, 1946, p. 5). In devising a plan of treatment, one must decide whether therapy should be supportive or uncovering, or whether it is necessary actively to modify certain aspects of the patient's life situation. In addition to such planning, the Chicago Institute group recommended the use of different techniques at various times as needed to fit the situation. Among the techniques used were: manipulating the frequency of interviews; more directive interviews, including directives to the patient concerning his daily life; interrupting treatment for various intervals as a means of preparing the patient for eventual termination of treatment; making use of the real life experiences of the patient; and regulating the transference relationship in terms of the needs of the individual case. In the last instance, the therapist may adopt a role that differs significantly from that encountered by the patient in relation to important figures in the past. In this regard, if the patient's father has been tyrannical, the therapist reacts in an opposite manner. Also emphasized is the significance of corrective emotional experiences occurring both in therapy and in the concurrent real life situations of the patient.

Although some use is also made of more traditional psychoanalytic techniques, such as free associations and dreams, the overall therapeutic approach does differ from classical psychoanalysis. It is evident that such an approach to psychotherapy is far from a simple routine application of specific techniques. Rather, it requires adequate knowledge of psychoanalytic theories of psychopathology, an accurate diagnostic appraisal of the individual, and a sensitive and flexible relationship with the patient.

Although the experimentation with therapeutic procedures and the search for more efficient and effective modes of conducting psychotherapy might be considered an extremely laudatory undertaking, the work of the Chicago group received the opposite reaction from their psychoanalytic colleagues. Many analysts did not approve of such innovative attempts, or saw them as too radical a departure from accepted procedures. In any event, the attempts at innovation apparently encountered considerable resistance, which was not analyzed. Thus, their impact was less than hoped for or anticipated. Instead of trying to perfect procedures in the hopes of shortening the time required for treatment, analysts have seemingly done the opposite. Whereas Freud decried the fact that some of his analyses took as long as a year, or occasionally more, analyses at present appear to require many years and to be increasing rather than decreasing in duration. This fact, combined with the relatively small number of analysts, greatly limits its social utility.

The preceding presentation hopefully has provided the reader with some indication of the varied development of analytically oriented theory and techniques. There is little question that psychoanalytic contributions have had a decided influence on the development of psychotherapy. A number of therapists have designated their therapy as analytically oriented therapy, even though they themselves have not been trained as psychoanalysts. This testifies to the influence of psychoanalysis and its derivatives on current psychotherapy, even though it frequently does not allow us to delimit precisely an individual therapist's specific orientation or actual therapeutic procedures. More recently, several variants of brief psychoanalytically oriented therapy have also appeared and will be described in the next chapter. There are, however, a number of approaches to psychotherapy that can be distinguished from analytic therapy. One such approach is known as "client-centered therapy."

CLIENT-CENTERED PSYCHOTHERAPY

The client-centered or nondirective therapy of Carl Rogers and his followers is reviewed here for several reasons. Although this form of therapy has roots and antecedents in the work of others, notably Rank, it was the first well-known therapy that was developed within the field of clinical psychology.

Out of a background of experience acquired at the Rochester Community Guidance Clinic, the Ohio State University, and the Counseling Center of the University of Chicago, Rogers steadfastly worked at developing and modifying his particular approach to therapy. Furthermore, serious attempts have been made to study and describe the process of therapy. Toward this end, a large number of therapeutic sessions were recorded and made available for analysis. More than any other therapeutic approach up to that time, client-centered therapy was marked by a zealous research orientation. The detailed research analysis of completely recorded therapy sessions was a significant contribution to research in this heretofore elusive and private body of data.

SOME BASIC TENETS OF CLIENT-CENTERED THERAPY

Client-centered therapy is a therapeutic approach that has undergone considerable change, reappraisal, and study. Some views emphasized earlier as being of great importance are now considered less so as a result of further experience. In general, there has been a decreasing emphasis on techniques of therapy and a correspondingly greater emphasis on the attitudes and feelings of both therapist and client. The primary orientation to therapy, however, has been a consistent one. This orientation revolves around the viewpoint that the client has basic potentialities within him for growth and development. The main function of the therapist is to provide an atmosphere in which the client feels free to explore himself, to acquire deeper understanding of himself, and gradually to reorganize his perceptions of himself and the world about him. The therapist refrains from offering advice, suggestions, or interpretations. Such views have resulted in the therapy being originally called "nondirective" and, later, "client-centered." Although other therapists have challenged the implication that only the Rogerian approach is client-centered, this orientation has been particularly emphasized by Rogers as a basic framework. In addition, emphasis has been placed on the fundamental importance of the therapist's deep emotional acceptance of the client's potentiality for constructive change and the therapist's qualities or therapeutic conditions deemed necessary for positive change.

Some of the major aspects of the process of client-centered therapy can be noted briefly as outlined particularly in two of the books by Rogers (1942, 1951). A condensed account of the steps in therapy is given most explicitly in Rogers's first book. This account of therapy is as follows:

1. The individual comes for help.
2. The therapeutic situation is usually defined. This means that the client

is informed that the therapist does not have the answers to his problems. Rather, therapy provides a situation whereby the client can work toward solving his own problems with the help of the therapist.

3. Free expression of the client's feeling in relation to his problem is encouraged by the therapist's friendly and accepting attitude.

4. Negative feelings can thus be expressed and are accepted and clarified by the therapist.

5. After rather full expression of negative feelings, the client begins to express more positive feelings and impulses.

6. The positive feelings are also accepted and clarified by the therapist. It is emphasized that both positive and negative feelings are accepted without praise or reproof, and that this acceptance gives the client "an opportunity for the first time in his life to understand himself as he is" (1942, p. 40).

7. The next step in therapy is the gradual understanding and acceptance of the self which can be received as insight.

8. Concomitant with the proceeding development is a process of clarifying possible courses of action, followed by

9. Positive action or behavior outside of the therapy situation.

10. Development of further insight and self-understanding.

11. Increasing constructive activity on the part of the client.

12. The client feels less need for help and recognizes that therapy must end.

As might also be expected from our previous discussion of Roger's theory of personality, the self-concept has received considerable emphasis in client-centered psychotherapy. Because the self-concept, or how the individual views himself, is completely within the person's awareness, it can be ascertained and utilized in attempting to appraise changes resulting from psychotherapy. In therapy, some reorganization of self supposedly takes place as the client's perceptions are modified and changed. What emerges hopefully in successful therapy is a more realistic and better integrated self-attitude. In general, as therapy proceeds there are fewer negative self-references and relatively more positive self-references.

The importance of the concept of self in client-centered therapy is clearly stated by Rogers in discussing the therapist's role:

> Psychotherapy deals primarily with the organization and the functioning of the self. There are many elements of experience which the self cannot face, cannot clearly perceive, because to face them or admit them would be inconsistent with and threatening to the current organization of self. In client-centered therapy the client finds in the counselor a genuine alter ego in an operational and technical sense—a self which has temporarily divested itself (so far as possible) of its own selfhood, except for the one quality of endeavoring to

understand. In the therapeutic experience, to see one's own attitudes, confusions, ambivalences, feelings, and perceptions accurately expressed by another, but stripped of their complications of emotion, is to see oneself objectively, and paves the way for acceptance into the self of all those elements which are now more clearly perceived. Reorganization of the self and more integrated functioning of the self are thus furthered (Rogers, 1951b, pp. 40–41).

The above quotation also helps to highlight the singular role of the therapist whose own personal values and personality traits recede into the background and allow the client freely to express and explore his own personality attributes.

THE NECESSARY CONDITIONS FOR THERAPEUTIC CHANGE

Over the past years, Rogers has also been interested in those factors or conditions that appear to be necessary in order to facilitate positive changes in the client. Different statements concerning the necessary variables have from time to time been offered (Rogers, 1957). In more recent years, however, these basic conditions have more or less been limited to three: Accurate Empathy, Unconditional Positive Regard or Nonpossessive Warmth, and Genuineness or Congruence (Truax and Carkhuff, 1967). As can be noted, these necessary conditions for change through psychotherapy refer to qualities or attributes of the therapist.

Since we have already discussed these three necessary conditions in Chapter 2, it is not necessary to dwell on them at any length here. Accurate empathy involves basically the therapist's ability to be sensitive to the client's own experience or the latter's private world as if it were his own, "but without ever losing the 'as if' quality" (Rogers, 1957, p. 99). The therapist should also be able to communicate this understanding to the client. Unconditional positive regard or warmth refers to the positive valuing of the client for himself, as a separate individual apart from conditions of worth. Genuineness, or congruence, refers to the therapist being a genuine and integrated person in the therapeutic relationship. He must be himself, without deception or facade. Over the years, various techniques and scales have been developed in the attempt to evaluate these therapeutic conditions and to relate them to outcome and process variables in psychotherapy. The volume by Truax and Carkhuff (1967) summarized much of the earlier work and reviews of the work since then also have been published (Mitchell, Bozarth, & Krauft, 1977; Parloff, Waskow, & Wolfe, 1978; Traux & Mitchell, 1971).

The most frequent procedure for evaluating the level of therapeutic conditions provided by the therapist was to take brief segments of tape-recorded therapy sessions. In much of this work, segments of 4 minutes in length drawn randomly from sessions at different times were used and rated by judges in terms of specific rating scales developed for this purpose.

In general, the results of early studies summarized by Truax and Carkhuff (1967) tended to show a positive relationship between moderate or high levels of the three therapeutic conditions and various criteria of outcome. Furthermore, in a study of 14 patients diagnosed as schizophrenic, patients who received high levels of the therapeutic conditions showed positive change, whereas those who received low levels showed a decrement in psychological functioning (Rogers, Gendlin, Kiesler, & Truax, 1967). The latter was a rather novel finding in the psychotherapeutic literature and thus received attention.

Nevertheless, despite such positive findings, other research results were not as supportive of the importance of therapeutic conditions. Contrary to expectations, some of these conditions were reported to correlate negatively with criteria of outcome. In one study, nonpossessive warmth correlated negatively with outcome (Truax, Wargo, Frank, Imber, Battle, Hoehn-Saric, Nash, & Stone, 1966), whereas in another, patients who received low levels of genuineness showed the greatest improvement (Truax, Carkhuff, & Kodman, 1965). Despite such perplexing findings, Truax and Mitchell (1971) in a review of the literature up through the year 1970 came to a very positive conclusion:

> The studies taken together suggest that therapists or counselors who are accurately empathic, nonpossessively warm in attitude, and genuine, are indeed effective. Also, these findings seem to hold with a wide variety of therapists and counselors, regardless of their training or theoretic orientation, and with a wide variety of clients or patients, . . . (p. 310).

Unfortunately, this positive view has failed to receive support in the years that followed its publication. In one study which was published in the same year as the aforementioned review, genuiness was found to correlate negatively with accurate empathy and nonpossessive warmth (−.66 and −.65) and all three conditions failed to correlate significantly with a variety of outcome measures (Garfield & Bergin, 1971). The more recent reviews, moreover, tend to be more cautious and less sweeping in their statements concerning the importance of the therapeutic conditions, although there is some variation in the appraisals. Mitchel et al. (1977) note several of the inadequacies of the existing research and offer a cautious conclusion:

> Briefly, our feeling is that many earlier conclusions need reformulation, that some qualification is necessary, and that much of the earlier and more recent data, when taken together, prove to be surprisingly inconclusive with respect to a number of issues. By the same token, we feel that none of the previous conclusions need to be discarded completely (p. 498).

Gurman (1977) evaluated studies in which the clients themselves were asked to rate their therapists on such variables as empathy and the like. This is in contrast to the procedures previously described in which segments of tape-recorded sessions are rated by independent judges. Gurman's analysis led him to reach a more positive view of the matter. However, as pointed out by Parloff *et al.* (1978), the studies analyzed by Gurman contain several methodological errors which seriously limit the conclusions that can be drawn from them. Parloff and his collaborators (1978) in a thorough review of research on therapist variables in relation to process and outcome in psychotherapy offered the following observation:

> Most reviewers of the large body of studies in this area are now content to acknowledge that after some 20 years of effort the evidence for the therapeutic conditions hypothesis is not persuasive. The associations found are modest and suggest that a more complex association exists between outcome and therapist 'skills' than originally hypothesized (p. 251).

The above comments should not be interpreted to signify that the personal qualities of the therapist or the quality of the relationship between therapist and client is of no consequence. Most therapists (and clients) will tell you otherwise. A desirable relationship would appear to be necessary for progress in psychotherapy. However, the relationship is only one among probably many variables which conceivably may account for therapeutic progress. The client-centered hypothesis that the three conditions of therapist—empathy, warmth, and genuineness—were the *necessary and sufficient* conditions for positive outcome in psychotherapy is what has been found wanting. The situation is undoubtedly more complex than this hypothesis would suggest. Nevertheless, the client-centered therapists and researchers offered hypotheses which stimulated a significant amount of research. It should be stressed again that client-centered therapists attempted to define their concepts operationally and to study them by means of research. Thus, their work can be more easily evaluated and found wanting than is true of therapeutic schools whose concepts are difficult to evaluate and whose research is limited. Consequently, the work of the client-centered therapists merits considerable praise. Only in this way can concepts be tested, revised, discarded, or supported.

DIAGNOSIS IN CLIENT-CENTERED THERAPY

The view taken by Rogers and his followers of the role of diagnosis in therapy is somewhat different from that held by many other therapists. Earlier,

Rogers's view was that diagnostic study was necessary only in making decisions as to treatment in difficult cases. Somewhat later, he stated that diagnosis "is not only unnecessary but in some ways is detrimental or unwise" (1951, p. 223). One reason was that it fosters the role of responsibility on the part of the therapist, thereby increasing the dependency of the client on the therapist. Another reason concerns the social implications of control by the therapist over the patient's decision in important areas of his life. From this point of view, the directive or authoritative use of psychological tests is definitely inconsistent with the basic philosophy of client-centered therapy and interferes with the patient's growth of self (Rogers, 1946).

Needless to say, this attitude toward diagnosis was criticized by other psychologists (Ellis, 1948; Hunt, 1948; Louttit, 1948). Among the objections raised were the need to evaluate the problems of the client before embarking on therapy and the necessity for deciding what kind of help is needed. It was also said that client-centered therapy implies a universality of effectiveness, since the diagnostic status of the client is not important. This view, therefore, was not widely shared, although what different clinicians mean by the term, diagnosis, varies widely.

RESEARCH IN CLIENT-CENTERED PSYCHOTHERAPY

Before completing our discussion of client-centered psychotherapy, we should mention again the contribution of Rogers and his co-workers to research methodology in psychotherapy. In an area like psychotherapy, which has been viewed more frequently as an art than as a science, the client-centered group contributed significantly toward a more systematic appraisal of the processes and outcomes of therapy.

Much of the literature on psychotherapy consists essentially of clinical accounts of what occurs in therapy. The earlier statistical reports on the outcomes of therapy also depended in great part upon the subjective evaluations submitted by individual psychotherapists. As a consequence, until quite recently, there was little research of a truly scientific character conducted in the field of psychotherapy. When a particular psychotherapist holds to a particular method of therapy, he usually does so on the basis of personal faith or experience rather than on the basis of research evidence of efficacy. Any attempts to refine procedures in psychotherapy, to explore systematically specific problems and hypotheses, to objectify processes and outcomes, and to communicate as explicitly as possible what is being done are to be regarded as significant innovations and contributions. In the opinion of the writer, the client-centered group has made such contributions to research methodology in psychotherapy.

REFERENCES

Adler, A. *The practice and theory of individual psychology*. (Rev. ed.) London: Kegan Paul, Trench, Trubner and Co., 1929.

Adler, K. Techniques that shorten psychotherapy: Illustrated with five cases. *Journal of Individual Psychology*, 1972, *28*, 155–168.

Alexander, F. *Fundamentals of psychoanalysis*. New York: W. W. Norton, 1948.

Alexander, F., & French, T. *Psychoanalytic therapy*. New York: Ronald Press, 1946.

Eiduson, B. T. The two classes of information in psychiatry. *Archives of General Psychiatry*, 1968, *18*, 405–419.

Ellis, A. A critique of the theoretical contribution of nondirective therapy. *Journal of Clinical Psychology*, 1948, *4*, 248–255.

Fiester, A. R., & Rudestam, K. W. A multivariate analysis of the early dropout process. *Journal of Consulting and Clinical Psychology*, 1975, *43*, 528–535.

Ford, D. H., & Urban, H. B. *Systems of psychotherapy. A comparative study*. New York: Wiley, 1963.

Freud, S. *The basic writings of Sigmund Freud*. New York: Modern Library, 1938.

Freud, S. *An Outline of Psychoanalysis*. New York: W. W. Norton, 1949.

Freud, S. The dynamics of the transference. In *Collected Papers*. Vol. 2. London: Hogarth Press and the Institute of Psychoanalysis, 1950. (a)

Freud, S. Recommendations for physicians on the psychoanalytic method of treatment. In *Collected Papers*. Vol. 2. London: Hogarth Press and the Institute of Psychoanalysis, 1950. (b)

Freud, S. Further recommendations in the technique of psychoanalysis. In *Collected Papers*. Vol. 2. London: Hogarth Press and the Institute of Psychoanalysis, 1950. (c)

Freud, S. Further recommendations in the technique of psychoanalysis. Observations on transference love. In *Collected Papers*. Vol. 2. London: Hogarth Press and the Institute of Psychoanalysis, 1950. (d)

Freud, S. *Collected Papers. Vol. 3*. London: Hogarth Press and the Institute of Psychoanalysis, 1950. (e)

Freud, S. *Collected Papers. Vol. 2*. London: Hogarth Press and the Institute of Psychoanalysis, 1950. (f)

Freud, S. On psychotherapy. In *Collected Papers. Vol. 1*. London: Hogarth Press and the Institute of Psychoanalysis, 1950. (g)

Fromm-Reichmann, F. *Principles of intensive psychotherapy*. Chicago: University of Chicago Press, 1950.

Garfield, S. L. Interpretation and the interpersonal interaction in psychotherapy. In E. F. Hammer (Ed.), *Use of interpretation in treatment*. New York: Grune and Stratton, 1968.

Garfield, S. L. Research on client variables in psychotherapy. In S. L. Garfield and A. E. Bergin (Eds.), *Handbook of psychotherapy and behavior change*. (2nd ed.). New York: Wiley, 1978.

Garfield, S. L. *Psychotherapy: An eclectic approach*. New York: Wiley, 1980.

Garfield, S. L., & Affleck, D. C. An appraisal of duration of stay in outpatient psychotherapy. *Journal of Nervous and Mental Disease*, 1959, *129*, 492–498.

Garfield, S. L., & Bergin, A. E. Therapeutic conditions and outcome. *Journal of Abnormal Psychology*, 1971, *77*, 108–114.

Gurman, A. S. The patient's perception of the therapeutic relationship. In A. S. Gurman and A. M. Razin (Eds.), *Effective psychotherapy. A handbook of research*. New York: Pergamon, 1977.

Hammer, E. F. *Use of interpretation in treatment*. New York: Grune and Stratton, 1968.

Hartmann, H. *Essays on ego psychology*. New York: International Universities Press, 1964.

Horney, K. *The neurotic personality of our time*. New York: W. W. Norton, 1937.

Horney, K. *New ways in psychoanalysis.* New York: W. W. Norton, 1939.

Hunt, W. A. Diagnosis and nondirective therapy. *Journal of Clinical Psychology,* 1948, *4,* 232–236.

Kadushin, C. *Why people go to psychiatrists.* New York: Atherton, 1969.

Kernberg, O. *The borderline conditions and pathological narcissism.* New York: Aronson, 1975.

Kernberg, O. F., Burstein, C. S., Coyne, R., Appelbaum, D. A., Horwitz, H., & Voth, T. J. Psychotherapy and psychoanalysis: Final report of the Menninger Foundation's psychotherapy research project. *Bulletin of the Menninger Clinic,* 1972, *36,* 1–276.

Kirman, W. J. Case history 5. Modern psychoanalytic treatment of depression. In G. S. Belkin (Ed.), *Contemporary psychotherapies.* Chicago: Rand McNally, 1980.

Knight, R. P. The present status of organized psychoanalysis in the United States. *Journal of American Psychoanalytical Association,* 1953, *1,* 197–221.

Kohut, H. *Analysis of the self.* New York: International Universities Press, 1971.

Kubie, L. S. *Practical and theoretical aspects of psychoanalysis.* New York: International Universities Press, 1950.

Levine, M. *Psychotherapy in medical practice.* New York: Macmillan, 1948.

Lorand, S. (Ed.), *Psychoanalysis today.* New York: International Universities Press, 1944.

Louttit, C. M. Training for nondirective counseling: A critique. *Journal of Clinical Psychology,* 1948, *4,* 236–240.

Luborsky, L., & Spence, D. P. Quantitative research on psychoanalytic therapy. In S. L. Garfield and A. E. Bergin (Eds.), *Handbook of psychotherapy and behavior change.* (2nd ed.). New York: Wiley, 1978.

Marmor, J., & Woods, S. M. (Eds.), *The interface between the psychodynamic and behavioral therapies.* New York: Plenum, 1980.

Mitchell, K. M., Bozarth, J. D., & Krauft, C. C. A reappraisal of the therapeutic effectiveness of accurate empathy, nonpossessive warmth, and genuineness. In A. S. Gurman and A. M. Razin (Eds.), *Effective psychotherapy: A handbook of research.* New York: Pergamon Press, 1977.

Obendorf, C. P. Results of psychoanalytic therapy. *International Journal of Psychoanalysis,* 1943, *24,* 107–114.

Obendorf, C. P., Greenacre, P., & Kubie, L. Symposium on the evaluation of therapeutic results. *International Journal of Psychoanalysis.* 1948, *29,* 7–33.

Parloff, M. B., Waskow, I. E., Wolfe, B. E. Research on therapist variables in relation to process and outcome. In S. L. Garfield and A. E. Bergin (Eds.), *Handbook of psychotherapy and behavior change.* (2nd ed.). New York: Wiley, 1978.

Rachman, A. W., & Kauff, P. F. Directory of post-graduate psychotherapy training facilities. *JSAS Catalog of Selected Documents in Psychology,* 1972, *2,* 116.

Rado, S. Recent advances of psychoanalytic therapy. In *Psychiatric Treatment.* Vol. 21. Proceedings of the Association for Research in Nervous and Mental Disease. Baltimore: Williams and Wilkins, 1953.

Rogers, C. R. *Counseling and psychotherapy.* Boston: Houghton Mifflin, 1942.

Rogers, C. R. Psychometric tests and client-centered counseling. *Educational & Psychological Measurement,* 1946, *6,* 139–144.

Rogers, C. R. *Client-centered therapy.* Boston: Houghton Mifflin, 1951.

Rogers, C. R. The necessary and sufficient conditions of therapeutic personality change. *Journal of Consulting Psychology,* 1957, *21,* 95–103.

Rogers, C. R., Gendlin, E. T., Kiesler, D. J., & Truax, C. B. (Eds.), *The therapeutic relationship and its impact.* Madison, WI: University of Wisconsin Press, 1967.

Rogers, L. S. Drop-out rates and results of psychotherapy in government-aided mental Hygiene clinics. *Journal of Clinical Psychology,* 1960, *16,* 89–92.

Rosenthal, D., & Frank, J. D. The fate of psychiatric clinic outpatients assigned to psychotherapy. *Journal of Nervous and Mental Disease,* 1958, *127,* 330–343.

Snyder, W. U. Interpretation in relationship therapy. In E. F. Hammer (Ed.), Use of interpretation in treatment. New York: Grune and Stratton, 1968.

Spotnitz, H. *Psychotherapy of pre-oedipal conditions.* New York: Jason Aronson, 1976.

Sullivan, H. S. *The interpersonal theory of psychiatry.* New York: W. W. Norton, 1953.

Thompson, C. Transference as a therapeutic instrument. In B. Glueck (Ed.), *Current therapies of personality disorders.* New York: Grune and Stratton, 1946.

Thompson, C. *Psychoanalysis: Evaluation and development.* New York: Hermitage House, 1950.

Truax, C. B., & Carkhuff, R. R. *Toward effective counseling and psychotherapy.* Chicago: Aldine, 1967.

Traux, C. B., Carkhuff, R. R., & Kodman, F., Jr. Relationship between therapist-offered conditions and patient change in group psychotherapy. *Journal of Clinical Psychology,* 1965, *21,* 327–329.

Truax, C. B., & Mitchell, K. M. Research on certain therapist interpersonal skills in relation to process and outcome. In A. E. Bergin and S. L. Garfield (Eds.), *Handbook of psychotherapy and behavior change.* New York: Wiley, 1971.

Truax, C. B., Wargo, D. G., Frank, J. D., Imber, S. D., Battle, C. C., Hoehn-Saric, R., Nash, E. H., & Stone, A. R. The therapist's contribution to accurate empathy, nonpossessive warmth, and genuineness in psychotherapy. *Journal of Clinical Psychology,* 1966, *22,* 331–334.

Wachtel, P. L. *Psychoanalysis and Behavior Therapy.* New York: Basic Books, 1977.

Wolman, B. B. (Ed.), *Psychoanalytic techniques.* New York: Basic Books, 1967.

Variations in
Psychotherapy—
Other Approaches

The psychotherapeutic systems or approaches discussed in the previous chapter are among the best known in this field. However, they by no means exhaust the number of approaches available for appraisal. Among those available the author has chosen a few for presentation in this chapter. These have been selected for diverse reasons. Some have attracted particular interest from practitioners in the field, some seem intriguing on their own account, some appear to utilize premises or procedures that are diametrically opposed to others, and some have been selected to illustrate further the great diversity that exists among current types of psychotherapy. Actually, each of the therapeutic approaches selected fits several of the criteria mentioned. After briefly reviewing these approaches, in the next chapter we shall discuss those procedures deriving from theories of learning, and which most frequently are referred to as "behavior therapies." Descriptions of still other approaches are available in other sources (Binder, Binder and Rimland, 1976; Burton, 1972; Morse and Watson, 1977; Patterson, 1966).

RATIONAL-EMOTIVE PSYCHOTHERAPY

An approach to psychotherapy, which differs in many respects from those already reviewed, is rational-emotive psychotherapy developed by Albert Ellis

(1958, 1962). This approach has gained a body of loyal followers and devotees, due, perhaps, to dissatisfaction with other approaches and the efforts of its energetic leader. Thus, a number of brief workshops and institutes have been held in various parts of the country to provide training and acquaint interested individuals with the rationale and procedures of rational-emotive psychotherapy.

First labeled rational psychotherapy, this approach appeared to stem from Ellis's dissatisfaction with conventional analytically oriented psychotherapy. After his own personal analysis, and after practicing psychoanalysis and psychoanalytically oriented psychotherapy for many years, Ellis went on to develop the approach named "rational-emotive therapy." The basic premise in this approach is that clients can be helped to lead more satisfying lives by being taught to organize and discipline their thinking, or, in other words, to think rationally.

According to Ellis (1958), the human being possesses four basic processes—perception, movement, thinking, and emoting—and all of these are integrally interrelated. Because of the interrelations of thought and emotion, each may affect the other. "Rational psychotherapy is based on the assumption that thought and emotion are not two entirely different processes, but that they significantly overlap in many respects and that, therefore, disordered emotions can often (though not always) be ameliorated by changing one's thinking" (Ellis, 1958, p. 36). What is frequently called emotion is actually a certain kind of thinking, usually of a biased or strongly evaluative kind. It is further hypothesized that thinking and emoting differ mainly in that thinking is a mode of discrimination that generally is more tranquil, less somatically involved, and less active than is emotion. Through the process of living and social acculturation, thinking and emoting become closely intertwined "so that one's thinking *becomes* one's emotion and emoting *becomes* one's thought" (Ellis, 1958, p. 36). Furthermore, because of the importance of language in human behavior, both thought and emotion involve "self-talk or internalized sentences; and that, for all practical purposes, the sentences that human beings keep telling themselves *are* or *become* their thoughts and emotions" (Ellis, 1958, p. 36).

The above represents some of the basic postulates underlying this particular orientation to psychotherapy. As is apparent from these postulates, the focus in therapy is on helping the client to see that his difficulties result largely from faulty thinking and expectations, and then getting him to think more rationally. In other words, the individual's disturbed behavior, or neurosis, is directly related to his illogical or irrational thinking. Furthermore, exploring and understanding the origins of this faulty thinking, as is implied in analytically oriented therapy, will not necessarily help the individual in modifying his behavior. Rather, more attention has to be paid to how disturbed individuals perpetuate their irrational thinking and how the latter can be modified. Thus, clients have to be shown that their self-verbalizations are the main source of their emotional difficulties, and that they are capable of controlling their emotions by more rational thinking. More specifically, the therapist in his interactions with the client consistently points out to the latter his faulty thinking, demonstrates how it is responsible for his current maladjustment, and teaches him how to rethink and reverbalize his faulty sentences in a more logical manner.

One illustration of this process is referred to as the *ABC* sequence of rational-emotive therapy. *A* represents the activating event or stimulus which tends to activate or begin a sequence of events. *B* refers to the belief system which influences how the person appraises the situation, the cognitive response. *C* represents the consequence which follows. In this sequence, it is point *B* which is considered the most important part of the sequence, for the individual's cognitions or beliefs influence how he or she interpret the activating situation and the response to it.

According to Ellis (1958), the therapist, in addition to dealing specifically and concretely with the client's distorted and illogical thinking, should also "demonstrate to this client what, *in general,* are the main irrational ideas that human beings are prone to follow and what more rational philosophies of living may usually be substituted for them" (p. 39). If this is not done, the client may eventually wind up with a different group of illogical ideas. Consequently, Ellis has listed a number of illogical ideas which, if held by individuals in our culture, appear to lead to personal difficulties. A few of these can be mentioned briefly. One is the idea that a person must be loved or approved for everything he does, rather than on securing approval for appropriate achievement, or loving instead of being loved. Another is the idea that much human misery is externally caused, instead of the idea that unhappiness is caused or sustained by the view that one takes of things rather than by the things themselves. A final illustrative idea is that one has little control over one's emotions and feelings, rather than the opposite, particularly if the individual works at controlling his emotions and practices.

Thus, the emphasis in rational-emotive psychotherapy is to get the client to face up to his illogical thinking, which is the cause of his difficulties, and to become more rational. Traditional therapeutic approaches, according to this view, demonstrate to the client that he does think illogically and point out how he developed in this manner. Nevertheless, they frequently do not show him how he currently maintains his illogical thinking and how he may change by developing rational philosophies of living and applying these to his life situation.

In rational-emotive therapy, the therapist tends to function in two main ways. First, he keeps pounding away at the illogical ideas and superstitions that lie at the basis of the client's fears. For example, if an individual is fearful of being imperfect, he must be shown in a variety of ways how such fears are really irrational, for no one is perfect. Second, the therapist encourages and persuades the client to engage in activities that will act as a counterforce to the ideas held by the client. If, for example, the client believes that no one will go out with him, attempts will be made to actually secure experiences in life which counter this false belief. Thus, assignments and practical tasks are also utilized in the therapy as aids in actually overcoming the client's illogical beliefs and fears. Once the basic irrational thinking is overcome, new difficulties are not anticipated. "For once an individual truly surrenders ideas of perfectionism, of the horror of failing at something, of the dire need to be approved by others, of the notion that the world owes him a living, and so on, what else is there for him to be fearful or disturbed about?" (Ellis, 1958, p. 46).

These, then, are the basic suppositions and views of rational-emotive psychotherapy. Ellis admits that the therapy is not effective for all potential clients. It does not appear to be suitable for clients who are not bright enough to engage in rational analyses, for those who are too emotionally disturbed, or are too inflexible or too prejudiced against logic and reason. For these reasons, the therapist must also be able to use other approaches. Ellis does believe, however, that his approach to therapy will prove to be more effective with more types of clients than "any of the nonrational or semirational therapies now being widely employed" (Ellis, 1958, p. 49).

Although rational-emotive therapy has attained a certain amount of popularity and has been considered a pioneer among the cognitive therapies, Ellis and other rational-emotive therapists have reported little in the way of systematic studies evaluating the effectiveness of the therapy (e.g., Bard, 1980). Ellis (1957) himself published one paper in which he reported that rational-emotive therapy secured better results than either orthodox psychoanalysis or psychoanalytically oriented psychotherapy. In this instance, however, Ellis was both the therapist and the evaluator of outcome, and one cannot take these results at face value.

More recently, Ellis (1977) published a paper on the research data supporting "the clinical and personality hypotheses of RET and other modes of cognitive-behavior therapy" (p. 2). In this rather lengthy paper, Ellis states: "I have written it to show that this particular system of psychotherapy has immense—indeed, almost awesome—research backing." (p. 3). Unfortunately, neither the present writer nor several highly respected individuals in the cognitive-behavioral area agree with Ellis' appraisal (Ewart and Thoreson, 1977; Mahoney, 1977; Meichenbaum, 1977b). The hypotheses formulated by Ellis are in many instances overly general, and although 22 pages of references are listed, most of these were not designed to test the therapy in any way and were carried out for different purposes by different investigators. Furthermore, Ellis selected only what he saw as confirmative studies and did not include potentially negative studies. The studies mentioned were for the most part only listed and not discussed or evaluated. Only one reference was made to the evaluation of outcome in rational-emotive therapy (DiGuiseppe, Miller, and Trexler, 1977) and the latter review contained only a few directly pertinent studies. Investigations of other cognitive-behavioral approaches cannot be taken as direct evidence of the efficacy of rational-emotive therapy. As stated by Ewart and Thoresen (1977) in their appraisal of Ellis' assertion, "The problem is that we simply cannot accept Ellis' claim that his methods are supported by large numbers of well designed, scientific studies" (p. 55). It appears, therefore, that more systematic and reliable data are required before we can adequately appraise the effectiveness of this form of therapy.

THE COGNITIVE THERAPY OF A. T. BECK

More recently, rational-emotive therapy has been viewed as just one of a number of cognitive therapies. Although these therapies may differ somewhat in their theoretical and procedural emphasis, they appear to share a common emphasis on the importance of cognitions as factors in human maladjustment. If cognitions or beliefs are viewed as possible causes of psychological disorders, it seems reasonable to hypothesize that modifying such beliefs may have positive therapeutic effects. Ellis' form of therapy is one illustration of this view. Another well-known example is the cognitive therapy of A. T. Beck (1976), Professor of Psychiatry at the University of Pennsylvania.

Beck, a trained psychoanalyst, eventually thought it might be possible and feasible to utilize conscious rational thinking on the part of the patient as an approach to therapy.

> This new approach—cognitive therapy—suggests that the individual's problems are de-
> rived largely from certain distortions of reality based on erroneous premises and assumptions.
> These incorrect conceptions originated in defective learning during the person's cognitive
> development. Regardless of their origin, it is relatively simple to state the formula for treat-
> ment: The therapist helps a patient to unravel his distortions in thinking and to learn alterna-
> tive, more realistic ways to formulate his experiences (Beck, 1976, p. 3).

Although the above formulation is quite similar to that of rational-emotive therapy, there are certain features of Beck's approach that differ in some respects from that of Ellis. Part of this may be due to the personal styles of these two individuals. Ellis appears to dominate his therapy sessions in a very forceful and sometimes dominating manner, whereas Beck differs in this regard. Beck focuses on the internal communications or introspections that occur within the individual, and which frequently are not verbalized. The patient, therefore, has to be helped to focus on such unverbalized or unreported thoughts, since generally they communicate in a different manner in conversing with other people. Beck also noticed that these unreported thoughts generally preceded an emotional state. He therefore instructed patients to try to recall the thoughts they had just prior to experiencing unpleasant feelings or sensations. "This instruction helped them to sharpen their awareness of their thoughts, and eventually they were able to identify the thoughts *prior* to experiencing the emotions" (Beck, 1976, p. 33).

Because these hitherto unexpressed thoughts appeared to emerge automatically and very rapidly after the therapist's instructions, Beck called them "automatic thoughts" and felt they allowed one to comprehend the emotional states and disturbance of the patient. Generally, these thoughts were very specific, came out in a telegraphic style, and were regarded by the patient as reasonable and plausible—even though they may not have seemed so to others. These thoughts also were seen as not only unique to the patient, but similar to those of patients with similar disorders. Thus, in cases of depression, the patient's cognitions center around a negative conception of self, a negative interpretation of the person's life experience, and a pessimistic or nihilistic view of the future.

Similar to many other approaches to psychotherapy, Beck also emphasizes the importance of a collaborative therapeutic relationship between therapist and patient. Thus, "the patient and therapist should reach a consensus regarding what problems require help, the goal of therapy, and how they plan to reach that goal" (Beck, 1976, p. 220). In this sense also, Beck appears to take a less authoritative stance than does Ellis, although both focus on distorted cognitions and beliefs. Even though cognitive modification is considered the essence of all cognitive approaches, Beck and others also use a variety of other procedures. Activities may be used to clearly demonstrate to the patient her distorted thoughts. Thus, in cases of depression, for example, where cognitive therapy has been applied with some success (Rush, Beck, Kovacs, & Hollon, 1977), successful performance of selected tasks has a positive effect on the patient and aids in the task of cognitive restructuring. Graded task assignments may be used to give the patient a feeling of successful experiences. The patient may also be asked to keep a record of his activities and to note those which have resulted in pleasure or success. Homework assignments are also made at each session and the patient may also be asked to keep a log of all automatic thoughts, writing down the negative cognition in one column and a rational response in another column.

Beck's cognitive therapy has become one of the more recognized cognitive approaches and some favorable appraisals have also been published (Kovacs,

Rush, Beck, & Hollon, 1981; Rush *et al.,* 1977; Shaw, 1977). Although the latter are still limited, such efforts are certainly commendable. In addition, Beck and some of his collaborators have prepared a detailed training manual for his therapeutic approach, which is a distinctive and innovative contribution, not only for training, but also for evaluating the therapy. As a result of this and the previous use of the therapy in treating cases of depression, Beck's cognitive therapy is one of two forms of psychotherapy being evaluated in an important collaborative study of the treatment of depression sponsored by the National Institute of Mental Health.

Although Beck's form of therapy has been designated as a cognitive therapy, both his therapy and rational-emotive therapy have included procedures which can also be termed behavioral. Social-learning approaches such as Bandura's (1969, 1977), also tend to emphasize both cognitive and performance aspects. Thus, there has occurred some blurring between cognitive and behavioral therapeutic approaches, and the term, cognitive-behavioral, has come into recent usage (Kendall and Hollon, 1979; Meichenbaum, 1977a). This seems like a sensible development since both cognitions and behavior are interrelated aspects of human functioning. We shall come back to this matter later when we discuss behavioral approaches to therapy.

REALITY THERAPY

Another interesting approach to psychotherapy is that developed by William Glasser and G. H. Harrington, and referred to as reality therapy. Like some of the other therapy systems already discussed, reality therapy also was developed as a result of dissatisfaction with the more traditional analytically oriented depth therapies. The basic concepts of reality therapy have been presented in rather concise form in a brief book by Glasser (1965). Although the book is challenging and provocative in many respects, unfortunately little in the way of systematic evaluation or research has been obtained. Nevertheless, some attempts at assessing the efficacy of treatment have been made and the methods have been used in several different settings with rather difficult patients.

Although Glasser himself is a psychiatrist, he is critical of current conceptions of mental illness and advocates doing away with the common psychiatric labels such as psychosis and neurosis, which tend to categorize and stereotype human beings. Instead, the emphasis is placed on describing the individual's behavior. From the standpoint of reality therapy, the actions or behaviors of a person, which might conventionally be labeled as neurotic or psychotic, are best described as *irresponsible.* Helping the person to become responsible is the goal of therapy, and this, in turn, is related to some other basic concepts in reality therapy.

According to this orientation, "everyone who needs psychiatric treatment suffers from one basic inadequacy: he is unable to fulfill his essential needs" (Glasser, 1965, p. 5). The patient's problem or symptom is a manifestation of his inability to fulfill his needs and represents his attempt at solving this problem. Furthermore, in their unsuccessful attempts to fulfill their needs, "all patients have a common characteristic: *they all deny the reality of the world around them*" (Glasser, 1965, p. 6). Regardless of the specific behaviors manifested, whether it be delinquency, fears, delusions, or suicide, there is some degree of denial of reality evident. Therapy, therefore, must attempt to help the patient meet successfully the demands of the real world in which he lives. He must learn to fulfill his needs in the real world since he has not been successful in accomplishing this previously. In reality therapy, therefore, the therapist must not only strive to help the individual accept the real world, but he must also help him fulfill his needs in the real world so that there will be no reason in the future to deny its existence.

In discussing the basic needs that all people appear to have, two in particular are stressed. These are *"the need to love and be loved and the need to feel that we are worthwhile to ourselves and to others"* (Glasser, 1965, p. 9). Other needs are, of course, recognized, but are not deemed to be of major concern to psychiatry. The two needs mentioned, however, do appear to be of importance and the inability to fulfill them leads to disturbed behavior. It is also emphasized that in order to fulfill these needs the individual must be *involved* with other people. "At all times in our lives we must have at least one person who cares about us and whom we care for ourselves" (Glasser, 1965, p. 7). If this essential person is lacking, then the individual will not be successful in fulfilling his needs. There must be this involvement with another person—and the latter must be in touch with reality and able to satisfy his own needs in the world. This last statement also is directly applicable to the therapist.

The need to love and be loved exists throughout our life and requires little elaboration. The need to feel worthwhile, while viewed as a separate need, is usually closely related to the previous one. It is theoretically possible to love and be loved, however, and not feel that one is worthwhile. An illustration of this is that of the child who is loved in an overindulgent manner and who receives approval even when his behavior is bad. Since the child knows the difference between good and bad behavior, receiving love for behavior he knows is bad prevents him from feeling worthwhile. In order to be worthwhile, the individual must maintain a satisfactory or acceptable standard of behavior. This means that values, morals, or standards of right and wrong behavior are closely related to fulfilling the need for self-worth.

If a person is unable to fulfill one or both of these basic needs, some discomfort or symptom results. Generally, the earlier and more satisfactorily a person learns to satisfy his needs, the better his adjustment. In most people's lives, however, their situations change and new means of need satisfaction have to be learned. In each instance, this requires involvement with other people, and those individuals who seek help generally lack this kind of relationship. "Therefore, to obtain help in therapy the patient must gain or regain involvement, first with the therapist, and then with others. His problem and the accompanying symptoms will disappear once he is able to become involved and fulfill his needs" (Glasser, 1965, pp. 12–13). It should be pointed out, also, that the focus in treatment is on the present and the past is largely ignored. In a similar way, the emphasis is on conscious experiences rather than unconscious factors.

Another related and basic concept of reality therapy is that of responsibility. The latter is defined "as the ability to fulfill one's needs, and to do so *in a way that does not deprive others of the ability to fulfill their needs*" (Glasser, 1965, p. 13). A responsible individual also does things that give him a feeling of self-worth and of being worthwhile to others. If a responsible person says he will do something, he will strive to accomplish it. The ability to become responsible is learned throughout life, and those who do not learn this manifest problems. Such individuals, as mentioned previously, are irresponsible rather than mentally ill. The task of therapy is to help the individual become more responsible in order that he may be able to satisfy his needs. Individuals learn responsibility through involvements with responsible human beings. In most instances, responsible behavior is learned in relation to the parents who provide both love and discipline and allow the individual to engage in such behavior when he appears ready to do so. In many instances, however, there are people whose circumstances are such that they fail to develop responsible behavior and must be helped to do so.

Reality therapy, in line with what has been presented, consists of three separate but interwoven procedures. The first is involvement. The therapist has to become sufficiently involved with the patient in order for the latter to begin to face reality and to see that his behavior is unrealistic. Second, the therapist must reject those aspects of the patient's behavior that are unrealistic, but at the same time be accepting of the patient and maintain his involvement with him. Finally, the therapist attempts to teach the patient more successful and realistic ways of fulfilling his needs.

According to Glasser, although the therapist has a difficult task in quickly building a firm emotional relationship with someone who has had difficulties in establishing such relationships, he is aided by the fact that the patient actually is desperate for such involvement. The ability of the therapist to become involved with the patient is the major skill of the therapist in this form of therapy. It is, however, difficult to describe verbally. The patient may offer resistance to therapy and will test out the sincerity and responsibility of the therapist. The latter must not be found wanting in these respects, or no involvement will take place. The model of the therapist in reality therapy is somewhat different from that usually depicted for other types of therapy. "The therapist must be a very responsible person—tough, interested, human, and sensitive. He must be able to fulfill his own needs and must be willing to discuss his own struggles so that the patient can see that acting responsibly is possible though sometimes difficult" (Glasser, 1965, p. 22). According to this view, the therapist has to be a strong person, able to withstand the demands and criticisms of the patient. He must never condone irresponsible actions or give in to expediency; and he must constantly point out reality to the patient. The therapist must also understand the patient, be able to accept him uncritically and not be overwhelmed by the patient's irrational behavior. The therapist thus has to be able to become emotionally involved with the patient. Once involvement is obtained, the patient can then begin to face reality.

In essence, then, the therapist conveys his interest, acceptance, and involvement with the patient, but he also confronts him with reality and demands responsible behavior. The patient is no longer allowed to evade the recognition of what he does and his responsibility for his behavior. Essentially, these patterns of the therapist deepen the relationship "because now someone cares enough about the patient to make him face a truth that he has spent his life trying to avoid: *he is responsible for his behavior*" (Glasser, 1965, p. 27). The patient is continually confronted with reality, and he is not allowed to excuse his behavior. Although, conceivably, this may appear to some as a rather harsh confrontation by the therapist, Glasser views it differently. "The patient thus finds a man who cares enough about him to reject behavior which will not help him to fulfill his needs" (Glasser, 1965, p. 27). This is a point that is stressed continuously by Glasser in his book. The emphasis on reality actually is considered to reflect the therapist's sincere interest and involvement with the patient rather than, as might be interpreted by others, a form of potentially critical rejection.

The emphasis and focus in reality therapy is on the behavior of the patient. While the therapist may listen to the patient's opinions, views, and attitudes, he continually stresses his concern with the patient's behavior. Behavioral change is the goal, and such change leads to changes in attitudes, and so on. Behavior which reflects responsibility on the part of the patient is praised; that which does not, brings forth disapproval. In reality therapy, the discussion is not overly involved with the patient's past or with his problem per se. Rather, the focus is on the present and topics of current concern—interests, hopes, fears, and, particularly, the patient's values. This reflects the therapist's basic interest in the patient as a person. *"When values, standards, and responsibility are in the background, all discussion is relevant to therapy"* (Glasser, 1965, p. 31). Furthermore, the stress is on *what* the patient is doing, not *why* he is doing it.

Reality therapy thus differs in several ways from more traditional psychodynamic forms of psychotherapy. Conceptions of mental illness, probing into the past, concerns with transference, and unconscious motivations are all disregarded. Instead, emphasis is placed on moral problems, on the present, and on teaching the patient how to behave in a better manner, one that will enable him to fulfill his needs. The methods of reality therapy have been utilized in treating delinquent girls in an institutional setting, in working with chronic patients in a Veterans Administration Hospital, and in private practice. Actually, although the first two groups of patients are usually seen as very difficult to treat, the control possible in institutional settings apparently allows the therapist considerable influence in attempts at modifying behavior. Although mainly clinical attempts at evaluation of treatment have been performed thus far, the results were encouraging. For example, of 370 girls treated at the Ventura School for Girls, in California, only 43 have been returnees to the school, a rather impressive result for this type of population. As Glasser himself admits, however, more systematic research data are needed in order to more adequately evaluate this approach to psychotherapy. Unfortunately, very little has been reported.

EXISTENTIAL APPROACHES TO PSYCHOTHERAPY

Somewhat in contrast to the other systems of psychotherapy presented, are developments usually referred to as existential therapies. This particular orientation to psychotherapy differs in several interesting ways from most of those already discussed. In the first place, with its roots in existential doctrine, there is a greater philosophical emphasis in this approach to therapy than is true of most others. Second, there appears to be less concern with the actual techniques of therapy than is characteristic of most psychotherapies. Not only do adherents of this view write relatively little about the actual techniques of therapy, but they are quite critical of any real concern with techniques. From their point of view, such concerns are likely to interfere with the essence of therapy. Finally, they show a greater involvement with spiritual issues and problems of value than is true of most other approaches. Although the differences just mentioned are quite apparent, occasionally one may also note some similarities between certain emphases mentioned by some of the existential psychotherapists and those expressed by other approaches. For example, the emphasis on values does have something in common with Glasser's reality therapy, and some of the existentialists have also emphasized the responsibility of the client (Frankl, 1965). Surprisingly, one also finds some similarities between existential points of view and procedures used by behavior therapists; but, let us postpone such comparisons until we describe this approach in more detail.

The existential orientations to psychotherapy were derived from existential philosophy and from the phenomenological movement in philosophy. A brief account of this development has been provided by May (1958a) and is also available in the works by Ford and Urban (1963), Hall and Lindzey (1978), and Patterson (1966). Important contributors to this movement, philosophically, were the phenomenologist Husserl, and such existentialists as Kierkegaard, Jaspers, Heidegger, and Marcel. While Sartre is perhaps better known to Americans, the ensuing developments in existential psychotherapy are more directly linked to the ideas of those mentioned above than to Sartre (Sonneman, 1954). For a number of reasons, including the nature of the material, the writer's inadequacies in the area of philosophy, and the primary concern of this chapter with psychotherapy, little attention will be paid to the more formal philosophical aspects of existential therapies. More detailed accounts are available elsewhere for the interested reader (Frankl, 1965; May, 1961; May, Angel, & Ellenberger, 1958; Sonneman, 1954).

The emphasis in existential philosophy and psychology is on the nature of man, his existence, and the meaning of this existence for the individual.[6] The person's being and existence is a fluid and changing one, it is not a static essence or substance. The individual also has the capacity for awareness, of being aware of himself and of what he is doing. There is a constant emphasis on the ever changing and dynamic quality of the person's existence. "He does not exist; he is not *a* being; rather he is coming into being, emerging, becoming, evolving toward something" (Ford and Urban, 1963, p. 448). The present experience and existence, as well as the direction and goals of the person, are judged important and receive emphasis. Such emphases as well as attempts to link the individual and his current situation, instead of artifically splitting the two, lead to a use of hyphenated words or expressions to convey the particular meaning implied. Thus, there are references to the-person-who-is-behaving, being-in-the-world, falling-out-of-being, being-with, being-for-itself, and so on.

The emphasis on phenomenology also underlines the attempt to understand what transpires from the point of view of the subjective observer. The

---

[6] Most of the writing referred to in this section reflects the language usage of the time and I found it awkward to change. The reader should understand that the usage of "man" here refers to humankind. (Author)

objective is to avoid abstractions but to strive to ascertain what is existentially real, or what is immediately experienced—to understand the person as he exists in his world. The "focus is on man's most immediate experience, his own existence. . . . Existence has been opposed to essence, which is an abstraction and which has been the concern of traditional science" (Patterson, 1966, p. 444). The existential point of view thus emphasizes the person's experience as he exists and interacts with his world.

Unfortunately, there is no really systematic or unified existential point of view that can be succinctly presented. Rather, there are a number of different existential philosophers and a variety of existential approaches to psychotherapy. Furthermore, as noted, little attention is paid to therapeutic techniques. There is, therefore, variation within this movement. Binswanger, Boss, May, and Frankl are among those who have been particularly interested in the application of existential viewpoints to psychiatry, psychology, and psychotherapy. A number of existential therapists appear to utilize psychoanalytic techniques, but somehow adapt them within the framework of an existential point of view. The following quotation from Binswanger may illustrate this:

> Regardless of whether the existential analyst is predominantly psychoanalytic or predominantly jungian in orientation, he will always stand on the same plane with his patients—the plane of common existence. He will therefore not degrade the patient to an object toward which he is subject, but he will see in him an existential partner. He will therefore not consider the bond between the two partners to be as that of two electric batteries—a 'psychic contact'—but as an encounter on what Martin Buber calls the 'sharp edge of existence,' an existence which *essentially* 'is in the world,' not merely as a self but also as a being-together with one another—relatedness and love. Also what has, since Freud, been called transference is, in the existential-analytic sense, a kind of encounter. For encounter is a being-with-others in *genuine presence,* that is to say, in the present which is altogether continuous with the *past* and bears within it the possibilities of a *future* (Binswanger, 1956, pp. 146–147).

It may be worthwhile also to refer to some of the general characteristics that May (1958b) believes distinguish existential therapists from others. In the first place, existential therapists place comparatively little stress on techniques and see them as subordinate to the major goal of understanding the client. Consequently, a variety of techniques may be used, and their use will be determined by what appears to be most effective in revealing the existence of the particular client at this time in his life. A second characteristic is the emphasis on the present reality, including that of the therapist and patient. Thus, such phenomena as transference are not viewed as distortions or projections deriving from the patient's past, but, instead, as parts of the patient's current relationship in the here and now. A third characteristic is that the therapist does not view the client as a generalized object to which he applies his knowledge and techniques. Rather, the therapist attempts to understand and experience the "being" of the patient as a unique person. Closely related is the attempt of the therapist to avoid behavior that would destroy "presence," or the encounter between therapist and client. A reliance on techniques or treating the patient as an object may, at times, diminish the therapist's anxiety but will interfere with the reality of the relationship. Another characteristic emphasis of the existentialists is that the goal of therapy is to increase the client's awareness of his own existence, and that he eventually experience his existence as real. The patient should attain a sense of self-direction and personal involvement, rather than feeling he is an object. Finally, existential therapy should help the client develop an attitude of commitment. Knowledge alone is insufficient and comes as a consequence of commitment. "The patient cannot permit himself to get insight or knowledge until he is ready to decide, takes a *decisive* orientation to life, and has made the preliminary decisions along the way" (May, 1958b, p. 87).

The material just presented represents some of the main emphases of existential psychotherapy. Although the varied statements concerning this approach are sometimes rather diffuse and difficult to comprehend concretely, the ideas and emphases presented do indicate the essential nature of this orientation and how it tends to differ from others. We shall delay any further comments or appraisal until we have examined one other and more specific existential approach known as "Logotherapy."

LOGOTHERAPY

Although logotherapy appears to have developed as the separate creation of the psychiatrist Victor E. Frankl, it is included here as a variant of the existential approach to psychotherapy. Frankl shares many of the common concerns and emphases of other existentialists and does refer to them, but he has presented his own formulations and in many ways is more specific and systematic than most of the others. What follows is derived mainly from his book, *The Doctor and the Soul* (Frankl, 1965). Again, the objective will not be to present an exhaustive account of Frankl's views, but rather to discuss briefly some of his more important conceptions with particular reference to psychotherapy. For those who desire a more extended, but yet rather condensed account, the presentation by Patterson (1966) can be recommended.

According to Frankl, man lives in three basic dimensions—the somatic, the mental, and the spiritual. The spiritual dimension has tended to be ignored, but it is what makes us human. People increasingly are concerned with the meaning of their lives, and this may be interpreted by therapists as a symptom of disturbance. It may only be a sign of spiritual distress, however, and in order for a proper diagnosis to be made, the spiritual side of man must be comprehended. Whereas psychoanalysis speaks of the pleasure principle or the "will-to-pleasure" and individual psychology of the "will-to-power," little has been said of the "will-to-meaning," that which is the most human phenomena of all. Furthermore, such meaning has to be highly specific and personal. Logotherapy not only recognizes the spiritual side of man but starts from there.

Frankl acknowledges the past importance of psychoanalysis and Adlerian individual psychology, but believes that each has been one-sided in its emphasis, and has omitted attention to the spiritual side of man. The aim of logotherapy is not to take the place of existing psychotherapies, but to complement them. "That is to say, there are cases in which ordinary psychotherapy must be applied and yet a complete cure can be effected only by logotherapy" (Frankl, 1965, p. xii). There are also instances, however, where what is called "existential frustration" may lead to neurotic symptomatology. Despair over the meaning of life may thus be called an "existential neurosis." This is a new type of neurosis called "noögenic neurosis." For such cases, logotherapy is considered to be a specific therapy. Other healers, however, such as the surgeon or the medical practitioner also may need to minister to patients who have spiritual problems as well as strictly medical ones.

The largest section of Frankl's book, *The Doctor and the Soul,* bears the heading, "From Psychoanalysis to Existential Analysis." This in turn has two main subdivisions. The first deals with general existential analysis and discusses some of the main concerns of the existentialists, including the meaning of life and the meaning of death, suffering, work, and love. Such concerns are not symptoms of maladjustment, but rather, the true expression "of the state of being human, the mark of the most human nature in man" (Frankl, 1965, p. 26). Only man, alone, is capable of raising the question of the meaning of his own existence. Existential analysis is also concerned with making men conscious of their responsibility, "since being responsible is one of the essential grounds of human existence" (Frankl, 1965, p. 25). The second subdivision of this section—special existential analysis—is concerned more specifically with abnormal conditions—anxiety neurosis, obsessional neurosis, melancholia, and schizophrenia. Neurotic symptoms have a fourfold root and are "grounded" in what are viewed as the four different layers or dimensions of man's being. These are the physical or physiological, the psychological, the social, and the spiritual. The latter, alone, provides the point of approach for existential analysis. "For only where neurosis is understood as a product of decision can there be the freedom to which existential analysis attempts to appeal" (Frankl, 1965, p. 177). The other dimensions offer no basis for existential freedom. On the physiological level, for example, the only possible treatment would be drugs.

There is no need here to discuss the different types of psychopathology as seen from the viewpoint of existential analysis. Nevertheless, a few comments on schizophrenia may serve to illustrate the application of such a viewpoint to psychotic behavior. One basic aspect of the disorder is that the schizophrenic experiences himself as an object. "The schizophrenic experiences himself as if he, the subject, were transformed into an object. He experiences psychic acts as if they were being rendered in the passive mood" (Frankl, 1965, p. 209). The primary delusional feeling in schizophrenia is viewed as "the experience of pure objectives." The schizophrenic individual, from this point of view, is limited in two existential factors: consciousness and responsibility. As a consequence, he can not feel himself as really "existent."

Finally, some mention should be made of two specific techniques of therapy which have been developed by Frankl. In contrast to much of the writing on existential therapy, the accounts of these techniques are quite specific and bear some relationship to methods used by others. The first technique is called "paradoxical intention." In this procedure the patient is instructed to actually attempt or try to perform that activity which is anxiety provoking and which he is fearful will occur. His fear is replaced by a paradoxical wish. If, for example, a person is afraid of fainting, he is instructed to try to faint as urgently as possible. Paradoxically, the individual is unable to accomplish that which he fears. Attempts are also made to accomplish this in as humorous fashion as possible, thus enabling the patient to detach himself from his symptom. Thus, someone who is afraid of trembling in front of his instructor can say to himself: "Oh, here is the instructor! Now I'll show him what a good trembler I am—I'll really show him how nicely I can tremble" (Frankl, 1965, p. 226). This procedure resembles that of Dunlap's "negative practice," and in some ways also, perhaps, that of implosion or flooding, a form of behavior therapy which we will discuss in the next chapter. But, Frankl emphasizes that paradoxical intention is not as superficial as it may appear. It appears to affect a deeper level, involving the capacity to detach oneself from the world as well as oneself.

The second technique of logotherapy is "de-reflection." This technique is intended to counteract the neurotic's inclination for self-observation and "crippling hyperreflection," just as paradoxical intention is supposed to overcome the patient's anticipatory anxiety. The aim is to divert the patient's attention from a preoccupation with certain personal concerns to other more constructive matters. Ideally, the patient learns to ignore his symptoms through de-reflection, although this particular technique is not as clearly described as is paradoxical intention. Perhaps a brief reference to a clinical example will make it more comprehensible. A woman was overly concerned with the act of swallowing her food and worried that it would "go down the wrong way" or that she might choke. She was taught to trust the automatic functioning of her body, and to see that *it* did the swallowing for her. Thus, her attention and concern were de-reflected. Frankl makes the following statement concerning this procedure:

> As we see, de-reflection can only be attained to the degree to which the patient's awareness is directed toward positive aspects. The patient must be de-reflected *from* his disturbance *to* the task at hand or the partner involved. He must be reoriented toward his specific vocation and mission in life. In other words, he must be confronted with the logos of his existence! (Frankl, 1965, p. 258.)

In conclusion, a few general comments may be offered concerning the existential approaches to psychotherapy. It can be noted that somewhat similar emphases have been presented by other psychologists, referred to as phenomenologists or as humanistic. Examples here are Snygg and Combs (1949), Abraham Maslow (1968) and Carl Rogers, although there are a number of others. This emphasis on "being" and existence appears to reflect both a discontentedness with contemporary cultural values as well as a dissatisfaction with conventional theories in psychology. The concern with the person's own experiencing or awareness of his existence and the meaning of this existence appear to be points of importance for many. Nevertheless, although this orientation has considerable appeal for those who see psychology as too mechanistic and neglecting the feelings and experiences of the human person, its final influence would appear to be limited by its unsystematic character and limited empirical data.

ADDITIONAL PSYCHOTHERAPEUTIC APPROACHES

Several important psychotherapeutic approaches have been discussed in the previous chapter and in the preceding pages of this chapter. From what has been presented, it should be apparent that wide differences exist among contemporary schools of psychotherapy in their theoretical emphases and procedures. In addition to the various therapies already mentioned, there are many others. Greatly influenced by the work of Rank were the relationship therapies developed by Taft (1933) and Allen (1942). Frohman (1948) developed his method, "Brief Psychotherapy," which usually required 20–30 therapeutic hours. In general, his was a somewhat eclectic approach in which various aspects of other approaches were utilized to suit the individual case. It is interesting that today, the designation, brief therapy, is used to characterize a variety of short-term therapies. The "Active Psychotherapy" of Herzberg (1946) is another interesting type of therapy in which the therapist prescribes certain tasks for the patient to perform. According to Herzberg, the set tasks do not allow the patient to procrastinate in therapy or to be as comfortable as he might be in psychoanalysis. Although the therapist plays an active role in this type of therapy, it is believed that the patient's independence is fostered by the carrying out and completion of various tasks. Other techniques, including those from psychoanalysis, are also utilized. The length of therapy, however, is found to be considerably shortened as contrasted with psychoanalysis. Specific tasks or "homework" in psychotherapy also have been utilized by several other recent approaches to psychotherapy, including reality therapy, rational-emotive psychotherapy, other cognitive therapies, and behavior therapy.

Another type of therapy that was quite distinctive was developed by Karpman (1949) and given the name of "Objective Psychotherapy." Although a psychoanalytic orientation is utilized, the techniques of therapy are different. After a few preliminary interviews the patient is asked to answer a series of questions taken from his own autobiography or from data secured by the therapist. Generally, three separate series of questions are used at different times, and when the answers to each are given, the therapist prepares a typed "memorandum" for the patient. The memorandum includes an organized presentation of the significant aspects of the material obtained from the patient and tentative interpretations from the therapist. At the end, a final "memorandum as a whole" is prepared. Through this process an attempt is made to provide the patient with insights about himself. Brief interviews are also held several times a week with the patient, but a very close relationship is avoided. Although Karpman considered his method as more superficial than psychoanalysis, he also believed it was more appropriate for the mild neuroses and the psychoses. He used it with institutionalized patients and claimed considerable success with criminals.

Since the approach developed by Karpman made some use of written material, mention can be made also of one of the techniques used by Phillips and Wiener (1966) and referred to as "Writing Therapy." This method has been used with college students and obviously presupposes some ability to write with a reasonable degree of clarity. The client is given a notebook that contains an explanation of the therapy and instructions and suggestions concerning her participation in therapy. She is given a regular weekly appointment, at which time she submits her notebook and receives in return the written comments of her therapist. The authors of this method point out that in addition to its efficiency, the procedure can be particularly useful in the training of beginning therapists. The latter have more time to reflect on what the client has related in her written material, and they can also consult with their supervisors about any aspects that may cause them uncertainty or concern. Phillips and Wiener (1966) provide some case excerpts in their book, which illustrate the actual written material provided by the client and the therapist. Their overall orientation emphasizes behavior and a structured approach, of which the writing therapy is merely one variant. In their case illustrations data are provided which indicate definite improvement in the clients treated by the writing therapy; however, the authors stress that these results are based on college students and one must be cautious in generalizing from them to other populations.

BRIEF PSYCHOTHERAPY

In recent years a greater concern with attempts to meet adequately the mental health needs of our population has produced a greater interest in brief therapies. As has been apparent from our previous discussions, many forms of traditional psychotherapy have required a rather lengthy period of therapy and have usually preferred rather intelligent, stable, and relatively well-integrated clients. Such an approach to psychotherapy, however, not only limits the number of persons who can be helped, but also ignores certain groups in our society who clearly have adjustment difficulties and are in need of help. As a result of such concerns, a number of attempts have been made at devising and utilizing relatively brief types of psychotherapy, even briefer than the approach of Frohman (1948), mentioned previously. Before discussing some of these, it is worth reviewing some of the empirical studies on the average length of treatment in outpatient psychotherapy and related findings. Such studies offer an important insight into what usually occurs in the psychotherapeutic treatment of clients in actual situations and reveal problems which are usually given little attention in most of the books on psychotherapy.

Because of the influence of the psychoanalytic or psychodynamic model in psychotherapy, psychotherapy has generally been viewed as a process which requires at least a moderate length of time. This has clearly been the expectation reflected in much of the traditional accounts of psychotherapy. It is quite surprising, therefore, that when one looks at the reports of outpatient clinics, the median length of treatment appears to range most frequently from six to eight interviews, certainly not an unusually large number of contacts! A review of reports from Veterans Administration outpatient clinics, medical school clinics, and community clinics reveals that by the eighth interview, 50% or more of the patients have terminated their psychotherapy (Craig and Huffine, 1976; Eiduson, 1968; Garfield, 1978; Rogers, 1960). We thus have an interesting discrepancy between theoretical expectations concerning the length of psychotherapy and what actually takes place for a significant number of people who actually begin psychotherapy in outpatient clinic settings. Unfortunately, comparable data from private practitioners on premature terminations and average length of therapy are lacking.

Although the reports of some clinics are not always clear, it does appear that the relatively brief average length of psychotherapy in most clinics is caused by the client's failure to keep his appointments and to drop out of therapy prematurely. A variety of reasons have been offered as possible explanations for this phenomenon. These have included inadequate motivation, lack of psychological mindedness or sophistication, inaccurate or faulty expectations concerning treatment, defensiveness on the part of the client, and disharmony between therapist and client. The variables most consistently found to be related to continuation in psychotherapy, however, have been those related to social class (Garfield, 1978). Lower class individuals, particularly those with limited education, have tended to drop out of psychotherapy at a disproportionate rate.

Such findings, although ignored for a time, have led to a variety of recommendations. One proposed solution to this problem is to intensify our efforts at patient selection so that only those clients who are really "suitable" or qualified are offered treatment. In practice, this would mean that we would tend to limit psychotherapy largely to those who are bright, verbal, educated, successful, and only minimally disturbed. Another solution proposed by some other workers (Heitler, 1976; Hoehn-Saric, Frank, Imber, Nash, Stone, & Battle, 1964; Strupp & Bloxom, 1973; Truax & Carkhuff, 1967) is to prepare the new client for psychotherapy by letting him listen to a psychotherapy session or to be told something about role requirements, expectations, and the like. A third solution is to attempt to modify conventional therapeutic methods in order to better meet the needs of the "less desirable clients" as well as to develop briefer and more efficient methods of psychotherapy. With regard to the latter, several developments and innovations have appeared to which we will refer briefly.

Several forms of brief psychotherapy have been developed which utilize a psychoanalytic framework. Among these is the emergency and brief psychotherapy developed by Bellak and Small (1965). A number of the emphases can be noted because several are quite similar to those emphasized by other workers in this area, whether or not they use a similar theoretical frame of reference.

One feature is providing emergency services on an around-the-clock basis so that individuals in a crisis can obtain immediate help. There are several reasons for providing service at a time of crisis. Some individuals who seek help at such times may be disinclined to do so when the crisis eases. Treatment at such times may also be efficient in that the individual, helped over the crisis situation, is able to reintegrate himself and return to his previous level of adjustment with relatively few sessions. In addition, intervention at times of crisis may also serve a preventative function in forestalling the emergence of a more chronic or severe pattern of adjustment.

Although the designation, brief psychotherapy, has been used to refer to varying amounts of psychotherapy, ranging from only a few interviews to periods of therapy of up to 1 year (Sifneos, 1965), the number of interviews used by Bellak and Small ranged from one to six. Because of the brevity of treatment, the therapist must be particularly alert to the behavior and communications of the client, must assess quickly the patient's strengths, weaknesses, and life situation, and come to some formulation of the problem. "In brief psychotherapy, the therapist does not have time for insight to develop; he must foster insight. He does not have time to wait for working through, he must stimulate working through. And where these basic aspects of the therapeutic process are not forthcoming, he must invent alternatives" (Bellak and Small, 1965, p. 6).

As already mentioned, this particular approach to brief therapy is based on psychoanalytic theory. Thus, basic Freudian concepts of psychic determinism, unconscious motivation, and the like are used as a frame of reference for interpreting the behavior of the client and aspects of the therapeutic process. Nevertheless, the goals and procedures in brief therapy differ from psychoanalysis and psychoanalytic psychotherapy. The goal of brief psychotherapy is the removal or amelioration of the symptoms that cause the client distress. Brief psychotherapy attempts "to improve the individual psychodynamic situation" to a degree that the individual can continue functioning and "nature" can continue the healing process. To this end, the therapist will usually play a more active role than is true of more traditional analytically oriented therapies. While interpretation is used in this form of brief therapy, its use is modified by demands of the current situation, and interpretation may be utilized along with more direct types of intervention. A different use is also made of transference. Positive transference is sought, encouraged, and maintained in this type of therapy and attempts are made to depict the therapist as a benign, helpful, and intervening person. Such therapeutic intervention may also depart from the more conventional therapies in utilizing tasks and activities outside of the therapy situation to foster the goals of therapy.

A brief form of emergency therapy would appear to be indicated in obvious crisis situations where the individual is acutely upset, experiencing severe discomfort, or where there is a threat to the life of the patient or others. Brief therapy may also be used with individuals who do not require long-term psychotherapy, are not amenable to such therapy, who cannot afford it, and so on.

Another form of psychoanalytically oriented brief psychotherapy has been reported by Sifneos (1965, 1981). In terms of the great demand for service and the typical waiting lists which develop in outpatient settings, an attempt was made to deal more quickly with those who had "developed circumscribed neurotic difficulties and symptoms." This brief therapy approach, while utilizing the theoretical principles of psychoanalysis, differs technically in several ways from traditional psychoanalytic therapy. The length of therapy varies from 2 to 12 months, sessions are held weekly, and the therapist concentrates on that area of the patient's conflicts which appear to underlie his symptoms. Involvement with so-called deep-seated characterological problems, such as dependency or passivity, are avoided. The role of the therapist is compared to that of "an unemotionally involved teacher," although it is difficult to see how the therapist remains unemotionally involved in such therapy which may last as long as a year. Even in this form of therapy, however, considerable emphasis is placed on the proper selection of patients for therapy. Patients who fulfill three out of the following five criteria are considered good candidates: (1) above average intelligence; (2) have had one meaningful relationship with another person and facing an emotional crisis; (3) able to interact with the evaluating psychiatrist and express some affect; (4) motivated to work hard during psychotherapy and not expect miracles; (5) patient should have a specific major complaint. Patients who fulfill three of the above criteria are then referred to the clinic director for an additional evaluation. In this interview the patient is informed that he has been selected out of a larger number of applicants for this form of therapy. He is told about the length of therapy, and his motivation is assessed further. In the latter instance, the patient is asked to state his expectations concerning the outcome of therapy and what sacrifices he is willing to make in order to secure or pay for his treatment.

It seems apparent from the previous statement that the patients selected for this type of brief psychotherapy have to meet some exacting criteria and that many prospective patients will not be offered therapy. Certainly it is not a therapy designed for lower-class individuals, and therapy that lasts a year would not be viewed as brief by many mental health workers.

Another form of brief or short-term psychotherapy was described in a series of papers by a group working at the Langley Porter Neuropsychiatric Institute in San Francisco (Harris, Kalis, and Freeman, 1963, 1964; Kalis, Freeman, and Harris, 1964). This approach was derived from several sources including a project concerned with precipitating stress. The latter was concerned with factors that led patients to request psychiatric help and how these factors were related to the patients' personalities. In the process of conducting this study, the investigators discovered that the clinical approach used provided a focus for short-term psychotherapy.

Before describing some of the features of this form of short-term psychotherapy, some general observations provided by Harris, Kalis, and Freeman

(1964) should be noted. Brief therapy is not considered the definitive treatment for all patients. Nevertheless, it served as a satisfactory therapeutic intake procedure for most patients, and for a significant number of them it "promoted a return to a functioning position" in seven or less therapy visits. For the remaining patients, where additional therapy appeared indicated, the brief therapy experience also appeared to serve a useful function. It helped in the delineation of the patient's problem and in the assessment and clarification of his motivation for therapy.

This rather innovative approach to brief psychotherapy has a number of interesting features which can be mentioned. The first is the emphasis on what is termed the selected focus of the therapy. One aspect of this concerns the matter of finding out why the patient is seeking help at this particular time. Thus, the focus is on the current crisis which does not allow the patient to function as he did previously. A second important emphasis concerns timing. Like the emergency therapy of Bellak and Small, therapy should be available when the patient in time of stress seeks help. At such times, conflicts are active and are judged to be more amenable to therapeutic intervention. Therapy, by helping the patient surmount the crisis and becoming more comfortable, may also help restore him to his usual level of functioning. After the initial focusing on the reasons for seeking therapy at this time, a period of rather free discussion may be encouraged. This allows the therapist to gain some awareness of the dynamic elements of the current crisis. Viewing the crisis or current stress as disruptive of the previous equilibrium of the patient, the therapist then attempts to work through and resolve factors derivative of the conflict involved or related to the stress of current disruption. Such exploration and working through is believed to facilitate the "establishment of a new adaptive balance." Although such matters as transference are considered important, they are not specifically analyzed during therapy. Rather, what is emphasized is the possible importance of the therapist's acceptance of short-term goals and therapy, his respect for the strengths of the patient, and the impact of these attitudes on the patient. Finally, the therapy requires more activity and directiveness on the part of the therapist than more traditional long-term therapy. This is manifested in the therapist's selective focusing on the current problem and in giving various kinds of support and suggestions.

Like many other reports of therapy, no systematic or quantified appraisals of this type of therapy are provided in the descriptive reports of the therapy. But, in view of the brevity of this form of psychotherapy and the current need for therapeutic services, this type of approach merits further application and evaluation.

Other reports of brief psychotherapy were also published in the 1960's indicating the growing interest in brief therapy (Haskell, Pugatch, and McNair, 1969; Jacobson, 1965; Jacobson, Wilner, Morley, Schneider, Strickler, and

Sommer, 1965; Malan, 1963; Rosenbaum, 1964; Swartz, 1969). Many of these also emphasize the current crisis or current problems as the focal point of therapy. Some also have a clear limit as to the length of therapy and are referred to as time-limited therapy. In this approach, therapy is arbitrarily limited to a specific number of sessions, and this information is given to the client at the beginning of therapy. Actually, to the extent that any brief therapy has a specific time limit (and this is told the client), the therapy is a time-limited one. The theoretical orientation may vary, but to the extent a specific number of interviews are specified at the start of therapy, the therapy is time-limited. Thus, in one series of investigations time-limited, client-centered therapy was compared to unlimited client-centered therapy and Adlerian therapy, and the results secured with the former were fully as good as with the unlimited forms of therapy (Schlien, 1957; Schlein, Mosak, and Dreikurs, 1962). In another study reported by Muench (1965), somewhat comparable findings were also secured. In the latter study, there was initially some opposition by the staff to carry out a controlled study of time-limited and brief therapy, since it was believed that it would be unfair to many clients to have their therapy arbitrarily limited in this way. After the study was completed, however, this particular staff decided to offer only ten interview time-limited psychotherapy in the future. It is believed by a number of therapists that imposing a time limit in advance not only reduces the length of therapy, but that it gives the client a precise goal and motivates him to utilize the therapeutic time more constructively.

Because of the need for services and the shortage of professional personnel, there appears to have been a wide increase in the use of brief therapies in clinical settings (Budman, 1981; Malan, 1976; Mann, 1973). Since these forms of therapy also report favorable results, it is likely that they will be used increasingly in the future, and that further experimentation will be tried in order to develop efficient procedures for helping a variety of clients with their problems (Butcher and Koss, 1978; Levine, 1966; White, Burke, and Havens, 1981).

REFERENCES

Allen, F. H. *Psychotherapy with children.* New York: W. W. Norton, 1942.

Bandura, A. *Principles of behavior modification.* New York: Holt, Rinehart & Winston, 1969.

Bandura, A. Self-efficacy: Toward a unifying theory of behavioral change. *Psychological Review,* 1977, *84,* 191–215.

Bard, J. A. *Rational-emotive therapy in practice.* Champaign, IL: Research Press, 1980.

Beck, A. T. *Cognitive therapy and the emotional disorders.* New York: International Universities Press, 1976.

Bellak, L., & Small, L. *Emergency psychotherapy and brief psychotherapy.* New York: Grune and Stratton, 1965.

Binder, V., Binder, A., & Rimland, B. *Modern therapies.* Englewood Cliffs, NJ: Prentice-Hall, 1976.

Binswanger, L. Existential analysis and psychotherapy. In F. Fromm-Reichmann and J. L. Moreno (Eds.), *Progress in psychotherapy 1956.* New York: Grune and Stratton, 1956.

Budman, S. H. *Forms of brief therapy.* New York: Guilford, 1981.

Burton, A. et al. *Twelve therapists.* San Francisco: Jossey-Bass, 1972.

Butcher, J. N., & Koss, M. P. Research on brief and crisis-oriented therapies. In S. L. Garfield and A. E. Bergin (Eds.). *Handbook of psychotherapy and behavior change.* (2nd ed.). New York: Wiley, 1978.

Craig, T., & Huffine, C. Correlates of patient attendance in an inner-city mental health clinic. *The American Journal of Psychiatry,* 1976, *133,* 61–64.

DiGuiseppe, R. A., Muller, N. J., & Trexler, L. D. A review of rational-emotive psychotherapy outcome studies. *The Counseling Psychologist,* 1977, *7,* 64–72.

Eiduson, B. T. The two classes of information in psychiatry. *Archives of General Psychiatry,* 1968, *18,* 405–419.

Ellis, A. Outcome of employing three techniques of psychotherapy. *Journal of Clinical Psychology,* 1957, *13,* 344–350.

Ellis, A. Rational psychotherapy. *The Journal of General Psychology,* 1958, *59,* 35–49.

Ellis, A. *Reason and emotion in psychotherapy.* New York: Lyle Stuart, 1962.

Ellis, A. Rational-emotive therapy: Research data that supports the clinical and personality hypotheses of RET and other modes of cognitive-behavior therapy. *The Counseling Psychologist,* 1977, *7,* 2–42.

Ewart, C. K., & Thoresen, C. E. The rational-emotive manifesto. *The Counseling Psychologist,* 1977, *7,* 52–56.

Ford, D. H., & Urban, H. B. *Systems of psychotherapy. A comparative study.* New York: Wiley, 1963.

Frankl, V. E. *The doctor and the soul.* (2nd ed.). New York: Alfred A. Knopf, 1965.

Frohman, B. S. *Brief psychotherapy.* Philadelphia: Lea & Febinger, 1948.

Garfield, S. L. Research on client variables in psychotherapy. In S. L. Garfield and A. E. Bergin (Eds.), *Handbook of psychotherapy and behavior change.* (2nd ed.). New York: Wiley, 1978.

Glasser, W. *Reality therapy.* New York: Harper and Row, 1965.

Hall, C. S., & Lindzey, G. *Theories of personality.* (3rd ed.). New York: Wiley, 1978.

Harris, M. R., Kalis, B. L., & Freeman, E. H. Precipitating stress: An approach to brief therapy. *American Journal of Psychotherapy,* 1963, *17,* 465–471.

Harris, M. R., Kalis, B. L., & Freeman, E. H. An approach to short-term psychotherapy. *Mind,* 1964, *2,* 198–206.

Haskell, D., Pugatch, D., & McNair, D. M. Time-limited psychotherapy for whom. *Archives of General Psychiatry,* 1969, *21,* 546–552.

Heitler, J. B. Preparatory techniques in initiating expressive psychotherapy with lower-class, unsophisticated patients. *Psychological Bulletin,* 1976, *83,* 339–352.

Herzberg, A. *Active psychotherapy.* New York: Grune & Stratton, 1946.

Hoehn-Saric, R., Frank, J. D., Imber, S. D., Nash, E. H., Stone, A. R., & Battle, C. C. Systematic preparation of patients for psychotherapy. I. Effects on therapy behavior and outcome. *Journal of Psychiatric Research,* 1964, *2,* 267–281.

Jacobson, G. F. Crisis theory and treatment strategy: Some sociocultural and psychodynamic considerations. *Journal of Nervous and Mental Disease,* 1965, *141,* 209–218.

Jacobson, G. F., Wilner, D. M., Morley, W. E., Schneider, S., Strickler, M., & Sommer, G. The scope and practice of an early-access brief-treatment psychiatric center. *American Journal of Psychiatry,* 1965, *121,* 1176–1182.

Kalis, B. L., Freeman, E. H., & Harris, M. R. Influence of previous help-seeking experiences on application for psychotherapy. *Mental Hygiene,* 1964, *48,* 267–272.

Karpman, B. Objective psychotherapy. *Journal of Clinical Psychology*, 1949, *5*, 193–342.

Kendall, P. C., & Hollon, S. C. *Cognitive-behavioral interventions. Theory, research, and procedures*. New York: Academic Press, 1979.

Kovacs, M., Rush, A. J., Beck, A. T., & Hollon, S. D. Depressed outpatients treated with cognitive therapy or pharmacotherapy: A one-year follow-up. *Archives of General Psychiatry*, 1981, *38*, 33–39.

Levine, R. A. Stand-patism versus change in psychiatric clinic practice. *American Journal of Psychiatry*, 1966, *123*, 71–77.

Mahoney, M. J. A critical analysis of rational-emotive theory and therapy. *The Counseling Psychologist*, 1977, *7*, 44–46.

Malan, D. H. *A study of brief psychotherapy*. New York: Plenum Press, 1963.

Malan, D. H. *Toward the validation of dynamic psychotherapy*. New York: Plenum Press, 1976.

Mann, J. *Time-limited psychotherapy*. Cambridge: Harvard University Press, 1973.

Maslow, A. H. *Toward a psychology of being*. (2nd ed.). New York: Van Nostrand Reinhold, 1968.

May, R. The origins and significance of the existential movement in psychology. In R. May, E. Angel, and H. F. Ellenberger, (Eds.), *Existence. A new dimension in psychiatry and psychology*. New York: Basic Books, 1958. (a)

May, R., Contributions of existential psychotherapy. In R. May, E. Angel, and H. F. Ellenberger (Eds.), *Existence. A new dimension in psychiatry and psychology*. New York: Basic Books, 1958. (b)

May, R. (Ed.), *Existential psychology*. New York: Random House, 1961.

May, R., Angel, E., & Ellenberger, H. F. (Eds.), *Existence. A new dimension in psychiatry and psychology*. New York: Basic Books, 1958.

Meichenbaum, D. H. *Cognitive-behavior modification: An integrative approach*. New York: Plenum, 1977. (a)

Meichenbaum, D. Dr. Ellis, please stand up. *The Counseling Psychologist*, 1977, *7*, 43–44. (b)

Morse, S. J., & Watson, R. I., Jr. *Psychotherapies. A comparative casebook*. New York: Holt, Rinehart and Winston, 1977.

Muench, G. A. An investigation of the efficacy of time-limited psychotherapy. *Journal of Counseling Psychology*, 1965, *12*, 294–299.

Patterson, C. H. *Theories of counseling and psychotherapy*. New York: Harper and Row, 1966.

Phillips, E. L., & Wiener, D. N. *Short-term psychotherapy and structured behavior change*. New York: McGraw-Hill, 1966.

Rogers, L. S. Drop-out rates and results of psychotherapy in government-aided mental hygiene clinics. *Journal of Clinical Psychology*, 1960, *16*, 89–92.

Rosenbaum, C. P. Events of early therapy and brief therapy. *Archives of General Psychiatry*, 1964, *10*, 506–512.

Rush, A. J., Beck, A. T., Kovacs, M., & Hollon, S. D. Comparative efficacy of cognitive therapy and pharmacotherapy in the treatment of depressed outpatients. *Cognitive Therapy and Research*, 1977, *1*, 17–37.

Schlien, J. M. Time-limited psychotherapy: An experimental investigation of practical values and theoretical implications. *Journal of Counseling Psychology*, 1957, *4*, 318–323.

Schlien, J. M., Mosak, H. H., & Dreikurs, R. Effect of time limits: A comparison of two psychotherapies. *Journal of Counseling Psychology*, 1962, *9*, 31–34.

Shaw, B. F. Comparison of cognitive therapy and behavior therapy in the treatment of depression. *Journal of Consulting and Clinical Psychology*, 1977, *45*, 543–551.

Sifneos, P. E. Seven-years experience with short-term dynamic psychotherapy. *Proceedings of the 6th International Congress of Psychotherapy*. Selected Lectures. Basel: S. Karger, 1965.

Sifneos, P. E. *Short-term dynamic psychotherapy: Evaluation and technique*. New York: Plenum Press, 1979.

Sifneos, P. E. Short-term anxiety provoking psychotherapy: Its history, technique, outcome, and instruction. In S. H. Budman (Ed.), *Forms of brief therapy*. New York: Guilford Press, 1981.

Snygg, D., & Combs, A. W. *Individual Behavior*. New York: Harper & Brothers, 1949.

Sonneman, U. *Existence and therapy*. New York: Grune and Stratton, 1954.

Strupp, H. H., & Bloxom, A. L. Preparing lower-class patients for group psychotherapy: Development and evaluation of a role-induction film. *Journal of Consulting and Clinical Psychology,* 1973, *41,* 373–384.

Swartz, J. Time-limited brief psychotherapy. *Seminars in Psychiatry,* 1969, *1,* 380–388.

Taft, J. *Dynamics of therapy*. New York: Macmillan, 1933.

Truax, C. B., & Carkhuff, R. R. *Toward effective counseling and psychotherapy*. Chicago: Aldine, 1967.

White, H. S., Burke, J. D., Jr., & Havens, L. L. Choosing a method of short-term therapy. A developmental approach. In S. H. Budman (Ed.), *Forms of brief therapy*. New York: Guilford Press, 1981.

Wilson, G. T. Behavior therapy as a short-term therapeutic approach. In S. H. Budman (Ed.), *Forms of brief therapy*. New York: Guilford Press, 1981.

Behavioral
Therapies

The approaches to therapy that will be discussed in this chapter differ in a number of significant ways from those previously described. In the first place, and probably most important, behavioral therapies have tried to base their techniques on psychological theories of learning. Also, as is implied in their designation, the emphasis tends to be placed on behavior rather than on inferred personality constructs. From this point of view, then, the individual's "symptoms" are seen as learned behaviors, and the appropriate approach is to try to change or modify such problem behaviors directly rather than to treat them indirectly as manifestations of underlying problems.

Although the behavioral therapies have attained popularity only in the last 20 years or so, there were early attempts at the use of such procedures during the 1920's. J. B. Watson, the early champion of Behaviorism, reported the famous case of "Little Albert," in which a 9-month-old boy developed a conditioned fear of animals. Previously, this child had played with animals and displayed no fear of them. But, after a number of trials where a loud noise was introduced as the child was about to touch a white rat, the child became fearful of the animal and this fear generalized to other animals (Watson and Rayner, 1920). A few years later, Mary Cover Jones (1924) reported her successful attempts at removing children's fears. The basic procedure was to have the child engaged in some pleasurable activity, such as eating, and then to introduce the feared object at some distance from the child. Gradually the feared object was brought closer and closer to the child, who eventually reacted to it without fear.

The response to these early experiments in the modification of behavior was limited, even though there were isolated reports of application of comparable procedures and principles. Mowrer and Mowrer (1938), for example, utilized such principles in treating enuresis, and Salter (1949) published a book describing the use of classical conditioning in the treatment of various types of behavioral disorders. Nevertheless, there was no widespread or enthusiastic acceptance of the theory or practice of behavior modification. In part, this may have been related to the limited status and development of clinical psychology during this period. The popularity of psychoanalysis and psychoanalytic psychotherapy may have also acted as a counterforce to learning theory approaches to therapy. Whatever the explanation, behavioral therapies developed very slowly, even though there were several papers in the 1940's that pointed out the relationship between learning theory and psychotherapy. In 1950, Dollard and Miller attempted to reformulate psychoanalytic concepts into learning terminology.

The person whose work appears to have had the greatest impact on the more recent growth and acceptance of behavior therapy is Joseph Wolpe. His book, *Psychotherapy by Reciprocal Inhibition,* published in 1958, generated considerable interest in behavioral methods of psychotherapy. Although Wolpe himself was trained as a psychiatrist in South Africa, he became dissatisfied with traditional procedures and carried out his own animal studies pertaining to "experimental neurosis." It was in part related to these studies that he developed his own views on therapy based on what he termed reciprocal inhibition—more frequently referred to nowadays as systematic desensitization. Wolpe became an effective proponent and leader of the behavioral approach to psychotherapy and the "movement" has progressed remarkably in the past 25 years.

At the present time, the behavior therapies represent an extremely active and vigorous orientation to psychotherapy and there is a considerable variety of methods, procedures, theories, and innovations grouped together under this rubric. Here we shall review some of the different behavioral approaches to psychotherapy and compare them with other forms of therapy. As mentioned in Chapter 2, most behavioral approaches have links with theories of learning, although this is not always direct. Similarly, there is a focus on behavior rather than on personality variables or inferred attributes or conflicts. The attempts at treatment deal more directly with the modification of observable behaviors and generally the therapeutic relationship, interpretation, and similar phenomena which are emphasized in analytically oriented and other comparable forms of traditional psychotherapy receive little emphasis. Finally, behavior therapists demonstrate greater interest in research and in relating their work to other areas of scientific psychology than is true of other therapeutic orientations. They also are more open in presenting and discussing the results of their therapeutic interventions.

WOLPE'S RECIPROCAL INHIBITION

As indicated, there are many behavioral procedures, and they can be variously categorized. For purposes of convenience, some of the best known procedures which, at the same time, reflect different learning principles, will be used to illustrate this approach to psychotherapy. Probably the best known work is that of Wolpe (1958, 1969). According to Wolpe, neurotic behaviors are basically conditioned (learned) maladaptive behaviors and thus can be modified by deconditioning. A related view is that anxiety is central to neurotic disturbance and the individual can be helped by creating conditions that inhibit anxiety. The reciprocal inhibition principle of psychotherapy states that "if a response inhibitory of anxiety can be made to occur in the presence of anxiety-evoking stimuli it will weaken the bond between these stimuli and the anxiety" (Wolpe, 1964, p. 10). A number of responses are potentially capable of inhibiting anxiety. As noted in the reference to the early work of Mary Cover Jones, eating is one such potential response. Wolpe lists several others, including relaxation, assertion, and sexual response. For example, if an individual tends to be anxious in expressing himself in his interpersonal relations, assertive responses can be used to counteract or inhibit the anxiety. The client is encouraged to express himself and his views, and as he continues to behave in this fashion, the assertive behavior inhibits the anxiety. Over a period of time, the assertion "habit" would gradually inhibit the anxiety response. Somewhat similar illustrations could be provided for sexual and other types of response, which also could be used as inhibitors of anxiety.

Another type of response that can be used to inhibit anxiety, and which has been rather widely used, is that of relaxation. Impressed by Jacobson's work on relaxation and its potential value as an inhibitor of anxiety, Wolpe used instruction in relaxation as part of a procedure that became known as *systematic desensitization.* In this procedure, a part of each of the first few sessions is spent in training the client to relax. Material is also secured from the client concerning the specific fears or phobias he has, and then lists of activities pertaining to each are organized into a hierarchy. For example, if an individual is fearful of entering an elevator, a hierarchy can be built up consisting of images that arouse minimal amounts of anxiety—walking in the street a block away from the elevator—to those that produce intense anxiety—getting in the elevator and proceeding rapidly downward. Once a hierarchy of scenes is assembled for each particular fear or phobia, the procedure employed is quite similar to that used by Jones. After the client is relaxed, he imagines the scene that arouses the smallest amount of fear or anxiety, and if he can imagine this scene with little or no anxiety, he proceeds to the next scene in the hierarchy. If he encounters anxiety in visualizing a particular scene in the hierarchy, the client usually signals the therapist and the activity is stopped. The client is then relaxed once more and the scene repeated until he can visualize it without any apprehension. The client then proceeds through the remainder of the hierarchy until the most anxiety-provoking scene can be imagined without any anxiety. If the client has more than one fear or phobia, a similar procedure is carried out with the others. According to Wolpe (1969), most individuals who can successfully carry out these procedures in their imagination can also encounter the real life situation without any appreciable anxiety. There are some individuals, however, who carry through the visualizations without improvement in actually meeting the feared stimuli. In such instances, the desensitization must be carried out in the actual situation.

In systematic desensitization, therefore, the client is gradually led by means of relaxation to imagine scenes or stimuli of increasing intensity until those that are most anxiety-provoking can be visualized and later experienced without anxiety. The initial anxiety response apparently becomes inhibited through this process of desensitization or counter-conditioning. The literature on systematic desensitization is now large, and while there are still some differences of opinion concerning the processes or variables which make for changes in behavior, the results of this form of therapy are quite positive. Before discussing such matters, however, let us continue our description of this type of therapy.

The principles of reciprocal inhibition have also been utilized in the area of sexual difficulties. In such instances, sexual responses are utilized to inhibit anxiety responses which have been conditioned to sexual situations. "By manipulating the conditions of sexual approaches so that anxiety is never permitted to be strong, reciprocal inhibition of anxiety by sexual arousal is effected, and the anxiety response habit is progressively weakened. It is usually possible to overcome impotence or premature ejaculation in a few weeks" (Wolpe, 1964, p. 12).

As indicated, the procedures and rationale of reciprocal inhibition and systematic desensitization have received wide application and have been used with groups as well as with children. A brief case excerpt taken from an account by Lazarus (1960) serves to illustrate this approach in the case of a 9½-year-old girl. Carol had apparently adjusted well until about 2 months after her ninth birthday. At that time she became enuretic, was afraid of the dark, and had night terrors. At school she developed severe abdominal pains which led to her mother being called to the school. Prior to the onset of her anxieties, three traumatic incidents occurred in succession within a few weeks: a friend drowned in a pool, her next door playmate died as a result of illness, and she saw a man killed in an auto accident. After a brief interlude of somewhat conventional therapy or consultation with the mother, the girl's behavior improved noticeably while on vacation. Upon returning home, however, the symptoms worsened. Carol wet the bed each night and became hysterical when taken to school. She also insisted on having her mother near her at all times; and when she returned for therapy she anxiously clung to her mother and insisted that her mother be present during the therapy interviews. On the basis of information secured from the history, interviews, and projective testing, it appeared that the girl's central fear was the possibility of losing her mother through death. Consequently, it was decided to treat this specific area of unadaptive anxiety through systematic desensitization. The child was given training in relaxation, and the following anxiety hierarchy was constructed:

> Separation from the mother for 1 week
> Separation from the mother for 2 days
> Separation from the mother for 1 day
> Separation from the mother for ½ day
> Separation from the mother for 1 hour
> Separation from the mother for 15 minutes
> Separation from the mother for 5 minutes (Lazarus, 1960, p. 118)

According to Lazarus, it took only five sessions spread over a period of ten days to fully desensitize the girl to her anxiety concerning the possible loss of her mother. Within a few days of the beginning of therapy, she went to school with no difficulty. "This was followed by an immediate dissipation of all her other neurotic conditions. A 15-month follow-up enquiry revealed that apart from very occasional enuretic incidents, she had maintained an eminently satisfactory level of adjustment" (Lazarus, 1960, p. 118).

The application of such procedures to cases with neurotic disorders have produced good therapeutic results according to Wolpe and others. Based on several criteria of improvement, but emphasizing the symptoms which brought the individual into therapy, Wolpe (1958) judged 89.5% of 210 patients he had treated to have recovered or to have shown marked improvement. Furthermore, these cases required an average of around thirty interviews. In a follow-up of forty-five of these cases for periods ranging from 2 to 7 years, only one relapse was reported. In a somewhat similar clinical study of 408 cases, Lazarus (1963) reported an improvement rate of 78%. Although this effort of leading behavior therapists to appraise the efficacy of their therapeutic efforts is commendable, such evaluations can only be regarded as suggestive. The evaluations were made by the therapists and no control groups were used.

Since these early clinical reports, a large number of studies have been carried out and summaries of this research are available in several sources

(Kazdin and Wilson, 1978; Marks, 1978; Ross, 1978). Only a few studies will be referred to for illustrative purposes.

Gelder, Marks, and Wolff (1967) compared the effectiveness of desensitization with individual and group psychotherapy. Although only a few patients in each group received drugs, another limiting factor was the relative inexperience of the psychiatrists who conducted behavior therapy. Nevertheless, better results were secured by means of desensitization. Based on ratings provided by both patients and therapists, and also in terms of the length of treatment, desensitization appeared more effective than either of the other two therapies. This finding was particularly true of the improvement in the patients' main phobias and the results were maintained in a follow-up investigation. An additional follow-up study revealed not only that the improvement concerning phobic behavior was generally maintained, but that other more general improvement in these patients' behavior also took place.

One additional point, which is of some theoretical interest, can also be made here. This concerns the matter of symptom substitution. According to psychoanalytic and related theories, such behavioral manifestation as phobias (extreme avoidance behaviors) are considered to be symptoms of some underlying and repressed conflict. Consequently, from this point of view if one treats and removes the symptom alone, the conflict is not resolved and some substitute symptom is expected to appear. In the study by Gelder, Marks, and Wolff (1967), no evidence of symptom substitution was secured in the second follow-up investigation some 16 months after treatment was terminated, and this appears to be the case in most studies (Bandura, 1969; Beech, 1969; Nolan, Mattis, and Holliday, 1970).

A number of controlled studies in recent years have been carried out with individuals who were recruited for the investigations rather than with individuals actively seeking help with their problems. As Lazarus (1971) has pointed out, such selected volunteers may differ "from psychiatric patients who seek out therapists and actively ask for help" (p. 16). Nevertheless, because some of these studies exemplify worthwhile research procedures in the area of psychotherapy, reference will be made to one well-known and well-designed study of this type. The study was carried out by Paul (1966), and a follow-up study was also performed 2 years later (Paul, 1967). Three groups of fifteen subjects each received individually systematic desensitization, insight-oriented psychotherapy, or what was termed "attention-placebo treatment." Twenty-nine subjects made up an untreated control group. Because the attention-placebo treatment was a novel one, a brief description of it is merited. This treatment "was used to determine the extent of improvement from nonspecific treatment effects, such as expectation of relief, therapeutic relationship (attention, warmth, and interest of the therapist), suggestion, and faith" (Paul, 1966, p. 22). In this procedure the subject's problem was first discussed briefly and then the treatment "rationale" was explained. In brief, the subject was told that his emotional reactions were a result of previous experiences, and that his anxiety could be overcome by specific training under stress. The latter involved the taking of a "fast-acting tranquilizer" and working at a stressful task. The subject was told that the drug would inhibit anxiety and that with practice on the assigned task, "his mind and body would gradually develop a tolerance for stress" (Paul, 1966, p. 22), and he would no longer experience anxiety under stress. The "tranquilizing drug" was actually a placebo, a 2-gram capsule of sodium bicarbonate. The "stressful" task was actually nonstressful and involved responding to specific auditory signals.

After the subject indicated that he understood and accepted the rationale, he was given the drug to swallow. The therapist then left the room for 10 minutes so the drug could take effect. The therapist then returned, checked the subject's pupillary response and his pulse, and proceeded with the administration of the stressful task. Five minutes before the end of the period, the task was stopped and the subject's reactions discussed. The therapist told him that the treatment was progressing well, and the pupillary response and pulse were rechecked. It was believed by the investigator that this procedure was an excellent attention-placebo treatment because anywhere from 35–45 minutes of each session was taken up by activities that precluded any verbal interaction between therapist and subject.

The subjects of the study were selected from a population of 710 undergraduate students enrolled in a course in public speaking. All students completed a battery of personality and anxiety scales, and those selected were rated high on performance anxiety and were considered to be motivated for treatment. The subjects' anxiety was considered to be strong to severe in most cases and to be of 2 to 20 years duration. In addition to high anxiety in relation to public speaking, the subjects also reported many of the common signs of anxiety, for example, nausea, "black-out," tremors, excessive perspiration, tension, headache, and so on. Before the pretreatment test speech certain measures of anxiety and physiological arousal were taken and ratings made on a behavioral check list of performance anxiety with high reliability. These were repeated prior to the posttreatment test speech. Five experienced therapists with a predominantly Neo-Freudian and Rogerian orientation were utilized in the study. Since these therapists generally utilized insight-oriented psychotherapy as their general approach and had no experience in systematic desensitization, each of them received intensive training with this procedure and practiced it with a number of persons before working with the subjects in the study. Each subject received five 50-minute therapy sessions over a 6-week period.

Now that the major outlines of the study have been sketched out, let us proceed to the results. In terms of the measures taken before the pretreatment and posttreatment test speeches, all three treatment groups improved significantly over the no-treatment control group on the behavioral checklist and on the Anxiety Differential, a measure of the "immediate cognitive experience of anxiety." The group receiving desensitization was the only one to secure a significant reduction in the measures of physiological arousal over the no-treatment group. On all measures, the desensitization group achieved consistently superior results than the other two groups. On none of these measures, furthermore, were there any significant differences secured between the groups receiving insight-oriented psychotherapy and attention-placebo treatment. When certain criteria were applied in analyzing each case individually, the percentage of "significantly improved" cases ranged from 87 to 100% on the different measures for the desensitization group, from 53 to 60% for the insight-oriented group, and from 47 to 73% for the attention-placebo group. Thus, on this series of measures, the results of desensitization were superior to those for insight-oriented psychotherapy, and those for the latter approximated the results secured from the attention-placebo treatment. The findings on the readministration of the various personality and anxiety scales, while not as marked as these results, were in the same direction.

As indicated, Paul (1967) also conducted a 2-year follow-up study and was able to contact a large percentage of his subjects. Basically, the same pattern of results were secured with the battery of personality and anxiety scales as were secured at the end of the initial investigation. Desensitization still had the best results, while insight-oriented psychotherapy and attention-placebo were roughly comparable. Furthermore, there was no evidence to indicate either significant relapses on the part of those treated by systematic desensitization or the occurrence of symptom substitution.

The results of Paul's research received considerable attention from behavior therapists because they indicated the relative superiority of desensitization over so-called insight-oriented psychotherapy and because the study was one of the best designed in the psychotherapy literature at that time. Concurrently, however, some limitations of the study have also drawn critical comments from others. The subjects, although having various symptoms of anxiety, were essentially "normal college students" who were not actively seeking help for their symptoms. A second criticism concerns the limited amount of time provided for therapy—five sessions. Many therapists believe that one can do very little in such a brief time and that the study clearly was not a fair test of the effectiveness of insight-oriented therapy, characteristically a therapy requiring considerable time. Although one should not overgeneralize on the basis of the results of such a study, there are some aspects of Paul's study that are quite intriguing. The relative comparability of the results secured for the insight-oriented and the attention-placebo therapy does draw attention to the issue of nonspecific factors in psychotherapy and the role they play in verbal psychotherapy. Another possible issue raised by the findings concerns the relative efficiency of the different forms of psychotherapy. Did the brief format favor desensitization since insight-oriented therapy requires time for change to be accomplished? It is interesting that whereas all of the therapists in Paul's study considered five sessions to be adequate for desensitization, three of the five therapists felt that more than five sessions were required for the insight-oriented therapy.

ASSERTION AND SOCIAL SKILLS TRAINING

Another behavioral procedure is that of assertion therapy or training. Wolpe includes it under reciprocal inhibition, with the assertive responses being viewed as inhibiting anxiety. However, as Beech (1969) points out, "the response of being self-assertive is not simply a means of inhibiting anxiety in certain interpersonal situations, but is an important new habit which will be preserved outside the therapeutic setting" (p. 127). To the extent that the newly acquired assertive behavior becomes part of the person's response repertoire, it may be viewed differently than the relaxation used during therapy which supposedly does not become a habit. No matter how the matter is viewed, assertion training has received recognition as a particular form of behavioral therapy where the problem appears to be a lack of adequate assertiveness. The assumption is made that the individual's lack of assertiveness, his inability to express his feelings, or the overly strong controls he exerts over his behavior have occurred in relation to anxiety associated with assertive responses in the past. In assertion training there appear to be at least two features. One concerns the inhibition of anxiety that is associated with specific situations. The second pertains to the positive reinforcement received from assertive behavior. "Thus, the counter-conditioning of anxiety and the operant conditioning of the motor act take place simultaneously, facilitating each other" (Wolpe, 1969, p. 62).

Although one can note the possible relationship of prior learning on the individual's inability to assert himself appropriately, the procedures used by Wolpe (1958, 1969) to overcome such difficulties do not appear to follow very clearly or specifically from theories of learning. Actually, the patient is provided with information concerning how his difficulty hampers him in life situations, and is told that once he begins to express himself, assertive behavior will become easier for him to perform. Some "exhortation and repeated promptings" may also be necessary. Generally, at the start, some explanation is given of how anxiety inhibits the individual's assertiveness and how he may also have underlying feelings of anger and resentment toward others in such situations. By being able to express his resentment, the individual is told that he also will suppress his anxiety. Specific ways of applying such information is then discussed with the patient and he is urged to try these new possibilities under appropriate circumstances. "Not only is he told that it will result in his feeling better, but his attention is focused on the enormity of any injustices being perpetrated on him, and in addition he is shown how undignified and unattractive to others it is for him to behave in his accustomed spineless way" (Wolpe, 1958, p. 117). Wolpe also points out that in advising the patient with reference to assertive behavior one must use judgment. Assertive behavior should be encouraged only when the anxiety evoked is unadaptive—that is, when anxiety occurs even though the assertive response will bring no negative consequences. On the contrary, such behavior should not be advised when the consequences would be detrimental to the patient—for example, telling the boss what one really thinks of him.

Wolpe also mentions that he utilizes what he first referred to as a kind of psychodrama with certain patients who have difficulty practicing assertive behavior in their everyday situation. In essence, this refers to the enactment of certain behaviors or roles in therapy which the client is asked to perform. This type of performance has frequently been referred to as "role-playing," or among behavior therapists, as "behavioral rehearsal." In such instances, the therapist may take the role of a particular person toward whom the patient is unable to be properly assertive, and the patient is instructed to express his inhibited feelings toward that person. In this type of role playing or behavioral rehearsal, the patient must be encouraged to behave with sufficient affect so that he really plays the part and does not merely go through the motions. The patient can repeat his statements and his behaviors until his performance is judged to be adequate. There are obviously all kinds of possibilities in this kind of role-playing procedure, and it can be adapted for a variety of purposes. It should be pointed out of course, that other therapists besides Wolpe make use of this and similar procedures. In any event, the behavioral rehearsals are seen as helping to propel the individual to behave properly in his interactions with the real people who previously caused him to be anxious and to inhibit his assertiveness. The practice in actually being assertive appears to make it somewhat easier for the individual to behave this way in real life and is more effective than merely talking about the problem.

More recently, behavior therapists have emphasized the application of their procedures to the improvement of a variety of social skills. Clinical and research programs have been reported in the areas of dating behaviors, shyness, and social interaction, among others, and procedures in this area have been used with some apparent success with children (Combs and Slaby, 1977; Ross, 1978), college students (Curran, 1975, 1977), and with chronic mental patients (Hersen and Bellack, 1981; Paul and Lentz, 1977). One of the important emphases in this work is the viewing of the individual's problem as a deficit in social skills instead of as a symptom of some particular personality disorder. Careful assessment of the individual is important, for in some instances more than a simple deficit in skills may be involved. Nevertheless, a direct attempt to improve skills in the social area may prove beneficial in the total treatment of the individual. In less severe cases, it can help to increase self-confidence and greater positive social interaction. In the case of more severely withdrawn and isolated patients, it may play a role in reducing social avoidance behaviors.

AVERSION THERAPY

Another type of behavior therapy is aversion therapy. In this approach to therapy, an attempt is made to decondition specific and undesirable behavior patterns or habits. Thus, aversion therapy has been used in the treatment of obsessions, compulsions, fetishes, homosexuality, alcoholism, and related problems. According to Wolpe (1969), however, except in certain cases of drug addiction, aversion therapy is usually not the behavioral treatment of first choice. According to him, the compulsive or other behavior is found to have a basis in neurotic anxiety and this should be deconditioned first. Nevertheless, others have utilized some form of aversion therapy with varying degrees of success.

Aversion therapy consists of presenting to the individual some stimulus which will produce a strong avoidance response, and this must be done in the context of the undesired response. In theory, when a strong avoidance response is produced, the undesirable response will be inhibited. By repeating this procedure, one produces a conditioned aversion to the response considered undesirable. "In other words, a measure of conditioned inhibition of that response will be established—a weakening of the habit—of the bond between the response and its stimulus. At the same time, the stimulus is likely to be to some extent conditioned to the response constellation which the shock evoked" (Wolpe, 1969, p. 201).

Although a variety of aversive stimuli can be used in aversion therapy, electric shock has probably been the most popular. It is relatively easy to administer, can be administered at precise time intervals, and can be given without undue danger. With the appropriate pairing of the shock with the undesirable behavior, thought, or other stimulus, an aversive response can be gradually built up. Several interesting case reports have been published with apparently positive results. One case, described by Wolpe (1969), concerned a woman who had irresistable impulses to eat certain foods that were not good for her. She was instructed to close her eyes and to imagine one of these particular foods. When she had formed a clear mental image of the selected food she signaled the therapist and immediately received a severe electric shock to her forearm. Ten shocks were given at each session. After a couple of sessions, thinking of these foods brought up an image of the shock equipment, and in turn a feeling of anxiety. After five sessions, she felt free of her compulsive cravings for the first time in 16 years.

One additional case, that of a 33-year-old man with an unusual fetish, is also worth mentioning (Raymond, 1960). This individual was referred for a possible prefrontal leucotomy (a type of brain surgery) after he had "attacked a perambulator" (baby carriage). This was actually the twelfth such incident known to the police. He was first apprehended and charged by the police some 6 years earlier when he slashed two empty prams and then set them on fire. At that time he also admitted five other incidents of damaging prams which had been investigated by the police, although he later admitted that he usually made two or three such attacks per week. He was placed in a mental hospital for about a month and then transferred to a neurosis unit where he was judged to be unsuited for psychotherapy and also dangerous. Sometime later, he was also in difficulty for smearing mucus on a handbag and damaging a pram. At that time, he was admitted again to a mental hospital where he remained for about 16 months. After his discharge, several more incidents and charges occurred including driving his motorcycle into a perambulator, which contained a baby in it, and damaging the carriage. These led eventually to the referral mentioned earlier.

This individual apparently had impulses to inflict damage on perambulators and handbags since the age of 10. He had received many hours of analytical treatment and was able to recall two childhood incidents that appeared related to his disorder; but this recall had not influenced his subsequent behavior. Handbags and perambulators seemed to have taken on sexual meaning and arousal quality for him. Masturbation took place with phantasies of damaging them, and intercourse with his wife was only possible with the help of phantasies of handbags and prams. At the time of referral, the man was married, the father of two children, and, outside of the difficulties discussed, was considered to be a good husband and father.

In the light of the patient's previous history, it was thought that he might conceivably respond to the aversion therapy used with alcoholics. The aim of the treatment was explained to the patient, and although skeptical, he was willing to try it. Consequently, the treatment was begun. "A collection of handbags, perambulators, and colored illustrations was obtained and these were shown to the patient after he had received an injection of apomorphine and just before nausea was produced. The treatment was given two-hourly, day and night, no food was allowed, and at night amphetamine was used to keep him awake" (Raymond, 1960, p. 306). At the end of 1 week, the treatment was temporarily suspended and the patient was allowed to go home to attend to his personal affairs. After 8 days, he returned and stated he had been able to have sexual relations with his wife for the first time without the use of his old phantasies. The treatment began again, with some discussion of his difficulties and his views of handbags and perambulators. After 5 days of additional treatment, the patient stated the mere sight of these objects made him sick. At this time he was confined to bed, the objects were with him continually, and the aversive treatment was given at irregular intervals. "On the evening of the ninth day he rang his bell and was found to be sobbing uncontrollably. He kept repeating, 'Take them away,' and appeared to be impervious to anything which was said to him" (Raymond, 1960, p. 306). The next day he voluntarily gave up a number of photographic negatives of perambulators which he had carried on him for years but which he said he would no longer need.

The patient was discharged from the hospital but agreed to a "booster" treatment 6 months later, even though he did not believe it was necessary. Nineteen months after he first received aversion therapy, this individual still appeared to be getting along well. He had had no further trouble with the police, his probation officer reported him as progressing noticeably, his marital relations had "greatly improved," the old phantasies were no longer required, and he had been promoted to a more responsible position.

One additional and very fascinating case report can be alluded to briefly before continuing our discussion, although the interested reader should read the original report. This concerns the case of a 9-month-old infant who was unable to retain his food because of chronic ruminative vomiting, thus endangering his very life. This case is also noteworthy for illustrating the ingenuity of the psychologist in adapting specific techniques and procedures in his therapeutic work with this child (Lang and Melamed, 1969).

In this case, the conditioning procedures were only undertaken after other treatments were either ruled out by diagnostic procedures or had been tried without success. The infant was hospitalized bacause of its inability to retain food and chronic rumination. He had been hospitalized three times previously because of this condition and his failure to gain weight. Although this infant had attained a weight of 17 pounds at the age of 6 months, by the time Lang and Melamed were called into the case, his weight was down to 12 pounds, he was in critical condition, and was being fed through a nasogastric pump. A variety of diagnostic tests had been done without finding any organic cause for the condition and a variety of treatment approaches had been unsuccessful.

The infant was first observed by the psychologists for 2 days during and after normal feeding periods. Most of the food was regurgitated within 10 minutes of each feeding. In order to obtain a clearer picture of the patterning of the infant's response, electromyograph (EMG) activity was monitored at three sites—on the underside of the chin, the upper chest at the base of the throat, and straddling the esophagus. In this way a precise picture of the patterning of the infant's muscular responses associated with vomiting could be ascertained, and the schedule for aversive conditioning worked out accordingly. "The authors were concerned with eliminating the inappropriate vomiting, without causing any fundamental disturbance in the feeding behavior of the child" (Lang and Melamed, 1969, p. 4). It was fortunate that the child did not vomit during feeding, and that sucking behavior, which usually preceded the vomiting, could be distinguished on the EMG.

After 2 days of observation and monitoring, the conditioning procedures were started. A brief but repeated shock was administered as soon as vomiting occurred and was continued until the response was terminated. Based on the observation of a nurse and the confirmation by the EMG, an attempt was made to administer shock "at the first sign of reverse peristalsis," and a tone was presented coincident with each presentation of shock. After two sessions, shock was rarely required. "Few shocks were administered after the first day of treatment, and both the time spent vomiting and the average length of each vomiting period were abruptly reduced" (Lang and Melamed, 1969, p. 4–5). By the sixth session, the infant no longer exhibited any vomiting during the testing procedures, and he was discharged from the hospital 6 days after the last conditioning trial. The infant's activity level had increased, he showed a steady gain in weight, he became more interested in his environment, and responded to those around him. One month after discharge he was eating well, looked healthy, and weighed 21 pounds. One year after treatment he continued to be a healthy and alert child. Thus, the application of aversive conditioning in this case not only seemingly saved the child's life, but led to healthy growth and improved social behavior, with no evidence of symptom substitution.

Aversive therapy in various forms has also been used for a variety of problems including homosexuality, alcoholism, and drug addiction. The use of drugs, which produce nausea in the treatment of alcoholism, has produced somewhat inconsistent results, and apparently is not as widely used today. In some instances, however, the aversive conditioning procedures used have been faultily applied. Particularly important is the timing of the onset of the nauseous effects of the drug. Another difficult behavior to modify, that of homosexuality, has also been treated by aversion therapy with some success. Feldman and MacCulloch's work (Feldman, 1966; Feldman and MacCulloch, 1965, 1967) has been among the best in this regard. They utilized slide pictures of males and females and the administration of electric shock when male pictures were presented but not when those of females were shown. The total procedure thus attempts to build up an avoidance reaction to males and an approach reaction to females, and therefore, relies on more than just aversive conditioning. In a follow-up study of twenty-five successfully treated patients, they found that 52% had maintained a heterosexual orientation for 1 year, a rather impressive result.

The results of electric aversion therapy in twenty-four patients with serious sexual problems who were followed up 2 years after treatment, can also be mentioned (Marks, Gelder, and Bancroft, 1970). The patients consisted of twelve so-called simple transvestites and fetishists, seven transsexual transvestites, and five sadomasochists. There were other symptoms for some of these patients but they need not be mentioned here. The transsexual patients are distinguished from the simple transvestites by wanting to have the body of a woman and lead the life of a woman. Unlike the simple transvestite, they may not always be aroused sexually by women's clothing. In most instances, the majority of patients had had their difficulties for a number of years. A program was worked out for each of the patients using the relevant stimuli and associating them with electric shock. The average number of sessions for the transvestites and the sadomasochists was 18 with a mean number of 259 shock trials. The average number of sessions for the transsexuals was 21 with a mean of 469 shock trials.

There appeared to be a clear difference in the results obtained for the different groups. Since the transvestites, fetishists, and sadomasochists seemingly had similar results, the results for these seventeen patients were compared with those of the seven transsexuals. In general, the latter group showed relatively little response to the treatment, whereas the former groups responded positively. There was comparatively little change in terms of attitudes and improvement in heterosexuality. Thus, the main result of the aversion treatment appeared to be a nontemporary reduction of deviant behavior in most of the transvestites, fetishists, and sadomasochists, but not in the transsexuals. The authors also note that there was no evidence of symptom substitution in those patients whose deviant behavior diminished. At the same time, it was noted that improvement with reference to deviant behavior was not necessarily followed by improved social or sexual relationships. In contrast to some reports by other behavior therapists, these results seem more related to the specific symptoms treated and apparently did not have a more generalized effect on the overall behavior and adjustment of the patients. Unlike the reports of Feldman and MacCulloch (1965, 1967) these patients did not show an increase in their heterosexual behavior, and it may be related to the fact that no attention was paid to conditioning for positive attitudes toward the opposite sex.

Although this writer has had relatively little enthusiasm for the use of aversive techniques, the dramatic report by Lang and Melamed (1969) referred to earlier, has caused him to rethink his views and to modify them accordingly. Although by no means a panacea for aberrant behavior, such techniques may be useful in selected cases when used judiciously and with proper controls. Except for emergency cases where children are involved, proper discussion with the client and the latter's permission would be minimal requirements.

IMPLOSIVE THERAPY AND FLOODING

Another variant of behavior therapy appears to utilize an approach that is the opposite of systematic desensitization. Although Wolpe (1969) makes reference to some earlier uses of this approach, it has usually been associated with the work of Stampfl (Hogan and Kirchner, 1967; Marks, 1978; Stampfl, 1967; Stampfl and Levis, 1967). The rationale behind implosive therapy (or a less emotionally intense variant of it called flooding) appears to be somewhat the opposite of that for desensitization. Whereas the latter begins with stimuli or situations which produce minimal anxiety and gradually builds up to more intense stimuli, implosive therapy utilizes stimuli of great intensity. Theoretically, also, instead of relying on a response that is antagonistic to anxiety, implosive therapy utilizes an extinction paradigm. The belief is that as the anxiety-provoking stimulus is encountered with the nonoccurrence of any anticipated and feared outcome, the anxiety is extinguished. Another important difference in the case of implosion (but not flooding) is that this approach to therapy attempts to incorporate aspects of psychodynamic personality theory, whereas most behavior and learning based therapies do not.

Implosive therapy utilizes the situations or stimuli which the client states he is fearful of or which cause him anxiety. Although these cues may produce considerably more anxiety than those commonly at the bottom of the graded hierarchy of fears used in systematic desensitization, it is hypothesized that those with the highest anxiety loading are avoided or repressed by the patient. Thus, while implosive therapy emphasizes exposing the patient to imagined or visualized cues which are quite anxiety provoking, to a certain extent this form of therapy also uses some form of gradation with less threatening stimuli presented first. As the patient works with these stimuli, he may gradually recall others of a more threatening nature which he has forgotten, or the therapist, himself, may infer such stimuli from his knowledge of the patient's history and psychodynamic theory. It does appear, however, that the patient is exposed to more emotionally upsetting and threatening material early in therapy than is the case with Wolpe's procedure.

In implosive therapy, the therapist usually has a few diagnostic interviews with the patient in order to secure basic information about his problems and to provide some basis for understanding some of the dynamics related to his difficulty. Generally, additional information will be forthcoming during the process of therapy. The patient is then given instruction concerning the implosive procedures. He is asked to play-act or to act out various scenes, which the therapist will present to him. "Every effort is made to encourage the patient to 'lose himself' in the part that he is playing and 'live' the scenes with genuine emotion and affect. He is asked, much like an actor, to portray certain feelings and emotions and to experience them as an important part of the process" (Levis, 1966, p. 29). The scenes utilized for this enactment pertain to situations or stimuli which supposedly are anxiety provoking for the patient. In describing the scenes, the therapist is expected to become visibly involved and dramatic. An attempt is also made by the therapist to attain as high a level of anxiety in the patient as possible. When such a level of anxiety is achieved, the patient is kept at this level until there is some indication of its spontaneous reduction. The reduction in anxiety is considered to be related to the process of extinction. Such procedures are repeated, and as the patient manifests reduction in his anxiety in response to these scenes, new variations are introduced in order to elicit more anxiety. The procedure continues until a significant reduction in anxiety has occurred. The patient himself is also given an opportunity to act out these scenes by himself, and to rehearse in his imagination these scenes in the time between the various treatment sessions. This type of assignment supposedly provides additional extinction trials.

Thus, what appears to occur in implosive therapy is the vivid description of anxiety eliciting situations which the patient is encouraged to visualize in imagery. In a sense, the therapist forces the patient to be exposed to anxiety-provoking cues that he may tend to avoid outside of the treatment session. "Therefore, with the avoidance response circumvented, greater exposure to the cues will occur, and subsequently greater extinction will be effected" (Levis, 1966, p. 31).

There is a greater emphasis on emotional tone in implosive therapy than is the case with systematic desensitization. The therapist will actively and vividly describe the situation that is upsetting to the client and in some ways may be compared to the director of a movie. Also, as mentioned before, whereas most behavior therapists tend to be theoretically opposed to psycho-analytic concepts, the advocates of implosive therapy may use such concepts in their work. Thus, when the symptom-contingent cues, which have been mentioned or secured from the client, have been extinguished, cues are introduced to be worked within therapy which are hypothesized on the basis of the client's history and psychoanalytic theory. Such cues are assumed to be even more anxiety provoking than those previously dealt with and in many instances to be repressed. They "are believed mainly to incorporate the dynamic areas thought relevant to the basic problems of the patient" (Levis, 1966, p. 31). Such cues usually involve the expression of hostility and aggression toward parental figures, experiences of rejection, deprivation, guilt, and concerns about sex.

Several studies have been carried out to evaluate the effectiveness of implosive therapy. One early study dealt with female college students who had a fear of rats (Hogan and Kirchner, 1967). Twenty-two controls and twenty-one experimental subjects who were afraid to pick up a white rat in a pretest were studied. Only one session of therapy was used with the implosive therapy subjects imagining such scenes as rats nibbling at their fingers, being attacked by a disease-ridden sewer rat, or even swallowing a rat which might destroy various internal organs. The controls, on the other hand, were asked to imagine various neutral or pleasant scenes. At a posttest, fourteen of the twenty-one experimental subjects were able to pick up a rat whereas only two of the twenty-two controls were successful in doing this. Hodgson and Rachman (1970) attempted a partial replication of this study, but did not secure similarly positive results.

Other studies have attempted to compare the relative efficacy of flooding and desensitization in the treatment of phobias. In one study, nine agoraphobics and seven patients with specific phobias were treated by means of a crossover design (Boulougouris, Marks, and Marset, 1971). Patients were randomly allocated to six sessions of desensitization in phantasy followed by six sessions of flooding in phantasy, or vice versa. Each session was 50 minutes. The fifth and sixth session of either treatment was followed immediately by 70 minutes of practice in either of the treatments. The patients were seen two to three times weekly with all receiving one treatment first and the other second. The desensitization procedures followed those described by Wolpe and Lazarus (1966), but the flooding procedure dealt only with fears actually mentioned by the patient. The same therapist conducted all of the therapy with a given patient. Various appraisals were made during and after therapy. In general, while both therapies produced significant reduction in the primary phobic reactions, flooding or implosion was superior to desensitization.

A somewhat different study has been reported by Hussain (1971). This was also a crossover study that compared flooding and desensitization, but a drug was utilized which produces relaxation, thiopental sodium (Pentothal), and a saline solution. In this investigation, forty patients with a diagnosis of phobic anxiety neurosis were divided into four groups as follows: (1) Implosive therapy—thiopental sodium first, saline second; (2) implosive therapy—saline first; (3) desensitization—thiopental sodium first; (4) desensitization—saline first. Thus, the crossover design involved the drug and saline with each of the behavioral approaches. Therapy for each condition consisted of six 45-minute sessions. Therapists' and patients' ratings of the severity of the phobia and of anxiety were the criteria measures used. The most marked effects were secured by the combination of flooding and the drug. Flooding and saline produced comparatively little effect. During desensitization under either condition the improvement was moderate and approximately equal. These results are interesting and offer a number of possibilities for interpretation. In this study, flooding without the drug appeared to have little effect. There was, however, a strong interaction effect between the two, which was not apparent in the case of desensitization. On the other hand, desensitization with saline appeared to be more effective than flooding under comparable conditions. Hussain himself believes the results are consistent with the view of Baum (1969a, b)—that the prevention of the avoidance response is effective because it leads to the learning of relaxation in response to the stimuli that produced anxiety. Relaxing the patient pharmacologically appeared to facilitate elimination of the avoidance response. Nevertheless, six sessions of implosive therapy without the drug did not appear to lead to much change. Baum (1970) later also concluded that relaxation does not completely explain the extinction of avoidance reactions.

Although the research on implosion and flooding is not as extensive as that of systematic desensitization, enough work has been reported to offer some tentative generalizations. As is true of research in other areas of psychotherapy, many of the studies can be faulted because of brief periods of treatment, inadequate and small number of subjects, failure to control for expectancy effects, and the like (Ayer, 1972; Morganstern, 1973). There are also conflicting findings in the published literature. Morganstern (1973) in his review of the literature available at that time concluded that due to the limitations in the research, interpretations were exceedingly difficult. However, he did not find the evidence to be convincing in demonstrating the efficacy of implosion or flooding, or in showing that these procedures were more effective than systematic desensitization. He also questioned "the desirability of having a client undergo such stress and trauma in the name of treatment, when systematic desensitization is at least as effective a procedure" (Morganstern, 1973, p. 332).

The lack of a difference in outcome between flooding and systematic desensitization is also contained in other reports (Gelder, Bancroft, Gath, Johnson, and Mathews, 1973; Mathews, Johnston, Shaw, and Gelder, 1974). Although some individuals believe that flooding may require less time, it is difficult to really make a case for its superiority. Marks (1978) believes that exposure to the evoking or anxiety-producing stimulus is the critical variable and not the level of anxiety produced by either flooding or systematic desensitization. Thus, both flooding and systematic desensitization have been viewed as essentially variants of exposure treatment. Whether the individual is exposed gradually to the feared stimulus in imagination via systematic desensitization, or more directly and emotionally by means of implosion, the crucial element is coming into contact with the aversive stimulus and experiencing no negative reactions. In fact, results of several studies summarized by Marks (1978) would indicate that the most effective procedure is *in vivo* exposure, that is, interacting with the fear-evoking stimulus in reality instead of fantasy.

OPERANT CONDITIONING

Other forms of behavioral modification have utilized the principles of operant conditioning, and the procedures developed have been used in a variety of situations with a large range of clinical problems. Interestingly enough, not only have the procedures used with pigeons and rats in the laboratory been applied with some success in modifying the disturbed behaviors of humans, but in a number of instances operant principles have been used with severely disturbed individuals who have either been resistant to other approaches or have been given up as hopeless cases. Thus, operant conditioning has been used in treatment programs designed for chronic institutionalized psychotic patients, severely withdrawn or autistic children, and hyperactive and severely retarded individuals (Kazdin, 1978; Ross, 1978).

One of the early reports concerning the use of operant conditioning and related procedures to modify the behavior of psychotic patients was made by Ayllon (1963). In this study, Ayllon reports the modification of some specific behaviors as carried out in an experimental ward in a hospital setting. The staff of the ward consisted of psychiatric nurses and aids who carried out the program of environmental manipulation under the direction of the experimenter. Systematic observations were made. Food was available for the patients only at the dining room, and the entrance to it could be controlled. Thus, in this setting the experimenter and his staff could exert control, by means of reinforcement and similar procedures, over the behavior of the patients.

The particular patient who was studied in this report was a 47-year-old female patient who had been hospitalized for 9 years with a diagnosis of schizophrenia. It was noted that the ward staff spent considerable time taking care of this patient, and that there were three problem behaviors which the staff had been unable to modify. These behaviors included stealing food, the hoarding of ward towels, and the wearing of excessive clothing. This patient, for example, would put on a half dozen dresses, several pairs of stockings, sweaters, and other articles of clothing. In order to modify the patient's behavior in a systematic manner, each of the patient's target behaviors was treated separately.

At the time of the experiment the patient weighed over 250 pounds, which the medical staff regarded as detrimental to her health. A special diet had been prescribed but the patient did not follow this. The patient in addition to eating her regular meals, stole food from the food counter and from other patients. All attempts at trying to discourage her in this behavior had been unsuccessful. Under the experimental regime, the patient was seated alone at a table in the dining room. Whenever the patient approached another table or picked up extra food from the dining room counter, she was removed from the dining room. Thus the patient might miss a meal as a result of attempting to steal food. When this type of withdrawal of positive reinforcement was made dependent upon the patient's stealing, the latter response was eliminated in 2 weeks. Furthermore, since the patient no longer indulged in extra eating, she did eat mainly the diet prescribed for her. As a result she showed a significant weight loss. Her previous low weight during her hospitalization was 230 pounds. At the conclusion of 14 months of this type of treatment, her weight had stabilized at 180 pounds.

A different procedure, called Stimulus Satiation, was used to modify the patient's hoarding behavior. During her years of hospitalization, the patient hoarded at any given time anywhere from nineteen to twenty-nine towels which she kept in her room. Again, the various attempts made by the nursing staff to discourage this type of behavior had been unsuccessful, and as they removed the towels from her room, she seemed to be able to replenish the supply. Under the experimental program, the removal of towels from the patient's room was discontinued. Instead, the program of stimulus satiation was instituted. At various times throughout the day, the nurses took a towel to the patient when she was in her room and handed it to her without comment. The first week she was given an average of seven towels daily, but by the third week, the number was increased to sixty. When the number kept in her room reached 625, the patient started taking a few of them out. From that point on, no more towels were given to her and during the next year, the mean number of towels found in her room was 1.5 per week. The principle behind this program was that a reinforcer loses its effect when an excessive amount is made available. When the number of towels reached the high mark of 625, the objects seemed to lose their positive attraction, and, in fact, to be perceived as negative stimuli. The change in the patient's attitudes and behavior is reflected in the following account:

> During the first few weeks of satiation, the patient was observed patting her cheeks with a few towels, apparently enjoying them. Later, the patient was observed spending much of her time folding and stacking the approximately 600 towels in her room. A variety

of remarks were made by the patient regarding receipt of towels. All verbal statements made by the patient were recorded by the nurse. The following represent typical remarks made during this experiment. First week: As the nurse entered the patient's room carrying a towel, the patient would smile and say, 'Oh, you found it for me, thank you.' 'Second week: When the number of towels given to patient increased rapidly, she told the nurses, 'Don't give me no more towels. I've got enough.' Third week: 'Take them towels away . . . I can't sit here all night and fold towels.' Fourth and fifth weeks: 'Get these dirty towels out of here.' Sixth week: After she had started taking the towels out of her room, she remarked to the nurse, 'I can't drag any more of these towels, I just can't do it' (Ayllon, 1963, p. 57).

The final experiment in this series dealt with the wearing of excessive clothing. In addition to several types of garments, the patient wrapped sheets and towels around her body, plus other items. It was decided in this case to use food reinforcement as a means of modifying the target behavior. By weighing the patient, the amount of clothes could be estimated. The patient was allowed a particular weight allowance beyond her body weight, but when her total weight exceeded this, she was informed that she weighed too much and consequently, she missed a meal. By manipulating the weight allowance allowed over a 14-week period, the weight of the patient's clothes was reduced from 25 to 3 pounds. At the conclusion of this treatment, the patient typically stepped on the scale wearing the normal amount of clothing that women generally wear. Some concomitant changes that took place are also worth noting. As this patient began to dress in a normal fashion, she began to participate in some of the social events of the hospital. Previous to this, she had been quite seclusive and spent most of the time in her room. About this time also, the patient's parents visited her and insisted on taking her home for a visit. This was the first time during the patient's 9 years of hospitalization that this had occurred. The parents remarked that previously they had not wanted to take the patient out because her excessive clothes and weight made her look like a "circus freak."

The above description is an interesting account of a pioneering effort at applying principles of operant conditioning to actually improve the behavior of a chronic and seriously disturbed patient. Specific behavioral goals were selected and appropriate programs of behavior modification were instituted. In terms of the objectives of the program, the latter was successful and significant and positive changes in behavior were obtained. However, concerns have been expressed that the individual in such cases is manipulated and treated as an object. The goals of treatment and behavior change were those of the experimenter or the staff of the hospital, and not necessarily those of the patient. This is clearly an important issue and one that is not always easy to resolve, particularly when we are dealing with seriously disturbed individuals who may not be capable of making informed decisions.

OPERANT CONDITIONING AND PATIENTS' RIGHTS

Another important issue concerns the withholding of certain necessities of life from institutionalized patients as a means of behavior modification. As Kazdin (1978) points out: "Developing a technology of behavior change has made salient the potential conflict between the rights and values of individuals and society. The conflict is especially pronounced in cases where individual freedoms are guaranteed by the United States Constitution and the state intervenes and restricts freedom in the name of treatment or rehabilitation" (p. 574).

As a result of such concerns, there have been considerable professional and legal pronouncements concerning the rights of patients in relation to treatment. One of the most important legal decisions was handed down in the case of *Wyatt v. Stickney* which concerned the institutional treatment of psychotic patients as well as those who are mentally retarded. Kazdin (1978), who has published a very concise and useful summary of the legal issues raised by operant conditioning programs, comments in the following manner on this decision:

> One aspect of this decision specified that patients are entitled by right to various items and activities that sometimes are used as reinforcing events. The court specified that patients are entitled to a comfortable bed, a balanced meal, a place for personal belongings, opportunities to attend religious services, to interact with the opposite sex, to be outdoors frequently, to receive visitors, and so on (p. 575).

Clearly, such legal decisions place restrictions on what types of operant conditioning programs may be used with hospitalized patients, even if they are seen as being of potential benefit to the patients involved. Many previously conducted programs would not be condoned today. Nevertheless, the matter of patients' human rights has to be seen as taking priority over other considerations, and should be considered seriously in planning operant or other types of programs. Now let us look at some additional examples in which operant conditioning has been applied.

OTHER PROGRAMS

In one study, an "operant-interpersonal method," was used with twelve very chronic psychotic patients, and comparable patients were administered other therapies (King, Armitage, and Tilton, 1960). The subjects were individually matched on severity of illness and length of hospitalization. One group of twelve subjects received verbal therapy equal in amount to that received by the operant-interpersonal method. Twelve subjects received recreational therapy for 3 to 5 hours per week, and one group did not receive any special treatment. All forty-eight subjects were transferred to a single day room in which they were the sole occupants.

A Multiple Operant Problem-Solving apparatus was constructed for the experimental program. This was built into an 8' × 8' panel and included levers that had to be depressed by the patients in order to receive rewards of candy and cigarettes, which were dispensed into a tray. The procedure emphasized motor behavior and the task progressed from simple to complex. Initially, the patients individually made simple operant responses in the presence of a therapist in order to receive their rewards. As these procedures were mastered, more complex psychomotor, verbal, and interpersonal components were incorporated systematically into the procedure, depending on the patient's progress. At the point of maximum complexity, the situation required each patient to communicate with other patients and to enter into cooperative relationships in order to solve problems. It should be remembered that these were patients in whom communication and cooperative social behavior were at a low level.

The operant-interpersonal method was found to be more effective than the control methods in promoting clinical improvement based on ward observations and interviews. The experimental group of subjects exhibited also a higher level of verbalization, a greater desire to leave the ward, decreased enuresis, and secured more transfers to better wards. The patients who received verbal therapy actually seemed to show an increase in their verbal withdrawal.

Other programs developed for hospitalized psychotic patients have utilized a variety of tasks and reinforcements to modify the behaviors of these individuals. For adults, rewards used have included candy, cigarettes, passes, privileges, and even psychotherapy. For children, candy, toys, and trips have been most frequently used. Tokens and token economies have also been utilized in a number of therapeutic endeavors (Ayllon and Azrin, 1968; Kazdin, 1977) and with different groups of children in school situations. When the individual completes a desired task or responds with an approved behavior he is given a token; later, various rewards can be purchased with a specified number of tokens. A token economy may be instituted on a given ward in an institution. In such an instance the patients must perform certain tasks or behaviors in order to receive the tokens which have become the official medium of exchange for this miniature society. Various commodities or activities can only be purchased by means of the tokens. In this type of situation, considerable control is lodged in the hands of the staff in order to secure desired behavioral change. It is also of obvious importance that all personnel receive adequate instruction in the treatment procedures so that only the desired behaviors are reinforced.

A variety of operant as well as other types of conditioning programs have been developed and used with severely disturbed children. Whether such children are referred to as psychotic, schizophrenic, or autistic, they clearly show very disturbed patterns of social behavior. Children described as autistic generally display a significant lack of development or impairment in speech; they are seen as isolated and detached from people and frequently exhibit compulsive repetitive behaviors. It is exceedingly difficult to communicate or relate to such children because they seem to ignore these efforts completely. There have been many discussions and controversies concerning the etiology of such disturbance, but these issues need not concern us here. Such children, however, have generally been very difficult to treat by conventional psychiatric and psychotherapeutic means and their prognosis has been considered poor. Nevertheless, there have been several experimental programs utilizing principles of behavior modification that have produced rather remarkable changes in behavior, including reduction in self-destructive behavior and improvement in social communication (Lovaas and Bucher, 1974). In most of these instances, the children have been treated in inpatient settings, which have allowed the experimenter or the therapist considerable control in regulating and modifying the environmental contingencies for the child's behavior. Such possibilities for control as well as change are not usually possible when the child is seen for relatively brief periods on an outpatient basis. Maintenance of gains secured in one such program depended on the disposition of the child after treatment. Those who returned to parents who were trained to continue the operant procedures maintained their improvement whereas whose who were assigned to a state hospital failed to maintain their gains (Lovaas, Kaegel, Simmons, and Long, 1973).

In many programs, the therapist begins with an emphasis on material things as reinforcers, but an attempt is usually made at a later stage to utilize some type of social reinforcement. Although the use of candy or other kinds of material reward may be effective in modifying a child's behavior in the controlled hospital setting, such a situation cannot be maintained consistently in real life. Of greater importance is the reinforcing values of social rewards from significant persons in the individual's environment. Consequently, programs of this type will try to introduce social reinforcement as early as possible so that the child will respond to the praise or smile of the adult and perceive this as a reward for his behavior.

Another important aspect of these programs is that the behavior of the child and the influence of various stimuli have been monitored with some precision in a systematic manner. Consequently, as different environmental stimuli are introduced, one can evaluate their relative effectiveness or ineffectiveness. A particular treatment program can be instituted and the resulting behaviors noted and plotted on a graph. After a given length of time, the particular program can be stopped, but the monitoring of behavior continued. The treatment program can then be reinstituted and the effectiveness of the program appraised. This particular design is sometimes referred to as an "ABAB" design. If desired changes in behavior are secured in the first treatment phase, if these behaviors then diminish during the cessation of treatment, and if the behaviors are manifested again with the resumption of treatment, one then has some basis for stating that the behavior change is actually a function of the treatment program.

The variety of treatment procedures that can be used, the need for selecting reinforcers appropriate to specific cases, the importance of constant surveillance of the way the child is responding to the treatment program, the need for proper training and supervision of ward staff, as well as the problems encountered in the residential treatment of severely disturbed children, have been vividly recounted by Browning and Stover (1971). Working in a state hospital setting, these psychologists set up a treatment program which made abundant use of operant conditioning principles as well as others. The book can be recommended to prospective clinical psychologists regardless of theoretical persuasion because it illustrates beautifully how the scientist-practitioner model can actually function.

In their program at the Children's Treatment Center in Madison, Wisconsin, Browning, Stover, and their co-workers used a wide variety of reinforcements, and were attentive to the problem of the children's learning to respond to such special discriminative cues as frowns, smiles, and the like. They have paid particular attention to strengthening the effects of social reinforcers which will be available to the child in his natural environment and to the incremental steps which are involved in shaping the more complex behaviors which children need to develop. These are not simple procedures, but, in the former instance, require analysis of the activity or objects which are rewarding for a given child and the development of a close relationship between the staff person and the child.

The procedures and activities developed for modifying the behavior of disturbed children and the methods used in monitoring and evaluating the effectiveness of the procedures used in this program are too varied and detailed to be described here. Nevertheless, the published report indicates the ingenuity, patience, and labor that are required to develop an effective program for working with such children. Even getting disturbed children to engage in apparently simple normal behaviors, let alone to develop more complex behaviors, requires some planning and effort. The following excerpt illustrates the shaping procedures used in one relatively simple instance:

Another youngster was terrified of swings. The child had daily sessions of sitting beside and on the lap of the staff member at decreasing distances from the swing. During these sessions, she would be rewarded with small preferred candies. Within one week she was eating the candies beside the swing, then on the lap of staff while swinging, then on the swing by herself, and within two weeks she was being pushed gleefully on the swing. The candy reinforcers were gradually deleted, since the swing itself had now acquired reward value (Browning and Stover, 1971, p. 135).

A few other well known programs also can be mentioned briefly before we conclude this section. Patterson (1971, 1974) and his collaborators have developed programs for children with conduct disorders which involve training the parents of these children, and in some instances implementing procedures in the school classroom. Another well-known program for delinquent boys, Achievement Place, uses therapeutic family-style homes based largely on operant principles embodied in a token economy (Phillips, Phillips, Fixsen, and Wolf, 1971). The boys in the program earn points for certain behaviors which can be exchanged for a variety of privileges. Later, the privileges or rewards are provided without such points, and socially desired behaviors receive social reinforcement. If the individual progresses, he is returned home. The results secured in terms of several criteria including subsequent acts of delinquency were quite positive as compared with control groups, although the individuals had not been randomly assigned to the various groups (Ross, 1978).

The outstanding illustration of the application of social-learning principles, including operant procedures, is provided in the study reported by Paul and Lentz (1977). Directed by Gordon Paul, this project attempted to compare a social-learning approach with a regular state hospital program and with a program of milieu therapy. Although planned initially as a program for hospitalized mental patients, in general, it turned out to be a program for very chronic hospitalized schizophrenic patients.

All of the patients were of low socioeconomic status, they averaged 17 years of hospitalization, and about one-half had previously received electroconvulsive shock treatments. Such patients generally would be regarded as patients with very poor prognoses for responding to treatment. Furthermore, the great majority had had no contact with family or friends during the previous year. Without going into additional descriptive detail, it can be mentioned that most of the patients could not take care of their personal needs in terms of feeding, bathing, and the like. Designing a program to run for a period of years with such patients is clearly a difficult and challenging undertaking.

The full report of this project is contained in a volume of over 500 pages and we can mention only a few highlights here. The project was undertaken in a state mental hospital, considered above average in comparison with other similar institutions, and in a regional mental health center, both in

Illinois. The 28 patients in the state hospital received the usual care provided such patients which consisted of medication, unstructured time, and to a lesser extent, classes, meetings, occupational therapy, and the like. The patients in the milieu therapy and social-learning groups, who were housed in the regional mental health center, participated in more organized programs with much less unstructured time. In these two groups, classes, meetings and focused activities took up almost 59% of the patients' time, unstructured time amounted to 11.6% of the total time, and drug administration, 3.1%. The corresponding figures were 4.9, 64, and 6.3% for those in the state hospital. In the hospital, authority for patient care was vested in the superintendant and the medical staff, whereas in the other two programs all individual staff members, regardless of status and discipline, were officially viewed as change agents and were encouraged to make decisions. As mentioned in the report, "all staff operations emphasized cross-training and competency criteria rather than profession or position identification" (Paul and Lentz, 1977, p. 30).

Both the milieu and social-learning programs were conducted in identical 28-bed coed units by the same staff and had some features in common. They emphasized resocialization, instrumental role performance, reduction or elimination of extreme bizarre behaviors, and provision of support in the community when the patient was released (at least one person capable of providing significant support). They also viewed the individual as a resident rather than a patient, expected improvement, indicated that residents were responsible people, encouraged social interaction, stressed communication skills, provided some training and practice in vocational skills, and brought residents into contact with the outside world. There were thus very clear procedures and objectives in these programs with an emphasis on helping the individual as much as possible to become a self-sustaining member of his/her community.

Despite such similarities, however, there were important differences between these two psychosocial programs, and detailed manuals were developed as guides for each of the programs. For the social-learning program, "the principles and techniques of instrumental and associative learning and the basic features of token economics were extended to a comprehensive, integrated program" (Paul and Lentz, 1977, p. 33). Thus, emphasis was placed on the law of effect (frequency of response is a function of the effect of the response), association by contiguity, and the development of new behaviors. A token economy was instituted and, in general, emphasis was placed on rewarding positive behaviors immediately, never reinforcing undesirable behavior, etc. The program was conceived as a 24-hour program, 7 days a week. Detailed schedules were prepared, and detailed observational records were maintained, particularly of social interactions, as a means of evaluating the actual operations and application of the program. Emphasis was placed on appropriate interactions between staff and residents and these were system-atically monitored. The residents were not viewed as "sick" people who had to be treated by medical personnel, since the emphasis was otherwise and only the part-time services of a physician were used. Most of the staff in fact were not professional people, but included aides, practical nurses, B.A.-level psychologists, and the like. They were trained and given supervision as required.

Some of the results secured from this project are quite impressive. Although each of the three programs used a comparable number of staff, the outcomes for the milieu and the social-learning programs were clearly superior to those of the traditional program. Ninety percent of the patients in the social-learning program were released from the regional center to community homes, with an additional 7.5% able to assume an independent, self-supporting existence. The comparable figures for the milieu therapy were 71 and 6.5% (over a 6-year period, some patients were discharged and replaced by others, so the numbers for each program exceed the original 28). For the state hospital, only 45 percent were released, and none were released for independent living. Considering all aspects, the social learning program was indicated as being the most efficient and economical, and the state hospital as the most expensive. Thus, both psychosocial programs were found to be superior to the traditional hospital program, and the social learning program was somewhat superior to the milieu program.

Although a number of individuals have been critical of the use of operant procedures as demeaning to the individual, as treating only symptomatic behaviors, and as authoritarian and dehumanizing, the fact remains that they have been used with some success with individuals who have not responded to other forms of treatment. Even though a number of the cases will never be restored to fully normal functioning, their level of institutional adjustment and independent functioning has been raised, and in some instances rather remarkable improvement has been obtained. It should also be stressed that the proper application of operant and other learning principles is not a simple mechanical procedure. The psychologist needs to observe the behavior of the individual, his interactions with others, the contingencies related to the emission of certain behaviors, and the kinds of reinforcements which might be used in helping to improve the individual's behavior. Once a behavioral analysis is made, certain types of programs can be formulated, tried out, and modified as needed. Systematic records of behaviors and contingencies can also be obtained to monitor the program and to evaluate its effectiveness. Such activities are far from mechanical. In addition, observers, technicians, and other treatment personnel require specific training in order to function properly in the program. Thus, although a variety of personnel can be trained to participate in such programs and to carry out specific functions, the plan-ning, overseeing, and evaluation of the treatment program requires a high level of training and sophistication. Such programs also require a high degree of patience, because a large number of trials may be required before the desired behavior is elicited from seriously disturbed individuals.

COGNITIVE-BEHAVIORAL THERAPY

A recent development, to which some brief reference was made earlier, is that of combining cognitive with behavioral approaches. Although this has been hailed by some as a necessary and significant step forward, integrating two important emphases in psychotherapy, some behaviorists have reacted negatively (Ledgwidge, 1978, 1979; Skinner, 1977; Wolpe, 1976). Let us take a brief look at this development.

It may be recalled that behavior therapy has been differentiated from most other therapies by its reliance on theories of learning. More than any other recognized form of therapy, behavior therapy has emphasized research and the applications of knowledge derived from experimental psychology. The recent emphasis on a cognitive-behavioral orientation may stem in part from research and related developments in the area of cognitive psychology. As indicated earlier, Bandura (1969) particularly emphasized the role of cognitive mediational processes in behavior modification. More recently, a number of behavior therapists have also indicated the importance of cognitive and symbolic processes in learning and in behavior change generally (Goldfried and Davison, 1976; Kendall and Hollon, 1979; Mahoney and Arnhoff, 1978; Meichenbaum, 1977). Somewhat separate from this development within behavior therapy or within a behavioral orientation has been the development of those approaches discussed in the previous chapter which tended to be called cognitive therapies, e.g., rational-emotive therapy. Most of the therapies in the latter category were not derived from a learning theory orientation or from the psychology laboratory, but were the development of individual clinicians dissatisfied with the more conventional therapeutic systems they had been using. However, since they also appeared to emphasize the importance of perceptions, beliefs, problem solving, and related processes, there has been a merging of these movements. Ellis (1977), as noted earlier, uses research on other cognitive-behavioral approaches to buttress the claims of his therapy, and Beck's therapy has been called both a cognitive and a cognitive-behavioral therapy.

What particular therapeutic approaches are called or labeled is not really of great importance. The important considerations pertain to identifying the procedures or variables which actually secure clearly demonstrated positive changes. Certainly, cognitive activities of a wide variety occur and play an important role in the behavior and adjustment of the human being. We perceive, we anticipate, we make value judgments, we have biases, and so on. All of these processes or attributions may influence our behavior. It is not merely the environmental stimuli which produce certain behaviors, but also how the stimuli are perceived by the organism.

What seems quite apparent in the critical responses of some behaviorists to cognitive emphases is a fear of the use of mentalistic concepts and a weakening of strictly behavioral emphases and formulations. Behavioral approaches have been viewed by them as distinctly positive and productive contributions which can only be diluted or tarnished by bringing in cognitive emphases. Cognitive-behaviorists on the other hand, take the view, as already indicated, that categorically neglecting clients' cognitions is to neglect variables of potential importance and perhaps to reduce the potential efficacy of therapy (Mahoney and Kazdin, 1979).

Although it is difficult to predict how this conflict will be resolved, a variety of cognitive emphases and procedures have been added by a number of behaviorally oriented clinicians. Such features as cognitive or rational restructuring, stress innoculation, self-regulation and self-control procedures, as well as others, have been described and reported in the literature. A description of a number of these are contained in the volume by Kendall and Hollon (1979) and in general treatises on behavior therapy (e.g., Goldfried and Davison, 1976). Bandura's (1977) effective presentation of the importance of the client's view of his/her self-efficacy as an important variable in treatment outcome has also had a positive impact on the development of a cognitive-behavioral approach to behavior modification. Although some comparative studies of the relative effectiveness of the two different approaches (behavioral versus cognitive-behavioral) have found little difference between the two (Ledgwidge, 1978), it is too early to draw any definitive conclusions at this time. Whether or not one or the other of these approaches will be found to be more effective with specific kinds of patients and disorders remains to be seen. However, it is difficult to conceive of a purely behavioral therapy in which cognitions on the part of the client are totally excluded.

OTHER BEHAVIORAL APPROACHES

We have reviewed some of the major behavioral approaches to therapy. The procedures discussed have been applied to a variety of clinical problems with varying amounts of apparent success. Still other applications of learning theories and combinations of methods have also been made (Bandura, 1977; Craighead *et al.*, 1981; Goldfried and Davison, 1976; Kendall and Hollon, 1979; Ross, 1978; Yates, 1975). The various methods have been used with children and with groups, and in the past 20 years or so have constituted an important addition to the psychotherapeutic armamentarium of the clinical psychologist as well as other professions. Before going on to some final summary statements about these procedures, a few additional comments about other related methods derived from learning theories can be made.

Modeling has also been used in working with disturbed children and frequently has been combined with some of the other procedures. A comprehensive account of this work is contained in a recent review by Rosenthal and Bandura (1978). Modeling principles and treatment procedures have been applied to the establishment of new patterns of behavior, to the elimination of fears and inhibitions, and to facilitating the expression of preexisting modes of response. As was noted in Chapter 2, individuals are able to acquire vicariously by means of observation a variety of behaviors without a long trial and error process.

Bandura and colleagues have reported several studies in which modeling has been used in the elimination of anxieties and fears. In one study (Bandura, Grusec, and Menlove, 1967), children who exhibited a marked avoidance of dogs were assigned to one of four treatment groups. In two somewhat varying groups the children observed a fearless peer model demonstrate increasingly more fear-provoking interactions with a dog. Over a period of eight sessions the threatening or aversive properties of the modeled performance were increased by varying the restraints on the dog, the intimacy of the interactions of the model with the dog, and the length of the interaction. Two other groups of children were utilized as controls. In one the children were exposed to the dog in a positive context but without the model. In the other, neither the dog nor the model was used. Following completion of these procedures, and also 1 month later, a series of graded tests were administered which included approaching and petting different dogs, releasing them from a playpen, feeding them, spending a fixed amount of time alone in the room with the dog, and, finally, climbing into the playpen with each dog, petting it, and remaining alone with it. The two groups that had been exposed to the modeling procedures showed significantly more approach behavior to the dogs, and two-thirds of them were able to remain alone in the playpen with the dog.

A related and comparable experiment, but employing movies of single and multiple models, also secured significantly positive results for the children exposed to the models (Bandura and Menlove, 1968). Particularly impressive was the increase in the approach behavior of the children in the control group who were exposed to the multiple modeling procedure after the initial experiment was completed. In another study with subjects with snake phobias, the use of a live model plus guided participation on the part of the subjects yielded markedly better results than did symbolic modeling with a film or systematic desensitization, although all three groups secured better results than an untreated control group (Bandura, Blanchard, and Ritter, 1969).

Modeling also was used along with other behavioral approaches by Lovaas and his co-workers in his work with autistic and schizophrenic children (Lovaas, 1967; Lovaas, Berberich, Perloff, and Schaeffer, 1966; Lovaas, Freitag, Nelson, and Whalen, 1967). As mentioned before, such children have severe deficits in social behavior and speech and are very difficult to work with. Lovaas used positive reinforcement, modeling, punishment, and other procedures. To a large extent the program was based on the view that positive change can be secured through establishing stimulus conditions that make the child amenable to social influences. This means that these heretofore unresponsive children must learn to attend to a variety of environmental stimuli and that selected social and related cues must acquire reinforcing properties.

Several procedures were used by Lovaas in his attempts to foster the acquisition of language. Particular attention was devoted to having a child attend to the task at hand. Thus the therapist would sit directly in front of the child so that the latter could not ignore the responses that were being modeled for him. The child was not permitted to avoid the task, and he might be physically restrained, spoken to in a sharp manner, or slapped on the thigh if these were necessary to hold his attention. In addition, food rewards and expressions of affection and social approval were made contingent upon the child's imitation of the model. Other aspects stressed were that the capabilities of the disturbed child must not be overtaxed and that the sequence of learning must be appropriate and planned by stages. In teaching a mute child to talk, for example, the therapist rewards any sounds that are made initially by the child. When some progress has been made, the child may be rewarded only if he produces a verbal response within a certain time after the therapist has given him his cue. Thus, a step by step procedure is utilized which combines modeling, reinforcement, and guided performance. The child proceeds from random vocalizations to imitating the sounds of the therapist, to verbalizing words, and continues hopefully until he can utilize speech in social situations. Obviously, this process is not an easy one, but once initial progress is made, the subsequent progress appears to proceed more quickly. The progress in language acquisition which these nonverbal children manifested in the program was quite impressive.

CONCLUDING COMMENTS

The developments in the behavioral therapies have constituted the most challenging and exciting movement in the field of psychotherapy in recent years. In their behalf it can be noted that the techniques and procedures used are relatively explicit, the time required for the behavioral therapies are generally very much less than that required for interpretive psychodynamic therapy, many of the techniques and methods have been derived from or related to basic psychological theory and research, some kind of quantitative evaluations of these behavioral methods are usually provided, a more rigorous research orientation is characteristic of this approach, some of the most difficult and neglected cases have been treated by means of behavioral approaches, and the results obtained appear to be at least as good as those reported with other therapies (Sloane, Staples, Cristol, Yorkston, and Whipple, 1975; Smith, Glass and Miller, 1980). Certainly, this is an impressive accomplishment, and the inquiring and innovative attitudes manifested by workers in the area of behavioral modification are most welcome.

At the same time, one should also remember that these therapeutic approaches are still at a relatively early stage of development. We need to know much more about what procedures work best with what types of clients and under what kinds of conditions. In spite of the theoretical rationale given for some of the procedures, the actual operations of the therapist at times appears rather far removed from them (Breger and McGaugh, 1965; Klein, Dittman, Parloff, and Gill, 1969). In some of the illustrations given it does appear that some of the common or nonspecific factors mentioned in Chapter 8 also operate and exert their influence (Garfield, 1980; Kazdin and Wilcoxon, 1976; Wilkins, 1971). The confidence of the therapist in his methods, the explanation of the therapist concerning how the therapy works, the linkage of this form of therapy to scientific developments in psychology, and the reports of previously obtained successes by this means of therapy may all have some positive influence on outcome. Furthermore, the opportunity to tell an interested, knowledgable, and nonjudgmental person about one's difficulties, the arousal of hope, and the presence of such variables as suggestion and reassurance would all appear to operate in varying degrees with these as well as other therapies. Consequently, additional research in which careful attention is devoted to the appraisal of the influence of such variables on outcome may shed further light on the significance of all of the variables operating in behavioral therapy. Several reports support this view and the related one that some of the operations specified in systematic desensitization may not be of critical importance. For example, several studies have shown that omitting relaxation does not significantly impair the results of desensitization (Agras, Leitenberg, Barlow, Curtis, Edwards, and Wright, 1971; Aponte and Aponte, 1971; Cooke, 1968), and one study has indicated that neither relaxation nor a graded hierarchy was necessary in reducing phobic behavior as long as the subjects were exposed in imagination to the feared object without negative reinforcement (Wolpin and Raines, 1966). Some other studies also suggest that creating expectancy conditions for change (Marcia, Rubin, and Efran, 1969) and providing therapeutically oriented instructions which indicate that a positive outcome is likely (Leitenberg, Agras, Barlow, and Oliveau, 1969; Oliveau, Agras, Leitenberg, Moore, and Wright, 1969) may also be therapeutic variables of some importance.

It should be emphasized that the preceding comments have reference to some of the theoretical ideas underlying behavioral approaches to the modification of behavior and not necessarily to the effectiveness of these procedures. The results secured by means of the various behavioral therapies clearly indicate that there is much of value to be gained from applying and studying these therapies. Of particular value, in the author's opinion, is the model offered by a number of outstanding behavioral therapists in utilizing psychological knowledge to devise a number of specific procedures for working with the particular problems presented by a given case, instead of applying the same approach to every case. As additional knowledge and research findings are secured with these techniques, we can anticipate some changes in procedures, and possibly some combination of behavioral and other approaches (Garfield, 1980; Goldfried, 1980; Marmor and Woods, 1980). As long as a research orientation continues to pervade the behavioral therapies, the latter should continue to show positive accomplishments.

REFERENCES

Agras, W. S. Leitenberg, H., Barlow, D. H., Curtis, N., Edwards, J., & Wright, D. Relaxation in systematic desensitization. *Archives of General Psychiatry,* 1971, *25,* 511–514.

Aponte, J. F., & Aponte, C. E. Group preprogrammed systematic desensitization without the simultaneous presentation of aversive scenes with relaxation training. *Behaviour Research and Therapy,* 1971, *9,* 337–346.

Ayer, W. A. Implosive therapy: A review. *Psychotherapy: Theory, Research and Practice,* 1972, *9,* 242–250.

Ayllon, T. Intensive treatment of psychotic behavior by stimulus satiation and food reinforcement. *Behaviour Research and Therapy,* 1963, *1,* 53–61.

Ayllon, T., & Azrin, N. J. *The token economy: A motivational system for therapy and rehabilitation.* New York: Appleton-Century-Crofts, 1968.

Bandura, A. *Principles of behavior modification.* New York: Holt, Rinehart and Winston, 1969.

Bandura, A. Self-efficacy: Toward a unifying theory of behavioral change. *Psychological Review,* 1977, *84,* 191–215.

Bandura, A., & Menlove, F. L. Factors determining vicarious extinction of avoidance behavior through symbolic modeling. *Journal of Personality and Social Psychology,* 1968, *8,* 99–108.

Bandura, A., Grusec, J., & Menlove, F. Vicarious extinction of avoidance behavior. *Journal of Personality and Social Psychology,* 1967, *5,* 16–23.

Bandura, A., Blanchard, E. B., & Ritter, B. The relative efficacy of desensitization and modeling approaches for inducing behavioral, affective, and attitudinal changes. *Journal of Personality and Social Psychology,* 1969, *13,* 173–199.

Baum, M. Extinction of an avoidance response following response prevention: Some parametric investigation. *Canadian Journal of Psychology,* 1969, *23,* 1–10.(a)

Baum, M. Extinction of an avoidance response motivated by intense fear: Social facilitation of the action of response prevention (flooding) in rats. *Behaviour Research and Therapy,* 1969, *7,* 57–62.(b)

Baum, M. Extinction of avoidance responding through response prevention (flooding). *Psychological Bulletin,* 1970, *74,* 276–284.

Beech, H. R. *Changing man's behaviour.* Baltimore, MD: Penguin Books, 1969.

Boulougouris, J. C., Marks, I. M., & Marset, P. Superiority of flooding (implosion) to desensitization for reducing pathological fear. *Behaviour Research and Therapy,* 1971, *9,* 7–16.

Breger, L., & McGaugh, J. L. Critique and reformulation of "Learning Theory" approaches to psychotherapy and neuroses. *Psychological Bulletin,* 1965, *63,* 338–358.

Browning, R. M., & Stover, D. O. *Behavior modification in child treatment.* Chicago: Aldine-Atherton, 1971.

Combs, M. L., & Slaby, D. A. Social skills training with children. In B. B. Lahey and A. E. Kazdin (Eds.), *Advances in clinical child psychology.* Vol 1. New York: Plenum, 1977.

Cooke, G. Evaluation of the efficacy of the components of reciprocal inhibition psychotherapy. *Journal of Abnormal Psychology,* 1968, *73,* 464–467.

Craighead, W. I., Kazdin, A. E., & Mahoney, M. J. (Eds.), *Behavior Modification. Principles, issues, and applications.* (2nd ed.). Boston: Houghton Mifflin, 1981.

Curran, J. P. An evaluation of a skills training program and a systematic desensitization program in reducing dating anxiety. *Behavior Research and Therapy,* 1975, *13,* 65–68.

Curran, J. P. Skills training as an approach to the treatment of heterosexual-social anxiety: A review. *Psychological Bulletin,* 1977, *84,* 140–157.

Dollard, J., & Miller, N. E. *Personality and psychotherapy.* New York: McGraw-Hill, 1950.

Ellis, A. Rational-Emotive therapy: Research data that supports the clinical and personality hypotheses of RET and other modes of cognitive-behavior therapy. *The Counseling Psychologist,* 1977, *7,* 2–42.

Feldman, M. P. Aversion therapy for sexual deviations: A critical review. *Psychological Bulletin,* 1966, *65,* 65–79.

Feldman, M. P., & MacCulloch, M. J. The application of anticipatory avoidance learning to the treatment of homosexuality. I. Theory, Technique and preliminary results. *Behaviour Research and Therapy,* 1965, *2,* 165–183.

Feldman, M. P., & MacCulloch, M. J. The management of a series of 43 homosexual patients treated by aversion therapy. *British Medical Journal,* 1967, *2,* 594–597.

Garfield, S. L. *Psychotherapy: An eclectic approach.* New York: Wiley, 1980.

Gelder, M. G., Marks, I. M., & Wolff, H. H. Desensitization and psychotherapy in the treatment of phobic states: A controlled inquiry. *British Journal of Psychiatry,* 1967, *113,* 53–73.

Gelder, M. G., Bancroft, J. H. J., Gath, D. H., Johnston, D. W., Mathews, A. M., & Shaw,

P. M. Specific and non-specific factors in behavior therapy. *The British Journal of Psychiatry,* 1973, *123,* 445–462.

Goldfried, M. R. Toward the delineation of therapeutic change principles. *American Psychologist,* 1980, *35,* 991–999.

Goldfried, M. R., & Davison, G. C. *Clinical behavior therapy.* New York: Holt, Rinehart & Winston, 1976.

Hersen, M., & Bellack, A. S. Treatment of chronic mental patients. In W. I. Craighead, A. E. Kazdin, and M. J. Mahoney (Eds.), *Behavior modification. Principles, issues and applications.* (2nd ed.). Boston: Houghton Mifflin, 1981.

Hodgson, R. J., & Rachman, S. An experimental investigation of the implosion technique. *Behaviour Research and Therapy,* 1970, *8,* 21–27.

Hogan, R. A., & Kirchner, J. H. Preliminary report of the extinction of learned fears via short-term implosive therapy. *Journal of Abnormal Psychology,* 1967, *72,* 106–109.

Hussain, M. Z. Desensitization and flooding (implosion) in treatment of phobias. *American Journal of Psychiatry,* 1971, *127,* 85–91.

Jones, M. C. The elimination of children's fears. *Journal of Experimental Psychology,* 1924, *7,* 383–390.

Kazdin, A. E. *The token economy: A review and evaluation.* New York: Plenum, 1977.

Kazdin, A. E. The application of operant techniques in treatment, rehabilitation, and education. In S. L. Garfield and A. E. Bergin (Eds.), *Handbook of psychotherapy and behavior change.* (2nd ed.). New York, 1978.

Kazdin, A. E., & Wilcoxon, L. A. Systematic desensitization and non-specific treatment effects: A methodological evaluation. *Psychological Bulletin,* 1976, *83,* 729–758.

Kazdin, A. E., & Wilson, G. T. *Evaluation of behavior therapy: Issues, evidence, and research evidence.* Cambridge, MA: Ballinger, 1978.

Kendall, P. C., & Hollon, S. D. *Cognitive-behavioral interventions. Theory, research, and procedures.* New York: Academic Press, 1979.

King, G. F., Armitage, S. G., & Tilton, J. R. A therapeutic approach to schizophrenics of extreme pathology: An operant-interpersonal method. *Journal of Abnormal and Social Psychology,* 1960, *61,* 276–286.

Klein, M. H., Dittman, A. T., Parloff, M. B., & Gill, M. M. Behavior therapy: Observations and reflections. *Journal of Consulting and Clinical Psychology,* 1969, *33,* 259–266.

Lang, P. J., & Melamed, B. G. Case report: Avoidance conditioning therapy of an infant with chronic ruminative vomiting. *Journal of Abnormal Psychology,* 1969, *74,* 1–8.

Lazarus, A. A. The elimination of children's phobias by deconditioning. In H. J. Eysenck (Ed.), *Behaviour therapy and neuroses.* New York: Pergamon Press, 1960.

Lazarus, A. A. The results of behavior therapy in 126 cases of severe neurosis. *Behaviour Research and Therapy,* 1963, *1,* 65–78.

Lazarus, A. A. *Behavior therapy and beyond.* New York: McGraw-Hill, 1971.

Ledwidge, B. Cognitive behavior modification: A step in the wrong direction? *Psychological Bulletin,* 1978, *85,* 353–375.

Ledwidge, B. Cognitive behavior modification or new ways to change minds: Reply to Mahoney and Kazdin. *Psychological Bulletin,* 1979, *86,* 1050–1053.

Leitenberg, H., Agras, W. S., Barlow, D. H., & Oliveau, D. C. Contribution of selective positive reinforcement and therapeutic instructions to systematic desensitization therapy. *Journal of Abnormal Psychology,* 1969, *74,* 113–118.

Levis, D. J. Implosive therapy: Part II. The subhuman analogue, the strategy, and the technique. In S. G. Armitage (Ed.), *Behavior modification techniques in the treatment of emotional disorders.* Battle Creek, MI: V. A. Publication, 1966, Pp. 22–37.

Lovaas, O. I. A behavior therapy approach to the treatment of childhood schizophrenia. In

J. P. Hill (Ed.), *Minnesota symposia on child psychology.* Vol. 1. Minneapolis: University of Minnesota Press, 1967.

Lovaas, O. I., & Bucher, B. D. (Eds.), *Perspectives in behavior modification with deviant children.* Englewood Cliffs, NJ: Prentice-Hall, 1974.

Lovaas, O. I., Berberich, J. P., Perloff, B. F., & Schaeffer, B. Acquisition of imitative speech by schizophrenic children. *Science,* 1966, *151,* 705–707.

Lovaas, O. I., Freitag, L., Nelson, K., & Whalen, C. The establishment of imitation and its use for the development of complex behavior in schizophrenic children. *Behaviour Research and Therapy,* 1967, *5,* 171–181.

Lovaas, O. I., Kaegel, R., Simmons, J. A., & Long, J. S. Some generalizations and follow-up measures on autistic children in behavior therapy. *Journal of Applied Behavior Analysis,* 1973, *6,* 131–166.

Mahoney, M. J., & Arnkoff, D. B. Cognitive and self-control therapies. In S. L. Garfield and A. E. Bergin (Eds.), *Handbook of psychotherapy and behavior change. 2nd Edition.* New York: Wiley, 1978.

Mahoney, M. J., & Kazdin, A. E. Cognitive behavior modification: Misconceptions and premature evacuation. *Psychological Bulletin,* 1979, *86,* 1044–1049.

Marcia, J. E., Rubin, B. M., & Efran, J. S. Systematic desensitization: Expectancy change or counterconditioning? *Journal of Abnormal Psychology,* 1969, *74,* 382–387.

Marks, I. Behavioral psychotherapy of adult neurosis. In S. L. Garfield and A. E. Bergin (Eds.), *Handbook of psychotherapy and behavior change.* (2nd ed.). New York: Wiley, 1978.

Marks, I., Gelder, M., & Bancroft, J. Sexual deviants two years after electric aversion. *British Journal of Psychiatry,* 1970, *117,* 173–185.

Marmor, J., & Woods, S. M. (Eds.), *The interface between the psychodynamic and behavioral therapies.* New York: Plenum, 1980.

Mathews, A. M., Johnston, D. W., Shaw, P. M., & Gelder, M. G. Process variables and the prediction of outcome in behavior therapy. *British Journal of Psychiatry,* 1974, *125,* 256–264.

Meichenbaum, D. *Cognitive-behavior modification: An integrative approach.* New York: Plenum Press, 1977.

Morganstern, K. P. Implosive therapy and flooding procedures: A critical review. *Psychological Bulletin,* 1973, *79,* 318–334.

Mowrer, O. H., & Mowrer, W. Enuresis: A method for its study and treatment. *American Journal of Orthopsychiatry,* 1938, *8,* 436–459.

Nolan, J. D., Mattis, P. R., & Holliday, W. C. Long-term effects of behavior therapy: A 12-month follow-up. *Journal of Abnormal Psychology,* 1970, *76,* 88–92.

Oliveau, D. C., Agras, W. S., Leitenberg, H., Moore, R. C., & Wright, D. E. Systematic desensitization, therapeutically oriented instructions and selective positive reinforcement. *Behaviour Research and Therapy,* 1969, *7,* 27–33.

Patterson, G. R. Behavioral intervention procedures in the classroom and in the home. In A. E. Bergin and S. L. Garfield (Eds.), *Handbook of psychotherapy and behavior change: An empirical analysis.* New York: Wiley, 1971.

Patterson, G. R. Intervention for boys with conduct problems: Multiple settings, treatment, and criteria. *Journal of Consulting and Clinical Psychology,* 1974, *42,* 471–481.

Paul, G. L. *Insight versus desensitization in psychotherapy.* Stanford, CA: Stanford University Press, 1966.

Paul, G. L. Insight versus desensitization in psychotherapy two years after termination. *Journal of Consulting Psychology,* 1967, *31,* 333–348.

Paul, G. L., & Lentz, R. J. *Psychosocial treatment of chronic mental patients: Milieu vs. social-learning programs.* Cambridge, MA: Harvard University Press, 1977.

Phillips, E. L., Phillips, E. A., Fixsen, D. L., & Wolf, M. M. Achievement Place: Modification of the behaviors of pre-delinquent boys within a token economy. *Journal of Applied Behavior Analysis,* 1971, *4,* 45–59.

Raymond, M. J. Case of fetishism treated by aversion therapy. In H. J. Eysenck (Ed.), *Behaviour therapy and the neuroses.* New York: Pergamon Press, 1960.

Rosenthal, T., & Bandura, A. Psychological modeling: Theory and practice. In S. L. Garfield and A. E. Bergin (Eds.), *Handbook of psychotherapy and behavior change.* (2nd ed.). New York: Wiley, 1978.

Ross, A. O. Behavior therapy with children. In S. L. Garfield and A. E. Bergin (Eds.), *Handbook of psychotherapy and behavior change.* (2nd ed.). New York: Wiley, 1978.

Salter, A. *Conditioned reflex therapy.* New York: Farrar, Straus, 1949.

Skinner, B. F. Why I am not a cognitive psychologist. *Behaviorism,* 1977, *5,* 1–10.

Sloane, R. B., Staples, F. R., Cristol, A. H., Yorkston, N. J., & Whipple, K. *Psychotherapy versus behavior therapy.* Cambridge, MA: Harvard University Press, 1975.

Smith, M. L., Glass, G. V., & Miller, T. I. *The benefits of psychotherapy.* Baltimore, MD: The Johns Hopkins University Press., 1980.

Stampfl, T. G. Implosive therapy: The theory. In S. G. Armitage (Ed.), *Behavior modification techniques in the treatment of emotional disorders.* Battle Creek, MI: Veterans Administration Publication, 1967.

Stampfl, T. G., & Levis, D. J. Essentials of implosive therapy: A learning-theory-based psychodynamic behavioral therapy. *Journal of Abnormal Psychology,* 1967, *72,* 496–503.

Watson, J. B., & Rayner, R. Conditioned emotional reactions. *Journal of Experimental Psychology,* 1920, *3,* 1–14.

Wilkins, W. Desensitization: Social and cognitive factors underlying Wolpe's procedure. *Psychological Bulletin,* 1971, *76,* 311–317.

Wolpe, J. *Psychotherapy by reciprocal inhibition.* Stanford, CA: Stanford University Press, 1958.

Wolpe, J. The comparative clinical status of conditioning therapies and psychoanalysis. In J. Wolpe, A. Salter, and L. J. Reyna (Eds.), *The conditioning therapies.* New York: Holt, Rinehart and Winston, 1964.

Wolpe, J. *The practice of behavior therapy.* New York: Pergamon Press, 1969.

Wolpe, J. Behavior therapy and its malcontents—II. Multimodal eclecticism, cognitive exclusivisms and "exposure" empiricism *Journal of Behavior Therapy and Experimental Psychiatry,* 1976, *7,* 109–116.

Wolpe, J., & Lazarus, A. A. Behavior therapy techniques. Oxford: Pergamon Press, 1966.

Wolpin, M., & Raines, J. Visual imagery, expected roles and extinction as possible factors in reducing fear and avoidance behavior. *Behaviour Research and Therapy,* 1966, *4,* 25–37.

Yates, A. J. *Theory and practice in behavior therapy.* New York: Wiley, 1975.

Chapter
Twelve

Group
Psychotherapy

In the preceding chapters we have reviewed some of the important concepts and views in psychotherapy. These have evolved primarily from work with individual adult patients. Psychotherapy, however, has not been limited solely to such situations. In this chapter, therapeutic and related procedures with groups will be discussed.

INTRODUCTION

Psychotherapy with groups has gradually evolved as a means of treatment since shortly after the beginning of the twentieth century (Thomas, 1943). Part of this development was related to the simple matter of expedience. Since there were large numbers of patients who conceivably might be helped by psychotherapy, and since there were relatively few therapists available, a group procedure, by which one therapist was able to treat a number of patients at the same time was considered a worthwhile approach. During World War II, group psychotherapy was given much official support in the armed services for this reason. Although it is unquestionably true that in a group setting, one therapist can treat a dozen patients instead of only a single patient, this has not been considered the only basis for recommending the use of group psychotherapy. Group therapy has evolved as a specific form of psychotherapy in its own right, and in recent years a variety of procedures have achieved relative popularity.

344

Many of the views discussed in the preceding chapter with reference to individual therapy apply also to group therapy, but group therapy, too, has its own theories and techniques as well. There is analytic group therapy, which utilizes a psychoanalytic point of view; there is group therapy along nondirective lines, rational-emotive groups, existential groups, gestalt groups, as well as many others (Gazda, 1975; Yalom, 1975). Some of the research on group dynamics has also been applied to clinical work with groups.

One of the first attempts at some form of group psychotherapy is credited to Dr. Joseph H. Pratt (1907), who established a group method of treating patients with tuberculosis in 1905. The type of psychotherapy utilized by Pratt and several others who followed him has sometimes been called a repressive-inspirational kind of psychotherapy (Thomas, 1943). In this approach, no real attempt was made to analyze or discuss the dynamic factors surrounding the individual's difficulties. There was, however, a recognition of the emotional support that the patient receives from the therapist and also from the other members of the group who have similar symptoms or problems. Some of the material discussed was of a frankly inspirational nature; for example, patients were told to dispel negative feelings by thinking of something pleasant. (It is interesting to note that a somewhat comparable procedure has also been used more recently by cognitive and behavioral therapists.) Frequently, literature or poetry of an "uplifting" sort was read to the group. Another technique was to have successful or "star" members of the group relate their own experiences to the group. Such patients were given special recognition in terms of seating arrangements and were also allowed to sit on the platform with the physician. The patients were encouraged to talk to one another, exchange experiences, and attempt to help each other. Without question, success in this setting depended upon such mechanisms as suggestion, desire for approval from the physician, the realization that others have similar problems, and the social support received from the group.

This type of group therapy or class method was utilized by others with a variety of medical patients, including cases of peptic ulcer, essential hypertension, diabetes, and other disorders (Slavson, 1950; Thomas, 1943). In many ways, these groups of medical patients signified an early recognition of the importance of psychological factors in somatic illness, an emphasis which has emerged again recently in what has been termed behavioral medicine. While this was a positive contribution in terms of emphasizing the totality of the patient as a person, the emphasis on the group meetings was somewhat adjunctive to the medical treatment. In many instances, for example, the patients not only received medical care, but also discussed their treatment in the group meetings. The results of these group meetings were judged to be highly satisfactory, but it is difficult to make an adequate appraisal of their specific effectiveness. In several important respects, however, the techniques utilized resembled those of suggestion and persuasion, as well as some of the elements of a revival meeting, rather than the more sophisticated procedures emphasized in present day group approaches.

An interesting analysis of the possible dynamic factors operating in these earlier attempts at group meetings was given by Slavson (1950):

> As we examine the fairly widespread use of "the class method," we see clearly that the basic dynamics operating in these groups are suggestion, temporary ego-strengthening, rivalry, and the desire to please the father (which is a modified form of transference). Each feels that if someone else can accomplish something—in this case, improvement— so can he. He is further placed in rivalry with those of the patients who "make the grade." Those who are moved up to the front benches and finally accepted in the inner (family) circle on the platform next to the therapist (father) are the envy of the others, who are thus motivated to attain a similar status (sibling rivalry). Here also submission to the father for the bounty (affection) he bestows is ever present. If one improves (pleases the father), he is accepted and loved by the father (doctor) (Slavson, 1950, p. 5).

Beginning in the 1930's some innovations in group therapy were introduced which bear a close relationship to current developments in this area. Thereafter, many different types of group therapy were introduced.

VARIETIES OF GROUP THERAPY

PSYCHOANALYTIC GROUP PSYCHOTHERAPY

Further developments in group therapy along psychoanalytic lines were reported by Wender (1940) and Schilder (1939, 1951). Wender's therapy was developed in a private institution and was seen as related to the total activities of the hospital. According to Wender, group psychotherapy was a technique of treatment in which the group interaction allows for the release of unconscious emotional difficulties.

> The premise of group psychotherapy is that the human individual is a "group animal," seeking a satisfying niche in his social setting: that he is a social product, whose inhibitions and repressions are motivated by the mores of the group; that difficulties in adjustment and failure to express his emotional troubles are the result of his inability to face the group and to find his place in it. He must repress his thinking and adapt to the demands of a complex group, and his failure to achieve this adaptation produces a neurosis or a psychosis. Place this individual who has failed in the more complex setting into a small group which is friendly to him and which is composed of others suffering from allied disturbances, and he will become enabled—when he learns to understand the problems of the others— to associate himself with them, to release his aggressive tendencies, his hates, his loves,

and his wishes, without accompanying sense of guilt. By working out his difficulties and achieving adjustment in the small group, he becomes able to face the large group (the world) and to handle his emotional problems, social or other, on a normal basis (Wender, 1940, p. 708).

Although Wender's theoretical orientation was psychoanalysis, he believed a group therapy approach necessitated a more active role for the therapist. The transference relationship was also viewed as different in the group situation. The therapist not only has relationships to all the patients, but there are transference relationships between the group members. The main factors in the group psychotherapy process were noted by Wender as being: (1) Intellectualization, or insight; (2) patient to patient transference; (3) catharsis; and (4) group interaction, which includes such phenomena as identification in the group and sharing of common experiences. In this approach, group lectures were given once or twice weekly. Each of the patients was evaluated and received several individual interviews prior to his entrance in the group. This material was then modified or disguised and used as an illustrative case for discussion in the group. The group discussion was then seen as leading to an understanding of the problem and to a sense of kinship among the members. The objective of the sessions was to give the individual some understanding of personality dynamics and adjustment mechanisms. "The patients are urged to be honest with themselves and to delve into their own unconscious thinking after the various mechanisms have been discussed" (Wender, 1940, p. 714).

Schilder's (1939, 1951) approach to group psychotherapy followed much more the traditional psychoanalytic pattern. He worked with small groups of four to six patients, and the method of free association was utilized extensively. In contrast to some of the other approaches, there was no special list of topics to be discussed in a prescribed order or any formal lectures to be presented to the group. Group interviews instead developed from the patient's associations and problems. At a later stage, patients were asked to write an autobiography dealing primarily with family relations and sexual development. In Schilder's approach, the patients seen in the group were also seen regularly in individual sessions.

Other group therapy procedures utilizing a psychoanalytic frame of reference were developed by Slavson (1947a, 1950, 1964, 1970), Ackerman (1947), Wolf (1975), and others. Slavson, who was one of the most active contributors to the field of group psychotherapy described different forms of group therapy for different kinds of clinical populations. Some were for preschool children, another for older children, and still other types were for use with adolescents and adults. Although all the group procedures were based on a similar theoretical orientation, the techniques varied in significant ways. The type designated as "interview group therapy," for use with adolescents and adults, most nearly approximates some of the other group procedures already mentioned. The group therapy for children utilized play and various kinds of activities. Another type of therapy introduced by Slavson and termed "activity group therapy" will be discussed later.

Using a psychoanalytic frame of reference, Slavson developed specific applications to group therapy and also utilized it for purposes of selecting members who would respond to group therapy. Probably more than anyone else, Slavson emphasized the importance of the selection of group members. He believed that the members of the group should have similar or common nuclear problems. Clinical diagnosis and symptomatology are not considered adequate for selecting group members. Additional criteria included such matters as interest in treatment, intelligence, and the intensity of the individual disturbance. Slavson (1964) specified four general criteria for selection: capacity for minimal primary relations; degree of sexual disturbance; minimal ego strength; and minimal superego development. He also listed several categories of patients with positive prognosis for his type of therapy, as well as several categories with negative prognosis. Examples of the former are children with behavior disorders, character disorders, adolescents, and mild psychoneurotics. On the other hand, he felt that most severe or fully developed neurotic adults, such as anxiety neurotics, obsessive compulsives, and the like, as well as psychopathic personalities, have very poor prognoses.

Slavson held some views that disagreed somewhat with those of others. One such view was that no real group formation develops in group therapy. "In fact, the greatest single therapeutic value of such groups is the very absence of group formation. There is compresence, interaction, interstimulation, emotional infection, and intensification, and other dynamics that always occur when people are in an intimate relation" (Slavson, 1947a, p. 27). By this, Slavson meant that the group in therapy is not a fixed one in terms of organization and roles for each of the members, as is true with many groups. The therapy group, rather, is a flexible one in which the patient is permitted to act out freely, to express his feelings, and to react in whatever way he desires. This does not mean, however, that the therapy group does not afford specific therapeutic advantages. The chief value of the group is that it permits the "acting out of instinctual drives," which is accelerated by the stimulating effect of the other members. According to Slavson, the patients reveal their problems more easily and therapy is speeded up. The group atmosphere is an accepting one and the individual is correspondingly freer to act. "It is always the individual, and not the group as such, that remains the center of the therapist's attention. The group is merely a means for activating individuals and supplying the kind of experience that helps modify feelings and attitudes" (Slavson, 1947a, p. 28).

Contrary to the position of Slavson, Ackerman (1947) reported some success in an analytic group therapy with psychoneurotic adults. In addition to presenting material from such sessions, he provided a clear appraisal of the specific values of group psychotherapy as compared with individual analysis. From his point of view, conventional analysis has difficulty in the areas of social reality and interpersonal values. In the group situation, however, tangible social reality is ever present in the form of ideas, values, and interpersonal patterns of the group. Inasmuch as the patient's contact with this social reality is immediate and tangible, the "therapeutic process moves back and forth between this social reality and the emotional life of each individual patient" (Ackerman, 1947, p. 153). In this regard it is mentioned that frequently patients who have had a successful psychoanalysis have some difficulty in translating their analytic insights into constructive forms of social reaction. Ackerman believes that greater support for this type of development is provided in the group situation and that group therapy could be a valuable supplement to psychoanalytic treatment.

Ackerman also emphasizes the fact that the therapist plays an active role in group therapy and that there is greater opportunity for the patient's "acting out" than is offered in individual therapy. His comparison of group therapy and individual therapy is summed up in the following statement.

> Group psychotherapy, operating on an interpersonal level different from that in psychoanalysis, yet gains much from applying psychoanalytic insight to the dynamics of group living. On the whole, Group Therapy is a more real experience than is individual therapy. It is less bound to the irrationalities of the unconscious and is weighted on the side of social reality. Its greatest effectiveness seems to be in the area of reintegration of ego-adaptive patterns with resulting improvement of social functioning (Ackerman, 1947, pp. 154–155).

Although a number of psychoanalytically oriented therapists may designate their therapy as psychoanalytic, this does not mean that they conduct their therapy in exactly the same way or emphasize the same aspects of psychoanalysis. For example, Wolf (1975) appears to emphasize more traditional features of psychoanalysis in his work than do other psychoanalytic group therapists.

> Psychoanalysis in groups is the use of analytic means—free association, the analysis of dreams and fantasies and the working through of resistance and transference—in the treatment of eight to ten patients in a group setting. Psychoanalysis in groups entails an understanding of unconscious processes and motivation. It seeks out the historical basis for current behavior in order to resolve its persistence in the present. It requires the working out and working through of repetitive and compulsive psychopathologic maneuvers. Psychoanalysis in groups pursues the latent as well as the manifest in patient interaction and

function. The search for unconscious processes is achieved by the promotion of the freedom
to express any thought, fantasy or feeling. The pursuit of unconscious motives moves patients
away from attending only to the present and toward an understanding of intrapsychic processes, historical determinants and the working through of transference distortions. (Wolf,
1975, pp. 102–103).

Rosenbaum (1976), another psychoanalytic therapist, states that the group
therapy he practices "is regressive and reconstructive and is based on psychoanalysis" (p. 48). He states that such group therapy offers the client "an
opportunity to explore his uniqueness" (p. 49). However, afterward, the individual "must decide how to use his uniqueness in the struggles of contemporary life" (p. 49). One may question whether this is a satisfactory outcome
since it is doubtful that an individual seeks therapy mainly to "explore his
uniqueness."

DIDACTIC GROUP THERAPY

Another type of group therapy has sometimes been referred to as "didactic
or pedagogical group psychotherapy," (Klapman, 1946, 1947) and consists
of a series of lectures on specific topics. In addition, a textbook can be used
both for study by the patients and for reading and discussion in group sessions.
Representative topics for the lectures and meetings include "the nature of
mental illness, relationship of society to mental patients, attitudes toward
mental illness, mental mechanisms, conflicts, how we think, and so on." Other
devices such as the reading of case histories and discussion of autobiographies
are also used. When controversial subjects come up in the therapy sessions,
they can be handled through patient symposia and debates.

In addition to the more formal lectures there is opportunity for questions
and discussions from the participants. The therapist acts as the leader of
the discussions and may amplify, interpret, or correct statements made by
the group members. This type of therapy has been used with psychotic patients
in institutions and also with other patients in private practice.

Like others, Klapman believes there is a reciprocal or complementary relationship between individual and group psychotherapy for adults. Patients
with whom positive transference might be difficult in individual therapy may
be able to overcome resistances more quickly after group experience. It is a
fairly common experience that many patients voluntarily approach the group
therapist after a few sessions and ask for some form of personal interview.
Klapman also feels that "it is quite probable that group treatment is more
effective in certain areas that have remained relatively untouched by individual
treatment. It seems reasonable that correction of deficiencies in social attitudes

is best accomplished in a social setting. In any case, the rapidity with which a positive working relationship is formed with the patient in group psychotherapy, which is often carried over to individual interviews, indicates its strong catalytic action" (Klapman, 1947, pp. 244-245). He is frank to admit, however, that truly objective appraisals of the effectiveness of the therapy are still lacking.

ACTIVITY GROUP THERAPY

This therapy was developed by Slavson and his colleagues at the Jewish Board of Guardians in New York City, and was considered a group treatment for certain types of children (Slavson, 1947b, 1950; Slavson and Schiffer, 1975). In activity group therapy, the therapist assumes a warm and permissive role. Various kinds of activities are provided for the individual participants, and the therapist allows the children free activity, but is available for help and materials. The members of the group have free access to various art and craft materials and tools. At the end of the session a treat consisting of candy, fruit, and milk is usually provided. The therapist participates with the children in this activity. Occasionally, also, the group goes on tours or special visits. The unique features are the permissive atmosphere and the unobtrusive role of the therapist.

It is believed that activity group therapy is best suited to children with behavior problems and defects in character development. Although the groups need to be carefully selected, the basis for selection differs from that utilized by Slavson in interview group therapy. In the activity group, an attempt is made to select individuals who complement each other, rather than having all with the same clinical syndrome. "Group balance" is the aim; thus, withdrawn and aggressive patients can be included together since it is believed they can actually help one another. The group members are usually fairly similar in age, although individual factors enter into consideration. A very immature child may be placed with group members somewhat younger than he is. No interpretations are offered by the therapist. "The purpose of these groups is to give substitute satisfactions through the free acting out of impulses, gratifying experiences, recognition of achievement, and unconditional love and acceptance from an adult" (Slavson, 1947a, p. 32). It is asserted that through these activities the child is free to grow at his own pace and overcome basic character difficulties. Slavson and his co-workers claimed good results with this type of therapy, but others have stated that it "cannot treat children who lack a minimal capacity to relate themselves to people or to being themselves under control in favorable circumstances" (Hammer and Kaplan, 1967, p. 27).

PSYCHODRAMA

Another distinctive type of group therapy was developed by Moreno (1946). In this approach, patients take part in a dramatic production. Various scenes taken from past life or situations to be encountered in the future are set up and patients are called upon to enact specific roles. In addition, other patients referred to as "auxiliary egos," also interact with the patient, called the protagonist, who is going to play the main role in the dramatic production. The players are thus encouraged to act out behaviorally their own role in relation to important problem areas. In addition, the individual may be asked to enact the role of an important figure in his own life and thus gain some understanding of the reactions of others to him. Other patients form an audience and also participate in the session.

The setting for psychodrama is fairly specific. In most instances, a special stage with three different levels is utilized. The director of the drama is usually the therapist. More specific theoretical and dynamic aspects of psychodrama have been set forth by Moreno (1946; Moreno and Elefthery, 1975), but a number of therapists make use of role-playing and related procedures without recourse to Moreno's views. The main values apparently stem from the fact that the participants actually engage in a dramatic sequence and thus specifically act out and experience some of their problems. The principles of spontaneity and catharsis are emphasized, as well as the fact that the dramatic situations approximate real-life situations. In addition, a discussion may follow the actual dramatic incident.

Moreno utilized this approach with many different kinds of groups and felt that the most positive results were obtained with normal groups. He also believed that the group should be made up of individuals with diverse pathologies. Earlier, he stated that hospital settings were artificial, and the results in such settings were bound to be limited. More recently, a more positive view toward working with hospitalized patients has been expressed (Moreno and Elefthery, 1975). Finally, it can be noted that Moreno's emphasis on action has influenced several more recent approaches such as Gestalt groups and transactional analysis.

GROUP-CENTERED THERAPY

Although the theoretical orientation of this group therapy is that of client-centered therapy, there are some differences between the individual and group approaches (Hobbs, 1951). One important difference "lies in the fact that

the group situation brings into focus the adequacy of interpersonal relationships and provides an immediate opportunity for discovering new and more
satisfying ways of relating to people" (Hobbs, 1951, p. 289). An opportunity
is afforded for the individual to come into closer contact with others and
gradually to become aware of those aspects of self which are important in
his relations with others. In some ways, too, the group setting is similar to
the earlier setting in which the individual's personality has developed. The
individual can learn what it means to give and receive emotional support
and understanding in a new and more mature way. In the group, the individual
also may give help to others at the same time that he receives help, and
this may be a therapeutic experience in itself. Mentioned also is the fact
that some people find it easier to talk and express themselves in the group
situation than in a one-to-one relationship. The final point of difference relates
to the matter of values. It is a cardinal point in client-centered therapy that
the therapist does not impose his own set of values on the client. This is
also true in group-centered therapy but here the client is exposed to the
many value systems expressed by the group members. He is, however, free
to appraise this material and still make the final choice for himself.

According to Hobbs (1951), optimum groups consist of about six members
and the therapist. This may vary slightly in either direction, but too large a
number might leave a number of people on the periphery of the group interac-
tive process. As a rule, groups have met about twice a week and the selective
criteria have been broad. One of the main criteria is whether or not the
individual chooses to join a group by herself. However, extremely hostile or
aggressive persons interfere with the atmosphere of acceptance and freedom
from threat which the group-centered therapist tries to create. Therefore, such
individuals usually would not be included in a group.

From what we have already noted about client-centered therapy, it should
be clear that the therapist in this group therapy does not have prepared
material for discussion by the group. The group is free to bring forth and
discuss any problems of significance to them. The therapist also does not
actively interpret material, as in some of the other group therapies. His main
activities are acceptance of the feelings of the group members, reflection of
feelings, clarification of the attitudes and feelings presented in the group,
and restatement of content. The latter has been found to be particularly effective in group therapy (Hobbs, 1951).

The fact that the group members also have a therapeutic role and influence
in relation to other members has been noted. This is considered a unique
aspect of group therapy. When the members participate in a manner that is
judged to be therapeutically positive, the therapist allows the activity to continue. But, if group members block feelings which are about to be expressed
or in any way produce a threat to the free expression of feelings, the therapist

intercedes in the process. He is thus not simply a passive spectator. The recent emphasis continues to be on the growth potential of the client in a caring environment and on the personal qualities of the therapist (Meador, 1975).

Following the patterns established by client-centered therapy, practitioners of group-centered therapy have a research orientation often lacking in other group therapists. Several studies have been carried out relating to the process and outcomes of this form of group therapy, and, as we noted previously, the importance of empathy, genuineness, and warmth to psychotherapy process and outcome has been emphasized (Truax and Carkhuff, 1967).

OTHER FORMS OF GROUP THERAPY

In addition to the variations in group psychotherapy already mentioned, there have been other modifications and adaptations of group procedures in various settings. During World War II, the armed forces utilized group therapy in many different ways in diverse military situations. Group psychotherapy of a didactic sort was used rather widely. Frequently a series of lectures was given on selected topics to a large group of patients. After each lecture, the group was divided into several smaller groups, each with a leader. The lecture was used as a takeoff for free discussion in the smaller groups. In other settings a questions box was provided for anonymous questions. The therapist in the group meeting attempted to answer the questions and stimulate discussion about them.

Partly as a result of the use of group psychotherapy in military hospitals and centers, there has been a steady expansion of group therapy in civilian hospitals since World War II. This has been evident in veterans and state hospitals where thousands of psychotic patients have been in need of treatment. As a result, group therapy procedures have been utilized with acutely disturbed and chronic psychotic patients (Feifel and Schwartz, 1953; McCann and Almada, 1950; Powdermaker and Frank, 1953). Although the research results of the use of group therapy with such patients raises considerable doubts about its efficacy (Parloff and Dies, 1977), there is also a desire to do something for these patients. Thus, various therapy programs are carried out with varied explanations provided in support of them.

To illustrate what has been mentioned, some notes from a group psychotherapy session conducted in a psychiatric hospital may offer a glimpse of what can occur in such a session. The group therapy employed was essentially eclectic in nature and attempted to provide a setting for selected patients to discuss their problems, explore some aspects of their personality, and extend their social relationships. The group was composed of six patients diagnosed as psychotic, but who had improved enough to be placed on open wards, that is, they could come and go as they pleased on the hospital grounds. The notes are from the third meeting of the group. The discussion revolved around the hospital and the patients' attitudes toward many aspects of the institution.

During this session there was a great deal of discussion by the patients with much of it centering around the hospital. Jones brought up his fears about "going nuts" when he had been placed on a locked ward in another institution. He was very fearful about his behaving like the other patients who were there, e.g., some of them wouldn't talk to him, some acted crazy, etc. He was very much disturbed about this at the time and didn't know what to do. He sometimes experiences similar feelings on the ward here. Various patients tell him things and he doesn't know whom to believe. One patient states that he is a guinea pig, while another says that he was railroaded here. At this point Brown broke in to state, "You know you don't believe all that stuff." However, there was some agreement among the patients about their concern over the behavior of other patients and their fear of being sent to the disturbed ward. Jones is very much afraid of the disturbed ward although he has never been there. His own concern about himself is reflected in his fear that he will some day be sent there. Black, who is anxious to go home, wanted to know why certain disturbed patients were able to leave the hospital ahead of him. When he was on 9 (the disturbed ward), "one guy bumped his head against the wall and now he is out of the hospital." One of the other patients remarked facetiously that perhaps if he bumped his head he would get to leave.

A discussion followed this in which the therapist emphasized the individual nature of each case. It was pointed out that some patients might be retained longer in the hospital if the staff felt that they could be helped further. Brown then expressed some of his fears when he was first hospitalized. There was some discussion and expression of feeling relative to the patients' being locked up upon their admittance to the hospital. The therapist explained why they had to be evaluated before being assigned to a different ward or given ground privileges. Green then recounted some of his experiences. He stated that he came here voluntarily and was asked just a few questions upon arrival. One question was, "Would you try to harm yourself?" He said, he thought about it for a while because the thought had never occurred to him and then he said, "no." However, he was placed on the disturbed ward for two days, apparently for observation, and felt that being there had had a bad effect on him. He also complained about the practice of sending patients to the disturbed ward for any minor misconduct and stated that if the doctor would talk to such a patient a little bit to find out why he was reacting in that particular way, perhaps he wouldn't have to send him to Ward 9.

All of the patients felt that if more things were explained to them when they were in the hospital, it would be better, e.g., why they are transferred to a certain ward, etc. The therapist allowed the patients to ventilate their feelings on this matter and then added that perhaps the hospital staff were overly cautious in safeguarding the patients' welfare, although more explanation could be given to the patient. There followed a discussion about the different kinds of problems revealed by the patients and the variations in patient behavior. It was pointed out that as they improved they might naturally see more differences between themselves and others who were not as well. Jones's fears were discussed in relation to his own insecurities and some of his personal characteristics. Both Brown and Smith gave

comments of a supportive nature. Smith, in a somewhat satisfied way, told Jones that he
had to develop confidence in himself. Shortly afterward, the time was up and the session
was closed.

Numerous types of group therapy programs were thus instituted in hospital
settings since there were few other available therapies for patients and even
those that were in use had limited success. The psychotherapy groups were
viewed as adjunctive therapies along with other procedures such as recreational therapy and occupational therapy. Even if the various therapies did
not have pronounced effects, it was considered desirable to have patients
involved in activities which required purpose and social interaction. Left to
themselves, a number of patients would become isolated and inactive, with
the possibility of further deterioration or impairment. In some instances, pa-
tient-staff councils were set up as a means of keeping patients involved in
decisions affecting their hospital life. One form of group therapy, Round-
Table psychotherapy, was instituted in a state hospital whereby patients were
encouraged to discuss their problems and receive help from each other
(McCann and Almada, 1950). The members of the round-table could also
recommend the transfer of patients and even release from the hospital. Although positive results were reported for this program, it seems to have
had little additional evaluation or impact.

Even from our brief presentation of developments in group therapy, it
should be clear that a variety of types of group psychotherapy were developed
for use with different categories of problem behavior. However, in the 1960's,
other developments appeared which, in some instances, were quite radically
different from most of the older ones and groups of one sort or another
reached a peak of popularity. Let us next turn to some of these developments.

RECENT DEVELOPMENTS

In the past, the various forms of therapeutic group activities have been
described primarily as group psychotherapy and the populations to be served
were viewed mainly as disturbed individuals with problems, whether they
were referred to as clients or patients. The "new" groups, on the other hand,
have dealt with individuals who have not been formally described as disturbed,
and the objectives of the group procedures, while perhaps overlapping the
objectives of the more traditional group therapy, have been somewhat different
(Yalom, 1975). Because this movement has attained such popularity, it is
worth discussing.

The sources of the current group movement appear to be diverse. The expansion of group therapy in the post World War II years has been only one of the possible influences on this movement. Other potential contributing factors appear to be related to certain changes in values which have affected some segments of our society. Such philosophical or value orientations as openness, the awareness and expression of feelings, relating to others, and personal growth have been the kinds of emphases that have guided these developments in the small-group field. Of importance historically are group procedures such as sensitivity training, human relations groups, and leadership training—activities designed for essentially normal people to increase their personal effectiveness and interactions with others, and which were essentially outside the clinical field. Somehow, these activities have merged and over-lapped with other developments and with some of the more traditional group therapeutic activities, with the result that diverse groups of leaders and partici-pants have been involved in a variety of group interactions bearing novel labels. One commentator on this development expressed it this way: "An ill-defined set of techniques has been broadly applied to groups of 'normals,' patients, and parapatients by leaders who are 'normals,' professionals, and paraprofessionals" (Parloff, 1970, p. 267). He went on to say that, "While there is little agreement regarding the definition or characteristics of groups variously labeled as personal growth, human relations, sensory awareness, sensitivity training, self-awareness, leadership training, love-ins, psychological karate, and so on, it is generally agreed that they represent a potent force for great benefit or great mischief" (Parloff, 1970, p. 267).

Because the various encounter and sensitivity groups at present may include both "patients" and "normals" and are conducted by professional psychothera-pists as well as nonprofessionals, it is sometimes difficult to distinguish clearly the differences between such groups and therapy groups. Theoretically, the various nontherapy groups are aimed at normal people, and the objectives include increased self-awareness, the expression and release of feeling, per-sonal growth, the attainment of intense emotional or peak experiences, in-creased authenticity, openness, joy, and self-realization (Parloff, 1970). Clearly, some of these objectives overlap with some of those that might be sought by means of psychotherapy. Mintz (1971), for example, is a psychologist and analyst who conducts both individual therapy and marathon groups. Furthermore, a large number of the participants in her marathon groups are individuals who have had personal psychotherapy or are currently in therapy. It seems clear from this information as well as the description of the clients in her groups that many of them would not ordinarily be viewed as nonpatients. Furthermore, the use of psychoanalytic theory and the attempts at the recall or reliving of past traumatic experiences also have their counter-parts in group psychotherapy. Thus, it is not always easy to separate clearly the new group movement from the earlier attempts at group therapy. Nevertheless, there appears to be a greater emphasis on openness, body contact, sensory awareness, emotional expression, and the use of structured situations or "games" than is true in most forms of therapy.

Encounter and sensitivity groups are believed to differ in other respects also from some of the more typical group psychotherapies. They generally last for a fixed and specified time, generally several hours a day for several days. The emphasis is usually on the here and now, with a focus on the dynamics of the group or the style and pattern of group interactions. Traditionally, the T-groups of the National Training Laboratories at Bethel, Maine, and the Group Relations Conferences of the Tavistock Clinic in London have focussed on the group process. Furthermore, these groups have espoused an educational rather than a therapeutic function (Lubin and Eddy, 1970; Rioch, 1970). But, as Parloff (1970) has pointed out, the more recent groups of this type have been "primarily concerned with the behavior, feelings, fantasies, and motivations of the individual" (p. 270). This appears to be particularly true of the marathon group, one form of encounter group. The marathon group, which runs continuously, except for time devoted to sleep, is a particularly intensive form of group encounter that lasts usually about 24 hours. To accommodate normally employed participants, a typical group may begin on a Friday evening or a Saturday afternoon and terminate on Sunday afternoon or evening. Because marathon groups exemplify many of the features of encounter groups and are a particularly intense form of group interaction, let us proceed to a brief description of some of the characteristics of such groups, keeping in mind that there is no standard format for them.

As mentioned, a marathon group meets for a specified period of time, usually a weekend, and thus may be considered a form of time-limited therapy. The number of participants usually consists of eight to twelve members, although it may vary depending on the predilections of the leader and whether or not a co-leader is used (Mintz, 1971; Rachman, 1969–70). The physical setting may also vary from an office to a specially selected retreat with a swimming pool. Some specify an informal living room setting, but even in the office situation, pillows, mattresses, and couches will be provided together with snacks and nonalcoholic beverages. To a large extent the groups are self-selected, although some minimal screening may occur. The particular orientation of the marathon and the types of procedures used may vary. Some, like those used at Synanon, on the West Coast, with ex-drug users, meet without a formal leader and utilize critical confrontations among the participants. In some groups the activities are well structured and the leader may play a dominant role. In others, the situation is essentially unstructured, although specific exercises or games may be suggested or introduced by the leader as he/she deems appropriate for individual or group participation. In many cases, the leader may also be a participant in the group, revealing his own emotions and feelings as stimulated by the interactions of the group. Thus, the leader may also function as a model of openness for the other group members. An attempt is made to create an atmosphere where social facades will be dropped and each of the participants can feel free to express his deepest feelings. "The group does not deal with anything except its chosen task, which usually is the expression and exploration of immediate feelings" (Mintz, 1971, p. 1). Descriptions of marathon groups also emphasize the importance of the atmosphere which is created in order to reduce defensiveness and increase verbal and emotional expression. "Stress is placed on the immediate dropping of facades, defenses, interpersonal maneuvers, and masks. Defensive maneuvers are immediately challenged by the therapist and the group" (Rachman, 1969–1970, p. 59).

A variety of exercises or games are utilized in the marathon groups. Some may emphasize body contact and sensory awareness, while others do not. Furthermore, some may be used as exercises for the entire group, while some are used by one or more participants as a particular occasion arises. Mintz (1971) has described a number of these games and a brief description of some of them follows.

One game is called "secrets." The group participants are asked to think of the most shameful secret that they possess and to imagine what the reaction of the group would be to the disclosure of the secret. As these silent fantasies continue, they apparently become less disturbing, a process akin to that of desensitization. The participants are not asked to reveal their secrets, but some do and supposedly are surprised to discover that the group's reaction is noncritical and supporting. Another game to facilitate interpersonal contact is that of "feedback." Each group member is asked to select three individuals whom he likes and three toward whom he feels critical. The participants are encouraged to give the bases for their feelings and to explore the extent to which their feelings are influenced by distorted perceptions or prejudices. Later, when the participants know each other better, they are asked to disclose the changes in their initial reactions. Still another game is "opening the fist." First, partners are chosen and one partner is asked to extend his fist, tightly closed. The remaining partner attempts to open the fist using any means that he wants, verbal or physical. The partner with the closed fist can choose to resist or comply. According to Mintz (1971), "Most people resist obstinately when physical force is used, but comply readily to persuasion or cajolery" (p. 52).

Another category of games is referred to as "conflict games." These may be used after the group has engaged in some of the others already mentioned and the participants have begun to respond in a more open or genuine manner. For some of these games it is essential that pillows or mattresses be on the floor and that an upholstered couch also be available. One of the mildest of the conflict games is "thumb-wrestling." In this game, the participants clasp hands with their thumbs upright and each tries to pin down the thumb of the other. A more vigorous game is "arm-wrestling." Here the two opponents lie on the floor, head to head, with their right arms resting on their elbows and their hands clasped. At a given count each attempts to pin down the other's arm. "The encounter becomes more meaningful if the opponents are asked to look into one another's eyes, and it is sometimes suggested that they also release feelings by making whichever sounds they wish" (Mintz, 1971, p. 55). It is believed that the physical intimacy and the opportunity for using physical strength without hurting anyone allows these physical activities to become very meaningful. Related games are "arm-squeezing," "hand-slapping" and "hand-pressing." These three types of exercises are considered to be useful in evoking and releasing pent-up feelings from the past and thus bringing them into the current experiential situation. Again, according to Mintz, "They can be used in a variety of ways, but I have found them most dramatically effective in offering myself as a mother symbol and bringing out feelings of rage which have been choked back since childhood" (pp. 57–58).

As the preceding statement suggests, the participant or leader may make personal interpretations or draw symbolic meaning from these physical encounters. In "hand-pressing," the therapist or a selected individual offers his hands clasped together with finger and thumbnails protected within the hands. The other person is then allowed to press them together as hard as possible. In this game, the person who is doing the hand-pressing is asked to close his eyes and when physical contact is established, he is asked what his mother used to call him as a boy and what he used to call her.[7] He and the woman whose hands he is pressing then speak to one another using childhood names. An attempt is made to recapture the pronunciation and intonation as given by the individual, and he is instructed to say to his mother whatever it was he wanted to say but never did. According to some reports, the results of such a technique can be quite unusual with the participant becoming angry, cursing his mother, and squeezing the hands with vigor. Such episodes seem to offer emotional release or catharsis. Another related game is "couch-pounding" in which an individual is encouraged to vent his aggressive feelings by pounding a couch.

Role-playing is also utilized in a variety of ways and since this procedure is relatively well known, little need be said about it here. Many variations are possible in terms of the roles that different members may play and the kinds of problem situations that may be enacted.

---

[7] Because Mintz is a woman, it appears understandable that she might follow such a procedure. Conceivably, a male therapist or leader would modify the procedure accordingly.

Mintz (1971) describes still other games utilized in encounter or marathon groups. In several of these games there is clearly an element of symbolism involved. One such set of games includes "breaking out of the circle" and "breaking into the circle." In the first mentioned game, the group forms a circle and a participant is placed in the middle with the task of breaking out. According to Mintz, "He usually understands at once that this is a symbolic challenge to find ways of breaking out of his emotional prison" (p. 71). If, in fact, the marathon participant sees this exercise symbolically, then he may feel somewhat elated at a successful breakthrough. Breaking into the circle utilizes an opposite symbolism and may be used when a participant feels that he is somehow voted out or excluded from the world. The games which are entitled "fall-catch game," "passing-around," and "lifting and rocking" are by this time rather well known since they have been described in a variety of publications including the popular media. Again, a certain amount of symbolism is attached to these games. For example, in the fall-catch game, one person stands a few feet back from the other and facing in the same direction. The person in front falls backward and is caught by the person behind him. Much is made of this game in terms of the matter of trust. Lifting and rocking is another game that is used either to satisfy the dependency needs of an individual participant or to convey the feeling of being lifted and cherished by the group. "People who are lifted and rocked almost always feel much closer to the group afterward and they become extremely receptive to the affection and concern shown within the group in its later phases" (Mintz, 1971, p. 73).

The games described in the preceding section are representative of the exercises utilized in encounter and marathon groups. How they will be used, and at what points in the group process, will vary from leader to leader or group to group. As already indicated, the purpose of these games is to increase sensory awareness, to help tear away the so-called social facades of the participants, to increase interpersonal interaction, and also, on a somewhat symbolic level, to deal with such matters as trust, rage, or other important feelings. If the reports of such activities can be taken at face value, these games may produce meaningful emotional responses on the part of the participants and contribute also to the feeling of group sharing and intimacy.

While the new forms of groups became very popular, and apparently for some people a way of life, criticism has also been directed at them. Among the aspects causing concern have been the lack of adequate screening of participants, the lack of professional training on the part of some group leaders, the overemphasis on the expression of feelings and physical contact on the part of participants, the use of nudity in some marathons, and the scarcity of adequate research evaluation of the effects of the various groups. Although there is some agreement that the participants in marathon groups can attain a degree of uplift and euphoria during the life of such groups, there is some question as to the durability of such uplifting feelings and concern about how the participants adjust to the "reentry" to their regular life situation. Few really systematic studies have been carried out and follow-up studies after a reasonable period of time have been conspicuous by their absence. Particular concern has been expressed at the possibility that severely disturbed individuals may be attracted to such groups and psychologically harmed by them. Although many professional therapists who lead marathon groups tend to label such concerns as unfounded and exaggerated, the available reports of marathon-induced disturbance and the scarcity of systematic follow-up studies do present important issues demanding attention (Hartley, Roback, and Abramowitz, 1976; Lieberman, Yalom, and Miles, 1973; Parloff, 1970; Saretsky, 1971; Yalom and Lieberman, 1971).

Among the difficulties encountered in trying to evaluate the effectiveness of groups are the variation in goals, participants, procedures, and group leaders. As a consequence, it is impossible to reach some overall generalization concerning the efficacy of groups. Although some attempts have been made to evaluate specific groups with specific types of clients, the diversity that exists needs to be kept in mind. Evaluation of the significance of the changes secured also constitutes a problem. For example, one review of the effectiveness of T-Group experiences in managerial training states "that while T-Group training seems to produce observable changes in behavior, the utility of these changes for the performance of individuals in their organizational roles remains to be demonstrated" (Campbell and Dunnette, 1968, p. 73). With regard to evaluations of such objectives as enhanced interpersonal skills and sense of well being, the reports are generally positive, but methodological limitations do not allow one to accept such reports fully. Most of the evaluations are global judgments provided by the participants, usually a short time after the termination of the group. As Parloff (1970) points out, apart from the matter of response bias, these reports suffer from an absence of control groups, no pre- and post-measures, and the use of global appraisals rather than measures of specific types of changes. Parloff summarizes the findings in the following manner:

> In summary, participants in encounter groups report favorable reactions and are frequently described by others as showing improved interpersonal skills. The evidence is meager that such participants undergo significant attitude change or personality change, and evidence that group training improves organizational efficiency is not compelling. What is clearest is that these groups provide an intensive affective experience for many participants (Parloff, 1970, p. 279).

As already indicated, there have been some concerns expressed regarding the potential dangers of encounter groups for some individuals and there have been several reports about individuals who have been upset enough after their encounter experience to seek personal therapy (Lazarus, 1971; Parloff, 1970). There have also been case reports of individuals who have developed psychotic or potentially psychotic behaviors as a result of such participation (Jaffe and Scherl, 1969). In reviewing some of the studies pertaining to outcome, Parloff (1970) points out the variability in the reports of such negative outcome. Depending on the type of group and leader as well as the source of information, the extent of severe emotional disturbance reported ranges from less than 1 percent to 19 percent of the participants. Some similar observations have been made by others, who have also mentioned the weaknesses in many of the studies (Hartley, Roback, and Abramowitz, 1976). The reports from encounter group leaders generally indicate a much smaller number of negative outcomes than those from other sources and it is difficult to evaluate the differences in these findings. Nevertheless, if marathon and encounter groups are considered to have some potency, as appears likely, then one would have to anticipate both positive and negative outcomes, and a search for the significant variables which affect outcome would need to be instituted.

More recently a well-controlled large-scale study of encounter groups was reported and the findings on casualties are worth noting (Lieberman, Yalom, and Miles, 1973; Yalom and Lieberman, 1971). In this investigation, 209 Stanford University undergraduates became participants in 18 encounter groups which met for 30 hours. The participants received three academic credits and completed a large battery of self-report questionnaires before beginning the groups, after each meeting, at the termination of the group experience, and after a 6-month follow-up period. Some of the groups had spaced meetings, for example, ten 3-hour meetings, while others followed the marathon format of a few extended meetings. Each meeting was tape-recorded and rated by two trained observers. Leaders were selected from a variety of ideological schools including N.T.L. sensitivity or T-Groups, Gestalt Therapy of the Esalen-Fritz Perls variety, Psychodrama, Psychoanalytic, Transactional Analysis, Sensory Awareness Focus (Esalen derivative), Marathon (Rogerian; eclectic personal growth), Synanon, and others, including two leaderless groups utilizing the Bell and Howell encounter tape (Peer Program). Because these labels and school derivations did not describe accurately the behavior of the group leaders, a different system of classifying these behaviors was devised by the investigators based on the data available.

The group leaders selected were highly recommended and experienced individuals, several of whom have national reputations. They were asked to lead the encounter groups in their regular manner and were paid for their services. After random assignments to the 18 groups, 170 students completed the group experience and 39 dropped out. Seventy-five control subjects were also studied. A casualty was defined as "an individual who, as a direct result of his experience in the encounter group, became more psychologically distressed or employed more maladaptive mechanisms of defense, or both; furthermore this negative change was not a transient but an enduring one, as judged eight months after the group experience" (Yalom and Lieberman, 1971, pp. 17–18). A number of sources and procedures were used to identify a high-risk group which could then be studied more intensively. These included requests for psychiatric aid during the group, dropouts, peer and leader evaluations, individuals who showed a large drop on a measure of self-esteem and those who entered psychotherapy subsequent to the group experience. A list of 104 suspected casualties was compiled and 8 months after the termination of the group each suspect was contacted by phone. If, after a 15- to 20-minute telephone interview, there was any suspicion that the individual had had a possibly destructive experience, he was invited in for an intensive interview, or if impossible, the interview was conducted by telephone.

A fairly stringent definition of a casualty was employed. Not only must the participant have undergone some psychological decompensation, but the disturbance must have been persistent and be clearly related to the group experience. For example, one of the student participants committed suicide after his second group meeting. In this instance, after careful consideration of all the data available, the investigators decided that the encounter group experience could not be considered the cause of his suicide and he was not considered a casualty. This individual had a long history of psychiatric disturbance and had sought help from a number of sources. He had participated in a number of local encounter groups, and concurrent with his participation in the experimental group procedure he was receiving both individual and group therapy and was also in another encounter group in a neighboring "growth institute."

Because of the fact that the group leaders knew they were being observed and evaluated and also because 25 of the 104 casualty suspects could not be reached by telephone, the investigators believe their incidence of casualties was probably a conservative estimate. In any event, sixteen casualties were identified, 9.4% of those who completed the group. The type and severity of psychological casualty varied over a wide range of disturbance. Three students exhibited psychotic decompensations and several of them had depressive and/or anxiety symptoms, including one individual with a depression that lasted 6 months and which was accompanied by a 40 pound weight loss and suicidal ideation. "Others suffered some disruption of their self-system: they felt empty, self-negating, inadequate, shameful, unacceptable, more discouraged about ever growing or changing" (Yalom and Lieberman, 1971, p. 19). Still others noted a deterioration of their interpersonal life.

There are a number of other interesting and provocative findings from this investigation, but only a few additional ones can be cited here. One of these is that peers were better able to identify casualties than were the encounter group leaders. Not only were some of the severe casualties completely missed by the leaders, but only three casualties were identified by them in contrast to twelve by their peers. Another interesting finding was the unequal distribution of casualties among the different groups. Six groups had no casualties, while three had two casualties and one had three. On the basis of factor analyses of leader behavior as rated by observers and participants, four basic dimensions of leader behavior were derived which accounted for 70% of the variance of total leader behavior. By means of statistical clustering, all of the group leaders could be classified into seven categories. One type, labeled "Aggressive Stimulators" and composed of the gestalt leaders, the two Synanon leaders, and one psychodrama leader, produced seven of the sixteen casualties. These leaders were perceived as the most charismatic of the leaders and were characterized as intrusive, confrontive, challenging, authoritarian, and self-revealing. Another type, by contrast, designated as "Love Leaders" had only one casualty in their three groups. This type, composed of a N.T.L. T-Group leader, a marathon eclectic leader, and a transactional analytic leader, were described as "caring, individually focused leaders, who gave love as well as information and ideas about how to change" (Yalom and Lieberman, 1971, p. 21). It can also be mentioned that the two leaderless groups that were directed by the Bell and Howell encounter tape had no casualties. Hence, it appears that certain types of groups, led by certain types of leaders, may have a higher risk rate than others. Finally, the findings also suggest that certain individuals may be more likely to suffer psychological harm than others:

> The entire picture is a consistent one: individuals with generally less favorable mental health with greater growth needs and higher anticipations for their group experience and yet who lacked self-esteem and the interpersonal skills to operate effectively in the group situation were more likely to become casualties" (Yalom and Lieberman, 1971, p. 28).

It should also be mentioned that many of the participants reported significant and far-reaching personal gains from their group participation. This is more in keeping with the rather glowing accounts reported by encounter group leaders and a large number of participants. From the accounts provided by a number of these individuals it appears as if the group experience can be an intense, emotional, mystical, and even a conversion experience for numerous participants. However, several appraisals of the outcome of such groups suggest that the gains secured tended to be temporary and to disappear over time. (Bednar and Kaul, 1978; Jones and Medvene, 1975; Lieberman *et al.,* 1973; Treppa and Fiecke, 1972). Furthermore, for some, the group experience can be a potentially upsetting or destructive one.

Although the writer believes that the popularity of encounter and related groups is on the decline, this is an impression, for data on such matters are not available. However, a number of issues still remain. One of these concerns the actual function or purpose of encounter groups. Are they a form of psychotherapy? Should they be used, as suggested by some, as mainly adjuncts to more conventional forms of psychotherapy? (Saretsky, 1971). Or, are they meant to provide some kind of growth or exhilarating experience for relatively well-integrated individuals? Although some attempts have been made to distinguish between encounter groups, growth groups, T-Groups or training groups, and therapy groups (Appley and Winder, 1973; Yalom, 1975), it is not always possible to do so and the interactions that take place may not always correspond to the names given them.

Although various types of group approaches have been developed and used for a number of years, the evaluation of their effectiveness has been a complicated and difficult matter. Many of the earlier appraisals suffered from inadequate research designs, lack of control groups, and limited measures for appraising change. Studies such as those of Lieberman, Yalom, and Miles (1973) on encounter groups are a rarity. Consequently, it is difficult to form a considered judgment on the efficacy of group psychotherapy in general, or of specific types of group therapy. Recent reviews of the research findings on group psychotherapy emphasize problems with the research data and difficulties in drawing conclusions concerning the efficacy of the group treatments. Brief excerpts from three recent views seem to share similar conclusions concerning the modest support available for group therapy.

> In brief, this ten-year survey of group psychotherapy outcome studies does not provide compelling endorsement of the contribution of group therapy to the treatment of schizophrenics, psychoneurotics, juvenile or adult offenders, or addicts (Parloff and Dies, 1977, p. 312).

> Although it may not be the best question to ask, there is a large body of research that indicates that group treatments "work." This conclusion must be qualified, however, since it is empirically and intuitively obvious that not all groups have had uniformly beneficial results. We have seen non-rejections of the null hypothesis in the research, and evidence of casualties as well. The conclusion must be qualified on other grounds as well; that is, group treatments have been shown to be somewhat effective in helping people achieve more positive and perhaps more healthy evaluations of themselves and others. These improvements are most frequently reported on measures reflecting self-concept assessment, attitude change, and positive personality developments . . . it seems most appropriate to view these measures as reflecting a nonspecific factor of improvement based on more favorable subjective evaluations that may or may not be accompanied by observable behavior changes. (Bednar and Kaul, 1978, p. 792.)

The gross deficiencies in this literature as a whole make it hard to evaluate the positive or negative findings and, worse yet, impossible to build upon smaller studies to accumulate adequate knowledge in the future. (Hartman, 1979, p. 465.)

Although each of the above reviewers focuses on somewhat different features of the research, and one may appear somewhat more positive (or negative) than the others, they all agree on the inadequacies of existing research and the need for better designed studies to answer important questions, namely, how effective are certain procedures with certain types of individuals, and what features of group therapy are the effective ingredients of change?

REFERENCES

Ackerman, N. W. Interview group psychotherapy with psychoneurotic adults. In S. R. Slavson (Ed.), *The practice of group therapy.* New York: International Universities Press, 1947. Pp. 135–155.

Appley, D. G., and Winder, A. E. *T-groups and therapy groups in a changing society.* San Francisco: Jossey-Bass, 1973.

Bednar, R. L., and Kaul, T. J. Experiential group research: Current perspectives. In S. L. Garfield & A. E. Bergin (Eds.), *Handbook of psychotherapy and behavior change.* (2nd ed.). New York: Wiley, 1978.

Campbell, J. P., and Dunnette, M. D. Effectiveness of T-Group experiences in managerial training and development. *Psychological Bulletin,* 1968, *70,* 73–104.

Feifel, H., and Schwartz, A. D. Group psychotherapy with acutely disturbed psychotic patients. *Journal of Consulting Psychology,* 1953, *17,* 113–121.

Gazda, G. M. (Ed.). *Basic approaches to group psychotherapy and group counseling.* (2nd ed.). Springfield, IL: Charles C. Thomas, 1975.

Hammer, M. and Kaplan, A. M. *The practice of psychotherapy with children.* Homewood, IL: Dorsey Press, 1967.

Hartley, D., Roback, H. B., and Abramowitz, S. I. Deterioration effects in encounter groups. *American Psychologist,* 1976, *31,* 247–255.

Hartman, J. J. Small group methods of personal change. *Annual Review of Psychology,* 1979, *30,* 453–476.

Hobbs, N. Group-centered psychotherapy. In C. R. Rogers (Ed.), *Client-centered therapy.* Boston: Houghton Mifflin, 1951. Pp. 278–319.

Jaffe, S. L., and Scherl, D. J. Acute psychosis precipitated by the T-Group experiences. *Archives of General Psychiatry,* 1969, *21,* 443–448.

Jones, D., and Medvene, A. Self-actualization effects of a marathon growth group. *Journal of Counseling Psychology,* 1975, *22,* 39–43.

Klapman, J. W. *Group psychotherapy: Theory and practice.* New York: Grune and Stratton, 1946.

Klapman, J. W. Didactic group psychotherapy with psychotic patients. In S. R. Slavson (Ed.), *The practice of group therapy.* New York: International Universities Press, 1947. Pp. 242–259.

Lazarus, A. A. *Behavior therapy and beyond.* New York: McGraw-Hill, 1971.

Lieberman, M. A., Yalom, I. D., and Miles, M. B. *Encounter groups: First facts.* New York: Basic Books, 1973.

Lubin, B., and Eddy, W. B. The laboratory training model: Rationale, method, and some thoughts for the future. *International Journal of Group Psychotherapy,* 1970, *20,* 305–339.

McCann, W. H., and Almada, A. A. Round-table psychotherapy: A technique in group psychotherapy. *Journal of Consulting Psychology,* 1950, *14,* 421–435.

Meador, B. D. Client-centered group therapy. In G. M. Gazda (Ed.), *Basic approaches to group psychotherapy and counseling.* (2nd ed.). Springfield, IL: Charles C. Thomas, 1975.

Mintz, E. E. *Marathon groups: Reality and symbol.* New York: Appleton-Century-Crofts, 1971.

Moreno, J. L. *Psychodrama.* Vol. 1 (2nd rev. ed.). New York: Beacon House, 1946.

Moreno, J. L., and Elefthery, D. G. An introduction to group psychodrama. In G. M. Gazda (Ed.), *Basic approaches to group psychotherapy and counseling.* (2nd ed.). Springfield, IL: Charles C. Thomas, 1975.

Parloff, M. B. Group therapy and the small-group field: An encounter. *International Journal of Group Psychotherapy,* 1970, *20,* 267–304.

Parloff, M. B., and Dies, R. R. Group psychotherapy outcome research 1966–1975. *International Journal of Group Psychotherapy,* 1977, *27,* 281–319.

Powdermaker, F. B., and Frank, J. D. *Group psychotherapy.* Cambridge: Harvard University Press, 1953.

Pratt, J. H. The class method of treating consumption in the homes of the poor. *Journal of the American Medical Association,* 1907, *49,* 755.

Rachman, A. W. Marathon group psychotherapy: Its origins, significance, and direction. *The Journal of Group Psychoanalysis and Process,* 1969/70, *2,* 57–74.

Rioch, M. J. Group relations: Rationale and technique. *International Journal of Group Psychotherapy,* 1970, *20,* 240–355.

Rosenbaum, M. Group psychotherapy. In M. Rosenbaum and A. Snadowsky (Eds.), *The intensive group experience. A Guide.* New York: The Free Press, 1976.

Saretsky, L. Feedback and measurements. In E. E. Mintz (Ed.), *Marathon groups: Reality and symbol.* New York: Appleton-Century-Crofts, 1971.

Schilder, P. Results and problems of group psychotherapy in severe neuroses. *Mental Hygiene,* 1939, *23,* 87–98.

Schilder, P. *Psychotherapy.* (Rev. ed.). New York: W. W. Norton, 1951.

Slavson, S. R. General principles and dynamics. In S. R. Slavson (Ed.), *The practice of group therapy.* New York: International Universities Press, 1947. Pp. 19–39. (a)

Slavson, S. R. (Ed.). *The practice of group therapy.* New York: International Universities Press, 1947. (b)

Slavson, S. R. *Analytic group psychotherapy.* New York: Columbia University Press, 1950.

Slavson, S. R. *A textbook in analytic group psychotherapy.* New York: International Universities Press, 1964.

Slavson, S. R. *An introduction to group therapy.* New York: International Universities Press, 1970.

Slavson, S. R., and Schiffer, M. *Group psychotherapies for children: A textbook.* New York: International Universities Press, 1975.

Thomas, G. W. Group psychotherapy: A review of the recent literature. *Psychosomatic Medicine,* 1943, *5,* 166–180.

Treppa, J. A., and Fricke, L. Effects of a marathon experience. *Journal of Counseling Psychology,* 1972, *19,* 466–467.

Truax, C. B., and Carkhuff, R. R. *Toward effective counseling and psychotherapy.* Chicago: Aldine, 1967.

Wender, L. Group psychotherapy: A study of its applications. *Psychiatric Quarterly,* 1940, *14,* 708–718.

Wolf, A. Psychoanalysis in groups. In G. M. Gazda (Ed.), *Basic approaches to group psychotherapy and group counseling.* (2nd ed.). Springfield, IL: Charles C. Thomas, 1975.

Yalom, I. D. *The theory and practice of group psychotherapy.* (2nd ed.). New York: Basic Books, 1975.

Yalom, I. D., and Lieberman, M. A. A study of encounter group casualties. *Archives of General Psychiatry,* 1971, *25,* 16–30.

Chapter Thirteen

Child and Family Psychotherapy

In the preceding chapters we have reviewed a number of different types and forms of psychotherapy, both individual and group. Although in the chapters on behavior therapy and group therapy reference was made to the uses of such therapy with children, the emphasis generally was on therapy with adults. In the present chapter, however, our attention will be focused largely on therapies developed exclusively for use with children or in which children have been a point of primary concern.

PSYCHOTHERAPY WITH CHILDREN

Because of the important differences between the child and the adult, some of the psychotherapeutic techniques developed for adults have not been completely feasible for use with children. Some of these differences illuminate the problems involved. In the first place, the personality of the child has not yet reached mature development. From the Freudian viewpoint, for example, the child's ego or superego may not be fully developed, and this poses a different therapeutic problem from that of the neurotic adult who may exhibit overly strong superego controls as one of his difficulties. In therapy with children, therefore, we are dealing with personalities which differ significantly from those encountered in therapy with adults.

A second important difference lies in the relative dependence of the child on his parents or parental figures in his home. Children, by the very nature of their dependence on adults for the satisfaction of their needs, can do little about modifying their current life situation. If the latter contributes significantly to the difficulties, a therapeutic program which does nothing to alter the situation may fall far short of success. In contrast to the child, the adult may have greater mobility and control in relation to external factors in her environment. Furthermore, if one accepts the premise that childhood events and experiences are important determinants of personality, the situational differences between adult and child are further highlighted. In the adult these events lie in the past, while for the child they are important factors in his current day to day living. Realistic attempts at psychotherapy would have to take such considerations into account. If parental figures play a significant role in the life of the child, then some attempt may have to be made to alter or influence their impact on the child along more constructive lines. Otherwise, the child is daily exposed to those forces which theoretically produce his personality difficulties. For this reason, a number of child psychologists and psychiatrists hold that therapeutic work with parents is an important aspect of therapy with children.

In addition to these considerations, there are others that suggest differences in therapeutic work with children as contrasted with adults. The child's intellectual and verbal development has not reached the level of the adult. Thus, the exclusively verbal approach of traditional types of adult therapy, with interpretations and symbolic analyses, may be ill-suited for the young child. Conversely, the child is inclined to be more physically active and to express himself in play and related activities. She may also indulge more freely in fantasy activities and theoretically repressed or unconscious components of her personality may be closer to the surface. As a consequence, these may be glimpsed more readily through the avenue of imaginative play and art activities.

Finally there are differences in how the individual comes to therapy and in issues of confidentiality. As will be discussed shortly, the decision to seek psychological treatment for a particular child is usually instituted by adults, most frequently parents or teachers who perceive some type of problem. Issues arise also in terms of the confidentiality of what takes place in therapy. Some clinicians believe the child's therapist should not communicate material derived from the therapy sessions to the parents lest this interfere with the therapeutic relationship and the child's trust in the therapist. Others, however, do not see this stance as completely realistic since parents want to be informed in a general (and sometimes not so general) way as to how therapy is progressing. Some authors suggest that the actual play activities and productions of the child should be kept in confidence. "However, the therapist's impressions about the child should not necessarily be kept confidential from the parent but can be conveyed with tact, and in keeping with one's assessment of how the parent will use such information" (Cooper & Wanermen, 1977, p. 99).

For such reasons, therapeutic work with children differs in several ways from that with adults. We have already alluded to one form of therapeutic work with children, the activity group therapy of Slavson, and indicated how it differs from other group therapies. In the following pages, we shall review briefly a few other forms of psychotherapy which have been developed primarily for work with children.

ANALYTIC CHILD THERAPIES

Several psychoanalytic theories and procedures have been adapted and developed for use with children. The interest in them has grown steadily and an annual series of volumes devoted to psychoanalytic investigations of children, *The Psychoanalytic Study of the Child,* has appeared regularly. Here we shall review briefly the two best known analytic child therapies.

One approach has been developed by Anna Freud (1946a,b, 1965), the daughter of the founder of psychoanalysis. According to her, the traditional analytic techniques used with adults were not directly applicable with children. In adult psychoanalysis, for example, the individual is aware of some difficulties in his adjustment, has some confidence in analysis, and usually has some desire for improvement. In the case of the child, the situation is different. The decision for treatment comes not from him, but from the parents. Moreover, the child may not perceive that difficulties or suffering lie within himself, "and so the situation lacks everything which seems indispensable in the case of the adult: insight into malady, voluntary decision, and the will towards cure" (Freud, 1946b, p. 5).

For these reasons, Anna Freud has held the view that most children need a period of preparation prior to the actual analytic work. This may vary considerably, depending on the problem involved. Certain general aims are usually sought in this preparatory period. In one illustrative case, Miss Freud mentions three such aims. One was to make herself interesting to the child. In this situation she did nothing but follow along with what the child did or wanted to do. A second aim was to prove herself useful to the child in several different ways, including such things as typing letters for him and making things for him. The third aim was to demonstrate that the analysis and the analyst had practical advantages to the child. In this connection the analyst takes the side of the child against others and even protects him from punishment. The child is thus made somewhat dependent on the analyst and enters into a transference relationship. Miss Freud emphasizes, however, that this preparatory period is not to be confused with the real analytic work to follow, which has as its goal the bringing into awareness of unconscious material. More recently, it is believed that the preparatory period can be shortened by attending more to the ego defenses of the child.

Other differences in terms of technique also occur in the analytic work with children. In contrast to adult cases, informational material relating to the child's past history and current adjustment must be secured from the parents rather than from the child directly. Drawings also are utilized frequently as a means of communication by the child. The use of play is mentioned by Miss Freud, too, but is not described in detail. The techniques of dream and daydream interpretations are also utilized and are similar to those used in analytic work with adults.

Anna Freud emphasizes how her use of play differs from that of the other well-known analytic approach developed by Melanie Klein (1949). Whereas Klein views the play of a child as roughly the equivalent of the adult's free associations, Freud does not agree. She does feel that the child, in most instances, cannot associate freely for any length of time but does not agree that each play activity should be interpreted as indicating some dynamic or symbolic aspect of the child's problem. Related to this is the fact that she views the transference relationship in child analysis as differing from that of the adult. According to her, there is an educational as well as a strictly therapeutic purpose in child analysis. Although the child enters into a lively relation with the analyst and gives many evidences of transference relationships, she is not capable of forming a transference neurosis—that is, she does not completely transfer her neurotic trends to the analytic situation as is believed to occur in classical psychoanalysis. One reason for this is that the child, unlike the adult, is unable to establish new patterns of love relationships because the older or existing relationships still exist. The original objects, the parents, are still real and interact with the child every day, as well as providing the child with her gratifications and denials. Although the analyst shares the child's relationships and attitudes, there is no necessity for the child to give up the original relationships for that with the analyst. Another reason is found in the behavior of the analyst. In work with adults the analyst tries to remain impersonal and in the background. In work with children the role is quite different, as we have already noted. It is for these reasons that the child cannot duplicate in the transference relationship her actual neurosis. Rather, it is still manifested in her actual home situation. As a consequence, Anna Freud feels that the analyst is dependent upon the parents for information as to what is occurring in the child's life and thus in a sense shares the therapeutic work with them.

Melanie Klein's (1948, 1949) approach to child analysis, sometimes referred to as the English School, differs noticeably from that of Anna Freud. The former does not believe that a preparation period is necessary prior to analysis or that work with parents is essential for therapeutic success. Instead, active analytic work with the child can be started at once.

Since the child's main avenue of expression is play, Klein utilizes it in analysis and interprets its symbolic significance to the child. Toys, drawing material, string, and water are provided for the child's use. In addition, considerable freedom is allowed the child in his play activities.

The most unusual aspect of Klein's approach is her extensive symbolic interpretation of the child's play activity. Play is judged to be the equivalent of free association by the adult. In addition, she assumes that the child's unconscious is close to consciousness and, as a consequence, interpretations of unconscious motivations or conflicts can be given and understood very early in therapy. From her point of view, such interpretative work is necessary to get at the basis of the child's disturbed feelings, give him some relief from anxiety, and thus allow treatment to continue.

The interpretations given by Klein are quite direct and utilize classical Freudian theory as well as modifications based on her own experience. As a result, many relate to the symbolic manifestations of sexual and aggressive impulses. For example, when the child bumps two toy cars together, his play may be interpreted as referring to the sexual relations between the parents. When an object or toy figure is overturned, it may be viewed as an aggressive representation against the father.

The type and rapidity of interpretation offered by Klein are illustrated in one of her discussions of the case of a girl slightly under 4 years of age. On the basis of the child's behavior during the first analytic hour, Klein felt she was able to form some idea of one of the girl's basic difficulties. The child insisted that flowers be removed from a vase. "She threw a little toy man out of a cart into which she had previously put him and heaped abuse on him; she wanted a certain man with a high hat that figured in a picture-book she had brought with her to be taken out of it; and she declared that the cushions in the room had been thrown into disorder by a dog. My immediate interpretation of these utterances in the sense that she desired to do away with her father's penis, because it was playing havoc with her mother (as represented by the vase, the cart, the picture-book and the cushion), at once diminished her anxiety and she left me in a much more friendly mood than she had come. . . ." (Klein, 1949, pp. 47–48).

Although the use of play activities has been accepted by many child therapists, the interpretative approach of Klein has met with considerable skepticism and doubt. Anna Freud (1946b), in particular, has been critical of Klein's procedures. There is no need to discuss these criticisms here, beyond noting that in general they challenge the validity of many of Klein's assumptions and techniques. Klein, on the other hand, has attempted to answer some of

Freud's criticisms and has made some countercharges of her own. According to her, Anna Freud's therapeutic approach emphasizes the conscious ego aspects of the child's personality difficulties and neglects the unconscious aspects (Klein, 1948). In contrast, Klein states her approach deals more directly with the basic unconscious conflicts. She also defends her use of interpretations by stating that they are based on her understanding of the particular case being treated. Although Melanie Klein has attained some following in England, her approach does not appear to have gained much acceptance in the United States. In contrast, Anna Freud's approach has been more positively received (Lesser, 1972).

RELATIONSHIP THERAPY

What is referred to as "relationship therapy" was influenced by the theoretical views of Otto Rank (Karpf, 1953). Nevertheless, proponents of this therapy, while following Rank's conceptions of the therapeutic process, do not necessarily subscribe to all of his theoretical views (Rogers, 1939). This point of view was at first most accepted and developed by a group within the field of social casework (Taft, 1933). Relationship therapy was also identified in the past with the Philadelphia Child Guidance Clinic and the work of Dr. Frederick H. Allen. It appears that the views emphasized in this approach to therapy have also had a broad influence on the therapeutic work of others and that certain features have been incorporated into the work of many therapists. Certainly the early work of Rogers (1939, 1942) was greatly influenced by this point of view and there is much similarity between the two.

As the name implies, the emphasis in relationship therapy is on the dynamics of the relationship which develops between the therapist and the child. Although it can be assumed that no therapy can function effectively without some sound relationship between the participants, the way the relationship is utilized may distinguish one form of therapy from another. In relationship therapy, the emphasis is on the immediate experience of the patient in therapy. This is contrasted with an authoritative use of the relationship, in which the client is told what to do, and with the psychoanalytic use of it to explore the individual's past in terms of making unconscious processes conscious.

The therapist begins where the patient is and seeks to help him to draw on his own capacities toward a more creative acceptance and use of the self he has. While maintaining an interest in understanding what has been wrong, the therapeutic focus is on what the individual can begin to do about what was, and, more important, still is wrong. Therapy emerges, then, from an experience in living, not in isolation but within a relationship with

another from whom the patient can eventually differentiate himself as he comes to perceive
and accept his own self as separate and distinct (Allen, 1942, p. 49).

This emphasis on the present experience as a living reality for the patient
was a keynote of Allen's therapy. The past is given significance only as it is
brought into the immediate reality in relationship to the therapist. While the
child will react in his characteristic manner, being aggressive, fearful, demanding, or placating, the therapist maintains his own integrity throughout. "It is
the therapist who provides a steady background, through his acceptance of
the patient's projections without, however, becoming in actuality what the
patient tries to make him" (Allen, 1942, p. 60).

The child is provided the opportunity of selecting what toys and other
equipment he wants to play with and how he will use the time allotted to
him. Within certain limits, he is allowed freedom in his play activities. The
limitations imposed relate to destruction of equipment, aggressive actions
toward the therapist, and the specific time allowed for therapy. These limitations are imposed for obvious reasons, and also because of their significance
in therapy. In essence, they are manifestations of reality, provide an indication
of the therapist's strength, and allow the child to assert and clarify his own
self in relation to another person. The specific meaningfulness of this, of
course, will vary, depending upon the problem of the child. For example, a
child who has been allowed to dominate the parents excessively may have
a distorted view of his own strength, accompanied by strong feelings of anxiety
and guilt. In therapy, the presence of the therapist and the imposed limitations
are actually reassuring to the child and allow him to test his assertiveness
realistically. Through this process, a clearer and more harmonious differentiation of self can emerge as indicated in the following example:

> In George there was a close connection between fear and badness. In the midst of
> making considerable noise he said to the therapist: "you are scared, you are a bad boy."
> The aggressiveness continued, and the therapist had to limit its concrete expression: "George,
> you feel as bad as you want, but there are some things you can't do." George was both
> angry and anxious and said, "You shut up. I am not bad. I don't want to be bad." But it
> was important for him to discover he could feel angry and want to be bad, yet accept
> some limits as to what he did with that feeling (Allen, 1942, p. 82).

Within the limits mentioned above, the emphasis in Allen's therapy is on
the freedom which allows the child to acquire selfhood. Only as the child
himself participates actively in the therapeutic process, can significant changes
take place. While play activities and equipment are used, it is pointed out
that play, per se, is not the important therapeutic activity. Rather, it is the

expression of the child's feelings as he relates to another. It is to these, too, that the therapist primarily reacts.

Allen stressed also the clarification of self in the therapeutic process. This is related to his views of child development, in which the process of individuation or differentiation is an essential element. The aim of therapy is to increase and clarify this differentiation and emergence of self which has been impeded or blocked in the child's past life experiences. This process begins with the first appointment, when the child leaves the mother and begins to participate in the new relationship which is therapy. The therapist, while friendly, accepting, and understanding, at the same time provides a consistent frame of reference within which the child can explore his own self.

Although Allen's book focuses primarily on the treatment of the child, it is clear that he viewed this as only one part of the total treatment process. In part this is related to his views concerning the development of the child's difficulties. Frequently the mother has not been able to allow the child to develop satisfactorily and needs to see her role clarified. When, for example, a child is unnecessarily tied to the mother emotionally, the process whereby the child can achieve differentiation of self would appear to involve also some clarification of the mother's part in this development. Essentially, then, if the factors which create difficulties are a function of the relationship between parent and child, the therapy process must try to improve the situation as far as both participants are concerned.

As a consequence, it was customary for the mother to be seen by a social case worker at the same time that the child was seen by his therapist. This form of therapy thus differs from some of the others discussed here, although this particular procedure is followed in a number of child guidance clinics with varying orientations. The fact that the mother and child go to separate therapists in different rooms is thought to highlight the process of separation and differentiation of self. The reunion of the two after the therapy hour also demonstrates that therapy does not signify a permanent separation, but allows for an eventual healthier relationship.

Although many features of the therapy are similar to client-centered therapy, the therapist in relationship therapy appears to take a somewhat more active role. In the case materials cited by Allen (1942), there are some specific examples of interpretation by the therapist which perhaps would not be found in client-centered therapy. The emphasis on the emergence of a new self in therapy is similar to that of client-centered therapy, but the orientation does differ somewhat in terms of how the concepts of individuation and differentiation are viewed. In contrast to the analytic therapies, the length of time for relationship therapy appears much shorter, although it varies, of course, from case to case. It would appear, also that some of the emphases on the relationship in therapy have also been utilized and incorporated by therapists with varying orientations.

CLIENT-CENTERED PLAY THERAPY

Play therapy with children from the client-centered point of view is another approach to child therapy. While showing some kinship to relationship therapy, it developed from the work of Rogers and his associates. Because of the essentially similar orientation between this approach to play therapy and client-centered therapy, our account will be exceedingly brief. More detailed descriptions of client-centered play therapy with excerpts from actual therapy sessions are available in the accounts by Axline (1947, 1948, 1965), Dorfman (1951), and Moustakas (1973).

Basic belief in the capacity of the child for growth and self-help has led to some specific views in relation to play therapy. One of these relates to therapeutic work with the child only, even though the family or environmental situation is a poor one. Apparently successful therapeutic results have been achieved in this fashion. The view is advanced that if the child changes in therapy, his environmental situation also changes as others react more positively to the change in the child. "Whatever the explanation may be, the fact remains that many children have benefited from play therapy without concurrent parent therapy" (Dorfman, 1951, p. 239). But, as noted previously, it is standard procedure in many children's clinics to involve one or both parents in some kind of therapeutic work and the recent growth of family therapy extends this emphasis further.

The role of the therapist in accepting the child and allowing him to use the time as he sees fit is also stressed (Moustakas, 1973). Emphasis is placed on the current feelings of the child, and no attempt is made to interpret his behavior or to force him into socially approved methods of response. Therapy proceeds at the child's pace. If he wants to remain silent for the entire treatment hour, his feelings are respected. In fact, improvement in social adjustment has been reported with children who participated very little in activities with the therapist, yet apparently profited from their experience (Dorfman, 1951). The therapist must be able to accept such preferences on the part of the child even though they may not be what he usually expects in the treatment hour and they are painful to endure for most therapists.

The matter of limits in therapy has also received some attention. While no limits are placed on the child's verbal expression of feelings, some limits are placed on his behavior or physical expression of feelings, similar to those already described for relationship therapy. "The therapist establishes only those limitations that are necessary to anchor the therapy to the world of reality and to make the child aware of his responsibility in the relationship" (Axline, 1947, pp. 75–76).

OTHER APPROACHES TO PLAY THERAPY

The previous use of play may be described as a free use of play in that the child is allowed to select the toys and engage in the activities that he desires. In other forms of therapy, however, the specific toys and play activities have been suggested or arranged by the therapist. This type of situation has frequently been termed the "controlled" use of play (Newall, 1941). One such type of therapy, "release therapy," was developed by Levy (1938, 1939). In this form of therapy, specific toys were utilized for specific problems. Levy was interested at one time in sibling rivalry and related problems, and used detachable dolls. These dolls could represent siblings and other family figures, and the child was encouraged to use them in a play situation. The therapist might set up a family situation in play and allow the child to release his negative feelings toward the new baby, the older sibling, or any other member of the family. In this fashion, release in relation to a specific problem was obtained.

Release therapy was used also with children who suffered from night terrors, tics, speech disturbances, temper tantrums, and related difficulties. Levy stressed that this therapeutic approach was limited to the resolving of specific problems and that more intensive therapy was required with the more seriously neurotic child (Levy, 1939, 1943). The criteria for selecting children for release therapy were as follows: (1) The presenting problem should involve a definite symptom precipitated by a specific event; (2) the problem should be of relatively short duration and the child preferably should not be over 10 years of age; (3) the child should be suffering from an event that occurred in the past and not from something going on at the time of treatment.

In general, there is little interpretative activity on the part of the therapist in release therapy. This is particularly true of very young children, who apparently improve without knowing why they came to the therapist or without relating improvement to the treatment. In one case, the child spent most of her time throwing clay on the floor and stepping on it; playing with water and spilling it; cutting, throwing, and hitting objects. The therapist gave no interpretations, and yet after nineteen such sessions considerable improvement was noted. "Release therapy in this type of child, by overcoming anxieties that had to do with dirt, orderliness, and hostile expressions, made possible an expansion of personality, presumably bound down by a discipline too early or too severe" (Levy, 1939, p. 717). The statements, of course, represent Levy's interpretation of what was involved. Without some type of controlled study, however, the explanation given has to be viewed as hypothetical.

Other child therapists have utilized play in somewhat related fashion (Conn, 1939, 1948; Schaefer, 1976; Solomon, 1938, 1948). In some cases, specific play is encouraged relating to possible traumatic incidents or problem relationships as obtained from the child's history (Solomon, 1940). Sometimes therapy is focused to a great extent on a number of concrete problems situations which the therapist helps the child to recreate by setting the stage for the play activity (Conn, 1939). In these latter instances, the therapist is also quite active in the play situation, particularly in asking the child questions relating to the reasons for the dolls' behavior, his feelings, and similar material. While there are variations in the way these techniques are used, this latter use of play apparently is applied where difficulties have arisen from specific events or where a few situations or behavioral patterns are deemed of primary significance in the child's adjustment. Needless to say, this use of play is quite different from the use of play in relationship or client-centered therapy where there is no such structuring of the situation. It would appear, also, that in the controlled use of play much less emphasis is placed on the relationship of the child to the therapist. But, Solomon, who has been identified with a somewhat controlled type of therapy called "Active Play Therapy" (Solomon, 1938), has emphasized the importance of the therapeutic relationship. He has also introduced a doll representing the therapist as one means of facilitating this relationship and believes this "lessens the dangers and increases the effectiveness of treatment" (Solomon, 1940, p. 781). In any event, the therapists who have used some such form of controlled play therapy feel it is a brief and worthwhile technique for selected problems.

Various workers in the field of child therapy have described the kinds of toys and play equipment which are deemed appropriate for therapeutic purposes (Schaefer, 1976). A fairly extensive list is provided by Axline (1947) and suggestions for the playroom and equipment are offered by Hammer and Kaplan (1967). Among those which are commonly used are clay, paints, water, finger paints, blocks, guns, and material which can be manipulated. Allen (1942) feels that the material for play need not be too elaborate and should not be so interesting that the child loses himself in play to the neglect of his relationship with the therapist. The play materials serve a wide variety of needs and purposes. Guns, toy soldiers, and similar material allow children to express their aggressive feelings and may be of special significance to children who need to have their feelings of power developed. In a similar fashion, dolls and household toys provide the child with an opportunity for bringing important relationships into his play. It has been noted frequently that a child may use a doll to portray some unacceptable aspect of himself.

Puppets have also been utilized in play therapy and provide opportunities for children to portray significant events and relationships in their lives.

It is apparent from what has been presented that there have been many different adaptations and uses of play for therapeutic purposes. Some are quite lengthy procedures which theoretically attempt to get at the bases of the disturbed behavior; others are fairly brief and aim for behavioral improvement in relation to specific kinds of problems. While some attempts have been made to appraise therapeutic programs in the past (Dorfman, 1951; Hoch, 1948; Lebo, 1953; Levy, 1943; Slavson, 1947), most of them have been rather limited in scope and methodology. Levitt (1957a) made an attempt to appraise the results of psychotherapy with children and surveyed the results of over thirty studies. Using primarily clinicians' judgments as the criterion for improvement, the average percentage of improvement at the end of treatment was found to be approximately 67% and at follow-up the corresponding figure was 78%. On the other hand, an estimate of improvement secured for a comparable group of cases which did not accept treatment was approximately the same. Such comparisons obviously do not make a very strong case for the effectiveness of psychotherapy. One of the critical problems in evaluating treatment programs with children is that they are developing over time and one needs to know if it is treatment or development that is responsible for change.

Levitt, Beiser, and Robertson (1959) later carried out a follow-up evaluation of 327 children treated at the Institute of Juvenile Research who were compared with a control group of 142 children who had been accepted for treatment but who, for some reason, had failed to begin treatment. The results were essentially the same as those mentioned previously. No really significant differences were obtained between the treated and the control subjects. Although the type of control group used by Levitt in his studies has been criticized by some (Hood-Williams, 1960), few investigations have been able to devise a better control group, without withholding treatment completely from one group, which is a difficult procedure to put into practice. Furthermore, Levitt (1957b) in a specific study comparing children who continued in treatment with those who refused treatment, did not secure any but chance differences between them on sixty-one different variables.

More recently, Levitt (1971) summarized the results of 47 reports of outcome studies with children spanning a 35-year period and including over 9000 cases. The percentage improved was about the same as in the earlier study and, in general, the same conclusions were drawn.

A more recent review of research on psychotherapy with children tends in general to agree with the conclusions reached by Levitt (Barrett, Hampe, & Miller, 1978). The latter authors also point to the limited amount of research conducted in this area in recent years. Although clinical research with children is complicated by the normal process of maturation in the child, the appropriate research procedures must be devised and applied.

It would appear that conventional psychotherapy with children in clinic settings has not yet convincingly demonstrated its effectiveness and that practitioners in this area must either provide research support for their practices or be open to new procedures. As Levitt (1971) pointed out, a number of traditional beliefs and practices in child guidance rest on very little empirical evidence and are thus open to challenge.

OTHER THERAPEUTIC APPROACHES WITH CHILDREN

Although conventional procedures in play therapy with children still appear to hold an important place in many child guidance clinics, a number of new developments have taken place. Of great importance has been the increasingly wider application of behavioral methods which was discussed in a previous chapter. As noted there, a variety of behavioral procedures have been used with disturbed children and the behavior therapists have been both innovative and research oriented. A few other interesting and related developments also can be mentioned here.

One of the innovative trends in the work with children has been a shift away from working with the child in a clinic setting to attempts at behavioral intervention in the classroom and in the home. There are a number of advantages apparent in this kind of shift. One is that the intervention and behavioral modification take place in the setting where the problem is occurring and to which the child must adjust. A second is that the significant adults involved in the child's adjustment become participants in the treatment program and also have their behavior altered. This allows the psychologist to increase his impact by utilizing others as change agents as well as, perhaps, having some generalizable effect on these adults in their handling of other children.

Much of this work has tended to utilize an operant conditioning framework with the view that the child is to a great extent "under the control of reinforcing contingencies supplied by the environment" (Patterson, 1971, p. 751). The significant persons in the child's environment are viewed as the dispensers of the reinforcers influencing the child's behavior and presumably are the persons who shape and maintain the child's deviant behavior. Consequently, in this type of approach "it is necessary to arrange reinforcement schedules provided by the parent, teacher, or peer group that will alter the deviant behavior but, in addition, to arrange reinforcing contingencies for simultaneously maintaining the behavior of these dispensers" (Patterson, 1971, p. 752).

Since it is believed that the deviant behaviors of the child are being reinforced, unwittingly or not, by the parents or other persons, one must institute some training program for them. Although other therapeutic approaches have also placed some emphasis on working with the parents, the particular procedures used in behavioral intervention are quite different. The focus is on the parent or teacher learning to observe the behaviors emitted by the child and the reinforcing behaviors they or others provide. Such training can take place in the laboratory, the home, or the school. Training need not be limited to the matter of observation alone, but may include the charting and graphing of the occurrence of specific behaviors, the reducing of reinforcement for deviant behaviors, and the reinforcing of positive behaviors.

A concise summary and evaluation of some of the work in this area was prepared by Patterson (1971). Clearly, many different procedures have been tried with apparently positive results. Although some parents exhibit difficulty in collecting the necessary observational data and modifying their patterns of reinforcement, such problems can be overcome by daily telephone calls to prompt the desired behavior. Group training has also been used by several workers and a description of one such program is provided by Patterson (1971):

> In these procedures, two weeks' baseline observation data are collected in the home, describing family interaction. Following this, the parents respond to a programmed textbook that outlines social learning theory (Patterson and Gullion, 1968). Contingent on their completing this assignment, the professional staff then spends one hour in helping them pinpoint one or two child behaviors and setting up a schedule for the parents to observe their child's behavior. Daily telephone calls serve both to prompt continued cooperation and to reinforce it when it occurs. Several days of consistently good data earn for the parents the right to enter the group.
>
> The group consists of three to five families, all of which contain at least one child whose behavior represents some extreme of antisocial behavior. Each parent is given thirty minutes in which to present his current data, describe the program used last week, and outline the current management problem. A timing device provides the necessary stimulus control: those parents who have no data (a rare occurrence) must wait until last. All of the group members participate in planning behavior-management programs for each other and in examining the data that are being passed around. Home observations are again made at four and at eight weeks. If at the four-week probe the data show that progress has been made, then arrangements are made for observers to go to the school and to begin collecting the baseline observations that will serve as a basis for classroom intervention programs. However, it is made clear to the parents that they must "earn" this additional involvement. After termination of all programs the families are followed up, systematically, for at least a six-month period (Patterson, 1971, p. 756).

Patterson (1974) has reported the results obtained with such a therapeutic program in which the parents of 27 children with conduct problems were trained to implement the program. The parents were given at least a month of training along the lines described above. In slightly over one-half of the cases, the classroom was also used. Besides being reinforced for appropriate behaviors in the classroom, the child brought home a work card to the parents on the basis of which certain consequences, previously contracted, were handed out.

The procedures were considered moderately successful in reducing the negative behaviors. For example, 1 year after the end of treatment, the total of deviant behavior at home was considered to be within the normal range. However, immediately after the end of treatment, negative behaviors increased for about one-half of the children. So-called "booster shots" of additional treatment were required to bring these levels down to those existing at the end of treatment.

The results of several studies indicate that at least a number of parents do reinforce, by means of attention and related responses, the very behaviors which they consider troublesome and fail to reinforce adequately more socially desired behaviors. By means of proper training and supervision the parents can become relatively effective change agents and it would appear also that as a result of the changes a better climate within the family ensues.

Somewhat similar procedures have been used to help train teachers to respond more appropriately to classroom behavior. Teachers, like parents, respond differentially to the children in their classes and frequently it is the disruptive child who gets the attention of the teacher. In one study, for example, one teacher reinforced appropriate behavior in the classroom ten times as frequently as another teacher, while the latter reinforced inappropriate behaviors over four times as frequently as the former (Madsen, Becker, and Thomas, 1968). A particular problem here is that the teacher's behavior also requires reinforcement. When monitored and reinforced by psychologists, teachers respond to these programs of operant conditioning; however, their attention and reinforcing behavior appears to decline when their own social reinforcement is withdrawn (Brown, Montgomery, and Barclay, 1969). Even though there are such problems, as well as others, a number of innovative attempts have been made by behaviorally oriented psychologists to intervene in the classroom to effect positive behavioral change in children. Various devices have been devised and installed in experimental classrooms such as lights and radio signals to signal the child that he has earned some type of reward. Tokens and the accumulations of points to obtain specific objects have also been used (Lahey & Drabman, 1981).

FAMILY AND MARITAL THERAPY

Somewhat in contrast to the operant work with parents has been the interest in therapeutic work with families along psychodynamic lines or from views of the family as a social system. There have been different approaches to family therapy (Ackerman, 1958; Bell, 1961, 1975; Boszormenyi-Nagy and Framo, 1965; Erickson and Hogan, 1972; Greenberg, Glick, Match, and Riback, 1964; Satir, 1967), but they have shared a common emphasis on the dynamics and importance of the family interactions. Among these views is the one that the individual cannot be viewed as an isolated organism, but that he and his particular pathology are formed, shaped, and reside in a family context. From this orientation the disturbed individual or his pathology may be, or should be, viewed as a symptom of a disturbance within the family. Consequently, the focus of treatment is on the family unit and its interactions.

There appears to be little question that the family is a significant social unit and that it exerts an important influence on the behavior of its members. There is also face validity in the idea that simply treating an individual without also changing or modifying the most important influences on his social behavior might be less than adequate for effective change. The family dynamics, coalitions, conflicts, and similar features are usually quite apparent when a therapist works with a family, and one does get a real feel for the way family conflicts may contribute to the disturbed person's difficulties. However, until quite recently, very little empirical research was done regarding the effectiveness of family therapy, let alone what type of interventions may be most effective. Rittenhouse (1970), for example, reviewed *Psychological Abstracts* for the decade 1960–1969, and was not able to find one adequate study of this type. A critical review of the literature 2 years later came to a somewhat similar conclusion (Wells, Dilkes, & Trivelli, 1972). Only 18 studies were found which met the minimal requirements of including three or more families and explicitly stating the outcome criteria used. Of these 18 studies, only two were considered to have adequate methodology. The situation, however, appears to be changing rapidly, for a more recent review of the research literature of family therapy was much more optimistic and positive (Gurman & Kniskern, 1978). Clearly, the field of family therapy is growing and developing, and we will return later to discuss some of the research findings on effectiveness. Let us now turn to an examination of some of the developments in family and marital therapy.

FAMILY THERAPY

Family therapy became visible as a therapeutic approach in the 1950's when several different individuals began to see potential benefits in working with families as opposed to exclusive reliance on individual therapy. Previously, social agencies had dealt with families in terms of what Ackerman (1954) referred to as social therapy, concentrating primarily on reality-oriented social and occupational aid. Emotional problems were viewed in psychodynamic terms and individual therapy was seen as the preferred treatment. However, as more psychotherapists became sensitive to important changes in marital and family relationships that appeared related to changes an individual was undergoing during individual psychotherapy, a greater interest in the former became evident. For example, it was not infrequently noted that when a child or spouse supposedly improved in individual therapy, the mother or other spouse, respectively, appeared to become worse.

The historical accounts of the development of family therapy are somewhat conflicting (Erickson & Hogan, 1972; Gurman & Kniskern, 1978; Jackson & Satir, 1961). However, there does not appear to have been one single or uniform source of development. Some of the first work developed from clinical involvement with problems of children (Bell, 1967), some from work with families which had a schizophrenic member (Olson, 1970), and some seemed to be extensions of working with parents or marital couples (Ackerman, 1954). Like the other forms of psychotherapy discussed in previous chapters, there are now a number of different types of family therapy, most of them deriving from the initial formulations of a particular individual (Erickson & Hogan, 1972; Olson, 1970). Although there is no completely agreed upon or systematic classification of the various forms of family therapy, some commonly used categorizations have been: psychoanalytic, social systems (or sometimes structural or strategic), and behavioral. In some instances the major categories used have been "behavioral" and "nonbehavioral" (Gurman & Kniskern, 1978). These appear to be very crude categorizations which do not really tell one a great deal about the actual operations or procedures used. Consequently, we will not be unduly concerned about such categorizations, but will examine briefly some of the emphases and approaches in family therapy.

BELL'S "FAMILY GROUP THERAPY"

One of the pioneers in the area of family therapy was the psychologist, John E. Bell. His presentation of "Family Group Therapy" at the meeting of the Eastern Psychological Association in 1953 was one of the earliest on family therapy (Erickson & Hogan, 1972), although the paper he presented was not published until much later (Bell, 1967). In general, Bell found that very young children tended to be a distraction and thus he would not include children below the age of 8 years, even though his initial focus was on problems of children.

Bell's therapy starts with an interview with the parents in which the history of the child's problem and development are obtained and the parents are informed as to the method of therapy. The parents are told that the therapist will function like a referee to see that all family members are given an opportunity to participate and express their views. It was also mentioned that the therapist will give support to the child so as to encourage him/her to feel free to express important feelings, although all family members will be allowed opportunities for similar expression. The parents are also reassured about the possible increase in the child's expression of hostility during therapy and how this is a necessary prelude to the more positive expression of feelings later. This session is then followed by the first session with the family. The children are informed about the previous interview with the parents and that the family meetings are being held because the family is not as happy as it should be. They are then informed of the unique role of the therapist in this special situation which allows them to express freely their feelings about the family.

The second stage of therapy is referred to as the *child-centered phase* for the child is encouraged to discuss what he believes is making the family an unhappy one. Sometimes this takes considerable encouragement and the parents also have to be encouraged not to be too active verbally or to complain about the child. Generally, children will complain about various aspects of their daily living—this can include almost anything from parental nagging to staying out late to inadequate weekly allowance. Usually, the child is asked how he would solve the problem being discussed, and within limits, the parents may be encouraged to cooperate in accepting his suggestion. Decisions, of course, can be modified later based on subsequent experience. If the parents "go along readily, the child exhausts his demands in a few weeks and therapy enters the next stage" (Bell, 1967, p. 29).

The *parent-centered phase* follows when according to the child everything is going well. According to Bell, the parents then begin to offer criticisms about the child's behavior. Although this criticism at first may center on problems outside the home, for example, at school, the therapist tries to relate the issue to matters at home. The parents may express considerable hostility and the therapist may respond to this in several ways, e.g., the child must also be allowed to express his/her views, the normalcy of the child's behavior if it falls within developmental norms, and helping the child to express his/ her reasons for the behavior. The parents' expression of hostility usually leads to a similar response on the part of the child. However, in this instance the child may express hostile feelings or fears which have never been expressed before. Although the expression of negative affect on both sides may at times be intense, this type of cathartic release seems to have a positive effect on family relations at home with more tolerance and understanding.

The final stage is called the *family-centered phase* and is indicated by a number of possible effects. These include the disappearance or diminution of the referral problems, a more positive mood including laughter during the sessions, the fact that more positive family interactions and activities are occurring, and an indication that therapy is no longer required. When this occurs, then the end of therapy is at hand. Throughout, however, the therapist plays an active interpretative role.

Unlike Bell's approach to family therapy, which was presented in a very concise and deceptively simple manner, many of the other approaches appear to reflect the personality of the originator or to be less systematically or concisely described. In many accounts of the development of family therapy, one gets the distinct impression of a number of influential, strong, or charismatic individuals who have been important leaders in the field (Gurman & Kniskern, 1978; Hoffman, 1981). However, it is not an easy task to describe adequately these different therapeutic approaches, or would it be a simple or necessarily desirable procedure for most of us to try to emulate these particular and unusual individuals. Thus, although an attempt will be made to offer some brief descriptions of a few of the other well-known approaches to family therapy, these descriptions will have to be only partial glimpses of the therapies described.

MINUCHIN'S STRUCTURAL THERAPY

Salvador Minuchin (1974), the Director of the Family Therapy Training Center at the Philadelphia Child Guidance Clinic, is one of the leading figures in family therapy today and is associated with what is called the structural approach. From this orientation, therapy has the general purpose of changing or modifying the current family organization, which is dysfunctional, so it approximates that of the normal family. According to Minuchin, a positively functioning or organized family has boundaries that are clearly marked. The marital subsystem of the family, for example, should have closed boundaries to protect the privacy of the marital partners and to allow them to interact in mutually supportive and creative ways. The subsystem of the parents should also have boundaries which clearly separate it from other family members, but which will allow normal access for the needs of children, etc. The sibling subsystem should have boundaries which keep the children from interference by adults and allow them reasonable privacy and the exploration of their own interests.

If the boundaries of the subsystems are overly rigid or overly diffuse, difficulties are more likely to arise. In the latter instance the system may become overloaded and be unable to adapt to changing or stressful situations. Where the boundaries become rigid, communication among subsystems becomes impeded and the normal protective functions of the family cannot operate. The therapist in his meetings with the family notes how the family deviates from normal expectations, and his/her goal is to change the organization of the family in order that it begins to resemble a normal or better functioning family. "When the structure of the family group is transformed, the positions of members in that group are altered accordingly. As a result, each individual's experiences change" (Minuchin, 1974, p. 2). The therapist thus "often functions as a boundary maker, clarifying diffuse boundaries and opening inappropriately rigid boundaries. His assessment of family subsystems and boundary functioning provides a rapid diagnostic picture of the family, which orients his therapeutic interventions" (Minuchin, 1974, p. 56).

Minuchin plays a very active role in his therapy, constantly observing the behavior and interactions of the family members, attending to particular individuals at particular times, asking questions, changing seating arrangements, and the like. "Structured family therapy is a therapy of action" (Minuchin, 1974, p. 14). The emphasis is also on the present and not on past events, for the latter are reflected in the present activities which the therapist observes. It is also the present interactions which need to be modified.

The target of therapeutic intervention is thus the family system and not individual pathology as such. As Minuchin views the process, he joins this system in order to modify it. In order to join the family the therapist tries to emphasize those aspects of his personality and his own experience that are syntonic with the families'. However, it is pointed out that the therapist retains the freedom to be spontaneous and to probe aspects of the family interaction. He cannot allow himself to become submerged within the family, thus losing his potential role of change agent.

The structure of the family is revealed by the arrangements made within the family that govern the transactions of its members. By "joining" the family, the therapist observes how the family members relate to him and to each other. Each may play certain roles within the family and there may be certain groupings or coalitions within the family. The therapist, however, is more than an observer. He is an active participant as well as director of the process. He initially probes the family structure as part of the evaluation of the family used to locate areas of potential flexibility and change. In this process, Minuchin utilizes his conception of boundaries and subsystems to depict family organization, at the beginning, and throughout therapy.

As mentioned previously, Minuchin is also a very active participant in the therapy process. He may align himself with one or more members to increase or decrease the barriers between different subsystems, to encourage certain behaviors, to confront individuals, and may meet only with some subsystem of the family and not with others. He may have some members act out certain interactions, he may have one or more members observe the remaining family members through a one-way mirror, or he may, himself, leave the family and observe them. Minuchin may give the family homework assignments, and he may enter the home if deemed necessary.

It should be apparent from the preceding comments that although Minuchin has developed a certain conceptual scheme for looking at families and their interactions, the way therapy is conducted is very much influenced by his own personality and experience. Despite this, however, he shares an apparent similarity of view with many other family therapists. He, too, views the identified patient's symptoms as "a system-maintaining or system-maintained device" (Minuchin, 1974, p. 110). The therapist's task, therefore, is to facilitate the family system. By joining the family system the therapist evaluates the family structure and then attempts to intervene in ways that will encourage or allow the transformation of this system. The transformation of the family system allows family members to interact in new ways which may lead to better functioning for all members of the family.

In this process of family therapy, therefore, the therapist joins and acts as leader of the family. Based on his structural analysis of the family, the therapist may support one individual or subsystem, confront another, use humor, interpret behaviors, and the like. These interventions tend to upset the current equilibrium of the family and are regarded as the first step in the process of change. As therapy proceeds, the focus is on restructuring the family. "Restructuring operations are the highlights of therapy. They are the dramatic interventions that create movement toward the therapeutic goals" (Minuchin, 1974, p. 139). However, the restructuring operations must reflect the sensitivity of the therapist to the family and the therapeutic relationship that has been formed. Thus, such operations must allow for periods of consolidation as the family changes. Throughout, the therapist must be sensitive to both individual and family needs. He may need to provide support to an individual member at a given period, but also must not be seen as unduly taking sides with some family members against other members. He must also guard against being drawn into family conflicts in such a way that his objectivity and leadership role are impaired.

It seems evident from what has been described of Minuchin's structural family therapy that it requires considerable activity and direction on the part of the therapist. He/she cannot be a simple observer or reflector of what goes on in the therapy sessions. Furthermore, as the therapy progresses and things begin to change within the family, the therapist has constantly to be alert to these changes and to modify his/her behavior accordingly.

Minuchin has also attempted to make some evaluation of the effectiveness of his therapy and published a report on 23 families in which the identified patient had psychosomatic problems (Minuchin, Baker, Rossman, Liebman, Milman, & Todd, 1975). Although there was no comparison group as a control, which limits the confidence one can have in the results obtained, nevertheless, the results were impressive. Using objective measures such as weight gain and blood sugar levels in the cases of anorexia nervosa and asthma, positive improvement was reported for all cases.

OTHER APPROACHES TO FAMILY THERAPY

There are a number of other family therapists who have contributed in noteworthy ways to the development and popularity of family therapy. The interest of several individuals in a family approach to treatment grew out of their work with schizophrenic patients (Hoffman, 1981; Olson, 1970). Bowen (1965) worked with families of hospitalized schizophrenics because of his original interest concerning the nature and origins of schizophrenia, and went so far as to invite a number of these families to actually live in the hospital. A group in Palo Alto, California also studied communication problems within families that had a schizophrenic member, and provided several leaders in the field of family therapy such as Jay Haley and Virginia Satir. A particular emphasis on communication problems in disturbed families was one feature of this work.

Still others such as Ackerman (1958) and Boszormenyi-Nagy (1965) attempted to combine a psychoanalytic approach with attention to the family system and related concepts. Boszormenyi-Nagy directed a family project involving hospitalized schizophrenic patients in which the therapy was labeled as intensive and lasted up to 4 years in length. In this approach, the identified patient was seen for individual analytically oriented therapy and the entire family met for an hour a week with a team of two therapists, one of whom was the identified patient's therapist. Even though the context or emphasis in the family meetings was the family, psychodynamic formulations were used to view the family interactions as well as the dynamics of the individuals involved.

> It is erroneous to assume that the context of conjoint family therapy is unsuitable for deep exploration of the individual members' fantasies. The experienced family therapist will find a key, for instance, in the many 'slips of the tongue' which reveal the conflicting aspects of relationships as well as the members' confusion between relationships and identifications. . . . For an optimal exploration of the intrapsychic and interactional dimensions the family's relationship with the therapist as well as the intermember transference relationships have to be such that *spontaneous free play* can be given to the repetitious acting-out patterns, just as a capacity for free association is fundamental to psychoanalysis (Boszormenyi-Nagy, 1965, pp. 95–96).

As the preceding quotation indicates, a psychoanalytic frame of reference is used in this form of family therapy. In terms of some of the case material presented by Boszormenyi-Nagy, it is apparent that family members may present accounts of their dreams and similar material. This approach, therefore, differs noticeably from those of Bell and of Minuchin which were discussed earlier. Whereas Minuchin would focus on the current boundaries and interactions of the family members and play an active role himself in the process by means of alignment, support, and confrontation, a therapist following the lead of Boszormenyi-Nagy would appear to take on the more traditional role of the psychodynamic therapist.

Much attention also appears to be paid to the early experience of the identified patient's parents who are stimulated to recall the difficulties experienced with their parents as an important factor entering into the current family problems and contributing to the pathology of the identified patient. In this sense a misfortune or injustice performed in the past to one or both parents is considered to be causally related to the symptoms of the identified patient. By getting to the source of the difficulty, and by interpretation of the past difficulties, the need for the symptom may be diminished. In essence, the identified patient's pathology is intimately related to these past events and represents a partial but unhealthy response to it. Supposedly, however, it acts as a device to avoid fractionation or disintegration of the family. When the "proper" explanations of the family members' behavior are accepted, a different and more compassionate view of each other is considered possible.

Unfortunately, as is typical of many of these types of family therapy, little in the way of systematic and controlled evaluation of the therapy's effectiveness has been conducted. Although changes may indeed take place in the identified patient and/or other family members, it is difficult to evaluate adequately if such changes are due primarily or solely to the therapeutic interventions. Human beings are not static organisms, and they may change over time for a variety of reasons. In children, in particular, changes may occur as a result of development and maturation. Consequently, reasonable conclusions concerning the efficacy of a particular therapeutic approach generally can only be drawn from well-designed controlled studies of outcome. Relatively few such studies have been conducted in the area of family therapy. In their comprehensive review of research on family and marital therapy, Gurman & Kniskern (1978) list only 11 controlled studies of so-called nonbehavioral family therapy. This reflects both the recency of the development of family therapy and the lack of adequate research in this area. Part of this may be due to the fact that psychologists have become involved in family therapy relatively recently. Furthermore, two of the 11 studies referred to above did include behavioral aspects. In the 16 comparisons made in these 11 studies, 8 favored family therapy, 1 favored the control group, and in 7 there were no significant differences.

Before concluding this section, something more can be added about behavioral approaches to family therapy. Some of the work in this area, namely that of Patterson (1971, 1974) was discussed earlier. Such work, however, has focused on the parents primarily with the goal of changing the child's behavior. Generally, this does not involve the entire family together in what has been termed conjoint family therapy. Rather, the focus is to a large extent on working with parents in an educational manner with an emphasis on training them to apply principles of reinforcement (LeBow, 1972).

One approach which combines a behavioral and systems approach to the treatment of delinquent behavior is worth particular mention. This program was developed by James F. Alexander and his associates (Alexander & Barton, 1980). This model hypothesizes that deviant social behaviors result primarily from patterns of interdependent behaviors to which all family members contribute. From this point of view, in normal or "adaptive" families stress is responded to by effective problem-solving sequences of behavior. Maladaptive families, however, in responding to stress, tend to develop interactions where "all family members reciprocally generate increasingly maladaptive behavior in one another" (Alexander & Barton, 1980, p. 55). The latter tends to result in "coercive interactions" or breakdowns in the family system leading to a variety of negative or acting-out behaviors such as running away or physical abuse. The behavioral point of view is readily apparent in the following statement: "Rather than isolating processes that have been hypothesized to be maladaptive, the systems-behavioral approach has studied families with delinquent children and adaptive families to observe directly the difference in interaction patterns that produce and maintain maladaptive outcomes, on the one hand, and adaptive outcomes, on the other". (Alexander & Barton, 1980). Once identified, these patterns become the focus of the therapeutic interventions.

In contrast to most other family therapy approaches, Alexander's (1973) approach was based on systematic observations of delinquent and normal families and is the result of a series of well-planned, systematic, and cumulative studies. An attempt was made to use methods of appraisal that would satisfy necessary research criteria but also be clinically meaningful. Although adhering to the behavioral emphasis of defining activities in operational terms and in using objective criteria for evaluating change, Alexander also attempted to incorporate an equal emphasis on the family system. "That is, the measures had to reflect the systems theory assumption that quite different behaviors can serve the same interpersonal function, and thus must be coded in the same way" (Alexander & Barton, 1980, p. 57). This goes beyond a simple categorizing of similar behaviors to focus on the impact that supposedly different behaviors may have on members of the family. Thus, a verbal comment, a frown, or other response may all have a similar negative impact on specific others. One must look beyond similar surface behaviors to observe the effects on family interactions. Adopting this systems-behavioral approach, Alexander also utilized two concepts from the field of group dynamics to appraise interaction in normal and delinquent families, defensiveness and supportiveness. What follows is a brief report of some of the research performed by Alexander and his collaborators.

In the first published study, Alexander (1973) compared defensiveness and supportiveness among dyads in normal and delinquent families. Not only was the pattern of supportiveness between normal parent and child dyads significantly higher, and the pattern of defensiveness significantly lower than in the comparable delinquent dyads, but there was also a clear reciprocity of such patterns of interaction. Thus, when members in a family behave in a defensive or supportive manner, the others tend to reciprocate in kind, but more importantly, the two types of reciprocity are of different kinds in the two types of families. In delinquent families, defensive reciprocity dominates and appears to be related to the problems experienced.

Based on the findings secured, Alexander proceeded to develop some therapeutic procedures. In addition to teaching effective communication skills and procedures for contingency contracting, the therapists were trained to emphasize supportive communications. Those families in the systems-behavioral family treatment condition showed a significant increase in their ratio of supportive to defensive communications whereas families receiving individual counseling or no treatment did not show significant changes.

As a result of these encouraging results, Alexander and his collaborators went on to develop more comprehensive procedures which would go beyond mere changes in communication patterns and change family patterns in a more significant manner. These procedures were rather complex and will not be described here. In essence, emphasis was placed on reducing the rigidity of the existing family systems, changing the family members' existing attributions, aiding them in seeing the interdependence of their behaviors, and in fostering generalization of what they learned. A variety of behavioral and self-control techniques were also used. In further studies, the families receiving the behavioral-systems therapy showed considerably less recidivism than did groups receiving alternate therapies or no treatment, and the siblings of the identified patients also showed fewer referrals to the juvenile court than did the siblings in the other groups.

The research of Alexander and his colleagues is a model of systematic hypothesizing, research appraisal, and effective therapeutic planning which is all too rare in the area of family therapy specifically and psychotherapy generally. It also represents a systematic attempt to go beyond a single theoretical orientation and to emphasize operational definitions of concepts and procedures, as well as to conduct controlled studies which lead to further modification and improvement of the therapeutic procedures.

MARITAL THERAPY

Another form of therapy which has received increased recognition in recent years is that of marital or couples therapy. Although marital counseling and therapy developed separately from that of family therapy, there has been a gradual drawing together of these two types of therapy. There are obviously some similarities and overlap among the two designated forms of therapy. Add an additional person to the marital couple and marital therapy becomes family therapy.

The term "marital therapy" has been used in the past to designate almost any therapy in which marital problems were a focus of the therapy. Thus, one spouse seen in individual therapy or both marital partners seen individually by the same therapist or by different therapists were all viewed as receiving marital therapy. More recently, however, marital therapy has referred to a form of therapy where both marital partners are receiving therapy conjointly, and where serious conflicts in the marital relationship have led to the couple's seeking therapy.

The requirements for getting married may not be as stringent as getting into graduate school, but maintaining a satisfactory marital relationship is not really a simple matter. This appears to be particularly true in the past two decades or so when sex roles and related marital roles have been undergoing significant change (Paolino & McCardy, 1978). The rapid increase in the rate of divorce in the United States and what appears to be an increasing number of marital couples seeking marital counseling or therapy are perhaps symptomatic of such problems. The reasons for seeking therapy are many, ranging from sexual problems and arguments to physical abuse and considerations of divorce. Usually, however, a couple does not seek therapeutic help until the marital conflict is quite serious and the marriage appears to be threatened.

As is true of the other forms of therapy already discussed, marital therapy also has many varieties including psychoanalytic, behavioral, systems theory, and several others (Paolino & McCardy, 1978; Ryle, 1979; Vincent, 1980). Since we have already discussed such varieties of family therapy, there is little need for any extensive elaboration here. The same types of emphasis are found in the corresponding marital therapies. Transference reactions, interpretations, and early parent-child relationships tend to be stressed in analytic marital therapy (Ryle, 1979), whereas reinforcement, contracting of desirable behaviors, modeling, and other behavioral procedures have been used in behavioral marital therapy. Systems theory approaches tend to emphasize the communication and system maintenance aspects of the marital relationship. There are also instances of more recent developments in which aspects of more than one orientation may be combined in a rather systematic manner. Thus Weiss (1980) has attempted to combine a cognitive-behavioral and systems approach which he has called "Strategic Behavioral Marital Therapy."

As was true of other types of therapy, much of the early outcome research on marital therapy was uncontrolled. However, in their review of the research findings on marital therapy, Gurman and Kniskern (1978) list five controlled studies of conjoint marital therapy, largely emphasizing communications training. Although no follow-up appraisals were reported, the findings in these five studies favored the treated groups. Also, in a larger number of studies comparing marital therapy to other types of therapy such as individual or group therapy, marital therapies secured more favorable outcomes in about 70% of the comparisons.

As is true in the area of psychotherapy generally, meaningful criteria of outcome are required but are not easy to devise. In the area of marital problems, for example, such social criteria as separation, reconciliation or divorce have no precise or uniform positive or negative value—they may reflect positive outcomes in some instances and negative outcomes in others. However, although we clearly need more definitive studies with adequate follow-up evaluations, the author's bias is clearly in favor of conjoint marital therapy where the problem is basically that of the marital relationship. Otherwise, the problem is not dealt with directly and the therapist who treats only one partner does not have an opportunity to really observe what the difficulties are. In essence the therapist gets only selected perceptions and accounts as the inputs to therapy, and this does not seem adequate or desirable.

REFERENCES

Ackerman, N. Interpersonal disturbanced in the family: Some unsolved problems in psychotherapy. *Psychiatry,* 1954, *17,* 359–368.
Ackerman, N. W. *The psychodynamics of family life; diagnosis and treatment of family relationships.* New York: Basic Books, 1958.
Alexander, J. F. Defensive and supportive communications in normal and deviant families. *Journal of Consulting and Clinical Psychology,* 1973, *40,* 223–231.
Alexander, J. F., and Barton, C. Systems-behavioral interventions with delinquent families: Clinical, methodological, and conceptual considerations. In J. P. Vincent (Ed.), *Advances in family intervention, assessment and theory.* Vol. 1. Greenwich, Conn.: JAI Press, 1980.
Allen, F. H. *Psychotherapy with children.* New York: W. W. Norton, 1942.
Axline, V. M. *Play therapy.* Boston: Houghton Mifflin, 1947.
Axline, V. M. Some observations of play therapy. *Journal of Consulting Psychology,* 1948, *12,* 209–216.
Axline, V. M. *Dibs: In search of self.* New York: Houghton Mifflin, 1965.
Barrett, C. L., Hampe, I. E., and Miller, L. Research on psychotherapy with children. In S. L.

Garfield and A. E. Bergin (Eds.), *Handbook of psychotherapy and behavior change.* (2nd ed.). New York: Wiley, 1978.

Bell, J. E. *Family group therapy.* Public Health Monographs No. 64. Washington, D.C.: U.S. Government Printing Office, 1961.

Bell, J. E. Family group therapy—A new treatment method for children. *Family Process,* 1967, *6,* 254–263.

Bell, J. E. *Family therapy.* New York: Jason Aronson, 1975.

Boszormenyi-Nagy, I. Intensive family therapy as process. In I. Boszormeny-Nagy and J. L. Framo (Eds.), *Intensive family therapy. Theoretical and practical aspects.* New York: Hoeber Medical Division, Harper & Row, 1965.

Boszormenyi-Nagy, I., and Framo, J. L. (Eds.), *Intensive family therapy. Theoretical and practical aspects.* New York: Hoeber Medical Division, Harper & Row, 1965.

Bowen, M. Family psychotherapy with schizophrenia in the hospital and in private practice. In I. Boszormenyi-Nagy and J. L. Framo (Eds.), *Intensive family therapy. Theoretical and practical aspects.* New York: Hoeber Medical Division, Harper & Row, 1965.

Brown, J., Montgomery, R., and Barclay, J. An example of psychologist management of teacher reinforcement procedures in the elementary classroom. *Psychology in the Schools,* 1969, *6,* 336–340.

Conn, J. H. The child reveals himself through play. *Mental Hygiene,* 1939, *23,* 49–69.

Conn, J. H. The play-interview as an investigative and therapeutic procedure. *Nervous Child,* 1948, *7,* 257–286.

Cooper, S., and Wanerman, L. *Children in treatment. A primer for beginning therapists.* New York: Brunner/Mazel, 1977.

Dorfman, E. Play therapy. In C. R. Rogers (Ed.), *Client-centered therapy.* Boston: Houghton Mifflin, 1951. Pp. 235–277.

Erickson, G. D., and Hogan, T. P. *Family therapy. An introduction to theory and technique.* Monterey, CA: Brooks/Cole, 1972.

Freud, A. *The ego and the mechanisms of defense.* New York: International Universities Press, 1946. (a)

Freud, A. *The psychoanalytic treatment of children.* London: Imago Publishing Co., 1946. (b)

Freud, A. *Normality and pathology in childhood: Assessments of development.* New York: International Universities Press, 1965.

Greenberg, I. M., Glick, I., Match, S., and Riback, S. S. Family therapy: Indications and rationale. *Archives of General Psychiatry,* 1964, *10,* 7–24.

Gurman, A. S., and Kniskern, D. P. Research on marital and family therapy. In S. L. Garfield and A. E. Bergin (Eds.), *Handbook of psychotherapy and behavior change.* (2nd ed.). New York: Wiley, 1978.

Hammer, M., and Kaplan, A. M. *The practice of psychotherapy with children.* Homewood, IL: Dorsey Press, 1967.

Hoch, P. H. (Ed.) *Failures in psychiatric treatment.* New York: Grune and Stratton, 1948.

Hoffman, L. *Foundations of family therapy.* New York: Basic Books, 1981.

Hood-Williams, J. The results of psychotherapy with children: A reevaluation. *Journal of Consulting Psychology,* 1960, *24,* 84–88.

Jackson, D. D., and Satir, V. A review of psychiatric developments in family diagnosis and family therapy. In N. W. Ackerman, F. L. Beatman, and S. N. Sherman (Eds.), *Exploring the base for family therapy.* New York: Family Service Association of America, 1961.

Karpf, F. B. *The psychology and psychotherapy of Otto Rank.* New York: Philosophical Library, 1953.

Klein, M. *Contributions to psychoanalysis. 1921–1945.* London: Hogarth Press, 1948.

Klein, M. *The psychoanalysis of children.* (3rd ed.). London: Hogarth Press, 1949.

Lahey, B. B., and Drabman, R. S. Behavior modification in the classroom. In W. E. Craighead, A. E. Kazdin and M. J. Mahoney (Eds.), *Behavior modification. Principles, issues, and applications*. (2nd ed.). Boston: Houghton Mifflin, 1981.

Lebo, D. The present status of research on nondirective play therapy. *Journal of Consulting Psychology*, 1953, *17*, 177–183.

LeBow, M. D. Behavior modification for the family. In G. D. Erickson and T. P. Hogan (Eds.), *Family therapy. An introduction to theory and technique*. Monterey, CA: Brooks/Cole, 1972.

Lesser, S. R. Psychoanalysis with children. In B. B. Wolman (Ed.), *Manual of child psychopathology*. New York: McGraw-Hill, 1972.

Levitt, E. E. The results of psychotherapy with children: An evaluation. *Journal of Consulting Psychology*, 1957, *21*, 189–196. (a)

Levitt, E. E. A comparison of "remainers" and "defectors" among child clinic patients. *Journal of Consulting Psychology*, 1957, *21*, 316. (b)

Levitt, E. E. Research on psychotherapy with children. In A. E. Bergin and S. L. Garfield (Eds.), *Handbook of psychotherapy and behavior change*. New York: Wiley, 1971. Pp. 474–494.

Levitt, E. E., Beiser, H. R., and Robertson, R. E. A follow-up evaluation of cases treated at a community child guidance clinic. *The American Journal of Orthopsychiatry*, 1959, *29*, 337–349.

Levy, D. M. Release therapy in young children. *Psychiatry*, 1938, *1*, 387–390.

Levy, D. M. Trends in therapy. III: Release therapy. *American Journal of Orthopsychiatry*, 1939, *9*, 713–736.

Levy, D. M. *Maternal overprotection*. New York: Columbia University Press, 1943.

Madsen, C. H., Jr., Becker, W. C., and Thomas, D. R. Rules, praise, and ignoring: Elements of elementary classroom control. *Journal of Applied Behavior Analysis*, 1968, *1*, 139–150.

Minuchin, S. *Families and family therapy*. Cambridge, MA: Harvard University Press, 1974.

Minuchin, S., Baker, L., Rosman, B., Liebman, R., Milman, L., and Todd, T. A conceptual model of psychosomatic illness in children. *Archives of General Psychiatry*, 1975, *32*, 1031–1038.

Moustakas, C. *Children in play therapy*. New York: Jason Aronson, 1973.

Newall, H. W. Play therapy in child psychiatry. *American Journal of Orthopsychiatry*, 1941, *11*, 245–251.

Olson, D. H. Marital and family therapy: Integrative review and critique. *Journal of Marriage and the Family*, 1970, *32*, 501–538.

Patterson, G. R. Behavioral intervention procedures in the classroom and in the home. In A. E. Bergin and S. L. Garfield (Eds.), *The handbook of psychotherapy and behavior change*. New York: Wiley, 1971. Pp. 751–775.

Patterson, G. R. Intervention for boys with conduct problems. Multiple settings, treatment and criteria. *Journal of Consulting and Clinical Psychology*, 1974, *42*, 471–481.

Paolino, T. J., and McCardy, B. M. (Eds.) *Marriage and marital therapy: Psychoanalytic, behavioral and theory systems perspectives*. New York: Brunner/Mazel, 1978.

Rittenhouse, J. D. Endurance of effect: Family unit treatment compared to identified patient treatment. *Proceedings, 78th Annual Convention, APA*, 1970. Pp. 535–536.

Rogers, C. R. *The clinical treatment of the problem child*. Boston: Houghton Mifflin, 1939.

Rogers, C. R. *Counseling and psychotherapy*. Boston: Houghton Mifflin, 1942.

Ryle, A. Couple therapy. In S. Walrond-Skinner (Ed.), *Family and marital psychotherapy. A critical approach*. London: Routledge & Kegan Paul, 1979.

Satir, V. M. *Conjoint family therapy: a guide to theory and technique*. (Rev. ed.). Palo Alto, CA: Science and Behavior Books, 1967.

Schaefer, C. E. (Ed.) *Therapeutic use of child's play*. New York: Jason Aronson, 1976.

Slavson, S. R. General principles and dynamics. In S. R. Slavson (Ed.), *The practice of group therapy*. New York: International Universities Press, 1947. Pp. 19–39.

Solomon, J. C. Active play therapy. *American Journal of Orthopsychiatry,* 1938, *8,* 479–498.

Solomon, J. C. Active play therapy: Further experiences. *American Journal of Orthopsychiatry,* 1940, *10,* 763–781.

Solomon, J. C. Trends in orthopsychiatric therapy. IV: Play technique. *American Journal of Orthopsychiatry,* 1948, *18,* 402–413.

Taft, J. *The dynamics of therapy in a controlled situation.* New York: Macmillan, 1933.

Vincent, J. P. (Ed.) *Advances in family intervention, assessment and theory.* Vol. 1. Greenwich, Conn.: JAI Press, 1980.

Weiss, R. L. Strategic behavioral marital therapy: Toward a model for assessment and intervention. In J. P. Vincent (Ed.), *Advances in family intervention, assessment and theory.* Vol. 1. Greenwich, Conn.: JAI Press, 1980.

Wells, R. A., Dilkes, T. C., and Trivelli, N. The results of family therapy: A critical review of the literature. *Family Process,* 1972, *7,* 189–207.

Psychotherapy: Research and Evaluation

In the previous six chapters a variety of psychotherapeutic approaches have been described. Although only a sample of the existing approaches and methods of psychotherapy were presented, probably enough varieties were included to amaze or bewilder the reader. Some references were also made to research appraisals of some of the different forms of psychotherapy discussed. In this chapter, however, we shall focus exclusively on the topic of research in psychotherapy, an area of particular importance in terms of the contributions made by clinical psychologists. However, before we proceed, a few words should be said with regard to forms of treatment other than psychotherapy.

Psychotherapy and behavioral change procedures have been emphasized in this book because these activities constitute the main forms of treatment provided by clinical psychologists. These are activities which we share with a number of other professions. However, other treatments exist. Particularly in the last 15 years, a number of drugs and medications have been developed and used in treating patients with a variety of problems. For example, pharmacological treatments have been developed to help individuals with anxiety, depression, psychotic behavior and the like (Goodwin, 1980; Honigfeld & Howard, 1978). Such treatments fall within the province of medicine. Psychiatrists also use other somatic treatments such as electroconvulsive therapy.

Psychologists, of course, are not prepared or qualified to administer such treatments. These treatments also have positive and negative effects, and have been used with and without psychotherapy (Goodwin, 1980; Hollon & Beck, 1978). No attempt will be made here to describe or evaluate these psychiatric treatments, since this is beyond the aim of the present book and the competence of the author. The main reason for mentioning this topic is to avoid any possible misinterpretation about the role of psychotherapy in the treatment of mental and emotional disorders. Psychotherapy, the primary treatment of psychologists, is not the only treatment available, and studies comparing the possible efficacy of the different treatments for specific disorders are reviewed elsewhere (Hollon & Beck, 1978). Now, however, let us discuss the problems of research in psychotherapy.

RESEARCH IN PSYCHOTHERAPY

During the past 30 years there has been a significant increase in both the quantity and quality of research conducted in the area of psychotherapy. This clearly is associated with the expansion of clinical psychology during this period and the leading role clinical psychologists have played in research of this type. Since psychotherapy is not a simple process which is fully understood, it is desirable to discuss some of the difficulties encountered in conducting research on the process and outcome of psychotherapy.

In conducting any research, the more clearly one can define and quantify the variables being studied, the greater the probability of securing meaningful and reliable results. Likewise, the simpler the variables under study are, the greater the chances for securing clearcut results. On all these counts, psychotherapy presents many problems to the would-be researcher. Let us consider some of them.

In the first place, many individuals use the term, psychotherapy, without specifying very clearly or in operational terms what is meant by it. For example, do two individuals who state that they engage in psychoanalytically oriented psychotherapy perform the same operations in their practice of psychotherapy? If we proceed beyond the general designation of psychotherapy and attempt to study the designated operations or processes of psychotherapy, we encounter a similar problem. Do such operations or constructs as interpretation, the attainment of insight, empathy, or transference, mean the same thing to all therapists when they describe what is taking place in psychotherapy? The use of such constructs without further operational definition or amplification clearly presents problems when research on such variables is contemplated.

Keeping in mind the kinds of difficulties just mentioned, there are at least three main factors, along with their possible interactions, that need to be considered in trying to evaluate outcome in psychotherapy. Here, I have reference to therapist characteristics, client characteristics, and outcome variables. In any research aimed at evaluating outcome in psychotherapy, detailed attention must be paid to these rather complicated sources of relevant data. In the case of the therapist, for example, one needs to consider his training, his theoretical orientation, his experience, his personality, his preferences for working with certain kinds of clients, his techniques, and so on. In the case of the client, one might consider such features as his symptoms, his degree of disturbance or impairment, his interest and motivation for therapy, his actual life situation, his age and sophistication, his expectations concerning therapy, and the duration of his difficulties as being of some consequence as far as the outcome of psychotherapy is concerned. The possible interaction effects between certain types of therapists and certain kinds of clients also appears to have some obvious influence on outcome. For example, some clients may relate better to certain therapists than to others and, conversely, some therapists may work more effectively with specific kinds of clients than with others. Thus, possible interaction effects would also need to be considered in outcome research.

Finally, there is the critical and complicated problem associated with the criteria to be used in assessing change or improvement. What criteria can be used for this purpose? Can one use an overall judgment of outcome provided by the therapist? Can the same standard measures of appraisal be used for all clients undergoing psychotherapy, or must criteria be developed or adapted for each individual client? Can changes resulting from psychotherapy be measured quantitatively, reliably, and validly? Are some types of change more important than others? If so, who decides this matter? Can different therapies with disparate goals be appraised in the same manner with the same procedures? At what time intervals should change be appraised? What period of follow-up is required to make changes meaningful? These are the kinds of problems that have to be considered in evaluating outcome in psychotherapy. Thus, appraising possible improvement resulting from psychotherapy is not a simple task and the complexities of the problem need to be kept in mind in evaluating the studies that have been reported in this area.

Much of the research in the past has tended to neglect such considerations, and, instead, has perpetuated what Kiesler (1966, 1971) has termed "uniformity" myths. That is, the three major variables of client, therapist, and outcome have been treated as uniform variables. The client, or patient, for example, was perceived as representing a homogeneous group of patients, and the therapist as representing a more or less homogeneous group of therapists. The importance of individual differences among clients and therapists tended to be neglected. Research based on the grouping together of a diversity of clients treated by a variety of therapists and using inadequate criteria of outcome necessarily has produced conflicting and frequently meaningless results. Because of such practices, as well as the difficulties in carrying out well-designed and controlled studies on outcome, much of the data on the effectiveness of psychotherapeutic approaches has been open to criticism.

Among the common inadequacies in much of the previous research was the poor description of the patient samples used. Apart from problems of lack of reliability of diagnosis was the tendency to lump patients under broad rubrics such as neurosis. In more recent times, studies have also been conducted on volunteers or other individuals who have not been very seriously disturbed. Consequently, generalization from such studies to specific clinical problems has been limited.

Although behavioral therapists in the past appeared to emphasize their therapeutic procedures and to pay relatively little attention to the personal qualities of the therapist, this has changed in recent years (Alexander & Barton, 1980; Goldfried & Davison, 1976; Wilson & Evans, 1977). Thus, most therapeutic schools today would acknowledge that the skill and personal attributes of the therapist are of some consequence. Nevertheless, with the exception of the client-centered therapists, who developed scales to measure therapist qualities expressed in the therapy sessions, few research studies have paid much attention to this issue. To a significant extent, therapists used in a number of research studies have been those who can be "persuaded" to participate or "volunteer" for research projects. These frequently have been psychiatric residents, clinical or counseling psychology interns, or graduate students receiving practicum training. This has been particularly true of specifically designed studies rather than studies of general outcome in a clinical setting. However, more recent studies have improved in this regard.

CRITERIA OF OUTCOME

The criteria used for evaluating outcome in psychotherapy is also a complicated matter worth further mention. In a large number of studies, particularly in the past, the main criterion used was the judgment or rating of the therapist. Although one can agree with the view that the therapist is the one who is best acquainted with the patient and the latter's progress in therapy, there are also some possible reasons to question the objectivity and validity of the therapist's evaluation. The therapist, after all, is not a disinterested participant. The outcome of therapy also reflects on the therapist's skill. Another problem is that such ratings of outcome are made at the end of therapy, and the therapist's memory of the initial status of the patient may be somewhat clouded. It has also been suggested that the therapist's final rating of outcome at the end of therapy may be greatly influenced by the overall adjustment level of the patient, rather than indicating the degree of change supposedly secured by means of therapy. That is, patients who enter therapy with minimal disturbance and who change relatively little may be rated as very much improved, whereas more severely disturbed individuals who actually change more, but who at the end of treatment are still far from an optimum level of adjustment, may not receive high ratings of improvement (Mintz, 1972).

Another frequently used criterion of outcome consists of ratings of improvement secured from patients. Somewhat similar issues are raised by such ratings as were mentioned for the ratings by therapists. Although an appraisal of outcome by the consumer of the psychological services provided should be sought and certainly considered, the patient also is not a fully objective evaluator. The patient may feel positive toward the therapist despite very modest improvement, and may also want to justify the time and money invested in therapy. Thus, the ratings may be more positive than otherwise. Some patients, of course, may respond in an opposite manner. In either case, the evaluation may be somewhat suspect. Finally, the type of rating scale used to evaluate outcome is also a factor in the possible value of ratings of both patients and therapists. Crude scales of outcome using such categories as "*Improved,*" "*Slightly Improved,*" and "*Greatly Improved,*" leave much to be desired in terms of how these rating categories are interpreted. Furthermore, if only patients' and therapists' ratings are used, there is no feasible procedure for estimating the reliability of such ratings.

Because of the potential limitations of such ratings of outcome, a number of other methods have been used. One procedure used in two well-known recent studies is that of securing ratings from an impartial clinical evaluator (Sloane, Staples, Cristol, Yorkston, & Whipple, 1975; Strupp & Hadley, 1979). This individual will usually be assigned the task of evaluating the client prior to therapy and again at termination and follow-up. Thus, in addition to an overall global appraisal of improvement at the end of therapy, the differences in the ratings made at the different appraisal points can also be made. One criticism made of such ratings is that the evaluator's ratings are based to a large extent on the information received from the patient. This may account for the fact that the correlations obtained between clients' ratings and evaluators' ratings frequently are higher than the correlations secured between therapist and client or therapist and evaluator (Horenstein, Houston, & Holmes, 1973; Ryan & Gizynski, 1971; Sloane et al., 1975). Another criticism of such ratings is the one already mentioned, namely, that the descriptive terms used in the rating scale generally lack operational definition and consequently are of limited value.

Psychological tests of many types have also been used in past evaluations of psychotherapy. They have some apparent advantages over simple ratings. They can be more objective, are standardized, and have normative data. Tests can be given before and after therapy, and the changes in scores noted. At the same time, there are also apparent problems in relying on psychological tests. Some, like the projective tests, present problems of reliability and validity because of the emphasis on clinical interpretation. Personality questionnaires also tend to deal with generalized traits or diagnostic syndromes, which may be lacking in suitability for the individual case. Furthermore, although looking at the difference in test scores obtained before and after treatment would appear to be a simple index of change, and preferable to global ratings secured at the end of therapy, such difference scores also present problems. For example, individuals who at the beginning of therapy are minimally maladjusted have less room to show a positive increase in test scores than those who are more disturbed and have lower scores. There is also a phenomenon known as regression toward the mean which states that upon retesting, the test scores of individuals will tend to regress to the mean score of the distribution. Consequently, high scores may decline and low scores may increase toward the mean. Fortunately, there are some statistical procedures which can be used to correct for such phenomena, but many previous studies did not use them.

With the rise of the behavioral therapies, researchers with this orientation have emphasized behavioral measures of outcome. Thus, if an individual has a fear of going on an airplane, the best criterion is the apparent removal of this fear as manifested by the individual's taking an airplane trip without any evident fear of flying. Such criteria of outcome are obviously very meaningful and, in the author's opinion, have been neglected in much psychotherapy research. However, not all clients have such specific problems which lend themselves to behavioral appraisal, nor is it always easy to secure valid observations of the behavior or problem in question. Furthermore, as was noted in the chapter on behavioral assessment, some of the behavioral measures used are employed in the treatment situation and the generalization to the real situation may be different.

It should be apparent, therefore, that there are no fully adequate measures for appraising outcome in psychotherapy. This should be kept in mind in evaluating the various reports on this topic. Researchers in the field have become sensitive to this problem and although there is no unanimity on this matter, a number of them have recommended that a variety of different types of measures be utilized (Strupp & Hadley, 1977; Waskow & Parloff, 1975). In this way, the limitations of any particular measure would not influence unduly the results obtained. Another point stressed is that different assessment procedures essentially represent different vantage points and that all need to be considered. Thus, Strupp and Hadley (1977) state that three viewpoints need to be considered, the patients', the mental health professional worker's, and that of society. In the case of the individual patient, his/her feelings and perceptions of adequacy and well being would be considered. In the case of the professional, judgments of mental health based on behavioral observation, psychological tests, and other clinical appraisals, integrated by the clinician in terms of theoretical views of personality and normal functioning would suffice. And, from society's vantage point, the emphasis would be on the behavior of the individual in terms of expected social roles and mores.

Although this tripartite view of evaluating outcome as well as similar schemes for comprehensive appraisal clearly appear more attractive than procedures which utilize only one or two types of measures, they are not complete solutions. For example, how does one reconcile significant discrepancies among the different vantage points when they are obtained? It is stated that the three vantage points need to be evaluated and integrated—but who will be designated to perform this important function? If it is another professional psychotherapist, then this one particular point of view might be overrepresented and emphasized.

OTHER RESEARCH CONSIDERATIONS

Two other considerations in conducting or evaluating research in psychotherapy have been emphasized by the author and can be mentioned briefly here (Garfield, 1980, 1981). One concerns the importance of proper control groups; the other pertains to the clinical significance of the results secured. It seems evident that a control group is necessary if one is to evaluate adequately the results of any treatment. Otherwise, we cannot be sure if the changes secured by the treatment are due to the treatment or to extraneous variables such as the passage of time or some fortuitous event such as getting married or divorced, receiving a promotion, recovery from physical illness, the departure of the client's mother-in-law, or the like. In the past, the emphasis was placed on a no-treatment control group and any differences noted between the treatment and control groups were ascribed to the treatment. Although such an arrangement meets the general requirements of a control group, it is not always possible to arrange. For example, if the therapy requires a moderate or considerable time period for completion, there are some real problems in maintaining a no-treatment control group. It is not really ethical to withhold therapy for long periods of time from patients who are disturbed and in need of treatment. Even if the therapy is relatively brief, it is not always possible to retain a control group. Many of the patients randomly assigned to the control group may decide to seek treatment elsewhere or to forego further participation in the project. In such instances, it may be extremely difficult to replace such patients with similarly comparable patients. Such attrition of control group patients also may limit the value of the control group since those patients who remain in the study can no longer be regarded as a representative or unselected sample.

A variation of the no-treatment control group is the wait-list control group. This has been used in studies of relatively brief therapy, where the control patients are told they will be placed on a waiting list but that they will be guaranteed treatment within a specified period—whatever the length of treatment is. In the study by Sloane *et al.* (1975), to which reference has been made previously, the wait-list control group was promised treatment within 4 months, the length of the two psychotherapies evaluated. Since these patients also maintained contact with a research assistant during the waiting period, this wait-list control condition has also been viewed as a "minimal treatment" condition.

Although the use of a no-treatment or wait-list control group is of definite importance in evaluating the effects of psychotherapy, some researchers have stated that such a control group is not completely adequate. Paul (1967), for example, has advocated the use of what he has designated as an "attention-placebo" control group to control for the effects of variables not directly linked to the forms of therapy being investigated. In other words, are the more positive effects secured by the psychotherapy patients actually due to the theoretical variables postulated for psychotherapy or are they due to such general variables as the opportunity to talk to someone and the like? The point made here is similar to that made earlier in the testing of new drugs. Some individuals appear to respond well to the taking of pills or medication, even though the latter may be pharmacologically ineffective. Consequently, in the evaluation of drugs the usual control is a placebo, an inert pill that closely resembles the active drug in appearance and taste (Shapiro & Morris, 1978). Only if the real drug clearly is more effective than the placebo is it considered to have therapeutic effectiveness. If both are equally effective, the positive effects are usually ascribed to nonpharmacological variables such as being seen by a physician and being given apparent treatment, suggestion, or other variable.

Because of such a view, it has been recommended that an attention-placebo control group be used in addition to a no-treatment group if it is at all possible. Such a control group would be told they are to receive therapy and would meet regularly with a therapist. However, the sessions might be somewhat general discussions or interactions which did not overlap the specific therapy being evaluated. If the group receiving psychotherapy does no better than the attention-placebo group despite improving more than the no-treatment group, the usual interpretation would be that the positive effects are essentially "placebo effects," and could be secured by interpersonal interactions other than psychotherapy. On the other hand, if the therapy group is clearly superior to both control groups, then a strong case can be made for the effectiveness of psychotherapy. However, it is not easy to devise an attention-placebo group which is really creditable, and there are some potential ethical considerations involved. All of these factors indicate that designing an adequate study with suitable control groups is a rather difficult undertaking.

The final point to be mentioned here concerns the issue of clinical versus statistical significance. Tests of statistical significance are used in research investigations to determine if the findings secured are due merely to chance. If they are, the results are considered as nonsignificant, that is, the experimental hypothesis has not been supported or a particular treatment has not produced a noticeable effect. The opposite, of course, would be true if the findings are found to be statistically significant and, therefore, as probably not due to chance.

What statistical tests of significance signify, therefore, is the probability that a certain outcome is due to a chance occurrence. It is quite common today to use a .05 level of significance as an acceptable probability level for estimating the statistical significance of the results secured. Thus, when such a level of statistical significance is secured, the investigator may conclude that his/her findings are significant. This means that there are only five chances out of a hundred that the results might have been obtained by chance. It is, of course, possible that the findings could have been secured by chance 5% of the time. However, the odds are against this by a ratio of twenty to one. The results, therefore, are judged to be significant.

The use of the term, significant, in this context refers only to the probability of chance findings. It is a statistical interpretation. In evaluating outcome in psychotherapy, however, we must also evaluate the *clinical significance* of the findings obtained. An obtained result may be statistically significant, that is, not due to chance, but its practical significance may be minimal or great. It is well to keep in mind also that statistical tests of significance are affected by the size of the sample used. With a very large sample, low correlations or small differences may be statistically significant (Garfield, 1978b). For example, a particular enrichment program provided to a large sample of school children may be found to produce a statistically significant gain of 4.5 points in IQ. However, for practical purposes the gain may be considered as insignificant in terms of the cost of the program. In a similar fashion, in evaluating research on the effectiveness of psychotherapy, we must go beyond the estimate of statistical significance and evaluate the results in terms of their clinical effectiveness or social worth. We shall return to this issue later in this chapter.

RESEARCH ON THE EFFECTIVENESS OF PSYCHOTHERAPY

Now that we have considered some of the difficulties in carrying out research to evaluate psychotherapy and should be sensitive to possible limitations in some of the published research in this area, let us review some of this material.

As indicated earlier, prior to the 1950's, there was very little research conducted on psychotherapy (Bergin, 1971). However, in 1952 the British psychologist, Hans Eysenck, published an article on the effects of psychotherapy which had a very strong impact on the field. In this article, Eysenck reviewed and evaluated the results of twenty-four studies, of which five were evaluations of psychoanalysis and the remainder were classified as studies of "eclectic" therapy. Although there were obvious difficulties in equating patients, the results presented by Eysenck were considered to be based on supposedly comparable groups of "neurotic" patients. The therapeutic results in these studies were also compared with data provided by Landis (1937) for hospitalized neurotic patients who purportedly received little or no therapy and were discharged from state hospitals as recovered or improved, and with the results reported by Denker (1946) for 500 patients treated by nonpsychiatric physicians. The latter two groups were selected essentially as control groups.

According to the data summarized by Eysenck, the proportion of cases improved by psychoanalysis ranged from 39 to 67% in the different reports with an average for all cases of 44%. The corresponding indices for the "eclectic" psychotherapies ranged from 40 to 77% with a mean of 64%. On this basis, the results of psychoanalytic treatment were viewed as not as satisfactory as those of the eclectic therapies. If, however, those patients who dropped out of psychoanalytic treatment before its completion are excluded from the calculations, then the percentage of cases improved via psychoanalysis rises to an average of 66%, which approximates the average of the eclectic cases. The interesting and rather disturbing point made by Eysenck, however, was not that the eclectic and psychoanalytic therapies may not show greatly divergent results, but that the results of all the psychotherapies did not exceed the results obtained from hospitalization with practically no psychotherapy or from superficial treatment by physicians with no training in psychotherapy. On the basis of these results, Eysenck even went so far as to question whether psychologists should be trained to engage in psychotherapy.

Needless to say, Eysenck's paper aroused considerable dismay and heated responses from a number of psychologists who quickly pointed out the deficiencies in the reports reviewed by Eysenck, as well as those in his review.

Because of their importance to all research on outcome, some of the limitations in this work can be mentioned here. The comparability of the patients treated in the various studies is open to serious question. The classification of "neurosis" is simply too broad and unreliable a one on which to base any serious conclusions. Furthermore, the patients in one so-called control group were hospitalized and their comparability with the other groups cannot be adequately ascertained. The variability among the different groups of therapists presents similar problems to those just mentioned for the patients.

The matter of the criteria of improvement used also presents problems. In most instances, the judgment of extent of improvement was left to the therapist. Here, again, one has to raise the problem of comparability and reliability of clinical judgment. When two different therapists judge a similar percentage of their patients to be improved, can we assume that these percentages are actually comparable or reflect the same *degree* of improvement? For that matter, what are the criteria used to determine a patient's improvement? Certainly a great many different aspects of the individual's personality and his social adjustment can be used and have been used in evaluating therapy. Examples of such indices are as follows: diminution or disappearance of symptoms, obtaining a job or a promotion, improvement in ability to socialize, verbalizing insight into one's problems, self reports of feeling better, being able to do things previously thought impossible, more mature behavior, better organized defenses, reorganization of the personality, and remaining out of the hospital.

It should be obvious that the examples of criteria listed above vary tremendously and may have different degrees of significance as far as a particular individual is concerned. Furthermore, even where attempts are made to use the same criteria in a subjective manner, there remains the problem of the variability and bias of the judgments made by different therapists. As a consequence, we can raise the question of whether or not two judgments of "improvement" in psychotherapy are in any degree equivalent in meaning or significance. In a study of clinical case records by the writer, for example (Garfield and Kurz, 1952), over 25 different evaluative terms were used by the therapists in recording their evaluations of 103 cases. These included such categories as "improved, greatly improved, slightly improved, much improvement, some improvement, maximum improvement, fair adjustment, symptomatic improvement, further treatment not required, seems to have adjusted, recovered, treatment completed successfully, and so forth." As one can see from this sample of therapeutic appraisals, it would be extremely difficult on this basis to compare the relative success of treatment among the various therapists.

Problems of this type are apparent in Eysenck's tabulations of the results from the various studies reviewed by him. Eysenck himself, in appraising the reported results of the Berlin Psychoanalytic Institute, decided that their category of "Improved" should be included in his category of "Slightly Improved." Bergin (1971), however, in reviewing the same materials, comes to a different conclusion and believes that such cases should be viewed as improved rather than as slightly improved. Since the cases judged to be "Slightly Improved" were not counted by Eysenck in his percentage of improvement resulting from therapy, one's decision here is crucial for how effective psychotherapy is judged to be. Whereas Eysenck (1952) came up with a 39% improvement rate for the Berlin Institute, Bergin (1971) came up with a 91% rate of improvement! Clearly, no scientific conclusions are possible from such data. It is interesting, however, that Bergin's appraisal of outcome in the 19 studies of eclectic therapy was practically identical to that of Eysenck's—an improvement rate of 65% as compared to a rate of 64%.

Eysenck (1961, 1966) published two additional reviews of outcome in psychotherapy. His conclusions based on these later appraisals of psychotherapy are essentially the same as his earlier ones although they are based on many additional studies, including some controlled ones which are more sophisticated than those reported earlier. In general, psychotherapy as traditionally practiced was not found to be any more efficacious than no treatment. "Civilian neurotics who are treated by psychotherapy recover or improve to approximately the same extent as similar neurotics receiving no psychotherapy" (Eysenck, 1966, p. 39). At least, one cannot accuse Eysenck of beating around the bush or being ambiguous. He also states that neurotic patients treated by the behavioral approaches based on learning theory improve significantly more quickly than patients treated by conventional psychotherapies. Thus, according to Eysenck, the research literature provides little support for the effectiveness of psychotherapy, with the exception of those approaches based on learning theory. Although the number of studies has increased, there apparently has been little increase in the amount of positive support for psychotherapy.

Although there were a number of reactions to the reviews of psychotherapy outcome by Eysenck (DeCharms, Levy, and Wertheimer, 1954; Eysenck, 1966; Luborsky, 1954; Rosenzweig, 1954), the first really substantive response to Eysenck's appraisal based on alternative reviews of the research literature was provided by Meltzoff and Kornreich (1970). These authors stated that they were able to find many more studies in the published literature that reported findings that favored psychotherapy than was the case in the reviews published by Eysenck. Meltzoff and Kornreich analyzed the findings from 101 studies and stated that in 80% of them, the results were positive for psychotherapy. Thus, their conclusions were the opposite of those reached by Eysenck.

Since that time there have been several additional reviews. In 1971, Bergin published his appraisal of the literature on outcome in psychotherapy. We have already made reference to the fact that Bergin reanalyzed some of the material reviewed by Eysenck, interpreted the measures of outcome differently, and reached a different conclusion on this material. Bergin also analyzed the data from 48 more recent studies and concluded that the results indicated that psychotherapy showed a "modestly positive" effect. He also differed very noticeably from Eysenck in his estimate of the "spontaneous remission" rate, that is, the percentage of people who improve without therapy. Bergin's estimate in this regard was around 30%, less than one-half the spontaneous remission rate posited by Eysenck.

Rachman (1971, 1973), a colleague of Eysenck, also prepared reviews of this literature, and perhaps not unexpectedly, tended to agree with Eysenck's conclusions and to be quite critical of those presented by Bergin. Rachman was particularly critical of Bergin's estimate of spontaneous remission and the studies upon which it was based. Because the studies reporting positive findings for the effectiveness of psychotherapy were found to have serious methodological shortcomings, Rachman agreed with Eysenck in concluding that the efficacy of psychotherapy, excluding behavior therapy, had yet to be demonstrated.

The next review of outcome studies was published a few years later by Luborsky, Singer, and Luborsky (1975). Utilizing certain methodological criteria of adequacy, these authors rated each study and finally selected 33 studies that at least met minimal requirements. In each of these studies, a given type of psychotherapy was compared with some type of control group. In 20 of the 33 studies, the comparisons showed psychotherapy to be significantly more effective than the control condition. In 13 of the studies no differences were found between the psychotherapy and control groups, and in no studies was the control group superior to the group receiving psychotherapy. Although these authors interpreted the results of their analysis as indicating that psychotherapy was effective, the results while favoring psychotherapy over no treatment, are not truly impressive. In almost 40% of the comparisons, psychotherapy did not show an effect significantly greater than no therapy. However, on an overall basis, the conclusions were in agreement with those of Meltzoff and Kornreich (1970) and those of Bergin as being positive toward psychotherapy and as differing from those of Eysenck (1961,1966) and Rachman (1971,1973). However, additional reviews have appeared since that time.

Bergin and Lambert (1978) prepared a review which was essentially an updating of Bergin's earlier review. This time, while reaffirming an improvement rate for psychotherapy of approximately 65%, on the basis of a different sample of studies, they offered an estimate of the spontaneous remission rate of 43%. They emphasized that this was a crude estimate and that there was noticeable variability from study to study. The effects of psychotherapy, therefore, were relatively modest, but improvement was obtained more quickly by means of psychotherapy than with no treatment.

A year before the Bergin and Lambert (1978) review appeared, a preliminary report of the largest-scale review of the effects of psychotherapy was published, based on 375 studies, both published and unpublished (Smith & Glass, 1977). These individuals also applied a new statistical method of analyzing research findings called meta-analysis. This procedure was considered to allow for a more objective evaluation of a group of research studies since it minimized the subjective judgment of the individuals reviewing and evaluating the studies. Without going into detail, it can be mentioned that explicit criteria can be set up for coding and classifying studies, and that, apart from a few basic considerations such as the presence of a control or comparison group and random assignment of subjects to treatment or control groups, all studies can be included. Statistical comparisons can then be made of studies of certain types or with certain characteristics. Thus, a larger number of studies can be compared and evaluated. Furthermore, meta-analysis allows one to secure an "effect size" or quantitative estimate of the effects of treatment. The effect size is the difference between the mean score of the treatment group and that of the control group divided by the standard deviation of the control group. In this way, the relative outcomes on different measures can be compared and outcomes on groups of studies can be combined.

In their preliminary report based on 375 studies, Smith and Glass (1977) secured an effect size of .65 standard deviation for the effectiveness of psychotherapy. To put it another way, the outcome scores of the average person at the end of therapy exceeded the scores of 75% of the controls. These findings were interpreted by Smith and Glass as indicating that psychotherapy was effective. This report, although received positively by some workers in the field (Parloff, 1979; Strupp, 1978) was strongly criticized by others (Gallo, 1978; Rimland, 1979; Strahan, 1978). Eysenck (1978) was particularly critical of the studies used upon which the conclusions were drawn, referring to "garbage in, garbage out."

The final report, entitled *The Effects of Psychotherapy,* was based on 475 studies analyzed by means of meta-analysis (Smith, Glass, & Miller, 1980). This time an effect size of .80 standard deviation was obtained, indicating that the average result of the psychotherapy clients exceeded 85% of those in the control groups. Smith, Glass, and Miller interpreted this effect size as demonstrating that psychotherapy was clearly effective. In comparison with the research results secured in other social science areas, the positive results for psychotherapy were considered as truly impressive—"The results show unequivocally that psychotherapy is effective" (Smith, Glass, & Miller, 1980, p. 124). With certain reservations, it was stated also that in general, there were no large differences in effectiveness found between the major forms of psychotherapy. Since the general conclusions drawn from this review and analysis were based on the largest amount of research data on outcome in psychotherapy ever assembled, one would feel that the effectiveness of psychotherapy was clearly and, perhaps, finally demonstrated. However, as might be inferred from earlier parts of this presentation, this has not been the case. Before discussing this issue further, one additional comprehensive review of the effects of psychotherapy needs to be mentioned.

In the same year that the book by Smith, Glass, and Miller (1980) appeared, there appeared also the book by Rachman and Wilson (1980), *The Effectiveness of Psychological Therapy*. Both of these authors are behaviorally oriented and reference has already been made to earlier reviews by Rachman (1971, 1973). In addition to general problems of research methodology, the book reviewed the research on various forms of psychotherapy. The authors were very critical of the conclusions drawn previously by Bergin (1971) and by Smith and Glass (1977) in their preliminary report of the meta-analysis of psychotherapy. They faulted these reports for their reliance on poorly conducted studies and for their failure to review well-conducted studies of behavior therapy. On the basis of their own analysis, they concluded first of all that there was still no sound data to support the efficacy of psychoanalysis. In general, it is very difficult to disagree with this conclusion for there has been a real dearth of systematic studies evaluating the results of psychoanalysis and no such studies were included in the analysis by Smith, Glass, and Miller. For other forms of psychotherapy generally, including psychoanalytically oriented and eclectic psychotherapy, Rachman and Wilson felt that there was slight evidence in support of such therapies but that the negative data were even larger. With regard to client-centered therapy, they expressed the disappointment that others have also expressed that the postulated therapeutic conditions have failed to live up to earlier expectations. However, they also reviewed a number of outcome studies on behavioral and cognitive therapies which they concluded showed the best results.

EVALUATING THE RESEARCH FINDINGS ON THE EFFECTIVENESS OF PSYCHOTHERAPY

We have now reviewed the major reviews of the research literature pertaining to outcome in psychotherapy as well as having made reference to research findings or the lack thereof in the previous chapters dealing with different forms of psychotherapy. As is probably evident by now, it is not easy to come to some overall conclusions concerning the effectiveness of psychotherapy. There are gaps in our knowledge, there are numerous conflicting findings in the research literature, and different experts in the field seem to interpret the body of existing data in different ways and to reach varying conclusions. This must be extremely confusing to the beginning student in the field or to one who aspires to a career in clinical psychology or to some allied mental health field. The author will do his best to interpret and evaluate this material and to offer some tentative conclusions of his own. The reader, however, should be aware by this time that not all workers in the field of psychotherapy and behavior change will necessarily agree with the views presented by the author.

There are a few interpretations or conclusions that can be mentioned quite briefly at the outset. The first one is that not all of the diverse forms of psychotherapy have had any systematic appraisal of their worth. The lack of such research on psychoanalysis has already been commented upon, although the same could be said of many other more recent or lesser known forms, e.g., existential therapy, reality therapy, and the like. Consequently, there are many current therapies for which there are no supporting research evidence. This does not mean that these forms of psychotherapy are not effective forms of therapy, but that they have not been adequately evaluated in terms of effectiveness. Decisions by individuals to practice or secure such forms of therapy are based on personal reasons of one kind or another, rather than on the basis of empirical evidence.

A second interpretation that can be made is that the existing research literature can be evaluated quite differently depending upon the reviewer's methodological and theoretical views. In terms of the reviews discussed in the preceding pages, it is apparent that the behaviorally oriented psychologists tend to interpret the research findings somewhat differently than do the other reviewers. The behaviorists find the existing research data to be less adequate methodologically and the support for the effectiveness of psychotherapy to be less convincing than do the other reviewers. They also appear to reject strongly the conclusion reached by practically all other reviewers that there are no marked differences between the forms of psychotherapy that have been compared. They contend that there is stronger support for behavioral forms of therapy than for others.

On the basis of what has just been stated, it is clear that there is no unanimity concerning the efficacy of psychotherapy and there have been many heated debates on the topic. It has also become very evident, particularly in recent years, that the issue is not simply a scientific or professional one, but one which has important social and political implications in terms of insurance coverage for psychotherapeutic services. For a variety of reasons, therefore, it is important to attempt some appraisal of psychotherapy's effectiveness.

First, it may be worthwhile to offer some general comments on issues raised in the various reviews of outcome mentioned earlier. Several of the reviewers, for example, have accused other reviewers of failing to perform an adequate search of the existing research literature. Thus, Meltzoff and Kornreich (1970) stated they found many more studies reporting positive findings for psychotherapy than Eysenck had found. Rachman and Wilson (1980) accused Smith and Glass (1977) of failing to include a number of well-conducted studies on behavior therapy. Smith, Glass, and Miller (1980) have accused most other reviewers of omitting many studies from their reviews and also of not specifying the bases for the selection and exclusion of studies. Luborsky, Singer and Luborsky (1975) specified their inclusion criteria and, as a result of their criteria, reviewed a relatively small number of studies. These comments basically dealt with two issues—the possible bias in selecting studies for review and the adequacy of the studies available for review. Here, personal judgment may enter into decisions, and conceivably, wise men (and women) may differ.

The first issue can be set aside, I believe, since there are enough studies available for review and the general patterns are discernable. The adequacy of the studies reviewed, however, is an issue of central importance, and a previous section of this chapter was devoted to this topic. This issue has been heightened by the meta-analyses of Smith and her colleagues (Smith & Glass, 1977; Smith et al., 1980). Although 475 studies were analyzed, one of the primary criticisms of the report is that many very weak and flawed studies were included and mixed with some adequate studies. For example, a significant percentage of the total studies included in the meta-analysis were doctoral dissertations and unpublished studies. These tend generally to be viewed as of lesser value or quality than research studies which have gone through an editorial review process and have been accepted for publication. The response of Smith and her colleagues is that the studies can be classified according to quality and comparisons made. They also point out that the better studies actually show somewhat more positive results than the weaker ones, so their conclusions should not be faulted.

Nevertheless, there are some other aspects of many of the studies analyzed by Smith et al. that have also been questioned. A large number of the studies were conducted on young samples of volunteer subjects in academic settings. The average age of all individuals included in the meta-analysis was 23 years. How well can the results be expected to generalize to older patients seen in actual clinical settings? A related issue is that 70% of the problems treated were phobic behaviors of some sort, whereas only 3% were cases of depression. The samples in the investigations reviewed were thus highly selected ones. Furthermore, a large number of the therapists were in training and consequently were not fully trained or experienced. The rebuttal to these criticisms by Smith and her collaborators is that all such variations in these variables can be analyzed statistically and their effects noted. In most instances, the effects are small or negligible. However, where studies with different types of therapists and patients are compared, are such comparisons truly meaningful? It would seem that only direct comparisons in the same study would provide appropriate answers.

There would appear to be little question that many of the studies reviewed by Smith *et al.* (1980), as well as by others, are studies which have important limitations in terms of the samples of clients treated, the type of problem treated, the kind of therapists used, and the criteria of outcome employed. Consequently, definitive conclusions would not appear possible. However, selecting studies on the basis of certain methodological criteria are said to be open to bias and to overemphasize methodology (Smith *et al.,* 1980; Glass & Kliegl, 1983). Nevertheless, although such misuses of selection criteria are possible, even those who are positive toward meta-analysis believe some selection is necessary (Strube & Hartmann, 1983). The author tends to agree with this view. Perhaps research psychologists are overly imbued with the importance of methodology, but to overlook such considerations does not seem wise either. How can one take seriously a study with obvious flaws or limitations?

Consequently, one can offer some tentative generalizations based on the existing research, and also offer some suggestions for future research. In terms of existing studies it seems reasonable to state that perhaps around 65% of those who undergo psychotherapy receive some benefit from it. However, having offered this generalization, some cautions need to be added. This is an overly broad generalization. Psychotherapy is a general term used to designate a variety of different procedures and approaches which have been applied to a variety of disorders and problems. Since not all approaches have been evaluated, the generalization cannot be applied to all of them. For the most part, and within the limitations of relying on general terms, most of the evaluative research has been conducted on some types of dynamically oriented therapy of relatively brief duration, some so-called eclectic therapies, a variety of behavioral therapies, and client-centered therapy. In a similar vein, not all patients are benefited by receiving psychotherapy, and predicting what patients will respond best is still difficult to do with any large degree of success (Garfield, 1978a).

It is evident, therefore, that while one can say that psychotherapy helps more than it fails to help (or harms), one probably should agree with Bergin (1971; Bergin & Lambert, 1978) that the effects are modest in most cases. If one examines a number of studies and looks closely at the gains secured by means of psychotherapy, it is apparent that the extent or amount of gain varies. A small number of clients show marked gains and are considered to be "recovered" from their disturbance. For example, in a large-scale study of brief therapy, 17% of the patients rated themselves as "recovered" after therapy, the most positive rating on the rating scale used (Avnet, 1965). In this study, the therapists also gave the same rating to 10.5% of the patients. Thus, although approximately three-fourths of the patients were judged to be "improved," only a small percentage of the patients were deemed to have "recovered." Comparable findings can be noted in other studies as well (Emmelkamp & Kuipers, 1979; Sloane et al., 1975). Taking all of those who are considered to have shown improvement, the trend is for a small number to show great improvement, a larger number to show small or moderate improvement, and a lesser number who show no improvement or get worse.

On the basis of such findings, the author has recommended that future research should be devoted to trying to discover what variables are operative in those cases where unusually positive results are secured (Garfield, 1981). The hypothetically postulated variables operating in such instances are not known. They might be patient variables, therapist variables, interaction variables or some other combination of variables. However, if we could discover or isolate those factors which appear to be the important ones for securing significant change, we might be able to improve our therapeutic procedures and our therapeutic outcomes.

At present, the conclusions we can reach are somewhat limited. We can state that on the average psychotherapy is of some modest benefit and that it may shorten the time of the discomfort suffered by the individuals who receive therapy as compared with those who do not. A behavioral approach using exposure treatment seems the most effective for phobias and related disorders, and cognitive-behavioral approaches appear promising for moderate cases of depression. A variety of brief therapies seem to get as good results as longer-term therapies although much of the research has limitations. Finally, we have to be cautious in speaking of the effectiveness of psychotherapy in general since there are many types of therapy, patients differ widely, and therapists also differ in terms of a variety of variables. Research in psychotherapy is still a relatively recent development, and although conducting well-designed high quality research is difficult and time consuming, we should anticipate some progress in the future.

REFERENCES

Alexander, J. F., & Barton, C. Systems-behavioral interventions with delinquent families: Clinical, methodological, and conceptual considerations. In J. P. Vincent (Ed.), *Advances in family intervention, assessment and theory.* Vol. I. Greenwich, Conn.: Jai Press, 1980.

Avnet, H. H. How effective is short-term therapy. In L. R. Wolberg (Ed.), *Short-term psychotherapy.* New York: Grune and Stratton, 1965.

Bergin, A. E. The evaluation of therapeutic outcomes. In A. E. Bergin & S. L. Garfield (Eds.), *Handbook of psychotherapy and behavior change: An empirical analysis.* New York: Wiley, 1971.

Bergin, A. E. & Lambert, M. J. The evaluation of therapeutic outcomes. In S. L. Garfield & A. E. Bergin (Eds.), *Handbook of psychotherapy and behavior change.* (2nd ed.). New York: Wiley, 1978.

DeCharms, R., Levy, J., & Wertheimer, M. A note on attempted evaluations of psychotherapy. *Journal of Clinical Psychology,* 1954, *10,* 233–235.

Denker, P. G. Results of treatment of psychoneuroses by the general practitioner—a follow-up of 500 cases. *New York State Journal of Medicine,* 1946, *46,* 2164–2166.

Emmelkamp, P. M. G., & Kuipers, A. C. M. Agoraphobia: A follow-up study four years after treatment. *British Journal of Psychiatry,* 1979, *134,* 352–355.

Eysenck, H. J. The effects of psychotherapy: An evaluation. *Journal of Consulting Psychology,* 1952, *16,* 319–324.

Eysenck, H. J. The effects of psychotherapy. In H. J. Eysenck (Ed.), *Handbook of Abnormal Psychology.* New York: Basic Books, 1961.

Eysenck, H. J. *The effects of psychotherapy.* New York: International Science Press, 1966.

Eysenck, H. J. An exercise in mega-silliness. *American Psychologist,* 1978, *33,* 517 (Comment).

Gallo, P. S., Jr. Meta-analysis—A mixed metaphor? *American Psychologist,* 1978, *33,* 515–517 (Comment).

Garfield, S. L. Research on client variables in psychotherapy. In S. L. Garfield & A. E. Bergin (Eds.), *Handbook of psychotherapy and behavior change.* (2nd ed.). New York: Wiley, 1978. (a)

Garfield, S. L. Research problems in clinical diagnosis. *Journal of Consulting and Clinical Psychology,* 1978, *46,* 596–607. (b)

Garfield, S. L. *Psychotherapy: An eclectic approach.* New York: Wiley, 1980.

Garfield, S. L. Evaluating the psychotherapies. *Behavior Therapy,* 1981, *12,* 295–307.

Garfield, S. L. & Kutz, M. Evaluation of treatment and related procedures in 1,216 cases referred to a mental hygiene clinic. *Psychiatric Quarterly,* 1952, *26,* 414–424.

Glass, G. V., & Kliegl, R. M. An apology for research integration in the study of psychotherapy. *Journal of Consulting and Clinical Psychology,* 1983, *51,* 28–41.

Goldfried, M. R., & Davison, G. C. *Clinical behavior therapy.* New York: Holt, Rinehart and Winston, 1976.

Goodwin, D. W. Biological psychiatry. In A. E. Kazdin, A. S. Bellack, & M. Hersen (Eds.), *New perspectives in abnormal psychology.* New York: Oxford University Press, 1980.

Hollon, S. D., & Beck, A. T. Psychotherapy and drug therapy: Comparisons and combinations. In S. L. Garfield & A. E. Bergin (Eds.), *Handbook of psychotherapy and behavior change.* (2nd ed.). New York: Wiley, 1978.

Honigfeld, G., & Howard, A. *Psychiatric drugs. A desk reference.* (2nd ed.). New York: Academic Press, 1978.

Horenstein, D., Houston, B., & Holmes, D. Clients', therapists' and judges' evaluations of psychotherapy. *Journal of Counseling Psychology,* 1973, *20,* 149–153.

Kiesler, D. J. Some myths of psychotherapy research and the search for a paradigm. *Psychological Bulletin,* 1966, *65,* 110–136.

Kiesler, D. J. Experimental design in psychotherapy research. In A. E. Bergin & S. L. Garfield (Eds.), *Handbook of psychotherapy and behavior change.* New York: Wiley, 1971.

Landis, C. A statistical evaluation of psychotherapeutic methods. In L. E. Hinsie (Ed.), *Concepts and problems of psychotherapy.* New York: Columbia University Press, 1937.

Luborsky, L. A note on Eysenck's article, "The effects of psychotherapy: An evaluation." *British Journal of Psychology,* 1954, *45,* 129–131.

Luborsky, L., Singer, B., & Luborsky, L. Comparative studies of psychotherapies. *Archives of General Psychiatry,* 1975, *32,* 995–1008.

Meltzoff, J., & Kornreich, M. *Research in psychotherapy.* New York: Atherton Press, 1970.

Mintz, J. What is "success" in psychotherapy? *Journal of Abnormal Psychology,* 1972, *80,* 11–19.

Parloff, M. B. Can psychotherapy research guide the policy-maker? A little knowledge may be a dangerous thing. *American Psychologist,* 1979, *34,* 296–306.

Paul, G. L. Insight versus desensitization in psychotherapy two years after termination. *Journal of Consulting Psychology,* 1967, *31,* 333–348.

Rachman, S. *The effects of psychotherapy.* Oxford: Pergamon, 1971.

Rachman, S. The effects of psychological treatment. In H. Eysenck (Ed.), *Handbook of Abnormal Psychology.* New York: Basic Books, 1973.

Rachman, S. J., & Wilson, G. T. *The effects of psychological therapy.* (2nd ed.). New York: Pergamon, 1980.

Rimland, B. Death knell for psychotherapy? *American Psychologist,* 1979, *34,* 192 (Comment).

Rosenzweig, S. A transevaluation of psychotherapy—a reply to Hans Eysenck. *Journal of Abnormal and Social Psychology,* 1954, *49,* 298–304.

Ryan, V., & Gizynski, M. Behavior therapy in retrospect: Patients' feelings about their behavior therapists. *Journal of Consulting and Clinical Psychology,* 1971, *37,* 1–9.

Shapiro, A. K., & Morris, L. A. Placebo effects in medical and psychological therapies. In S. L. Garfield & A. E. Bergin (Eds.), *Handbook of psychotherapy and behavior change.* (2nd ed.). New York: Wiley, 1978.

Sloane, R. B., Staples, F. R., Cristol, A. H., Yorkston, N. J., & Whipple, K. *Psychotherapy versus behavior therapy.* Cambridge, Mass.: Harvard University Press, 1975.

Smith, M. L., & Glass, G. V. Meta-analysis of psychotherapy outcome studies. *American Psychologist,* 1977, *32,* 752–760.

Smith, M. L., Glass, G. V., & Miller, T. I. *The benefits of psychotherapy.* Baltimore: The Johns Hopkins University Press, 1980.

Strahan, R. F. Six ways of looking at an elephant. *American Psychologist,* 1978, *33,* 693 (Comment).

Strube, M. J., & Hartmann, D. P. Meta-analysis: Techniques, applications, and functions. *Journal of Consulting and Clinical Psychology,* 1983, *51,* 14–27.

Strupp, H. H. Psychotherapy research and practice: An overview. In S. L. Garfield & A. E. Bergin (Eds.), *Handbook of psychotherapy and behavior change.* (2nd ed.). New York: Wiley, 1978.

Strupp, H. H., & Hadley, S. W. A tripartite model of mental health and therapeutic outcomes: With special reference to negative effects in psychotherapy. *American Psychologist,* 1977, *32,* 187–196.

Strupp, H. H., & Hadley, S. W. Specific vs. non-specific factors in psychotherapy. A controlled study of outcome. *Archives of General Psychiatry,* 1979, *36,* 1125–1136.

Waskow, I. E., & Parloff, M. D. *Psychotherapy change measures.* Washington, D.C.: National Institute of Mental Health, 1975.

Wilson, G. T., & Evans, I. M. The therapist-client relationship in behavior therapy. In A. S. Gurman & A. M. Razin (Eds.), *Effective psychotherapy: A handbook of research.* New York: Pergamon Press, 1977.

Community
Psychology
and Mental
Health

Until fairly recently, the emphasis in the mental health movement was essentially on illness and disturbance rather than health and adjustment. Viewed as mentally ill, people with serious problems of adjustment were treated by physicians in hospitals and allied medical institutions. It is true that the child guidance clinics established in the early part of this century, did place an emphasis on prevention. To a large extent, however, these clinics also mainly offered the severely or moderately ill child and his family one-to-one therapy. Eventually, professionals and lay persons alike expressed increasing dissatisfaction with the mental health care practices and facilities. Mental hospitals, public or private, tended to be large institutions, often located in isolated areas, that devoted much of their effort to custodial care. Criticism was directed at such institutions because an individual who became a patient was removed some distance from his home and his family and severed community ties. Hence, the eventual return of the patient to his home and his readjustment to a normal life and role in the community was made more difficult. Studies of length of institutionalization and hospital discharge also indicated that the longer the individual remained in the hospital, the smaller were his chances for an eventual discharge.

421

THE JOINT COMMISSION ON MENTAL ILLNESS AND HEALTH

As a result of persistent attacks on long-established mental health care practices, the United States Congress in 1955 sponsored the establishment of a Joint Commission on Mental Illness and Health to conduct an objective and comprehensive study of mental illness and its treatment. One and one-quarter million dollars was provided by Congress to fund this project. The Joint Commission was requested specifically to make a thorough study of the available resources and current practices in the field of mental health, and to come up with recommendations pertinent to the entire problem of mental health.

The Joint Commission assembled a large multidisciplinary staff and invited the participation of thirty-six national organizations concerned with the problems of mental health. The American Psychological Association was one of the participating organizations. The investigations of the Joint Commission covered a period of about 5 years and resulted in a report consisting of eleven volumes, including its official summary report, *Action for Mental Health* (Joint Commission on Mental Illness and Health, 1961). A number of the findings and recommendations were provocative and important, and deserve mention.

One of the problems illuminated was the small existing supply of professional manpower in the mental health field. It was clearly apparent that there was a shortage of such professional personnel as psychiatrists, clinical psychologists, and psychiatric social workers in relation to the large number of people who were in need of mental health services. In 1960, when the population of the United States was around 160 million people, the membership of the American Psychiatric Association was approximately 12,000 or one psychiatrist for every 13,000 people. At that time the American Psychological Association had close to 20,000 members, of whom it was estimated that no more than 6000 were involved in some aspect of clinical psychology. In addition, there was an imbalance between the needs of certain segments of our society and the availability of mental health services.

At the same time, it was apparent that it would be difficult to increase significantly the output of psychiatrists and clinical psychologists. Both programs of training are expensive and lengthy. To become a psychiatrist requires 3 or 4 years of premedical training in college, 4 years of medical school, 1 year of internship, and/or 3 years of residency training in psychiatry. Thus, if one wants to increase the supply of psychiatrists, one will have to wait at least 11 years to secure an increase if the conventional programs are followed. A somewhat comparable situation held for the Ph.D. programs in clinical psychology. Although most university programs required a minimum of 4 years for completion, the average time to secure the Ph.D. degree exceeded 5 years. Furthermore, the total annual output of the Ph.D.'s in clinical psychology was relatively small at that time. Even in the early 1970's only 500 to 600 Ph.D.'s were graduated annually, and since some of them accept university positions emphasizing research and teaching, a small number are available to provide direct clinical services.

Another problem mentioned earlier is that the supply of services is not distributed equally throughout our population. The large urban centers in our country have a high percentage of the supply of mental health personnel, whereas most of the rural and less densely populated sections have less in the way of such resources. In a similar fashion, well-to-do individuals can secure the services they desire, whereas the poor cannot. The state hospitals, with the most serious cases of personality disorder, generally have chronic shortages of professional staff, and the most distinguished members of the mental health professions do not practice there. As the report of the Joint Commission indicated, the "vast majority of psychiatrists go into private practice" (1961, p. 146), and their availability for service is limited to those who can afford their fees. As Hollingshead and Redlich (1958) reported in their survey of the New Haven, Connecticut, area, the most intensive and long-term psychotherapy is provided primarily to clients from the middle and upper social classes. Lower-class individuals tend more frequently to be diagnosed as schizophrenic and to be sent to a state hospital. Similar findings on a national scale were also secured in surveys conducted for the Joint Commission.

These findings highlighted the problem of unequal utilization of resources and the need for change and new programs if the mental health needs of our people were to be met more adequately. Certainly, it did appear that those in least need of treatment secured the most expensive and intensive treatment. Closely related to this problem was one presented by psychoanalysis. Although this form of psychotherapy was highly regarded in the past by many clinical psychologists and psychiatrists alike, it is a form of therapy that requires up to five sessions a week for several years. As a consequence, it is very expensive and relatively few individuals can be treated in this manner. "In sum, then, psychoanalysis is adapted neither to the treatment of the psychoses nor to mass application of any kind. It is principally effective for a limited number of carefully selected patients who are not totally incapacitated by their illness and do not require hospitalization" (Joint Commission on Mental Illness and Health, 1961, p. 80).

Another aspect of the problem is that a concerted attack on problems of mental health and personal adjustment must include more than just an increase in the number of practitioners. In the long run, of potentially greater importance are research into the possible causes of such disturbance and programs of effective prevention. In the latter instance, the public health model (in which such procedures as education, vaccination, sanitation, diet, and so forth have been used to prevent and reduce the incidence of disease) may be the appropriate one.

Thus, the report of the Joint Commission underlined some of the problems and needs pertaining to the broad field of mental health in this country. A number of recommendations were also made, a few of which can be mentioned here for their specific relevance to our present discussion. One of the recommendations was that the Congress of the United States should give increased support to basic and diversified research in the field of mental health. Recommendations were also offered for increased training in the mental health area for a variety of workers and at different levels of skills. Furthermore, since surveys authorized by the Joint Commission indicated that over two-thirds of those with personal problems consulted either clergymen or physicians as contrasted with only 18% who consulted psychologists or psychiatrists (Gurin, Veroff, & Fields, 1960), specific recommendations were made for providing special training and consultation for such groups. In addition, it was recommended that a variety of mental health services be provided in the community where people live. Instead of sending people away to isolated institutions, the emphasis was placed on community mental health centers.

THE COMMUNITY MENTAL HEALTH CENTER

As a result of the Joint Commission's recommendations for the establishment of comprehensive community mental health centers, Congress in 1962 appropriated funds to assist the states in evaluating their needs and facilities for the purpose of developing plans for mental health programs. In 1963, Congress authorized additional funds to help support the cost of constructing mental health centers within the framework of the mental health plans proposed by the states. This act, the Community Mental Health Centers Act, provided up to two-thirds of the funds necessary for the construction of facilities for these new mental health centers. Furthermore, communities were defined as sensibly delineated *catchment areas* which contained from 75,000 to 200,000 persons. The programs, in essence, were to take care of the mental health needs of this defined community and the people of the community or their representatives were to participate in the planning of these programs. Two years later, in 1965, funds were also authorized to help in the staffing of these new community mental health centers.

Under the Community Mental Health Centers Act of 1963 certain guidelines were provided by the Public Health Service for these centers to ensure comprehensive services. Five "essential" and five additional services were specified. The five "essential" services were: (1) inpatient care; (2) outpatient services; (3) partial hospitalization; (4) emergency twenty-four-hour service, and (5) consultation and education. Inpatient and outpatient treatment are traditional services which require little elaboration. Partial hospitalization includes day treatment for those who can return home in the evening and evening or overnight care for those individuals who are able to work or study during daytime hours. Emergency care emphasized the availability of the other three services on an around-the-clock basis and also in order to provide continuity of service. Consultation and education were to be available to community agencies and professional personnel in order to have a broader impact on community services, to link the mental health center more effectively with other agencies in the community, and to help with early detection of problems and prevention. The additional services consisted of diagnostic services, rehabilitative services, precare and aftercare services, training for all types of mental health personnel, and research and evaluation. The latter included the evaluation of the effectiveness of the programs as well as research on the problems of mental illness.

The enabling legislation for a community mental health program resulted in the establishment of several hundred such centers. Nevertheless, the mere creation of centers has not always led to innovative and creative attempts at dealing with problems of personal and social adjustment. Many traditional diagnostic and treatment activities and programs were simply transferred to new settings with some limited additional services added. Thus, while the report of the Joint Commission was critical of many traditional modes of treatment and of the relative neglect of certain segments of our society with mental health needs, many of the community mental health centers were not fully responsive to such problems. This is not to say that no innovative and effective programs were developed. Rather, the appearance of a large number of new community mental health centers has not produced any revolution in the handling of mental health problems (Smith and Hobbs, 1966). To a certain extent, it appears as if the federal guide lines for community mental health centers tended to rigidify practices with a resulting uniformity of activities in which mainly traditional services are provided. Certainly, community consultation and education as well as research have received only minor emphasis. That significant progress is still required is quite clear from the results secured from a mental health survey reported by Ryan (1969) for the city of Boston. Some of the most significant findings can be summarized briefly.

One interesting finding was that about 150 individuals per 1000 were identified by someone as being emotionally disturbed. Of those who are judged to be emotionally disturbed, perhaps nine will apply for help at one of the outpatient psychiatric clinics in Boston—of these, four may be accepted for treatment. Of the total 150 persons identified, another 5 or 6 will appear so disturbed that they will be sent to a mental hospital. One of the 150 will be treated by a psychiatrist in private practice. Consequently, only about 10 of the 150 cases will receive some kind of professional mental health care or treatment. Of the remaining 140, the majority will be cared for by the family doctor or other nonpsychiatric physicians, social agencies, or churches. Together, all of the resources mentioned thus far may provide some kind of help or support for about two-thirds of those who are identified as emotionally disturbed, although only a small percentage are actually seen by mental health professionals. On the other hand, one-third of this identified group receives no service at all. As Ryan states:

> For some of these persons, of course, it would be difficult to try to provide help, since they are unsure, or reluctant to admit, that they have a problem or a need for help. But even more important than the question of the motivation of disturbed persons is the issue of resources. Realistically, nothing is "left over" to help this one-third of the disturbed population. There is no place, there are no people, there is no time available to them (Ryan, 1969, p. 12).

The Boston survey highlights the continuing problem of trying to cope with extensive social needs with limited resources. One additional finding on the patients who receive treatment from psychiatrists illustrates another aspect of the problem: "These patients cover a relatively narrow age range, half of them falling between the ages of twenty-two and thirty-six. About two-thirds are female; four out of five have gone to college or are now college students; and occupations are generally consistent with education, reflecting a class level in the middle and upper ranges" (Ryan, 1969, p. 15). Furthermore, a majority of those receiving private psychiatric treatment live in a small area of the city. "About one-quarter of all Bostonians who are private patients are young women in their twenties and early thirties who live within an area of less than 100 blocks" (Ryan, 1969, pp. 15). 16). Actually a group of 3000 young college-educated women make up one-quarter of the Boston patients in private psychiatric treatment.

COMMUNITY PSYCHOLOGY: ORIENTATION AND EMPHASES

On the basis of what has been discussed thus far, it is apparent that the designation, community mental health center, may be applied to centers which differ noticeably in how they go about meeting their program objectives. Only in some instances do we find programs that truly are innovative, involve large or significant segments of the community, are engaged in a variety of efforts in the community, utilize new types of personnel, and generally differ from the traditional clinical settings. Too often we find mainly traditionally trained personnel performing traditional functions, and the word "community" merely refers to the title or locus of the center. Yet increasingly in recent years, the terms "community mental health" and "community psychology" have taken on a somewhat broader, if still imprecise meaning. In a general way the emphasis on community in these instances has signalled a change in the activities, roles, and conceptualizations of the psychologist and others involved in this development. Some see community psychology as a separate specialty within psychology, whereas others see it as an important new emphasis within clinical psychology. It should be clear, however, that other psychologists, particularly social psychologists, and other disciplines including social work, psychiatry, and sociology also can lay fair claim to this area.

The need to provide more efficient services as well as to reach the large numbers of people who were not being served well by conventional mental health facilities or personnel has led to some significant new developments in recent years (Beigel and Levenson, 1972; Golann and Eisdorfer, 1972; Zax and Specter, 1974). Although consistent with many of the emphases contained in the report of the Joint Commission, these developments appear to have taken place in response to a generally greater concern for the welfare of the poor and disadvantaged members of our society and to have a broader social focus. Examples of such emphases have been the emergence of such specialties as social psychiatry, community psychology, and human ecology.

"It is a grand commentary on the creative energies of mental health professionals that once the momentum for change developed, a barrage of activity ensued which attempted to transcend professional territoriality, cross disciplinary barriers, and overcome narrowly delineated latitudes of concern" (Roen, 1971, p. 777). In general, the emphasis in this movement represented a shift from an exclusive concern with the nature of the individual and intrapsychic problems to a concentration on the problems that individuals face in coping with their social and physical environment. This latter emphasis was apparent both in preventative efforts (Golann and Eisdorfer, 1972) and in developing programs for patients discharged from mental hospitals (Beigel and Levenson, 1972).

While there are some clearly identified emphases in the community movement, the field contains a variety of goals, values, and points of view, with theories, methods, and procedures still to be adequately defined and validated. Some of the more important ideas underlying the field have been summarized by Roen (1971) as follows:

1. The environmental context is always relevant and social realities are often prepotent in determining and changing behavior.

2. Mental health professionals are accountable to the communities they serve.

3. Social approaches to amelioration can be effective.

4. Prevention is the most valued answer to the mass problem of mental disorder.

5. Help for a problem is best offered in close proximity to where it became visible and through indigenous resources.

6. Optimal programming requires community participation, if not control.

7. The more urgent needs of local populations or groups should order program priorities and determine the characteristics of facilities.

8. Regaining or enhancing competence are important objectives of treatment.

9. Since milieu can be structured to facilitate mental health, intervening at the level of social system is a preferred strategy.

10. Services should reach out to recalcitrant high-risk groups and be rendered parsimoniously, efficiently, and equitably.

11. The accidental or developmental stresses and strains of life are strategic points of entry for preventive intervention.

12. Since the causative chain in mental disorder seems linked to the stresses of debilitating social problems, social reform is an important professional goal.

13. Professionals can be better deployed and the manpower pool effectively enhanced by training nonprofessionals to perform helping tasks.

14. Careful planning, innovative programming, and the formulation of new conceptual models are to be encouraged.

15. Since psychological disorder is practically legion, public education about mental health should be a high priority activity. (Roen, 1971, pp. 777–778.)

Several important changes in viewpoint and focus are apparent in the points enumerated above. The emphasis on the environment in attempts to modify behavior, the importance of prevention of disorder, the significance of community participation in mental health programming, the need for reaching out to work with high risk populations, the importance of intervention attempts at periods of crisis, a concern with social systems, and the use of "nonprofessionals" are all emphases which signify a change from traditional practices in the mental health field. Some additional discussion of each of these should help to clarify the thrust of community psychology and mental health as well as their implications for practice and training in clinical psychology.

The emphasis on the importance of the environment in influencing the behavior of the individual represents an important change from the previous preoccupation of mental health workers with the psychodynamics and intrapsychic economy of patients. As indicated in previous sections of this book, conventional psychodiagnostic study focused primarily on the appraisal of the individual's psychological makeup, and psychotherapy reflected a similar emphasis on changing the individual. While the importance of the individual's family and home situation was not infrequently mentioned, such variables tended not to be dealt with directly. Change was sought in the patient or client. The community approach tends to reverse this emphasis by focusing greater attention on the environment in which the individual lives and by attempts at intervening or modifying the environment or the social systems which are part of it. Clearly, this change has important theoretical and practical implications for how mental health workers function.

A related concern is that of intervention at the level of social systems. Each individual is a member of or participates in a number of social systems— family, school, neighborhood, working organization, church, and so on. Conceivably, many of these social systems exert some influence on the behavior and adjustment of the individuals who make up the social system. Within this context, the influence of a social system may be positive or negative, strong or weak, and it may be more efficacious to influence the social system in terms of its impact on the individuals concerned than to work solely with individuals. Interventions of this type may also contain aspects of prevention. For example, instead of waiting for referrals of children who manifest serious learning or behavioral difficulties in school and then offering them treatment, it could be more efficient to establish a regular consultative relationship with the school system in order to identify a child's problems before they become serious. In this way not only may some potential problems be averted, but the teacher may be offered information and procedures by means of which the child's behavior may be modified. The attitudes of school personnel toward problem behavior also may be influenced and a more favorable climate for positive personal development be established.

Similar kinds of interventions are possible with such social units as the family, the police department, welfare agencies, and the like. One novel program, for example, was developed where selected policemen in one precinct were trained to handle family problems. Since a large number of the calls to the precinct police involved family disturbances and altercations, it seemed reasonable to set up a training program for policemen and to provide them with professional consultation and supervision for handling these problems in the best manner possible. The policemen who participated in this program were quickly perceived by their colleagues as "experts" in family problems and were called on by them to handle such matters when they appeared to be of a serious nature. In this manner, family disputes could be handled more expeditiously by influencing an existing social system or network (the police) which actually came into firsthand contact with such problems.

Another related group of concerns pertains to community involvement and participation in the establishment of priorities and goals of the mental health program. In the past, mental health professionals for the most part determined what the activities of the clinical setting would be, what clients would be treated, and similar matters. The community was not involved in what were deemed to be professional concerns pertaining to the objectives and programs of the mental health facility. In the new look in community mental health centers the community representatives are seen as joint participants in this venture or even as the group which has the final say in decisions pertaining to the characteristics of the enterprise. For example, in the formation of one community mental health center in Chicago the community council decided on the nature of the center and its primary functions. Instead of setting up a center that would provide a variety of treatment services, the community representatives decided to place their primary emphasis on work with children (Kellam, Branch, Agrawal, & Grabill, 1972). As a consequence, a program for working with all of the children entering the first grade was given the top priority.

Another emphasis implicit in the community mental health movement is that of reaching out to provide services for high-risk groups in the community who might not otherwise seek or be offered services. Many of those who might profit from psychological intervention are poor and uneducated. They are not as sophisticated in regard to psychological problems, treatment, or resources for help as are better educated members of the wider community. Many of these individuals may not seek professional help because of the stigma they believe is associated with mental illness (Hollingshead and Redlich, 1958). In many instances they are not brought to the attention of mental health caretakers until the problems are relatively severe. A traditional clinic which waits for its clients to be referred from other community agencies or to present themselves at the clinic may either not see them or will have contact with them only when the difficulty has become serious enough that others have to intervene. This is obviously an inefficient and inhumane method of handling problems. Consequently, the need for reaching out to make contact with potentially high-risk groups in the community has been recognized as an important aspect of community mental health. Among the potential high-risk groups are families where one parent is absent from the home or where one member is psychotic, families with excessive discord, and families where the parent or parents are unable to provide adequate supervision or models for their children or where the children are not attending school.

Still another aspect deserving mention concerns intervention at the time of crisis. There are several reasons for considering treatment or preventative attempts at times of crisis as particularly effective mental health efforts. At times of crisis there is a greater felt need for help and a potentially greater responsiveness to attempts at intervention. If treatment efforts can be brought to bear on the individual at such a time, there may be a greater chance for positive outcome. On the other hand, if treatment is delayed unnecessarily and individuals are placed on waiting lists with long periods before services are provided, the motivation for treatment is diminished and the optimum time for instituting such efforts is lost. Times of crisis are also feasible periods for instituting preventive programs to diminish the possibility of more serious disturbance (Caplan, 1964). If an individual can be helped at such times he may be able to overcome the crisis situation quickly and forestall the possibility of more chronic disturbance. Preventative programs can also be developed to help individuals over normal developmental crises which all of us face (Caplan and Grunebaum, 1967). These may include developmental problems associated with entering school, adolescence, the sexual role, marriage, parenthood, loss of a loved one, and retirement. While programs of this type have not been developed in very large numbers, crisis intervention treatment programs have been instituted in a number of clinical settings (Kalis, 1970; Kalis, Harris, Prestwood, and Freeman, 1961). Walk-in clinics or emergency clinics and services have been developed which provide immediate treatment at the time of crisis and in which the focus of treatment is the resolution of the crisis and the quick restoration of the individual to his previous level of functioning. Generally, this type of program is limited to a specific number of treatments, usually six to eight and clinical reports thus far are encouraging (Darbonne, 1967; Harris, Kalis, and Freeman, 1963; Jacobson, 1965). Other innovations of this type include around-the-clock clinical services and the availability of emergency help by means of the telephone. The latter has been used particularly as one approach to the problem of preventing suicide, and where a number of volunteers have received special training to participate in such programs.

One of the most significant, and also controversial developments in the community mental health movement has been that concerning the training and use of "nonprofessional" personnel. As indicated previously, one means of improving the manpower situation is to deploy the current professional manpower as effectively as possible. Using professionals to train, supervise, and utilize other types of personnel in the mental health endeavor is a means to this end. There are many functions currently carried out by professional workers that others could be trained to perform. Among these are interviewing, certain kinds of counseling, psychotherapy and behavior modification procedures, and the administration of psychological tests. Some workers have also believed that personnel selected from the community in which the clinic is situated and sharing a common background with the people in the community may be better able to communicate and empathize with the clients the clinic serves (Garfield, 1969). In some instances, clients speak a foreign language and "indigenous" workers who speak that language may have to be employed. In any event, a number of programs have been developed to meet such needs and we can refer to a few of them to illustrate the diversity evident in these undertakings.

One of the pioneering efforts in this area was that of Margaret Rioch

(Rioch, 1967; Rioch, Elkes, and Flint, 1965) and her associates at the National Institute of Mental Health. Middle-aged housewives with a college degree were solicited for a new program to train nonprofessionals to engage in psychotherapy. The rationale was that here was an untapped resource of intelligent people whose children would be grown and who might be interested in a second career in the mental health field. Eight women were selected from among forty-nine applicants and underwent a program of largely practical training in psychotherapy. The program was planned on a half-time basis extending over a period of 2 years, with practicum training and placements in mental health clinics. The trainees were systematically evaluated throughout the program and for several years after the completion of training. In fact, few psychotherapists or counselors have been so thoroughly studied with a variety of criteria—including evaluations by employers and supervisors—as were these novel trainees. On the whole, these "nonprofessional" psychotherapists have performed about as well as psychotherapists from the mental health professions (Freeman and Golann, 1965; Golann, Breiter, and Magoon, 1966; Magoon and Golann, 1966). After graduation from the program, all eight of the women were employed. "Five are employed in a mental health clinic or center; one on an NIMH experimental ward; one in a university counseling center, one in a college" (Rioch, 1967, p. 121).

Still other programs have been set up by agencies themselves to train individuals to perform specific functions within the agency. In one program at the Philadelphia State Hospital college graduates were trained to provide "social interaction therapy" at the hospital. Again, this is a practically oriented on-the-job type of training program. Most of the graduates of this program have been employed to provide therapeutic services on the wards of state hospitals where the patients previously tended to receive mainly custodial care (Sanders, 1967). At another state hospital in Colorado, a 6-month program was organized for training psychiatric technicians to perform a variety of functions within the hospital setting. Truax and Carkhuff (1967) also developed a 100-hour training program in psychotherapy utilizing tapes of psychotherapy sessions. The results of this approach in one study of five volunteer hospital personnel consisting of three aides, an industrial therapist, and one volunteer worker were seen as promising. A group of chronic hospital patients treated by five volunteer therapists who received this training secured more positive gains than did a control group (Carkhuff and Truax, 1965).

A very novel program which for a while used nonprofessional personnel exclusively was developed in a mental health center in the Southwest. Because of an extreme shortage of mental health personnel in this locality, the lone mental health worker, a psychiatric nurse who functioned as the state mental health consultant, was able to secure community support for setting up a center staffed completely by nonprofessionals. The staff consisted of individuals with varying backgrounds. One was a middle-aged housewife with a college degree in social studies, two were previously employed as secretaries, and one was a former army officer. These individuals received some instruction and regular supervisory consultation from psychologists and psychiatrists who flew in weekly from the state university medical school. At the time the writer visited this center, programs had been developed for emotionally disturbed children, mentally retarded individuals, alcoholism, and suicide prevention. Community volunteers also acted as assistants to these nonprofessional mental health workers. Another nonprofessional with consultation from a trained researcher was attempting to collect data for evaluating the effectiveness of these programs. Community leaders, without whose support the effort could not have succeeded, were obviously pleased with the activities of their mental health center.

As indicated previously, the attempts to train and utilize nonprofessionals have not been without some controversy and problems. While many professionals have provided enthusiastic leadership and participated in the training of such workers, others have been hesitant or reluctant. Certainly, such developments are threatening to many professional people and some are seriously concerned with the quality of service that will be offered by individuals with limited training. Most individuals tend to be jealous of their own professional turf, and possible competition is not well received, particularly when individuals with lesser training may be perceived to be performing rather well. Using nonprofessionals in clearly limited and demarcated areas is not especially threatening. However, when such individuals perform functions that are essentially similar to those performed by professionals, the situation becomes more threatening. Nevertheless, with on-the-job training and supervision, with adequate selection of potential workers, and with the proper delineation of functions and responsibilities, it appears that many individuals with less than full professional training can be utilized to provide a larger amount and variety of mental health services. At the same time, some problems exist for these new types of mental health workers. They lack some type of professional or occupational identity, and frequently there is no career ladder provided for them by which they can advance to higher levels.

Before concluding this discussion, reference should be made to a recent review of 42 studies which compared the effectiveness of professional and paraprofessional helpers (Durlak, 1979). Although many of the studies have some design deficiencies and the studies "are limited to helpers functioning in narrowly-defined clinical roles with specific client populations, findings are consistent and provocative" (Durlak, 1979, p. 80). In general the results obtained by the paraprofessionals are as good or better than those obtained by the professional workers. This is clearly a provocative finding, and although it is easy to criticize many of the studies reviewed, one must not simply disregard the results secured. It would appear that some clinical functions performed by professional workers could be handled competently by selected nonprofessionals with the proper training and supervision.

INNOVATIVE PROGRAMS IN COMMUNITY MENTAL HEALTH

As a result of the emergence of community psychology, a number of attempts have been made to devise programs which reflect this orientation. Several such endeavors have been referred to briefly in the preceding section. Reference will be made here to some additional programs which have appeared to be particularly interesting or innovative.

PROJECT RE-ED

One of the pioneer programs of this type was called "Project Re-ED." Under the leadership of Nicholas Hobbs, a clinical psychologist, a cooperative program involving the states of Tennessee and North Carolina and Peabody College was initiated with support from the National Institute of Mental Health (Hobbs, 1966, 1968; Lewis, 1967). The program was seen as an alternative to existing programs for emotionally disturbed children. The basic idea was to use carefully selected teachers, give them special training, and provide consultative services from mental health professionals. Instead of a hospital or clinic setting, residential schools were to be used. Several reasons were given for choosing this model in place of the conventional psychiatric center. There will never be enough trained professionals to provide the services required; the cost of conventional centers is almost prohibitive; and conventional treatment programs have not been particularly effective in quickly getting children back to a suitable level of functioning in their home, school, and community.

Two such schools were set up to provide an intensive around-the-clock reeducation effort, one in Nashville, Tennessee and one in Durham, North Carolina. Emotionally disturbed children of average to superior intelligence were selected for the program. All of the children were either having serious difficulties in their regular schools or were unable to attend school. The Re-ED schools were staffed by "teacher-counselors" who received 9 months of graduate training leading to a masters degree. The teacher-counselors were selected in terms of their natural ability to work with children and were drawn from the teaching profession or from related fields. Consultants were available on the job from such fields as pediatrics, psychiatry, psychology, and education.

The central thrust of the program is on helping the children attain competence in coping with the every day reality problems of their current life. As was mentioned earlier, community psychology has stressed the development of competence in work and social relations as an objective instead of mainly treating pathological symptoms or intrapsychic distress. In Project Re-ED, the child is helped to attain competence in reading, in sports activities, in being able to go to school without fear, in how to react to other individuals, and a variety of other reality-oriented areas of current adjustment. The program recognizes also that the child has to live within and interact with other social systems which influence his adjustment. Consequently, efforts are made to work with the home, school, and neighborhood. In fact, Hobbs and his associates have been led to view "the problem of the child called disturbed as a manifestation of the breakdown of an ecological system composed of child, family, neighborhood, school, and community. The goal of mental health service for children would then not be to cure a child or to prepare him to cope with all possible life roles, but to restore to effective operation the small social system of which the child is an integral part" (Hobbs, 1968, p. 13).

THE ROCHESTER PROJECT

Another interesting mental health project, aimed at early detection of problems and possible prevention, has been carried out for a number of years by a group of psychologists at the University of Rochester (New York) in a public school system (Cowen and Zax, 1968; Cowen, Dorr, Trost, and Izzo, 1972; Zax and Cowen, 1967). The program developed from the view that any comprehensive and preventively oriented approach to mental health had to be concerned with the young child and his environment. In terms of the latter, the school plays a particularly important role in the life of the child. For most children entry into the school situation is an important milestone in separation from the home situation, in fostering independence, in relating to peers, and in socialization. Since the school therefore represents an important period of adjustment which all children experience, it is a good point for mental health intervention. Problems of emotional disturbance could be identified early and efforts made to work with problem children or to modify the school environment accordingly.

Several different aspects of a preventative program have been devised and studied by Cowen, Zax, and their collaborators over the years. One aspect was concerned with the early detection of potential problems. In this particular project, first-grade children were evaluated psychologically, were observed in the classroom, their mothers were interviewed by social workers, and reports were also received from teachers. On the basis of the information secured, children were divided into two groups. One group, designated as the Red-Tag was for youngsters who were already manifesting problem behavior or who appeared to be likely to exhibit disturbance. Approximately 35–40% of the children studied received the Red-Tag designation. All other children were labeled Non-Red-Tag. These children were then followed up to check the accuracy of these earlier designations. Generally, children who were labeled as Red-Tag in the first grade were performing less adequately and exhibiting greater signs of maladjustment on a variety of measures 3 years later than were the children not so designated (Cowen, Zax, Izzo, and Trost, 1966). The implication of this particular project is that problem or potentially problem children can be identified with some accuracy in the first year of school.

In addition, Cowen, Zax, and their co-workers have attempted to develop procedures aimed at prevention of disturbance. In addition to early diagnostic evaluation of the first-grade children, social work interviews were carried out with the mothers, consultative services were provided the teachers, there were after-school activity programs, and parent and teacher discussion groups. The program was evaluated during the last month of the third school year and a variety of criterion measures were used. The latter included such measures as attendance at school, grades, achievement test scores, teachers' behavior rating scales, peer evaluation instruments, and self-report and self-evaluation measures of adjustment. In this part of the study, an experimental group in one school which participated in the prevention program was compared with a control group selected from two comparable schools. Of the total of nineteen criterion measures used, seven differed significantly and all of these favored the experimental group. Thus, the results secured from this evaluation were rather promising.

A follow-up study performed on another group of children when they reached the seventh grade, however, did not secure as positive results. The children who had participated in the experimental program had lower grades and poorer attendance records than the children in the control group. However, the former were less anxious and did better on several achievement tests. "Thus the results of this fairly long-term follow-up did not lead to definitive conclusions. The relatively weak follow-up findings may be the result of program inadequacies or the high attrition rates. Whatever the reasons, the positive effects of the preventative program were not demonstrated to be enduring with respect to the measures used" (Zax and Specter, 1974, p. 191).

Partly because of these results, the program was altered in order to provide more direct service to children. As a result, a program utilizing nonprofessional "teacher aides" was developed. This program has gone through modifications over time and appears to have achieved some success. Essentially, the teacher-aides work with children referred by the teachers. Other modifications have included an after-school day-care program using college students and the training of school mental health professionals with reference to the objectives of the program. The program is noteworthy for its continuing attempts to appraise its effectiveness systematically and for creatively modifying the program in the light of the results secured.

It is of interest to mention also that the Rochester Primary Mental Health Project was used as a model in setting up a similar program using group behavioral reinforcement techniques (Durlak, 1977). In one school, the school counselor, the school nurse, and four teachers volunteered to serve as group leaders (aides). In a second school, the aides were largely college students. All received training in reinforcement procedures applicable to a group situation and received 1 hour of supervision per week. The children were seen for 1 hour per week for 8 weeks and a follow-up appraisal was made after 7 months. The children who participated in the program showed significant improvement on the two rating scales completed by teachers as compared with a control group.

A NEIGHBORHOOD SERVICE CENTER PROGRAM

Another well-known and unusual program, developed by the Lincoln Hospital Mental Health Services, utilized a Neighborhood Service Center (NSC) in a highly disadvantaged community in the southeast section of the Bronx in New York City (Riessman, 1967). The community was a very poor one economically and there was a dearth of services available to its members. Compared to the Bronx as a whole, the rate of unemployment, overcrowded housing, and public assistance was twice as high. The rates for juvenile offenses, venereal disease, and admission to state mental hospitals was also higher than the rest of the Bronx. Thus, the community served is a seriously disadvantaged one with many problems. Its members are not generally viewed as favorable cases for psychotherapy, or do they frequently seek out such services.

The NSC was located in a store-front, functioning at street level. It was intended to serve a radius of five blocks containing approximately 50,000 people. The staff consisted of five or six indigenous nonprofessionals from the neighborhood and one professional mental health specialist who functioned as the director. Because of its store-front character and location, as well as the neighborhood mental health aides, the center and its services were readily available.

The NSC differs from most other mental health centers and programs in a number of ways, although other programs may also stress prevention as one of their goals. Part of this difference, perhaps, is related to the two sources of support for the program. One was the Lincoln Hospital Mental Health Services, funded by the Department of Hospitals of New York City; the other was the Community Action Program of the federal Office of Economic Opportunity. Thus, the NSC program attempted to combine social action and mental health into one program. It was felt, however, that there are common or overlapping goals for both features of the program. The development of autonomy, self-determination, and coping skills among the residents of the neighborhood, for example, reflect objectives shared by both sources of support for the program.

The NSC program was viewed as having three basic goals:

1. Expediting and providing services relevant to mental health. This includes bringing new clients into the system of services, making service systems more responsive to clients, and providing additional new services.

2. Increasing social cohesion within the concentration area. An effort is made to produce community impact, particularly with regard to the development of various types of groups leading to the development of community action. Thus, the effort is to provide a sociotherapeutic approach oriented toward reducing powerlessness, building community ties, and group involvement.

3. Initiating various types of institutional change, particularly with regard to better coordination of services for the people in the community. An effort is made to change agency policies and practices with regard to service delivery and the development of comprehensive mental health services. This is a long-range goal and it is more connected, than are the first two goals, with other programs in the Lincoln Hospital Mental Health Services complex (Riessman, 1967, pp. 165–166).

The goals listed above and the means of their implementation can be elaborated upon briefly. With regard to service and preventive intervention, individual services to neighborhood residents are considered to provide the basis or "entering wedge" for the program. The target population to be served is that segment of the poor that has been least active and is in greatest need of services. By means of a service-oriented program it is hoped that these individuals can be encouraged to participate later in various informal social groups, task-oriented groups, and even in community action groups. Thus, service has both a direct objective, the improvement of mental health, and an indirect objective, community action.

The NSC differs markedly from conventional community mental health centers in the services it provides. The range of direct services is wide— from the giving of information, filling out forms, escorting of clients, helping people to move, and making home visits to personal counseling. The staff also attempts to expedite service from other agencies, refer clients to appropriate agencies, and to integrate and coordinate services. The NSC is presented to the neighborhood as a place where they can bring and be helped with any type of problem. People are free to walk into the center at the time they are faced with a problem or crisis and receive immediate assistance. Furthermore, the prospective client does not have to identify or label his problem as being appropriate for a particular kind of agency. In this instance, he does not have to label his problem as mental illness which appears to hold a particular stigma for lower-class individuals.

The rendering of services is also viewed as providing a realistic basis for the formation of groups. Clients with similar service needs, for example, managing a family on a welfare allotment, can meet together to discuss means of handling this problem. While the initial basis of group formation and participation might be a common need for service, later groups can be organized with a more specific task or community orientation. Community actions which might result from such group efforts therefore would tend to reflect the immediate needs of the people in the community, which again, is the focus of the NSC program. The basic strengths of this type of service program are considered to be its focus on specific neighborhood problems, the offering of a broad range of services, the expediting and integration of services, its tie-in with community action, and the fact that the services are geared specifically for low-income populations.

Some early statistics on the services provided may also be of interest. During the first six weeks of the program, 69% of the people seen were Puerto Rican, 18% were black, and 13% were non-Puerto Rican white. Over 50% of those seen were walk-ins. The main areas in which aid was sought were: housing 25%, welfare 22%, employment 23%, and family problems 8%. Somewhat over 6000 persons are seen at an individual center in a year, a fairly impressive number for a staff of six or seven. Certainly, most clinics of this size do not see anywhere near this number of clients. An additional note was that the operating expenses of the NSC were quite low—less than $50,000 for the salaries of the professional director, five mental health aides, the secretary, rent for the store, and all other expenses.

This program appeared to be unusually successful. The first center was opened in February of 1965 and a second began operations later that year. In 1968, the mental health program at Lincoln Hospital received an award from the American Psychiatric Association for its innovative program of providing psychiatric services to the community. However, despite this apparent success, various internal difficulties and struggles for power led to the closing of the center's operations in the spring of 1969. "The crises encountered at that center were precipitated directly by indigenous non-professionals employed in large numbers by the center" (Zax and Specter, 1974, p. 405).

Apparently, a number of factors were involved in producing the conflict, including bureaucratic delays, problems between professional and nonprofessional staff over performance evaluations, racial conflicts, and other matters. An account of this tragic conflict based on unpublished material is provided by Zax and Specter (1974). On a number of matters, however, a central aspect was the power conflict between the professional and nonprofessional staff. The latter resisted decisions made by the professionals, demanded increased status, and "their primary criterion for replacing the white supervisor became a racial one" (Zax and Specter, 1974, p. 407).

During the last year of the center's operation, several serious confrontations occurred. The nonprofessionals staged a sit-in in the office of the hospital business administrator and made a series of demands. The professionals, on the other hand, demanded more authority, and in response to small salary increases, staged a work stoppage. After a number of such confrontations there was a short period of quiet followed by a major crisis. Part of this was related to political fights in the community in which some of the black nonprofessional employees of the center were involved, but the apparent precipitating event was the firing of a black nonprofessional staff member. Although it appeared that most of the staff felt the dismissal was appropriate, those who were political leaders insisted that agreed-upon procedures had not been followed, and a whole series of accusations, including the allegation of racist practices were lodged against the administration.

What followed was tragic and disastrous: ". . . a work stoppage was declared, buildings were occupied, nonstrikers were locked out, and non-professionals took over as chiefs of the various services" (Zax and Specter, 1974, p. 408). Other activist groups, including the Black Panthers, joined in to support the strikers, although it appeared that the local community, which was 70% Puerto Rican, gave it little support. On March 6, 1969, the center was closed, and a program that was almost unique in its involvement with members of the community seemed to be out of business, in part at least, due to this involvement. Not all stories or experiments have happy endings, and community programs are no exception.

There have been a number of other interesting community mental health programs developed and instituted since the passage of the Community Mental Health Centers Legislation. Those that have been presented, however, should give the reader some idea of the developments that have taken place. Fortunately, there are a number of books which contain accounts of many additional programs, and those who are interested can pursue the matter further (Adelson and Kalis, 1970; Beigel and Levinson, 1972; Cook, 1970; Golann and Eisdorfer, 1972; Iscoe and Spielberger, 1970; Zax and Specter, 1974).

CONCLUDING COMMENTS

The topics discussed in this chapter contain most of the important emphases in community psychology and mental health. Potentially, these developments have important implications for the field of clinical psychology but it is still too early to know precisely what their final impact will be. Some of the emphases and activities have been incorporated into clinical psychology and have enlarged the role and functions of the clinical psychologist. This is already evident in the incorporation of didactic and practicum instruction in community psychology into graduate clinical programs, and the appearance of clinical programs with a community emphasis. There is, however, no complete unanimity concerning the value and importance of the community psychology movement. Some critics believe that the emphases on community, social environment, prevention, and helping the poor are all socially worthwhile, but that these are not the primary professional concerns of clinical psychologists. Most of the latter have been trained in assessment, psychotherapy, and research, and these are the functions they are qualified and prepared to perform. Although social causes and the prevention of disturbance are worthy goals, many individuals require diagnosis and treatment which the clinical psychologist can provide. Sociologists, social workers, public health workers, and the like can attempt to meet these other objectives. Other critics, or perhaps skeptics, express the view that the field of community psychology has lofty goals and aspirations, but little else. From this point of view there is no validated theory or technology for attaining the lofty goals posited by the community psychologists and little to show that their attempts at prevention are really bearing any fruit. To some sideline observers, the "community thing" is rather hazy and proposed by a bunch of "do-gooders." "Social reforms may be well and good, but what do they have to do with psychology?"

At the other end of the continuum are sincere and socially motivated individuals who believe that conventional efforts in the mental health enterprise are essentially limited stop-gap or patch-up efforts that do not get at the roots of the problem. Poverty, discrimination, deteriorating neighborhoods, lack of opportunity, inferior education, and similar factors are closely related to maladjustment and disturbance, and if real progress is to be made, then the important causes or predisposing conditions have to be eradicated. To use conventional procedures in an attempt to adjust deprived individuals to a "sick society" is, at best, an approach which is doomed to fail. What is required is environmental change and social reform. The psychologist, therefore, should devote at least some of his/her energies to attempts to change society for the better. In some instances this may mean helping the community to organize its efforts in attempting to modify the existing power structure and to improve the conditions of living. Discussions of this type and related attempts at community organization and change are clearly different from conventional mental health activities, and have tended to make some people suspicious of community psychology. Anything which appears to diverge from or attack existing institutions and practices will generally be viewed as threatening and some of this is evident in the reaction to the developments discussed here.

Although the situation in the field of mental health has changed rather noticeably in the past 20 years or so, some of the problems referred to earlier still remain. The number of trained professionals has increased markedly. In clinical psychology, for example, the number of doctorates has just about doubled in the last decade. Thus, the scarcity of trained manpower does not constitute the problem it did earlier. However, the concentration of professional workers in urban areas and the lack of such professionals in rural areas remains. Mental health services are not provided in equal amount or quality to all segments of the population. Furthermore, the emphasis on preventative efforts is still not what some leaders would describe as desirable and lags behind that for treatment. This is particularly true when the emphasis is placed on social factors which may play an important role in matters of human adjustment.

As is true of similar movements, community psychology presents a diverse range of viewpoints and emphases. At one end the emphasis is on the more traditional clinical concerns centered around the individual, whereas at the other end, the emphasis tends to be on environmental and social factors (Monahan and Vaux, 1980; Swift, 1980). Nevertheless, the community psychology emphasis and related movements have focused on important social problems and inequities, have highlighted some of the inadequacies of current mental health practices, have reemphasized the importance of prevention, and have increased the social sensitivity of a large number of workers in the field. These are positive contributions.

REFERENCES

Adelson, D., and Kalis, B. L. (Eds.) *Community psychology and mental health. Perspectives and challenges.* Scranton, PA: Chandler, 1970.

Beigel, A., and Levenson, A. I. *The community mental health center. Strategies and programs.* New York: Basic Books, 1972.

Caplan, G. *Principles of preventative psychiatry.* New York: Basic Books, 1964.

Caplan, G., and Grunebaum, H. Perspectives on primary prevention: A review. *Archives of General Psychiatry,* 1967, *17,* 331–346.

Carkhuff, R. R., and Truax, C. B. Lay mental health counseling. The effects of lay group counseling. *Journal of Consulting Psychology,* 1965, *29,* 426–431.

Cook, P. E. (Ed.) *Community psychology and community mental health. Introductory readings.* San Francisco: Holden-Day, 1970.

Cowen, E. L., Zax, M., Izzo, L. D., and Trost, M. A. Prevention of emotional disorders in the school setting: A further investigation. *Journal of Consulting Psychology,* 1966, *30,* 381–387.

Cowen, E. L., and Zax, M. Early detection and prevention of emotional disorder: Conceptualization and programming. In J. W. Carter, Jr. (Ed.), *Research contributions from psychology to community mental health.* New York: Behavioral Publications, 1968.

Cowen, E. L., Dorr, D. A., Trost, M. A., and Izzo, L. D. Follow-up study of maladapting school children seen by nonprofessionals. *Journal of Consulting and Clinical Psychology,* 1972, *39,* 235–238.

Darbonne, A. R. Crisis: A review of theory, practice, and research. *Psychotherapy: Theory, Research and Practice,* 1967, *4,* 49–56.

Durlak, J. A. Description and evaluation of a behaviorally oriented school-based preventive mental health program. *Journal of Consulting and Clinical Psychology,* 1977, *45,* 27–33.

Durlak, J. A. Comparative effectiveness of paraprofessional and professional helpers. *Psychological Bulletin,* 1979, *86,* 80–92.

Freeman, R. W., and Golann, S. E. Third year evaluations by co-workers of Mental Health Counselors. Paper presented at the American Psychological Association Convention, Chicago, September, 1965.

Garfield, S. L. New developments in the preparation of counselors. *Community Mental Health Journal,* 1969, *5,* 240–246.

Golann, S. E., Breiter, D. E., and Magoon, T. M. A filmed interview applied to the evaluation of mental health counselors. *Psychotherapy,* 1966, *3,* 21–24.

Golann, S. E., and Eisdorfer, C. (Eds.) *Handbook of community mental health.* New York: Appleton-Century-Crofts, 1972.

Gurin, G., Veroff, J., and Fields, S. *Americans view their mental health.* New York: Basic Books, 1960.

Harris, M. R., Kalis, B., and Freeman, E. Precipitating stress: An approach to brief therapy. *American Journal of Psychotherapy,* 1963, *17,* 465–471.

Hobbs, N. Helping disturbed children: Psychological and ecological strategies. *American Psychologist,* 1966, *21,* 1105–1115.

Hobbs, N. Reeducation, reality and community responsibility. In J. W. Carter, Jr. (Ed.), *Research contributions from psychology to community mental health.* New York: Behavioral Publications, 1968.

Hollingshead, A. B., and Redlich, F. C. *Social class and mental illness.* New York: Wiley, 1958.

Iscoe, I., and Spielberger, C. D. (Eds.) *Community psychology: Perspectives in training and research.* New York: Appleton-Century-Crofts, 1970.

Jacobson, G. F. Crisis theory and treatment strategy: Some sociocultural and psychodynamic considerations. *Journal of Nervous and Mental Disease,* 1965, *141,* 209–218.

Joint Commission on Mental Illness and Health. *Action for mental health.* New York: Basic Books, 1961.

Kalis, B. L. Crisis theory: Its relevance for community psychology and directions for development.

In D. Adelson and B. L. Kalis (Eds.), *Community psychology and mental health. Perspectives and challenges.* Scranton, PA: Chandler, 1970.

Kalis, B. L., Harris, M. R., Prestwood, A. R., and Freeman, E. H. Precipitating stress as a focus in psychotherapy. *Archives of General Psychiatry,* 1961, *5,* 219–226.

Kellam, S. G., Branch, J. D., Agrawal, K. C., and Grabill, M. E. Woodlawn Mental Health Center: An evolving strategy for planning in community mental health. In S. E. Golann and C. Eisdorfer (Eds.), *Handbook of community mental health.* New York: Appleton-Century-Crofts, 1972.

Lewis, W. W. Project Re-ED: Educational intervention in discordant child rearing systems. In E. L. Cowen, E. A. Gardner, and M. Zax (Eds.), *Emergent approaches to mental health problems.* New York: Appleton-Century-Crofts, 1967.

Magoon, T. M., and Golann, S. E. Nontraditionally trained women as mental health counselors/psychotherapists. *Personnel and Guidance Journal,* 1966, *44,* 788–793.

Monahan, J., and Vaux, A. Task Force Report: The macroenvironment and community mental health. *Community Mental Health Journal,* 1980, *16,* 14–26.

Riessman, F. A neighborhood-based mental health approach. In E. L. Cowen, E. A. Gardner, and M. Zax (Eds.), *Emergent approaches to mental health problems.* New York: Appleton-Century-Crofts, 1967.

Rioch, M. J. Pilot projects in training mental health counselors. In E. L. Cowen, E. A. Gardner, and M. Zax (Eds.), *Emergent approaches to mental health problems.* New York: Appleton-Century-Crofts, 1967.

Rioch, M. J., Elkes, C., and Flint, A. A. *National Institute of Mental Health project in training mental health counselors.* Washington, D.C.: U.S. Department of H.E.W. Public Health Service Publication No. 1254, 1965.

Roen, S. R. Evaluative research and community mental health. In A. E. Bergin and S. L. Garfield (Eds.), *Handbook of psychotherapy and behavior change.* New York: Wiley, 1971. Pp. 776–811.

Ryan, W. (Ed.) *Distress in the city.* Cleveland: The Press of Case Western Reserve University, 1969.

Sanders, R. New manpower for mental hospital service. In E. L. Cowen, E. A. Gardner, and M. Zax (Eds.), *Emergent approaches to mental health problems.* New York: Appleton-Century-Crofts, 1967.

Smith, M. B., and Hobbs, N. The community and the community mental health center. *American Psychologist,* 1966, *21,* 499–509.

Swift, C. Task Force Report: National Council of Community Mental Health Centers Task Force on Environmental Assessment. *Community Mental Health Journal,* 1980, *16,* 7–13.

Truax, C. B., and Carkhuff, R. R. *Toward effective counseling and psychotherapy.* Chicago: Aldine, 1967.

Zax, M., and Cowen, E. L. Early identification and prevention of emotional disturbance in a public school. In E. L. Cowen, E. A. Gardner, and M. Zax (Eds.), *Emergent approaches to mental health problems.* New York: Appleton-Century-Crofts, 1967.

Zax, M., and Specter, G. A. *An introduction to community psychology.* New York: Wiley, 1974.

Chapter
Sixteen

Professional
Problems and
Development

PROBLEMS, ROLES, AND RELATIONSHIPS

In this final chapter we will focus our presentation on the important issues that have characterized the professional development of clinical psychology. We shall discuss the relation of clinical psychology to the broader field of psychology, relationships with other professions, changing roles in clinical psychology, problems of legislation, matters of professional competence, standards of ethical performance, and current training.

CLINICAL PSYCHOLOGY AND PSYCHOLOGY

Throughout the development of clinical psychology as a special area of psychology, there has been evident some conflict in the relationship between clinical psychology and the parent field of psychology. One aspect of this problem is the relative emphasis placed on applied psychology in relation to the total efforts devoted to advancing the basic science of psychology. Although applied developments in psychology are almost as old as the development of the science itself, there has always been controversy about the relative emphasis given to these two areas. The "scientific" or "pure" psychologists have viewed with concern some of the developments in the applied areas of psychology. The importance and intensity of this feeling have varied from time to time. On the other hand, applied psychologists also have resented the disdainful attitudes of their scientific colleagues toward the applied areas of psychology.

Manifestations of this difference in value orientation have been apparent in the formation of special groups to represent the special interests of psychologists. As early as 1917, a group of psychologists interested in applied psychology met to discuss such matters as the certification of psychologists for clinical work. This problem produced controversy in the American Psychological Association (APA) and finally, in 1919, resulted in the formation of a section of clinical psychology within the APA (Watson, 1953). Shortly thereafter, a separate organization of consulting psychologists was formed, and in 1937 the American Association for Applied Psychology (AAAP) was established. This organization was created to meet the needs of those who were active in various fields of applied psychology, and clinical psychology was one of the areas included. The *Journal of Consulting Psychology* was published by the AAAP as its official journal and its pages contained many discussions of problems of a professional nature:

> Thus, there existed at the close of the thirties two major psychological societies—one dedicated to the advancement of psychology as a science and the other to its application. Generally speaking, members of the latter also had membership in the former but sincerely felt the essential nature of their applied organization (Watson, 1953, p. 338).

In 1945, however, the AAAP and a few other special psychological organizations were incorporated into a reorganized APA. This reorganization was a manifestation of the unity of psychology and was representative of a general consensus that American psychology could continue within one organizational framework as both a science and a profession. In the remodeled APA, consideration was given to the specialized interests of many different groups of psychologists who set up a large number of divisions, one of which was the Division of Clinical Psychology. Within this new structure, each division was given certain prerogatives with regard to setting membership requirements, selecting delegates to the APA Council of Representatives, and arranging programs at the annual meetings of the national association. In addition, a full-time position of executive secretary and a central office for the APA were established to take care of the increasing membership of the APA and the new problems, largely of a professional sort, that were arising in the postwar era.

As a result of these developments, an adequate reconciliation of science and profession, of pure and applied psychology, seemed to have been reached. However, from time to time, serious problems have been evident as a result of the conflict between scientific and professional emphases.

SCIENCE AND PROFESSION

Although all members of the APA acknowledge their basic allegiance to the science of psychology, the very fact that some are engaged primarily in daily clinical activities of a practical nature leads to a disparity in values. There are a number of reality considerations that draw the practitioner away from a purely scientific orientation. In the first place, she is confronted with practical problems, demanding immediate answers. Some recommendation must be made with regard to a given patient, even though really dependable knowledge may be lacking. A detached research point of view toward every problem encountered in the clinical situation would not help in caring for the immediate problems at hand. As a consequence, the clinical psychologist often must put aside her scientific role and participate as a professional practitioner.

Another consideration is that a number of theories and techniques which many clinicians use in their work do not stem directly from academic psychology. This can lead to a point of view which overemphasizes clinical experience and practical knowledge at the expense of research findings. Still another factor is that practical competence in the skills pertaining to clinical activities are valued more highly in a majority of clinical settings than are research skills, leading to a widening of the hiatus between experimental and clinical psychologists. The individual who strongly desires to be a practicing clinician identifies with his fellow mental health workers and seeks to perform in ways that are valued within this frame of reference.

On the other side of the picture, the experimental psychologist may look with suspicion and disfavor upon the clinical practitioner. He sees him as forsaking his birthright of research for "a mess of clinical pottage." The clinicians' use of techniques and procedures with questionable validity and their apparent lack of concern about such matters is one factor which leads experimental psychologists to view the former with some suspicion. Some academic psychologists also believe that a number of clinical psychologists are drawn into professional practice because of the financial rewards available. Others have expressed the view that it is a wasted effort to train individuals in research, only to have them go into clinical practice and forego research completely after receiving the Ph.D. degree.

Thus, there have been recurring stresses and strains as a result of differing value systems and of the different demands made of APA by the professional psychologists and the scientific ones. The former have emphasized the need for lobbying efforts and support of legislation in behalf of psychologists who are service providers. This has been viewed by the scientists as leading to increased association dues and an undue involvement with professional concerns and legal battles in terms of insurance payments for psychological services and the like. As a result, scientific concerns become less important.

As the number of clinical psychologists has increased and as some of them actually conducted organized political campaigns for offices within the APA, a practice frowned upon by many psychologists, the conflict at times became rather intense. As a result, at various periods proposals have been submitted to reorganize the association into a federated society, in which scientific and professional interests would be given greater autonomy to assess their own dues, publish their own journals, and pursue their particular interests (Policy and Planning Board, 1972). However, such proposals tended to be viewed as divisive and were not accepted. Nevertheless, quite recently, a compromise formula has been adopted for a trial period in which the scientific and professional representatives to the APA Council meet separately for part of the meeting, and jointly for the rest. Although many academic psychologists have been distressed by the way the APA had become politicized by some groups of clinicians, both groups of psychologists appear to have realized that in the long run, their interests are best served by one association. Practice which is not based on scientific or research findings is bound to be limited, and a science of psychology which has no relationship to applied problems will likewise suffer.

The conflict between science and profession is a particularly acute one for the clinical psychologists who adhere to the Boulder Model of the scientist-practitioner and who see this as providing the unique strength of clinical psychology. It is difficult to estimate the percentage of clinical psychologists who feel this way, but it is the writer's impression that it is the view of a significant number of clinical psychologists, particularly of those who contribute the bulk of the research in clinical psychology. Consequently, a possible split within the APA has been seen as a threat to the viability of clinical psychology as it has existed in this country since 1945, and also as a step that would be detrimental to the science of psychology. Thus far, such a split has been avoided.

CHANGING ROLES IN CLINICAL PSYCHOLOGY

As the profession of clinical psychology has developed rapidly in the period since World War II, so has the range in roles and functions of the clinical psychologist. There has emerged a large group of psychological practitioners which differs in important respects from its counterparts in the prewar period. As contrasted with the prewar clinical psychologist, the clinician in our current era is usually better trained, has a broader range of professional responsibility, and represents a larger and more powerful status group within the total field of psychology. Whereas the prewar clinician was essentially limited to psychometric testing, the present-day clinical psychologist, as we have noted, uses a wide variety of diagnostic procedures, engages actively and has contributed in important ways to the area of psychotherapy and behavior change, functions as a consultant, and participates in research. The programs of training have been essentially doctoral programs with practicum and internship requirements.

The large increase in the number of clinical psychologists since 1945 has led to clinical psychology becoming the largest specialty area in psychology. In each of the years, 1978, 1979, and 1980, approximately 35% of all doctorates in psychology were awarded to students specializing in clinical psychology (Doctorate Production Levels Off, 1981). This has also resulted in the majority of clinical psychologists working in clinical settings, with perhaps a quarter of them in academic settings. Over this period of time the clinical psychologists have established themselves as worthy professionals in the mental health field and are not the newcomers they felt themselves to be in the immediate postwar period. For example, when the author accepted a position in 1946 as chief psychologist in a V.A. Hospital, he frequently had to explain to staff members and others what a psychologist was and how his training differed from that of the psychiatrist. Today, the public's confusion concerning the difference between these two mental health professionals has all but disappeared.

LICENSING AND CERTIFICATION

Along with the increased range of activities and the expanded role of the clinical psychologist, there has been an evident and healthy concern on the part of American psychology with appropriate professional standards of practice and ethics. This has been manifested in a number of ways. One important indicator was the establishment of legal requirements that must be met before a psychologist can be certified to the public as a qualified psychologist and be allowed to practice independently. There are several different approaches to this problem. Before discussing them, however, let us examine the need for such legal action.

About 35 years ago, in most states, there was no legal definition of the practice or qualifications of a psychologist. As a consequence, anyone could set himself up in practice as a clinical, consulting, or any other kind of psychologist. Such an individual might have *no* training whatsoever in psychology, yet could advertise himself to the public at large as a psychologist and offer to perform a wide variety of psychological services. Furthermore, individuals seeking such services might patronize such "psychologists" in the absence of legal or other guides (Daniel and Louttit, 1953).

Because of this situation, psychologists were interested in both statutory and nonstatutory means of certifying psychologists with certain levels of competence. Certification was judged to be a way of promoting worthwhile standards within the profession as well as protecting the interests of the public at large. In the area of legislation, state laws can be drafted either to set up the requirements for professional practice or to limit the use of the title, "psychologist," to persons meeting certain educational and experiential requirements. A second and nonlegislative means of certifying the competency of a professional person usually involves specified educational requirements and the passing of an examination, upon successful completion of which a diploma is issued. The specialty boards in medicine are examples of the latter. If a physician wants to be certified as a specialist in psychiatry, obstetrics, or pediatrics, he must pass the examinations set up by the appropriate specialty board. For example, in psychiatry, it is the American Board of Psychiatry and Neurology that conducts the examinations and awards the diploma certifying this level of competence. Such certification of the individual's special skills has no real legal status, but simply indicates that the individual in question bears the stamp of approval of the particular professional organization or specialty board. If such certification becomes widely known and accepted, it can exert a definite influence on the standards required for the practice of that specialty. It should be remembered, however, that the student of medicine who passes his state examination for a *license* can *legally* practice any specialty.

Psychologists have attempted to utilize the two different means of regulating and certifying professional competence. First let us consider the attempts made in the area of legislation. Broadly speaking, legislation pertaining to the professional has been of two types: (1) certification, and (2) licensing. In certification the objective is to guarantee that the title "psychologist" or "certified psychologist" will be used only by people who meet certain standards. The standards set up can vary from state to state. Legal certification is, in essence, a certification of title rather than practice. In other words, a specific professional title can be assumed only by people who have met certain requirements. It usually does not define the activities that limit the practice of the professional field.

Licensing, as distinct from certification, is more inclusive and usually defines a profession in terms of the activities or functions of that profession. "Such a law requires a comprehensive and precise definition of the practice of the profession and prohibits anyone but persons licensed under the law to engage in such activities. This is the pattern of most Medical Practices Acts which begin with a definition of practice and restrict to licensed physicians the inclusive right to engage in such practices" (Sanford, 1955, p. 136). In this sense, licensing is a more restrictive form of legislation than is certification because it defines the actual functions of the profession and usually prohibits anyone who is not licensed, under penalty of law, from practicing the profession. Both types of legislation have been secured by psychologists.

LEGISLATION AND PROFESSIONAL CERTIFICATION

Because it obviously seems to be in the public interest to prescribe standards and safeguards for the practice of a profession such as psychology, it might appear that attempts at legislation would not be difficult. However, it has not turned out that way. As has been indicated, some of the functions engaged in by psychologists are also practiced by other professions. This has raised problems, particularly with respect to licensing. For example, if psychotherapy is listed as a function of the clinical psychologist, a restrictive licensing law could preclude other trained professional personnel from engaging in this activity. Although psychologists have not sought such restrictive legislation, nevertheless, their efforts to secure legal certification or licensing met with strong opposition from organized medical groups. Some of the reasons for this reaction have been mentioned earlier in several sections of this book. The main problem has centered around the independent practice of psychotherapy by psychologists. Medical groups in the past have insisted that such practice must be supervised by psychiatrists in order to ensure that sufficient consideration was given to the possible medical aspects of the cases treated. Because of this, as well as other reasons, there was considerable opposition to the legislative efforts of psychologists.

The American Psychological Association, while insisting on the rights of its members to pursue their own profession, has also given considerable thought to the problems involved and has published and periodically revised a code of ethics to ensure that adequate safeguards are observed in the practice of psychotherapy. Some of the pertinent principles adopted over the years in this regard are the following:

In clinical or consulting practice the psychologist must refer his client to an appropriate specialist when there is evidence of a difficulty with which the psychologist is not competent to deal (American Psychological Association, 1953, pp. 78–79).

The psychologist who engages in psychotherapy is obligated to assist his client in obtaining professional help for all important aspects of his problem which fall outside the boundaries of the psychologist's competence. Most frequently this principle will require that adequate provision be made for the diagnosis and treatment of medical problems (American Psychological Association, 1953, p. 79).

The psychologist recognizes the boundaries of his competence and the limitations of his techniques and does not offer services or use techniques that fail to meet professional standards established in particular fields. The psychologist who engages in practice assists his client in obtaining professional help for all important aspects of his problem that fall outside the boundaries of his own competence. This principle requires, for example, that provision be made for the diagnosis and treatment of relevant medical problems and for referral to or consultation with other specialists (American Psychological Association, 1963, p. 56).

Psychologists recognize the boundaries of their competence and the limitations of their techniques. They only provide services and only use techniques for which they are qualified by training and experience (American Psychological Association, 1981b, p. 634).

Although psychologists have taken their social role and professional responsibility quite seriously, and have attempted to set up proper standards and safeguards for the practice of their profession, as mentioned previously, they encountered considerable opposition from organized medical groups toward their independent practice. It is true that men and women are psychobiological organisms and that to concentrate solely on the "psyche" may lead to a disregard of the "soma" and the interrelationships between the two. If proper safeguards are observed, however, there is no reason that psychological therapy should be the exclusive concern of the medical profession. Other professions and fields of knowledge also have an interest in the problem and potential contributions to make. The conflict between the various professions in the long run may be at the expense of science and society.

In any event, the efforts of psychologists to secure legislation controlling the title and practice of psychology did not go unchallenged. In great part, as a result of this, legislation of one type or another had been enacted in only nine states by the end of 1955 (Washington Legislative Committee, 1955). In New York, for example, a licensing bill for psychologists was passed by both houses of the state legislature in 1951, but was finally vetoed by the governor primarily because of medical opposition (Combs, 1951). In some other states, proposed bills were defeated either in the legislature or in legislative committees.

Because of the importance of these matters there have been repeated attempts on the part of both the APA and the American Psychiatric Association to reach some understanding and agreement. At various times committees of both associations have met to discuss these problems, and various agreements reached. Although the relationship between the two associations has fluctuated from time to time, considerable progress has been made. Suffice it to say that the previous opposition has diminished and psychologists gradually succeeded in their attempts at securing legislation for certification or licensing. By 1973, such legislation existed in all but four of the states in the United States, and by the late 1970's all of the 50 states had passed such legislation.

However, a new problem has been encountered very recently which is known as the sunset procedure. This refers to "a procedure calling for automatic expiration of the existing state law regulating the profession unless a new law is enacted or the old law reenacted" (Cohen and Goldman, 1980, p. 51). The designation, sunset legislation, thus refers to legislation which is allowed to terminate in this manner. In three states, this has occurred to the legislation defining the practice of psychology, and new attempts have had to be made to restore the previous legislation.

Although the requirements for certification or licensing vary from state to state, most states require a doctoral degree, 1 or 2 years of professional experience, and the passing of written and/or oral examinations. Some states have two levels of certification, one requiring a doctorate and the other usually a master's degree. Waivers of the examination were also provided by some states if the individual is a diplomate of the American Board of Professional Psychology or has been certified previously in another state with similar examination requirements (American Association of State Psychology Boards, 1968).

THE AMERICAN BOARD OF PROFESSIONAL PSYCHOLOGY

In addition to securing legislation to ensure adequate standards of psychological practice, psychologists also have utilized professional certification as one means of specifying competency in certain applied fields of psychology. To meet this objective, a board was formed in 1947 whose current name is the American Board of Professional Psychology (ABPP). The board was entrusted with the task of examining and certifying individuals in specific areas of professional psychology. At present, these areas are Clinical Psychology, Counseling Psychology, Industrial Psychology, and School Psychology.

The board was formed as an independent corporation even though it was established by the APA. A number of considerations entered into this decision. In the case of possible legal action resulting from some decisions of the board, it would be better to have such action directed against the ABPP and not against the APA. The independence of the board also helps to highlight the special professional function of ABPP, and makes clear that membership in the APA does not imply competence to perform a specific professional function. In great part, this need for ABPP stemmed from the rapid growth of professional psychology in the postwar period of the 1940's and the resulting need to certify a high level of competency in those applied areas of psychology which involved offering services to the public for a fee.

Candidates for the ABPP diploma must have a Ph.D. degree in psychology that meets APA's standards for doctoral training and at least 4 years of acceptable experience. They must also pass an oral examination conducted by a panel of five diplomates, "at least two of whom share the candidate's theoretical orientation and approach, and at least three of whom hold diplomas in the candidate's specialty." The examination is based in part on sample protocols reflective of the candidate's usual practice, and "seeks to ascertain the candidate's awareness of the relevance of research and theory and his sensitivity to the ethical implications of his professional practice." The candidate is also observed in a field situation in which he interacts with a client, and is expected to demonstrate superior competence and impeccable ethical standards. The largest number of those who have taken the ABPP examination and received their diplomas have been clinical psychologists.

The examination of candidates and the awarding of diplomas by ABPP are means whereby the profession of psychology attempts to maintain standards and to assure the public at large of a highly acceptable level of competence for psychological specialists. At various intervals, a directory has been published of all diplomates in the various specialties of psychology and distributed to various agencies and organizations. Upon satisfactory completion of the examination, the candidate is awarded the diploma which states that she has met the requirements of the board and is certified as a professional psychologist in her specialty. An individual who has failed the examination, or any part of it, may be given an opportunity to take it again at a subsequent date. The diploma also may be revoked if the individual violates the ethical code of the profession and of the board.

The initial awarding of diplomas by ABPP antedated state certification and licensure in most states, and thus tended to be viewed as a significant mark of professional competence. However, a combination of events seemingly lessened its subsequent prestige and desirability. The gradual emergence of certification and licensure in the various states clearly was a competitive factor. Furthermore, meeting state requirements was mandatory for independent practice and these requirements were less stringent than those for the ABPP diploma. Finally, it is the author's view that there did not appear to be any particular rewards for securing the ABPP diploma. Only a relatively few positions such as that of director of clinical training in a university graduate program either required the diploma or indicated that it was a desirable asset. However, the board has continued to operate and diplomas are still awarded every year.

ETHICAL PRACTICE IN CLINICAL PSYCHOLOGY

We referred earlier to the APA code of ethical standards and professional conduct in reference both to legal certification and to the diplomate in professional psychology. Over the years, a number of separate committees of the APA have been set up to consider ethical standards and practices for various types of professional and scientific activities. Lists of standards have been developed and revised by these committees along with examples illustrating both violations and ethical conflicts which have arisen in the various areas of professional work. These standards, approved by the governing bodies of the APA, have then been published as official policy.

The first really significant publication was the volume, *Ethical Standards of Psychologists,* published in 1953, a collaborative effort of many psychologists. The standards adopted were derived empirically from intensive study of actual incidents occurring in the work of psychologists and were organized into six categories: public responsibility, client relationships, teaching, research, writing and publishing, and professional relationships. Each of these areas contained subsections that included specific ethical principles as well as lists of "incidents" related to the stated principles.

Subsequent versions of the *Ethical Standards of Psychologists* were much briefer statements. The most recent statement entitled "Ethical Principles of Psychologists," is but six pages in length (American Psychological Association, 1981). It lists 10 principles and is meant for all psychologists, not just professional or clinical psychologists. The first nine principles plus a few illustrative sections particularly relevant to clinical practice are listed below:

Principle 1
RESPONSIBILITY

In providing services, psychologists maintain the highest standards of their profession. They accept responsibility for the consequences of their acts and make every effort to ensure that their services are used appropriately.

As practitioners, psychologists know that they bear a heavy social responsibility because their recommendations and professional actions may alter the lives of others. They are alert to personal, social, organizational, financial, or political situations and pressures that might lead to misuse of their influence.

Principle 2
COMPETENCE

The maintenance of high standards of competence is a responsibility shared by all psychologists in the interest of the public and the profession as a whole. Psychologists recognize the boundaries of their competence and the limitations of their techniques. They only provide services and only use techniques for which they are qualified by training and experience.

In those areas in which recognized standards do not yet exist, psychologists take whatever precautions are necessary to protect the welfare of their clients. They maintain knowledge of current scientific and professional information related to the services they render.

Psychologists responsible for decisions involving individuals or policies based on test results have an understanding of psychological or educational measurement, validation problems, and test research.

Psychologists recognize that personal problems and conflicts may interfere with professional effectiveness. Accordingly, they refrain from undertaking any activity in which their personal problems are likely to lead to inadequate performance or harm to a client, colleague, student, or research participant. If engaged in such activity when they become aware of their personal problems, they seek competent professional assistance to determine whether they should suspend, terminate, or limit the scope of their professional and/or scientific activities.

Principle 3
MORAL AND LEGAL STANDARDS

Psychologists' moral and ethical standards of behavior are a personal matter to the same degree as they are for any other citizen, except as these may compromise the fulfillment of their professional responsibilities or reduce the public trust in psychology and psychologists. Regarding their own behavior, psychologists are sensitive to prevailing community standards and to the possible impact that conformity to or deviation from these standards may have upon the quality of their performance as psychologists. Psychologists are also aware of the possible impact of their public behavior upon the ability of colleagues to perform their professional duties.

In their professional roles, psychologists avoid any action that will violate or diminish the legal and civil rights of clients or of others who may be affected by their actions.

Principle 4
PUBLIC STATEMENTS

Public statements, announcements of services, advertising, and promotional activities of psychologists serve the purpose of helping the public make informed judgments and choices. Psychologists represent accurately and objectively their professional qualifications, affiliations, and functions, as well as those of the institutions or organizations with which they or the statements may be associated. In public statements providing psychological information or professional opinions or providing information about the availability of psychological products, publications, and services, psychologists base their statements on scientifically acceptable psychological findings and techniques with full recognition of the limits and uncertainties of such evidence.

When announcing or advertising professional services, psychologists may list the following information to describe the provider and services provided: name, highest relevant academic degree earned from a regionally accredited institution, date, type, and level of certification or licensure, diplomate status, APA membership status, address, telephone number, office hours, a brief listing of the type of psychological services offered, an appropriate presentation of fee information, foreign languages spoken, and policy with regard to third-party payments. Additional relevant or important consumer information may be included if not prohibited by other sections of these Ethical Principles.

Principle 5
CONFIDENTIALITY

Psychologists have a primary obligation to respect the confidentiality of information obtained from persons in the course of their work as psychologists. They reveal such information to others only with the consent of the person or the person's legal representative, except in those unusual circumstances in which not to do so would result in clear danger to the person or to others. Where appropriate, psychologists inform their clients of the legal limits of confidentiality.

Information obtained in clinical or consulting relationships, or evaluative data concerning children, students, employees, and others, is discussed only for professional purposes and only with persons clearly concerned with the case. Written and oral reports present only data germane to the purposes of the evaluation, and every effort is made to avoid undue invasion of privacy.

Psychologists make provisions for maintaining confidentiality in the storage and disposal of records.

When working with minors or other persons who are unable to give voluntary, informed consent, psychologists take special care to protect these persons' best interests.

Principle 6
WELFARE OF THE CONSUMER

Psychologists respect the integrity and protect the welfare of the people and groups with whom they work. When conflicts of interest arise between clients and psychologists' employing institutions, psychologists clarify the nature and direction of their loyalties and responsibilities and keep all parties informed of their commitments. Psychologists fully inform consumers as to the purpose and nature of an evaluative, treatment, educational, or training procedure, and they freely acknowledge that clients, students, or participants in research have freedom of choice with regard to participation.

Psychologists are continually cognizant of their own needs and of their potentially influential position vis-à-vis persons such as clients, students, and subordinates. They avoid exploiting the trust and dependency of such persons. Psychologists make every effort to avoid dual relationships that could impair their professional judgment or increase the risk of exploitation. Examples of such dual relationships include, but are not limited to, research with and treatment of employees, students, supervisees, close friends, or relatives. Sexual intimacies with clients are unethical.

Psychologists make advance financial arrangements that safeguard the best interests of and are clearly understood by their clients. They neither give nor receive any remuneration for referring clients for professional services. They contribute a portion of their services to work for which they receive little or no financial return.

Psychologists terminate a clinical or consulting relationship when it is reasonably clear that the consumer is not benefiting from it. They offer to help the consumer locate alternative sources of assistance.

Principle 7
PROFESSIONAL RELATIONSHIPS

Psychologists act with due regard for the needs, special competencies, and obligations of their colleagues in psychology and other professions. They respect the prerogatives' and obligations of the institutions or organizations with which these other colleagues are associated.

Psychologists understand the areas of competence of related professions. They make full use of all the professional, technical, and administrative resources that serve the best interests of consumers. The absence of formal relationships with other professional workers does not relieve psychologists of the responsibility of securing for their clients the best possible professional service, nor does it relieve them of the obligation to exercise foresight, diligence, and tact in obtaining the complementary or alternative assistance needed by clients.

Psychologists do not exploit their professional relationships with clients, supervisees, students, employees, or research participants sexually or otherwise. Psychologists do not condone or engage in sexual harassment. Sexual harassment is defined as deliberate or repeated comments, gestures, or physical contacts of a sexual nature that are unwanted by the recipient.

Principle 8
ASSESSMENT TECHNIQUES

In the development, publication, and utilization of psychological assessment techniques, psychologists make every effort to promote the welfare and best interests of the client. They guard against the misuse of assessment results. They respect the client's right to know the results, the interpretations made, and the bases for their conclusions and recommendations. Psychologists make every effort to maintain the security of tests and other assessment techniques within limits of legal mandates. They strive to ensure the appropriate use of assessment techniques by others.

In using assessment techniques, psychologists respect the right of clients to have full explanations of the nature and purpose of the techniques in language the clients can understand, unless an explicit exception to this right has been agreed upon in advance. When the explanations are to be provided by others, psychologists establish procedures for ensuring the adequacy of these explanations.

In reporting assessment results, psychologists indicate any reservations that exist regarding validity or reliability because of the circumstances of the assessment or the inappropriateness of the norms for the person tested. Psychologists strive to ensure that the results of assessments and their interpretations are not misused by others.

Principle 9
RESEARCH WITH HUMAN PARTICIPANTS

The decision to undertake research rests upon a considered judgment by the individual psychologist about how best to contribute to psychological science and human welfare. Having made the decision to conduct research, the psychologist considers alternative directions in which research energies and resources might be invested. On the basis of this consideration, the psychologist carries out the investigation with respect and concern for the dignity and welfare of the people who participate and with cognizance of federal and state regulations and professional standards governing the conduct of research with human participants.

In planning a study, the investigator has the responsibility to make a careful evaluation of its ethical acceptability. To the extent that the weighing of scientific and human values suggests a compromise of any principle, the investigator incurs a correspondingly serious obligation to seek ethical advice and to observe stringent safeguards to protect the rights of human participants.

As is evident from the preceding statements, psychologists have devoted serious attention to their professional responsibilities. The matter of ethics and professional responsibility does pervade all aspects of the psychologist's work and is as important as his technical knowledge and skills. Furthermore, the ethical standards devised have not been viewed as static pronouncements, but have been appraised and revised in the light of continued experience with them. A casebook illustrating and discussing the ethical issues involved also has been published (American Psychological Association, 1967). Cases in which ethical violations are alleged are usually referred to the appropriate committees of the state psychological associations, APA, or to the licensing boards.

THE INDEPENDENT PRACTICE OF CLINICAL PSYCHOLOGY

The matter of private practice has been discussed previously as a unique development in the postwar expansion of clinical psychology. In many ways this has been a primary problem around which matters of legislation and relationships with the medical profession have hinged. Since these issues have been discussed in other sections, there is no need for undue elaboration here. It is pertinent, however, to point out that the role of independent practitioner has been a relatively new one for psychologists. During the decade following World War II, only a small percentage of the membership of the Division of Clinical Psychology of the APA was engaged in full-time private practice (Report of the Committee on Private Practice, 1948, 1949; Sanford, 1952) and the increase over the years has been small, but steady. However, a fairly large number of clinical psychologists combine some part-time private practice with a full-time position.

An exact figure concerning the number of clinical psychologists in private practice is difficult to ascertain, but an authoritative survey of over 23,000 psychologists for the 1968 National Register of Scientific and Technical Personnel indicated that 1182 clinical psychologists were self-employed (Cates, 1970). According to the writer's calculations, this would indicate that approximately 17% of clinical psychologists were so employed at that time. This figure, incidentally, was the same as that secured by Kelly (1961) some years earlier in a survey of the members of the Division of Clinical Psychology of the APA. In a survey conducted in the early 1970's of a comparable sample of clinical psychologists, those primarily involved in private practice was slightly over 23% (Garfield and Kurtz, 1976). A more recent survey of a much smaller sample secured a figure of 31% in private practice (Norcross and Prochoska, 1982). Thus, this type of professional activity accounts for a significant minority of clinical psychologists.

The great majority of clinical psychologists have chosen some other mode of practice or employment—college or university teaching, practice in a clinic or hospital setting, medical school, and the like. Nevertheless, the profession itself, as we have noted, has insisted on its right to practice and develop as an independent profession with no control exercised by other professions. At the same time, the matter of adequate safeguards to be observed in the independent practice of psychology has also been emphasized. It may be added, however, that where clinical psychologists have practiced independently, or in groups, as consulting psychologists to industry, there has been relatively little controversy. It is in the area of the private clinical practice with clients with personality and behavioral disorders that much of the difficulty between psychologists and the medical profession has arisen in the past. Such conflicts have diminished, but to a certain extent have been rekindled over the matter of so-called third-party payments, that is, payments by insurance companies. Those health insurance policies that have included provisions for mental health services generally have referred to services provided by physicians or requested by physicians. Since psychologists are not physicians, they could not be reimbursed for such services unless a physician requested them.

The above-mentioned problem has led to considerable controversy, discussion, and legal battles which need not be detailed here. A number of health insurance companies have been reluctant to provide coverage for such services as psychotherapy because of the fear that the costs would be excessive. Supported by medical groups, some companies have balked at reimbursing psychologists for professional services unless authorized and requested by physicians. Psychologists, on the other hand, have advocated freedom of choice for the client in the selection of professional help for psychological problems. Some psychologists have even recommended that psychologists be considered as physicians for insurance purposes which seems ironic considering the criticism of the so-called "medical model" by psychologists.

There has been one celebrated case, referred to as the "Virginia Blues," which can be mentioned here (Kiesler and Pallak, 1980). In this case, the Virginia Academy of Clinical Psychologists brought suit against the insurance company, arguing in essence that insurance holders were being kept from using the services of qualified psychologists. The insurance company based their case on the arrangements made for the reimbursement of medical services by physicians, and refused to reimburse psychologists without both physician referral and supervision. The District Court upheld the insurance company; however, the U.S. Court of Appeals reversed the decision, ruling in favor of the psychologists. This is where the case rests pending a decision for further appeal. Thus, although there has been significant acceptance and recognition of the contribution and activities of clinical psychologists, economic competition and related matters still are sources of conflict. Furthermore, as the number of practitioners in all mental health fields has increased noticeably in the past 25 years or so, such competition can be expected to continue. However, psychologists have won important recognition by the courts.

TRAINING PROGRAMS IN CLINICAL PSYCHOLOGY

In Chapter 1, we reviewed some of the significant developments pertaining to training in clinical psychology during the postwar period. Included were the scientist-practitioner model, the more recent professional practitioner model with either the Ph.D. or Psy.D. degree, the internship requirement, and the formal accreditation of training programs by committees of the APA. Existing training programs have more or less followed these general outlines, although there have been, and continue to be, wide differences in the actual programs developed in specific universities and professional schools. In some universities a major emphasis throughout the clinical training program has been on theory and research methodology. In other settings a significant emphasis has been placed on training in psychotherapy. More recently in a few programs, the major emphasis has been on community psychology. In most programs, provisions also are made for at least some practicum or clerkship experience prior to the formal internship year. Initially, the internship took place in the third graduate year, but now many programs allow their students to take their internship during their fourth year or even after all other requirements are met.

At the present time, therefore, the student has more options for training available to her with a larger number of institutions providing graduate training than ever before. In 1981, there were 113 clinical psychology programs that were fully approved by the Committee on Accreditation of the APA. There were also eight programs that were provisionally approved and three that were on probation. There were also 24 approved programs in counseling psychology and 16 approved programs in school psychology (American Psychological Association, 1981a). In addition to these programs there are also a number of the recently developed professional programs which do not have current APA approval. Consequently, although there are more opportunities for graduate training available to the student interested in pursuing a career in clinical psychology or related areas than have existed previously, the quality and diversity of programs vary extensively. The requirements for admission and completion of the different programs also vary, and the prospective applicant should study the various catalogs and program descriptions and seek advice from her undergraduate faculty before deciding which programs best suit her future needs.

Although most programs may appear superficially similar in having course work in basic areas of psychology, personality, abnormal behavior, assessment, treatment, and research methodology, as well as providing practicum and internship experience, as mentioned, they differ in the quality and extent of such training. University programs tend to rely on full-time faculty, whereas the free-standing professional schools rely more on part-time faculty, who are largely practitioners in the community. At present, the overwhelming majority of clinical programs that are APA approved programs are university programs.

Graduate programs in clinical psychology and internship training centers alike are accredited each year by the APA. Every 5 years each program is visited by two or more psychologists who perform an on-site evaluation of the program, and a report of the visit is sent to the Committee on Accreditation of the APA. In the years between the visits each university or training center makes an annual report to the APA in which any changes in the program are given including changes in faculty, students who have graduated from the program, and similar matters. Clinical programs are generally evaluated in terms of the graduate curriculum, practicum training, size and quality of faculty, quality and progress of the students in the program, library, and other training facilities. Somewhat comparable criteria are used in the evaluation of internship centers. Lists of the approved university and internship programs in clinical psychology are published each year in a late issue of the *American Psychologist* so that prospective applicants and advisors can readily find out what programs have been approved.

Clinical psychology has been a very popular field for the past 30 years, and as a consequence it has not been easy to gain admission to a first-rate clinical psychology program. Many more applicants apply than can be admitted each year. The majority of university programs admitted from eight to fourteen students in past years. However, for several reasons, the number of admissions to these programs has undoubtedly decreased the past few years. In the first place, the federal programs for supporting clinical psychology training have had their funds greatly reduced. The federal government, after providing funding for general mental health training for approximately 35 years, has decided to phase out the programs previously administered by the National Institute of Mental Health. Furthermore, as mentioned in Chapter 1, the Veterans Administration, which formerly supported over 700 graduate students during the first 4 years of training, has shifted primarily to an internship program. Consequently, there has been a significant loss in federal stipends for graduate students in clinical psychology. Adding to the problem has been the financial situation encountered in recent years, by both private and public universities. After unprecedented expansion in the period following the second World War, the universities now find themselves in a very tight financial condition. The consequence of all this is that financial support for students desiring to enter graduate programs in clinical psychology and related fields is much less plentiful than it was in the past.

Despite the negative developments mentioned above, as indicated earlier, there are more institutions currently offering doctoral programs of one type or another than ever before, and there are still a large number of individuals who wish to receive graduate training. Furthermore, with the increase in training institutions, acceptance into some programs may be easier to secure than was true previously. Nevertheless, in most instances the prospective student would do well to have a creditable undergraduate academic record, good recommendations, a strong interest in clinical psychology, no observable serious personality defects, and good scores on the Graduate Record Examination and/or the Miller Analogies Test. Some universities also have specific course requirements concerning undergraduate preparation in psychology and related fields. As is true of admission to college generally, the better known and more prestigeful university programs are more difficult places in which to gain admission, although most universities receive more applications than they have openings for admission. Individuals who have less than a B average in their undergraduate work and undistinguished test scores will generally find it more difficult to gain admission to a graduate program in clinical psychology. Many schools, however, have special admissions criteria for minority students that take into account the educational deprivation most blacks and chicanos have experienced.

CURRENT ATTITUDES AND OPPORTUNITIES

Other aspects of the field have also changed in the past 30 to 40 years. The negative attitude toward mental health workers and mental health services has been replaced to some extent by a more positive view. In a survey conducted by the Survey Research Center at the University of Michigan in 1957, only 33% of the sample interviewed indicated that they would seek professional help for their problems. In a comparable survey in 1976, 46% of the sample replied in this manner (Veroff, Kulka, and Douvan, 1981). The later survey thus "revealed a substantial increase in people's acceptance of mental health professional help over the two decades. People are now more willing to accept the view that emotional problems should be referred to more specialized professional resources (mental health specialist) for treatment rather than to more general purpose professional help sources, such as doctors or clergy" (Veroff, Kulka, and Douvan, 1981, p. 73). Furthermore, the percentage of people who reported actually using professional help almost doubled during the time between the two surveys.

Paralleling this greater acceptance of the services of professional mental health workers in general has been the growth and acceptance of the field of clinical psychology. We have commented on this several times previously. However, growth and development also contribute to changes in a field and such has been the case with clinical psychology. The great shortage of clinical psychologists which existed 35 years ago does not exist today. During this period of time, as has been noted, training programs multiplied and increasing numbers of clinical psychologists were trained and entered the field. In the years 1978, 1979, and 1980, for example, approximately 1050 clinical students received their doctoral degrees each year (Doctorate Production Levels Off, 1981). In these 3 years alone, more clinical psychologists with doctoral degrees entered the field than comprised the entire field 35 years previously. Besides this, a large number of individuals with master's degrees also accept employment as clinical psychologists in many of our institutions. Consequently, at the present time there are relatively fewer positions available and more individuals available to fill them. This situation has been particularly apparent in our colleges and universities. What this appears to indicate, along with national and state economic problems, is a less favorable employment picture for clinical psychologists than was true in the past. Whether this is a temporary phenomenon or not, remains to be seen.

CLINICAL PSYCHOLOGY—SOME CONCLUDING REMARKS

We have come now to the end of our survey of clinical psychology. From a very modest beginning at the end of the last century, clinical psychology developed slowly until it became transformed by the events following World War II. It was during this latter period that the professional functions and roles of the clinical psychologist expanded and gave new significance and vitality to the field. The establishment and accreditation of university clinical training programs, the formation of ABPP, certification and licensure for psychologists, the code of ethics, the involvement in research, the increased number of clinical psychologists, and the overwhelming demands for their services have been noticeable developments during this period. This rather phenomenal expansion of American psychology has been characterized by an unusual amount of energy and activity on the part of a large number of psychologists interested in making psychology a truly worthwhile profession.

Although clinical psychologists have expanded greatly in number and public visibility, there have always been some stresses and conflicts evident during this period of growth. Possibly, some of this is inevitable as a result of a fast growing profession, some of whose functions overlap those of other, more established professions. At the same time, some of the conflicts appeared to be due to the particular combination of skills and values inherent in the field. Another factor of importance is that the field of clinical psychology in recent years has been a dynamic and rapidly changing one. As soon as one problem or issue is settled, or one role established, new ones appear on the horizon. To its credit, clinical psychology has not remained a static discipline, but one that has been sensitive to social influences and to the need for effective and efficient procedures. The scientific "conscience" developed in the clinical psychologist by his research training in the past has caused him to be dissatisfied frequently with some of his techniques and procedures, but it has also led to the attempted validation and improvement of his services.

At the present time, as we have noted, there are indications of a number of recent developments. These include a greater emphasis on behavioral approaches, the developments in community psychology, the use and training of new types of mental health workers at a variety of levels, and the emergence of health psychology and behavioral medicine. Many of these pose a challenge to established practices and beliefs, but they also reflect the desire of clinical psychologists to make their contribution to the better understanding and treatment of psychological health and disturbance. Despite the introduction of newer training models which emphasize professional practice over research skills, the research role and contribution of clinical psychologists remain as vital and important ones. Clinical psychologists, because of their unique background and skills, should continue to play a significant role in this important area of human concern.

REFERENCES

American Association of State Psychology Boards. Handbook for members of state psychology boards, 1968.

American Psychological Association, APA Approved Doctoral Programs in Clinical, Counseling, and School Psychology, 1981. *American Psychologist,* 1981, *36,* 1516–1518. (a)

American Psychological Association. Ethical principles of psychologists. *American Psychologist,* 1981, *36,* 633–638. (b)

American Psychological Association. *Ethical standards of psychologists.* Washington, D.C.: American Psychological Association, 1953.

American Psychological Association. Ethical standards of psychologists. *American Psychologist,* 1963, *18,* 56–60.

American Psychological Association. *Casebook on ethical standards of psychologists.* Washington, D.C.: American Psychological Association, 1967.

Cates, J. Psychology's manpower: Report on the 1968 National Register of Scientific and Technical Personnel. *American Psychologist,* 1970, *25,* 251–263.

Cohen, L. D., and Goldman, J. R. Sunset-Sunrise. *Professional Practice of Psychology,* 1980, *1,* 51–56.

Combs, A. W. A report of the 1951 licensing effort in New York State. *American Psychologist,* 1951, *6,* 541–548.

Daniel, R. S., and Loutit, C. M. *Professional problems in psychology.* New York: Prentice-Hall, 1953.

Doctorate production levels off. *APA Monitor,* September, 1981, p. 51.

Garfield, S. L., and Kurtz, R. M. Clinical psychologists in the 1970's. *American Psychologist,* 1976, *31,* 1–9.

Kelly, E. I. Clinical Psychology—1960. Report of survey findings. *Newsletter, Division of Clinical Psychology.* Winter, 1961, 1–11.

Kiesler, C. A., and Pallak, M. S. Editorial. The Virginia Blues. *American Psychologist,* 1980, *35,* 953–954.

Norcross, J. C., and Prochaska, J. O. A national survey of clinical psychologists: Affiliations and orientations. *The Clinical Psychologist,* 1982, *35,* No. 3, pp. 1, 4–6.

Policy and Planning Board. Structure and functions of APA: Guidelines for the future. *American Psychologist,* 1972, *27,* 1–10.

Report of the Committee on Private Practice. *Newsletter, Division of Clinical and Abnormal Psychology of the American Psychological Association,* 1948, *1,* No. 6, 5–6.

Report of the Committee on Private Practice. *Newsletter, Division of Clinical and Abnormal Psychology,* 1949, *2,* No. 7, 5–6.

Sanford, F. H. Annual report of the Executive Secretary: 1952. *American Psychologist,* 1952, *7,* 686–696.

Sanford, F. H. Psychology, psychiatry, and legislation. *American Psychologist,* 1955, *10,* 135–138.

Veroff, J., Kulka, R. A., and Douvan, E. *Mental health in America. Patterns of help-seeking from 1957 to 1976.* New York: Basic Books, 1981.

Washington Legislative Committee. Legislative activity in Washington. *American Psychologist,* 1955, *10,* 570–571.

Watson, R. I. A brief history of clinical psychology. *Psychological Bulletin,* 1953, *50,* 321–346.